PHILIPS'
MODERN
SCHOOL
ATLAS

Contents

Front Endpaper: Astronomical Geography

Edited By

B.M. Willett, *Cartographic Editor*

D. Gaylard, *Assistant Cartographic Editor*

and L. Prince-Smith, J. Russell, R. Smith and A. Wells
George Philip and Son Ltd., London.

Maps prepared by

George Philip Cartographic Services Ltd., London under the direction of A.G. Poynter, *Director of Cartography.*

© **1986 George Philip & Son, Ltd., London**

Eighty-second Edition

ISBN 0 540 05508 5 (Educational Edition)
0 540 05509 3

Printed in Great Britain by Redwood Offset, Trowbridge

THE SEASONS

The earth revolves around the sun once a year in an anti-clockwise direction. The earth is tilted at an angle of 66½ degrees to the plane of its orbit and always points into space in the same direction. In June the northern hemisphere is tilted towards the sun and it is the northern summer — days are longer and it is generally warmer. The southern hemisphere is pointing away from the sun. It is cooler and the days are shorter — the southern winter. In December the reverse is the case.

Equinox – One of the two times in the year when day and night are of equal length, owing to the Sun being overhead at the Equator.

Solstice – One of the two times in the year, midway between the two equinoxes, when the Sun is overhead at one of the Tropics (Cancer or Capricorn) and is at its highest latitude from the Equator (23½° North or South).

SHADOW

NORTHERN SPRING EQUINOX

POLAR ZONE
TEMPERATE ZONE
TROPICAL ZONE
TROPICAL ZONE
TEMPERATE ZONE

SOUTHERN AUTUMN EQUINOX

ORBIT

March 21st

NORTHERN SUMMER SOLSTICE

June 21st

SOUTHERN WINTER SOLSTICE

SHADOW

• Kingston   London •

• Nairobi
• Harare

SUN

ORBIT

NORTHERN WINTER SOLSTICE

December 21st

SOUTHERN SUMMER SOLSTICE

SHADOW

• Kingston

Hours of daylight in June
London 16½
Kingston 13
Nairobi 12
Harare 11

September 21st

Arctic Circle
Tropic of Cancer
Equator
Tropic of Capricorn

NORTHERN AUTUMN EQUINOX

SOUTHERN SPRING EQUINOX

SHADOW

ORBIT

Hours of daylight in December
Harare 13½
Nairobi 12
Kingston 11
London 8

On June 21st. the Arctic has 24 hours of daylight and the Antarctic total darkness. The opposite occurs on December 21st.

At the Equator the length of day and night are almost equal all of the year.

LENGTH OF DAY AND NIGHT ON THE EARTH

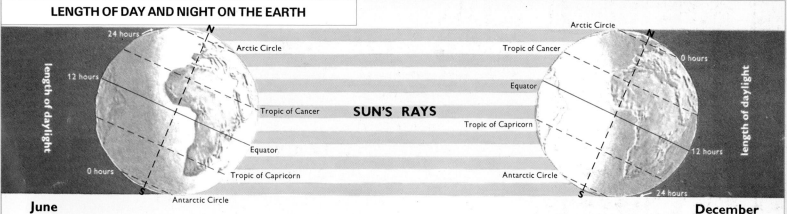

24 hours — N
length of daylight
12 hours
Arctic Circle
Tropic of Cancer
Equator
0 hours
Tropic of Capricorn
Antarctic Circle
S
June

SUN'S RAYS

Arctic Circle
Tropic of Cancer
N
0 hours
Equator
length of daylight
Tropic of Capricorn
Antarctic Circle
12 hours
S
24 hours
December

TIME

The Year – the time taken by the Earth to revolve around the Sun, or 365¼ days.

The Month – the approximate time taken by the Moon to revolve around the Earth. The twelve months of the year in fact vary from 28 (29 in a Leap Year) to 31 days.

The Week – an artificial period of 7 days, not based on astronomical time.

The Day – the time taken by the Earth to complete one rotation on its axis.

The Hour – 24 hours make one day. Usually the day is divided into hours A.M. (ante meridiem or before noon) and P.M. (post meridiem or after noon), although most timetables now use the 24-hour system, from midnight to midnight, for example, 1p.m. = 13.00 hours.

SUNRISE AND SUNSET

From the diagrams below it is possible to find out the time of sunrise or sunset on a given date and for latitudes between 60°N and 60°S.

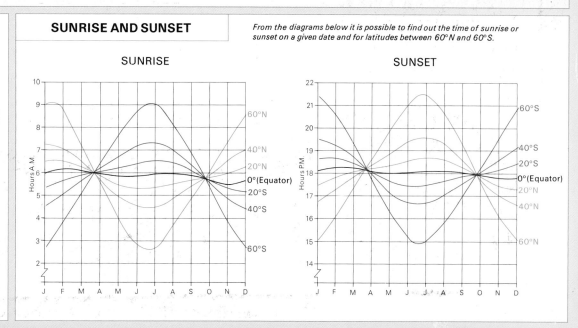

SUNRISE

Hours A.M.
60°N
40°N
20°N
0°(Equator)
20°S
40°S
60°S
J F M A M J J A S O N D

SUNSET

Hours P.M.
60°S
40°S
20°S
0°(Equator)
20°N
40°N
60°N
J F M A M J J A S O N D

Contents

General Reference

Settlement symbols in order of size

SETTLEMENTS

LONDON   ■ Osaka   ◉ Venice   ◎ Andropov   ◉ Toledo   ○ Cromer   ○ Interlaken

Settlement symbols and type styles vary according to the scale of each map and indicate the importance of towns on the map rather than specific population figures.

ADMINISTRATION

——— International Boundaries

– – – International Boundaries (Undemarcated or undefined)

International boundaries show the 'de facto' situation where there are rival claims to territory.

········ Internal Boundaries

COMMUNICATIONS

═══ Motorways in UK

⌒ Principal Roads

⌒·⌒ Tracks and Seasonal Roads

⊣---⊢ Road Tunnels

⌒ Principal Railways

--⌒-- Railways under construction

⊐---⊏ Railway Tunnels

≍ Passes

········· Principal Canals

——⊢ Principal Oil Pipelines

✧ Principal Airports

PHYSICAL FEATURES

⌒ Perennial Streams

······ Seasonal Streams

⊆⊃ Seasonal Lakes and Salt Flats

⌒ Swamps and Marshes

▭ Permanent Ice and Glaciers

∪ Wells in Desert

▲ 8848 Elevations in metres

▼ 8050 Sea Depths in metres

1134 Height of Lakes

1:4 000 000

50   0   50   100   150 km

GEOLOGY
1:16 000 000

SOUTHERN LIMIT OF GLACIATION

Tertiary — sand, clays
Mesozoic — chalk, clays, limestone, sandstone
Upper Palaeozoic — coal, limestone, sandstone
Lower Palaeozoic — sandstone, shales, slates
Pre-Cambrian — gneiss, quartzite, schists

Lavas
Granites
Major Faults

See pp. 106-107 for Geological Time Scale

Insets:

Shetland Is. — Unst, Fetlar, Yell, Out Skerries, Whalsay, Mainland, St. Magnus B., Bressay, Foula, Sumburgh Hd., Fair Isle

Orkney Is. — Westray, Rousay, Sanday, Stronsay, Mull Head, N. Ronaldsay, Start Point, Mainland, Hoy Sound, Hoy, Pentland Firth, Dunnet Hd., John o' Groats, Duncansby Hd., S. Ronaldsay

m
1000
400
200
100
0
50
100
200

Scotland — Highlands and Islands:

C. Wrath, L. Eriboll, Butt of Lewis, Pentland Firth, Stroma, N. Ronaldsay, Dunnet Hd., Duncansby Hd., Wick, Flannan Is., Eddrachillis B., Ben Hope 927, Thurso, Morven 705, Helmsdale, Lewis 799, B. More Assynt 998, L. Shin, B. Dearg 1081, L. Broom, Harris, North Minch, L. Shin, Dornoch Firth, Tarbat Ness, Moray Firth, Kinnairds Hd., St. Kilda, Outer Hebrides, North Uist, L. Gairloch, L. Torridon, Maree, B. Wyvis 1045, Cromarty Firth, Benbecula, Skye, North West Highlands, L. Carron, Inverness, Spey, South Uist, Cuillin Hills 1009, Carn Eige 1182, Glen Affric, L. Ness, Strath Spey, Don, Aberdeen, Girdle Ness, Canna, Rhum, L. Hourn, Glen Garry, Cairn Gorm 1245, Dee, Barra, Eigg, Morar, Glen Mor, Spean, Lochnagar 1154, North Esk, Muck, L. Shiel, Ben Nevis 1347, L. Linnhe, Grampian Mountains, Schiehallion 1081, Tummel, Pass of Killiecrankie, South Esk, Coll, Tiree, Mull, L. Laven 1214, L. Tay, Strathmore, Sidlaw Hills, Staffa, Ben More 966, Oban, Earn, Perth, Firth of Tay, Iona, L. Awe, L. Katrine, Ochil Hills, Fife Ness, Colonsay, L. Lomond 974, The Trossachs, Forth, L. Leven, Firth of Forth, Jura, L. Lomond, Lennox Hills, Glasgow, Edinburgh, Bass Rock, Islay, Sound of Jura, L. Fyne, Bute, Clyde, Pentland Hills, Moorfoot Hills, Lammermuir Hills, St. Abb's Hd., Gigha, Kintyre, Firth of Clyde, Arran, Goat Fell 874, Irvine, Southern Uplands, Ettrick, Tweed, Berwick

Ireland:

Lough Swilly, Malin Hd., Giant's Causeway, Sheep Haven, Bloody Foreland, Aran I., Rathlin I., Fair Hd., Mull of Kintyre, L. Foyle, Londonderry, Trostan 554, Mts. of Antrim, Gweebarra B., Derryveagh Mts., Finn, Errigal 752, Bluestack 676, Sperrin Mts., Sawel 683, L. Neagh, Belfast, Lagan, Belfast L., North Channel, Donegal Bay, Sligo Bay, Ox Mts., Erne, Blackwater, L. Erne, Upper L. Erne, Slieve Gullion, Mourne Mts., Slieve Donard 852, Dundrum B., Strangford L., Clogher Hd., Broad Haven, Erris Hd., Mullet Pen., Killala Bay, Nephina 806, L. Conn, L. Arrow, L. Allen, Moy, Carlingford L., Dundalk B., Blacksod B., Achill Hd., Achill I., Clew B., Mweelrea 819, Inishbofin, L. Mask, L. Corrib, L. Ree, Boyne, Slyne Hd., Connemara, Bertraghboy B., Kilkieran B., Galway Bay, Aran Is., St. Elva 345, Central Plain, Shannon, Bog of Allen, Dublin, Dublin B., Mal Bay, Slieve Bernagh, L. Derg, Slieve Bloom Mts. 529, Liffey, Ireland's Eye, Keeper 694, Wicklow, Lughnaquilla 926, Wicklow Mountains, Wicklow Hd., Loop Hd., Shannon, Limerick, Golden Vale, Galty Mts. 920, Mt. Leinster 796, Tralee B., Brandon Mt. 953, Slea Hd., Dingle B., Killarney, Macgillycuddy's Reeks 1041, Boggeragh Mts., Nagles Mts., Knockmealdown Mts., Comeragh Mts., Cahore Pt., Valentia I., Mts. of Kerry, St. Mishair, Caha Mts., Shehy Mts., Lee, Cork, Bandon, Wexford Harbour, Greenore Pt., Carnsore Pt., Waterford Harbour, Dungarvan Harbour, Youghal Harbour, Hook Hd., Bolus Hd., Kenmare, Bantry Bay, Cork Harbour, Old Head of Kinsale, Galley Hd., Mizen Hd., C. Clear, Clear I., Fastnet

England and Wales:

I. of Man, Pt. of Ayre, Calf of Man, Snaefell 620, St. Bees Hd., Solway Firth, Carlisle, Cumbrian Mts., Lake District, Scafell Pikes 978, Cross Fell 893, Pennines, Sunderland, Newcastle, S. Tyne, N. Tyne, Tyne, Cheviot Hills, The Cheviot 816, Coquet, Barrow-in-Furness, I. of Walney, Windermere, Whernside 737, Wensleydale, Swale, Ure, North York Moors 454, Robin Hood's Bay, Morecambe Bay, Forest of Bowland, Ribble, Fylde, Lune, Wharfe, Nidd, Vale of York, Yorkshire Wolds, Flamborough Hd., Bridlington B., Irish Sea, Leeds, Aire, Calder, Don, Hull, Humber, Spurn Hd., Holderness, Liverpool Bay, Gt. Ormes Head, Liverpool, Mersey, Manchester 636, Sheffield, Lincoln, Lincolnshire Wolds, Lincoln Heath, Holy I., Anglesey, Cheshire Plain, Chester, Stoke, Trent, Sherwood Forest, Lincoln Edge, Caernarfon Bay, Menai Strait, Snowdon 1085, Conwy, Dee, Clwyd, Derwent, The Wash, Braich-y-Pwll, Bardsey I., L. Bala, Berwyn, Cambrian Mountains, Cader Idris 892, Mawddach, Plynlimmon 752, Vale of Powys, Shrewsbury, The Wrekin 407, Cannock Chase, Charnwood Forest, Vale of Belvoir, The Fens, Norfolk Broads, Cardigan Bay, Teifi, Black Mt., Clee Hills, Teme, Birmingham, Avon, Rockingham Forest, Nene, Breckland, Wentworth, Yare, Norwich, Bure, Tremadoc Bay, Radnor Forest, Leominster, Northampton Uplands, Ouse, Waveney, Cam, Cambridge, Deben, Orwell, Mynydd Prescelly, Strumble Hd., Mynydd Eppynt, Black Mts. 811, Brecon Beacons 886, Forest of Dean, Gloucester, Cotswolds 330, Thame, Oxford, Chiltern Hills, Colne, London, Stour, Ipswich, The Naze, St. David's Hd., St. Brides B., Milford Haven, Carmarthen B., Gower, Worms Hd., Swansea, Cardiff, Vale of Glamorgan, Bristol, Mendip Hills, Avon, Salisbury Plain, Vale of White Horse, Berkshire Downs, Kennet, Marlborough Downs, Walbury Hill 297, Hampshire Downs, Reading, Thames, North Downs, Vale of Kent, Leith Hill 294, The Weald, Forest Ridges, Rother, Romney Marsh, North Foreland, Dover, Strait of Dover, Bristol Channel, Lundy, Barnstaple B., Exmoor, Dunkery Beacon 520, Brendon Hills, Quantock Hills, Vale of Taunton, The Parrett, Blackdown Hills, North Dorset Downs, Cranborne Chase, Salisbury, Hampshire Downs, South Downs, Beachy Hd., Celtic Sea, High Willhays 621, Dartmoor, Exe, Taw, North Dorset Downs, South Dorset Downs, Frome, I. of Purbeck, New Forest, Southampton, The Solent, Selsey Bill, Dungeness, Brown Willy 419, Bodmin Moor, Tor B., Lyme Bay, Portland Bill, The Needles, St. Catherine's Pt., I. of Wight, Camel, Plymouth, St. Ives B., Land's End, Mount's B., Whitsand Bay, Bolt Hd., Start Pt., Isles of Scilly, St. Mary's, Falmouth B., Lizard Point, English Channel

ATLANTIC OCEAN
NORTH SEA
Dogger Bank
IRISH SEA
St. George's Channel
CELTIC SEA
ENGLISH CHANNEL

1 : 4 000 000

50   0   50   100   150 km

Projection: *Conical with two standard parallels*
COPYRIGHT. GEORGE PHILIP & SON. LTD.

The DISTRICTS of Northern Ireland have been numbered and can be identified by reference to this table.

1	Londonderry	14	Craigavon
2	Limavady	15	Armagh
3	Coleraine	16	Newry & Mourne
4	Ballymoney	17	Banbridge
5	Moyle	18	Down
6	Larne	19	Lisburn
7	Ballymena	20	Antrim
8	Magherafelt	21	Newtownabbey
9	Cookstown	22	Carrickfergus
10	Strabane	23	North Down
11	Omagh	24	Ards
12	Fermanagh	25	Castlereagh
13	Dungannon	26	Belfast

Metropolitan Counties :-
On 1st April 1986 the administrative functions of the six metropolitan counties such as planning, education, transportation, libraries and social services were transferred to the city and town boroughs and various non-elected residual bodies.

ORKNEY
Kirkwall
59
HIGHLAND

SHETLAND
Lerwick
60

WESTERN ISLES
Stornoway

ATLANTIC OCEAN

HIGHLAND
Inverness
GRAMPIAN
Aberdeen

SCOTLAND

TAYSIDE
Dundee

CENTRAL
Stirling
FIFE
Glenrothes

STRATHCLYDE
Glasgow
Edinburgh
LOTHIAN

Newtown St. Boswells
BORDERS

DUMFRIES AND GALLOWAY
Dumfries
NORTHUMBERLAND
Newcastle
TYNE AND WEAR

NORTH SEA

Carlisle
Durham
DURHAM
CLEVELAND
Middlesbrough

CUMBRIA
Northallerton

ISLE OF MAN
Douglas

NORTH YORKSHIRE

DONEGAL
Lifford

NORTHERN IRELAND
Londonderry
Tyrone

Fermanagh
Monaghan
LEITRIM
Carrick-on-Shannon

SLIGO
Sligo

MAYO
Castlebar

Belfast
Down

Armagh
MONAGHAN
Cavan
Dundalk
LOUTH

CAVAN

ROSCOMMON
Roscommon
LONGFORD
Longford
MEATH
An Uaimh (Navan)
WESTMEATH
Mullingar

IRISH SEA

LANCASHIRE
Preston
WEST YORKSHIRE
Wakefield
Barnsley
SOUTH YORKSHIRE

HUMBERSIDE
Hull

GREATER MANCHESTER
MERSEYSIDE
Manchester
Liverpool

ENGLAND
Lincoln

GALWAY
Galway

IRELAND

OFFALY
Tullamore
KILDARE
Naas
DUBLIN
Dublin

Chester
CHESHIRE
DERBYSHIRE
Matlock
NOTTING-HAMSHIRE
Nottingham
LINCOLNSHIRE

Caernarfon
Mold
CLWYD
GWYNEDD

CLARE
Ennis

Port Laoise
LAOIS

WICKLOW
Wicklow

Kilkenny
KILKENNY
CARLOW
Carlow

Shrewsbury
SHROPSHIRE
Stafford
STAFFORD-SHIRE
WEST MIDLANDS
Birmingham
Leicester
LEICESTERSHIRE

NORTH-AMPTON-SHIRE
Northampton
CAMBRIDGE-SHIRE
Cambridge

NORFOLK
Norwich

WALES
POWYS

Llandrindod Wells
HEREFORD AND WORCESTER
Worcester
Warwick
WARWICK-SHIRE
Bedford
BEDFORD-SHIRE

SUFFOLK
Ipswich

LIMERICK
Limerick

TIPPERARY

Clonmel
WEXFORD
Wexford

DYFED
Carmarthen

Gloucester
GLOUCESTER-SHIRE
Oxford
OXFORDSHIRE
Aylesbury
BUCK-INGHAM-SHIRE
Hertford
HERTFORD-SHIRE

ESSEX
Chelmsford

Tralee
KERRY

WATERFORD
Waterford

St. George's Channel

WEST GLAMORGAN
Swansea
MID GLAMORGAN
Cardiff
SOUTH GLAMORGAN
GWENT
Cwmbran
AVON
Bristol
WILTSHIRE
Trowbridge
BERKSHIRE
Reading
GREATER LONDON
Kingston

Maidstone
SURREY
KENT

CORK
Cork

SOMERSET
Taunton
HAMPSHIRE
Winchester
WEST SUSSEX
EAST SUSSEX
Lewes

DEVON
Exeter
DORSET
Dorchester
Chichester
Newport
ISLE OF WIGHT

CORNWALL
Truro

ENGLISH CHANNEL

FRANCE

West from Greenwich   0   East from Greenwich

○ Norwich   Administrative headquarters
— MERSEYSIDE   Metropolitan counties
Antrim   Former Northern Ireland counties

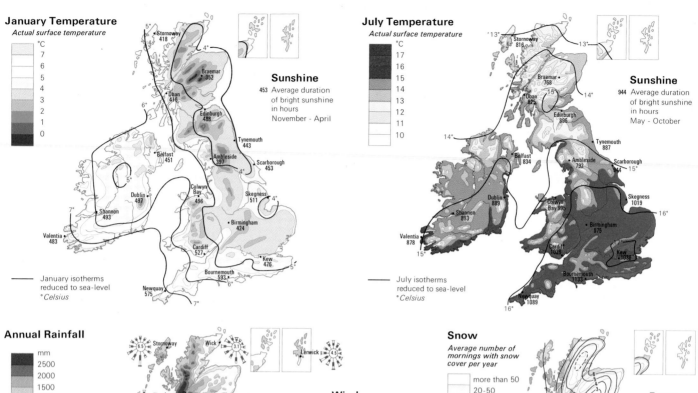

January Temperature
Actual surface temperature

°C
7
6
5
4
3
2
1
0

Sunshine
453 Average duration of bright sunshine in hours November – April

Stornoway 418
Braemar 352
Oban 416
Edinburgh 488
Tynemouth 443
Belfast 451
Ambleside 397
Scarborough 453
Dublin 497
Colwyn Bay 496
Skegness 511
Shannon 493
Birmingham 424
Valentia 483
Cardiff 527
Kew 476
Bournemouth 593
Newquay 575

— January isotherms reduced to sea-level °Celsius

July Temperature
Actual surface temperature

°C
17
16
15
14
13
12
11
10

Sunshine
944 Average duration of bright sunshine in hours May – October

Stornoway 816
Braemar 768
Oban 825
Edinburgh 896
Tynemouth 887
Belfast 834
Ambleside 792
Scarborough 944
Dublin 889
Colwyn Bay 995
Skegness 1019
Shannon 893
Birmingham 875
Valentia 878
Cardiff 1026
Kew 1038
Bournemouth 1133
Newquay 1089

— July isotherms reduced to sea-level °Celsius

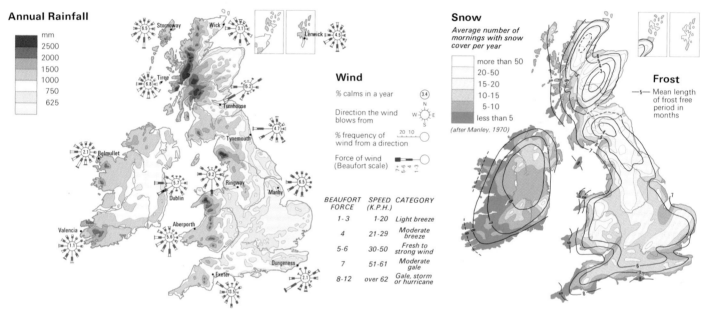

Annual Rainfall

mm
2500
2000
1500
1000
750
625

Stornoway Wick
Lerwick (4.5)
Tiree (6.8)
Turnhouse
Belmullet (2.1)
Tynemouth
Dublin (5.7)
Ringway (9.2)
Manby
(6.5)
Valencia (1.1)
Aberporth (5.6)
Dungeness
Exeter (13.5)
(6.5)
(6.5)
(3.1)
(15.2)
(4.7)
(2.1)

Wind
% calms in a year

Direction the wind blows from

% frequency of wind from a direction 20 10

Force of wind (Beaufort scale) 7+ 5 4 1-3

BEAUFORT FORCE	SPEED (K.P.H.)	CATEGORY
1-3	1-20	Light breeze
4	21-29	Moderate breeze
5-6	30-50	Fresh to strong wind
7	51-61	Moderate gale
8-12	over 62	Gale, storm or hurricane

Snow
Average number of mornings with snow cover per year

more than 50
20-50
15-20
10-15
5-10
less than 5

(after Manley, 1970)

Frost
—5— Mean length of frost free period in months

Variability of Rain
The percentage frequency with which rainfall varies from the normal rainfall regime in an area: the higher the percentage figure, the more variable the rainfall.

over 20%
18-20%
16-18%
14-16%
12-14%
10-12%
under 10%

(after Gregory, 1955)

Rainfall is least variable in the wetter northern and western areas and most variable in the drier eastern and southern areas

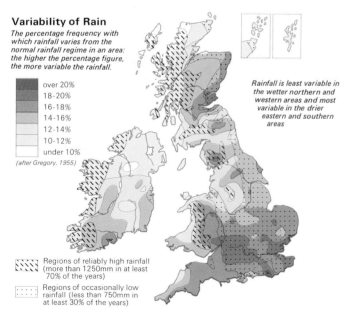

Regions of reliably high rainfall (more than 1250mm in at least 70% of the years)

Regions of occasionally low rainfall (less than 750mm in at least 30% of the years)

Synoptic Chart for a Typical Winter Depression

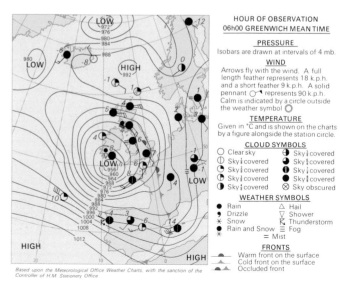

HOUR OF OBSERVATION
06h00 GREENWICH MEAN TIME

PRESSURE
Isobars are drawn at intervals of 4 mb.

WIND
Arrows fly with the wind. A full length feather represents 18 k.p.h. and a short feather 9 k.p.h. A solid pennant represents 90 k.p.h. Calm is indicated by a circle outside the weather symbol

TEMPERATURE
Given in °C and is shown on the charts by a figure alongside the station circle.

CLOUD SYMBOLS
Clear sky Sky ½ covered
Sky ¹⁄₁₀ covered Sky ⅝ covered
Sky ³⁄₁₀ covered Sky ¾ covered
Sky ⅜ covered Sky ⁹⁄₁₀ covered
Sky ⁴⁄₁₀ covered Sky obscured

WEATHER SYMBOLS
Rain △ Hail
Drizzle ▽ Shower
Snow Thunderstorm
Rain and Snow Fog
= Mist

FRONTS
Warm front on the surface
Cold front on the surface
Occluded front

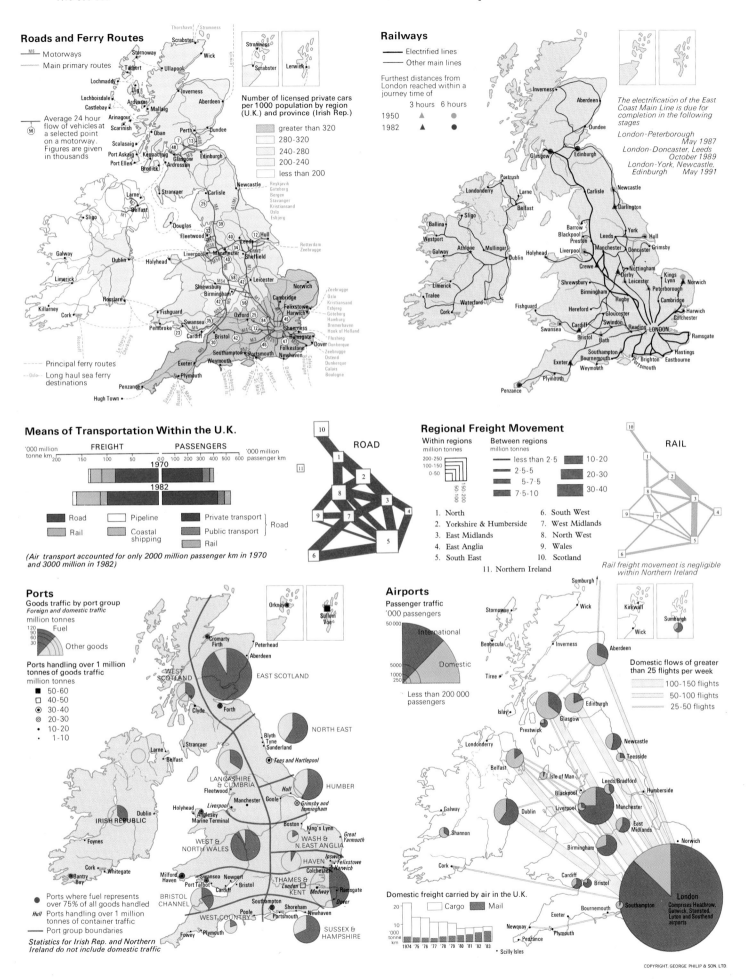

Roads and Ferry Routes

— M6 — Motorways
——— Main primary routes

Average 24 hour flow of vehicles at a selected point on a motorway. Figures are given in thousands

Number of licensed private cars per 1000 population by region (U.K.) and province (Irish Rep.)

greater than 320
280-320
240-280
200-240
less than 200

---- Principal ferry routes
--Oslo-- Long haul sea ferry destinations

Railways

——— Electrified lines
——— Other main lines

Furthest distances from London reached within a journey time of

	3 hours	6 hours
1950	▲	●
1982	▲	●

The electrification of the East Coast Main Line is due for completion in the following stages
London-Peterborough   May 1987
London-Doncaster, Leeds   October 1989
London-York, Newcastle, Edinburgh   May 1991

Means of Transportation Within the U.K.

FREIGHT   PASSENGERS
'000 million tonne km   200   150   100   50   0.0   100 200 300 400 500 600   '000 million passenger km

1970
1982

Road
Rail
Pipeline
Coastal shipping
Private transport ⎫
Public transport ⎬ Road
Rail ⎭

(Air transport accounted for only 2000 million passenger km in 1970 and 3000 million in 1982)

ROAD

Regional Freight Movement

Within regions   Between regions
million tonnes   million tonnes

200-250
100-150
0-50
150-200
50-100

——— less than 2·5   ▬ 10-20
——— 2·5-5   ▬ 20-30
▬ 5-7·5   ▬ 30-40
▬ 7·5-10

1. North   6. South West
2. Yorkshire & Humberside   7. West Midlands
3. East Midlands   8. North West
4. East Anglia   9. Wales
5. South East   10. Scotland
11. Northern Ireland

RAIL

Rail freight movement is negligible within Northern Ireland

Ports

Goods traffic by port group
Foreign and domestic traffic
million tonnes
120
90
60
30
Fuel
Other goods

Ports handling over 1 million tonnes of goods traffic
million tonnes
■ 50-60
□ 40-50
◉ 30-40
◎ 20-30
• 10-20
· 1-10

● Ports where fuel represents over 75% of all goods handled
Hull Ports handling over 1 million tonnes of container traffic
Port group boundaries

Statistics for Irish Rep. and Northern Ireland do not include domestic traffic

Airports

Passenger traffic
'000 passengers
50 000
International
5000
Domestic
1000
250
Less than 200 000 passengers

Domestic flows of greater than 25 flights per week
100-150 flights
50-100 flights
25-50 flights

London Comprises Heathrow, Gatwick, Stansted, Luton and Southend airports

Domestic freight carried by air in the U.K.
□ Cargo   ▨ Mail
20
10
'000 tonne km
'74 '75 '76 '77 '78 '79 '80 '81 '82 '83

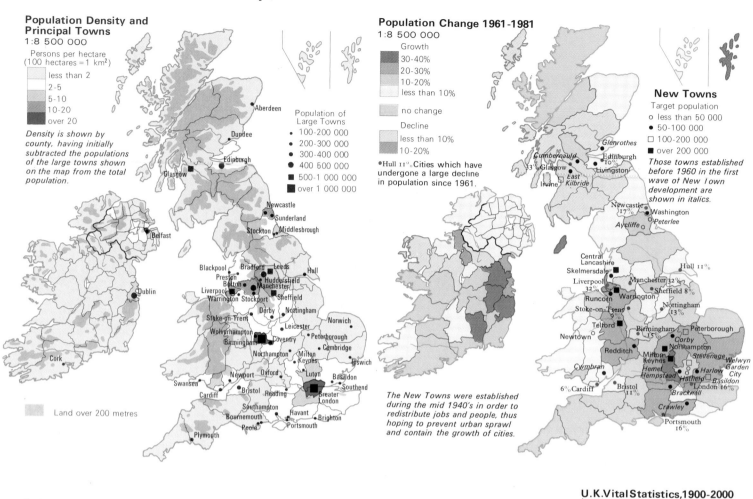

Population Density and Principal Towns
1:8 500 000

Persons per hectare
(100 hectares = 1 km²)
- less than 2
- 2-5
- 5-10
- 10-20
- over 20

Density is shown by county, having initially subtracted the populations of the large towns shown on the map from the total population.

Population of Large Towns
- • 100-200 000
- • 200-300 000
- • 300-400 000
- • 400 500 000
- ■ 500-1 000 000
- ■ over 1 000 000

Land over 200 metres

Aberdeen
Dundee
Edinburgh
Glasgow
Belfast
Dublin
Cork
Newcastle
Sunderland
Stockton
Middlesbrough
Blackpool
Bradford
Leeds
Hull
Preston
Bolton
Huddersfield
Liverpool
Manchester
Warrington
Stockport
Sheffield
Derby
Nottingham
Stoke-on-Trent
Leicester
Norwich
Wolverhampton
Peterborough
Birmingham
Coventry
Cambridge
Northampton
Milton Keynes
Ipswich
Newport
Oxford
Luton
Basildon
Swansea
Reading
Southend
Cardiff
Bristol
Greater London
Southampton
Bournemouth
Havant
Brighton
Plymouth
Poole
Portsmouth

Population Change 1961-1981
1:8 500 000

Growth
- 30-40%
- 20-30%
- 10-20%
- less than 10%

no change

Decline
- less than 10%
- 10-20%

•Hull 11%.Cities which have undergone a large decline in population since 1961.

The New Towns were established during the mid 1940's in order to redistribute jobs and people, thus hoping to prevent urban sprawl and contain the growth of cities.

New Towns
Target population
- ○ less than 50 000
- • 50-100 000
- □ 100-200 000
- ■ over 200 000

Those towns established before 1960 in the first wave of New Town development are shown in italics.

Glenrothes
Cumbernauld
Edinburgh
Livingston
Glasgow 33%
East Kilbride
Irvine
Newcastle 17%
Washington
Aycliffe
Peterlee
Central Lancashire
Skelmersdale
Hull 11%
Liverpool 32%
Manchester 32%
Runcorn
Warrington
Sheffield 8%
Stoke-on-Trent 9%
Nottingham 13%
Telford
Newtown
Birmingham 15%
Peterborough
Corby
Redditch
Northampton
Stevenage
Milton Keynes
Welwyn Garden City
Cwmbran
Hemet Hempstead
Harlow
Hatfield
Cardiff 6%
Bristol 11%
Brackmill
London 16%
Basildon
Crawley
Portsmouth 16%

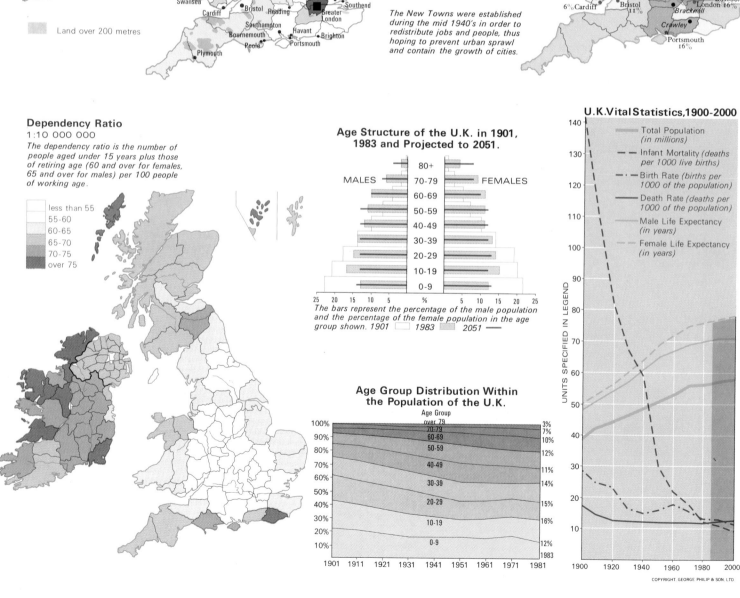

Dependency Ratio
1:10 000 000

The dependency ratio is the number of people aged under 15 years plus those of retiring age (60 and over for females, 65 and over for males) per 100 people of working age.

- less than 55
- 55-60
- 60-65
- 65-70
- 70-75
- over 75

Age Structure of the U.K. in 1901, 1983 and Projected to 2051.

MALES   FEMALES

80+
70-79
60-69
50-59
40-49
30-39
20-29
10-19
0-9

25 20 15 10 5   5 10 15 20 25
%

The bars represent the percentage of the male population and the percentage of the female population in the age group shown. 1901 ☐ 1983 ▨ 2051 ▬

Age Group Distribution Within the Population of the U.K.

Age Group
over 79 — 3%
70-79 — 7%
60-69 — 10%
50-59 — 12%
40-49 — 11%
30-39 — 14%
20-29 — 15%
10-19 — 16%
0-9 — 12%

100%
90%
80%
70%
60%
50%
40%
30%
20%
10%

1901 1911 1921 1931 1941 1951 1961 1971 1981 1983

U.K. Vital Statistics, 1900-2000

- Total Population (in millions)
- Infant Mortality (deaths per 1000 live births)
- Birth Rate (births per 1000 of the population)
- Death Rate (deaths per 1000 of the population)
- Male Life Expectancy (in years)
- Female Life Expectancy (in years)

UNITS SPECIFIED IN LEGEND

140
130
120
110
100
90
80
70
60
50
40
30
20
10

1900 1920 1940 1960 1980 2000

Agricultural Land Use Capability
1:10 000 000

NORTHERN IRELAND AND THE IRISH REPUBLIC
(Land Use Range)

- Wide
- Somewhat Limited
- Limited
- Very Limited
- Extremely Limited

GREAT BRITAIN
(Land Quality)

- First Class
- Good
- Good and Medium
- Medium
- Medium and Poor
- Poor
- Urban Areas

The land use capability classification assesses the value of land for agricultural purposes according to physical conditions and type of management.

Leading Agricultural Enterprises
1:10 000 000

- Crops
- Dairy
- Beef
- Sheep
- Pigs
- Horticulture
- Crofting

The leading enterprises shown on this map are those which use the most man-days in each district.

Principal Crops

		Production ('000 tonnes)
Wheat		10 801
Barley		7517
Oats		343
Potatoes		5493
Sugar Beet		7494
Fruit		3559
Hops		9

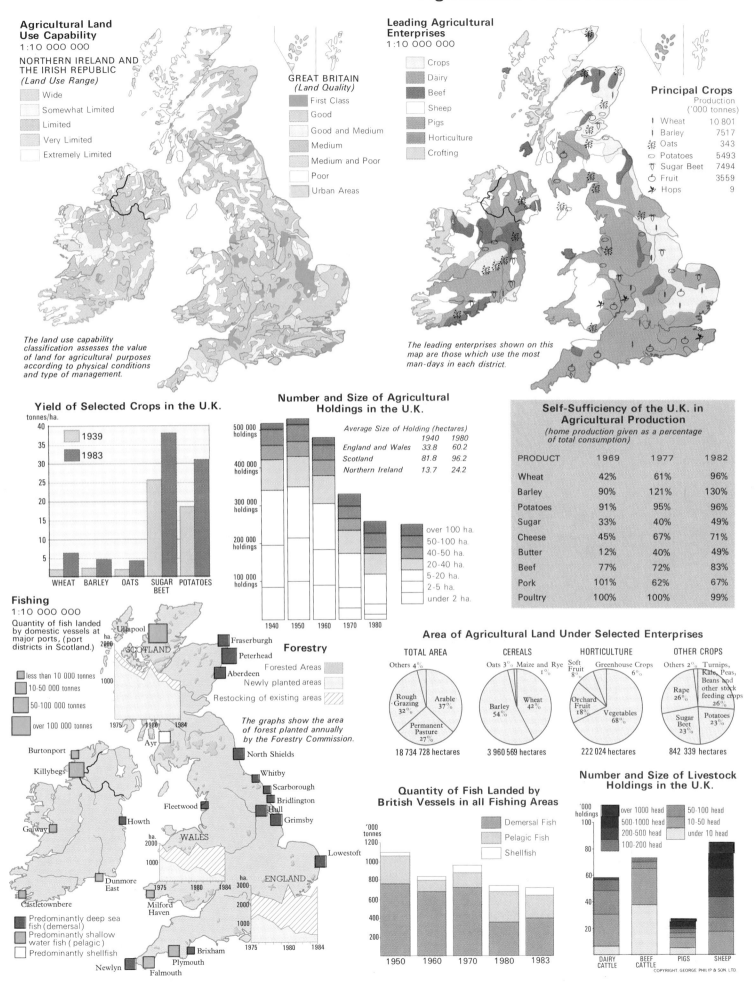

Yield of Selected Crops in the U.K.

tonnes/ha.

- 1939
- 1983

WHEAT, BARLEY, OATS, SUGAR BEET, POTATOES

Number and Size of Agricultural Holdings in the U.K.

Average Size of Holding (hectares)	1940	1980
England and Wales	33.8	60.2
Scotland	81.8	96.2
Northern Ireland	13.7	24.2

- over 100 ha.
- 50-100 ha.
- 40-50 ha.
- 20-40 ha.
- 5-20 ha.
- 2-5 ha.
- under 2 ha.

1940, 1950, 1960, 1970, 1980

Self-Sufficiency of the U.K. in Agricultural Production
(home production given as a percentage of total consumption)

PRODUCT	1969	1977	1982
Wheat	42%	61%	96%
Barley	90%	121%	130%
Potatoes	91%	95%	96%
Sugar	33%	40%	49%
Cheese	45%	67%	71%
Butter	12%	40%	49%
Beef	77%	72%	83%
Pork	101%	62%	67%
Poultry	100%	100%	99%

Fishing
1:10 000 000

Quantity of fish landed by domestic vessels at major ports, (port districts in Scotland.)

- less than 10 000 tonnes
- 10-50 000 tonnes
- 50-100 000 tonnes
- over 100 000 tonnes

Ullapool, SCOTLAND, Fraserburgh, Peterhead, Aberdeen, Ayr, Burtonport, Killybegs, Galway, Howth, Fleetwood, WALES, Milford Haven, Dunmore East, Castletownbere, North Shields, Whitby, Scarborough, Bridlington, Hull, Grimsby, ENGLAND, Lowestoft, Brixham, Plymouth, Newlyn, Falmouth

- Predominantly deep sea fish (demersal)
- Predominantly shallow water fish (pelagic)
- Predominantly shellfish

Forestry

- Forested Areas
- Newly planted areas
- Restocking of existing areas

The graphs show the area of forest planted annually by the Forestry Commission.

1975 1980 1984

Quantity of Fish Landed by British Vessels in all Fishing Areas

'000 tonnes

- Demersal Fish
- Pelagic Fish
- Shellfish

1950, 1960, 1970, 1980, 1983

Area of Agricultural Land Under Selected Enterprises

TOTAL AREA
- Others 4%
- Rough Grazing 32%
- Arable 37%
- Permanent Pasture 27%

18 734 728 hectares

CEREALS
- Oats 3%
- Maize and Rye 1%
- Barley 54%
- Wheat 42%

3 960 569 hectares

HORTICULTURE
- Soft Fruit 8%
- Greenhouse Crops 6%
- Orchard Fruit 18%
- Vegetables 68%

222 024 hectares

OTHER CROPS
- Others 2%
- Turnips, Kale, Peas, Beans and other stock feeding crops 26%
- Rape 26%
- Sugar Beet 23%
- Potatoes 23%

842 339 hectares

Number and Size of Livestock Holdings in the U.K.

'000 holdings

- over 1000 head
- 500-1000 head
- 200-500 head
- 100-200 head
- 50-100 head
- 10-50 head
- under 10 head

DAIRY CATTLE, BEEF CATTLE, PIGS, SHEEP

COPYRIGHT GEORGE PHILIP & SON. LTD.

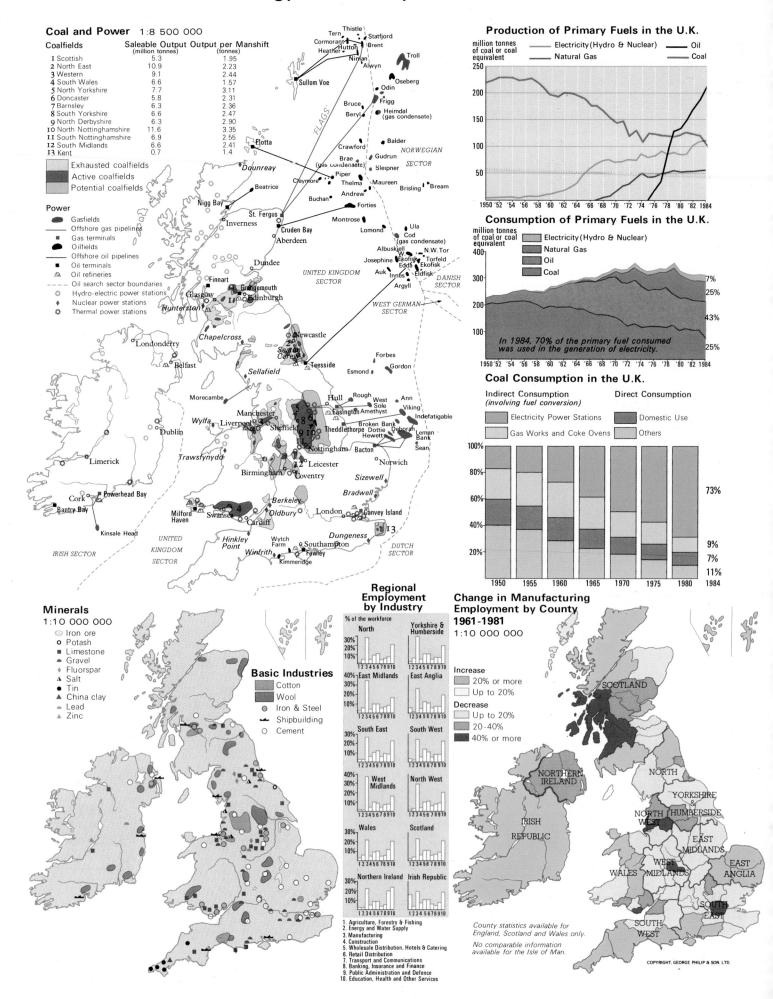

Coal and Power 1:8 500 000

Coalfields	Saleable Output (million tonnes)	Output per Manshift (tonnes)
1 Scottish	5.3	1.95
2 North East	10.9	2.23
3 Western	9.1	2.44
4 South Wales	6.6	1.57
5 North Yorkshire	7.7	3.11
6 Doncaster	5.8	2.31
7 Barnsley	6.3	2.36
8 South Yorkshire	6.6	2.47
9 North Derbyshire	6.3	2.90
10 North Nottinghamshire	11.6	3.35
11 South Nottinghamshire	6.9	2.55
12 South Midlands	6.6	2.41
13 Kent	0.7	1.4

- Exhausted coalfields
- Active coalfields
- Potential coalfields

Power

- Gasfields
- Offshore gas pipelines
- Gas terminals
- Oilfields
- Offshore oil pipelines
- Oil terminals
- Oil refineries
- Oil search sector boundaries
- Hydro-electric power stations
- Nuclear power stations
- Thermal power stations

Production of Primary Fuels in the U.K.

million tonnes of coal or coal equivalent

Electricity (Hydro & Nuclear) — Oil
Natural Gas — Coal

250 200 150 100 50
1950 '52 '54 '56 '58 '60 '62 '64 '66 '68 '70 '72 '74 '76 '78 '80 '82 1984

Consumption of Primary Fuels in the U.K.

million tonnes of coal or coal equivalent

- Electricity (Hydro & Nuclear) 7%
- Natural Gas 25%
- Oil 43%
- Coal 25%

400 300 200 100
In 1984, 70% of the primary fuel consumed was used in the generation of electricity.
1950 '52 '54 '56 '58 '60 '62 '64 '66 '68 '70 '72 '74 '76 '78 '80 '82 1984

Coal Consumption in the U.K.

Indirect Consumption *(involving fuel conversion)*
- Electricity Power Stations
- Gas Works and Coke Ovens

Direct Consumption
- Domestic Use
- Others

100% 80% 60% 40% 20%
1950 1955 1960 1965 1970 1975 1980 1984

73%
9%
7%
11%

Minerals 1:10 000 000

- Iron ore
- Potash
- Limestone
- Gravel
- Fluorspar
- Salt
- Tin
- China clay
- Lead
- Zinc

Basic Industries

- Cotton
- Wool
- Iron & Steel
- Shipbuilding
- Cement

Regional Employment by Industry

% of the workforce

North
Yorkshire & Humberside
East Midlands
East Anglia
South East
South West
West Midlands
North West
Wales
Scotland
Northern Ireland
Irish Republic

1. Agriculture, Forestry & Fishing
2. Energy and Water Supply
3. Manufacturing
4. Construction
5. Wholesale Distribution, Hotels & Catering
6. Retail Distribution
7. Transport and Communications
8. Banking, Insurance and Finance
9. Public Administration and Defence
10. Education, Health and Other Services

Change in Manufacturing Employment by County 1961-1981 1:10 000 000

Increase
- 20% or more
- Up to 20%

Decrease
- Up to 20%
- 20-40%
- 40% or more

SCOTLAND
NORTHERN IRELAND
IRISH REPUBLIC
NORTH
YORKSHIRE & HUMBERSIDE
NORTH WEST
EAST MIDLANDS
WALES
WEST MIDLANDS
EAST ANGLIA
SOUTH EAST
SOUTH WEST

County statistics available for England, Scotland and Wales only.
No comparable information available for the Isle of Man.

Employment in the U.K. by Industry

Numbers employed '000

25000
20000
15000
10000
5000

1931 1941 1951 1961 1971 1981 1984

62% Services
7% Transport
26% Manufacturing
3% Mining & Energy Supply
2% Agriculture, Forestry & Fishing

Unemployment Rates for Selected Regions

Unemployment Rate (%)

20 18 16 14 12 10 8 6 4 2

1964 1966 1968 1970 1972 1974 1976 1978 1980 1982 1984

— — England : North
- - - England : South East
- - - Northern Ireland
—— Irish Republic
—— Scotland
···· Wales

Leisure
1:8 500 000

National Parks
National Park Direction Areas (Scotland)
National Forest Parks
Areas of Outstanding Natural Beauty (England & Wales)
National Scenic Areas (Scotland)

Coastal Conservation Zones (Scotland)
Heritage Coasts (England & Wales)
Long Distance Footpaths
Navigable Waterways
Canals

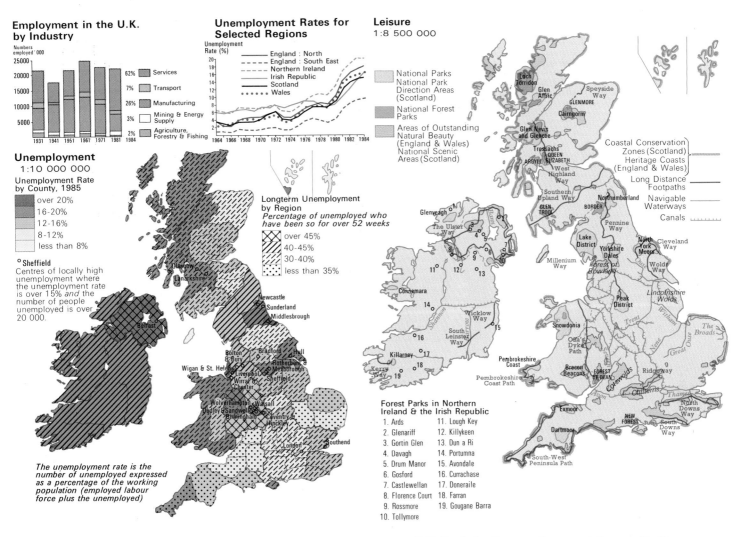

Unemployment
1:10 000 000

Unemployment Rate by County, 1985

over 20%
16-20%
12-16%
8-12%
less than 8%

○ Sheffield
Centres of locally high unemployment where the unemployment rate is over 15% *and* the number of people unemployed is over 20 000.

Longterm Unemployment by Region
Percentage of unemployed who have been so for over 52 weeks

over 45%
40-45%
30-40%
less than 35%

The unemployment rate is the number of unemployed expressed as a percentage of the working population (employed labour force plus the unemployed)

Forest Parks in Northern Ireland & the Irish Republic

1. Ards
2. Glenariff
3. Gortin Glen
4. Davagh
5. Drum Manor
6. Gosford
7. Castlewellan
8. Florence Court
9. Rossmore
10. Tollymore
11. Lough Key
12. Killykeen
13. Dun a Ri
14. Portumna
15. Avondale
16. Currachase
17. Doneraile
18. Farran
19. Gougane Barra

Top Ten Trading Partners with the U.K. by Value of Goods

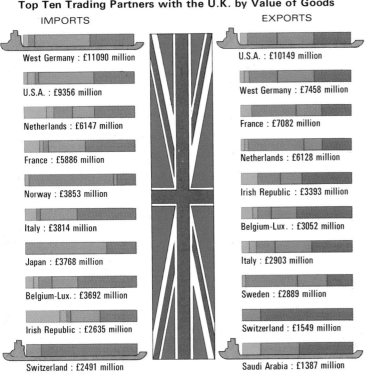

IMPORTS

West Germany : £11090 million
U.S.A. : £9356 million
Netherlands : £6147 million
France : £5886 million
Norway : £3853 million
Italy : £3814 million
Japan : £3768 million
Belgium-Lux. : £3692 million
Irish Republic : £2635 million
Switzerland : £2491 million

EXPORTS

U.S.A. : £10149 million
West Germany : £7458 million
France : £7082 million
Netherlands : £6128 million
Irish Republic : £3393 million
Belgium-Lux. : £3052 million
Italy : £2903 million
Sweden : £2889 million
Switzerland : £1549 million
Saudi Arabia : £1387 million

Food and drink
Raw materials
Fuel
Machinery and equipment
Manufactured goods

U.K. Trade by Country Group and Commodity Type
(percentages are given by value of trade)

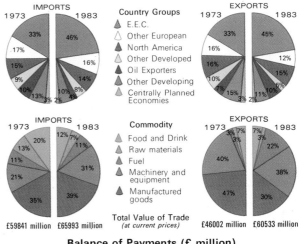

IMPORTS 1973 1983
33% 46%
17% 16%
15% 14%
9% 8%
10% 4%
13% 10%
3% 2%

EXPORTS 1973 1983
33% 45%
16% 12%
16% 15%
10% 6%
4% 10%
15% 11%
3% 2%

Country Groups
▲ E.E.C.
△ Other European
▲ North America
△ Other Developed
▲ Oil Exporters
▲ Other Developing
△ Centrally Planned Economies

IMPORTS 1973 1983
7% 12%
13% 7%
11% 11%
21% 31%
35% 39%
20%

Commodity
▲ Food and Drink
▲ Raw materials
▲ Fuel
▲ Machinery and equipment
▲ Manufactured goods

EXPORTS 1973 1983
3% 7%
7% 3%
40% 22%
47% 38%
30%

Total Value of Trade *(at current prices)*
£59841 million £65993 million
£46002 million £60533 million

Balance of Payments (£ million)

		1963	1973	1983
CREDITS	Visibles *(Exports)*	4331	11937	60625
	Invisibles	2515	8506	34975
	Total	6846	20443	95600
DEBITS	Visibles *(Imports)*	4450	14523	61341
	Invisibles	2271	6899	31343
	Total	6721	21422	92684
BALANCE		+125	−979	+2916

Visible trade involves transactions of goods while invisible trade involves transactions of money and services.

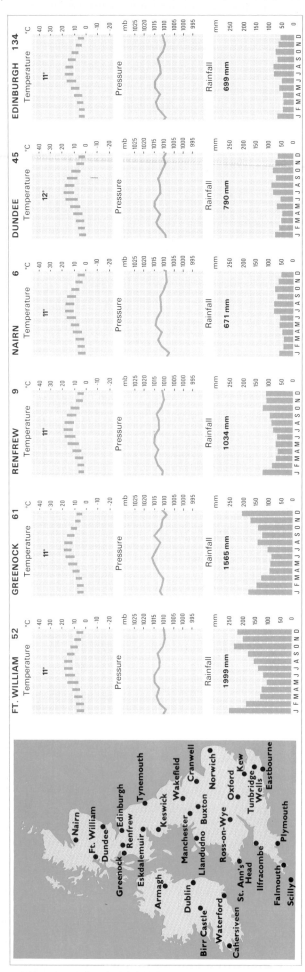

The climate graphs should be used in conjunction with the maps illustrating the climate of the British Isles on page 6. The stations have been selected to show climatic variations throughout the British Isles. On each graph the name of the station is followed by its height in metres above sea level, so that comparisons between stations can be made allowing for elevation. Temperature is shown by a bar, the top of the bar representing the mean monthly maximum and the bottom of the bar the mean monthly minimum temperature. A mid point between these is the mean monthly temperature; the mean annual range of temperature (in degrees Celsius) is given above the graph. The line on the pressure graphs shows the mean monthly pressure (in millibars reduced to sea level). The rainfall graphs show the average monthly rainfall and above them is given the average total annual rainfall (in millimetres).

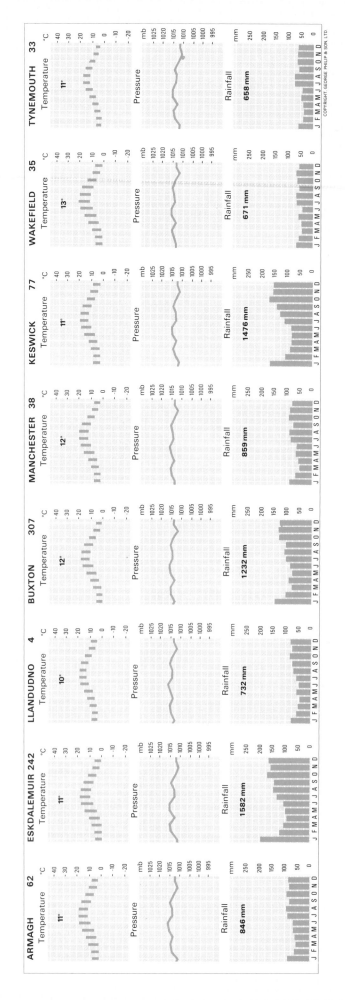

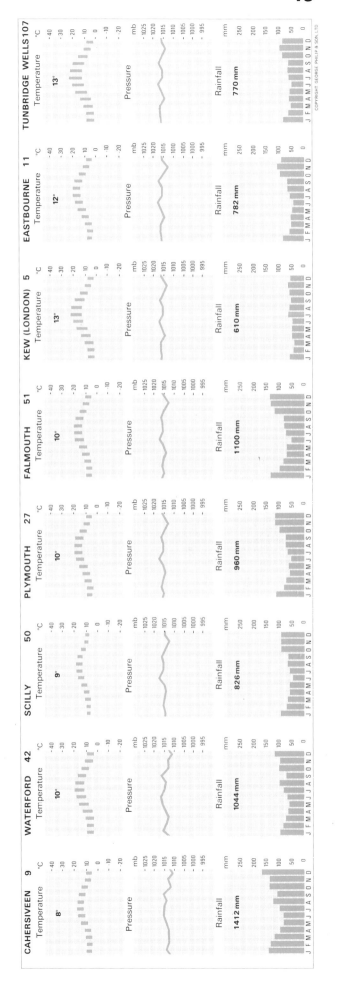

NORWICH 34 — Temperature 13° — Pressure — Rainfall 650 mm

CRANWELL 62 — Temperature 13° — Pressure — Rainfall 597 mm

OXFORD 63 — Temperature 13° — Pressure — Rainfall 653 mm

ILFRACOMBE 8 — Temperature 10° — Pressure — Rainfall 973 mm

ROSS-ON-WYE 68 — Temperature 12° — Pressure — Rainfall 709 mm

ST. ANN'S HEAD 43 — Temperature 9° — Pressure — Rainfall 945 mm

DUBLIN 16 — Temperature 10° — Pressure — Rainfall 696 mm

BIRR CASTLE 53 — Temperature 10° — Pressure — Rainfall 828 mm

TUNBRIDGE WELLS 107 — Temperature 13° — Pressure — Rainfall 770 mm

EASTBOURNE 11 — Temperature 12° — Pressure — Rainfall 782 mm

KEW (LONDON) 5 — Temperature 13° — Pressure — Rainfall 610 mm

FALMOUTH 51 — Temperature 10° — Pressure — Rainfall 1100 mm

PLYMOUTH 27 — Temperature 10° — Pressure — Rainfall 960 mm

SCILLY 50 — Temperature 9° — Pressure — Rainfall 826 mm

WATERFORD 42 — Temperature 10° — Pressure — Rainfall 1044 mm

CAHERSIVEEN 9 — Temperature 8° — Pressure — Rainfall 1412 mm

1:1 000 000

10   0   10   20   30   40 km

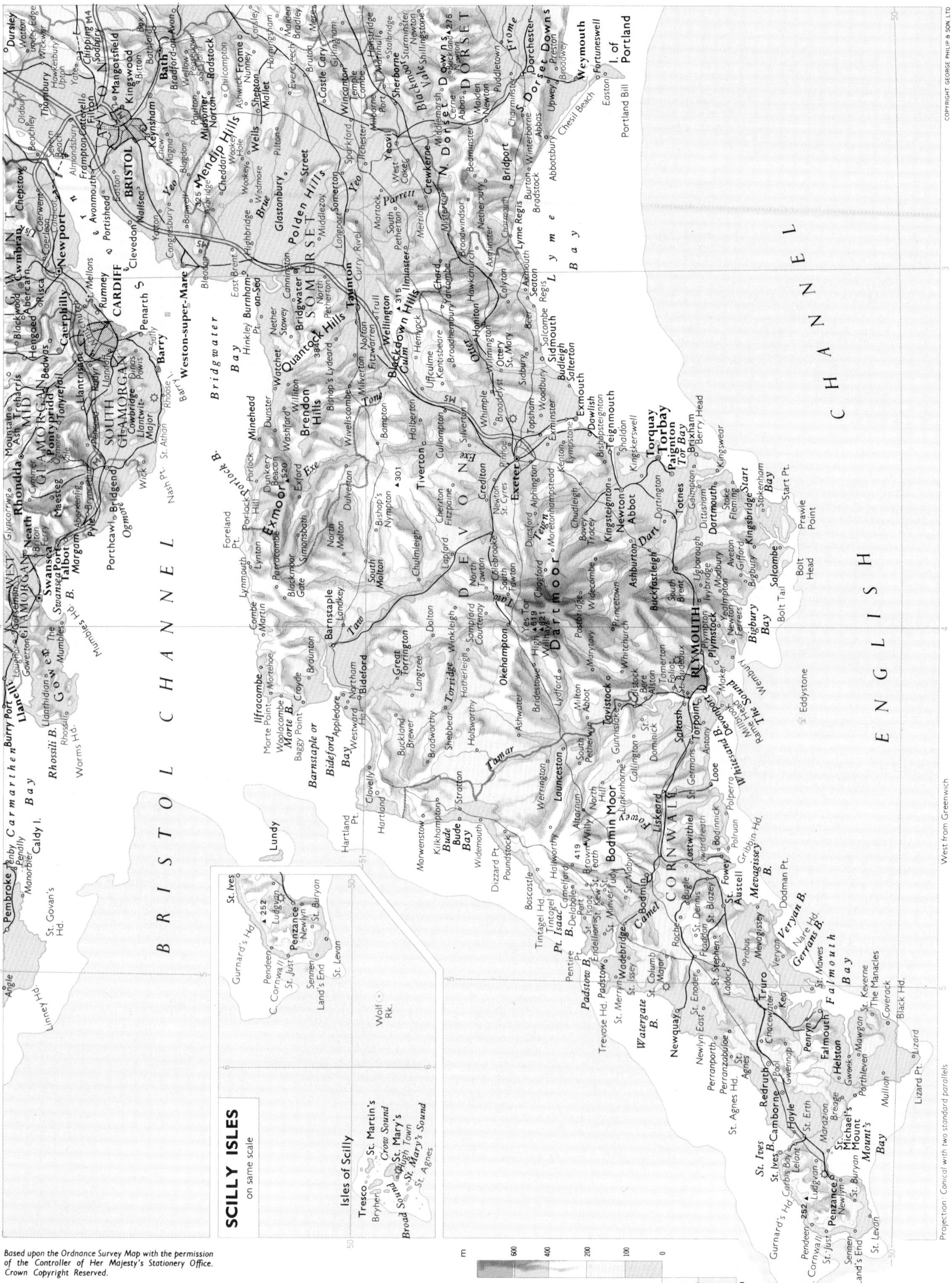

BRISTOL CHANNEL

ENGLISH CHANNEL

SCILLY ISLES
on same scale

Isles of Scilly

COPYRIGHT GEORGE PHILIP & SON, LTD.

West from Greenwich

Projection Conical with two standard parallels

m   600   400   200   100   0

0   50   m

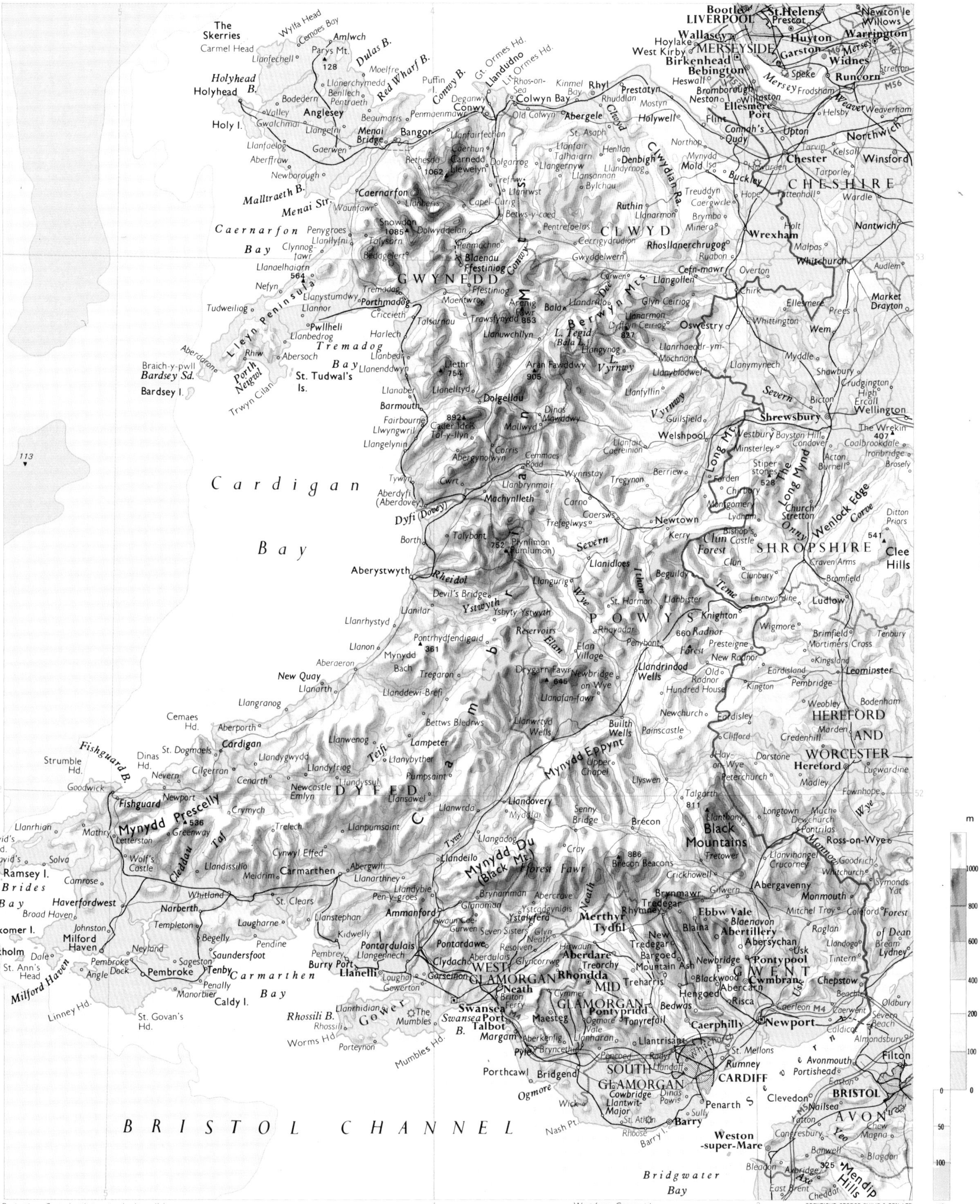

1:1 000 000

10 0 10 20 30 40 km

Cardigan

Bay

BRISTOL CHANNEL

GWYNEDD

CLWYD

POWYS

DYFED

WEST GLAMORGAN

MID GLAMORGAN

SOUTH GLAMORGAN

GWENT

SHROPSHIRE

HEREFORD AND WORCESTER

CHESHIRE

CARDIFF

Swansea

Newport

LIVERPOOL

MERSEYSIDE

Chester

Shrewsbury

Aberystwyth

Holyhead

Anglesey

Caernarfon

Bangor

Colwyn Bay

Wrexham

Carmarthen

Milford Haven

Haverfordwest

Fishguard

St. David's

Brecon Beacons

Black Mountains

Mynydd Eppynt

Menai Str.

Caernarfon Bay

Tremadog Bay

Carmarthen Bay

Milford Haven

St. Brides Bay

Bridgwater Bay

Mendip Hills

Projection: Conical with two standard parallels

West from Greenwich

m
1000
800
600
400
200
100
0
50
100
m

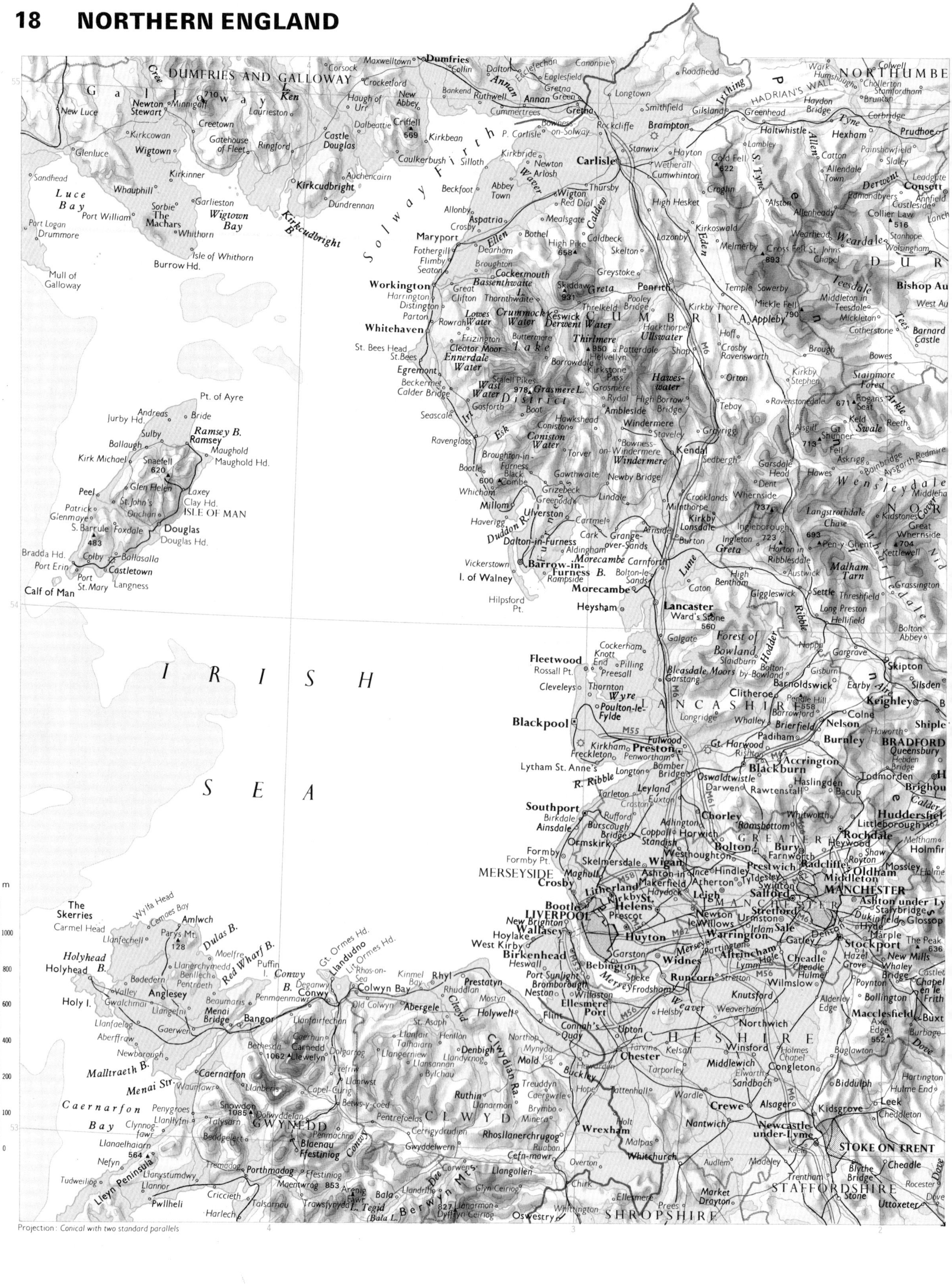

DUMFRIES AND GALLOWAY

NORTHUMBE...

HADRIAN'S WALL

Dumfries
Annan
Gretha
Carlisle
Brampton
Haltwhistle
Hexham
Prudhoe

Galloway
New Luce
Newton Stewart
Minnigaff
Wigtown
Kirkcowan
Glenluce
Kirkinner
Whauphill
Sorbie
Garlieston
Port William
Kirkcudbright
Dundrennan
Castle Douglas
Dalbeattie
Crocketford
Maxwelltown
Corsock
Crossmichael

Luce Bay
The Machars
Wigtown Bay
Whithorn
Isle of Whithorn
Burrow Hd.
Sandhead
Port Logan
Drummore
Mull of Galloway

Solway Firth
Kirkcudbright B.
Silloth
Abbey Town
Wigton
Maryport
Workington
Whitehaven
St. Bees Head
St. Bees
Egremont
Cleator Moor

CUMBRIA

Lake District
Keswick
Derwent Water
Bassenthwaite L.
Skiddaw 931
Thirlmere
Ullswater
Crummock Water
Buttermere
Ennerdale Water
Wast Water
Scafell Pikes 978
Grasmere L.
Ambleside
Windermere
Coniston Water
Kendal

Penrith
Appleby
Brough
Weardale
Teesdale
Bishop Au...
Barnard Castle
Cross Fell 893
Mickle Fell 790

Barrow-in-Furness
Morecambe
Heysham
Lancaster
Fleetwood
Cleveleys
Blackpool
Lytham St. Anne's
Southport
Formby
Crosby
LIVERPOOL
Bootle
Birkenhead
Wallasey
Hoylake
West Kirby

IRISH SEA

ISLE OF MAN
Pt. of Ayre
Ramsey
Ramsey B.
Snaefell 620
Peel
Douglas
Castletown
Port Erin
Port St. Mary
Calf of Man
Bradda Hd.

Preston
Blackburn
Burnley
BRADFORD
Bolton
Bury
Rochdale
Oldham
MANCHESTER
Salford
Wigan
Warrington
Stockport
Runcorn
Widnes
Northwich
CHESHIRE
Chester
Crewe
Nantwich
Wrexham
Whitchurch
Macclesfield
STOKE ON TRENT
STAFFORDSHIRE

GWYNEDD
CLWYD
Holyhead
Holy I.
Anglesey
Menai Bridge
Bangor
Caernarfon
Caernarfon Bay
Snowdon 1085
Carnedd Llewelyn 1062
Bala
Llangollen
Lleyn Peninsula
Pwllheli
Porthmadog
Blaenau Ffestiniog
Conwy
Colwyn Bay
Llandudno
Rhyl
Prestatyn
Holywell
Flint
Mold
Denbigh
Ruthin

SHROPSHIRE
Oswestry
Market Drayton

m
1000
800
600
400
200
100
50
0
m

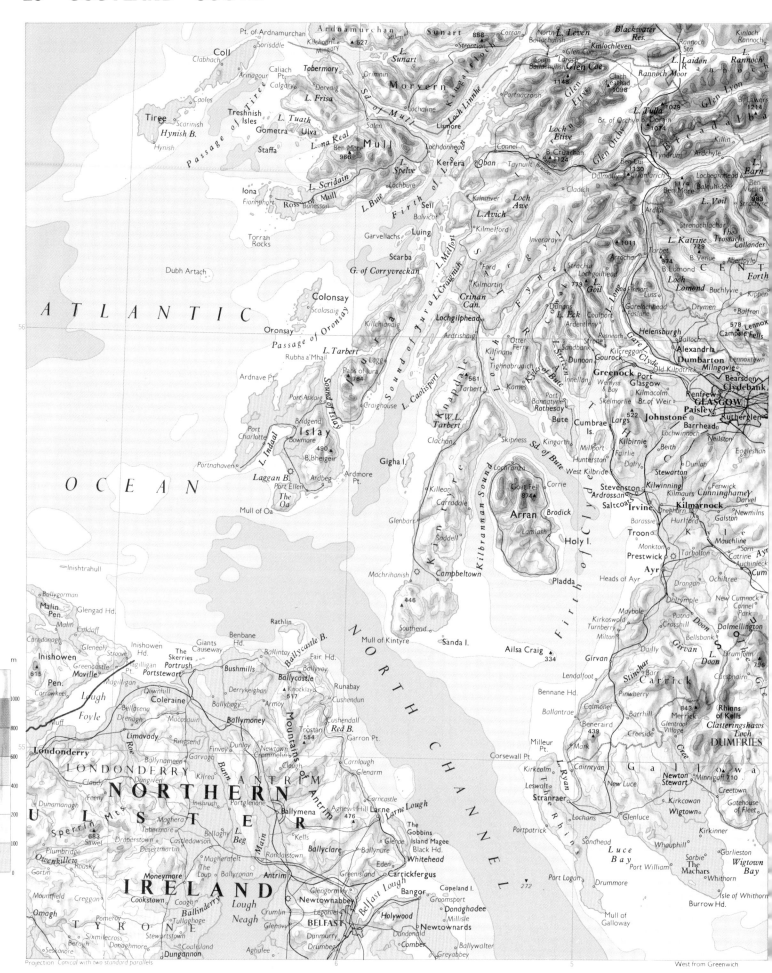

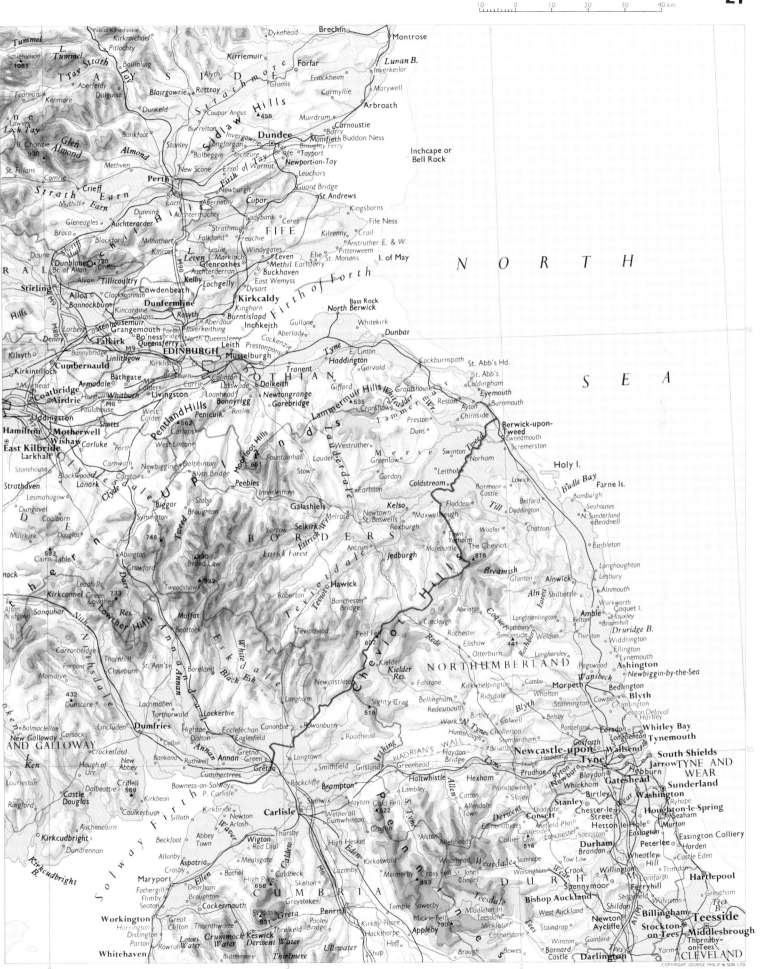

1:1 000 000

10 0 10 20 30 40 km

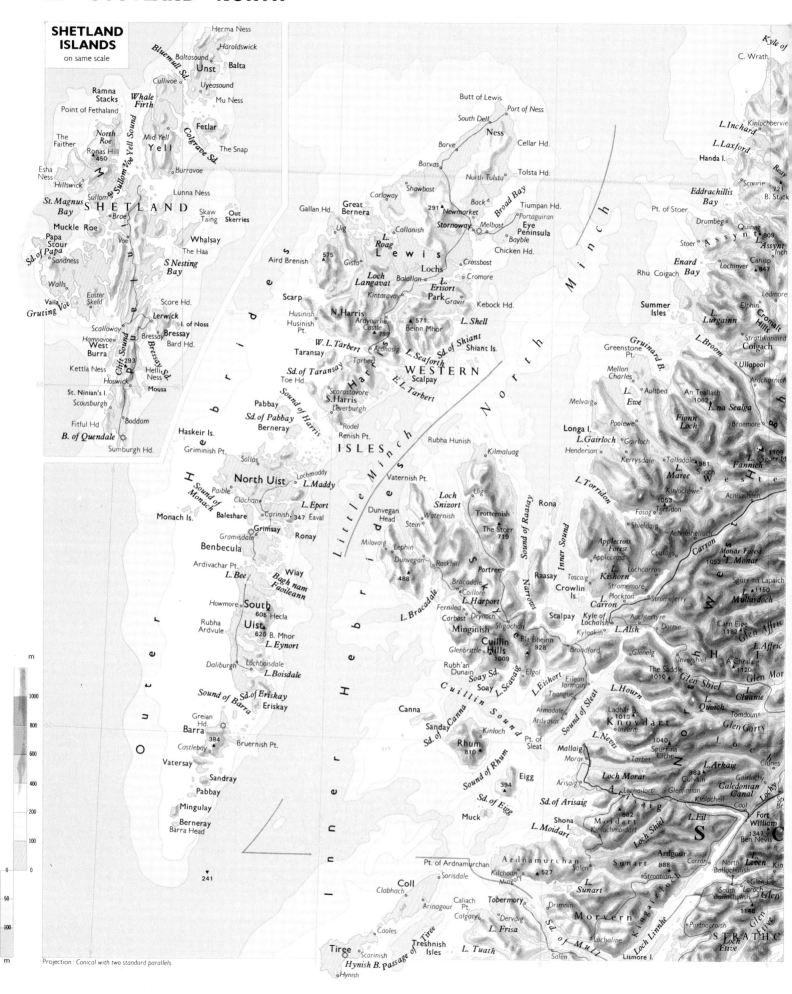

SHETLAND ISLANDS
on same scale

Herma Ness
Haroldswick
Baltasound
Balta
Bluemull Sd.
Cullivoe
Unst
Uyeasound
Mu Ness
Ramna Stacks
Whale Firth
Fetlar
Point of Fethaland
The Snap
The Faither
North Roe
Ronas Hill 450
Mid Yell
Yell
The Snap
Colgrave Sd.
Esha Ness
Hillswick
Sullom
Voe
Sullom Voe
Yell Sound
Burravoe
Lunna Ness
Skaw Taing
Out Skerries
SHETLAND
Brae
Voe
Muckle Roe
Papa Stour
Sandness
Sd. of Papa
Walls
Easter Skeld
Vaila Voe
Gruting
Whalsay
The Haa
S Nesting Bay
Score Hd.
Sandwick
I. of Noss
Lerwick
Bressay
Scalloway
Hamnavoe
Bressay Sd.
Bard Hd.
West Burra
Clift Sound
Helli Ness
Kettla Ness
Hoswick
Mousa
St. Ninian's I.
Scousburgh
Boddam
Fitful Hd.
B. of Quendale
Sumburgh Hd.

Kyle of
C. Wrath
Kinlochbervie
L. Inchard
L. Laxford
Handa I.
Rear
Scourie 121 B. Stack
Eddrachillis Bay
Pt. of Stoer
Drumbeg
Quinag 809
Stoer
Assynt
L. Assynt 847
Rhu Coigach
Lochinver
Canisp
Summer Isles
Elphin
Ledmore
Cromalt Hills
Lurgainn
L. Gairn
Strathkanaird
Coigach
Greenstone Pt.
Gruinard B.
L. Broom
Ullapool
Ardcharnich
Mellon Charles
L. Ewe
Aultbea
An Teallach 1062
Melvaig
Poolewe
Fionn Loch
L. na Sealga
Longa I.
L. Gairloch
Gairloch
Henderson
Kerrysdale
Talladale
981
L. Maree
1109
Sgurr M
Fannich
Slioch
1053
L. Torridon
Kinlochewe
Weste
Fasag
Torridon
Achnasheen
Shieldaig
1052 L. Monar
Applecross Forest
Coulags
Carron
Monar Forest
Applecross
Lochcarron
L. Monar
Kishorn
Stromeferry
1150
Carron
Plockton
Sgurr na Lapaich
Mullardoch
Scalpay
Kyle of Lochalsh
Carn Eige
1182
Auchtertyre
Glen Affric
Kyleakin
L. Alsh
Dornie
L. Affric
Broadford
Glenelg
Invershiel
A Chralaig
1120
Glen Mor
The Saddle
1010
Glen Shiel
L. Quoich
Cluanie
Tomdoun
Knoydart
Glen Garry
1040
Sgurr na Ciche
L. Arkaig
383
Gairlochy
Culvain
Caledonian Canal
Glenfinnan
Kinlocheil
882
Caol
Fort William
1347 Ben Nevis

Western Isles / Outer Hebrides

Butt of Lewis
Port of Ness
South Dell
Ness
Borve
Cellar Hd.
Barvas
North Tolsta
Tolsta Hd.
Carloway
Shawbost
Back
Tiumpan Hd.
Gallan Hd.
291 Newmarket
Broad Bay
Great Bernera
Stornoway
Portaguiran
Melbost
Eye Peninsula
Uig
Callanish
Bayble
L. Roag
Lewis
Chicken Hd.
575
Gisla
Lochs
Crossbost
Aird Brenish
Balallan
Cromore
Loch Langavat
L. Erisort
Scarp
Kintaravay
Park
Gravir
Husinish
N. Harris
Kebock Hd.
Husinish Pt.
Ardvourlie Castle
571
Beinn Mhor
L. Shell
799
W. L. Tarbert
Ardhasig
L. Seaforth
Sd. of Shiant
Taransay
Tarbert
Shiant Is.
Sd. of Taransay
WESTERN
Scalpay
Toe Hd.
E. L. Tarbert
Scarastavore
S. Harris
Leverburgh
Pabbay
Rodel
Sd. of Pabbay
Renish Pt.
Berneray
ISLES
Rubha Hunish
Haskeir Is.
Kilmaluag
Griminish Pt.
Vaternish Pt.
Sollas
North Uist
Lochmaddy
Uig
Trotternish
Paible
L. Maddy
Rona
Clachan
Dunvegan Head
Loch Snizort
Carinish
L. Eport
Waternish
The Storr 719
Monach Is.
Baleshare
347 Eaval
Stein
Grimsay
Milovaig
Lephin
Sound of Raasay
Gramsdale
Ronay
Dunvegan
Roskhill
Inner Sound
Benbecula
488
Portree
Ardivachar Pt.
Wiay
Bracadale
Raasay
Toscaig
L. Bee
Bagh nam Faoilleann
Coillore
Narrows
Crowlin Is.
Howmore
South Uist
605 Hecla
L. Harport
Stromemore
Fernilea
Carbost
Drynoch
Plockton
Rubha Ardvule
620 B. Mhor
Skye
Sligachan
Scalpay
L. Eynort
Carbost
Minginish
Bla Bheinn 928
Kyleakin
Daliburgh
Cuillin Hills 1009
Broadford
Lochboisdale
Glenbrittle
L. Boisdale
Rubh'an Dunain
Soay Sd.
Elgol
Eilean Iarmain
Sound of Eriskay
Soay
L. Scavaig
Teangue
Sd. of Eriskay
Eriskay
L. Eishort
Armadale
Greian Hd.
Ardvasar
Sound of Barra
Canna
Sound of Sleat
Barra
Cuillin Sound
L. Hourn
384
Sanday
Castlebay
Canna Sound
Vatersay
Kinloch
Pt. of Sleat
Mallaig
Bruernish Pt.
Sd. of Rhum
Rhum 810
Morar
Sandray
Eigg
Arisaig
Pabbay
Sound of Rhum
L. Arkaig
Mingulay
394
Sd. of Eigg
Berneray
Muck
Sd. of Arisaig
Barra Head
Shona I.
Moidart
Loch Morar
241
L. Moidart
Kinlochmoidart
L. Eil
Canna
Ardnamurchan
882
888
Pt. of Ardnamurchan
Sorisdale
Kilchoan
527
Salen
Coll
Mingary
Sunart
Ardgour
Clabhach
Strontian
Corran
Arinagour
L. Sunart
North Ballachulish
Tiree
Caliach Pt.
Calgary
Tobermory
Drimnin
Morvern
1148
Scarinish
Dervaig
L. Frisa
South Ballachulish
Hynish B.
passage of Tiree
L. Tuath
Lochaline
Loch Linnhe
STRATH
Hynish
Treshnish Isles
L. Tuath
Salen
Sd. of Mull
Lismore I.
Loch Etive

Scale (metres)

m
1000
800
600
400
200
100
0

m
0
50
100

1:1 000 000

10   0   10   20   30   40 km

ORKNEY ISLANDS
on same scale

Pentland Firth

NORTH

SEA

COPYRIGHT. GEORGE PHILIP & SON. LTD

Based upon the Ordnance Survey Map with the permission
of the Controller of Her Majesty's Stationery Office.
Crown Copyright Reserved.

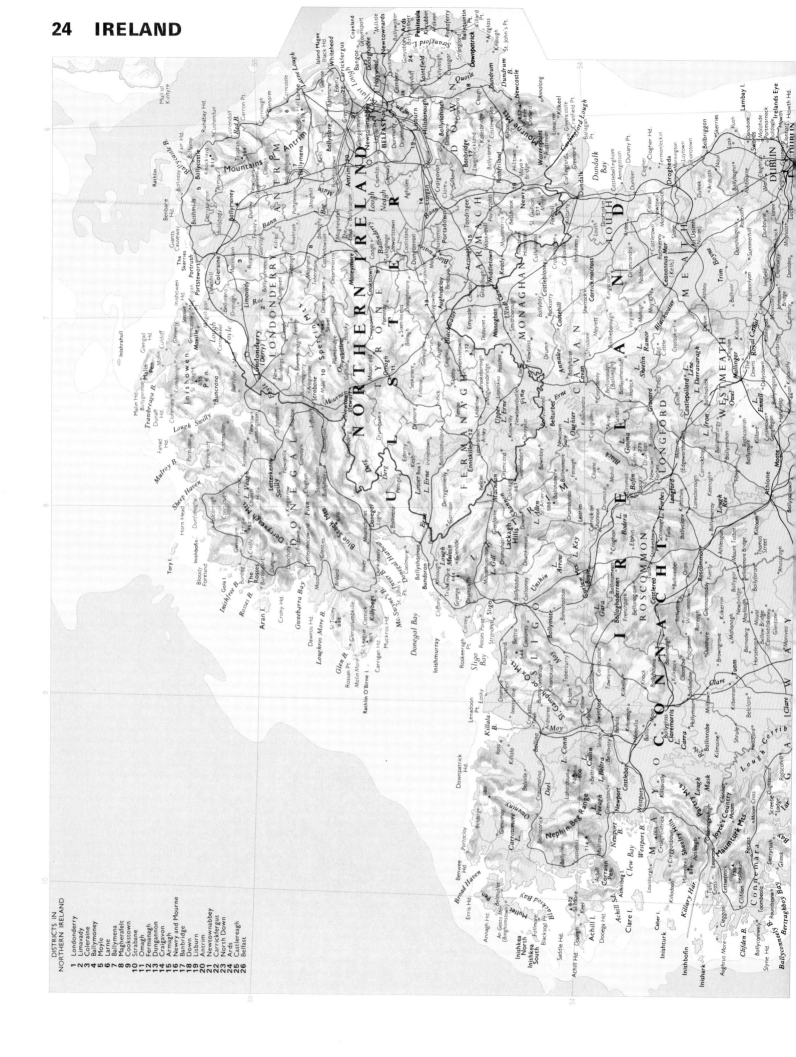

1:1 250 000

10 0 10 20 30 40 50 km

ATLANTIC OCEAN

LEINSTER

MUNSTER

CONNACHT

WICKLOW

WEXFORD

KILKENNY

TIPPERARY

WATERFORD

LIMERICK

CLARE

KERRY

CORK

OFFALY

LAOIS

KILDARE

Dún Laoghaire (Dunleary)

(Baile Átha Cliath)

Galway Bay

Galway

Cork

Cork Harbour

Bantry Bay

Dingle Bay

Kenmare R.

Macgillycuddy's Reeks

Comeragh Mts.

Knockmealdown Mts.

Galty Mts.

Dingle

Tralee

Killarney

Wexford

Waterford

Rosslare

Arklow

Wicklow

Bray

Aran Is.

Valentia I.

C. Clear

Fastnet Rock

West from Greenwich

Projection: Conical with two standard parallels

COPYRIGHT GEORGE PHILIP & SON LTD

m
1000
800
600
400
200
100
0

m
50
100

1:20 000 000

200   0   200   400   600   800 km

CASPIAN SEA

Ural Mountains

Tundra

Ob

Pechora

Vyichegda

Kama

Obshchiy Syrt

Volga Uplands

White Sea

Kola Peninsula

Kanin Peninsula

Mezen

N. Dvina

Onega

L. Onega

L. Ladoga

Rybinsk Res.

Volga

Oka

Don

Central Russian Uplands

Tsimlyansk Res.

Sea of Azov

Crimea

Manych

Terek

Caucasus
5633

Rion

Sevan

Ararat
5165

Van
L. Van

Kizil

Euphrates

BLACK SEA
2211

Anatolia
3916

Taurus

Cyprus 1951

Ukraine

Dnepr (Dnieper)

Bug

Pripyat (Pripet) Marshes

Dnestr (Dniester)

Prut

Danube

Siret

Carpathians

Transylvanian Alps

Wallachia

Balkans

Rhodope

Balkan Peninsula

Pindus

Morea

C. Matapan

5121

Ionian Is.

Ionian Sea

Aegean Sea

Crete

North Cape

Nordkinn

Lapland

Scandinavia

Kjølen

Glittertind
2469

Galdhöpiggen
2123

Vesterålen

Lofoten

Torne

Kemijoki

Finland

G. of Bothnia

G. of Finland

Neva

L. Chudskoye

Gotland

G. of Riga

Niemen

Wisła (Vistula)

Tatra
2655

Plain of Hungary

Danube

Tisza

Drava

Sava

Morava

Dinaric Alps

ADRIATIC SEA

Str. of Otranto

Calabria

Str. of Messina

Sicily
3263

Etna

Malta

MEDITERRANEAN SEA

NORWEGIAN SEA
3734

Iceland
2119

Hekla
1491

Öraefajökull

SOUTH EAST ICELAND

Faroe Bank

Rockall
4461

Rockall

Hebrides

British Isles

Ireland

Great Britain
1344

Ben Nevis

Shetland Is.

Orkney Is.

NORTH SEA

Dogger Bank

Helgoland

Jutland

Skagerrak

Kattegat

Vänern

Vättern

Mälaren

BALTIC SEA

North European Plain

Oder (Odra)

Elbe

Weser

Harz
1142

Erz Geb.

Bohemian For.

Sudetes

Moravian Heights

Black For.

Thüringer Wald

Rhine

Vosges

Ardennes

Meuse

Netherlands

German Bight

Dogger Bank

FISHER

VIKING

FORTIES

CROMARTY

FORTH

TYNE

HUMBER

THAMES

DOVER

Channel

WIGHT

PORTLAND

PLYMOUTH

Bristol Channel

Irish Sea

Snowdon
1085

Land's End

English Channel

Brittany

Seine

Loire

Gironde

Garonne

Bay of Biscay

FINISTERRE

SOLE

SHANNON

FASTNET

LUNDY

BAILEY

HEBRIDES

FAIR ISLE

FAEROES

Faroe Is.

Fisher Bank

Valentia I.

C. Clear

C. Finisterre

ATLANTIC OCEAN

Alps
4807
Mt. Blanc

Jura

Apennines
2914

Vesuvius
1277

Tyrrhenian Sea

Ligurian Sea

Corsica

Sardinia

C. Bonifacio

Rhône

G. of Lion

Central Massif
1886
Mt. Dore

Cévennes

Pyrenees
3404

Cantabrian Mts.

Old Castile

New Castile

Iberian Peninsula

Sierra Morena

Andalusia

Sierra Nevada
3478

Guadalquivir

C. St. Vincent

C. Trafalgar

Str. of Gibraltar

Rif

Maritime Atlas

Plateau of the Shotts

Ebro

Douro

Tagus

Guadiana

Projection Bonne   0° West from Greenwich 0° East from Greenwich

Sea areas named in ROCKALL weather forecasts

m 4000 2000 1000 400 200 0 200 2000 4000 m

1 : 20 000 000

200 0 200 400 600 800 km

COPYRIGHT GEORGE PHILIP & SON LTD

UNION OF SOVIET SOCIALIST REPUBLICS

Nizhniy Tagil
Sverdlovsk
Chelyabinsk
Magnitogorsk
Orenburg
Ufa
Kuybyshev
Perm
Ob
Kotlas
Kirov
Kazan
Ulyanovsk
Penza
Saratov
Tambov
Voronezh
Volgograd
Uralsk
Ural
Guryev

MOSCOW
Gorki
Ivanovo
Yaroslavl
Kostroma
Vologda
Rybinsk L.
Ryazan
Tula
Orel
Kursk
Kharkov
Dnepropetrovsk
Donetsk
Zaporozhye
Taganrog
Rostov
Voroshilovgrad
Krasnodar
Stavropol
Astrakhan
Don
Volga
Penza

N. Dvina
Arkhangelsk
Onega
L. Onega
White Sea
Murmansk

CASPIAN SEA
KAZAKHSTAN
Baku
AZERBAIJAN
Tbilisi
GEORGIA
ARMENIA
Yerevan
Tabriz
IRAN (PERSIA)
Baghdad
IRAQ
SYRIA
Aleppo (Halab)
Homs
Mosul
Erzurum
Diyarbakir
Euphrates
Tigris

RUSSIA
WHITE RUSSIA
Minsk
Smolensk
Vitebsk
Mogilev
Gomel
Chernigov
Kiev
Zhitomir
Lvov
Pripyat
Brest
Bialystok
Lublin
Kishinev
MOLDAVIA
Odessa
Nikolayev
Kherson
Krivoy Rog
Dnepr (Dnieper)
U. Dnestr (Dniestr)

Leningrad
L. Ladoga
Vyborg
Kronstadt
Chudskoye
ESTONIA
Tallinn
LATVIA
Riga
LITHUANIA
Vilnius
Kaunas
Kaliningrad

FINLAND
Helsinki
Tampere
Oulu

NORWAY
SWEDEN
Stockholm
Kiruna
Narvik
Lulea
Lule
Ume
Sundsvall
Gävle
Uppsala
Vänern
Vättern
Jönköping
Göteborg
Oslo
Bergen
Stavanger
Trondheim
Tromsö
Hammerfest
Hardanger Fd.
Sogne Fd.
Skagerrak
Kattegat
Gulf of Bothnia
BALTIC SEA

Hammerfest

DENMARK
COPENHAGEN
Aarhus
Aalborg
Malmö
Odense
Kiel

POLAND
WARSAW
Lódz
Kraków
Poznań
Wroclaw (Breslau)
Gdańsk
Szczecin
Bydgoszcz
Katowice
Wisla (Vistula)
Odra (Oder)

GERMANY
East
West
BERLIN
Hamburg
Bremen
Hanover
Magdeburg
Leipzig
Dresden
Halle
Karl-Marx-Stadt (Chemnitz)
Cologne
Dortmund
Essen
Düsseldorf
Frankfurt
Munich
Nuremberg
Stuttgart
Mannheim
Wiesbaden
Elbe
Weser
Rhine

CZECHOSLOVAKIA
PRAGUE
Bratislava
Brno
Ostrava

AUSTRIA
VIENNA
Graz
Salzburg
Linz

HUNGARY
BUDAPEST
Debrecen
Miskolc
Szeged
Pécs

ROMANIA
BUCHAREST
Cluj
Timişoara
Brasov
Galati
Ploiesti
Constanta
Danube

BULGARIA
Sofia
Plovdiv
Varna

YUGOSLAVIA
Belgrade
Zagreb
Sarajevo
Split
Ljubljana
Skopje
Niš

ALBANIA
Tiranë

GREECE
ATHENS
Thessaloníki
Pátrai
Kérkyra
Kríti (Crete)

SWITZERLAND
Bern
Zürich
Geneva
Basle
Lausanne

ITALY
ROME
Milan
Naples
Turin
Genoa
Venice
Bologna
Florence
Palermo
Catania
Messina
Bari
Taranto
Trieste
Verona
Sardinia
Sicily
Tiber
ADRIATIC SEA
Tyrrhenian Sea
Ionian Sea

FRANCE
PARIS
Marseilles
Lyons
Nantes
Bordeaux
Toulouse
Lille
Strasbourg
Nice
Dijon
Nancy
Rouen
Le Havre
St. Etienne
Limoges
Toulon
Metz
Reims
Seine
Loire
Rhône
Garonne
Cherbourg
Brest
Monaco
BAY OF BISCAY

BELGIUM
Brussels
Antwerp
LUX.

NETHERLANDS
Amsterdam
The Hague
Rotterdam
Groningen

UNITED KINGDOM
LONDON
ENGLAND
SCOTLAND
WALES
Glasgow
Edinburgh
Aberdeen
Dundee
Newcastle
Leeds
Sheffield
Manchester
Liverpool
Birmingham
Bristol
Cardiff
Swansea
Hull
Bradford
Nottingham
Plymouth
Southampton
Portsmouth
Norwich
N.I.
Belfast
Hebrides
Shetland Is.
Orkney Is.
I. of Man
English Channel
Is. of Scilly
Ushant

IRELAND
Dublin
Cork
C. Clear

ICELAND
Reykjavik
Faroe Is. (Don.)

ATLANTIC OCEAN
NORTH SEA
IRISH SEA
Arctic Circle

SPAIN
MADRID
Barcelona
Valencia
Sevilla
Zaragoza
Bilbao
Málaga
Murcia
Granada
Córdoba
Valladolid
Alicante
Cádiz
Oviedo
Gibraltar (Br.)
Balearic Is.
Mallorca (Majorca)
Menorca (Minorca)
Palma
Ebro
Duero
Guadiana
Tagus
Guadalquivir
La Coruña
Vigo
C. Finisterre
Andorra

PORTUGAL
Lisbon
Oporto
Douro

MOROCCO
Rabat
Fès
Meknès
Tangier
Str. of Gibraltar

ALGERIA
Algiers
Oran
Constantine
Annaba (Bône)

TUNISIA
Tunis
Sousse

MALTA
Valletta
Corsica
Ajaccio
Sardinia
Cagliari
Pantelleria (Ital.)

MEDITERRANEAN SEA
BLACK SEA
BALTIC SEA

TURKEY
ANATOLIA
Ankara
Istanbul
Izmir
Bursa
Konya
Adana
Kayseri
Samsun
Sevastopol
Sea of Azov

CYPRUS
Nicosia
Limassol

LONDON Capital Cities

Projection Bonne   West from Greenwich   0   East from Greenwich

JULY TEMPERATURE

ACTUAL SURFACE TEMPERATURE
°C
30
25
20
15
10
5
0

Prevailing Winds
Cold Current
Warm Current

North Atlantic Drift

Arctic Circle

JANUARY TEMPERATURE

ACTUAL SURFACE TEMPERATURE
°C
10
5
0
−5
−10
−15
−20

Prevailing Winds
Cold Current
Warm Current

North Atlantic Drift

Arctic Circle

NATURAL VEGETATION

Coniferous Forest
Broad-leaved Forest and Meadow
Evergreen Trees and Shrubs
Grassland
Steppe: Moorland and Semi-desert
Desert
Alpine and Tundra

Ural Mountains
Caucasus
Carpathians
Balkan Pen.
Pindus
Dinaric Alps
Apennines
Alps
Scandinavia
Pyrenees
Sa. Nevada

ANNUAL RAINFALL
mm
1 500
1 000
750
500
250

Helsinki
Bucharest
Athens
Moscow
Vienna
Marseilles
Bergen
Reykjavik
London
Lisbon

Average monthly temperature
Average monthly rainfall

1:20 000 000

200   0   200   400   600   800 km

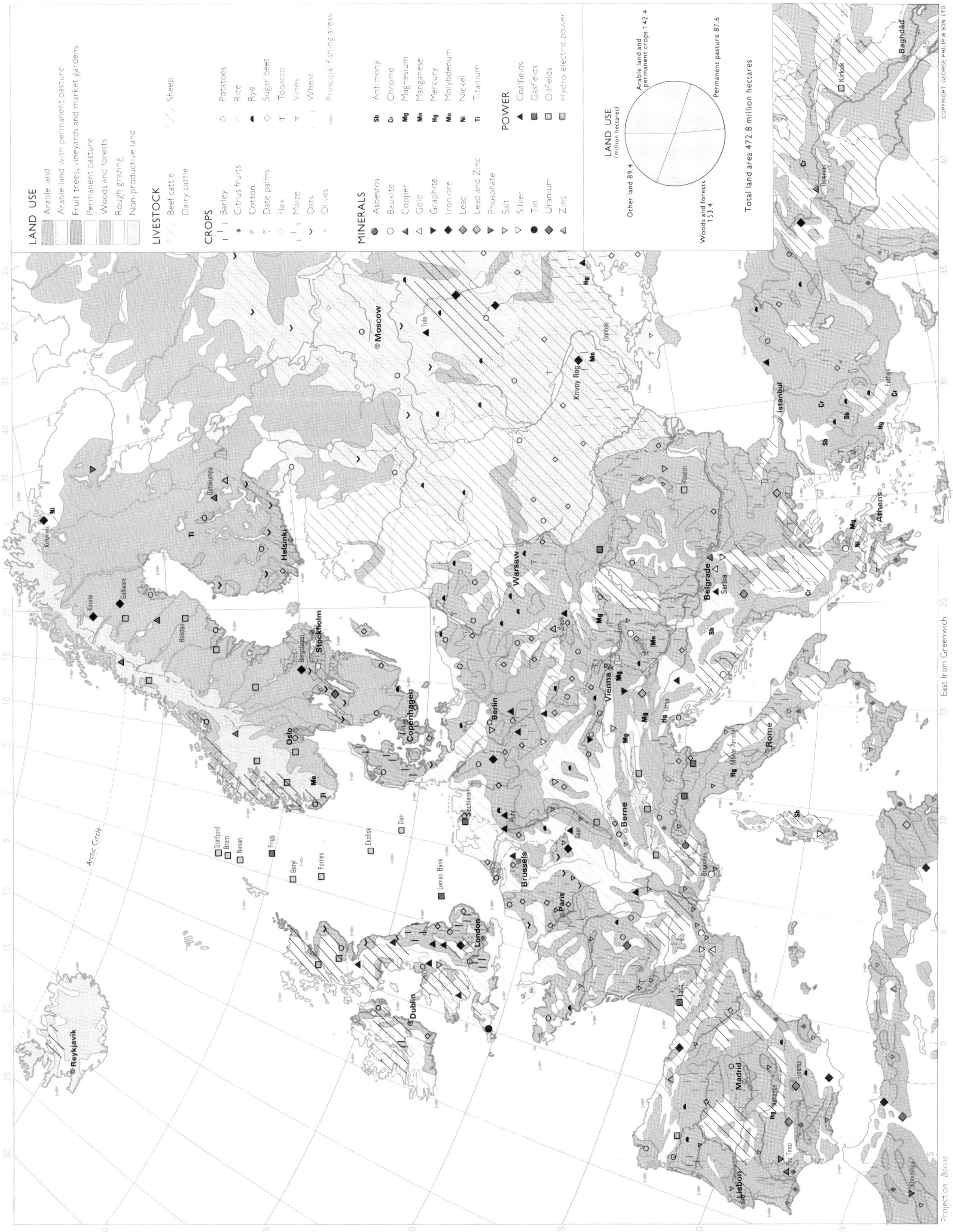

LAND USE

- Arable land
- Arable land with permanent pasture
- Fruit trees, vineyards and market gardens
- Permanent pasture
- Woods and forests
- Rough grazing
- Non-productive land

LIVESTOCK

- Beef cattle
- Dairy cattle
- Sheep

CROPS

Barley	◦ Potatoes
Citrus fruits	◦ Rice
Cotton	◦ Rye
Date palms	◊ Sugar beet
Flax	T Tobacco
Maize	▽ Vines
Oats	· Wheat
Olives	Principal fishing areas

MINERALS

◐ Asbestos	**Sb** Antimony
◦ Bauxite	**Cr** Chrome
◁ Copper	**Mg** Magnesium
△ Gold	**Mn** Manganese
▶ Graphite	**Hg** Mercury
◆ Iron ore	**Mo** Molybdenum
◇ Lead	**Ni** Nickel
◈ Lead and Zinc	**Ti** Titanium
▷ Phosphate	
▽ Salt	
▷ Silver	**POWER**
● Tin	▲ Coalfields
◆ Uranium	■ Gasfields
◁ Zinc	□ Oilfields
	▣ Hydro-electric power

LAND USE
(million hectares)

Arable land and permanent crops 142.4

Other land 89.4

Woods and forests 153.4

Permanent pasture 87.6

Total land area 472.8 million hectares

COPYRIGHT GEORGE PHILIP & SON LTD

Projection: Bonne   East from Greenwich

Arctic Circle

Place names: Reykjavik, Dublin, London, Brussels, Paris, Madrid, Lisbon, Berne, Rome, Berlin, Copenhagen, Oslo, Stockholm, Helsinki, Warsaw, Vienna, Belgrade, Istanbul, Athens, Moscow, Baghdad, Kirkuk, Kristiansund, Kiruna, Gällivare, Boliden, Outokumpu, Ruhr, Saar, Plzeň, Krivoy Rog, Tula, Statfjord, Brent, Ninian, Frigg, Beryl, Forties, Ekofisk, Dan, Leman Bank, Rio Tinto, Kirkuk

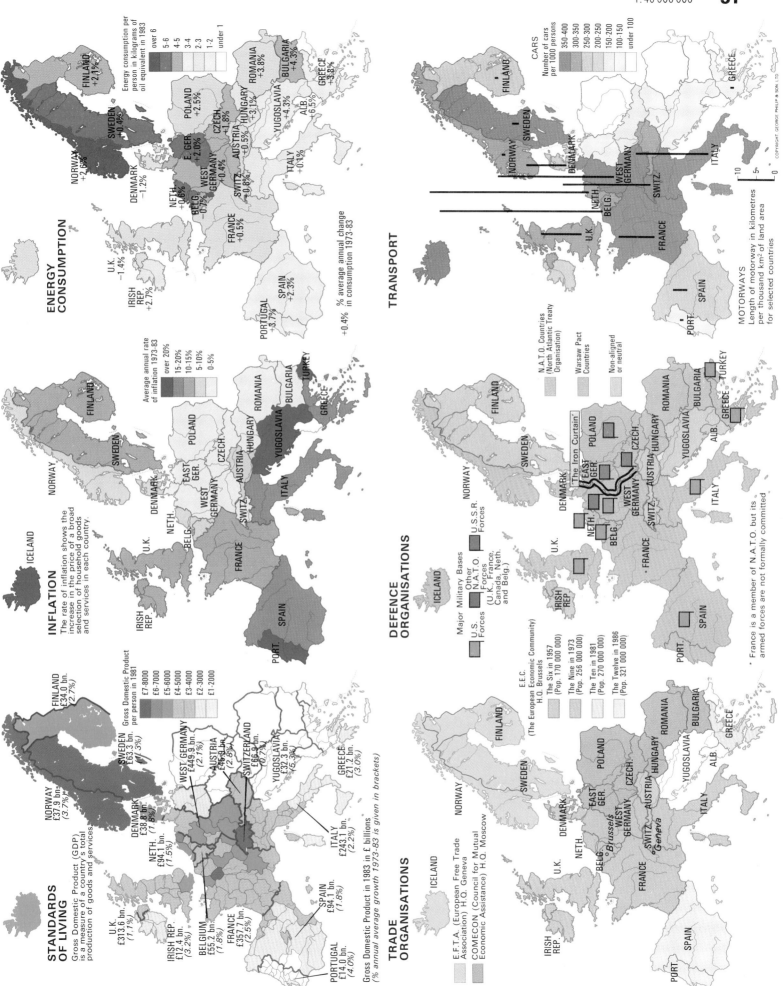

STANDARDS OF LIVING

Gross Domestic Product (GDP) is a measure of a country's total production of goods and services

NORWAY
£37.9 bn.
(3.7%)

FINLAND
£34.0 bn.
(2.7%)

SWEDEN
£63.3 bn.
(1.3%)

DENMARK
£38.8 bn.
(1.8%)

U.K.
£313.6 bn.
(1.1%)

IRISH REP.
£12.4 bn.
(3.2%)

NETH.
£94.1 bn.
(1.5%)

WEST GERMANY
£449.9 bn.
(2.1%)

BELGIUM
£55.2 bn.
(1.8%)

AUSTRIA
£46.9 bn.
(2.8%)

SWITZERLAND
£66.9 bn.
(0.7%)

YUGOSLAVIA
£32.3 bn.
(5.3%)

FRANCE
£357.1 bn.
(2.5%)

ITALY
£243.1 bn.
(2.2%)

SPAIN
£94.1 bn.
(1.8%)

PORTUGAL
£14.0 bn.
(4.0%)

GREECE
£21.2 bn.
(3.0%)

Gross Domestic Product (GDP)
per person in 1981

£7-8000
£6-7000
£5-6000
£4-5000
£3-4000
£2-3000
£1-2000

Gross Domestic Product in 1983 in £ billions
(% annual average growth 1973-83 is given in brackets)

TRADE ORGANISATIONS

E.F.T.A. (European Free Trade Association) H.Q. Geneva

COMECON (Council for Mutual Economic Assistance) H.Q. Moscow

E.E.C.
(The European Economic Community)
H.Q. Brussels

The Six in 1957
(Pop. 170 000 000)

The Nine in 1973
(Pop. 256 000 000)

The Ten in 1981
(Pop. 270 000 000)

The Twelve in 1986
(Pop. 321 000 000)

INFLATION

The rate of inflation shows the increase in the price of a broad selection of household goods and services in each country.

Average annual rate of inflation 1973-83

over 20%
15-20%
10-15%
5-10%
0-5%

DEFENCE ORGANISATIONS

Major Military Bases

U.S. Forces

Other N.A.T.O. Forces (U.K., France, Canada, Neth. and Belg.)

U.S.S.R. Forces

N.A.T.O. Countries (North Atlantic Treaty Organisation)

Warsaw Pact Countries

Non-aligned or neutral

'The Iron Curtain'

* France is a member of N.A.T.O. but its armed forces are not formally committed

ENERGY CONSUMPTION

NORWAY +2.6%

FINLAND +2.1%

SWEDEN +0.4%

DENMARK −1.2%

NETH. +0.6%

BELG. −0.7%

WEST GERMANY −0.4%

E. GER. +2.0%

POLAND +2.5%

CZECH. +1.8%

AUSTRIA +0.8%

SWITZ. +0.8%

HUNGARY +0.5%

ROMANIA +3.8%

BULGARIA +4.3%

YUGOSLAVIA +3.1%

ALB. +6.5%

GREECE +3.8%

ITALY +0.1%

FRANCE +0.5%

U.K. −1.4%

IRISH REP. +2.7%

SPAIN +2.3%

PORTUGAL +3.7%

Energy consumption per person in kilograms of oil equivalent in 1983

over 6
5-6
4-5
3-4
2-3
1-2
under 1

+0.4% % average annual change in consumption 1973-83

TRANSPORT

CARS

Number of cars per 1000 persons

350-400
300-350
250-300
200-250
150-200
100-150
under 100

MOTORWAYS
Length of motorway in kilometres per thousand km² of land area for selected countries

	Population					Growth			Land			Agriculture		
	Total	Density	Birth Rate	Death Rate	Life Expectancy	1965-73	1973-83	Urban	Area	Arable	Forest	Agricultural Population	Index of Production	Food intake
	th.	persons per km²	per th. popn.		yrs.	av. % per annum		%	th. km²	th. km²	th. km²	% of total popn.	1974-76 = 100	calories per day
Albania	2 901	107	26	6	71	2.6	2.1	38	27	7	12	58	130	3 063
Austria	7 552	91	12	12	73	0.4	0.2	56	83	16	33	7.9	113	3 426
Belgium*	9 877	329	12	11	73	0.4	0.1	89	30	8.3	7.0	2.7	104	3 774
Bulgaria	8 961	81	14	11	70	0.6	0.1	67	111	42	39	30	118	3 622
Czechoslovakia	15 459	124	15	12	70	0.3	0.6	65	125	52	46	8.8	117	3 395
Denmark	5 112	122	10	11	74	0.7	0.2	85	42	27	4.9	6.1	120	3 548
Finland	4 882	16	14	9	73	0.2	0.4	60	305	24	233	11	115	3 079
France	54 947	101	14	10	75	0.8	0.4	80	546	186	146	7.5	115	3 530
Germany,East	16 671	157	14	13	71	0.5	0.1	76	106	50	30	8.7	102	3 689
Germany,West	61 181	251	10	11	75	0.7	0.1	86	244	75	73	3.3	113	3 351
Greece	9 896	76	14	9	75	0.5	1.1	64	131	39	26	35	105	3 668
Hungary	10 665	116	12	14	70	0.3	0.3	55	92	53	16	14	126	3 484
Iceland	239	2.3	18	7	77	1.6	0.8	89	100	0.1	1.2	10	108	3 274
Ireland	3 535	51	19	9	73	0.8	1.3	56	69	9.7	3.3	19	106	3 699
Italy	56 983	194	11	10	76	0.6	0.3	71	294	124	64	9.5	113	3 688
Luxembourg*	363	140	12	11	69	0.9	0.2	78	2.6					
Malta	380	1 267	15	8	71	0.1	1.8	85	0.3	0.1		4.5	152	2 843
Netherlands	14 420	424	12	8	76	1.1	0.7	52	34	8.6	2.9	4.7	123	3 618
Norway	4 140	13	12	10	77	0.8	0.4	55	308	8.4	83	6.7	117	3 392
Poland	36 914	121	19	10	71	0.7	0.9	59	305	148	87	28	97	3 479
Portugal	10 164	110	14	9	71	0.2	1.1	30	92	36	36	24	84	3 205
Romania	22 897	100	15	10	71	1.2	0.8	51	230	105	63	45	117	3 346
Spain	38 717	76	13	7	75	1.0	1.0	76	499	205	156	15	108	3 296
Sweden	8 337	20	11	11	78	0.7	0.2	85	412	30	264	4.3	102	3 146
Switzerland	6 442	161	11	9	79	1.2	0.2	59	40	4.1	11	4.6	116	3 455
U.K.	55 624	230	13	12	74	0.4	0.1	91	242	70	21	1.8	120	3 249
Yugoslavia	22 963	90	17	10	69	0.9	0.8	45	255	78	93	34	116	3 550
U.S.S.R.	275 000	12	20	10	69	0.9	0.9	65	22 272	2 323	9 200	15	108	3 360

*Many figures for Luxembourg included in Belgium.

Population. This is the United Nations' estimate for the mid-year 1984 (thousands).

Population density. This is the quoted population total divided by the quoted land area (persons per square kilometre).

Birth Rates and Death Rates. These are the registered or United Nations' estimated rates per thousand population.

Life Expectancy. This figure indicates the number of years that a child born today can expect to live if the levels of death of today last throughout its life. The figure is an average of that for men and women. The figure for women is usually higher than that for men (U.K. male 70, female 76 years).

Population Growth. This shows the average annual percentage change in population for two periods 1965-1973 and 1973-1983.

Urbanization. This is the percentage of the total population living in urban areas. The definition of urban is that of the individual nation and usually includes quite small towns.

Land Area. This is the total area of the country minus the area covered by major lakes and rivers (thousand square kilometres).

Arable Land and Permanent Crops. This excludes fallow land but includes temporary pasture (thousand square kilometres).

Forest and Woodland. This includes natural and planted woodland and land recently cleared of timber which will be replanted (thousand square kilometres).

Agricultural Population. This is the percentage of the economically active population working in agriculture. It includes those people working also in forestry, hunting and fishing.

Index of Agricultural Production. The base period for this index is 1974-1976 and it shows the level of production in each country in 1983 in comparision with that of the earlier period. Only edible crops and meat are included.

Food Supply. The figures are the average intake per person in calories per day in the period 1979-1981.

Trade		Education		Health	Energy	Consumer Price Index	G.N.P		G.D.P. Part formed by		Loans & Debt		
Imports	Exports	Primary	Secondary	Popn. per doctor	Consumption in kgs of oil equiv. per capita	1970 = 100	US$ per capita	Growth per capita % per yr. 1973-82	Agric.	Indust.	end 1983 US$ millions	as % of GNP	
US$ per capita		% of age group							%				
		100	66		982								Albania
2 598	2 083	99	74	400	3 083	234	9 210	2.7	4	31	181	0.3	Austria
5 395	5 049	98	94	400	4 401	286	9 160	1.6	2	28	410	0.6	Belgium*
1 414	1 432	100	82	410	4 390		3 800		19	48			Bulgaria
1 105	1 112	89	46	360	4 691	123	5 000		7	61			Czechoslovakia
3 322	3 196	98	100	480	3 061	376	11 490	1.2	5	18	449	0.9	Denmark
2 549	2 768	98	98	530	4 649	443	10 440	2.2	8	29	178	0.4	Finland
1 888	1 698	100	87	580	3 429	398	10 390	2.2	4	28	3 790	0.8	France
1 376	1 490	94	88	520	5 370		6 800		9	73			Germany,East
2 489	2 758	100	94	450	4 156	199	11 420	2.3	2	36	2 767	0.5	Germany,West
960	486	100	81	430	1 790	959	3 970	2.4	16	21			Greece
760	803	100	73	400	2 968	216	2 150	5.6	15	37			Hungary
3 417	3 033	100		488	3 364	9 898	10 270	1.7					Iceland
2 730	2 720	100	95	780	2 354	640	4 810	1.3	11	35			Ireland
1 414	1 292	100	74	340	2 458	708	6 350	2.0	6	35	1 105	0.3	Italy
		100		495	9 000	266	12 190	2.3	2	33			Luxembourg*
1 887	1 037	100		383	1 180	99	3 710	9.1	3	37			Malta
4 309	4 569	98	98	540	5 397	249	9 910	0.9	4	26	1 268	1.0	Netherlands
3 355	4 568	99	95	520	8 087	346	13 820	3.2	4	35	526	1.0	Norway
269	304	100	75	570	3 133	383	3 700		30	42			Poland
767	510	100	50	540	1 194	637	2 190	1.9	8	32			Portugal
435	578	100	71	680	3 305		2 500		16	57			Romania
744	608	100	88	450	1 858	732	4 800	0.8	7	27			Spain
3 159	3 518	99	85	490	5 821	373	12 400	0.8	3	24	737	0.8	Sweden
4 577	4 016	100		410	3 794	200	16 390	0.8			286	0.3	Switzerland
1 775	1 628	100	83	650	3 461	515	9 050	1.0	2	29	1 432	0.3	U.K.
522	447	100	83	550	1 903	3 368	2 570	4.3	14	42			Yugoslavia
293	333	100	97	270	4 505		5 300		15	51			U.S.S.R.

Andorra, Land 0.5/Popn. 34; Faeroe Is. 1.4/45; Gibraltar 0.01/28; Liechtenstein 0.2/27; Monaco 0.0015/27; San Marino 0.06/22; Svalbard 62/3.

Trade. The trade figures are normally for the year 1983 or 1984. The total trade figures have been divided by the population and are a measure of the country's external trade (U.S. $ per capita).

Education. The ages of primary school are taken to be 6-11 years and secondary school 12-17 years. The percentage of the total school age group in this type of education is shown.

Energy. All forms of energy have been converted to their equivalent in oil. Firewood and other traditional forms used in developing countries are not included and so the energy consumption in those countries is understated (kilograms of oil equivalent per capita).

Consumer Price Index. The base year is 1970 which is 100 and the level of consumer prices in 1984 or 1985 are shown in relation to the base year. It is a measure of inflation.

G.N.P. (Gross National Product) This figure is an estimate of the average production per person measured in U.S. dollars and for 1983. The G.N.P. measures the value of goods and services produced in a country, plus the balance, positive or negative, of income from abroad, for example investments, interest on capital, money returned from foreign labour, etc. The rate of change is the average annual percentage change during the period 1973-1982 in the G.D.P. The G.D.P. (Gross Domestic Product) is the G.N.P. minus the foreign balances. The adjoining two columns show the percentage contribution to the G.D.P. made by the agricultural and mining and manufacturing sectors.

Loans and Debt. This figure in millions of U.S. dollars shows the external public debt at the end of 1983. This is then shown as a percentage of the annual G.N.P. The figures in red show official development assistance made by the developed countries and also as a percentage of the donor country's G.N.P.

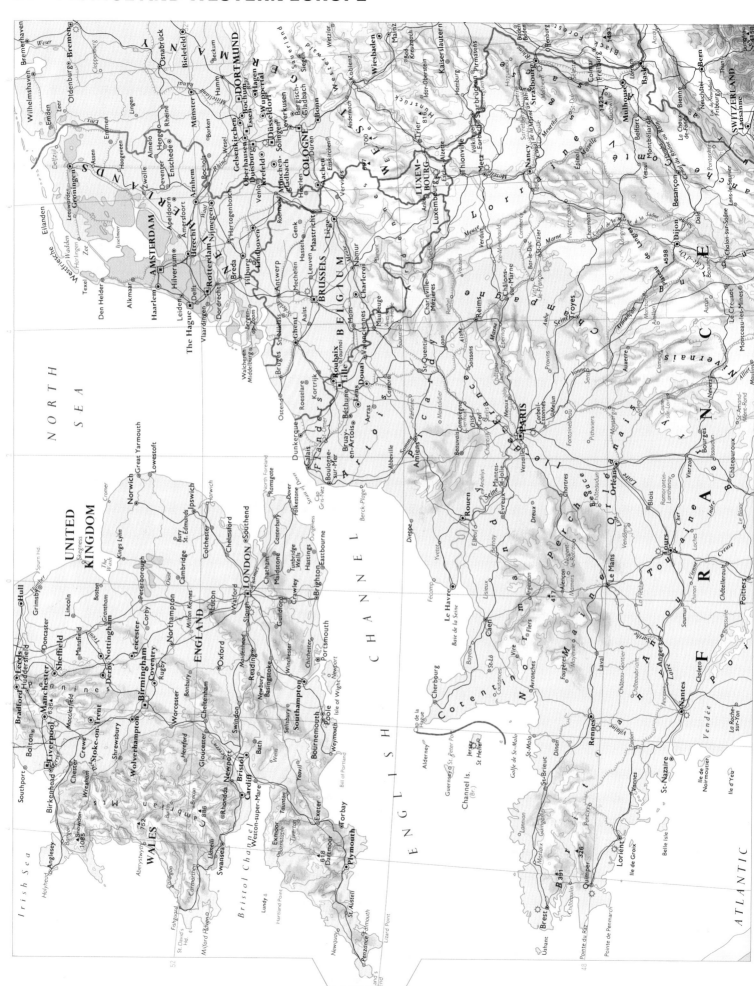

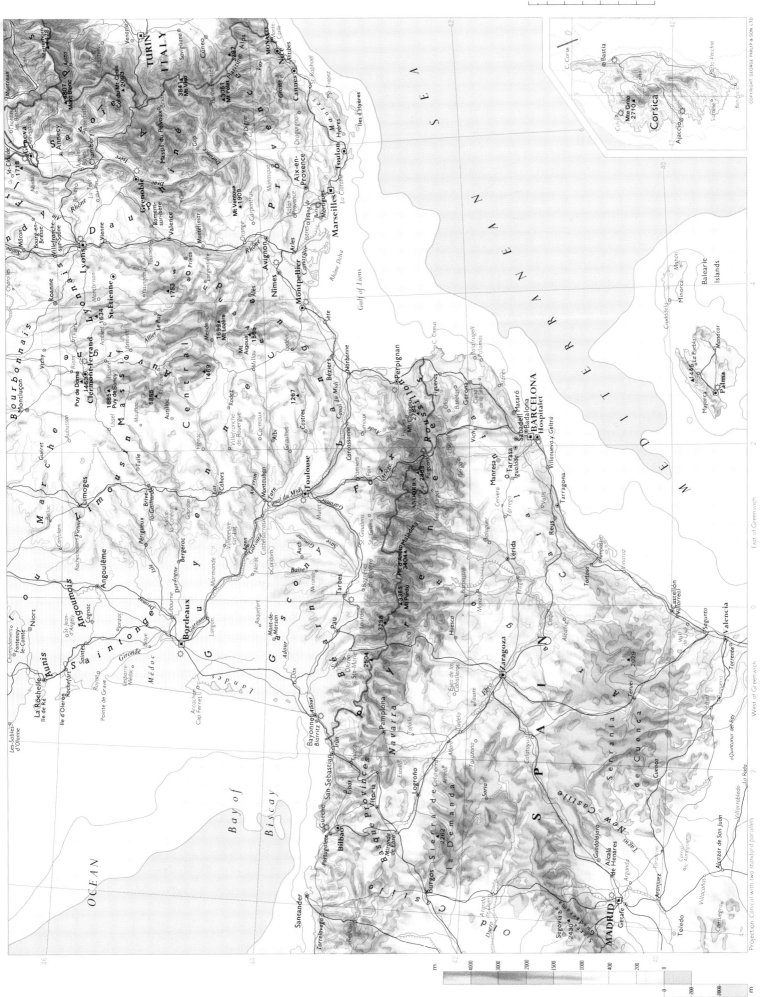

20 0 20 40 60 80 100 120 km

COPYRIGHT GEORGE PHILIP & SON LTD

C. Corse

Bastia

Corsica

Mte Cinto
2710▲

Ajaccio

Porto-Vecchio

Bonifacio

MEDITERRANEAN

SEA

Gulf of Lions

Balearic
Islands

Minorca

Mahón

Majorca

Palma

1445▲

ITALY

TURIN

4807 Mont Blanc

3841 Mt Viso

3051 Mt Pelat

Cuneo

Savigliano

MONACO

Nice

Antibes

Cannes

Ste Maxime

Iles d'Hyères

Hyères

Toulon

Marseilles

Aix-en-Provence

Mt Ventoux ▲1909

Grenoble

Lyons

Valence

Montélimar

Orange

Avignon

Arles

Nîmes

Montpellier

Sète

Béziers

Narbonne

Carcassonne

Perpignan

BARCELONA

Badalona

Hospitalet

Sabadell

Mataró

Tarrasa

Manresa

Gerona

Figueras

Tarragona

Reus

Lérida

Tortosa

Castellón

Villarreal

Sagunto

Valencia

Torrente

2029

Cuenca

MADRID

Getafe

Aranjuez

Toledo

Alcalá
de Henares

Guadalajara

Segovia

Soria

Logroño

Burgos

Miranda
de Ebro

Zaragoza

Tudela

Huesca

Pamplona

Bilbao

Portugalete

San Sebastián

Vitoria

Eibar

Santander

Torrelavega

Bordeaux

Bayonne

Biarritz

Pau

Tarbes

Lourdes

Toulouse

Montauban

Agen

Albi

Castres

Rodez

Montluçon

Vichy

Clermont-Ferrand

St-Étienne

Le Puy

Mende

1885 Puy de Sancy

Limoges

Périgueux

Brive

Tulle

Guéret

Angoulême

Cognac

Saintes

Rochefort

La Rochelle

Les-Sables-
d'Olonne

Niort

OCEAN

Bay

of

Biscay

Cap Ferret

Arcachon

Pointe de Grave

Ile d'Oléron

Ile de Ré

Geneva

St-Claude

Annecy

Chambéry

Mâcon

Bourg-en-
Bresse

Villefranche-
sur-Saône

Vienne

Roanne

Projection Conical with two standard parallels

East of Greenwich   West of Greenwich

m
4000 3000 2000 1500 1000 400 200 0

m
2000
0 200

1:2 000 000

10 0 10 20 30 40 50 60 70 80 km

NORTH SEA

FRISIAN ISLANDS

Schiermonnikoog
Terschelling
Vlieland
Ameland
Wadden Zee
Texel
Den Helder
Den Oever
Leeuwarden
Harlingen
Franeker
Dokkum
Delfzijl
Groningen
Hoogezand
Winschoten
Veendam
Emden
Ostfriesland
Jadebusen
Varel
Aurich
Wiesmoor
Westerstede
Leer
Papenburg
Bad Zwischenahn
Oldenburg
Friesoythe

FRIESLAND
Sneek
Workum
Lemmer
Heerenveen
Assen
Drachten
Stadskanaal
Cloppenburg
Löningen
Vechta
Quackenbruck
NIEDER SACHSEN
73

DRENTHE
Steenwijk
Hoogeveen
Emmeloord
Meppel
Emmen
Coevorden
Meppen
Bersenbruck
Damme
Bramsche

Noordoost Polder
Urk
Kampen
Zwolle
Nordhorn
Lingen
Ibbenbüren
Osnabrück
331

Den Burg
Enkhuizen
Alkmaar
Hoorn
Lelystad
Harderwijk
Nunspeet
Almelo
Oldenzaal
Rheine
Emsdetten
Lengerich
Greven

Castricum
Purmerend
Edam
Volendam
Marken
Deventer
OVERIJSSEL
107
Rijssen
Hengelo
Enschede
Gronau
Ahaus
Warendorf

Beverwijk
IJmuiden
Zaandam
AMSTERDAM
Huizen
Apeldoorn
GELDERLAND
Lochem
Berkel
Stadtlohn
Münster
Haarlem
Zandvoort
Heemstede
Bussum
Hilversum
Soest
Amersfoort
Ede
Zutphen
Dieren
Doetinchem
Wintterswijk
Coesfeld
Katwijk-aan-Zee
Leiden
Aalsmeer
UTRECHT
Arnhem
Emmerich
Bocholt
Borken
Dülmen
NORDRHEIN
Oelde
Beckum
Scheveningen
THE HAGUE
('s Gravenhage)
Voorburg
Alphen a/d Rijn
Zeist
Wageningen
Tiel
Waal
Nijmegen
Kleve
Rees
Wesel
Lüdinghausen
Ahlen

Hoek van Holland
Europoort
Delft
Rijswijk
Gouda
Lek
ROTTERDAM
Oss
s'Hertogenbosch
Goch
Rhein
Dorsten
Marl
Lippe
Recklinghausen
Lünen
Hamm
Werl
Soest

Vlaardingen
Schiedam
Sliedrecht
Gorinchem
Maas
Veghel
Boxtel
Kevelaer
Geldern
Niers
Bottrop
Oberhausen
Gelsenkirchen
Herne
Bochum
DORTMUND
Mühle

Goeree
Schouwen
Noord Beveland
Zierikzee
Overflakkee
Dordrecht
Waalwijk
BRABANT
Helmond
Venray
Duisburg
ESSEN
Mülheim
Witten
Menden
Ruhr
Neheim

Walcheren
Middelburg
Goes
Bergen-op-Zoom
Roosendaal
Breda
Tilburg
Eindhoven
Venlo
Krefeld
Moers
Hagen
Iserlohn

Flushing (Vlissingen)
West Schelde
Terneuzen
Essen
Turnhout
Valkenswaard
Weert
Roermond
Viersen
Mönchen-Gladbach
Neuss
DÜSSELDORF
Solingen
Remscheid
Wuppertal
Lüdenscheid
Plettenberg

Ostend (Oostende)
Zeebrugge
Knokke
Maldegem
Eeklo
Brasschaat
Schoten
ANTWERPEN
Merksem
Deurne
Mol
Geel
Maaseik
Erkelenz
WESTFALEN
Opladen
Bergisch Gladbach
Olpe
Siegen

Nieuwport
Bruges (Brugge)
St. Niklaas
Lokeren
Herentals
Nethe (Nete)
95
Genk
Sittard
Jülich
Leverkusen
COLOGNE (Köln)
Gummersbach
Sauerland
Diksmuide
Ghent
Wetteren
Aarschot
Demer
Hasselt
Geleen
Heerlen
Eschweiler
Brühl
Siegburg
Betzdorf
657

Roeselare
Aalst
Leuven
Maastricht
Tongeren
Aachen
Stolberg
Düren
Bonn
Ypres
Menin
Kortrijk
Oudenaarde
Ninove
157
BRUSSELS (Brussel Bruxelles)
Tienen
St. Trond
Herstal
Liège
Eupen
Euskirchen
Königswinter
Westerwald

Tourcoing
Mouscron
Ronse
Anderlecht
Halle
Wavre
BRABANT
Waterloo
Verviers
Spa
Schleiden
Remagen
Neuwied

Roubaix
Lille
Tournai
Ath
Soignies
Nivelles
BELGIUM
Namur
Huy
Seraing
Malmédy
694
Andernach
746
Koblenz
Bad Ems
Diez
Limburg

Lens
Orchies
Mons
La Louvière
Binche
Sambre
Charleroi
Cineya
Hohe Venn
St. Vith
Prüm
Gerolstein
Mayen
Cochem
RHEINLAND
Bingen
Wiesbaden
Mainz

Douai
Valenciennes
Denain
Thuin
Maubeuge
Dinant
313
652
697
Ernstberg 700
Daun
PFALZ
Zell
Bacharach
St. Goar
Boppard

Arras
PAS-DE-CALAIS
Cambrai
Solesmes
Avesnes
Philippeville
Rochefort
Marche
Houffalize
569
Bitburg
Wittlich
Bernkastel
Bad Kreuznach
816
Idar-Oberstein
687

Caudry
Bohain
Fourmies
Chimay
LUXEMBOURG
St. Hubert
Clervaux
Bastogne
LUXEMBOURG
Ettelbruck
549
Trier
Konz
Hunsrück

SOMME
St-Quentin
Guise
Hirson
Revin
Lesse
Neufchâteau
Semois
Bouillon
Ardennes
Saarburg
Dillingen
Merzig
St. Wendel
Kaiserslautern

Noyon
Chauny
Vervins
Laon
PICARDIE
Rethel
ARDENNES
Charleville-Mézières
Sedan
Virton
Longwy
Arlon
Differdange
Esch
Villerupt
Longuyon
MEURTHE ET MOSELLE
Thionville
SAAR
Sulzbach
Neunkirchen
Homburg
Zweibrücken
Neustadt

Compiègne
Soissons
Aisne
Le Chesne
Vouziers
Chiers
MEUSE
Verdun
Metz
Montigny
St. Avold
Sarreguemines
Völklingen
Saarbrücken
Forbach
MOSELLE
Pirmasens
Landau

Reims
Vesle
Plaine de Champagne
Marne
284
Suippes
Côtes
Meuse
Jœuf
Dieuze
Sarrelouis
Saarlouis

m
400
200
0

Projection: Conical with two standard parallels

East from Greenwich

COPYRIGHT GEORGE PHILIP & SON, LTD.

1:5 000 000

50   0   50   100   150   200 km

COPYRIGHT GEORGE PHILIP & SON LTD

East from Greenwich

West from Greenwich

Projection: Conical with two standard parallels

m 3000 2000 1500 1000 400 200 0

m 0 200

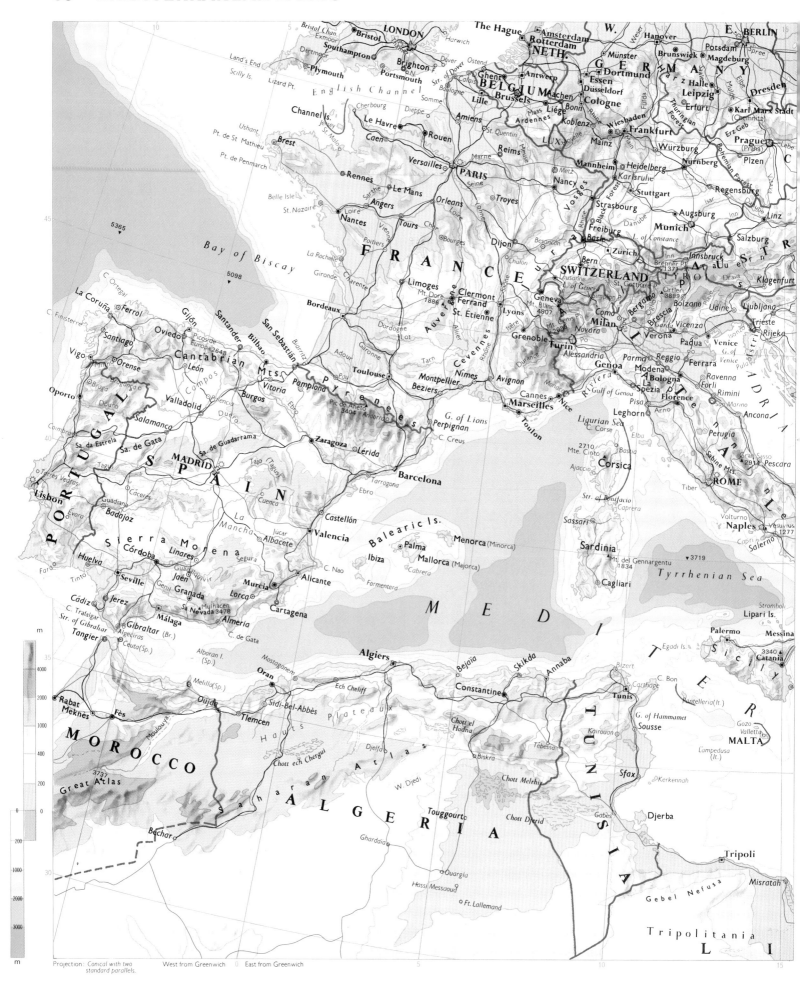

100   0   100   200   300   400 km

POLAND
Poznan
Łódź
Warsaw (Warszawa)
Wrocław
Radom
Lublin
Brest
Pripyat Marshes
Chernigov
Sumy
Kharkov
Volgograd

Wisła (Vistula)
Warta
der
Brno
Ostrava
Jablunka P.
Sněžka 1602
(Elbe)
Chorzów
Kraków
Przemysl
Lvov
Vinnitsa
Zhitomir
Kiev
Cherkassy
Poltava
Kremenchug
(Dnieper)
Voroshilovgrad
Shakhty
Tsimlyansk Reservoir

CZECHOSLOVAKIA
2655
Tatra
Košice
RUTHENIA
Chernovtsy
MOLDAVIA
U. S. S. R.
U K R A I N E
Dneprodzerzhinsk
Donetsk
Gorlovka
Makeyevka
Novocherkassk
Rostov
Don

Vienna
Bratislava
Miskolc
Pietrosul 2305
Iaşi
Kishinev
Kirovograd
Dnepropetrovsk
Krivoy Rog
Zaporozhye
Zhdanov
Taganrog

Bruck
Graz
HUNGARY
Budapest
Debrecen
Oradea
Pietrosul 2102
Sava
Siret
Odessa
Nikolayev
Kherson
Melitopol
Sea of Azov
Kerch & Str.
Krasnodar
Armavir
Stavropol
L. Manych Gudilo
Manych

Zagreb
Pécs
Szeged
Subotica
Arad
ROMANIA
Cluj
Negoiu 2535
Sibiu
Braşov
Galaţi
Brăila
G. of Karkinitsk
C. Tarkhankut
Crimea
Simferopol 1545
Novorossiysk

YUGOSLAVIA
Novi Sad
Timişoara
Transylvanian Alps
Iron Gate
Piteşti
Ploeşti
Bucharest (Bucureşti)
Constanţa
Sevastopol

BOSNIA
Belgrade
Craiova
Danube
Ruse
Tolbukhin
Varna
BLACK SEA
2211
Batumi

Sarajevo
Mostar
SERBIA
Niš
Pleven
Shipka P.
Sliven
Burgas
C. Ince
Trabzon

Zadar
Dinaric Alps
Durmitor 2522
MONTENEGRO
Novi Pazar
BULGARIA
Sofia
Stara Zagora
Maritsa
2565
Canik (Pontine) Mts.

Dubrovnik
Laštovo
Shkodër
Musala 2925
Plovdiv
Rhodope
Edirne
Zonguldak
Samsun
Sivas
Firat

ADRIATIC SEA
Mt. Gargano
Foggia
Bari
Brindisi
Tiranë
ALBANIA
Bitolj
Skopje
Vardar
Thessaloniki
Gökçeada
İstanbul
Bosporus
Üsküdar
Ankara
Kayseri
Erciyaş Dağ 3770

Taranto
G. of Taranto
Str. of Otranto
GREECE
Pindus
Áthos
Límnos
Sea of Marmara
İznik Gölü
Bursa
TURKEY
Eskişehir
Afyon
Tuz Gölü
Maraş
Gaziantep

Cosenza
La Sila 1929
Kérkira
Ionian Is.
Larísa
Vólos
N. Sporades
Lésvos
Aegean Sea
Balikesir
Menderes
Sakarya
Egridir Gölü
Konya
Seyhan
Adana
Aleppo

Reggio
Ionian Sea
Levkás
Kefallinía
Khíos
Sámos
Ikaría
Denizli
Beyşehir Gölü
Isparta
Taurus Mountains
Tarsus
Mersin
Antakya
SYRIA

Siracusa
C. Spartivento
Zákinthos
Olympia
Pátrai
Morea
Athens
Piraíevs
Síros
Andros
Kikládhes
Náxos
Dodecanese
Antalya
G. of Antalya
3086
Latakia
Hama
Homs

C. Passero
C. di Maria Leuca
C. Tainaron
Mílos
Thíra
Íos
Ródhos (Rhodes) 4486
Karpáthos
CYPRUS
Nicosia
Famagusta
Larnaca
Limassol
Troodos 1951
Tarabulus (Tripoli)
LEBANON
Beirut
Damascus

Str. of Messina
Andikíthira
Khaniá
Mt. Ídhi 2456
Iráklion
Crete
Kíthira
Mt. Hermon 2814
Jebel ed Druz
Haifa

5121
3174
Tel Aviv-Jaffa
ISRAEL
Jerusalem
Amman
JORDAN
Dead Sea -395
Gaza

4135
M E D I T E R R A N E A N   S E A
L. Burullus
Damietta
Port Said
El 'Arish

Beida (Al Bayda)
Darnah
G. of Bomba
Tobruk
G. of Salum
Mahalla el Kubra
Alexandria
Tanta
Ismailia
Bitter Lakes
Suez
Desert el Tih

Benghazi
Gulf of Sidra
Cyrenaica
Salum
CAIRO
EGYPT
El Faiyûm
Beni Suef
Nile
Sinai Pen. 2637
G. of Aqaba

LIBYA

Division between Greeks and Turks in Cyprus; Turks to the North.

MALTA
1:1 000 000
0   10 km

S.E. EUROPE
POLITICAL
1:25 000 000

Projection : Conical with two standard parallels

1:5 000 000

50 0 50 100 150 200 km

Kaposvár Szekszárd Mt. Bihor 1848 *Transylvania* Carpathians U.S.S.R.

Hódmezővásárhely White Criși Alba-Iulia Sfântu Gheorghe Bârlad Sasyk

Szeged Arad Mureș Deva Sibiu Brașov (Orașul Stalin) Focșani Galați Izmail

Pécs Subotica R O M A N I A

Baja Sombor Timișoara Banat Red Tower P. 350 Mt. Negoiu 2535 Mt. Omu 2507 Buzău Brăila Tulcea

Drava Kikinda Transylvanian Alps Râmnicu Vâlcea Ploești Buzău

Osijek Novi Sad Zrenjanin (Petrovgrad) Peleaga 2509 Parângul-Mare 2518 Tîrgu-Jiu Tîrgoviște Prahova Danube Dobrogea

Bosna Pancevo Orșova Iron Gate Jiu Pitești Dâmbovița Bucharest (București) Constanța

Belgrade (Beograd) Smederevo Turnu-Severin W a l l a c h i a Argeș Ialomița Trajan's Wall Călărași

Tuzla Drina Sava Morava Danube Craiova Slatina Olt Giurgiu Vedea Ruse (Ruschuk) Silistra Tutrakan

G O S L A V I A Kragujevac Morava Vidin Oryakhovo Șomovit Svishtov Tolbukhin C. Kaliakra

Sarajevo Cacak S E R B I A Timok Pleven Sumen (Kolarovgrad) Varna

Mostar Krusevac Niš 2168 Balkan Mountains Gabrovo Sliven Burgas B L A C K S E A

Govina Kopaonik Leskovac Južna Morava Dragoman Vezhen 2198 Shipka P. Tundzha

Durmitor 2522 Ibar Kosovska Mitrovica Sofia B U L G A R I A Stara Zagora Yambol

MONTENEGRO Pec Priština Pernik Trajan's Gate Maritsa Pazardzhik

Dubrovnik Titograd (Podgorica) White Drin Kyustendil Musala 2925 Plovdiv Khaskovo Edirne Istranca Mts. 1018 C. Igneada

1224 Shkoder Prizren Crna Gora R h o d o p e Arda TURKEY Bosporus

Shkodër Tar Pl. 2496 Kumanovo Struma M o u n t a i n s Dhidhimotikhon Istanbul Üsküdar

A L B A N I A Tetovo Skopje Mesta Ergene T H R A C E

C. Rodonit Korab 2764 Solunska 2540 M A C E D O N I A Vardar Petrich Xánthi Komotiní Enez Sea of Marmara Marmara Imrali

C. Palit 1269 Prilep Crna Drama Serrai Kaválla Alexandroúpolis Bandirma Bursa 2543

Durrës Tirane Jablanica Dojran D O N I Gelibolu (Gallipoli) G. of Saros Canakkale

Shkumbin Elbasan Bitola (Monastir) Edhessa M Polýros Mt. Áthos 2033 Gökçeada Çanakkale Troy Ida 1766 Balikesir 2181

Ohridsko L. Presp Florina A Véroia Singitikós G. G. of Toronaíos Dardanelles (Hellespont) Boz. Ada G. of Edremit Ayvalik TURKEY

Berat Çemani Tomorrit 2480 C Kastoria Kozáni G. of Thessaloniki Límnos A n a t o l i a

Vijose Vlóre Sazan Olympus 2917 Psevdhókavos Ayios Evstrátios Mytilíni 968 Izmir (Smyrna) 2157 Alaşehir

Brindisi Francavilla Smolikas 2637 E Ossa 1978 Pílion Lésvos Turgutlu

Lecce Galatina P i n d u s G R Larisa 1575 N. Sporades A E G E A N 2308 Menderes

C. Otranto Str. of Otranto Kérkira (Corfu) Ioánnina E E Trikkala THESSALY Volos G. of Volos Iliodhrómia Skíros Khíos (Chios) Samos G. of İzmir Aydin

C. St. Maria di Leuca E p i r u s M t s. Árta C Lamía Dhírfis 1743 Évvoia (Euboea) Khíos 1297 Menderes

Préveza Akhelóos Giona 2510 P. of Thermopylae Khalkís 1398 Ándros S E A Samos G. of Kerme 2294

I O N I A N Levkás (Sta. Maura) Mesolóngion Parnassós 2467 Mycenae Athens (Athinai) Ikaría İzmir

Kefallinía (Cephalonia) G. of Pátrai Gulf of Corinth Piraievs (Piraeus) Tínos Pátmos G. of Kerme

S E A Argostólion Pátrai Killíni Corinth Mýkonos Ermoúpolis Síros Kálimnos

Zákinthos Erimanthos 2224 2376 Mycenae Alfiós Kéa Kíthnos Sérifos Náxos 1001 Astipálaia Kos Ródhos

Zákinthos Pírgos PELOPONNESE Nauplion Sífnos KIKLÁDHES (Cyclades) Amorgós Tílos

Olympia Trípolis G. of Argolis Páros Mílos Thíra Ródhos (Rhodes) 4486 1215

Kiparissía G. Sparti Idhra D O D E K Kásos Karpáthos 1215

5121 Kalamáta Parnon Mts. Kíthira (Cerigo) N I S E

I T E R R A N E A N S E A G. of Messíni G. of Lakonía C. Malea

Yíthion C. Tainaron (Matapan)

Andíkithira C. Spátha Khanión B. C R E T E C. Lithinon

Khaniá Soudhas B. Rethimnon C. Dia Iraklion (Candia) Merabéllou B.

Lévka Óri 2452 Mt. Idhi 2456 Dhíkti 2148 Knossos Kásos

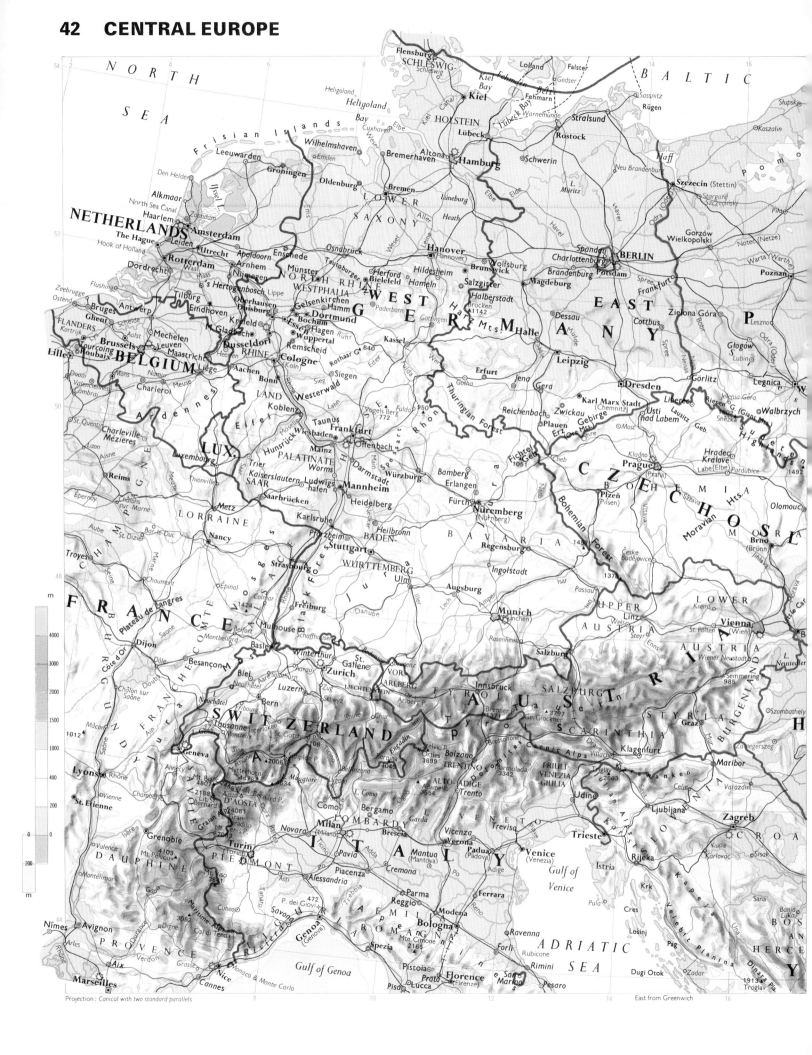

NORTH SEA

BALTIC

Flensburg
SCHLESWIG-
Lolland
Falster
Gedser
Rügen
Słupsk
Heligoland
Heligoland
Kiel Canal
Kiel
Fehmarn
Koszalin
HOLSTEIN
Lübeck Bay
Warnemünde
Stralsund
Cuxhaven
Wilhelmshaven
Bremerhaven
Altona
Hamburg
Schwerin
Rostock
Haff
Pom

Frisian Islands
Leeuwarden
Groningen
Emden
Bremen
Lüneburg
Elbe
Elde
L. Müritz
Neu Brandenburg
Szczecin (Stettin)
Stargard Szczeciński
Pila

Den Helder
Alkmaar
Oldenburg
LOWER
Heath
Havel
Gorzów Wielkopolski
Noteć (Netze)
Haarlem
North Sea Canal
Ijssel L.
Zaandam
SAXONY
Weser
Aller
Spandau
BERLIN
Warta Warth

NETHERLANDS
Amsterdam
Apeldoorn
Osnabrück
Hanover
Brunswick
Wolfsburg
Brandenburg
Charlottenburg
Potsdam
Spree
Frankfurt
Poznań

The Hague
Leiden
Utrecht
Enschede
Hannover
Hildesheim
Hamelin
Salzgitter
Magdeburg
EAST
P

Rotterdam
Arnhem
Nijmegen
NORTH RHINE
Herford
Bielefeld
Halberstadt
Dessau
Mulde
Cottbus
Zielona Góra
Odra (Oder)
Leszno

Dordrecht
Waal
Münster
WESTPHALIA
WEST
Brocken 1142
Halle
Leipzig
Głogów
Lubin

Zeebrugge
Flushing
's Hertogenbosch
Lippe
Oberhausen
Gelsenkirchen
Paderborn
G
E
Saale
Görlitz
Legnica
W

Ostend
Bruges
Antwerp
Ghent
Tilburg
Eindhoven
Krefeld
Duisburg
Dortmund
Hamm
Kassel
Erfurt
Jena
Gera
Dresden
Liberec
Walbrzych

FLANDERS
Kortrijk
Aalst
M. Gladbach
Essen
Bochum
Hagen
Wuppertal
Rothaar G. 840
R
M
Y
Reichenbach
Zwickau
Karl Marx Stadt (Chemnitz)
Jelenia Góra
Riesen G. (Giant Mts)
Sněžka 1492

Tourcoing
Roubaix
BELGIUM
Brussels
Leuven
Maastricht
Düsseldorf
Remscheid
Eder
RHINE
Cologne (Köln)
Siegen
Fulda
Thuringian Forest
Gotha
Plauen
Erz Geb.
Usti nad Labem
Most
Sudeten Highlands

Lille
Mons
Charleroi
Namur
Liège
Aachen
Bonn
LAND
Sieg
Siegen
Werra
950
E
Fichtel Geb. 1051
Cheb
Kladno
CZECHOSLO
Hradec Králové

Ardennes
Meuse
Eifel
Westerwald
Koblenz
Lahn
Vogels Berg 772
Rhön
Bamberg
Jura
Naab
Prague (Praha)
Labe (Elbe)
Pardubice
1492

St. Quentin
Charleville-Mézières
LUX.
Luxembourg
Trier
Moselle
Hunsrück
TAUNUS
Wiesbaden
Mainz
Frankfurt
Offenbach
Würzburg
Erlangen
Bohemian Forest 1457
Plzeň (Pilsen)
BOHEMIA
Vltava
Jihlava
Olomouc

Reims
Aisne
Thionville
Kaiserslautern
SAAR
PALATINATE
Worms
Darmstadt
Ludwigshafen
Mannheim
Fürth
Nuremberg (Nürnberg)
České Budějovice
1378
Sázava
Brno (Brünn)
SR

Épernay
Châlons sur Marne
Metz
Saarbrücken
Heidelberg
Neckar
Heilbronn
BAVARIA
Regensburg
Passau
MORAVIA
M

Troyes
Bar-le-Duc
St. Dizier
LORRAINE
Karlsruhe
Pforzheim
Stuttgart
BADEN-
Ingolstadt
Isar
LOWER
AUSTRIA
Krems

Aube
Nancy
Strasbourg
Black Forest
WÜRTTEMBERG
Augsburg
Lech
Danube
Munich (München)
Linz
St. Pölten
Vienna (Wien)
Morava

Chaumont
Épinal
Colmar
Freiburg
Ulm
Iller
Amper
UPPER
Steyr
Enns
AUSTRIA
Wiener Neustadt
Neusiedler

FRANCE
Plateau de Langres
Belfort
Mulhouse
Schaffhausen
Constance
Rosenheim
Salzburg
Semmering 985

Dijon
Montbéliard
Basle
Winterthur
St. Gallen
Bregenz
VOR-
ARLBERG
Innsbruck
SALZBURG
AUSTRIA
STYRIA
Graz
BURGENLAND
Szombathely

Côte d'or
Besançon
Doubs
Biel
Aarau
Zürich
Zug
LIECHTENSTEIN
Arlberg
Brenner P. 1371
SE
Wiener
Neusiedler L.

Saône
Dôle
Jura
Neuchâtel
Solothurn
Luzern
Schwyz
Rhine
Chur
TYROL
Gr. Glockner 3797
CARINTHIA
Klagenfurt
Maribor

Mâcon
1012
1424
Fribourg
Bern
Interlaken
St. Gotthard P.
Engadin
Bernina 4049
Ortles 3899
Dolomites
Marmolada 3342
FRIULI-VENEZIA GIULIA
Triglav 2863
Udine
Ljubljana
Zagreb
CROA

SWITZERLAND
Lausanne
Montreux
2108
Ticino
Bellinzona
Bolzano
TRENTINO
ALTO-ADIGE
Klis
Trieste
Rijeka

Geneva
Mt. Blanc 4807
Matterhorn 4478
Maggiore
Lugano
L. Como
Adamello 3554
Trento
VENETO
Venice (Venezia)
Istria
Krk

Lyons
Annecy
St. Bernard P.
2188
Gr. St. Bernard
Gran Paradiso 4061
Como
Bergamo
L. Garda
Vicenza
Treviso
Padua (Padova)
Gulf of Venice
Pula

DAUPHINE
Vienne
Chambéry
Graian Alps
D'AOSTA
2083
LOMBARDY
Milan (Milano)
Brescia
Verona
Mantua (Mantova)
Adige
Venice
Cres
Lošinj

St. Etienne
Grenoble
Mt. Pelvoux 4103
Turin (Torino)
PIEDMONT
Novara
Pavia
Adda
ITALY
Po
Rovigo
Ravenna
Dugi Otok
Zadar

Montélimar
Mt. Viso 3841
Cuneo
Asti
Alessandria
Piacenza
Cremona
Parma
Reggio
Modena
Ferrara
Forlì
Rimini
ADRIATIC SEA
Pula

Nîmes
Avignon
Digne
Maritime Alps 3052
P. dei Giovi 472
Tanaro
Trebbia
EMILIA
ROMAGNA
Bologna
Mte. Cimone 2165
Pesaro

Arles
Aix
PROVENCE
Grasse
Nice
Monaco & Monte Carlo
Col di Tenda
River Riviera
Genoa (Genova)
Spezia
Pistoia
Prato
Florence (Firenze)
Lucca
Pisa
San Marino
Troglav 1913

Marseilles
Cannes
Gulf of Genoa
Rubicone

Projection: Conical with two standard parallels
East from Greenwich

1:5 000 000

50   0   50   100   150   200 km

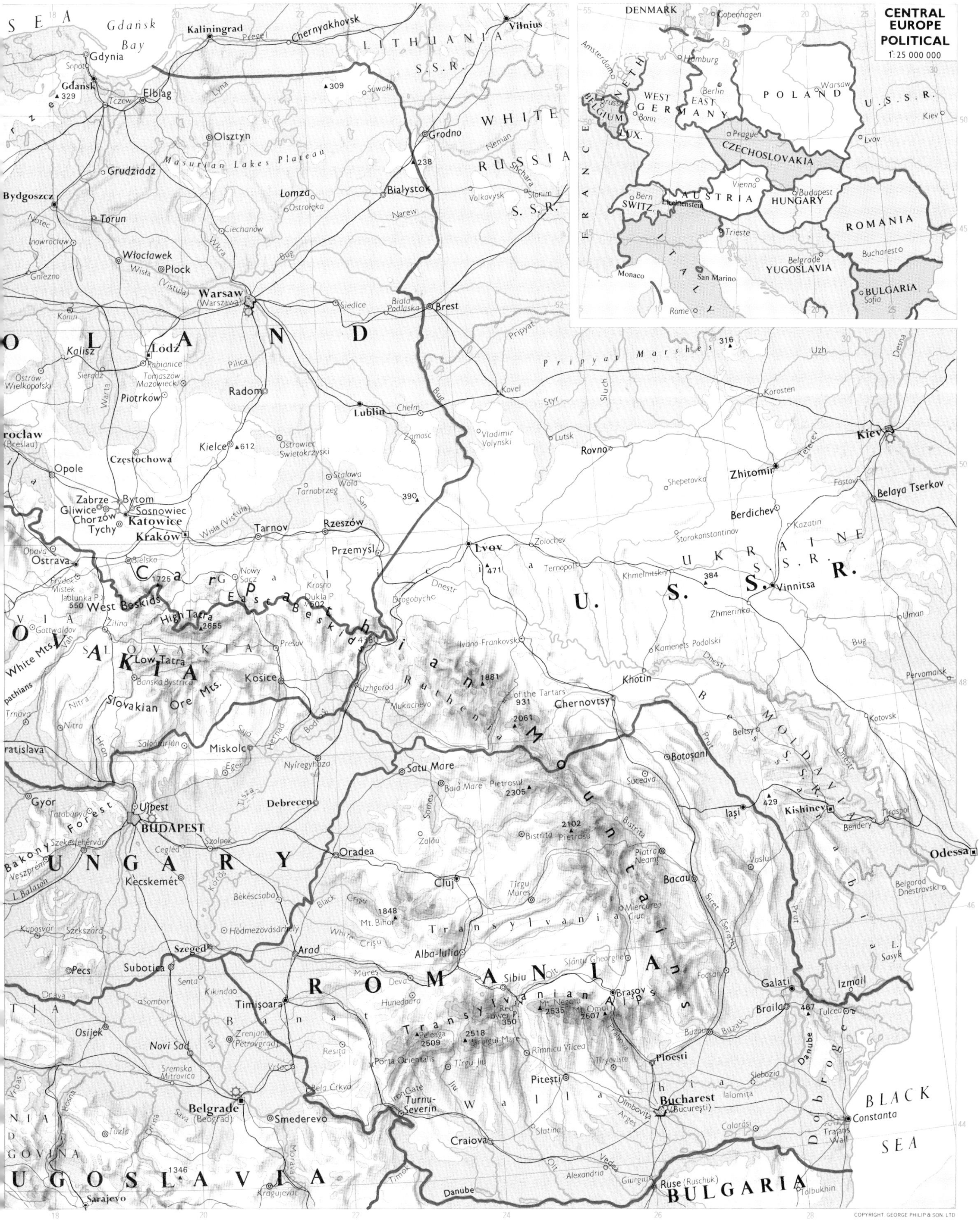

CENTRAL EUROPE POLITICAL
1:25 000 000

Inset map (Central Europe Political):
DENMARK
Copenhagen
NETH.
Amsterdam
Hamburg
Berlin
POLAND
Warsaw
U.S.S.R.
WEST GERMANY
EAST GERMANY
BELGIUM
Brussels
LUX.
Bonn
Prague
CZECHOSLOVAKIA
Lvov
Kiev
FRANCE
SWITZ.
Bern
Liechtenstein
AUSTRIA
Vienna
Budapest
HUNGARY
ROMANIA
Bucharest
ITALY
Trieste
Belgrade
YUGOSLAVIA
Monaco
San Marino
Rome
BULGARIA
Sofia

Main map labels:

SEA
Gdańsk Bay
Gdynia
Sopot
Gdańsk
△329
Elblag
Tczew
Kaliningrad
Pregel
Chernyakhovsk
LITHUANIA S.S.R.
Vilnius
Lyna
Suwalki
△309
WHITE
Grodno
Neman
238
RUSSIA
S.S.R.
Olsztyn
Masurian Lakes Plateau
Grudziadz
Lomza
Ostrołęka
Bialystok
Volkovysk
Shchara
Stonim
Bydgoszcz
Torun
Notec
Ciechanów
Narew
Inowrocław
Włocławek
Wisła (Vistula)
Płock
Wkra
Gniezno
Konin
Warsaw (Warszawa)
Siedlce
Biala Podlaska
Brest
Pripyat
Pripyat Marshes
△316
Uzh
Desna
POLAND
Łódź
Kalisz
Rabianice
Sieradz
Tomaszow Mazowiecki
Pilica
Radom
Kovel
Styr
Sluch
Korosten
Ostrów Wielkopolski
Piotrków
Warta
Chelm
Bug
Vladimir Volynski
Lublin
Zamosc
Lutsk
Rovno
Shepetovka
Zhitomir
Fastov
Kiev
Wrocław (Breslau)
Opole
Częstochowa
Kielce
△612
Ostrowiec Świetokrzyski
Stalowa Wola
390
San
Tarnobrzeg
Berdichev
Kazatin
Starokonstantinov
Belaya Tserkov
Zabrze
Gliwice
Chorzów
Bytom
Sosnowiec
Katowice
Tychy
Kraków
Wisła (Vistula)
Tarnov
Rzeszów
Lvov
Zolochev
Ternopol
Khmelnitsky
△384
Vinnitsa
UKRAINE S.S.R.
Przemyśl
Dnestr
Zhmerinka
U. S. S. R.
Ostrava
Bielsko
Carpathians
△1725
Nowy Sacz
Krosno
△607
Dukla P.
Drogobycho
Ivano-Frankovsk
Uman
Kamenets Podolski
Pervomaisk
Bug
Opava
Frydek Mistek
Jablunka P.
550 West Beskids
High Tatra
△2655
East Beskids
△790
Presov
Uzhgorod
Mukachevo
△1881
△931 of the Tartars
△2061
Khotin
Chernovtsy
Beltsy
Kotovsk
Gottwaldov
Žilina
SLOVAKIA
Low Tatra
Košice
Ruthenian Mountains
MOLDAVIA S.S.R.
White Mts.
Nitra
Slovakian Ore Mts.
Banská Bystrica
Sajo
Hernad
Miskolc
Eger
Nyíregyháza
Satu Mare
Baia Mare
Pietrosul
△2305
Suceava
Botoşani
Iaşi
△429
Kishinev
Bendery
Odessa
Tiraspol
Bratislava
Nitra
Hron
Salgótarján
Tisza
Debrecen
Somes
△2102
Pietrosu
Bistrita
Zalau
Bistrita
Győr
Tatabánya
Újpest
BUDAPEST
Cegléd
Szolnok
Oradea
Cluj
Tîrgu Mures
Bacau
Piatra Neamt
Vaslui
Belgorod Dnestrovski
Szekesfehervar
Kecskemét
Bekescsaba
Miercurea Ciuc
HUNGARY
Bakony Forest
Veszprém
Hódmezővásárhely
Black
Crişu
Mt. Bihor
△1848
White Crişu
Alba-Iulia
Transylvania
Sîntu Gheorghe
Focşani
Galati
Izmail
L. Balaton
Kaposvár
Szekszárd
Szeged
Arad
Mures
Deva
Sibiu
Brasov
Braila
467
Tulcea
Pécs
Subotica
Senta
Kikindao
Hunedoara
ROMANIA
Red Tower P. 350
Mt. Negoiu △2535
Mt. Omul △2507
Danube
Dobrogea
Novi Sad
Timişoara
Banat
Zrenjanin (Petrovgrad)
Reşita
Peleaga △2518
△2509 Parîngul Mare
Transylvanian Alps
Rîmnicu Vîlcea
Tîrgovişte
Ploesti
Buzau
Osijek
Drava
Sombor
Vrsac
Bela Crkva
Porta Orientalis
Tîrgu-Jiu
Jiu
Wallachia
Pitesti
Arges
Slobozia
Ialomiţa
BLACK
Belgrade (Beograd)
Smederevo
Iron Gate
Turnu-Severin
Olt
Slatina
Dîmbovita
Bucharest (Bucureşti)
Calarasi
Constanta
Trajans Wall
Morava
Craiova
Veder
Olt
Alexandria
Giurgiu
Ruse (Ruschuk)
Danube
Talbukhin
SEA
YUGOSLAVIA
△1346
Sarajevo
Kragujevac
Timok
BULGARIA
NIA
GOVINA
Tuzla
Bosna

18   20   22   24   26   28

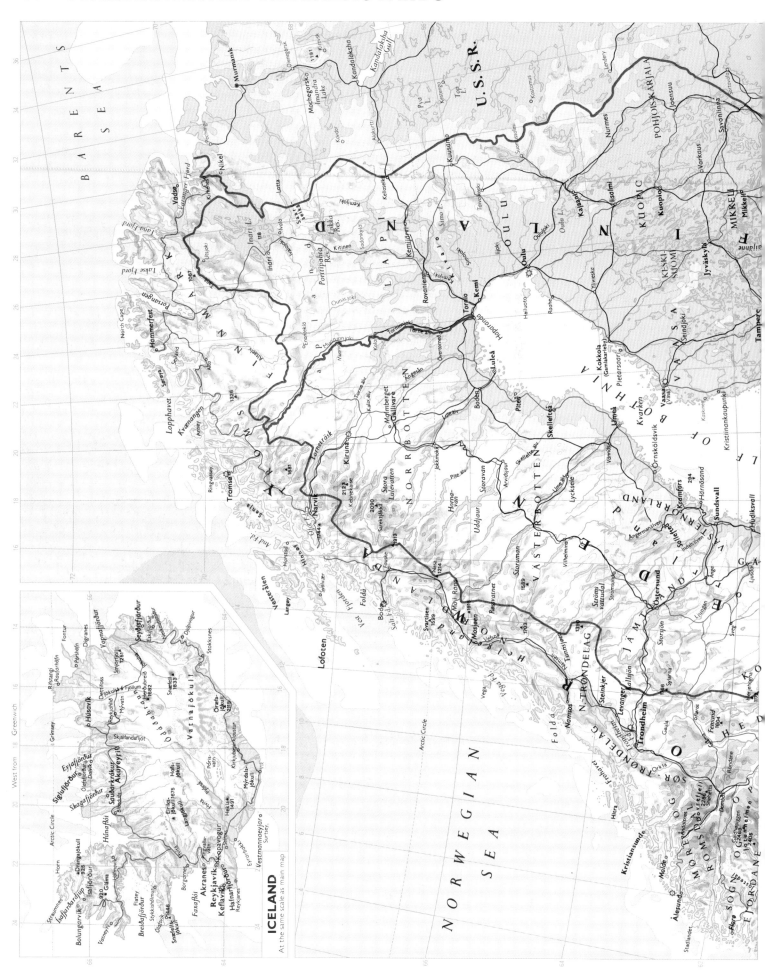

ICELAND

At the same scale as main map

1 : 6 000 000

50   0   50   100   150   200   250 km

COPYRIGHT GEORGE PHILIP & SON LTD

East from Greenwich

Projection: Conical with two standard parallels

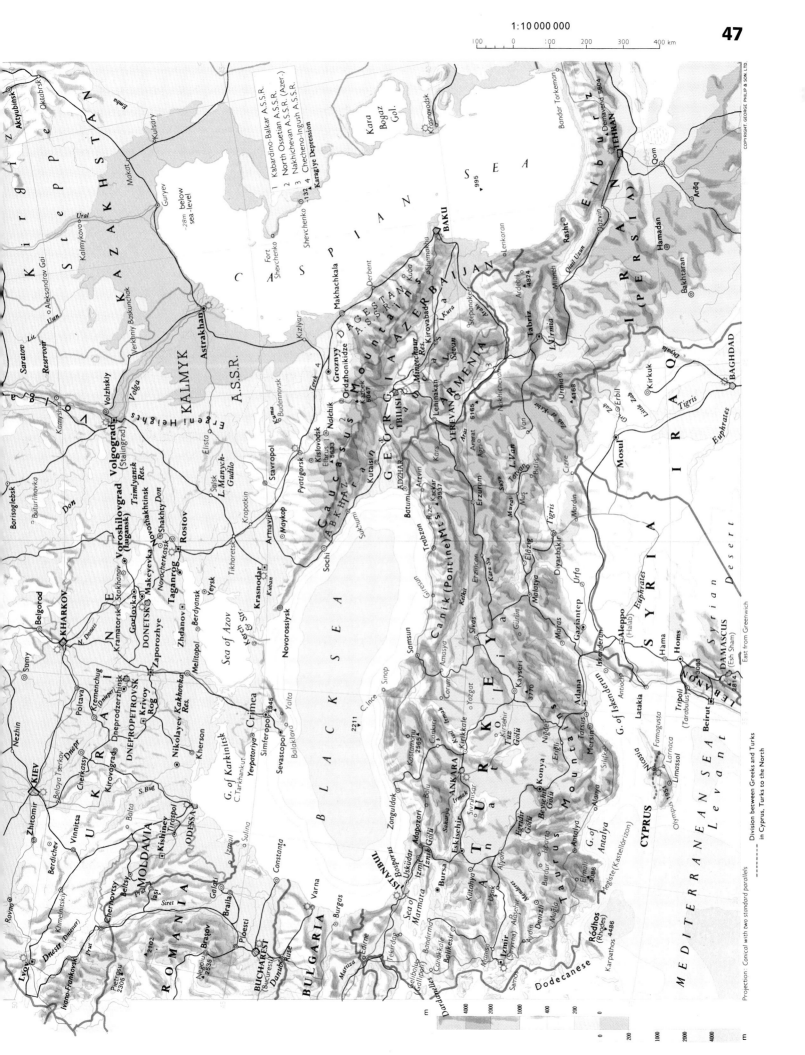

1:10 000 000

100   0   100   200   300   400 km

COPYRIGHT GEORGE PHILIP & SON, LTD.

Projection: Conical with two standard parallels

Division between Greeks and Turks
in Cyprus, Turks to the North

East from Greenwich

1 Kabardino-Balkar A.S.S.R.
2 North Ossetian A.S.S.R. (Azer.)
3 Nakhichevan A.S.S.R. (Azer.)
4 Checheno-Ingush A.S.S.R.
   Karagiye Depression

R.S.F.S.R.
1. Daghestan A.S.S.R.
2. Kabardino–Balkar A.S.S.R.
3. Mari A.S.S.R.
4. Mordovian A.S.S.R.
5. North Ossetian A.S.S.R.
6. Tatar A.S.S.R.
7. Udmurt A.S.S.R.
8. Chuvash A.S.S.R.
9. Checheno–Ingush A.S.S.R.
AZERBAIJAN
10. Nakhichevan A.S.S.R.
GEORGIA
11. Abkhaz A.S.S.R.
12. Adzhar A.S.S.R.

Projection: Conical Orthomorphic with two standard parallels

East from Greenwich

1:50 000 000

Projection: Bonne

1:50 000 000

500 0 500 1000 1500 2000 km

ARCTIC OCEAN

PACIFIC OCEAN

INDIAN OCEAN

U. S. S. R.

CHINESE REPUBLIC OF CHINA / TIBET

INNER MONGOLIA

MONGOLIA
Ulan Bator ⊙
Hovd

Bering Sea
Aleutian Is.
East C. (C. Dezhnev)
Wrangel I.
Chukchi Sea
Kolyma
Verkhoyansk
Yakutsk
New Siberian Is.
Laptev Sea
Lena
Lower Tunguska
Kara Sea
Novaya Zemlya
Severnaya Zemlya
Svalbard
Barents Sea
White Sea
● Murmansk
● Arkhangelsk
■ Moscow
■ Leningrad
Ural Mts.
Arctic Circle
Vistula
Danube
Dnieper
Don
Volga
Rhine
North Sea
Baltic Sea
Black Sea
BRITISH ISLES
ICELAND
■ **London**
■ **Paris**
■ **Rome**
■ **Berlin**
■ **Vienna** ● **Warsaw**
● **Belgrade**
● **Odessa**
● Rostov
Astrakhan
Caspian Sea
Aral Sea
Syr Darya
Amu Darya
● Tashkent
⊙ Samarkand
Ashkhabad
● Sverdlovsk ● Novosibirsk
Chelyabinsk ⊙ Omsk
Magnitogorsk
Orenburg
Semipalatinsk
● Alma Ata
⊙ Urumqi
Tarim
⊙ Kashi
L. Balkhash
Irkutsk
L. Baikal
⊙ Chita
● Krasnoyarsk
Angara
Tomsk
Yenisei
Ob
Irtysh
Igarka

Mediterranean Sea
■ **Athens**
● **Istanbul**
Ankara
Izmir
TURKEY
CYPRUS
Nicosia
Damascus
SYRIA
LEB. **Beirut**
ISRAEL **Jerusalem**
JORDAN **Amman**
■ **Baghdad**
IRAQ
Basra
Tigris
Euphrates
KUWAIT
Tehran ■
IRAN
⊙ Esfahan
Shiraz
⊙ Tabriz
Baku
Tbilisi
⊙ Mashhad
AFGHANISTAN
Herat ⊙ **Kabul**
Qandahar ⊙
Zahidan ⊙
BAHRAIN
QATAR
UNITED ARAB EMIRATES
Abu Dhabi
OMAN
Muscat
G. of Oman
Gulf
Kuria Muria Is.
SAUDI ARABIA
Riyadh
Medina
Jedda
Mecca
Red Sea
YEMEN **Sana**
SOUTH YEMEN **Aden**
G. of Aden
Socotra (South Yemen)

PAKISTAN
⊙ **Islamabad**
Karachi
Indus
KASHMIR
Lahore
Delhi ■
INDIA
Kanpur
Varanasi
Calcutta
Ahmadabad
Bombay
Hyderabad
Nagpur
Narmada
Godavari
Bangalore
Madras
Lakshadweep Is. (India)
Colombo
SRI LANKA
MALDIVES
Arabian Sea
NEPAL **Katmandu**
BHUTAN
BANGLA. **Dacca**
BURMA
Mandalay
Rangoon
Irrawaddy
Lhasa
Brahmaputra
Ganges
Bay of Bengal
Andaman Is. (India)
Nicobar Is. (India)

CHINA
Peking ■
Tientsin
Shenyang
Harbin
Dalian
Qingdao
Nanking
Shanghai
Wuhan
Sian
Lanzhou
Zhou
Chungking
Kunming
Yangtze
Huang
Yellow Sea
East China Sea
Canton
Hong Kong (Br.)
Macau (Port.)
Hainan
Fuzhou
Taipei
Taiwan
South China Sea
Tropic of Cancer

LAOS
Vientiane
THAILAND
Bangkok
VIETNAM
Hanoi
CAMBODIA
Phnom Penh
Ho Chi Minh City
Mekong
G. of Thailand
Str. of Malacca
Medan
Kuala Lumpur
MALAYSIA
PEN. MALAYSIA
SINGAPORE
Sumatra
Jakarta
Java
Palembang
Banjarmasin
Kuching
Borneo
BRUNEI
Sabah
Sarawak
Celebes Sea
Celebes
Sulu Sea
Sulu Is.
Zamboanga
Mindanao
Davao
PHILIPPINES
Luzon
Manila ■
Palawan
Moluccas
Halmahera
Ceram
Banda Sea
Flores
Surabaya
Ujung Pandang
Timor
New Guinea
Irian Jaya
Guam (U.S.)
Caroline Is.
Belau Is.
AUSTRALIA

Rwanda
Burundi
ZAIRE
UGANDA
KENYA
Nairobi
Kampala
TANZANIA
Dar es Salaam
Mombasa
ZAMBIA
MALAWI
ETHIOPIA
Addis Ababa
SOMALI REP.
Mogadishu
Djibouti
SUDAN
Khartoum
Juba
EGYPT
Cairo
Alexandria
Nile
Aswan
Port Sudan
LIBYA
AFRICA
SEYCHELLES
Amirantes
Equator

Peking Capital Cities

East from Greenwich

Projection: Bonne
COPYRIGHT GEORGE PHILIP & SON LTD

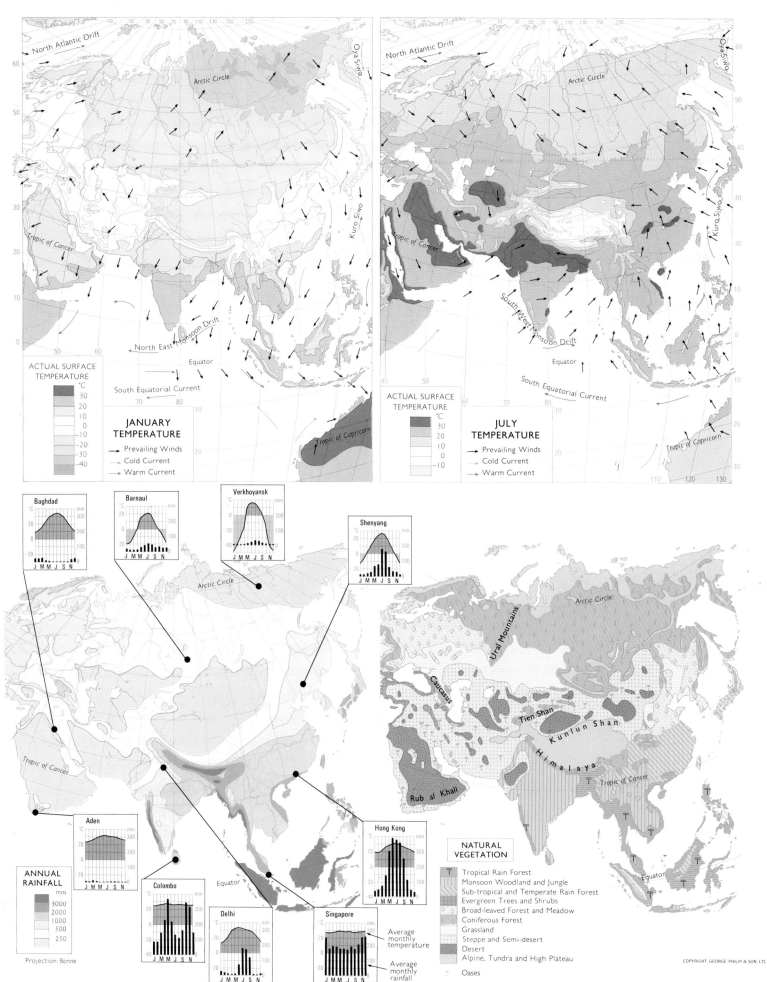

ACTUAL SURFACE TEMPERATURE
°C
30
20
10
0
−10
−20
−30
−40

JANUARY TEMPERATURE

→ Prevailing Winds
→ Cold Current
→ Warm Current

ACTUAL SURFACE TEMPERATURE
°C
30
20
10
0
−10

JULY TEMPERATURE

→ Prevailing Winds
→ Cold Current
→ Warm Current

Baghdad
Barnaul
Verkhoyansk
Shenyang

Aden
Colombo
Delhi
Singapore
Hong Kong

ANNUAL RAINFALL
mm
3000
2000
1000
500
250

Projection: Bonne

Average monthly temperature
Average monthly rainfall

NATURAL VEGETATION

T Tropical Rain Forest
Monsoon Woodland and Jungle
Sub-tropical and Temperate Rain Forest
Evergreen Trees and Shrubs
Broad-leaved Forest and Meadow
Coniferous Forest
Grassland
Steppe and Semi-desert
Desert
Alpine, Tundra and High Plateau

T Oases

COPYRIGHT. GEORGE PHILIP & SON. LTD

1:50 000 000

500 0 500 1000 1500 2000 km

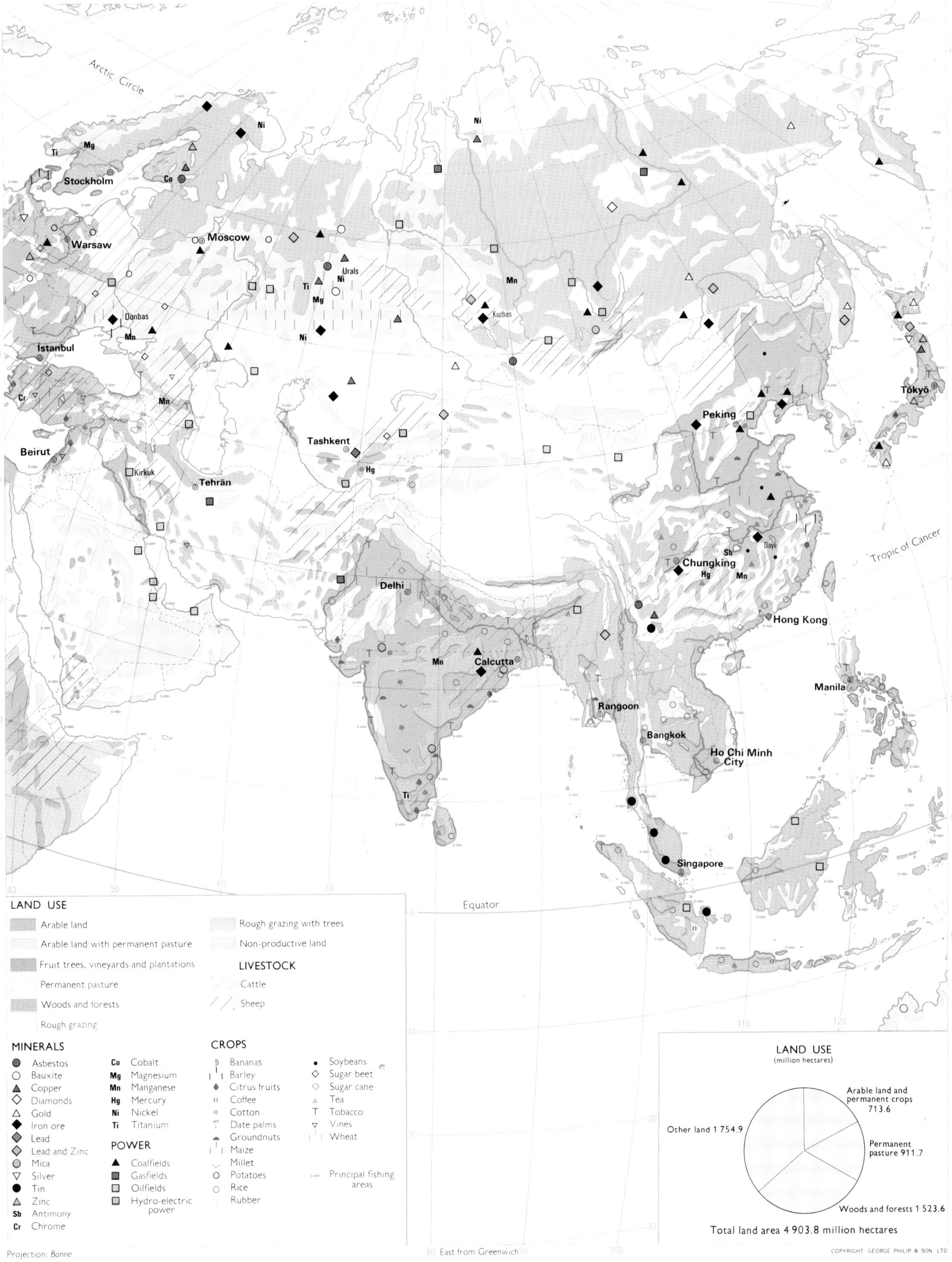

Arctic Circle

Ni

Ti Mg

Stockholm

Co

Ni

Mg

Mn

Warsaw

Moscow

Urals

Ti Ni

Mg

Donbas

Mn

Kuzbas

Ni

İstanbul

Mn

Ni

Mn

Ni

Beirut

Tashkent

Peking

Kirkuk

Hg

Tōkyō

Tehrān

Sb Daye

Chungking

Hg Mn

Delhi

Hong Kong

Mn

Calcutta

Manila

Rangoon

Bangkok

Ho Chi Minh City

Ti

Singapore

Tropic of Cancer

Equator

East from Greenwich

Projection: Bonne

LAND USE

Arable land

Arable land with permanent pasture

Fruit trees, vineyards and plantations

Permanent pasture

Woods and forests

Rough grazing

Rough grazing with trees

Non-productive land

LIVESTOCK

Cattle

Sheep

MINERALS

	Asbestos	**Co**	Cobalt
	Bauxite	**Mg**	Magnesium
	Copper	**Mn**	Manganese
	Diamonds	**Hg**	Mercury
	Gold	**Ni**	Nickel
	Iron ore	**Ti**	Titanium
	Lead		
	Lead and Zinc		
	Mica		
	Silver		
	Tin		
	Zinc		
Sb	Antimony		
Cr	Chrome		

POWER

Coalfields

Gasfields

Oilfields

Hydro-electric power

CROPS

	Bananas		Soybeans
	Barley		Sugar beet
	Citrus fruits		Sugar cane
	Coffee		Tea
	Cotton		Tobacco
	Date palms		Vines
	Groundnuts		Wheat
	Maize		
	Millet		Principal fishing areas
	Potatoes		
	Rice		
	Rubber		

LAND USE
(million hectares)

Arable land and permanent crops 713.6

Other land 1 754.9

Permanent pasture 911.7

Woods and forests 1 523.6

Total land area 4 903.8 million hectares

	Population						Growth			Land			Agriculture		
	Total	Density	Birth Rate	Death Rate	Life Expectancy	1965-73	1973-83	Urban	Area	Arable	Forest	Agricultural Population	Index of Production	Food intake
	th.	persons per km²	per th. popn.		yrs.	av. % per annum		%	th. km²	th. km²	th. km²	% of total popn.	1974-76 = 100	calories per day
Afghanistan	17 672	27	48	22	36	2.3	2.6	17	648	81	19	77	115	2 055
Bangladesh	96 730	722	47	19	50	2.6	2.4	17	134	91	21	83	125	1 837
Burma	37 614	57	39	14	55	2.3	2.0	29	658	101	322	50	150	2 420
Cambodia	7 149	40	30	40	31	1.8			177	30	134	72	104	1 922
China	1 051 551	113	22	8	67	2.7	1.5	21	9 326	1 009	1 282	57	145	2 426
Cyprus	657	73	20	9	74		0.6		9	4.3	1.7	33	113	3 378
Hong Kong	5 364	5 364	14	5	76	2.0	2.5	92	1	0.1	0.1	2.1	67	2 771
India	746 742	251	34	12	55	2.3	2.3	24	2 973	1 695	675	61	132	2 056
Indonesia	159 895	88	36	15	54	2.1	2.3	24	1 812	196	1 218	57	140	2 373
Iran	43 414	27	43	12	60	3.3	3.1	53	1 636	137	180	36	116	2 834
Iraq	15 158	35	47	13	59	3.3	3.6	69	434	55	15	38	136	2 789
Israel	4 194	210	24	7	74	3.1	2.3	90	20	4.2	1.2	6.2	121	3 062
Japan	120 018	323	13	6	77	1.2	0.9	76	371	48	252	9.2	99	2 852
Jordan	3 375	35	48	10	64	3.0	2.7	72	97	4.1	0.4	24	136	2 498
Korea, North	19 630	164	33	8	65	2.8	2.5	62	120	23	90	43	138	2 995
Korea, South	40 578	414	23	6	67	2.2	1.6	62	98	22	66	35	122	3 056
Laos	4 315	19	43	17	44	1.4	2.2	15	231	8.9	128	72	150	1 927
Lebanon	2 644	264	30	9	65	2.6	0.3	78	10	2.9	0.7	7.9	123	2 995
Malaysia	15 204	46	31	7	67	2.6	2.4	31	329	43	219	45	127	2 518
Mongolia	1 820	1.1	37	8	63	3.1	2.8	54	1 565	13	152	45	111	2 757
Nepal	16 107	118	45	21	46	2.0	2.6	7	137	23	45	92	117	1 933
Pakistan	93 286	120	42	10	50	3.1	3.0	29	779	203	29	52	132	2 180
Philippines	53 351	179	34	8	64	2.9	2.7	39	298	118	122	44	133	2 405
Saudi Arabia	10 824	5	46	14	56	4.0	4.7	71	2 150	11	16	58	36	2 947
Singapore	2 529	4 215	16	5	73	1.8	1.3	100	0.6	0.007	0.003	1.9	75	3 165
Sri Lanka	15 606	240	26	6	69	2.0	1.7	26	65	22	24	52	124	2 255
Syria	9 934	54	46	9	67	3.4	3.3	48	184	58	4.9	46	166	3 010
Taiwan	19 012	528	20	5	72				36	8.9	1.9	22	121	2 811
Thailand	50 396	98	31	8	63	2.9	2.3	18	512	190	158	74	134	2 330
Turkey	48 265	63	35	10	63	2.5	2.2	45	771	273	202	50	121	3 002
Vietnam	58 307	179	39	12	64	3.1	2.7	20	325	61	102	69	136	2 034
Yemen, North	6 386	33	49	24	44	2.6	2.9	18	195	28	16	74	79	2 478
Yemen, South	2 225	6.6	48	21	46	2.1	2.2	37	333	2	24	57	101	2 276
U.S.S.R.†														
Australia	15 544	2	16	7	76	2.1	1.3	86	7 618	465	1 060	5.2	122	3 055
New Zealand	3 233	12	16	8	74	1.4	0.6	83	269	4.7	100	8.6	117	3 572
Papua New Guinea	3 601	8	43	16	54	2.5	2.1	14	452	3.7	322	81	122	2 074

† See in Europe

Population. This is the United Nations' estimate for the mid-year 1984 (thousands).

Population density. This is the quoted population total divided by the quoted land area (persons per square kilometre).

Birth Rates and Death Rates. These are the registered or United Nations' estimated rates per thousand population.

Life Expectancy. This figure indicates the number of years that a child born today can expect to live if the levels of death of today last throughout its life. The figure is an average of that for men and women. The figure for women is usually higher than that for men (U.K. male 70, female 76 years).

Population Growth. This shows the average annual percentage change in population for two periods 1965-1973 and 1973-1983.

Urbanization. This is the percentage of the total population living in urban areas. The definition of urban is that of the individual nation and usually includes quite small towns.

Land Area. This is the total area of the country minus the area covered by major lakes and rivers (thousand square kilometres).

Arable Land and Permanent Crops. This excludes fallow land but includes temporary pasture (thousand square kilometres).

Forest and Woodland. This includes natural and planted woodland and land recently cleared of timber which will be replanted (thousand square kilometres).

Agricultural Population. This is the percentage of the economically active population working in agriculture. It includes those people working also in forestry, hunting and fishing.

Index of Agricultural Production. The base period for this index is 1974-1976 and it shows the level of production in each country in 1983 in comparision with that of the earlier period. Only edible crops and meat are included.

Food Supply. The figures are the average intake per person in calories per day in the period 1979-1981.

Trade		Education		Health	Energy	Consumer Price Index	G.N.P.		G.D.P. Part formed by		Loans & Debt		
Imports	Exports	Primary	Secondary	Popn. per doctor	Consumption in kgs of oil equiv. per capita		US$ per capita	Growth per capita % per yr. 1973-82	Agric.	Indust.	end 1983 US$ millions	as % of GNP	
US$ per capita		% of age group				1970 = 100			%				
41	42	35	12	16 730	46				63	20			Afghanistan
21	10	60	15	7 810	36	642	130	3.2	48	8	4 185	38	Bangladesh
6	8	84	20	4 680	65	327	180	3.6	47	11	2 226	36	Burma
				20 000	2 093								Cambodia
19	21	100	35	1 740	455		290	4.5	42	43			China
2 067	871	84		1 060	2 000	182	3 720		9	20			Cyprus
5 329	5 283	100	67	1 210	1 647	350	6 000	6.8	1	27	224	0.8	Hong Kong
18	11	79	30	3 690	182	323	260	1.8	32	19	21 277	11	India
87	137	100	33	11 530	204	159	560	4.6	24	36	21 685	29	Indonesia
283	476	97	40	6 090	976	699			17	22			Iran
	668	109	59	1 800	763				7	53			Iraq
2 036	1 190	95	74	370	1 932	683th	5 630	0.2	6	29	15 149	70	Israel
1 137	1 148	100	92	780	2 929	271	10 100	3.3	3	34	4 319	0.4	Japan
824	222	100	77	900	790	130	1 710	7.8	6	18	1 940	48	Jordan
		100		430	2 093								Korea, North
755	721	100	89	1 440	1 168	634	2 010	5.6	17	32	21 472		Korea, South
31	81	97	18	20 000	76								Laos
1 364	334	100	58	540	610				9	18	182		Lebanon
963	958	92	49	4 000	702	126	1 870	4.9	25	28	10 665	39	Malaysia
388	258	106	89	450	1 137		1 500		15	29			Mongolia
27	6	73	21	30 060	13	210	170	0.3	63	4	346	14	Nepal
63	35	44	14	3 480	197	184	390	2.9	27	18	9 755	31	Pakistan
153	96	100	64	7 970	252	351	760	2.9	23	29	10 385	30	Philippines
3 763	4 505	67	32	1 670	3 536	370	12 180	6.2	1	67			Saudi Arabia
11 394	9 567	100	66	1 150	4 757	220	6 620	6.5	1	32	1 244	7.6	Singapore
118	93	100	54	7 170	143	411	330	3.2	27	19	2 205	44	Sri Lanka
414	187	100	51	2 240	847	507	1 680	4.9	18	24	2 305	14	Syria
1 163	1 613	100	95	1 242		331	2 570						Taiwan
203	147	96	29	7 100	269	320	810	4.0	24	23	7 060	18	Thailand
224	147	100	39	1 630	599	269	1 230	1.4	21	28	15 396	30	Turkey
		100	48	4 190	90		170						Vietnam
250	6	59	7	11 670	116		510	3.5	28	8	1 574	38	Yemen, North
332	212	64	18	7 120	934		510	6.4	10	13	1 263	119	Yemen, South
													U.S.S.R.†
1 507	1 529	100	90	560	4 811	387	10 780	0.9	6	30	773	0.5	Australia
1 860	1 659	100	81	640	3 808	568	7 410	0.3	11	27	59	0.3	New Zealand
305	247	65	13	13 590	223	299	790	0.7	36	19	911	40	Papua New Guinea

† See in Europe

Bahrain Land 0.6/Popn. 400; Bhutan 47/1 338; Brunei 5.3/269/Kuwait 17.8/1 787;Macau 0.02/343; Maldives 0 3/173; Oman 212.5/1 181; Qatar 11/291; U.A.E. 83.6/1 255. American Samoa 0.2/34; Cocos Is.0.01/0.5; Cook Is 0.2/19; Fiji 18.3/686; Fr. Polynesia 3.7/160; Guam 0.6/112; Johnston I. 0.001/1; Kiribati 0.7/62; Midway I. 0.005/2; Nauru 0.02/8; New Caledonia 18.8/152; Niue I. 0.26/3; Norfolk I. 0.036/2; Pacific Is. 1.8/149; Samoa 2.9/159; Solomon Is.27.5/269; Tokelau 0.01/1.6; Tonga 0.7/107; Tuvalu 0.2/8; Vanuatu 14.8/128; Wake Is.0.008/2; Wallis & Futuna 0.2/10

Trade. The trade figures are normally for the year 1983 or 1984. The total trade figures have been divided by the population and are a measure of the country's external trade (U.S. $ per capita).

Education. The ages of primary school are taken to be 6-11 years and secondary school 12-17 years. The percentage of the total school age group in this type of education is shown.

Energy. All forms of energy have been converted to their equivalent in oil. Firewood and other traditional forms used in developing countries are not included and so the energy consumption in those countries is understated (kilograms of oil equivalent per capita).

Consumer Price Index. The base year is 1970 which is 100 and the level of consumer prices in 1984 or 1985 are shown in relation to the base year. It is a measure of inflation.

G.N.P. (Gross National Product) This figure is an estimate of the average production per person measured in U.S. dollars and for 1983. The G.N.P. measures the value of goods and services produced in a country, plus the balance, positive or negative, of income from abroad, for example investments, interest on capital, money returned from foreign labour, etc. The rate of change is the average annual percentage change during the period 1973-1982 in the G.D.P. The G.D.P. (Gross Domestic Product) is the G.N.P. minus the foreign balances. The adjoining two columns show the percentage contribution to the G.D.P. made by the agricultural and mining and manufacturing sectors.

Loans and Debt. This figure in millions of U.S. dollars shows the external public debt at the end of 1983. This is then shown as a percentage of the annual G.N.P. The figures in red show official development assistance made by the developed countries and also as a percentage of the donor country's G.N.P.

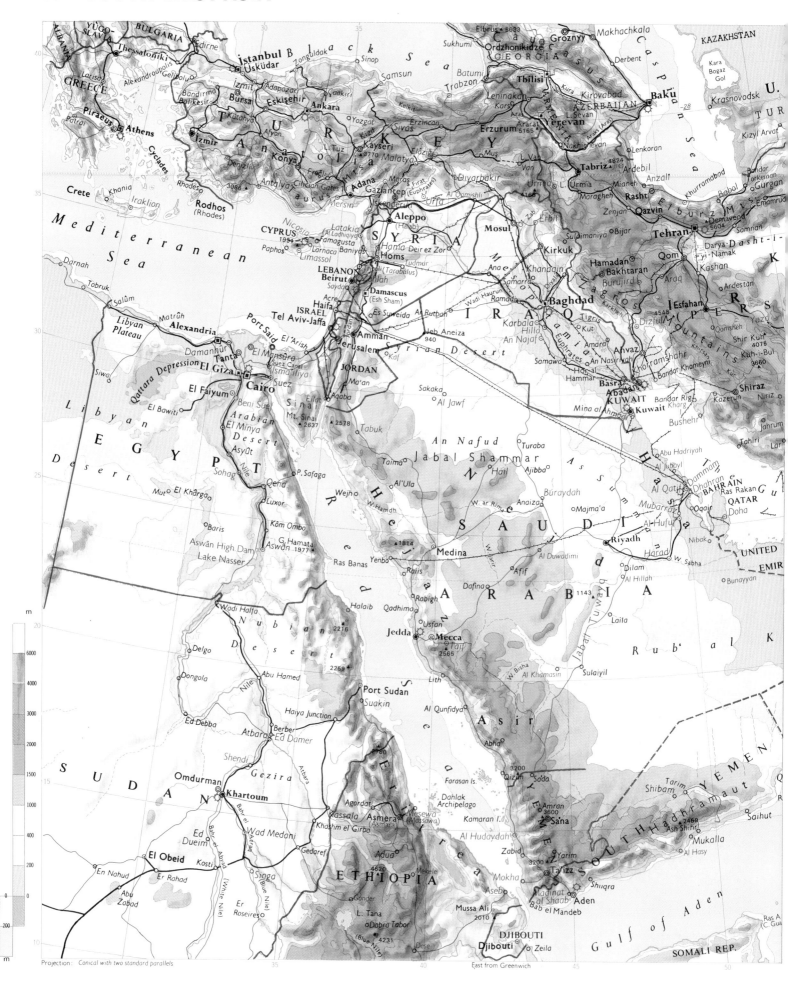

1:15 000 000

100   0   100   200   300   400   500   600 km

CHINA

S.S.R.   UZBEKISTAN   Samarkand
Tashauz   Bukhara   TADZHIKISTAN
KMENISTAN   Amu Darya   Dushanbe   Pamir
Kara Kum   Chardzhou   Kerki   Faizabad   Gilgit   Kashmir
Ashkhabad   Mary   Kushka   Kholm   Chitral   Srinagar
Nishapur   Sabzawar   Maimana   Baghlan   Kunar   Islamabad   Rawalpindi
Mashhad   Gharian   Charikar   Khyber Pass   Peshawar   Sialkot
hurasan   Birjand   AFGHANISTAN   Kabul   Jalalabad   Kohat   Lahore
Tabas   Daulatabad   3787   Qalat   Bannu
Kavir   Neh   Farah   Ghazni   Dera Ismail Khan   Multan
A   Zabul   Ft. Sandeman   Sutlej
Kerman   Saguch   3994   Zahidan   Qandahar   Kundar   Pishin   Dera Ghazi Khan   Bahawalpur
Saidabad   4419   Ladis   Nushki   Quetta   Sibi   Jacobabad   Sukkur
Bam   Kuh-i-Taftan 4042   Bolan Pass   Kalat   Shikarpur   Larkana
Khanu   Haliri   Bampur   Panjgur   Bela   Nawabshah
Bandar Abbas   Minab   Fanuch   Pasni   INDIA
Qishm   Kuhran 2163   Hyderabad
Lingeh   2057   Jask   Chahbar   Gwadar   Karachi
Dubai   Sharja   Gulf of Oman   MAKRAN
Abu Dhabi   As Sohar   Tropic of Cancer
ARAB   Al Khabura   Matrah   Muscat
ATES   J. ash Sham 3019   Sur   Ras al Hadd
OMAN   Izki   W. Andam   Arabian   Sea
Dawwah   Al Masira
hali   Al Khalaf   Gulf of Masira
Ras al Madraka
Dhofar   Sauqra Bay
1678   Kuria Muria
Salala   Is.
Marbat
amr Bay
as Fartak
Socotra (South Yemen)
The Brothers
sir
rdafui)

BEIRUT (Bayrut)   Djounie (Juniyah)   Mts J. Sannini 2628   Ba'labakk (Baalbek)
Bikfaiya
Zahlah
Aley   2462
Anti Lebanon
Saydā (Sidon)   Bisri   Khirbat Qanafar   Damascus (Esh Sham)
Jezzine   Bekaa Valley   Dareiya
Nabatiyé el Tahta   LEBANON   Hermon 2814   Qatana   SYRIA
Litani   Al Khiyam   Kiswe
Tyre (Sur)   Qiryat Shemona   Al Qunaytirah   Sanamein
Tibnin
Nahariya   Me'ona 1208   Tsefat (Safad)   Capernaum
Acre   GALILEE   L. Kinneret   Jizr'a
B. of Haifa   Migdal   Tiberias (Sea of Galilee) -209
Haifa   Mt. Carmel 546   Nazareth   Fiq
Tirat Karmel   Samar
Daliyat el Karmel   Afula   515   Dar'a
Caesarea   Taiyiba   Esdraelon   Arab   Irbid
Megiddo   Ramtha
Pardes Hanna   Umm el Fahm   Beit Shean
Hadera   Janin   Yabis 1198
Netanya   SAMARIA   Tubas   Jebel 'Ajlun   Al Mafraq
Anabta   Ajlun 1247
Tul Karm   Sumaria   Jarash
Ra'anana   940   Faria   Zarqa
Herzliya   Kefar Sava   881 Nablus   Damiya   Az Zarqa
TEL AVIV-JAFFA   Petah Tiqva   Shilo   1113   As Salt
Ramat Gan   1016   JORDAN   Amman
Holon   Wadi es Sir   802   Na'ur
Bat Yam   Lod (Lydda)   Jericho   Madaba
Rishon Le-Zion   Ramla   Hussein Br.
Rehovot   Ram Allah
Ashdod   Yavne   Soreq   Jerusalem   Dhiban
Gedera   Qumran   Muib
Ashqelon   Bethlehem   JUDAEA   Dead Sea
Qiryat Gat   1020 Hebron (El Khalil)   716
Gaza (Ghazzah)   Shiqma   Shephela
Gaza Strip   Lakhish   Az Zahiriya   Al Mazra
Khan Yunis   Mishmar Ha Negev   Masada
Rafah   Habesor   Judaean Wilderness   Al Karak
Beersheba   Arad
EGYPT   Dimona   395
Qezi'ot   NEGEV

East from Greenwich   35

THE HOLY LAND
Armistice boundaries between Arab States
and Israel, 1949-1974
1:1 500 000

10   0   10   20   30   40   50 km

U.S.S.R.

3020

BADGHIS
FARYAB
SAMANGAN
BALKH
JOUZJAN
BAGHLAN
TAKHAR
BADAKHSHAN
Range

Gunabad
Bala Murghab
Maimana
Tukzar
Kushka
Kohsan
Murghab
Herat
Hari Rud
Obeh
Daulat Yar
BAMIAN
Naiak
Koh-i-Baba
5143
Kabul
KABUL
Chitral
Disteghil Sar 7885
Aghil Pass 4779
Aghil Mountains
Rakaposhi 7788
K2 8611
Karakoram Pass 5575
Soda Plains
Gilgit
Skardu
8126
Saser 7672
Karakoram Range

HINDU KUSH
PARWAN
KAPISA
LAGHMAN
KUNAR
Dir
Desai Mountains
Nanga Parbat
Shyok

HERAT
Ghurian
Paropamisus Range
GHOR
Shindand
2886
4148
URUZGAN
3787
GHAZNI
Mukur
5143

Birjand
Neh
Anardara
Farah
Farah
FARAH
Washir
Girishk
Khash Desert
Khash
Khugiani
Qandahar
ZABUL
Qalat
PAKTIKA
3513

AFGHANISTAN

WARDAK
LOGAR
NANGARHAR
Jalalabad
Khyber Pass
Peshawar
Mardan
Wah
Baramula
Srinagar
135
Anantnag
Leh
KASHMIR
7026
Chushul
Bangong
Indus
Shipki La
Garyars

PAKTYA
Wazo
Gardez
Ghazni
PAKTIA

PERSIA (IRAN)

Daryacheh-ye-Sistan
Hamun-i-Helmand
NIMRUZ
Chahar Burjak
Rudbar
Landi
HELMAND
Dasht-i-Margo
Registan
Chaman
Khojak Pass
Bolan Pass
Quetta
3593
Mach
Sibi
Loralai
Mekhtar
Fort Sandeman
Gomal Pass
Zhob
Dera Ismail Khan
Bannu
Kohat
Thal
Gomal
Monzai
North Waziristan
Dargai

Zahidan
Ribat
Gaud-i-Zirreh
Chagai Hills
Nushki
Kalat
Dalbandin
Hamun-i-Mashkel
Nasirabad
Jacobabad
Shikarpur
Sukkur
Khairpur
Larkana
Khazdar
Dadu
SIND
BALUCHISTAN
Kirthar Range
Pab Hills
Siahan Range
Central Makran Range
Makran Coast Range
Turbat
Panjgur
Bela
Nal
Pasni
Gwadar
Chahbar
Dasht

ARABIAN SEA
Tropic of Cancer
C. Monze
Hab
KARACHI
Mouths of the Indus
Indus
Totta
Kotri
HYDERABAD
Tando Adam
Mirpur Khas
Nawabshah
Rann of Kutch

Islamabad
Rawalpindi
Jhelum
Mangla Dam
Mianwali
Khushab
Sargodha
Sagar Doab
Jhang Maghiana
Gujrat
Sialkot
Gujranwala
Wazirabad
Hafizabad
Lahore
Faisalabad (Lyallpur)
Amritsar
Jammu
Chamba
Pathankot
HIMACHAL PRADESH
Mandi
Simla
Bhakra Dam
Jullundur
Ludhiana
Chandigarh
Nangal Dam
Sutlej
PUNJAB
Kasur
Ferozepore
Fazilka
Okara
Sahiwal
Bari Doab
Multan
Khanewal
Dera Ghazi Khan
Rahimyar-Khan
Khanpur
Bahawalpur
Ahmadpur
Rajasthan Canal
Bikaner
Ratangarh
Churu
Sikar
1052
Nagaur
Phalodi
Great Indian (Thar) Desert
RAJASTHAN
387 R.
Barmer
Luni
Jodhpur
Pali
Marwar
Sirohi
1722
Udaipur
Deesa
Palanpur
Patan
Nathdwara
Sambhar
Ajmer
Beawar
Bhilwara
Bundi
Kota
Gandhi Sagar Dam
Tonk
Jaipur
Alwar
Bharatpur
Mathura
Agra
Dholpur
Gwalior
Firozabad
Etawah
Kanpur
Shivpuri
Baran 521
Guna
Lalitpur
Jhansi
Chhatarpur
Sagar
Damoh
Sutlej
Dehra Dun
Nanda Dev 7817
Hardwar
Saharanpur
Karnal
Muzaffarnagar
Panipat
Najibabad
Haldwani
Meerut
Rampur
Moradabad
Hapur
Amroha
Sambhal
HARYANA
Rohtak
Bhiwani
DELHI
Gurgaon
Rewari
Ghaziabad
Bulandshahr
Pilibhit
Shahjahanpur
Bareilly
Aligarh
Hathras
Mainpuri
Fatehgarh
UTTAR

GUJARAT
Bhuj
Little Rann
Mandvi
Mehsana
Nadiad
AHMADABAD
Dohad
Godhra
Jamnagar
Rajkot
Dwarka
Cambay
Vadodara
Ratlam
Ujjain
Dewas
Indore
Mhow
MADHYA PRADESH
Bhopal
Sehore
Jhabua
Shajapur
Dhar
Gwalior
Porbandar
Junagadh
1117
Amreli
Bhavnagar
Bharuch
Surat
Navsari
Gulf of Kutch
Gulf of Cambay
Veraval
Diu
DAMAN, DADRA & NAGAR HAVELI
Narmada
Tapti
Nandurbar
Khargon
Burhanpur
Khandwa
Betul
1353
Gadarwara
Jabalpur
Bhanrer Range
Satpura Range
Bhusawal
Dhule
Jalgaon
Akola
Amravati
Nagpur
Wardha
Bhandara
Gondia
Balaghat
Chhindwara
Gawilgarh Hills
Malegaon
Satmala Hills
Nasik
Deolali
1646
Ajanta Range
Aurangabad
Jalna
Parbhani
Hingoli
Adilabad
Chanda
Penganga
Wardha
Yeotmal
MAHARASHTRA
Thana
Ulhasnagar
BOMBAY
Kirkee
Pune (Poona)
Ahmadnagar
Godavari
Balaghat Range
Nizamabad
Bodhan
Karimnagar
796
Bir
Latur
1438
Satara
Pandharpur
Bhima
Solapur
Barsi
Ratnagiri
Kolhapur
Sangli
Miraj
Bijapur
Gulbarga
Bidar
Secunderabad
HYDERABAD
Warangal
ANDHRA PRADESH
Narayanpet
Mahbubnagar
Yadgir
Raichur
Krishna
917
Nallamalai Hills
Jamkhandi
Belgaum
Vengurla
Panaji (Panjim)
Marmagao
GOA
1053
Dharwad
Gadag
Tungabhadra
Kurnool
Adoni
Erramala Hills
Bellary
Proddatur
Ongole

Continuation Southwards on same scale

GOA
Dharwad
Gadag
Kurnool
Adoni
Bellary
Erramala Hills
Velikonda Ra.
Ongole
Penner
Nellore
Pulicat Lake
1100
Anantapur
Proddatur
Cuddapah
1151
Tirupati
Chittoor
Pulicat Lake
Madras
Davangere
Shimoga
Sagar
Bhadravati
KARNATAKA
Tumkur
1255
Kolar Gold Fields
Vellore
Kanchipuram
Mangalore
Hassan
Bangalore
Mandya
Mysore
Melagiri Hills
Salem
1628
Pondicherry
Mettur
Cuddalore
Western Ghats
Eastern Ghats
Cannanore
Calicut (Kozhikode)
2637
Coimbatore
Tiruppur
Erode
TAMIL NADU
Thanjavur
Kumbakonam
Nagappattinam
Trichur
Palghat
Pollachi
Tiruchchirappalli
Dindigul
Coromandel Coast
Cochin
Mattancheri
2698
Palni Hills
Karaikkudi
Madurai
Alleppey
KERALA
Cardamon Hills
Palk Strait
Jaffna
Palk Bay
Mannar
Quilon
Rajapalaiyam
Tuticorn
Gulf of Mannar
Adam's Bridge
Trivandrum
1654
Tirunelveli
Nagercoil
Cape Comorin
Malabar Coast
Anuradhapura
766
Trincomalee
Foul Pt.
Puttalam
Batticaloa
SRI LANKA
Kurunegala
Matale
Kandy
2524
Piducutalagala
Badulla
Colombo
Moratuwa
Kalutara
Adam's Peak 2243
Galle
Matara
Dondra Head
Negombo

ARABIAN SEA

Gulf of Kutch
Gulf of Cambay

m
6000
4000
3000
2000
1500
1000
400
200
0
m
200

62 64 66 68 70 72 74 76 78 80 82

Projection: Conical with two standard parallels

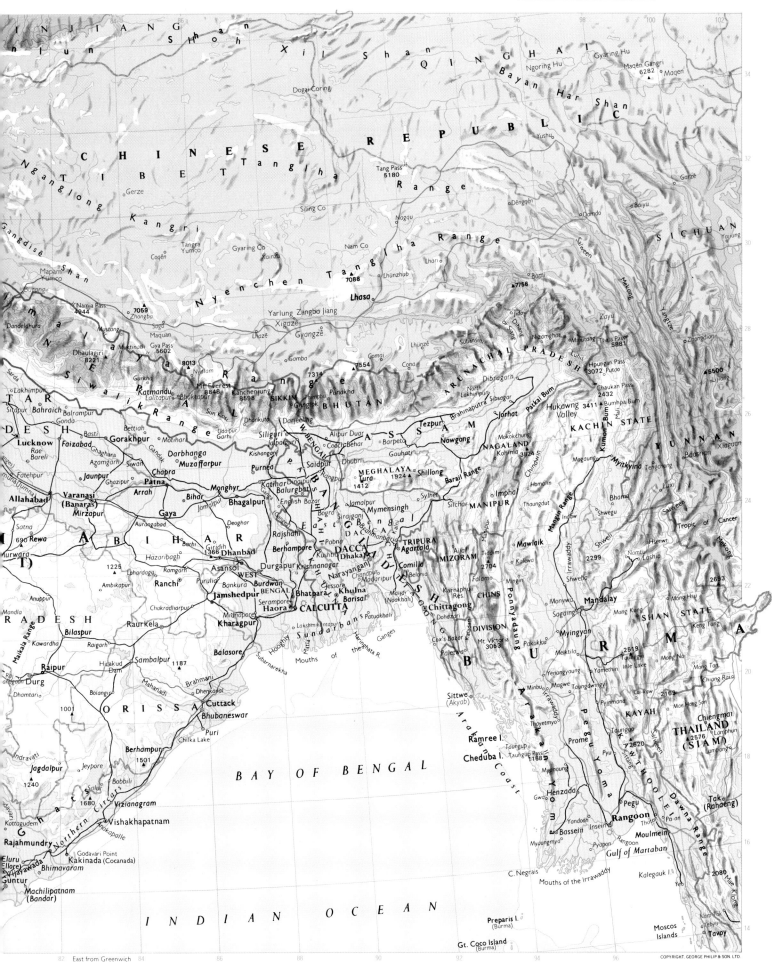

100   0   100   200   300   400 km

I N J I A N G

n l u n   S h a n

T a r i m   S h a n

X i l   S h a n

Q I N G H A I

Dogai Coring

Ngoring Hu

Gyaring Hu

Maqên Gangri
6282 • Maqen

C H I N E S E   R E P U B L I C

T I B E T   T a n g l h a   R a n g e

Bayan   Har   Shan

Garzê

N g a n g l o n g   K a n g r i

Gerze

Tang Pass
5180

Dêngqên

S I C H U A N

Yalung

Baiyu

Siling Co

Nagqu

Yushu

Qamdo

Mapam
Yumco

Burang

Tangra
Yumco

Gyaring Co

Nam Co

N y e n c h e n   T a n g l h a   R a n g e

Lhari

Bomi

7756▲

Zhongba

7059
4944

Namla Pass

Mustang

Coqên

Xainza

Lhünzhub

7088▲

Lhasa

Salween

Mekong

Yanetze

Zogandian

Dandeldhura

Saga

Maquan

Lhozê

Yarlung   Zangbo   Jiang

Xigazê

Gyangzê

Gomai

Jido

Sang

Dhang

Nizamghat

Zayu

Thala Pass
5881

5500
▲

Lijiang

Muktinath

Gya Pass
5602

Gamba

Cona

Lhünzê

Subansiri

Luhit

Hpungan Pass
3072 Putoo

Dhaulagiri
8221

8013
▲

N y d a m

Gurkha

Mt. Everest
8848

7314
▲

7554
▲

A r u n a c h a l   P r a d e s h

Dibrugarh

Chaukan Pass
2432

Ratmandu

Lalitapur

Bhaktapur

Kanchenjunga
8598

SIKKIM

Thimphu

Punakha

B H U T A N

North
Lakhimpur

Sibsagar

Brahmaputra

Jorhat

Pakai Bum

Hukawng
Valley

Bumha Bum

H i m a l a y a   S i w a l i k   R a n g e

Gangtok

Darjeeling

A S S A M

Tezpur

Mokokchung

KACHIN STATE

Kumon Bum   3411

Lakhimpur

Sitapur

Bahraich

Balrampur

Siliguri
(Jalpaiguri)

Alipur Duar

Cooch-Behar

Barpeta

Gauhati

Nowgong

N A G A L A N D

Kohima
3924

Chindwin

Mogaung

Myitkyina

Tengchong

Y U N N A N

Baoshan

Xiaguan

Gonda

Basti

Bettiah

Motihari

Kishanganj

Dhubri

Homalin

Luxi

T A R
D E S H

Lucknow

Rae
Bareli

Faizabad

Ghaghara

Azamgarh

Gorakhpur

Siwan

Gandak

Darbhanga

Muzaffarpur

Purnea

Katihar

Saidpur

Dinajpur

Rangpur

Dhubri

MEGHALAYA

Tura
1412

1924 ▲

Shillong

Barail Range

Sylhet

Silchar

M A N I P U R

Imphal

Thaungdut

Mangin   Range

Indaw

Shwegu

Bhamo

Shweli

Hsenwi

Namtu

Lashio

Fatehpur

Jaunpur

Ghazipur

Chapra

Patna

Arrah

Monghyr

Bihar

Bhagalpur

English Bazar

Balurghat

Jamalpur

Mymensingh

Kalni

Thaungdut

Tropic   of   Cancer

Allahabad

Varanasi
(Banaras)

Mirzapur

Gaya

Aurangabad

Deoghar

Rajshahi

Pabna

Bogra

Sirajganj

Dacca
DA

Comilla

T R I P U R A

Agartala

M I Z O R A M

Aijal

Tiddim
2704

Falam

Kalewa

Mawlaik

Monywa

2299

Mandalay

2693

Satna

Rewa
690

B I H A R

1366 Dhanbad

Barhi

Giridih

Hazaribagh

Berhampore

Durgapur

Krishnanagar

Narayanganj

Chandpur

Madaripur

Belonia

CHINS

Mingin

Sagaing

Mong Kung

S H A N   S T A T E

Keng Tung

Murwara

1225

Lohardaga

Ramgarh

Asansol

Purulia

Bankura

Burdwan

W E S T

B E N G A L

Bhatpara

Jessore

Khulna

Barisal

Majdi
(Noakhali)

Chittagong

Karnaphuli
Res.

DIVISION

2519

Tiddim
2704

Falam
2620

Myingyan

Meiktila

2163

Mong Nai

Mong Tau

Chiang Rai

Anuppur

Ambikapur

Ranchi

Chakradharpur

Jamshedpur

Serampore

Haora

CALCUTTA

Bhatpara

Midnapore

Barisal

Cox's Bazar

Dohazari

B U R M A

Mt. Victoria
3053

Pakokku

Pyu

Yenangyaung

Magwe

Taungdwingyi

Yamethin

Inle Lake

Lai-kaw

2576

KAYAH

Chiengmai

Lamphun

Lampang

Mandla

RADESH

Maikala   Range

Kawardha

Bilaspur

Raigarh

Raurkela

Kharagpur

Lakshmikantapur

Patuakhali

Palewa

Karnaphuli

Prome

Myingyan

Pyinmana

2176

THAILAND
(SIAM)

Indravati

Raipur

Durg

Dhamtari

Hirakud
Dam

Sambalpur

1187

Balasore

Subarnarekha

Sundarbans

Hooghly

Ganges

theneghata R.

Mouths   of   the

Arakan   Coast

Sittwe
(Akyab)

Ramree I.

Cheduba I.

Taungup

Taungup Pass
1188

Thayetmyo

A r a k a n   Y o m a

Minbu

Prome

Henzada

Pegu   Yoma

Taungoo

P e g u   Y o m a

Prome

Pyu

Salween

2620

Kawthoole

Dawna   Range

Dhamtario

Bolangir

Mahanadi

Brahmani

Dhenkanal

1001

O R I S S A

Cuttack

Bhubaneswar

Puri

Chilka Lake

Jagdalpur

1240

Berhampur

1501

Salur

Bobbili

Vizianagram

Indravati

1680

Kottagudem

Vishakhapatnam

Anakapalle

G h a t s

N o r t h e r n   C i r c a r s

B A Y   O F   B E N G A L

Ramree I.

Cheduba I.

C. Negrais

Mouths   of   the   Irrawaddy

Gwa

Bassein

Inseing

Rangoon

Myungmya

Pyapon

Thaton

Pa-an

Moulmein

Gulf   of   Martaban

Kalegauk I.

2080

Mae Klong

G

Rajahmundry

Godavari Point

Kakinada (Cocanada)

Eluru
(Ellore)

Vijayawada

Bhimavaram

Guntur

Machilipatnam
(Bandar)

I N D I A N   O C E A N

Preparis I.
(Burma)

Gt. Coco Island
(Burma)

Moscos
Islands

Tavoy

Nam Tok

KAZAKHSTAN

Karaganda
Karsakpay
Karkaralinsk

Semipalatinsk
Ust
Kamenogorsk
Rubtsovsk

UNION OF SOVIET SOCIALIST
Western Sayan
Munku Sardyk *3491*
Cheremkhovo
Angarsk
Irkutsk
455

Tannu Ola
Belukha *4506*
Zyryanovsk

Hatgal
Höysgöl Nuur

Lake Ralkhash
342
Taldy-Kurgan

Ayaguz
Lake Zaisan

Altay
Fuhai
Ulungur

Ulaangom
Uvs Nuur
Tesyn Gol

Hyargas Nuur
Har Us Nuur
Hovd

Dörôö Nuur
Ulyasutay

Selenge Orhon Gol
Tsetserleg
Altanbulag

Ulan Bator
Dzuunmod

M O N G O

Tarbagatai Ra.
Tacheng
Ala Kul
Karamay

Fuyun
4362

Buyanhongor

Alma Ata
Issyk Kul
Frunze
Dzhambul
Dzhetysuat
Bole
Yining

Dzungarian Gates
Usu

Dzungaria
Shan

Altai

Dalandzadgad

Namangan
Andizhan
KIRGIZIA
1609
Naryn

Pik Pobedy
7439

Ürümqi
5445
Qitai

Turpan
154

ZIZHIQU
4925

Gaxun Nur

G o
NEI

Linhe

Kashi

Aksu
Kuqa
Korla

Bosten (Bagrax) Hu
Kuruktag

Hami

NINGXIA
Wuhai
2514

Shache
Yecheng
Hotan
Yutian

XINJIANG
Takla Makan
1635

Tarim He
Tarim Basin

UYGUR

Lop Nor

Ruoqiang
Qiemo

Dunhuang
Anxi
Yumen

Altun Shan
Jiayuguan

Nan Shan
6346
Zhangye

Ala Shan
Alxa Zuoqi
Yinchuan
HUIZU
Wuwei
Wuzhong

ZIZHIQU
LANZHOU

Karakoram
K2 *8611*
8126
Karakoram Pass
5575

JAMMU & KASHMIR
Srinagar
Leh
Rutog

Da Qaidam
Qaidam Pendi
Golmud
Tianjun

Dulan
Qinghai Hu *3205*
Gonghe
Xining

Linxia
Pingliang

Nanda Devi
7817
Burang

Kunlun Shan
7723

XIZANG
Gar

Ngoring Hu *4237*
Gyaring Hu
Maqen

Min Xian
Tianshui
Baoji

Dehra Dun
Mapam Yumco

Bayan Har Shan
6094

Wudu
4113
Hanzhong

Meerut
DELHI
Moradabad
Bareilly
Aligarh

Zhongba

Tanglha Range
Siling Co *4495*
Amdo

Nam Co *4627*
Xainza

Nagqu

QINGHAI
Yushu
Yalong
Huang He

SI
CHUAN

Mianyang
Daxian

Agra
Gwalior
Jhansi

HIMALAYA
Dhaulagiri
8221

Nyenchen Tanglha Range
(TIBET)
Lhasa
Xiagaze
Lhaze

Yarlung Zangbo
Yamzho Yumco

Mekong
Qamdo

Nujiang Shan
Nu Jiang (Salween)

Shaluli Shan

Gatze
Daxue Shan
Gongga Shan *7600*

CHENGDU
Neijiang
Nanchong
Hechuan

KANPUR
LUCKNOW
Gorakhpur

NEPAL
Katmandu
Everest *8848*
Thimphu
BHUTAN

Namcha Barwa *7756*
Bomi

Zayu

Wutongqia
Luzhou
Yibin
CHUNG
Zigong

Allahabad
Patna
Varanasi

Koch Bihar
Brahmaputra

Dibrugarh
Tezpur
Gauhati

Zhongdian

Zunyi
Wu

INDIA
Jabalpur
Ranchi
Jamshedpur

Rajshahi
BANGLADESH
Asansol

Khasi Hills
Patkai Hills

Myitkyina
3411

Xichang
Lijiang
Zhaotong

GUIZHO

Tropic of Cancer
Gwalior

DACCA (Dhaka)
Narayanganj
Haora

Silchar
Imphal *3824*

Bhamo

Dongchuan
Xiaguan

Daliang Shan
Zhanyi
Anshun
Guiyang
Duyun

Raipur
NAGPUR

Khulna
CALCUTTA

CHITTAGONG

Arakan Yoma

Monywa

Luxi
Baoshan

KUNMING
Xingyi
Hechi

GUA
ZHUA

Warangal

Mahanadi
Cuttack

Indravati

B U R M A

Victoria *3053*
Akyab

Mandalay
2650

Jiangcheng

Y U N N A N
Gejiu
Shiping

Wenshan
Bose

Nanning
Pingxiang
ZIZ
Qinzhou

Vishakhapatnam

BAY OF BENGAL

Arakan Yoma
Irrawaddy
Pegu Yoma
Yamethin

Salween
Mekong
2163
THAILAND (SIAM)
Toungoo

Sra Da (Black)
3143

HANOI
Hod-Binh
VIETNAM
LAOS
Luang Prabang
HAIPHONG
Gulf of Tonkin

East from Greenwich

Projection: Bonne

m
6000
4000
3000
2000
1500
1000
400
200
0
200
m

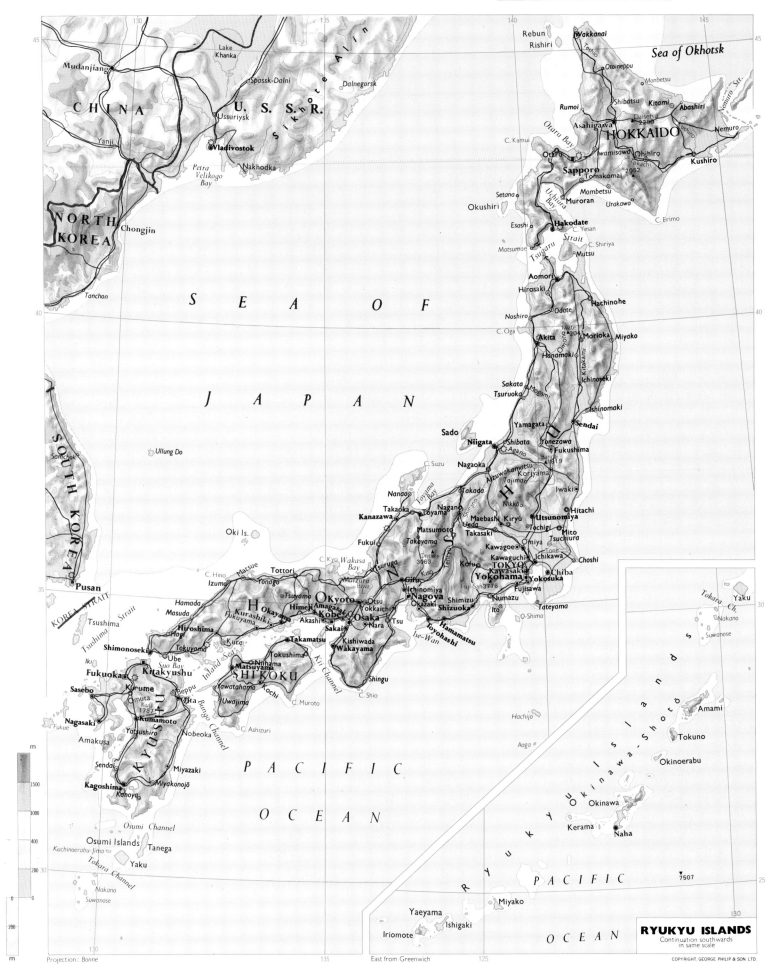

1 : 7 500 000

50 0 50 100 150 200 250 300 km

RYUKYU ISLANDS
Continuation southwards
in same scale

Projection: Bonne

East from Greenwich

COPYRIGHT. GEORGE. PHILIP & SON. LTD.

1:15 000 000

100 0 100 200 300 400 500 600 km

COPYRIGHT GEORGE PHILIP & SON LTD

PHILIPPINES

LUZON

MANILA
Quezon City
Batangas

San Carlos
Baguio

Catanduanes
Polillo Islands
Lamon Bay
Lipa
Calapan
Mindoro
Mindoro Str.

Marinduque
Tablas
Romblon
Masbate
Panay
Iloilo
Negros
Bacolod
Cebu
CEBU
Leyte
Calbayog
Catbalogan
Samar
Tacloban
San Bernardino Str.
Legazpi
Naga
Daet

Bohol
Dumaguete
Siquijor
Dipolog
Ozamis
Pagadian
Zamboanga
Isabela
Basilan
Jolo
Tawitawi

Cagayan de Oro
Butuan
Surigao
Dinagat
Agusan
Davao
Davao G.
General Santos
Cotabato
MINDANAO

SULU SEA
SULU

CELEBES SEA

Morotai
Halmahera
Gebe
Obi Is.
Bacan Gr.
Ternate
Equator

CERAM SEA
Ambon
Buru
Wahai
Banda Is.
BANDA SEA

MALUKU (Moluccas)

Talaud Is.
Sangihe Is.
Manado
Gorontalo
G. of Tomini
Peleng
Banggai Arch.
Sula Is.
Sanana
Mangole
Taliabu
Buton

SULAWESI (CELEBES)
Palu
Poso
Kolaka
Kendari
Muna
Baubau
Ujung Pandang
Watampone
G. of Bone
Str. of Makasar

Wetar
Alor
Flores
Ende
Maumere
Sumba
Sawu Sea
Waingapu
Kupang
Timor
Lesser Sunda Islands
FLORES SEA
Lombok
Sumbawa
Bali
Mataram
Denpasar
Kangean Is.

SOUTH CHINA SEA

Paracel Islands

Spratly I.
Amboyna I.

Palawan Islands

Puerto Princesa
Balabac Str.
SABAH (NORTH BORNEO)
Kota Kinabalu (Jesselton)
Kinabalu 4101
Sandakan
Kudat
Victoria
Weston
Bandar Seri Begawan
BRUNEI
Miri
Seria
SARAWAK
Kuching
Sibu
Kapuas Hulu Ra.

BORNEO
KALIMANTAN
Tarakan
Tanjungselor
Tanjungredep
Samarinda
Balikpapan
Muller Ra.
Schwaner Ra.
Pontianak
Singkawang
Sambas
Ketapang
Banjarmasin
Martapura
Palangkaraya
Sampit

Natuna Is. (Bunguran)
N. Bunguran Is.
Anambas Is.
Karimata Str.
Belitton Is.
Bangka
Karimata

MALAYSIA
PENINSULAR MALAYSIA
Kuala Lumpur
Shah Alam
Selangor
Kuala Terengganu
Kota Baharu
Kuantan
Ipoh
Taiping
Alor Setar
George Town
Pinang
Johor Baharu
SINGAPORE
Malacca
Strait of Malacca
Kota Tinggi
Seremban
Kluang

THAILAND (SIAM)
BANGKOK
Ayutthaya
Nakhon Sawan
Nakhon Ratchasima
Khon Kaen
Chonburi
Chanthaburi
Gulf of Thailand
Ko Samui
Surat Thani
Nakhon Si Thammarat
Songkhla (Singora)
Pattani
Hat Yai
Thale Luang
Phuket
Ko Phangan
Chumphon
Isthmus of Kra
Prachuap Khiri Khan
Phetchaburi

VIETNAM
HO CHI MINH CITY (SAIGON)
Da-Nang
Hue
Qui Nhon
Nha Trang
Da Lat
Phan Thiet
Phan Rang
Bien Hoa
My Tho
Can Tho
Vinh Loi
Phu Quoc
Quan Long

LAOS
Savannakhet
Pakse

CAMBODIA (KAMPUCHEA)
Phnom Penh
Battambang
Kompong Som
Kompong Cham
Sihanoukville
Tonle Sap
Phnom Dang Raek

BURMA
Moulmein
Tavoy
Mergui
Victoria Point
Mergui Archipelago
Bilauk Taung Ra.

INDONESIA
Greater Sunda Islands

SUMATRA (SUMATERA)
Medan
Pematang Siantar
Sibolga
Gunung Sitoli
Nias
Padang
Bukittinggi
Payakumbuh
Pekanbaru
Jambi
Palembang
Bengkulu
Bangka
Pangkalpinang
Lubuksikaping
Muaratebo
Rengat
Muarabungo
Barisan Mts.
Mentawai Is.
Siberut
N. Pagai
Enggano
Simeulue
Banda Aceh (Kutaraja)
Sabang
Tapaktuan

JAVA (JAWA)
JAKARTA
Bandung
Bogor
Cirebon
Semarang
Pekalongan
Tegal
Surakarta
Yogyakarta
Madiun
Kediri
Malang
SURABAYA
Madura
Bawean

INDIAN OCEAN

East from Greenwich

Projection: Mercator

m 2000 1500 1000 400 200 0

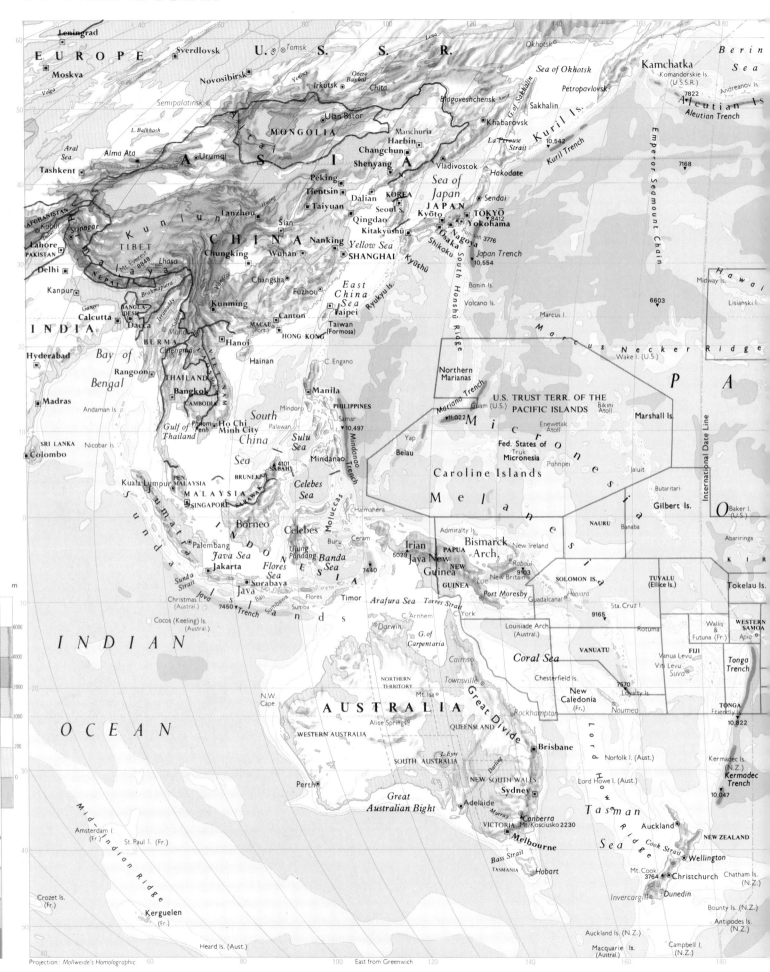

Projection: Mollweide's Homolographic   East from Greenwich

ALASKA

6050

Gulf of Alaska

Bristol Bay

Prince of Wales I.

Queen Charlotte Is.

Prince Rupert

Kitimat

Juneau

R O C K Y

Edmonton

Vancouver

Vancouver I.

Victoria

Seattle

Portland

Boise

Snake

C. Mendocino

San Francisco

4418

Los Angeles

San Diego

▼6741

▼6225

6050

Calgary

Regina

Winnipeg

L. Winnipeg

L. Superior

Minneapolis

CHICAGO

Denver

Salt Lake City

Kansas

Oklahoma

Dallas

Ciudad Juárez

Sierra Madre

Gulf of California

6225 ▼

Monterrey

M E X I C O

México

7680

Guadalajara

Revilla Gigedo Is. (Mexico)

Puebla 5700

Acapulco

St. Lawrence

Montréal

Quebec

Ottawa

Toronto

L. Huron

L. Michigan

Detroit

Buffalo

Pittsburgh

Cincinnati

Memphis

St. Louis

Missouri

Mississippi

San Antonio

Houston

New Orleans

San Antonio

Gulf of Mexico

Havana

Yucatan Channel

Mérida

Belize

GUATEMALA

Guatemala

EL SALVADOR

Salvador

HONDURAS

NICARAGUA

Managua

CENTRAL AMERICA

COSTA RICA

San José

Colón

PANAMA

Panama Canal

Boston

NEW YORK

Philadelphia

Baltimore

Washington

Atlanta

Jacksonville

C. Hatteras

C. Sable

Pr. Edward I.

Saint John

Newfoundland

Labrador

GREENLAND

C. Farewell

A T L A N T I C

O C E A N

Bermuda (U.K.)

BAHAMAS

CUBA

West Indies

Hispaniola 9200

HAITI

JAMAICA

Kingston

DOM. REP.

PUERTO RICO

Leeward Is.

Caribbean Sea

BARBADOS

Windward Is.

TRINIDAD & TOBAGO

Barranquilla

Maracaibo

Caracas

Orinoco

VENEZUELA

Medellín

Bogotá

Cali

COLOMBIA

Quito

ECUADOR

Guayaquil

C. Pariñas

Iquitos

Manaus

Amazon

BRAZIL

SOUTH

PERU

Trujillo

Lima

Cuzco

L. Titicaca

Arequipa

Illampu & Ancohuma 6550

La Paz

Peru-

6866

BOLIVIA

Iquique

Chile

8050

Antofagasta Trench

AMERICA

6369 ▼

Córdoba

Rosario

Valparaíso

Santiago

Buenos Aires

Concepción

ARGENTINA

URUGUAY

Montevideo

Río de la Plata

Asunción

PARAGUAY

Tucumán

Pto. Alegre

6960

Chile Rise

Arch. de Juan Fernández (Chile)

Sala-y-Gómez (Chile)

Easter Is. (Chile)

San Félix (Chile)

San Ambrosio (Chile)

Galápagos (Ecuador)

Cocos I.

Clipperton I. (Fr.)

East Pacific Ridge

Equator

Tropic of Cancer

Hawaiian Is. (U.S.A.)

Honolulu

Oahu

Hawaii

Johnston I. (U.S.)

Palmyra Is. (U.S.)

Teraina

Tabuaeran

Kiritimati

Jarvis I. (U.S.)

N.W. Christmas Island Ridge

Canderbury I.

Phoenix Is.

Malden I.

Starbuck I.

KIRIBATI

Pukapuka

Manihiki

Suwarrow Is.

Tongareva Penrhyn Is.

Vostok

Flint I.

Caroline I.

Marquesas Is.

Leeward Is.

Tuamotu Archipelago

Society Is.

Windward Is.

Tahiti

FRENCH POLYNESIA

Cook Islands

Manuae

Austral

Rarotonga

Tubuai Is. (Austral Is.)

Rapa Iti

Seamount Chain

Tuamotu Ridge

Pitcairn I. (U.K.)

Ducie I.

Tropic of Capricorn

P A C I F I C

O C E A N

N.W. Christmas I. Ridge

Laysan I.

Midway Ridge

NEW ZEALAND

Niue (N.Z.)

Rotuma

MER. SAMOA

Utunia

Chonos Arch.

G. of Penas

Punta Arenas

Str. of Magellan

Tierra del Fuego

C. Horn

Falkland Is. (U.K.)

South Georgia

6212 ▼

SOUTH

ATLANTIC

OCEAN

Pacific-Antarctic Ridge

Patagonia

Andes

Hudson Bay

N O R T H

C A N A D A

A M E R I C A

UNITED STATES

Appalachian Mts.

Rocky Mountains

West from Greenwich

COPYRIGHT GEORGE PHILIP & SON LTD.

Croker

Cobourg Pen.
Crocodile Is.
Bathurst I. Melville I.
Van Diemen
Gulf
Clarence Str. Arnhem
P. Darwin
Darwin

Anson B. Batchelor Rum Jungle Arnhem Land
Daly
Katherine Roper
Mataranka Limmer
Daly Birdum

C. Londonderry
C. Bougainville Cambridge G.
Admiralty G.
Joseph
Bonaparte
Gulf
Drysdale
Wyndham
Kununurra Victoria

Mt. Hann L. Argyle
776 Wave Hill Newcastle Waters
Kimberley
L. Woods Barkly

NORTHER

Mt. Ord
King Sd. 1007 King Leopold Ras. Durack Range Ord
C. Levêque
Lacepede Is. Hall's Creek
Derby Gordon Downs Hordern Tanami
Fitzroy Hills Desert TERRITO
Broome Fitzroy Crossing Sturt
Roebuck B. Murchison
Ras. Davenpo
Tennant Creek Ra.

TIMOR

SEA

Java Trench 6389

Ashmore
Reef

Scott Reef Bonaparte
Archipelago

Rowley
Shoals

Gregory
Lake

Great Sandy Desert
Sandover

Eighty Mile Beach
P. Hedland
Mount Goldsworthy Mt. Singleton
De Grey 808
Reynolds Ra.
Marble Bar L. Dora Mt. Ziel 998
Dampier Archipelago Karratha Throssell Ra. 1510
Dampier Roebourne Pilbara Nullagine Macdonnell Ras. Alice Springs
Barrow I. C. Fortescue L. Mackay L. Macdonald James Ra. Hugh
Exmouth G. Hamersley Ra. Mt. Bruce L. Disappointment Finke
N.W. Cape Onslow 1235 Ophthalmia Ra. Palmer
Exmouth Tom Price Newman Gibson Desert Sim
Learmonth Ashburton Paraburdoo Robertson Ra. Rawlinson Ra. L. Amadeus Des
Mount Whaleback Mt. Olga Ayers Rock
1069 868
Mt. Augustus WESTERN
1105 Musgrave Ranges Hamilton
L. McLeod Blackstone Ra. Mt. Woodroffe Alberga
Lyons 1849
Geographe Everard Ras.
Chan. Carnarvon Peak Hill Oodnadatta
Gascoyne Robinson L. Carnegie
Shark Wooramel Ra. L. Wells Warrina
Dirk B. Murchison AUSTRALIA 661
Hartog Denham Meekatharra L. Yeo Coober
Pedy
Great Victoria Desert Stuart
L. Austin Laverton SOUTH AUST
Tallering Mt. Magnet Sandstone Leonora
Peak 453 Oldea Tarcoola
Houtman Mullewa Leonora L. Carey
Abrolhos Northampton L. Monger L. Barlee L. Minigwal L. Everard
Geraldton L. Moore Menzies Rawlinna Deakin L. Gairdner
Dongara Kanowna Peneng Ceduna Nukey Bluff
Bonnie Rock Kalgoorlie-Boulder Nullarbor Plain 472
Bencubbin Coolgardie Hampton Tableland Head of Bight C. Adieu Streaky B.
Southern Cross L. Lefroy Eyre Nuyts Archipelago Anxious B. Eyre
Northam L. Cowan Penin.
Span York Kellerberrin The Norseman Great Australian Bight Coffin B. Penin. Kimba
Perth Johnston L. Dundas Port Lincoln Inves
Fremantle Lakes
Kwinana Narrogin Esperance C. Pasley
Pinjarra
Bunbury Collie Wagin Archipelago
Geographe B. Katanning of the Recherche
Busselton Bridgetown Stirling Ra.
Augusta Manjimup Mt Barker C. Knob
C. Leeuwin Albany
Flinders B.

Darling Ra.

INDIAN OCEAN

m
2000
1500
1000
400
200
0
200
2000
4000
6000
m

Projection: Bonne
115 120 125 130 East from Greenwich 135

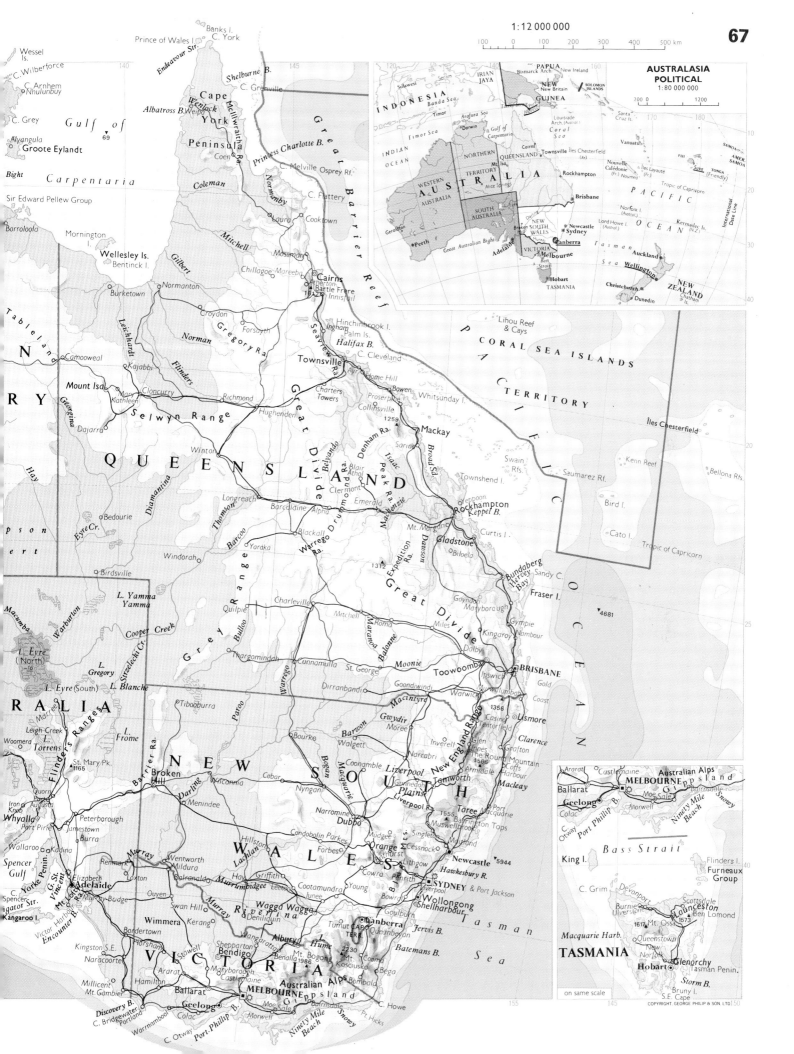

1:12 000 000
100   0   100   200   300   400   500 km

AUSTRALASIA POLITICAL
1:80 000 000
200   0   1200

Wessel Is.
C. Wilberforce
C. Arnhem
Nhulunbuy
C. Grey
Alyangula
Groote Eylandt
Sir Edward Pellew Group
Borroloola
Mornington I.
Wellesley Is.
Bentinck I.
Burketown
Camooweal
Mount Isa
Mary Kathleen
Cloncurry
Kajabbi
Dajarra
Hay
Bedourie
Eyre Cr.
Birdsville
L. Yamma Yamma
Macumba
Warburton
Cooper Creek
L. Eyre (North)
L. Eyre (South)
L. Gregory
L. Blanche
Matree
Leigh Creek
L. Torrens
Woomera
St. Mary Pk.
Quorn
Iron Knob
Port Augusta
Whyalla
Port Pirie
Jamestown
Burra
Peterborough
Wallaroo
Kadina
Spencer Gulf
Yorke Penin.
G. St. Vincent
Elizabeth
Adelaide
Mt. Lofty
Murray Bridge
Kangaroo I.
Kingston S.E.
Naracoorte
Millicent
Mt. Gambier

Gulf of Carpentaria
Bight

Prince of Wales I.
Banks I.
C. York
Endeavour Str.
Shelburne B.
C. Grenville
Cape York Peninsula
Albatross B. Weipa
Wenlock
Coen
Mcllwraith Ra.
Princess Charlotte B.
Coleman
Mitchell
Normanby
C. Melville
Osprey Rf.
C. Flattery
Laura
Cooktown
Normanton
Croydon
Forsayth
Gilbert
Norman
Chillagoe
Mareeba
Mossman
Cairns
Atherton
Bartle Frere
Innisfail
Hinchinbrook I.
Ingham
Palm Is.
Halifax B.
Seaview Ra.
C. Cleveland
Townsville
Ayr
Home Hill
Charters Towers
Bowen
Proserpine
Whitsunday I.
Collinsville
1259
Mackay
Sarina
Broad Sd.
Townshend I.
Swain Rfs.
Yeppoon
Keppel B.
Rockhampton
Mt. Morgan
Curtis I.
Gladstone
Biloela
Expedition Ra.
Bundaberg
Hervey Bay
Sandy C.
Fraser I.
Gayndah
Maryborough
Gympie
Nambour
Kingaroy
Dalby
Toowoomba
Ipswich
BRISBANE
Gold Coast
Warwick
Stanthorpe
Tenterfield
Casino
Lismore
Clarence
Grafton
Coffs Harbour

QUEENSLAND

Great Barrier Reef

Leichhardt
Flinders
Selwyn Range
Richmond
Hughenden
Winton
Great Divide
Belyando
Denham Ra.
Blair Athol
Clermont
Emerald
Drummond Ra.
Peak Ra.
Isaac
Mackenzie
Dawson
Longreach
Barcaldine
Alpha
Blackall
Thomson
Barcoo
Yaraka
Warrego Ra.
1312
Great Divide
Windorah
Charleville
Quilpie
Bulloo
Thargomindah
Cunnamulla
Mitchell
Maranoa
Roma
Miles
Balonne
St. George
Moonie
Goondiwindi
Dirranbandi
Macintyre
Gwydir
Moree
Warialda
Barwon
Bourke
Walgett
Narrabri
Inverell
Glen Innes
1586
The Round Mountain
Armidale
Tamworth
New England Range
Macleay
Port Macquarie
1555
Barrington Tops
Taree
Gloucester
Muswellbrook
Singleton
Maitland
Cessnock
Newcastle
5944
Hawkesbury R.
SYDNEY
& Port Jackson
Liverpool
Wollongong
Shellharbour

Grey Range
Diamantina
Eyre Cr.

SOUTH AUSTRALIA
RALIA

Flinders Ranges
L. Frome
Tiboobarra
Milparinka
Barrier Ra.
Broken Hill
Wilcannia
Menindee
Darling
Cobar
Nyngan
Bogan
Macquarie
Coonamble
Gilgandra
Dubbo
Narromine
Parkes
Forbes
Condobolin
Lachlan
Hillston
West Wyalong
Young
Cowra
Orange
Mudgee
Lithgow
Bathurst
Penrith
Liverpool Plains
Liverpool Ra.

NEW SOUTH WALES

Wentworth
Mildura
Renmark
Loxton
Swan Hill
Balranald
Hay
Murrumbidgee
Griffith
Leeton
Narrandera
Junee
Wagga Wagga
Riverina
Deniliquin
Cootamundra
Gundagai
Tumut
Cooma
Bombala
Bega
Batemans B.
C. Howe
Pt. Hicks

Murray
Ouyen
Kerang
Wimmera
Horsham
Stawell
Ararat
Ballarat
Bendigo
Castlemaine
Maryborough
Bordertown
Mt. Bogong 1986
Mt. Kosciusko 2230
Australian Alps
Shepparton
Wangaratta
Benalla
Albury
Hume
CAP. TERR.
CANBERRA
Queanbeyan
Jervis B.

VICTORIA
Colac
C. Otway
Port Phillip B.
MELBOURNE
Geelong
Moe
Sale
Morwell
Ninety Mile Beach
Snowy
Gippsland
Bairnsdale
Warrnambool
Discovery B.
C. Bridgewater
Portland
Hamilton

PAPUA
NEW GUINEA
INDONESIA
IRIAN JAYA
Timor
Timor Sea
Darwin
Arafura Sea
Gulf of Carpentaria
NORTHERN TERRITORY
QUEENSLAND
Townsville
Mt. Isa
Alice Springs
Rockhampton
WESTERN AUSTRALIA
Geraldton
SOUTH AUSTRALIA
Perth
AUSTRALIA
NEW SOUTH WALES
Broken Hill
Newcastle
Sydney
Adelaide
Canberra
Great Australian Bight
VICTORIA
Melbourne
Ban
Strait
Hobart
TASMANIA
New Britain
SOLOMON ISLANDS
Coral Sea
Îles Chesterfield (Fr)
Nouvelle Calédonie (Fr.) Nouméa
Vanuatu
Norfolk I. (Austral.)
Lord Howe I. (Austral.)
Tropic of Capricorn
FIJI
Suva
SAMOA
AMER. SAMOA
TONGA (Friendly)
PACIFIC OCEAN
Kermadec Is. (N.Z.)
Auckland
Tasman Sea
Wellington
NEW ZEALAND
Christchurch
Dunedin
Chatham Is.
International Date Line

CORAL SEA ISLANDS
TERRITORY
Lihou Reef & Cays
Îles Chesterfield
4681
Kenn Reef
Bellona Rfs.
Bird I.
Cato I.
Saumarez Rf.
Tropic of Capricorn

PACIFIC OCEAN

Tasman Sea

TASMANIA
Ararat
Castlemaine
Australian Alps
Ballarat
MELBOURNE
Geelong
Colac
C. Otway
Port Phillip B.
Moe
Sale
Morwell
Gippsland
Ninety Mile Beach
Snowy
Bass Strait
King I.
C. Grim
Devonport
Burnie
Ulverstone
Smithton
Queenstown
Macquarie Harb.
New Norfolk
Glenorchy
Hobart
Bruny I.
S.E. Cape
Storm B.
Tasman Penin.
1617 Mt. Ossa
1573
Launceston
Ben Lomond
Scottsdale
Flinders I.
Furneaux Group
on same scale
COPYRIGHT. GEORGE PHILIP & SON. LTD

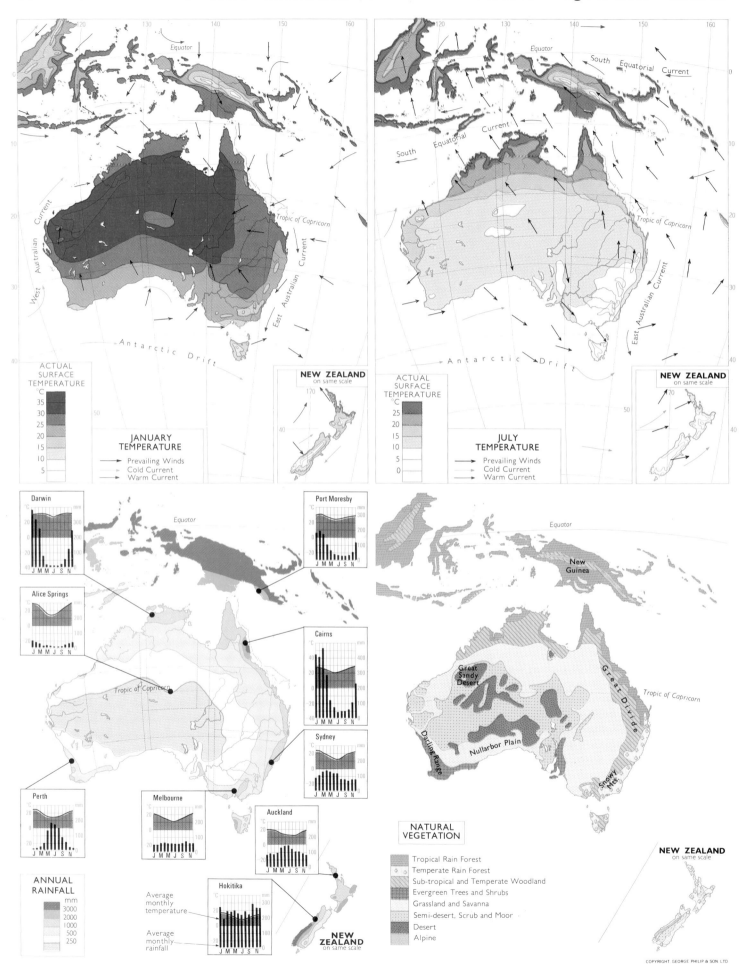

ACTUAL
SURFACE
TEMPERATURE
°C
35
30
25
20
15
10
5

JANUARY
TEMPERATURE

→ Prevailing Winds
▸ Cold Current
➤ Warm Current

NEW ZEALAND
on same scale

ACTUAL
SURFACE
TEMPERATURE
°C
25
20
15
10
5
0

JULY
TEMPERATURE

→ Prevailing Winds
▸ Cold Current
➤ Warm Current

NEW ZEALAND
on same scale

Darwin
Port Moresby
Alice Springs
Cairns
Sydney
Perth
Melbourne
Auckland
Hokitika

ANNUAL
RAINFALL
mm
3000
2000
1000
500
250

Average
monthly
temperature

Average
monthly
rainfall

NEW ZEALAND
on same scale

New
Guinea

Great
Sandy
Desert

Great Divide

Darling Range

Nullarbor Plain

Snowy Mts.

Tropic of Capricorn

NATURAL
VEGETATION

Tropical Rain Forest
Temperate Rain Forest
Sub-tropical and Temperate Woodland
Evergreen Trees and Shrubs
Grassland and Savanna
Semi-desert, Scrub and Moor
Desert
Alpine

NEW ZEALAND
on same scale

1:20 000 000

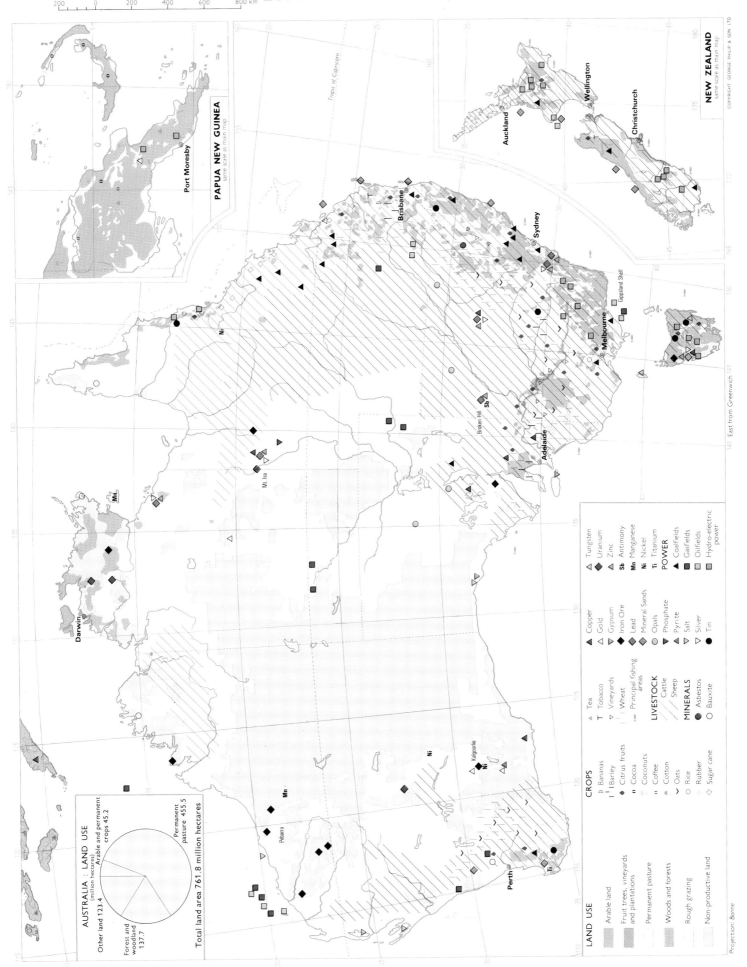

200   0   200   400   600   800 km

Tropic of Capricorn

PAPUA NEW GUINEA
same scale as main map

Port Moresby

NEW ZEALAND
same scale as main map

COPYRIGHT GEORGE PHILIP & SON LTD

Auckland
Wellington
Christchurch

Brisbane

Sydney

Gippsland Shelf

Melbourne

Broken Hill

Sb

Adelaide

Mt. Isa

Ni

Mn

Darwin

Mn

Ni

Kalgoorlie
Ni

Pilbarra

Perth

LAND USE

Arable land
Fruit trees, vineyards and plantations
Permanent pasture
Woods and forests
Rough grazing
Non-productive land

AUSTRALIA : LAND USE
(million hectares)

Arable and permanent crops 45.2

Other land 123.4

Permanent pasture 455.5

Forest and woodland 137.7

Total land area 761.8 million hectares

CROPS

⊲ Tea
Þ Bananas
I|I Barley
◆ Citrus fruits
○ Cocoa
○ Coconuts
○ Coffee
○ Cotton
⟩ Oats
○ Rice
◇ Rubber
◇ Sugar cane
⊲ Tobacco
▽ Vineyards
Ι Wheat
✓ Principal fishing areas

LIVESTOCK
Cattle
Sheep

MINERALS
● Asbestos
○ Bauxite
◀ Copper
△ Gold
◆ Gypsum
◆ Iron Ore
◆ Lead
◆ Mineral Sands
○ Opals
▼ Phosphate
▲ Pyrite
▽ Salt
▽ Silver
● Tin
△ Tungsten
◆ Uranium
Sb Antimony
◢ Manganese
Ni Nickel
Ti Titanium

POWER
◀ Coalfields
□ Gasfields
□ Oilfields
□ Hydro-electric power

Projection: Bonne

East from Greenwich

1:4 500 000

25   0   25   50   75   100   125   150   175   200 km

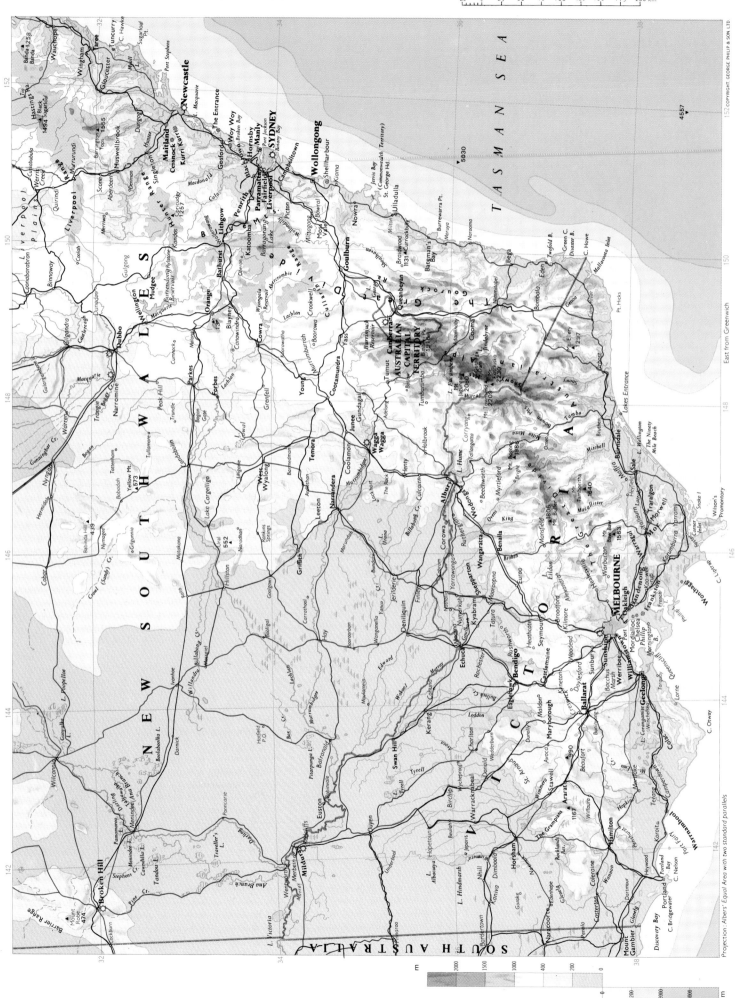

TASMAN SEA

NEW SOUTH WALES

Newcastle
Maitland
Cessnock
Kurri Kurri
SYDNEY
Parramatta
Liverpool
Penrith
Fairfield
Wollongong

Dubbo
Bathurst
Orange
Mudgee
Wellington

Goulburn
Queanbeyan
Canberra
AUSTRALIAN CAPITAL TERRITORY

Cooma

Narromine
Parkes
Forbes
West Wyalong
Temora
Wagga Wagga
Junee
Cootamundra
Young
Gundagai
Tumut

Griffith
Leeton
Narrandera
Coolamon
Albury
Wodonga

Broken Hill

Mildura

VICTORIA

Bendigo
Ballarat
Geelong
MELBOURNE
Dandenong
Frankston

Shepparton
Wangaratta
Benalla
Echuca

Warracknabeel
Horsham
Ararat
Stawell
Hamilton
The Grampians

SOUTH AUSTRALIA

Projection: Albers' Equal Area with two standard parallels

East from Greenwich

m 2000 1500 1000 400 200 0

COPYRIGHT GEORGE PHILIP & SON LTD.

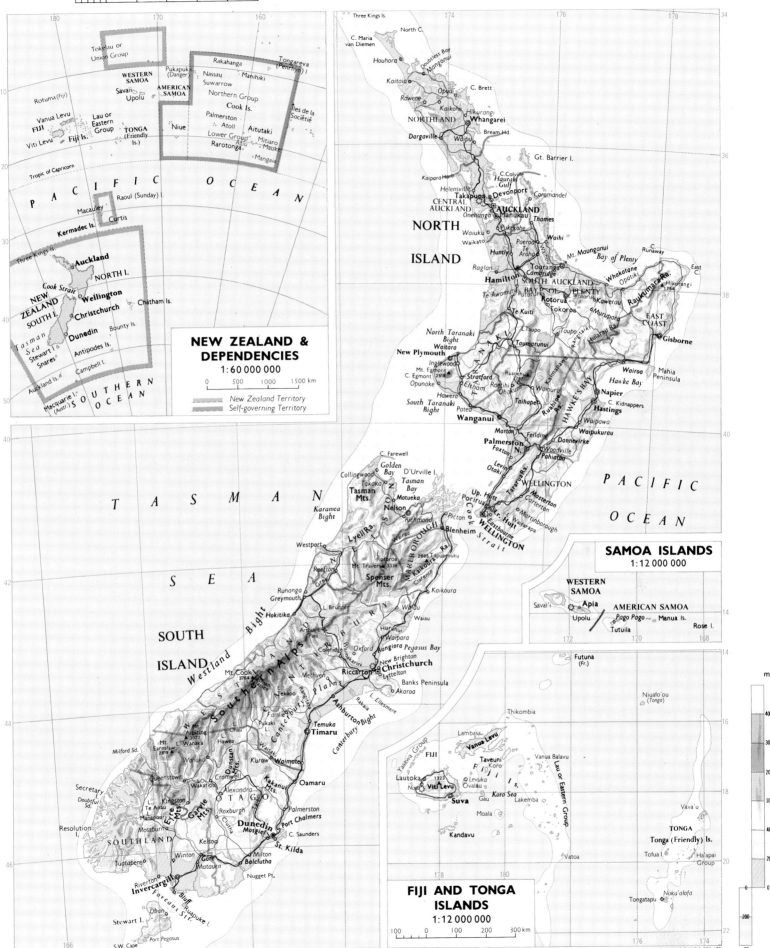

1 : 6 000 000

50   0   50   100   150   200   250 km

NEW ZEALAND & DEPENDENCIES
1 : 60 000 000

0   500   1000   1500 km

New Zealand Territory
Self-governing Territory

SAMOA ISLANDS
1 : 12 000 000

WESTERN SAMOA
Savai'i   Apia
Upolu   AMERICAN SAMOA
Pago Pago   Manua Is.
Tutuila   Rose I.

FIJI AND TONGA ISLANDS
1 : 12 000 000

100   0   100   200   300 km

Projection : Conical with two standard parallels

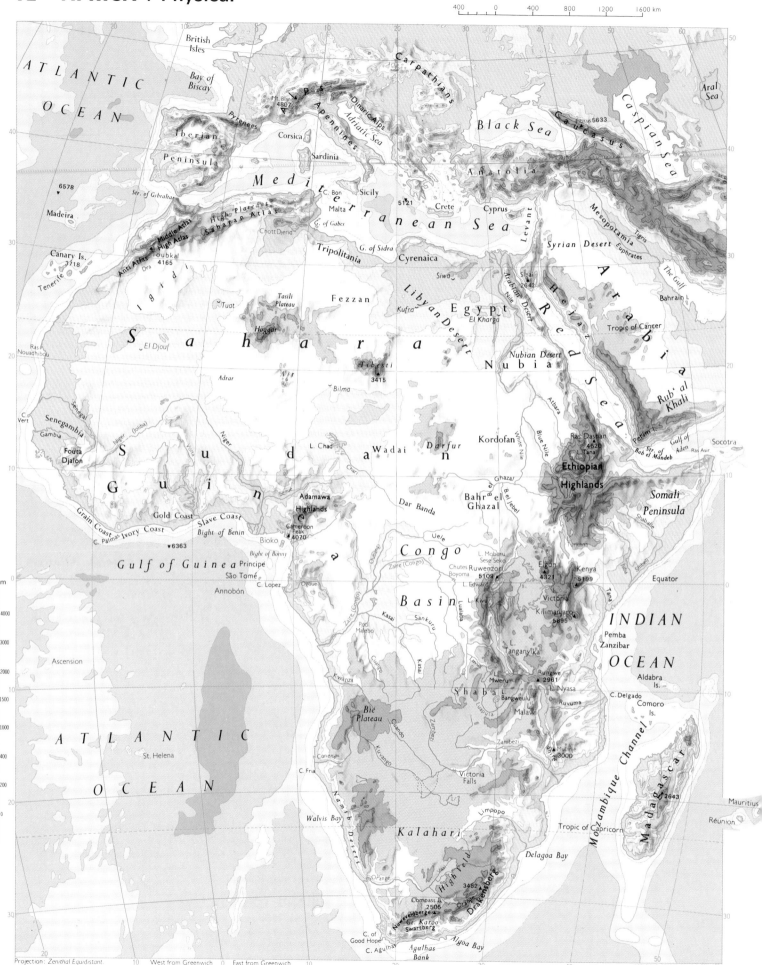

1 : 40 000 000

400   0   400   800   1200   1600 km

Projection: Zenithal Equidistant.   West from Greenwich   East from Greenwich   COPYRIGHT GEORGE PHILIP & SON LTD.

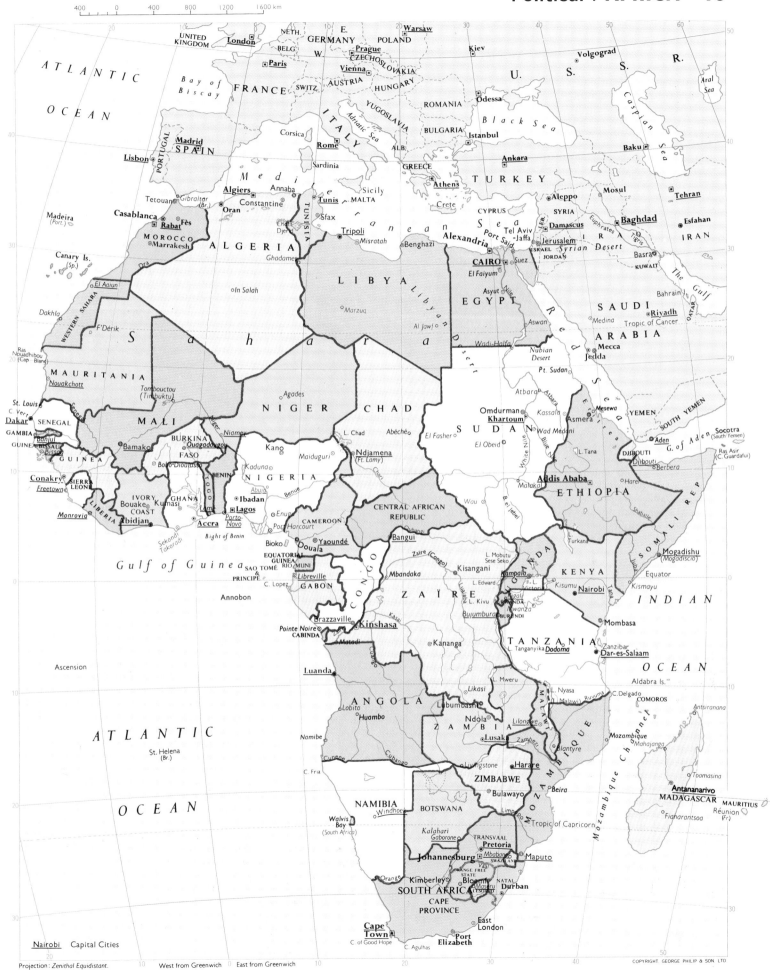

1 : 40 000 000

400   0   400   800   1200   1600 km

Nairobi   Capital Cities

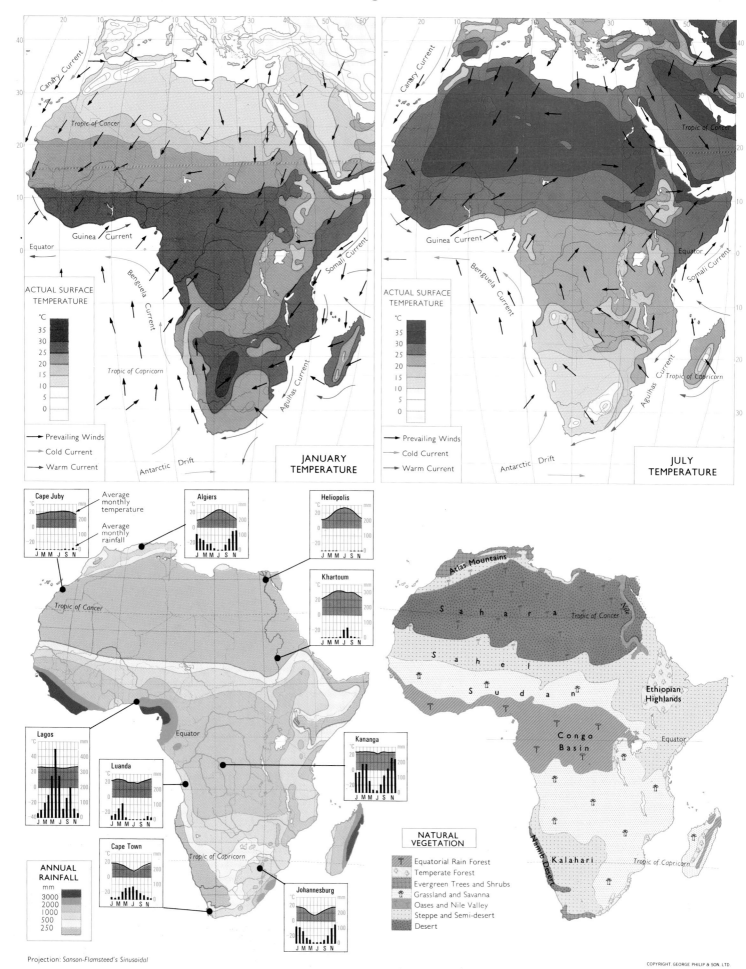

ACTUAL SURFACE
TEMPERATURE

°C
35
30
25
20
15
10
5
0

→ Prevailing Winds
→ Cold Current
→ Warm Current

Canary Current
Tropic of Cancer
Guinea Current
Equator
Benguela Current
Tropic of Capricorn
Somali Current
Agulhas Current
Antarctic Drift

JANUARY TEMPERATURE

ACTUAL SURFACE
TEMPERATURE

°C
35
30
25
20
15
10
5
0

→ Prevailing Winds
→ Cold Current
→ Warm Current

Canary Current
Tropic of Cancer
Guinea Current
Equator
Benguela Current
Somali Current
Agulhas Current
Tropic of Capricorn
Antarctic Drift

JULY TEMPERATURE

Cape Juby
Average monthly temperature
Average monthly rainfall

Algiers

Heliopolis

Khartoum

Lagos

Luanda

Kananga

Cape Town

Johannesburg

Tropic of Cancer
Equator
Tropic of Capricorn

ANNUAL RAINFALL

mm
3000
2000
1000
500
250

Atlas Mountains
Sahara
Nile
Tropic of Cancer
Sahel
Sudan
Ethiopian Highlands
Congo Basin
Equator
Kalahari
Namib Desert
Tropic of Capricorn

NATURAL VEGETATION

Equatorial Rain Forest
Temperate Forest
Evergreen Trees and Shrubs
Grassland and Savanna
Oases and Nile Valley
Steppe and Semi-desert
Desert

Projection: Sanson-Flamsteed's Sinusoidal

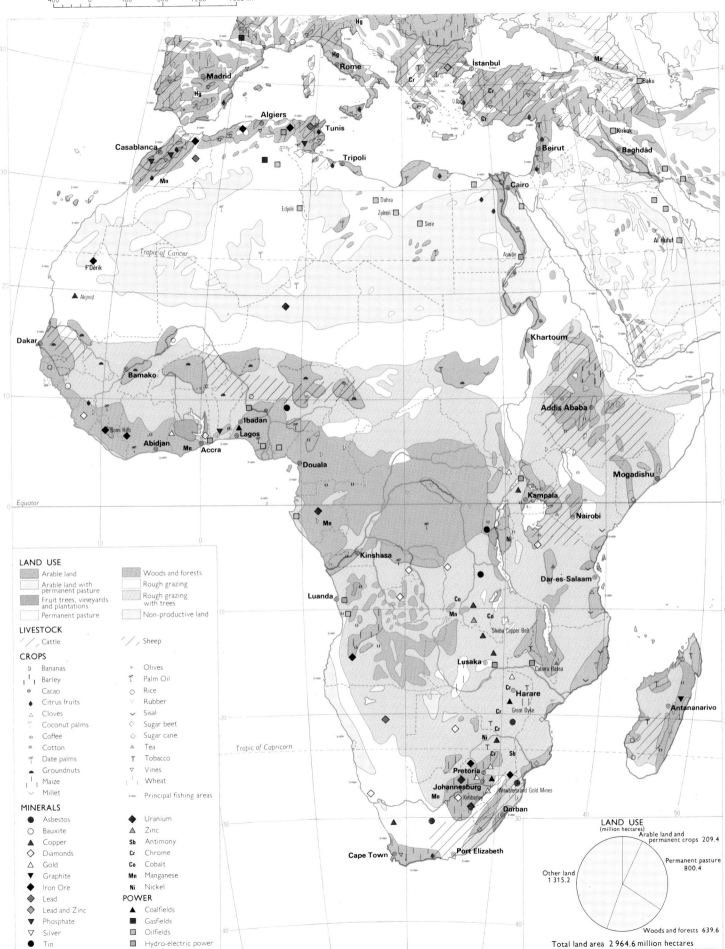

1 : 40 000 000

400 0 400 800 1200 1600 km

LAND USE

- Arable land
- Arable land with permanent pasture
- Fruit trees, vineyards and plantations
- Permanent pasture
- Woods and forests
- Rough grazing
- Rough grazing with trees
- Non-productive land

LIVESTOCK

- Cattle
- Sheep

CROPS

-) Bananas
- Barley
- o Cacao
- Citrus fruits
- Cloves
- Coconut palms
- Coffee
- Cotton
- Date palms
- Groundnuts
- Maize
- Millet
- Olives
- Palm Oil
- Rice
- Rubber
- Sisal
- Sugar beet
- Sugar cane
- Tea
- Tobacco
- Vines
- Wheat
- Principal fishing areas

MINERALS

- Asbestos
- Bauxite
- Copper
- Diamonds
- Gold
- Graphite
- Iron Ore
- Lead
- Lead and Zinc
- Phosphate
- Silver
- Tin
- Uranium
- Zinc
- Sb Antimony
- Cr Chrome
- Co Cobalt
- Mn Manganese
- Ni Nickel

POWER

- Coalfields
- Gasfields
- Oilfields
- Hydro-electric power

LAND USE
(million hectares)

Arable land and permanent crops 209.4

Permanent pasture 800.4

Other land 1 315.2

Woods and forests 639.6

Total land area 2 964.6 million hectares

Projection: *Zenithal Equidistant*

West from Greenwich 0 East from Greenwich

COPYRIGHT GEORGE PHILIP & SON LTD

	Population						Growth			Land			Agriculture		
	Total	Density	Birth Rate	Death Rate	Life Expectancy	1965-73	1973-83	Urban	Area	Arable	Forest	Agricultural Population	Index of Production	Food intake
	th.	persons per km²	per th. popn.		yrs.	av. % per annum		%	th. km²	th. km²	th. km²	% of total popn.	1974-76 = 100	calories per day
Algeria	21 272	8.9	47	13	57	2.9	3.1	46	2 382	75	44	47	98	2 586
Angola	8 540	6.8	48	24	43	2.2	2.6	23	1 247	35	536	56	83	2 353
Benin	3 825	34	51	25	48	2.6	2.8	16	111	18	39	45	119	2 174
Botswana	1 051	1.8	51	14	53		4.6	16	585	14	10	78	97	2 352
Burkina Faso	6 582	24	48	24	44	2.0	1.9	11	274	26	71	79	114	2 009
Burundi	4 537	175	42	20	47	1.4	2.2	2	26	13	0.6	82	118	2 353
Cameroon	9 467	20	43	19	54	2.4	3.1	39	469	70	254	79	100	2 295
Central Africa	2 508	4.0	45	24	48	1.6	2.3	44	623	20	397	86	107	2 117
Chad	4 901	3.9	44	24	43	1.8	2.1	20	1 259	32	203	81	114	1 823
Congo	1 695	5.0	45	20	63	2.6	3.1	55	342	6.7	213	32	113	2 433
Egypt	45 657	46	37	10	58	2.3	2.5	45	995	25	0	49	119	3 183
Ethiopia	35 420	32	49	23	43	2.6	2.7	15	1 101	140	265	77	128	2 149
Gabon	1 146	4.4	33	19	40		1.4		258	4.5	200	75	113	2 763
Gambia	630	63	48	30	34		3.7	18	10	1.6	2.0	77	73	2 251
Ghana	13 044	57	47	16	59	2.2	3.1	38	230	28	86	48	76	1 769
Guinea	5 301	22	47	25	37	1.8	2.0	26	246	16	105	79	107	1 880
Guinea-Bissau	875	31	41	22	41		4.6		28	2.9	11	80	92	2 176
Ivory Coast	9 474	30	46	20	52	4.6	4.6	44	318	40	89	78	137	2 613
Kenya	19 536	34	56	16	57	3.7	4.0	17	569	24	25	76	124	2 011
Lesotho	1 481	49	37	15	53	2.1	2.5	13	30	3.0	0	81	95	2 424
Liberia	2 109	22	50	21	49	2.8	3.3	38	96	3.7	38	68	111	2 276
Libya	3 624	2.1	38	13	56	4.1	4.3	61	1 760	21	6.2	12	112	3 812
Madagascar	9 731	17	45	18	49	2.4	2.6	20	582	30	132	81	110	2 491
Malawi	6 839	73	49	25	44	2.9	3.0	11	94	23	43	82	137	2 208
Mali	7 719	6.3	43	18	45	2.6	2.5	19	1 220	206	87	85	117	1 894
Mauritania	1 832	1.8	50	23	46	2.3	2.2	25	1 030	2.1	151	81	119	2 072
Morocco	22 848	51	45	14	52	2.4	2.6	43	446	84	52	49	113	2 607
Mozambique	13 693	17	45	17	46	2.3	2.6	17	784	31	152	61	77	1 881
Namibia	1 507	1.8	45	19	47		2.7		823	6.6	104	46	109	2 197
Niger	5 940	4.7	51	25	45	2.6	3.0	14	1 267	37	28	86	147	2 440
Nigeria	92 037	101	51	19	49	2.5	2.7	22	911	304	143	51	119	2 378
Rwanda	5 903	236	51	22	47	3.1	3.4	5	25	10	2.6	88	138	2 274
Senegal	6 352	33	55	23	46	2.4	2.8	34	192	52	53	73	75	2 346
Sierra Leone	3 536	49	48	32	38	1.7	2.1	23	72	18	21	63	120	1 938
Somalia	5 423	5.9	46	21	45	3.5	2.8	33	927	11	88	78	113	1 986
South Africa	31 586	26	38	15	64	2.6	2.4	35	1 221	136	46	28	91	2 862
Sudan	20 945	8.8	47	19	48	2.6	3.2	20	2 376	124	483	75	113	2 314
Swaziland	649	38	47	19	46		3.5	20	17	1.3	1.0	70	147	2 553
Tanzania	21 062	24	51	17	51	3.1	3.3	14	886	52	419	79	118	1 955
Togo	2 838	53	46	19	49	2.8	2.6	22	54	14	16	66	120	2 126
Tunisia	7 042	45	33	11	62	2.0	2.5	54	155	50	5.6	38	104	2 763
Uganda	15 150	76	50	16	49	3.5	2.8	7	200	58	60	79	119	1 784
Zaire	32 084	14	46	17	51	2.1	2.5	38	2 268	64	1 769	73	115	2 130
Zambia	6 445	8.7	48	17	51	3.0	3.2	47	741	52	206	65	93	2 146
Zimbabwe	7 980	21	47	14	56	3.4	3.2	24	387	28	238	57	90	2 108

For explanations see pages 54-55 or 86-87.

Trade		Education		Health	Energy	Consumer Price Index	G.N.P.		G.D.P. Part formed by		Loans & Debt		
Imports	Exports	Primary	Secondary	Popn. per doctor	Consumption in kgs of oil equiv. per capita	1970 = 100	US$ per capita	Growth per capita % per yr. 1973-82	Agric.	Indust.	end 1983 US$ millions	as % of GNP	
US$ per capita		% of age group							%				
484	602	93	36	2 630	982	265	2 400	2.4	6	41	12 942	28	Algeria
74	238				226								Angola
97	18	65	21	16 980	39		290	2.7	44	7	615	59	Benin
				7 378		245	920	5.0	12	34			Botswana
45	9	28	3	48 510	22		180	1.6	37	12	398	38	Burkina Faso
41	22	33	3	45 020	17	382	240		51	9	284	26	Burundi
117	93	100	19	13 990	128	448	800	4.6	29	19	1 883	27	Cameroon
53	45	70	14	26 750	35		280	1.3	31	18	215	33	Central Africa
23	12		3	47 640	30	145	80	7.7	41	17	129	44	Chad
488	646		69	5 510	216	383	1 230	3.6	8	46	1 487	76	Congo
224	70	78	54	970	532	459	700	6.6	22	28	15 229	49	Egypt
27	12	46	12	69 390	19	363	140	0.7	45	10	1 223	26	Ethiopia
755	1 748			2 560	941	440	4 250	4.7	5	50			Gabon
156	75			11 632	230	474	290	0.8					Gambia
200	160	76	34	7 160	111	24 648	320	3.8	61	10	1 095	28	Ghana
		33	16	17 110	54		300	0.5			1 216	69	Guinea
59	14			7 306	50		180	2.1					Guinea-Bissau
194	222	76	17	15 234	186	407	720	1.1	27	13	4 824	79	Ivory Coast
73	52	100	20	7 890	109	467	340	1.0	28	13	2 384	43	Kenya
		100	20	18 640		447	470	4.0	24	13	145	23	Lesotho
288	298	66	20	8 550	357	260	470	0.9	17	18	699	72	Liberia
2 155	4 189		67	660	2 769	167	7 500	0.3	2	56	85	0.4	Libya
41	43	100	14	10 220	59	594	290	2.5	33	19	1 490	52	Madagascar
47	33	62	4	41 460	45	182	210	1.1	38	15	719	55	Malawi
46	22	27	9	22 130	22	567	150	2.1	46	11	881	89	Mali
106	161	33	10	14 500	130	150	440	0.7	22	19	1 171	158	Mauritania
169	92	80	28	10 750	258	270	750	2.1	14	23	9 445	70	Morocco
65	18	100	6	39 140	95								Mozambique
							1 760	1.8					Namibia
79	59	23	5	38 790	43	352	240	2.8	50	14	631	49	Niger
151	127	98	16	12 550	150	466	760	0.7	20	32	11 757	18	Nigeria
48	14	70	2	31 340	35	265	270	2.3	46	17	220	14	Rwanda
164	86	48	12	13 780	151	461	440	0.7	18	28	1 496	61	Senegal
47	42	40	12	17 520	102	1 776	380	0.3	31	17	359	35	Sierra Leone
65	39	30	11	15 630	84	217	250	1.9	50	11	1 149	62	Somalia
472	314			1 906	2 278	482	2 450	0.5	7	44			South Africa
67	31	52	18	8 930	66	1 498	400	3.5	34	10	5 726	78	Sudan
				7 000		544	890	0	20	21			Swaziland
40	18	98	3	17 740	38	760	240	0.1	43	8	2 584	59	Tanzania
103	59	100	27	18 100	88	354	280	0.4	27	17	805	114	Togo
452	269	100	32	3 690	473	190	1 290	4.1	14	26	3 427	43	Tunisia
22	26	60	8	26 810	23	730	220	5.6	73	7	623	18	Uganda
16	36	90	23	13 940	77	1 813	160	4.2	26	16	4 022	92	Zaire
88	100	96	16	7 670	432	640	580	2.5	17	27	2 638	84	Zambia
120	136	100	23	5 900	491	192	740	3.3	16	31	1 497	28	Zimbabwe

British Indian Oc. Terr. Land 0.08/Popn. 2; Cape Verde 4.0/317; Comoros 2.2/443; Djibouti 22/354; Eq. Guinea 28/383; Mauritius 1.9/1 011; Reunion 2.5/555; St.Helena 0.3/6; Sao Tome 0.9/94; Seychelles 0.3/65; Western Sahara 266/151

NORTH ATLANTIC OCEAN

6578

SPAIN
Cádiz · Málaga
Gibraltar (Br.) · Sidi Bel Abbès · Oran · Mostaganem · ALGIERS (Alger) · Tizi-Ouzou · Béjaïa · Skikda · Annaba (Bône) · Bizerte · Tuni
Str. of Gibraltar · Ceuta (Sp.) · Melilla (Sp.) · Blida · Medéa · Constantine · Béja
Tangier · Tétouan · Oujda · Tlemçen · Saïda · Tiaret · Sétif · Aïn Beïda · Batna · Tébessa · Gafsa
Ksar er Kebir · Fès · Taza · Méchéria · El Bayadh · Biskra · Djelfa · Laghouat · Touggourt · El Oued · Médenine
Kenitra · Salé · Rabat · Meknès · Bou · Ghardaïa · Ouargla · Gabès
CASABLANCA · El Jadida · Khouribga · Settat · Béchar · Chett Djerid
Ras Beddouza (C. Cantin) · Safi · Marrakech · Ar Rachidya · Abadla · Ghadamès
Essaouira · 2235 · El Goléa · Hassi Inifel
C. Rhir · Agadir · 4165 · Taroudant · Beni Abbès · Timimoun · Bordj Omar Driss
Ifni · Dra · Adrar · In Salah · Ilizi · Ghat
Anti Atlas · Plateau du Tademait · Zaouiet Reggane · Arak · Idelès · Djanet

ALGERIA

Canary Is. (Span.)
Palma · Lanzarote · Fuerteventura
Tenerife · Gomera · Sta. Cruz · Gran Canaria · Las Palmas · C. Juby · Tarfaya (Villa Bens) · Tindouf · Chech · Erg · Tanezrouft · Hoggar (Ahaggar) · 2918 · Tahat · Tamanrasset
Hierro · El Aaiún · Bj. Fly Ste. Marie

WESTERN SAHARA
C. Bojador
Bir Moghreïn (Ft. Trinquet)
Dakhla · Pta. Durnford
Cintra · Zouérate · Poste Maurice Cortier (Bidon 5) · Tessalit · Iférouane · Tamgak Mts. · Agadès
Nouadhibou (Port Etienne) · Atar · Chinguetti · El Djouf · Adrar · Air (Azbine) · 1900 · Fachi
Nouadhibou · Akjoujt · Tidjikdja · Mabrouk · Arouane · Kidal

MAURITANIA
MALI
NIGER
Timris · Nouakchott · Boutilimit · Moudjeria · Kiffa · Néma · Tombouctou (Timbuktu) · Bamba · Bourem · Kidal
Boghé · Kaédi · M'bout · Goundam · Gao · Tahoua · Tanout · Boultoum
St. Louis · Selibaby · Nioro · Nara · Ansongo · Ménaka · Madaoua
Louga · Linguère · Kayes · Sokolo · Didieni · Kolokani · Douentza · Filingué · Maradi · Zinder · Nguru
Thiès · Diourbel · Tambacounda · Ségou · Mopti · Dori · Téra · Niamey · Dosso · Sokoto · Gusau · Katsina · Azare · Yob
DAKAR · Kaolack · Koulikoro · San · Ouahigouya · Niamey · Birnin-Kebbi · Gummi · Kano · Hadejia · Potiskum
GAMBIA · Georgetown · Kayes · Bamako · Sikasso · BURKINA FASO · Ouagadougou · Fada N'Gourma · Kaduna · Zaria · Bauchi
Banjul · Koïda · Kédougou · Siguiri · Bougouni · Koutiala · Dédougou · Koudougou · Tenkodogo · Kandi · Kontagora · Minna · Jos
Ziguinchor · GUINEA · Bafatá · Kankan · Bobo-Dioulasso · Bolgatanga · Bawku · Natitingou · BENIN · NIGERIA · Abuja · Shendam
Bissau · BISSAU · Fouta Djalon · Labé · Sikasso · Banfora · Gaoua · Wa · Mango · Kandi · Bida · Ilorin · Lafia · Wukari
Bissagos Is. · Boké · Télimélé · Kindia · Faranah · Kissidougou · Korhogo · Tamale · Sokodé · BENIN · Oshogbo · Iwo · Lokoja · Makurdi · Gushaka
GUINEA · 1948 · Kenema · IVORY COAST · Wa · Black Volta · TOGO · Ogbomosho · Ibadan · Owo · Benin City · Enugu · Bamenda · Foumban
SIERRA LEONE · Conakry · Dubreka · Kindia · Odienné · Katiola · Bouaké · Sunyani · Ho · Abomey · Abeokuta · Ijebu Ode · Onitsha · CAMEROON
Freetown · Makeni · Magburaka · Man · Daloa · Dimbokro · Kumasi · Nkawkaw · Kpalime · Porto Novo · Warri · Aba · Calabar · Nkongsamba
Sherbro I. · Bo · Kenema · Gagnoa · GHANA · Koforidua · Lomé · LAGOS · Cotonou · Port Harcourt · Limbe · Doula · Yaoundé
Bonthe · LIBERIA · Danané · Séguéla · Agboville · Oda · Keta · Accra · Tema · Bight of Benin · Niger Delta · 4070 · Rey Malabo · Bioko · Sanaga
Monrovia · Buchanan · Sassandra · Gagnoa · Abidjan · Grand Bassam · Cape Coast · Sekondi-Takoradi · Winneba
Greenville · San Pedro · C. Palmas · C. Three Points · EQUATORIAL GUINEA

Madeira (Port.) · Funchal

St. Louis · C. Vert · DAKAR · SENEGAL

Bight of Benin

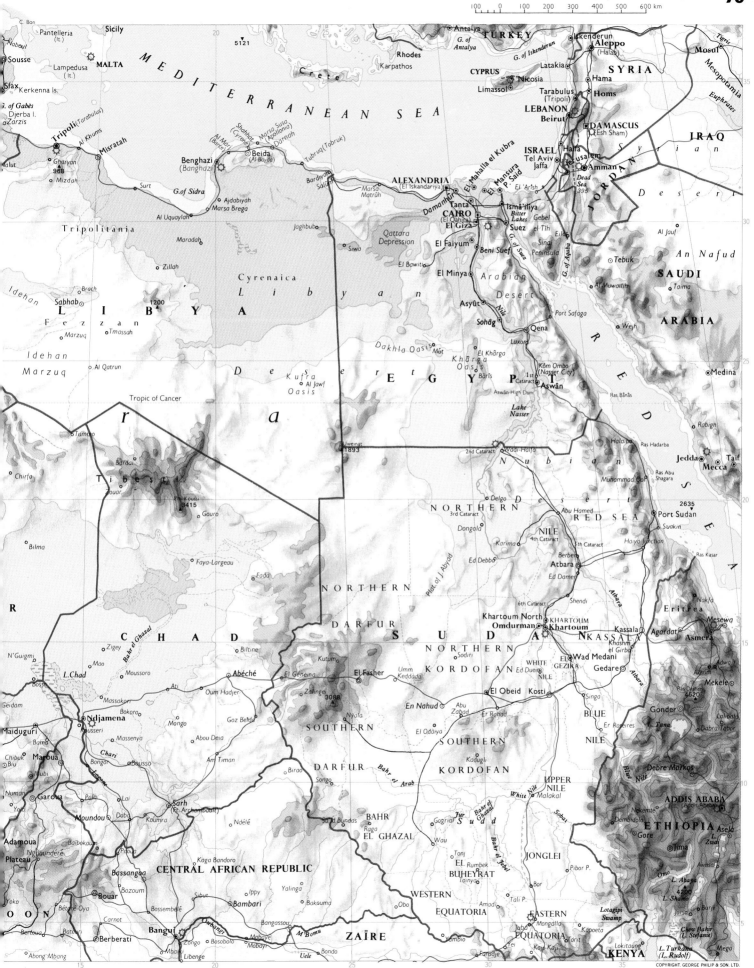

1:15 000 000

100 0 100 200 300 400 500 600 km

M E D I T E R R A N E A N   S E A

TURKEY
Antalya
G. of Antalya
Rhodes
Karpathos
Iskenderun
Aleppo
(Halab)
Mosul
Tigris
Latakia
G. of Iskenderun
SYRIA
CYPRUS
Nicosia
Limassol
Hama
Homs
Tarabulus
(Tripoli)
LEBANON
Beirut
DAMASCUS
(Esh Sham)
Mesopotamia
IRAQ
Euphrates

Crete
Sicily
Pantelleria (It.)
C. Bon
Naboul
MALTA
Lampedusa (It.)
Sousse
Sfax
Kerkenna Is.
5121

G. of Gabès
Djerba I.
Zarzis
Tripoli (Tarabulus)
Al Khums
Misratah
Gharyan
968
Mizdah
Nalut

Benghazi
(Banghazi)
Beida
(Al Bayda)
Al Marj
(Barce)
Shahhat
(Cyrene)
Marsa Susa
(Apollonia)
Darnah
Tubruq (Tobruk)
Bardiyah
Salum
ALEXANDRIA
(El Iskandariya)
Marsa Matruh
El Arish
El Mahalla el Kubra
Mansura
P. Said
Ismâ'iliya
Damanhur
Tanta
CAIRO
(El Qahira)
El Giza
Suez
Bitter Lakes
Gebel el Tih
ISRAEL
Haifa
Tel Aviv
Jaffa
Jerusalem
Amman
Dead Sea
-395
JORDAN
Syrian Desert
Al Jauf

Ajdabiyah
Marsa Brega
Al Uquaylah
Surt
G. of Sidra
Tripolitania
Maradah
Zillah
Jaghbub
Siwa
Qattara Depression
El Bawiti
El Faiyum
Beni Suef
El Minya
El Khârga
Asyût
Sohâg
Qena
Luxor
Kôm Ombo
(Nasser City)
Barîs
SAUDI
Tebuk
Al Muwailih
An Nafud
Taima
ARABIA
Port Safaga
Wejh

Cyrenaica
L i b y a n
Idehan
Sabhab
Brach
1200
Fezzan
Marzuq
Tmassah
Idehan Marzuq
Al Qatrun
D e s e r t
Kufra Oasis
Al Jawf
Oasis
Tropic of Cancer
Tummo
Bardai
Chirfa
Tibesti
Emi Koussi
3415
Zouar
Gouro

E G Y P T
Dakhla Oasis
Mût
El Khârga
Khârga Oasis
Aswân
1st Cataract
Aswân High Dam
Lake Nasser
Uweinat
1893
2nd Cataract
Wadi Halfa
Nubian
Desert
Delgo
Abu Hamed
NORTHERN
3rd Cataract
Dongola
Karima
4th Cataract
Ed Debba
5th Cataract
NILE
Berber
Atbara
Ed Damer

Ras Bânas
R E D   S E A
Ras Hadarba
Jedda
Mecca
Taif
Medina
Rabigh
2635
Port Sudan
Suakin
Haiya Junction
Ras Abu Shagara
Ras Kasar
Muhammad Qol
Halaib

R
Bilma
Faya-Largeau
Fada
Gouro
Chek el Abyad
Plat. of J. Abyad
6th Cataract
Shendi
Khartoum North
KHARTOUM
Omdurman
Khartoum
NORTHERN
DARFUR
S U D A N
Kutum
El Geneina
El Fasher
Zalingei
3088
Nyala
Biltine
Abéché
Oum Hadjer
Umm Keddada
Sodiri
NORTHERN
KORDOFAN
Ed Dueim
El Obeid
Kosti
En Nahud
Abu Zabad
Er Rahad
El Odaiya
Singa
SOUTHERN
KORDOFAN
Kadugli
WHITE
NILE
El Wad Medani
GEZIRA
Gedaref
Khashm el Girba
Kassala
Agardat
Asmera
Eritrea
Nakfa
Mesewa
Adwa
Axum
Mekele
4620
Ras Dashen
Gonder
L. Tana
BLUE
Debre Markos
Er Roseires
NILE
Debra Tabor
Lalibela

CHAD
Bahr el Ghazal
Zigey
Mao
Moussoro
Ati
Biltine
N'Guigmi
L. Chad
Bosso
Geidam
Maiduguri
Bama
Kousseri
Ndjamena
Massakori
Bokoro
Mongo
Massenya
Am Timan
Abou Deia
Goz Beïda
Birao
Songo
SOUTHERN
DARFUR
Bahr el Arab
Saïd Bundas
Raga
Wau
BAHR
EL GHAZAL
Tonj
Bahr el Arab
Bahr el Ghazal
Gogrial
Jur
JONGLEI
Amadi
WESTERN
EQUATORIA
Yambio
Obo
EASTERN
EQUATORIA
Juba
White Nile
Malakal
UPPER
NILE
Sobat
BLUE
NILE
ADDIS ABABA
(Addis Abeba)
ETHIOPIA
Dembidolo
Nekemte
Gore
Jima
Asela
Asgi
L. Zwai
L. Abaya
4200
L. Shamo
Awasa
L. Stefania
(L. Stefania)
Chew Bahir
(L. Stefania)

Chari
Maroua
Mubi
Chibuk
Biu
Numan
Yola
Garoua
Poli
Lai
Daba
Moundou
Koumra
Sarh
(Ft. Archambault)
Ndélé
Birao
Bangassou
Mbomou
CENTRAL AFRICAN REPUBLIC
Kaga Bandoro
Yalinga
Ippy
Bambari
Bakouma
Bangui
Sibut
Bossembélé
Bossangoa
Bozoum
Bouar
Baïbokoum
Bétaré-Oya
Bertoua
Abong Mbang
Adamaoua
Plateau
Ngaoundéré
Yoko
Carnot
Berbérati
Batouri
Nola
Zongo
Bosobolo
Libenge
Mobaye
Bondo
Uele
ZAÏRE
Yambio
M'Bomu
Tambura
Faradje
Aba
Kaji Kaji
Mongalla
Kapoeta
Lokichokio
Lotagipi Swamp
KENYA
L. Turkana
(L. Rudolf)
Mega
Moyale
Lokitaung
Jarso
Burji

Arabian Desert
Red Sea
Sinai Peninsula
G. of Aqaba
G. of Suez
Eilat

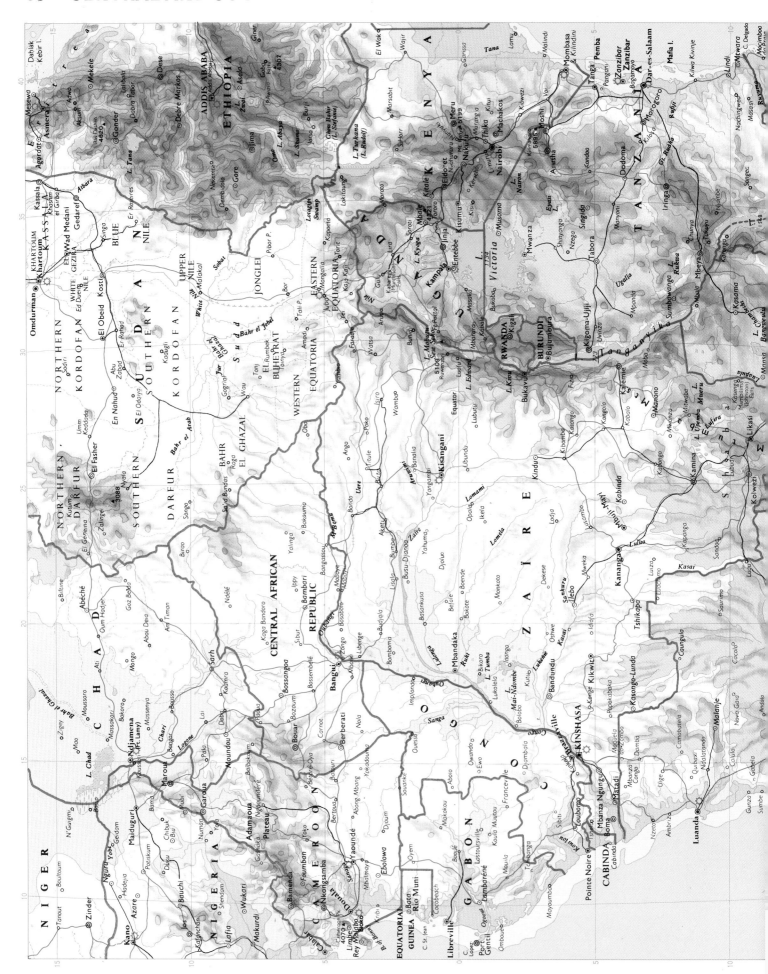

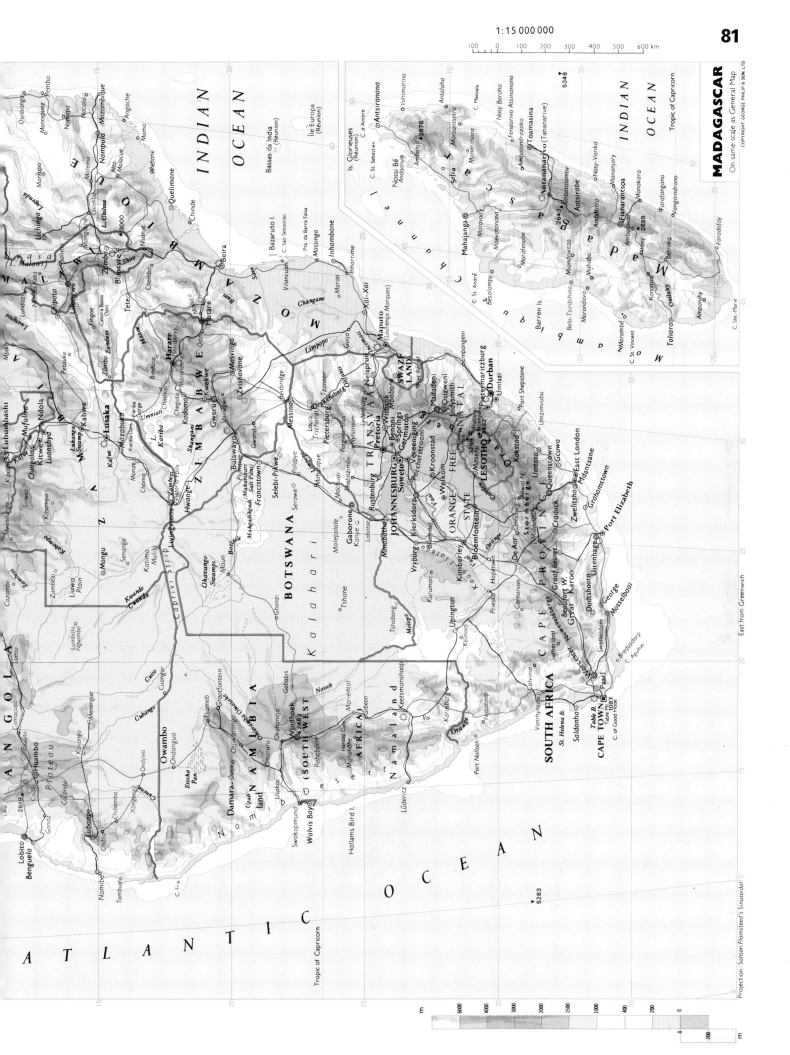

1:15 000 000

100   0   100   200   300   400   500   600 km

MADAGASCAR
On same scale as General Map

COPYRIGHT GEORGE PHILIP & SON LTD

INDIAN OCEAN

Tropic of Capricorn

Projection: Sanson Flamsteed's Sinusoidal

East from Greenwich

m   6000 4000 3000 2000 1500 1000 400 200 0

INDIAN OCEAN

ATLANTIC OCEAN

ANGOLA

ZAMBIA

NAMIBIA (SOUTH WEST AFRICA)

BOTSWANA

ZIMBABWE

MOÇAMBIQUE

MALAWI

SOUTH AFRICA

CAPE PROVINCE

ORANGE FREE STATE

TRANSVAAL

LESOTHO

SWAZILAND

NATAL

Tropic of Capricorn

1:35 000 000

400   0   400   800   1200 km

ARCTIC OCEAN

Asia

Wrangel I.

C. Barrow

Beaufort Sea

Greenland

Iceland

Denmark Strait

Peterman's Pk 2940

Gunnbjörns 3700 Fjeld

Mt. Forel 3360

Bering Strait

St. Lawrence

Nunivak I.

Bering Sea

Pr. of Wales

Brooks Range

Alaska Range

Porcupine

Axel Heiberg

Sverdrup Is.

Parry Is.

Queen Elizabeth Islands

Ellesmere I.

Kane Basin

Thule

3800

Nares Str.

Godthåb

Julianehåb

C. Farewell

Banks

Melville Magnetic N. Pole Pole Viscount

M'Clure Strait

Melville Sound

Prince of Wales I.

C. Bathurst

Bathurst I.

Devon I.

Lancaster Sound

Somerset I.

Bylot I.

Disko I.

Davis Strait

Baffin Bay

Baffin Island

Alaska Pen.

Kodiak I.

Gulf of Alaska

Mt. St. Elias 5489 Mt. Logan 6050

Alexander Archipelago

Queen Charlotte Islands

Mt. Waddington 3990 Queen Charlotte Sound

Vancouver I. Vancouver

Juan de Fuca Strait C. Flattery

Seattle

Portland

C. Blanco

C. Mendocino

San Francisco

PACIFIC OCEAN

Mendocino Seascarp

Murray Seascarp

Clarion Fracture Zone

Revilla Gigedo Is.

Tropic of Cancer

C. San Lúcas

Gulf of California

Lower California

6225

C. Corrientes

Guadalajara

C. Corrientes

Revilla

Yukon

Mackenzie Mts.

Coast Mountains

Peace

Liard

Mackenzie

Great Bear L.

Great Slave L.

Athabasca

Athabasca L.

Back

Debarib

Reindeer L.

Churchill

Nelson

Chesterfield Inlet

Arctic Circle

Boothia Pen.

Gulf of Boothia

Melville Pen.

Foxe Basin

Southampton I.

Foxe Channel

Hudson Strait

Resolution I. C. Chidley

Frobisher Bay

Cumberland Sound

2591

Hudson Bay

James Bay

Belcher Is.

Henrietta Maria

Ungava Peninsula

Wollaston

1676

Labrador

Hamilton Inlet

C. Harrison

Eastmain

L. Charles

Bulls Elk Strait C. Charles

50

Newfoundland

St. John's

C. Race

Edmonton

Calgary

Kicking Horse Pass

Crowsnest Pass

Yellowhead Pass

Mt. Robson 3954

Fraser

Columbia

N. Saskatchewan

S. Saskatchewan

Regina

Winnipeg

L. Winnipeg

Lake Winnipeg

Minneapolis

Missouri

Mississippi

Chicago

L. Superior

L. Michigan

L. Huron

Huron

Detroit

Hamilton

L. Erie

Niagara Falls

Toronto

Ottawa

L. Ontario

Montreal

Québec

St. Lawrence

Pt. Edward

C. Breton

Nova Scotia

Bay of Fundy

Halifax

Saint John

Sable I.

C. Sable

Laurentian Plateau

Gulf of St. Lawrence

Anticosti

50

Snake

Bitterroot Range

Bighorn Mountains

Mt. Rainier 4392

Columbia

Great Salt Lake

Wasatch Mountains

Rocky Mountains

Coast Range

Cascade Range

Sierra Nevada

Mt. Shasta 4317

Sacramento

San Joaquin

Mt. Whitney 4418

Mt. Elbert 4399

Denver

Colorado

Colorado Plateau

Grand Canyon

Gila

Los Angeles

Great Basin

4370 Blanca Pk.

N. Platte

S. Platte

Kansas City

St. Louis

Memphis

Ozark Plateau

Arkansas

Red

Dallas

Houston

Llano Estacado

Great Plains

Interior Plains

Minnesota

Mississippi

Alabama

New Orleans

Mississippi Delta

Gulf of Mexico

New York

Philadelphia

Washington

Chesapeake Bay

Mt. Washington 1917

Allegheny Mts.

Appalachian Mts.

Cumberland Plateau

2037

Atlanta

C. Hatteras

Florida

ATLANTIC OCEAN

Bermuda

6399

Bahama Islands

Florida Strait

Havana

Cuba

Greater Antilles

Jamaica

Hispaniola

Port-au-Prince

Milwaukee Deep 9200

Puerto Rico

Venezuela Basin

9200

Monterrey

Western Sierra Madre

Eastern Sierra Madre

Mexican Plateau

Mexico

Puebla

Popocatepetl 5452 5800

Orizaba

Isthmus of Tehuantepec

G. of Tehuantepec

Guatemala Trench 6662

Guatemala

Gulf of Campeche

Yucatán

Yucatán Peninsula

C. Catoche

Yucatán Strait

Yucatán Basin

Cayman Trough 7680

Gulf of Honduras

Coco

C. Gracias a Dios

L. Nicaragua

Panama Canal

3837

G. of Darién

G. of Panama

Colombian Basin

Caribbean Sea

Sa. Nevada de Sta. Marta

5800

G. of Venezuela

Maracaibo

L. Maracaibo

Sierra Nevada de Mérida

Andes

Magdalena

130   120   110   West from Greenwich   100   90   80

Projection: Bonne

m
4000
2000
1000
400
200
0
0
200
2000
4000
6000
8000
m

1 : 35 000 000

400   0   400   800   1200 km

ARCTIC OCEAN

GREENLAND (Denmark)

U.S.S.R.

Bering Strait

Bering Sea

Beaufort Sea

Queen Elizabeth Is.

Ellesmere I.

Denmark Strait

Reykjavik ICELAND

Baffin Bay

Davis Strait

C. Farvel

ALASKA
Yukon
Arctic Circle
Fairbanks
Anchorage
Gulf of Alaska

Porcupine

INUVIK

Victoria I.

KITIKMEOT

BAFFIN

Baffin I.

Goothaab

YUKON TERRITORY

Whitehorse

FORT SMITH

Mackenzie

Great Bear L.

NORTHWEST TERRITORIES

Back

KEEWATIN

Hudson Strait

NEWFOUNDLAND

Juneau

Yellowknife

Great Slave L.

Dubawnt

Hudson Bay

Liard

C A N A D A

Labrador

BRITISH COLUMBIA

Skeena

Finlay

Peace

Athabasca

L. Athabasca

Churchill

Nelson

Eastmain

QUÉBEC

St. John's

Fraser

ALBERTA

Edmonton
N. Saskatchewan

SASKATCHEWAN

MANITOBA

L. Winnipeg

ONTARIO

St. Lawrence

PR. EDWARD

Charlottetown

Victoria

Vancouver

Calgary

S. Saskatchewan

Regina

Winnipeg

L. Superior

Québec

Montréal

Fredericton

MAINE

NEW BRUNS. WICK

NOVA SCOTIA

Halifax

SPM

WASHINGTON
Seattle
Olympia

Portland

Salem

Columbia

OREGON

MONTANA
Helena

Missouri

NORTH DAKOTA
Bismarck

MINNESOTA

Minneapolis
St. Paul

WISCONSIN

Madison

Lansing

MICHIGAN

Huron

Toronto

L. Ontario

Buffalo

Detroit

Cleveland

PENNSYLVANIA

Ottawa

VER. N.H.
Montpelier
Concord

Albany

Boston
MASS. Providence R.I.
Hartford

NEW YORK

NEW YORK

IDAHO
Boise

Snake

WYOMING

Cheyenne

SOUTH DAKOTA
Pierre

Milwaukee

Chicago

Toledo

OHIO

Pittsburgh

Harrisburg

Philadelphia

NEW JERSEY

Trenton Dover

N. Platte

NEBRASKA

Lincoln

IOWA

Des Moines

ILLINOIS

INDIANA

Columbus

Cincinnati

Ohio

WEST VIRGINIA

Baltimore

Annapolis D.C. DEL.

Washington M.

Sacramento

San Francisco
San Jose

CALIFORNIA

NEVADA

Carson City

Salt Lake City

UTAH

Denver

COLORADO

Kansas City

Topeka

KANSAS

Jefferson City

MISSOURI

St. Louis

Springfield

Indianapolis

Frankfort

KENTUCKY

Charleston

Richmond

VIRGINIA

Raleigh

Las Vegas

Arkansas

Nashville

TENNESSEE

Tennessee

NORTH CAROLINA

Columbia

PACIFIC OCEAN

LOS ANGELES

San Diego

Santa Fe

ARIZONA

Phoenix

NEW MEXICO

Albuquerque

Oklahoma City

OKLAHOMA

Red River

Little Rock

ARKANSAS

Memphis

Mississippi

Birmingham

Atlanta

SOUTH CAROLINA

Tucson

Gila

Colorado

El Paso

Fort Worth

Dallas

MISSISSIPPI

Jackson

ALABAMA

Montgomery

GEORGIA

Jacksonville

ATLANTIC OCEAN

Bermuda

Rio Grande

TEXAS

Austin

LOUISIANA

Baton Rouge

New Orleans

Tallahassee

FLORIDA

Tropic of Cancer

MEXICO

Houston

Tampa

Miami

Str. of Florida

C. Sable

Nassau

BAHAMAS

Monterrey

Gulf of Mexico

Havana

CUBA

Caribbean Sea

DOMINICAN REP.

HAITI
Port-au-Prince

San Juan

PUERTO RICO

Guadalajara

JAMAICA

Kingston

Santo Domingo

MEXICO

Belmopan

BELIZE

GUATEMALA

Guatemala

HONDURAS

Tegucigalpa

Maracaibo

Barranquilla

VENEZUELA

EL SALVADOR

San Salvador

NICARAGUA

Managua

L. Nicaragua

Panamá

COSTA RICA

San José

PANAMA

Medellin

COLOMBIA

Bogotá

SOUTH AMERICA

Projection: Bonne

Washington Capital Cities

C   CONNECTICUT
D.   DELAWARE
D.C. DISTRICT OF COLUMBIA
M.   MARYLAND
MASS. MASSACHUSETTS

N.H. NEW HAMPSHIRE
N.J. NEW JERSEY
R.I. RHODE ISLAND
VER. VERMONT
SPM   ST. PIERRE ET MIQUELON

West from Greenwich

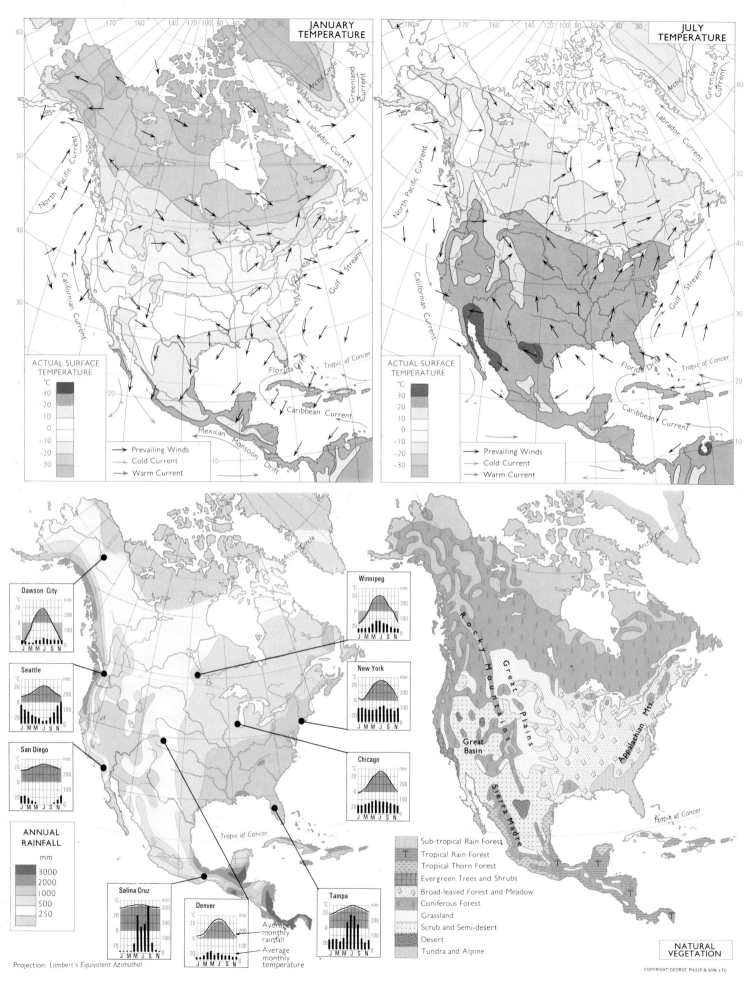

JANUARY TEMPERATURE

ACTUAL SURFACE TEMPERATURE
°C
30
20
10
0
-10
-20
-30

→ Prevailing Winds
→ Cold Current
→ Warm Current

North Pacific Current
Californian Current
Greenland Current
Labrador Current
Gulf Stream
Florida Drift
Tropic of Cancer
Caribbean Current
Mexican Monsoon Drift
Arctic Circle

JULY TEMPERATURE

ACTUAL SURFACE TEMPERATURE
°C
30
20
10
0
-10
-20
-30

→ Prevailing Winds
→ Cold Current
→ Warm Current

North Pacific Current
Californian Current
Greenland Current
Labrador Current
Gulf Stream
Florida Drift
Tropic of Cancer
Caribbean Current
Arctic Circle

ANNUAL RAINFALL

mm
3000
2000
1000
500
250

Dawson City
Seattle
San Diego
Salina Cruz
Denver
Winnipeg
New York
Chicago
Tampa

Average monthly rainfall
Average monthly temperature

Tropic of Cancer
Arctic Circle

Projection: Lambert's Equivalent Azimuthal

Rocky Mountains
Great Plains
Great Basin
Sierra Madre
Appalachian Mts.
Tropic of Cancer
Arctic Circle

Sub-tropical Rain Forest
Tropical Rain Forest
Tropical Thorn Forest
Evergreen Trees and Shrubs
Broad-leaved Forest and Meadow
Coniferous Forest
Grassland
Scrub and Semi-desert
Desert
Tundra and Alpine

NATURAL VEGETATION

COPYRIGHT GEORGE PHILIP & SON LTD.

1:32 000 000

400   0   400   800   1200 km

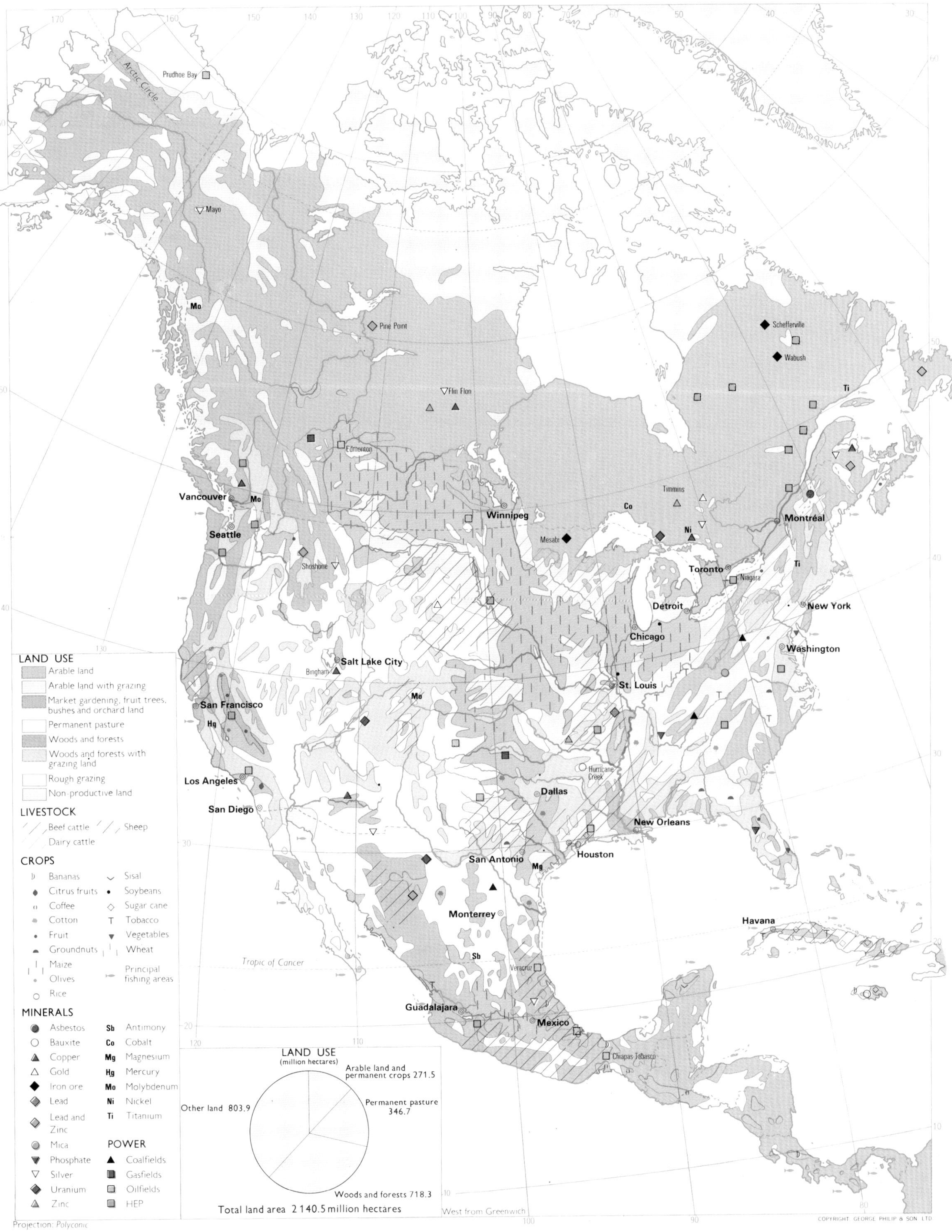

Prudhoe Bay

Arctic Circle

Mayo

Mo

Pine Point

Flin Flon

Schefferville

Wabush

Ti

Edmonton

Ti

Vancouver   Mo

Timmins

Co

Montréal

Seattle

Mesabi

Ni

Shoshone

Toronto

Niagara

Ti

Salt Lake City

Detroit

New York

Bingham

Chicago

Washington

San Francisco

St. Louis

Hg

Mo

Los Angeles

Hurricane
Creek

San Diego

Dallas

San Antonio

New Orleans

Houston

Mg

Monterrey

Havana

Sb

Guadalajara

Veracruz

Mexico

Tropic of Cancer

Chiapas Tabasco

LAND USE

- Arable land
- Arable land with grazing
- Market gardening, fruit trees, bushes and orchard land
- Permanent pasture
- Woods and forests
- Woods and forests with grazing land
- Rough grazing
- Non-productive land

LIVESTOCK

- Beef cattle   Sheep
- Dairy cattle

CROPS

▷	Bananas	∨	Sisal
◆	Citrus fruits	•	Soybeans
⌒	Coffee	◇	Sugar cane
⬡	Cotton	T	Tobacco
•	Fruit	▼	Vegetables
⌒	Groundnuts	∥	Wheat
‖	Maize		
∘	Olives		Principal fishing areas
○	Rice		

MINERALS

◑	Asbestos	**Sb**	Antimony
○	Bauxite	**Co**	Cobalt
▲	Copper	**Mg**	Magnesium
△	Gold	**Hg**	Mercury
◆	Iron ore	**Mo**	Molybdenum
◆	Lead	**Ni**	Nickel
◈	Lead and Zinc	**Ti**	Titanium
◉	Mica		
▼	Phosphate	**POWER**	
▽	Silver	▲	Coalfields
◆	Uranium	▦	Gasfields
△	Zinc	▢	Oilfields
		▣	HEP

LAND USE
(million hectares)

Arable land and permanent crops 271.5

Other land 803.9

Permanent pasture 346.7

Woods and forests 718.3

Total land area 2 140.5 million hectares

Projection: Polyconic

West from Greenwich

COPYRIGHT GEORGE PHILIP & SON LTD

	Population					Growth			Land			Agriculture		
	Total	Density	Birth Rate	Death Rate	Life Expectancy	1965-73	1973-83	Urban	Area	Arable	Forest	Agricultural Population	Index of Production	Food intake
	th.	persons per km²	per th. popn.		yrs.	av. % per annum		%	th. km²	th. km²	th. km²	% of total popn.	1974-76 =100	calories per day
Bahamas	226	23	24	5	67		1.3		10	0	3.2	8		2 200
Barbados	252	630	17	8	67		0.4		0.4	0.3	0	16	116	3 020
Canada	25 150	2.7	15	7	76	1.4	1.2	75	9 221	462	3 261	4	130	3 346
Costa Rica	2 534	50	30	4	74	3.0	2.4	45	51	6.3	16	33	118	2 653
Cuba	9 992	87	17	6	72	1.8	0.8	70	115	32	19	21	128	2 795
Dominican Rep.	6 102	127	35	9	63	2.9	2.4	54	48	15	6.3	55	115	2 131
El Salvador	5 388	257	28	6	64	3.4	3.0	42	21	7.3	1.3	49	103	2 155
Guadeloupe	331	184	20	7	71		0.4		1.8	0.4	0.7	14	90	2 491
Guatemala	7 740	72	39	7	60	3.0	3.1	40	108	18	44	53	115	2 138
Haiti	5 185	185	42	16	54	1.5	1.8	27	28	8.9	1.0	64	106	1 904
Honduras	4 232	38	47	12	60	2.9	3.5	38	112	18	39	61	141	2 135
Jamaica	2 290	208	28	6	70	1.5	1.3	52	11	2.7	3.0	19	101	2 542
Martinique	327	297	17	7			0.6		1.1	0.2	0.3	13	82	2 673
Mexico	76 792	40	38	6	66	3.3	2.9	69	1 923	235	474	34	131	2 890
Nicaragua	3 162	27	46	12	58	2.9	3.9	55	119	13	43	40	98	2 188
Panama	2 134	28	20	7	71	2.7	2.3	50	76	5.8	41	33	122	2 338
Puerto Rico	3 404	382	20	7	73		0.8		8.9	1.3	1.8	2.4	94	
Trinidad & Tobago	1 105	217	25	7	68	0.9	0.6	22	5.1	1.6	2.3	15	71	2 837
U.S.A.	236 681	26	16	9	75	1.1	1.0	74	9 127	1 906	2 845	1.9	98	3 641
Argentina	30 097	11	24	8	70	1.5	1.6	84	2 737	358	600	12	119	3 380
Bolivia	6 253	5.7	47	18	51	2.4	2.6	43	1 084	34	561	48	82	2 082
Brazil	132 580	16	32	9	64	2.5	2.3	71	8 456	746	5 701	36	133	2 580
Chile	11 878	16	23	6	70	1.9	1.7	82	749	55	155	17	112	2 759
Colombia	28 217	27	32	8	64	2.6	1.9	66	1 039	57	516	25	125	2 494
Ecuador	9 115	33	42	10	63	2.7	2.6	46	277	26	144	43	109	2 114
Guyana	936	4.8	28	7			0.8		197	4.9	164	20	102	2 359
Paraguay	3 278	8.3	37	8	65	2.7	2.5	41	397	19	205	48	143	2 839
Peru	19 198	15	38	12	58	2.8	2.4	67	1 280	35	704	35	100	2 195
Surinam	352	2.2	28	8					161	0.6	155	16	139	2 524
Uruguay	2 990	17	18	9	73	0.6	0.5	85	174	14	6.3	11	113	2 886
Venezuela	16 851	19	37	6	68	3.6	3.5	85	882	38	344	16	116	2 649

Population. This is the United Nations' estimate for the mid-year 1984 (thousands).

Population density. This is the quoted population total divided by the quoted land area (persons per square kilometre).

Birth Rates and Death Rates. These are the registered or United Nations' estimated rates per thousand population.

Life Expectancy. This figure indicates the number of years that a child born today can expect to live if the levels of death of today last throughout its life. The figure is an average of that for men and women. The figure for women is usually higher than that for men (U.K. male 70, female 76 years).

Population Growth. This shows the average annual percentage change in population for two periods 1965-1973 and 1973-1983.

Urbanization. This is the percentage of the total population living in urban areas. The definition of urban is that of the individual nation and usually includes quite small towns.

Land Area. This is the total area of the country minus the area covered by major lakes and rivers (thousand square kilometres).

Arable Land and Permanent Crops. This excludes fallow land but includes temporary pasture (thousand square kilometres).

Forest and Woodland. This includes natural and planted woodland and land recently cleared of timber which will be replanted (thousand square kilometres).

Agricultural Population. This is the percentage of the economically active population working in agriculture. It includes those people working also in forestry, hunting and fishing.

Index of Agricultural Production. The base period for this index is 1974-1976 and it shows the level of production in each country in 1983 in comparision with that of the earlier period. Only edible crops and meat are included.

Food Supply. The figures are the average intake per person in calories per day in the period 1979-1981.

Trade		Education		Health	Energy	Consumer Price Index	G.N.P		G.D.P.			Loans & Debt		
Imports	Exports	Primary	Secondary					Growth per capita	Part formed by					
				Popn. per doctor	Consumption in kgs of oil equiv. per capita		US$ per capita	% per yr. 1973-82	Agric.		Indust.	end 1983 US$ millions	as % of GNP	
US$ per capita		% of age group				1970 = 100				%				
13 152	10 361	99		1 200	5 400	243	4 060	0.5	4		12			Bahamas
2 636	1 564	100		1 300	1 060	544	3 930	2.9	7		13			Barbados
2 942	3 455	100	95	550	8 847	310	12 000	1.1	4		26	1 535	0.5	Canada
443	372	100	48	1 460	609	1 220	1 020	0.4	23		22	3 315	126	Costa Rica
815	618	100	72	720	1 042			1 400	4		43			Cuba
215	132	100	41	2 410	407	226	1 380	1.5	18		20	1 065	29	Dominican Rep
171	141	61	20	3 220	190	214	710	2.3	23		17			El Salvador
1 855	261			1 000	860	426	4 330	4.7	7		7			Guadeloupe
151	154	73	16	8 610	178	116	1 120	1.4	25		18	1 405	16	Guatemala
61	36	69	13	8 200	55	142	320	1.9	38		18	433	27	Haiti
188	169	99	32	3 120	204	300	670	0.7	25		18	1 570	56	Honduras
513	339	99	58	2 830	980	996	1 300	4.0	8		31	1 950	65	Jamaica
1 960	318			900	900	460	4 270	3.3	11		5			Martinique
146	306	100	54	2 000	1 332	4 092	2 240	3.2	8		30	66 732	49	Mexico
256	124	100	41	1 800	262		900	5.3	25		23	3 417	133	Nicaragua
668	120	100	63	980	2 082	231	2 070	2.5	10		14	2 986	74	Panama
		82		4 000	2 500	232	2 890	0.8	2		41			Puerto Rico
2 245	2 046	99	61	1 360	5 191	615	6 900	5.2	2		44	887	12	Trinidad & Tobago
1 376	921	100	97	520	7 030	278	14 090	1.5	3		29	8 698	0.2	U.S.A.
151	269	100	59	430	1 460	157th	2 030	1.1	9		29	24 593	32	Argentina
101	124	86	34	2000	292	4.8 mill	510	1.1	16		25	2 969	78	Bolivia
115	204	96	32	1 600	745	58 763	1 890	2.8	11		24	58 068	29	Brazil
269	308	100	59	1 930	755	265	1 870	1.4	7		29	6 827	39	Chile
181	112	125	46	1 710	786	1 888	1 470	2.7	19		27	6 899	18	Colombia
188	282	100	56	760	675	286	1 430	3.0	12		30	6 239	63	Ecuador
639	97	95		9 000	700	449	520	1.3	19		19			Guyana
146	82	100	36	1 310	187	407	1 140	6.8	28		19	1 161	29	Paraguay
97	163	100	59	1 390	550	37th	1 040	0.4	9		38	7 932	48	Peru
1 274	686	100		1 700	3 160	287	3 520	5.1	9		25			Surinam
265	352	100	63	540	776	74th	2 490	2.9	7		23	2 523	48	Uruguay
407	915	100	40	990	2 295	373	4 100	0	6		40	12 911	20	Venezuela

Antigua & Barbuda Land 0.4/Popn. 79; Belize 23/156; Bermuda 0.05/56; Br. Virgin Is. 0.2/13; Cayman Is. 0.3/19; Dominica 0.8/77; Greenland 342/53; Grenada 0.3/112; Montserrat 0.1/13; Netherlands Antilles 1/260; St. Christopher-Nevis 0.4/51; St Lucia 0.6/134; St Pierre & M. 0.2/6; St Vincent 0.3/104; Turks and Caicos Is. 0.4/8; U.S. Virgin Is. 0.3/103. Falkland Is. 12/2; Fr.Guiana 89/72.

Trade. The trade figures are normally for the year 1983 or 1984. The total trade figures have been divided by the population and are a measure of the country's external trade (U.S. $ per capita).

Education. The ages of primary school are taken to be 6-11 years and secondary school 12-17 years. The percentage of the total school age group in this type of education is shown.

Energy. All forms of energy have been converted to their equivalent in oil. Firewood and other traditional forms used in developing countries are not included and so the energy consumption in those countries is understated (kilograms of oil equivalent per capita).

Consumer Price Index. The base year is 1970 which is 100 and the level of consumer prices in 1984 or 1985 are shown in relation to the base year. It is a measure of inflation.

G.N.P. (Gross National Product) This figure is an estimate of the average production per person measured in U.S. dollars and for 1983. The G.N.P. measures the value of goods and services produced in a country, plus the balance, positive or negative, of income from abroad, for example investments, interest on capital, money returned from foreign labour, etc. The rate of change is the average annual percentage change during the period 1973-1982 in the G.D.P. The G.D.P. (Gross Domestic Product) is the G.N.P. minus the foreign balances. The adjoining two columns show the percentage contribution to the G.D.P. made by the agricultural and mining and manufacturing sectors.

Loans and Debt. This figure in millions of U.S. dollars shows the external public debt at the end of 1983. This is then shown as a percentage of the annual G.N.P. The figures in red show official development assistance made by the developed countries and also as a percentage of the donor country's G.N.P.

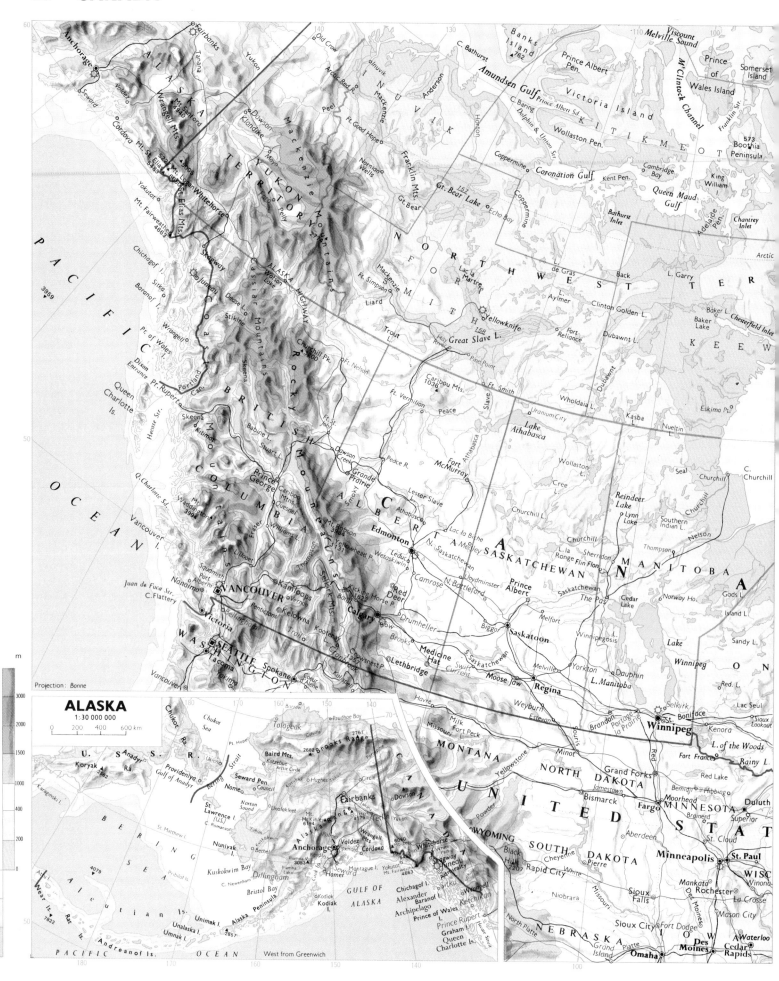

ALASKA

1 : 30 000 000

0   200   400   600 km

Projection: Bonne

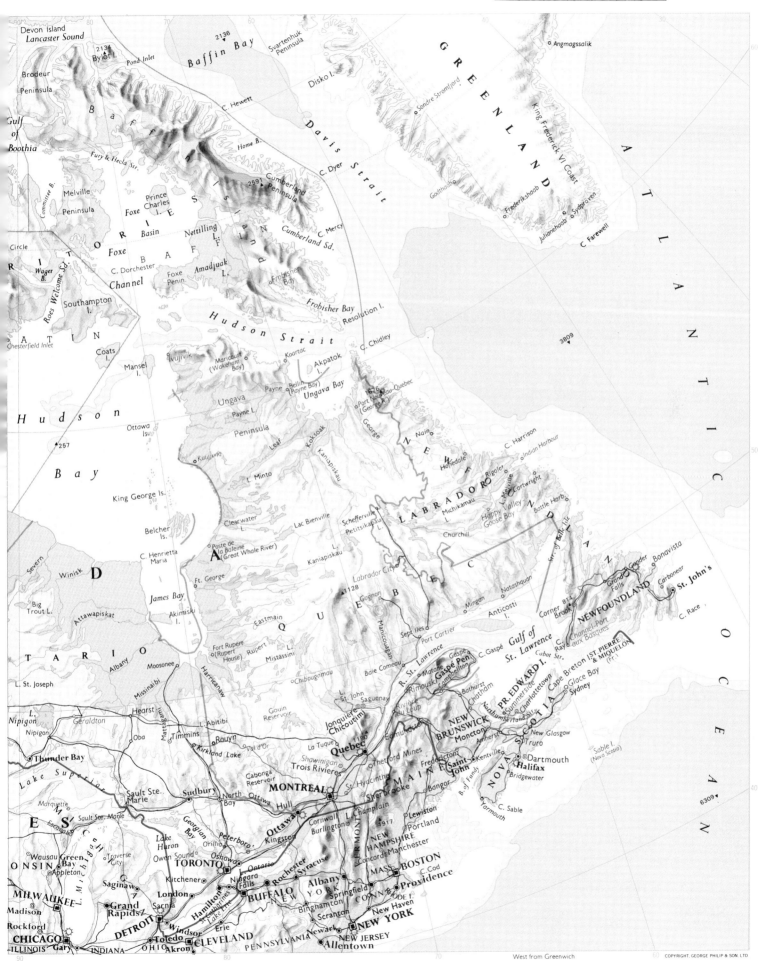

1:15 000 000

100   0   100   200   300   400   500   600 km

GREENLAND

ATLANTIC

Devon Island
Lancaster Sound
2134
Bylot I.
Pond Inlet
Brodeur
Peninsula
Gulf
of
Boothia
Baffin Bay
Svartenhuk Peninsula
Disko I.
C. Hewett
2136
Sondre Stromfjord
King Frederick VI Coast
Angmagssalik
Godthaab
Frederikshaab
Sydproven
Julianehaab
C. Farewell

Fury & Hecla Str.
Melville
Prince Charles
Foxe
Basin
Nettilling
L.
2591 Cumberland Peninsula
C. Dyer
Davis Strait
C. Mercy
Cumberland Sd.

Committee B.
Melville
Peninsula
Circle
Wager
B.
C. Dorchester
Foxe
Channel
Southampton
I.
Roes Welcome Sd.
Chesterfield Inlet
Coats
I.
Mansel
I.

VICTORIA
Foxe
Penin.
Amadjuak
L.
Frobisher
Bay
Frobisher Bay
Resolution I.

Hudson Strait
C. Chidley

Ivujivik
Koartac
Akpatok
I.
Maricourt
(Wakeham Bay)
Bellin
(Payne Bay)
Ungava Bay
1676
Port Nouveau-Quebec
(George R.)

Hudson
Payne
Ungava
Payne L.
Peninsula
Leaf
Koksoak
Kaniapiskau
George
Nain
NEW

Ottawa Isls.
257
Kuujjuaq
L. Minto
Hopedale
Rigolet
C. Harrison
Indian Harbour

Bay
King George Is.
Clearwater
Lac Bienville
Scheffervile
Petitsikapau
L.
Churchill
LABRADOR
L. Melville
Cartwright
Michikamau
L.
Happy Valley
Goose Bay
Battle Harb.
Str. of Belle Isle

Belcher
Isls.
C. Henrietta
Maria
Poste de
la Baleine
(Great Whale River)
A
Labrador City
1128
Gagnon
C
Natashquan
Gander
Bonavista
Carbonear
St. John's
C. Race

Severn
Winisk
D
Ft. George
James Bay
Akimiski
I.
Eastmain
Fort Rupert
(Rupert House)
Rupert
Mistassini
L.
QUEBEC
Gouin
Reservoir
Chibougamau
Mingan
Anticosti
I.
Corner
Brook
NEWFOUNDLAND
Grand
Falls
3809

Big
Trout L.
Attawapiskat
TARIO
Albany
Moosonee
Harricanaw
Eastmain
St. John
Sept Iles
Port Cartier
NEW
BRUNSWICK
Manicouagan
R. St. Lawrence
Gulf of
St. Lawrence
Cabot Str.
Cape Breton
ST. PIERRE
& MIQUELON
(Fr.)
Channel-Port
aux Basques
814

L. St. Joseph
L.
Nipigon
Geraldton
Hearst
L. Abitibi
La Tuque
Baie Comeau
Gaspé
Matane
Gaspé Pen.
Campbellton
Bathurst
PR. EDWARD I.
Summerside
Charlottetown
Glace Bay
Sydney
Sable I.
(Nova Scotia)

Nipigon
Thunder Bay
Lake Superior
Marquette
Oba
Timmins
Kirkland Lake
Val d'Or
Shawinigan
190
Jonquiere
Chicoutimi
Quebec
Trois Rivieres
Rimouski
Riviere
du Loup
Chatham
Moncton
Amherst
New Glasgow
NOVA
SCOTIA
Truro
Dartmouth
Halifax
Bridgewater
6309
C. Sable

Sault Ste.
Marie
Sudbury
North
Bay
Cabonga
Reservoir
MONTREAL
Ottawa
Hull
St. Hyacinthe
Sherbrooke
Thetford Mines
Edmundston
MAINE
Fredericton
Saint
John
B. of Fundy
Yarmouth

ES
ONSIN
Marquette
Escanaba
Sault Ste. Marie
Georgian Bay
Lake
Huron
Orillia
Peterboro.
Kingston
Cornwall
Burlington
L. Champlain
1917
NEW
HAMPSHIRE
Concord
Manchester
Bangor
Portland
Lewiston
C. Cod

Wausau
Green Bay
Appleton
Traverse City
Owen Sound
Orillia
TORONTO
L. Ontario
Rochester
Syracuse
Binghamton
VERMONT
Springfield
MASS.
BOSTON
Providence
RHODE I.

MILWAUKEE
Madison
Grand
Rapids
Saginaw
Kitchener
London
Sarnia
Hamilton
St. Catharines
BUFFALO
Niagara
Falls
NEW
YORK
Albany
CONN.
New Haven
New York

Rockford
CHICAGO
Gary
ILLINOIS
INDIANA
DETROIT
Windsor
Toledo
Akron
CLEVELAND
OHIO
Erie
L. Erie
PENNSYLVANIA
Scranton
Newark
NEW JERSEY
Allentown
NEW YORK

West from Greenwich

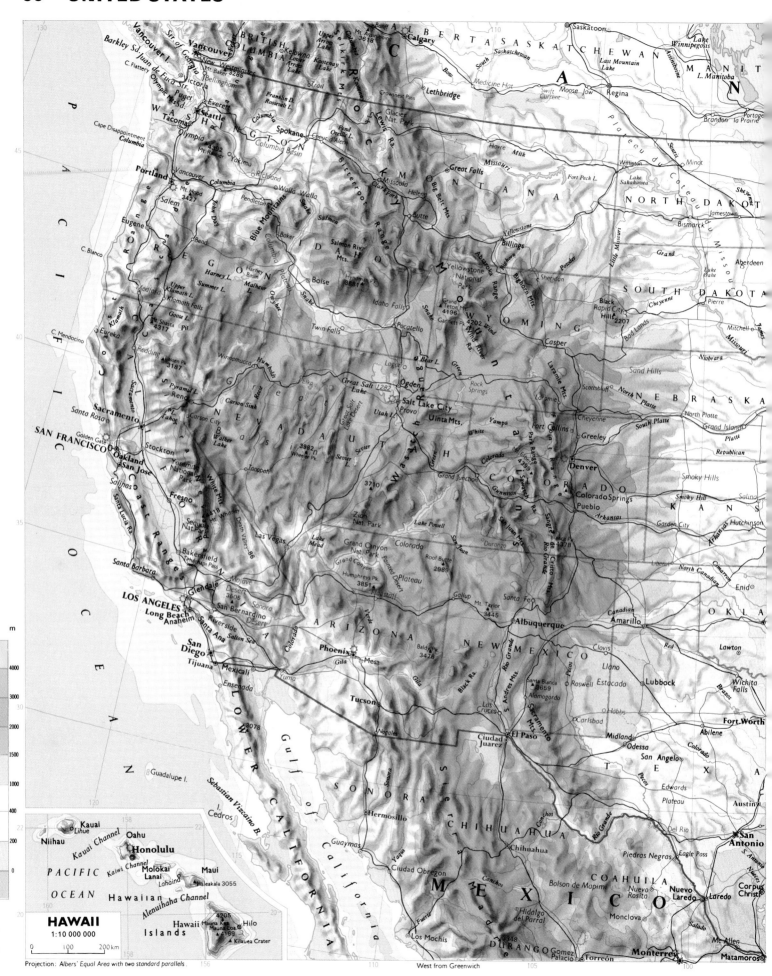

HAWAII
1:10 000 000

0   100   200 km

Projection: Albers' Equal Area with two standard parallels.   West from Greenwich

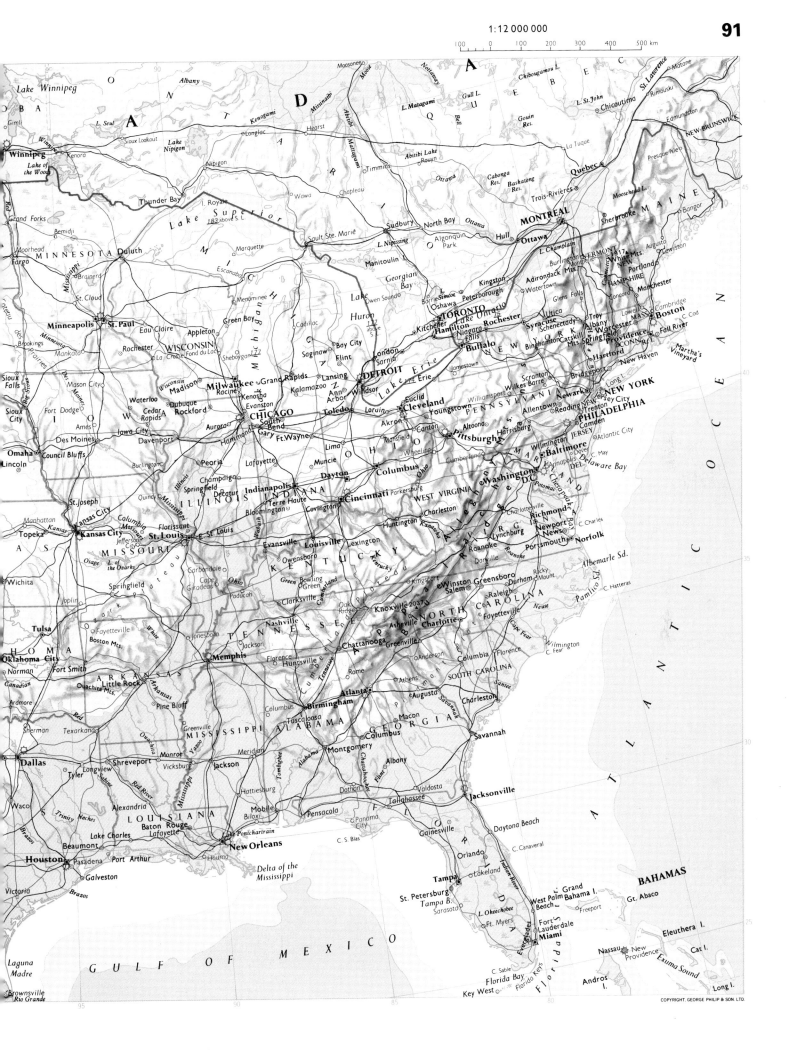

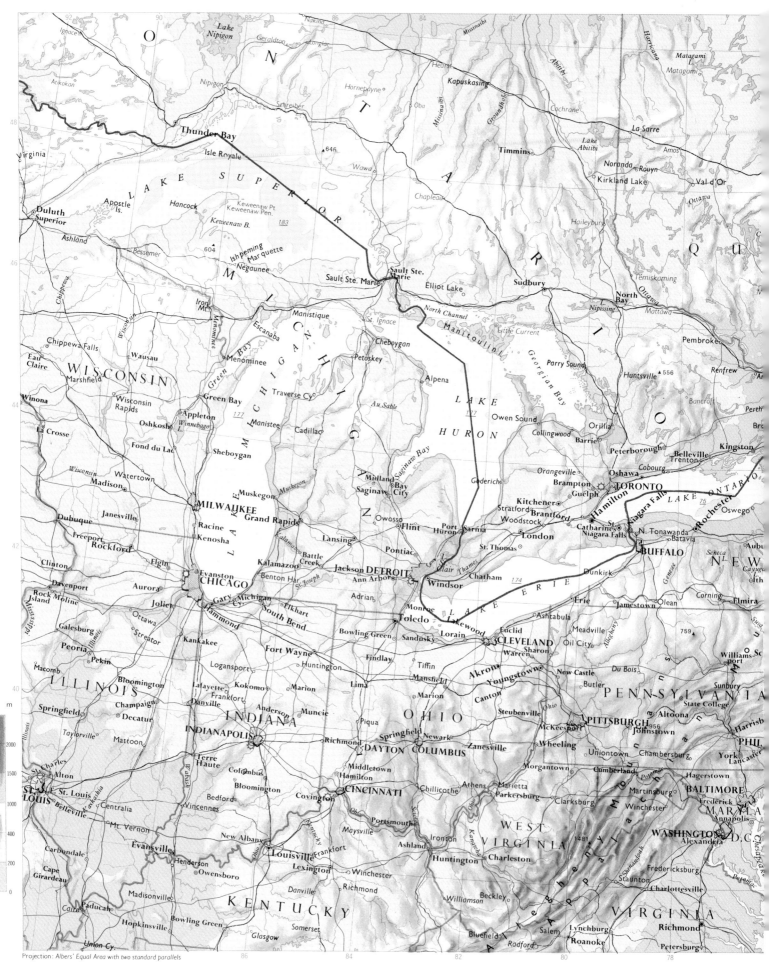

1:6 000 000

50 0 50 100 150 200 250 km

93

Port Cartier   West Pt.   *A n t i c o s t i I.*   Heath Pt.

Jupiter

Chibougamau
556 ▲ *Chibougamau L.*

Pipmuacan L.

Cap Chat
Matane   1310 ▲   Gaspé
Shickshock Mts.   C. Gaspé
Gaspé Peninsula

GULF OF ST. LAWRENCE

▼ 572

Gouin Res.

Dolbeau
St. Félicien   *Lac St. Jean*
Roberval   **Chicoutimi**
Jonquière   *Saguenay*

Rimouski
Dalhousie   *Chaleur Bay*
Campbellton   Bathurst

Magdalen Is. (Quebec)

C. North
632 ▲   **Cape Breton Island**

St. Lawrence

Rivière du Loup
Edmundston
Grand Falls   **N E W**

Miramichi B.   North Pt.   Tignish
Newcastle   **PRINCE EDWARD ISLAND**
Chatham   Summerside
Charlottetown   East Pt.

Glace Bay
SYDNEY
Bras d'Or L.

Baie St. Paul

Q U E B E C

La Tuque

Quebec
Levis   Montmagny

Presque Isle   **B R U N S W I C K**
819 ▲

Northumberland Str.
Chipman
Moncton   Springhill   New Glasgow
Grand L.   Stellarton
Sussex   Truro   *Chedabucto B.*
Canso

Grand'Mère
Shawinigan
960 ▲   **Trois Rivières**
Joliette   Victoriaville
St. Jérome   Thetford Mines
Sorel   Drummondville
Buckingham   **St. Hyacinthe**   Mégantic

Mt. Katahdin 1606 ▲
Moosehead L.

Houlton
Fredericton
Saint John
St. Stephen

Kentville
Digby   **N O V A**   Bridgewater
Bay of Fundy

Dartmouth
Halifax

Ottawa   **MONTREAL**
Hull   **Ottawa**   St. Jean   Sherbrooke
Cornwall   Valleyfield   Magog
Newport   **M A I N E**

Bangor   Grand Manan I.

St. John
Kennebec   *Penobscot*

L. Rossignol
Yarmouth   Shelburne
C. Sable

Ogdensburg
Plattsburg   *L. Champlain*
Burlington   Montpelier   Barre
Watertown   Adirondack Mts. 1629 ▲
L. George

Waterville
Augusta
1917   Auburn   Lewiston   Rockland
Berlin

Mt. Desert I.

Rome   Utica   Glen Falls
Oneida L.   Rutland
Syracuse   Schenectady   Troy
Y O R K   **Albany**   Pittsfield

Concord   Laconia
N E W H A M P S H I R E
Keene   **Manchester**
Bennington   Fitchburg   Nashua
Lawrence Lowell
Connecticut

Portland
Biddeford
Rochester   Dover
Portsmouth
Salem
Massachusetts

Cortland   Catskill Mts. 1281 ▲
Binghamton   *Hudson*
MASS   Newton   **BOSTON**   *Bay*
Worcester   Quincy   C. Cod
Holyoke   **Cambridge**
Springfield   Woonsocket   Brockton   *Cape Cod B.*
Hartford   Pawtucket
New Britain   **Providence**   Fall River   New Bedford
Waterbury   Meriden   R.I.   Newport   *Nantucket Sd.*

Poughkeepsie
Newburgh
Middletown   **New Haven**   New London   Block I.
Wilkes Barre   Bridgeport   Stamford   *Nantucket I.*
Martha's Vineyard

Hazleton   Paterson   Yonkers
Bethlehem   Newark   **NEW YORK**
Allentown   Jersey City   Elizabeth
Reading   *Long Island*

A T L A N T I C

O C E A N

PHILADELPHIA   Trenton
Camden   **NEW JERSEY**
Newark   Wilmington
Vineland
D E L A W A R E   Atlantic City
Dover

Salisbury

Cape May

Cape Charles

West from Greenwich   COPYRIGHT GEORGE PHILIP & SON. LTD.

San Diego
Tijuana
Ensenada
Mexicali
Yuma
Phoenix
Tucson
Nogales
Ciudad Juarez
El Paso
Agua Prieta
Villa Ahumada
3078
Pt. Baja
Sta. Rosalía
Pt. Sta. Eugenia
C. San Blas
Hermosillo
Tiburón
Guaymas
Empalme
Ciudad Obregón
Los Mochis
Guamúchil
Culiacan
C. San Lucas
2406
Mazatlán
Rosario
Tepic
Las Tres Marías
C. Corrientes
Guadalajara
Ameca
Colima Vol.
3960
Colima
Manzanillo
Zamora
L. de Chapala
Morelia
Toluca
Cuernavaca
Acapulco
Ometepec
Balsas
Chilpancingo
Iguala
Mexcala
Chihuahua
3200
Sta. Maria
Conchos
Rio Grande
Delicias
Hidalgo del Parral
Nazas
Torreón
Saltillo
Durango
Fuerte
Yaqui
Navojoa

Wichita Falls
Fort Worth
Dallas
Shreveport
Jackson
Birmingham
Montgomery
Abilene
Waco
Austin
San Angelo
Alexandria
Monroe
Alabama
Pensacola
Mobile
Baton Rouge
Lafayette
Houston
Beaumont
Lake Charles
Port Arthur
Galveston
New Orleans
C. San Blas
Mississippi Delta
San Antonio
Eagle Pass
Piedras Negras
2896
Nueva Rosita
Sabinas
Monclova
Falcon Res
Laredo
Nuevo Laredo
Matagorda I.
Corpus Christi
Padre I.
Brownsville
Reynosa
Rio Grande del Norte
Matamoros
Laguna de la Madre
GULF OF MEXICO

S. Pedro
Gómez Palacio
Concepción del Oro
3150
Fresnillo
Zacatecas
Matehuala
Ciudad Victoria
4064
San Luis Potosí
Aguascalientes
3353
León
Irapuato
Celaya
Querétaro
Pachuca
Ciudad Mante
Ciudad Madero
Tampico
C. Rojo
Tuxpan
Pahuco
MEXICO
Popocatepetl 5700
Puebla
Orizaba
Jalapa Enriquez
Veracruz
Gulf of Campeche
Coatzacoalcos
Minatitlán
Villahermosa
Ciudad del Carmen
3395
Oaxaca
Tuxtla Gutierrez
Juchitan
Salina Cruz
3139
Tonala
San Cristóbal
Isthmus of Tehuantepec
G. of Tehuantepec
Tapachula
Quezaltenang
4217
GUATEMALA
Sta. Ana
San Salvador
EL SALVADOR
San Miguel

Tropic of Cancer

Yucatan Str.
Progreso
Mérida
Valladolid
Peto
i. de Cozumel
Campeche
Yucatan
Laguna de Terminos
Chetumal
Belize
Belmopan
BELIZE
Turneffe Is.
Pto. Barrios
Gulf of Hond
Pto. Cortés
Tela
La Ceiba
S. Pedro Sula
HONDURAS
Zacapa
Comayagua
Tegucigalpa
Choluteca
NICARAG
G. of Fonseca
Leon
Managua
L. N
Nicoya Pen.
Puntarenas
San

PACIFIC OCEAN

PANAMA CANAL
1:1 000 000
0   10   20 km

Colón
Coco Solo
Fort Sherman
Cristóbal
Margarita
Puerto Pilón
Zorra
El Limón
Gatun Locks
Gatun Dam
Juan Gallegos
Frijoles
Escobal
Colorado
Darien
Buenos Aires
Madden L.
Madden Dam
Gamboa
The Gaillard Cut
Balboa Hill
350
Culebra
Paraiso
Pedro Miguel
Pedro Miguel Locks
Miraflores Locks
Corozal
Arraijan
Balboa
La Chorrera
Fort Clayton
Curundu
Fort Amador
PANAMA
Panama

JAMAICA
1:5 000 000
0   50 km

Montego Bay
Falmouth
St. Ann's Bay
Galina Point
Annotto Bay
Port Antonio
Savanna la Mar
Mandeville
KINGSTON
2256
Spanish Town
May Pen
Morant Point
Morant Bay
Portland Point

TRINIDAD AND TOBAGO
1:5 000 000
0   50 km

Charlotteville
Tobago
Scarborough
Port of Spain
940
Arima
Sangre Grande
Gulf of Paria
San Fernando
Point Fortin
Rio Claro
Princes Town
Siparia
Serpent's Mouth
TRINIDAD

LEEWARD ISLANDS
1:5 000 000
0   50 km

The Valley
Anguilla (Br.)
Marigot
St. Martin (Fr.)
St. Maarten (Neth.)
St. Barthélemy (Fr.)
Saba (Neth.)
St. Eustatius (Neth.)
Codrington
Barbuda
ANTIGUA & BARBUDA
St. Christopher (St. Kitts)
ST. CHRISTOPHER-NEVIS
Basseterre
Charlestown
Nevis
St. John's
Antigua
Redonda
Montserrat
Plymouth
GUADELOUPE (Fr.)
Grande Terre
Moule
Basse Terre
Ste Rose
Guadeloupe Passage
Désirade (Fr.)
Pointe-à-Pitre
Marie-Galante
I. des Saintes (Fr.)
Grand Bourg
Dominica Passage
Portsmouth
Morne Diablotin
DOMINICA (Windward Is.)
1490
Roseau

WINDWARD ISLANDS
1:5 000 000
0   50 km

Martinique Passage
Mt. Pelée 1397
Ste. Marie
St. Pierre
Fort de France
Le Francois
Lamentin
MARTINIQUE (Fr.)
Ste. Anne
St. Lucia Channel
Castries
Soufrière
ST. LUCIA
Vieux Fort
St. Vincent Passage
Soufrière
1178
Georgetown
ST. VINCENT
Kingstown
& Bequia
THE GRENADINES
Mustique
Canouan
Union
Carriacou
Ronde
The Grenadines
Hillsborough
St. 840
George's
GRENADA
Grenville
BARBADOS
Speightstown
Bridgetown

Projection: Bonne

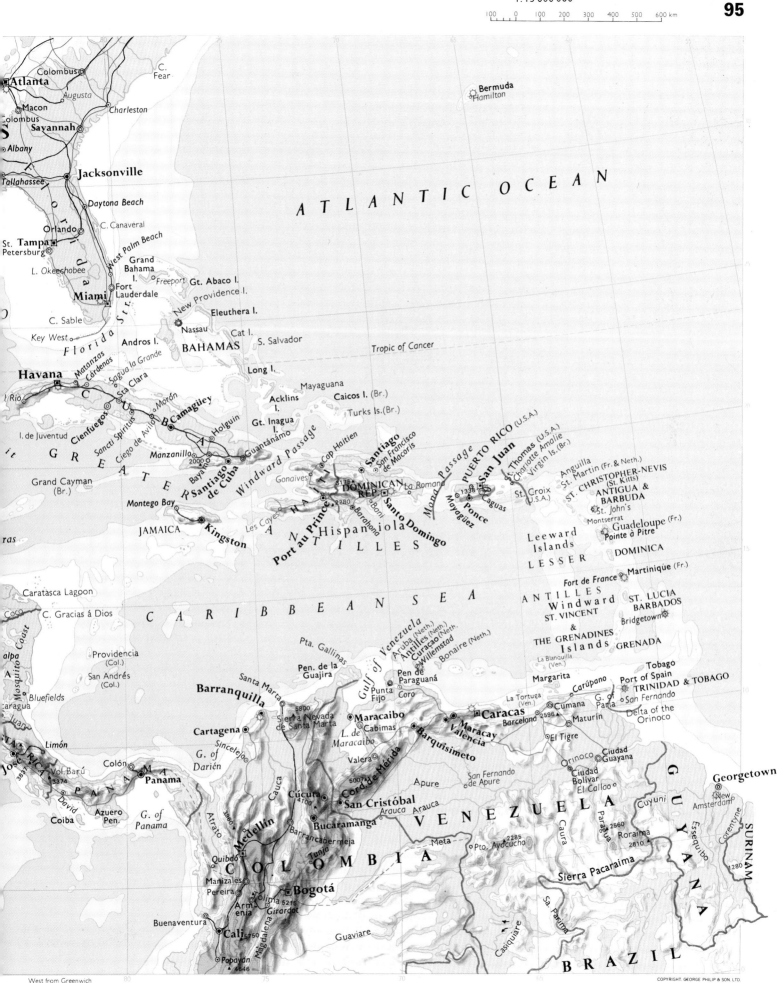

1:15 000 000

100   0   100   200   300   400   500   600 km

ATLANTIC OCEAN

Bermuda
Hamilton

Atlanta
Colombus
Macon   Charleston
Savannah
Albany

Jacksonville

Tallahassee
Daytona Beach
Orlando   C. Canaveral
St. Tampa   West Palm Beach
Petersburg   Grand
L. Okeechobee   Bahama
Miami   Freeport   Gt. Abaco I.
Fort   New Providence I.
Lauderdale
C. Sable   Eleuthera I.
Key West   Nassau   Cat I.
Andros I.   S. Salvador
BAHAMAS   Tropic of Cancer
Florida Str.
Long I.
Havana   Matanzas
Cárdenas   Sta Clara   Mayaguana
I. Rio   Sagua la Grande   Acklins I.   Caicos I. (Br.)
C   Morón   Gt. Inagua   Turks Is.(Br.)
GREATER   Camagüey   I.
Cienfuegos   B   Holguín   PUERTO RICO (U.S.A.)
Sancti Spiritus   Cap Haitien   Santiago   St. Thomas (U.S.A.)   Anguilla
I. de Juventud   Ciego de Avila   San Francisco   San Juan   Charlotte Amalie   St. Martin (Fr. & Neth.)
A   de Macoris   Virgin Is.(Br.)   ST. CHRISTOPHER-NEVIS
Manzanillo   Guantánamo   Mona   (St. Kitts)
2000   Gonaives   DOMINICAN   La Romana   Passage   St. Croix   ANTIGUA &
Grand Cayman   Bayamo   R   3175   REP.   (U.S.A.)   BARBUDA
(Br.)   Santiago   Les Cayes   2280   Mayagüez   St. John's
de Cuba   Windward Passage   Ponce   Montserrat
Montego Bay   Barahona   1338   Guadeloupe (Fr.)
Boni   Caguas   Pointe à Pitre
JAMAICA   Kingston   H   Santo Domingo   Leeward
Port au Prince   Hispaniola   Islands   DOMINICA
A   N   T   I   L   L   E   S   LESSER   Martinique (Fr.)

Caratasca Lagoon   Fort de France   ST. LUCIA
Coco   ANTILLES   BARBADOS
C. Gracias á Dios   CARIBBEAN SEA   Windward   ST. VINCENT   Bridgetown
alpa   ST. VINCENT   &
Mosquito Coast   Providencia   Pta. Gallinas   Aruba (Neth.)   THE GRENADINES   GRENADA
(Col.)   Antilles (Neth.)   Islands
Bluefields   San Andrés   Pen. de   Curaçao (Neth.)   La Blanquilla
aragua   (Col.)   la Guajira   Willemstad   Bonaire (Neth.)   (Ven.)   Tobago
uan   Gulf of Venezuela   Pen de   Margarita   Port of Spain   TRINIDAD & TOBAGO
Santa Marta   Paraguaná   La Tortuga   Carúpano   San Fernando
Barranquilla   Punta   Coro   (Ven.)   Cumana   G. of Paria
Fijo   Cumaná   Maturín   Delta of the
Cartagena   Sierra Nevada   Maracaibo   Barcelona   2596   Orinoco
de Santa Marta   5800   L. de   Caracas
Sincelejo   Cabimas   Maracay
Limón   G. of   L. de   Valencia   El Tigre   Ciudad
Jose   Darién   Maracaibo   Barquisimeto   Orinoco   Guayana
RICA   Colón   Valera   San Fernando   Ciudad
Vol. Barú   3374   Cord de Mérida   de Apure   Bolívar   El Callao
3837   PANAMA   5007   Apure   El Callao   Georgetown
David   Panama   Cúcuta   Orinoco   New
Azuero   G. of   4100   San Cristóbal   Pto. Ayacucho   Amsterdam
Coiba   Pen.   Panama   Arauca   Arauca   GUYANA   SURINAM
Medellín   3960   Bucaramanga   VENEZUELA   2560
Barrancabermeja   Meta   2285   Roraima   Corentyne
Quibdó   COLOMBIA   Pto. Ayacucho   2810   1280
Manizales   Tunja   Caura   Sierra Pacaraima
Pereira   Bogotá   Sa. Parima
Tolima 5215
Buenaventura   Armenia   Girardot   Guaviare
Cali 5750   Guaviare   Casiquiare
Popayán   BRAZIL
4646

West from Greenwich   COPYRIGHT. GEORGE PHILIP & SON. LTD.

1:30 000 000

200 0 200 400 600 800 1000 km

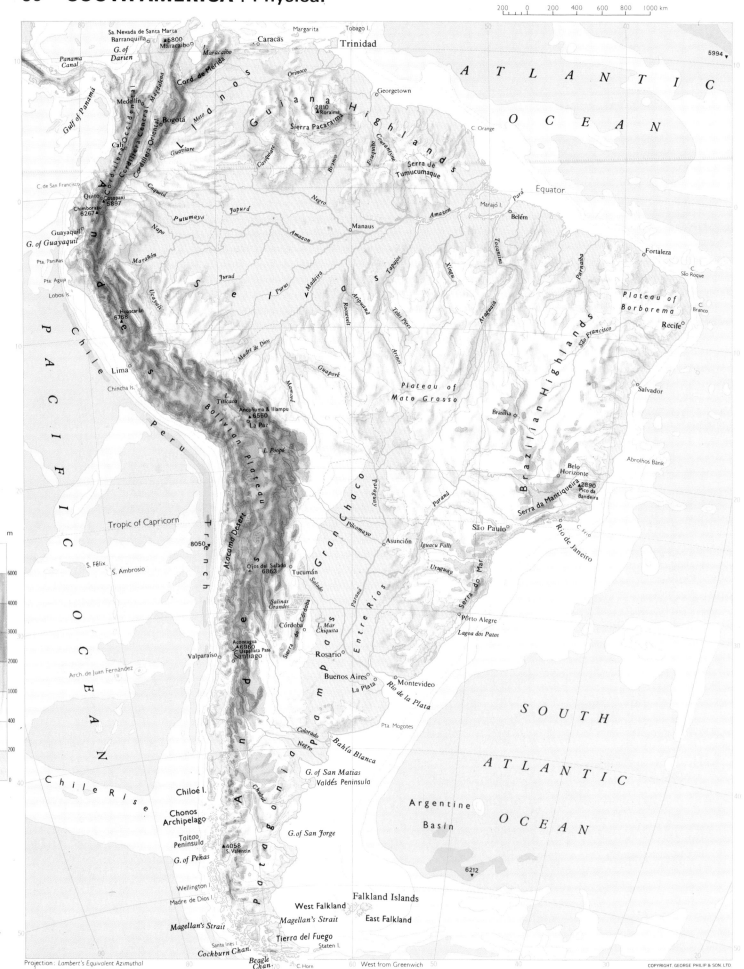

5994 ▼

ATLANTIC

OCEAN

Sa. Nevada de Santa Marta
Barranquilla ▲5800
Maracaibo
G. of
Darien
Panama
Canal
Gulf of Panamá
Medellin
Cali
Bogotá
C. de San Francisco
Quito
Cotopaxi
5897
Chimborazo
6267
Guayaquil
G. of Guayaquil
Pta. Pariñas
Pta. Aguja
Lobos Is.

Margarita   Tobago I.
Caracas   Trinidad
L. Maracaibo
Cord. de Mérida
Orinoco
Meta
Guaviare
Caquetá
Putumayo
Napo
Marañón
Juruá
Ucayali

Georgetown

Guiana   Highlands
Roraima ▲2810
Sierra Pacaraima
Serra de
Tumucumaque

C. Orange

Equator

Jutaí
Negro
Amazon
Manaus
Japurá
Amazon

Marajó I.   Pará
Belém

Fortaleza
C.
São Roque

Plateau of
Borborema
Recife
C.
Branco

Huascarán
6768

Lima
Chincha Is.

S

Purus   Madeira
Madre de Dios

e   l   v   a   s

Juruá

Aripuana
Roosevelt

Tapajos

Teles Pires

Xingu

Araguaia

Tocantins

Parnaiba

São Francisco

Brazilian   Highlands

Salvador

PACIFIC

Chile   Peru

Bolivian Plateau

L. Titicaca
Ancohuma & Illampu
▲6560
La Paz
L. Poopó

Guaporé
Mamoré

Plateau of
Mato Grosso

Brasília

Belo
Horizonte

Abrolhos Bank

Pico da
Bandeira ▲2890
Serra da Mantiqueira

Tropic of Capricorn

S. Félix
S. Ambrosio

8050
Atacama Desert
Trench

Ojos del Salado
6863
Tucumán

Gran   Chaco

Pilcomayo

Paraguay

Paraná

Asunción
Iguaçu Falls

Uruguay

São Paulo

Serra do Mar

Rio de Janeiro
C. Frio

OCEAN

Arch. de Juan Fernández

Salinas
Grandes
Sierra de Córdoba
Córdoba
Aconcagua
▲6960
Uspallata Pass
Santiago
Valparaíso

Salado

L. Mar
Chiquita

Rosario

Buenos Aires

Paraná
Entre Rios

La Plata

Montevideo
Río de la Plata

Pôrto Alegre
Lagoa dos Patos

SOUTH

ATLANTIC

Pta. Mogotes

Colorado
Negro
Bahía Blanca

P   a   m   p   a   s

Chiloé I.
Chonos
Archipelago
Taitao
Peninsula
G. of Peñas

Wellington I.
Madre de Dios I.

Patagonia

Chubut

G. of San Matias
Valdés Peninsula

G. of San Jorge

▲4058
S. Valentin

OCEAN

Argentine

Basin

6212
▼

Chile Rise

Magellan's Strait
Santa Inés I.
Cockburn Chan.

Falkland Islands
West Falkland
Magellan's Strait   East Falkland
Tierra del Fuego
Staten I.
Beagle
Chan.
C. Horn

West from Greenwich

m
6000
4000
3000
2000
1000
400
200
0
0
200
2000
4000
6000
8000
m

1:30 000 000

200   0   200   400   600   800   1000 km

NORTH

ATLANTIC

OCEAN

COSTA
RICA
San José

PANAMA
Panamá
G. of
Darién
G. of
Panamá

Colón

Barranquilla
Cartagena
Ciénaga
Cabimas
Maracaibo
Barquisimeto
Valencia
Cumaná
Punto Fijo
Port of Spain

TRINIDAD
AND
TOBAGO

Caracas
Maturín

Montería
Cúcuta
San
Cristóbal
Bucaramanga

VENEZUELA

Orinoco
Ciudad Guayana
Ciudad Bolívar

Georgetown

Medellín
Manizales
Pereira
Ibagué
Buenaventura
Cali
Popayán
Pasto

Bogotá

COLOMBIA

Orinoco

Branco

GUYANA

Paramaribo

SURINAM

FRENCH
GUIANA

Cayenne

C. Orange

Quito

ECUADOR

Putumayo

Macapá

Equator

Ilha de
Marajó

Belém
(Pará)

Guayaquil
G. de Guayaquil
Cuenca

Iquitos

Marañón

Japurá

Amazon

Manaus

Santarém

São Luís

Fortaleza (Ceará)

Piura
Chiclayo
Trujillo
Chimbote

Benjamim
Constant

Juruá

Purus

Madeira

Tapajós

Xingu

Bacabal

Teresina

C. de São Roque
Natal

Juazeiro do
Norte

João Pessoa
(Paraíba)

PERU

Ucayali

Pôrto Velho

Parnaíba

Recife
(Pernambuco)

Callao
Lima
Huancayo

Cuzco

Madre de Dios

Rio Branco

Guaporé

BRAZIL

Maceió

Ica

Arequipa

Titicaca

La Paz
Cochabamba

BOLIVIA

Santa Cruz

Cuiabá

São Francisco

Aracaju

Salvador
(Bahia)

Brasília

Goiânia

Montes Claros

Arica

Oruro
Sucre

Corumbá

Gov. Valadares

Iquique

Campo Grande

Uberaba

Belo
Horizonte

Vitória

Ribeirão
Prêto

Juiz de Fora

Campos

Tropic of Capricorn

Antofagasta

San Félix
(Chile)

San Ambrosio
(Chile)

PARAGUAY

Paraná

Bauru

Londrina

Campinas

Niterói

RIO DE JANEIRO

Salta

Paraguay

Asunción

Santos

São
Paulo

San Miguel
de Tucumán

Resistencia

Posadas

Ponta Grossa

Curitiba

Santiago
del Estero

Corrientes

Uruguay

Florianópolis

Pilcomayo

SOUTH

Juan Fernández
(Chile)

ARGENTINA

Córdoba

San Juan

Santa Fe
Paraná

Rosario

Pôrto
Alegre

ATLANTIC

Viña del Mar
Valparaíso

Mendoza

Mercedes

URUGUAY

Pelotas

Lagoa dos Patos

Santiago

BUENOS
AIRES

La
Plata

Montevideo

Rio de la Plata

OCEAN

Talcahuano
Concepción

Talca

Mar del Plata

Valdivia

Bahía Blanca

Colorado

Puerto Montt

Negro

Viedma

San Carlos
de Bariloche

Península
Valdés

Chiloé

Trelew

Chubut

Chonos
Arch.

Golfo
Comodoro Rivadavia
San Jorge

PACIFIC

CHILE

OCEAN

I. Wellington

FALKLAND ISLANDS
(ISLAS MALVINAS)
(U.K.)

Stanley

Río Gallegos

Strait of Magellan

Punta
Arenas

Tierra
del
Fuego

Cape Horn

70   West from Greenwich   60

BUENOS AIRES   Capital Cities

COPYRIGHT. GEORGE PHILIP & SON. LTD.

1:70 000 000

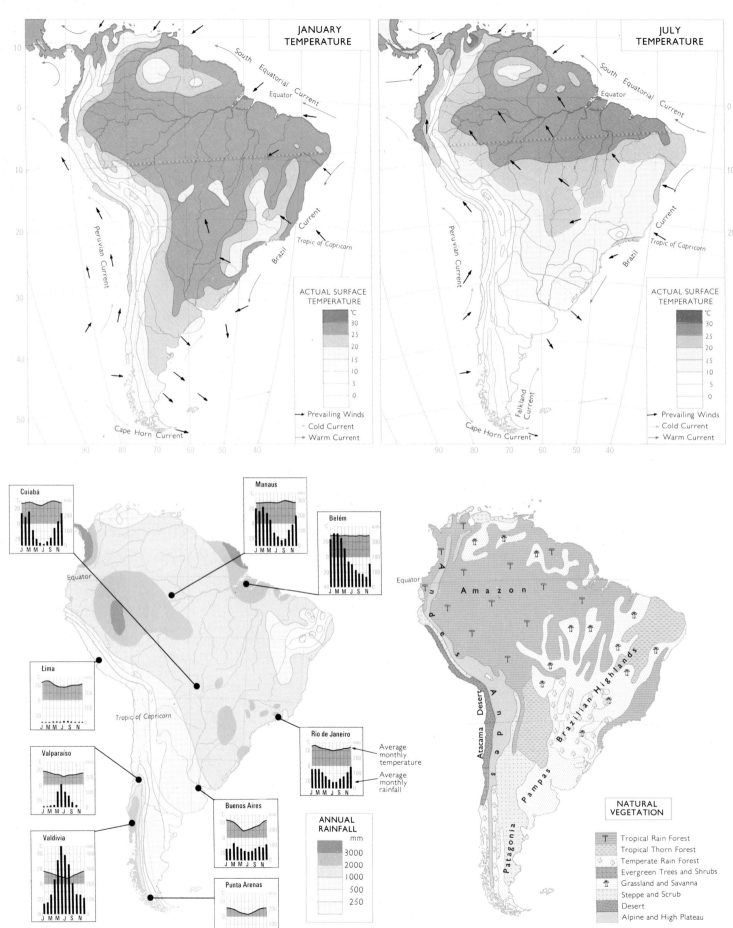

JANUARY
TEMPERATURE

JULY
TEMPERATURE

South Equatorial Current

Equator

Peruvian Current

Tropic of Capricorn

Brazil Current

Cape Horn Current

ACTUAL SURFACE
TEMPERATURE

°C
30
25
20
15
10
5
0

→ Prevailing Winds
→ Cold Current
→ Warm Current

Falkland Current

Cuiabá

Manaus

Belém

Equator

Lima

Tropic of Capricorn

Valparaíso

Valdivia

Buenos Aires

Rio de Janeiro

Average monthly temperature

Average monthly rainfall

Punta Arenas

ANNUAL
RAINFALL
mm
3000
2000
1000
500
250

Amazon

Andes

Atacama Desert

Brazilian Highlands

Pampas

Patagonia

Equator

NATURAL
VEGETATION

Tropical Rain Forest
Tropical Thorn Forest
Temperate Rain Forest
Evergreen Trees and Shrubs
Grassland and Savanna
Steppe and Scrub
Desert
Alpine and High Plateau

Projection: Lambert's Equivalent Azimuthal

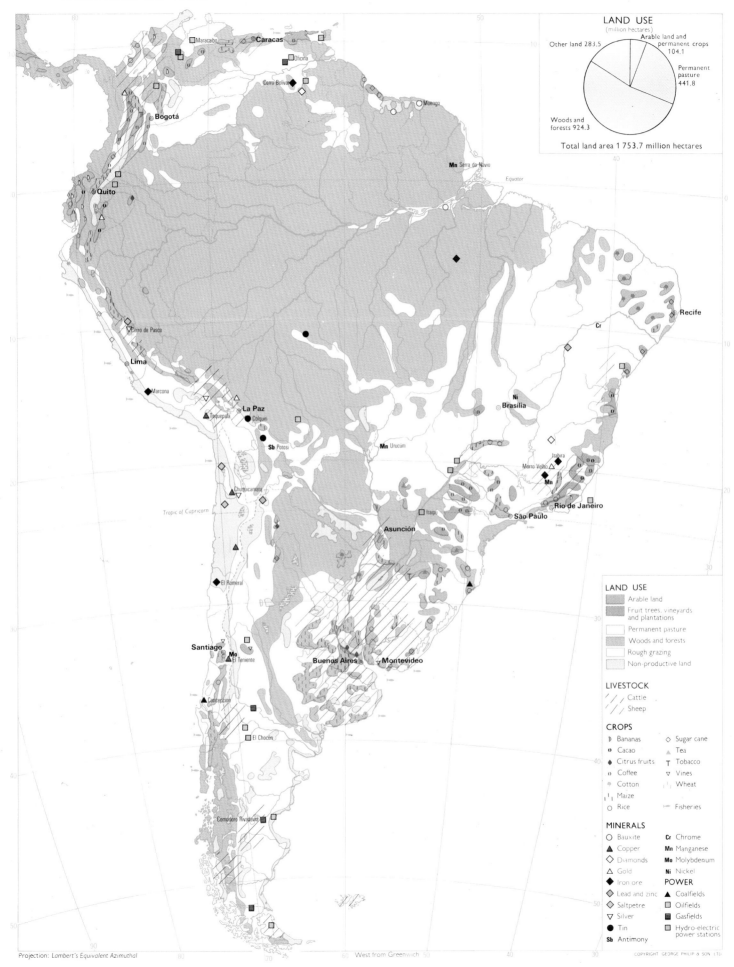

1:30 000 000

200   0   200   400   600   800   1000 km

LAND USE
(million hectares)

Other land 283.5

Arable land and permanent crops 104.1

Permanent pasture 441.8

Woods and forests 924.3

Total land area 1 753.7 million hectares

Maracaibo   Caracas   Oficina

Cerro Bolivar   Moengo

Bogotá

Mn Serra do Navio

Equator

Quito

Cerro de Pasco

Lima

Marcona

La Paz

Toquepala   Colquiri

Sb Potosí   Mn Urucum

Brasília   Ni

Chuquicamata   Itabira   Morro Velho   Mn

Tropic of Capricorn

Itaipu   Rio de Janeiro

El Romeral   São Paulo

Asunción

Santiago   Mo   El Teniente

Buenos Aires   Montevideo

Concepción

El Chocón

Comodoro Rivadavia

LAND USE
- Arable land
- Fruit trees, vineyards and plantations
- Permanent pasture
- Woods and forests
- Rough grazing
- Non-productive land

LIVESTOCK
- Cattle
- Sheep

CROPS
- D Bananas
- ᴑ Cacao
- Citrus fruits
- ᴑ Coffee
- Cotton
- Maize
- ○ Rice
- ◇ Sugar cane
- Tea
- T Tobacco
- ▽ Vines
- Wheat
- Fisheries

MINERALS
- ○ Bauxite
- ▲ Copper
- ◇ Diamonds
- △ Gold
- ◆ Iron ore
- ◇ Lead and zinc
- ◇ Saltpetre
- ▽ Silver
- ● Tin
- Sb Antimony
- Cr Chrome
- Mn Manganese
- Mo Molybdenum
- Ni Nickel

POWER
- ▲ Coalfields
- ▢ Oilfields
- ▤ Gasfields
- ▣ Hydro-electric power stations

Projection: Lambert's Equivalent Azimuthal

West from Greenwich

COPYRIGHT GEORGE PHILIP & SON LTD

Projection. Sanson-Flamsteed's Sinusoidal

1:16 000 000

200 100 0 200 400 600 km

A T L A N T I C

ATLANTIC

SURINAM

FR. GUIANA

Amsterdam
Nieuw Nickerie
Totnes
Paramaribo
Nieuw Amsterdam
Moengo
St. Laurent
Iracoubo
Cayenne
Brokopondo
Tafelberg 1280

C. Orange
Oiapoque
Amapá
Araguari

AMAPÁ

Ilha de Maracá
C. do Norte

Mouths of
the Amazon
Ilha Caviana

Equator

Serra
Tumucumaque
Jari
Serra do Navio
Macapá

C. Maguarinho
Souré
Vigia
Bragança
Ilha de Marajó

Belém (Pará)
Turiaçu

B. de São Marcos
São Luís (Maranhão)

Camocim

FORTALEZA (Ceará)

Rocas

Fernando de Noronha
(Braz.)

Cumina
Óbidos
Monte Alegre
Almeirim
Pôrto de Móz
Breves
Cametá
Baião

Amazon
Santarém
Altamira

Parintins
Juruti

Tapajós
Jamanxim
Curua
Iriri
Xingu
Xingu
Tocantins

PARÁ

Tucuruí

Rosário
Viana
Coroatá
Cudá
Caxias

Bacabal

Campo Maior
Ipu

Sobral
Quixadá
Crateús

Teresina

MARANHÃO

Marabá
Itaperatiba
Tocantinópolis

Carolina

Imperatriz

Floriano
Uruçui
Oeiras

Aracati
Macau

FORTALEZA (Ceará)

Iguatu

Mossoró
RIO GRANDE
DO NORTE
Natal
C. de São Roque

Caicó

Crato
Juàzeiro do
Norte
Campina Grande

PARAÍBA
João Pessoa
(Paraíba)

Pernambuco

Conceição do
Araguaia
Pedro Afonso

Araguaia
Tocantins

Chapada das Mangabeiras

Paulistana

Petrolina
Juàzeiro

Caruaru
1123
Pesqueira
Garanhuns

Olinda
RECIFE
(Pernambuco)

B R A Z I L

Sa. do Cachimbo

Serra formosa

Serra do Roncador

Ilha do Bananal

Pôrto Nacional

Remanso

PIAUÍ

Guribeba

Pôrto Nacional

Xique-Xique

Senhor do
Bonfim

Paulo Afonso
São Francisco

Arapiraca
ALAGOAS
Maceió

Penedo

SERGIPE
Aracaju

Jacobina

Serrinha
Feira de
Santana

Alagoinhas

GOIÁS

Barreiras

Itaberaba

Cachoeira
Santo Amaro

SALVADOR (Bahia)

B A H I A

São Francisco

Paraná

Caetité

Brumado
Contas

Jequié

Valença
B. de Todos os Santos

MATO GROSSO

Plateau of

Cuiabá
Mato Grosso
Rondonópolis

Ceres

1678

FED.
DIST.
BRASÍLIA

Goiás
Anápolis

Goiânia

Goiás

Paracatu
Januária
Monte Azul

Vitória da
Conquista
Itabuna
Ilhéus

Canavieiras

MATO GROSSO
DO SUL

Jataí
Rio Verde

Itiquira
Aporé

Coxim

Camapuã

B r a z i l i a n

Pirapora

Montes
Claros

Teófilo Otoni
Nanuque

Banka
Abrolhos

Taquari
Aquidauana

Campo Grande

Três Lagoas

Andradina
Araçatuba

Paranaíba

Patos de
Minas

Catalão

Araguari
Uberlândia

Ituiutaba

Uberaba

Araxá
1340

MINAS GERAIS

Diamantina

Gov. Valadares

Aimorés
Doce

São Mateus

ESPÍRITO
SANTO

Pico da
Bandeira
2890

Vitória
Cachoeira de Itapemirim

H i g h l a n d s

Barretos
S. José do
Rio Prêto

Franca

Ribeirão Prêto

Passos
Poços de
Caldas

Lavras

Formiga

BELO HORIZONTE
Nova
Ubá

Caratinga

Trindade
(Braz.)

Marília
SÃO
PAULO
Bauru

Assis

Piracicaba

São
Carlos

Campinas

2787
Petrópolis
RIO DE JANEIRO
Niterói

Juiz de Fora
Campos

V. Redonda

Pres.
Prudente

Paraná

Serra da Mantiqueira

Pedro Juan
Caballero
Ponta Pora

Greenwich

COPYRIGHT GEORGE PHILIP & SON LTD.

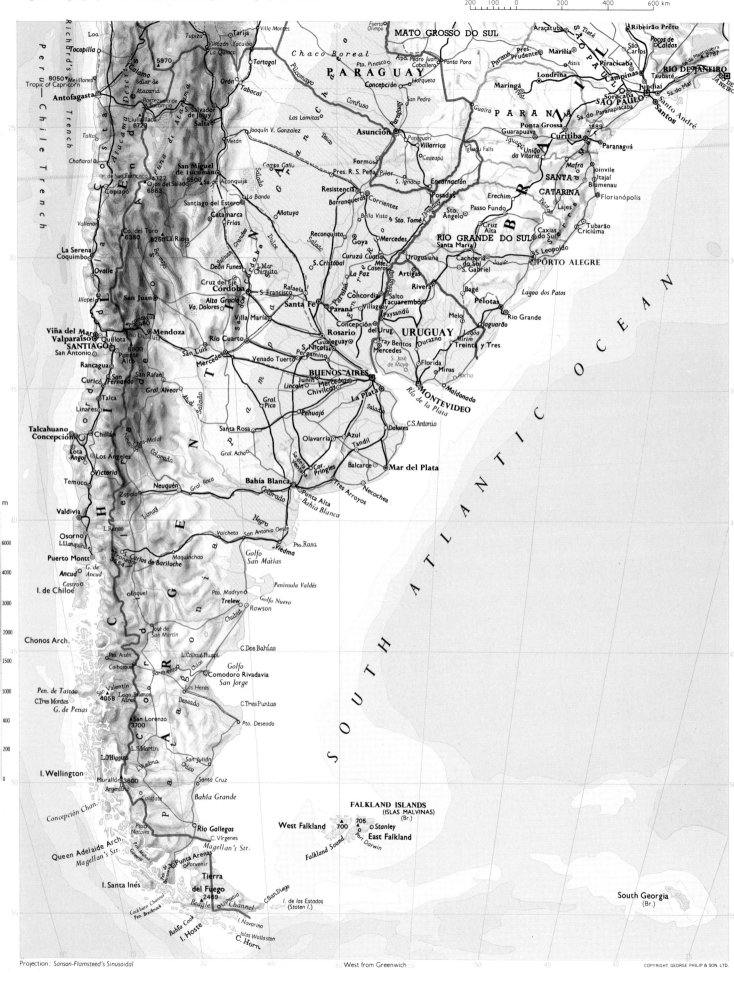

1:16 000 000

200 100 0 200 400 600 km

Projection: Sanson-Flamsteed's Sinusoidal

West from Greenwich

COPYRIGHT. GEORGE PHILIP & SON. LTD.

1 : 50 000 000

500   0   500   1000   1500   2000 km

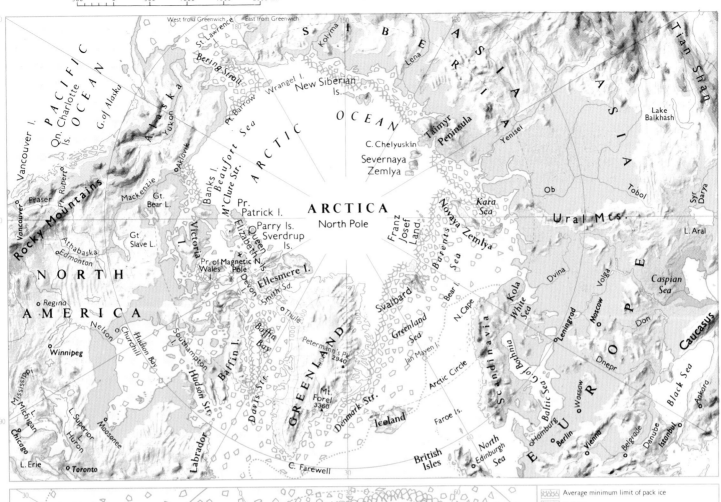

West from Greenwich   East from Greenwich

150

PACIFIC
OCEAN

Vancouver I.
Qn. Charlotte
Is.

G. of Alaska

Fraser
Vancouver

Rocky Mountains

Pr. Rupert

Alaska

Yukon

Aklavik

Mackenzie

Gt.
Bear L.

Banks I.

Beaufort
Sea

M'Clure Str.

Pr.
Patrick I.

Parry Is.
Sverdrup
Is.

Queen
Elizabeth Is.

Pr. of
Wales
I.

Magnetic N.
Pole

Devon
I.

Ellesmere I.

Smith Sd.

Thule

Pt. Barrow

Wrangel I.

New Siberian
Is.

Kolyma

Bering Strait

St. Lawrence I.

ARCTIC

OCEAN

ARCTICA
North Pole

C. Chelyuskin

Severnaya
Zemlya

Franz
Josef
Land

S   I   B   E   R   I   A

Lena

Taimyr
Peninsula

A   S   I   A

Tian Shan

Lake
Balkhash

Yenisei

Novaya Zemlya

Kara
Sea

Ob

Tobol

Ural Mts.

Syr
Darya

L. Aral

NORTH

AMERICA

Edmonton

Athabaska

Gt
Slave L.

Victoria
I.

Regina

Nelson

Winnipeg

Churchill

Hudson Bay

Southampton
I.

Baffin I.

Baffin
Bay

Davis Str.

Petermann's Pk.
2940

Mt.
Forel
3360

GREENLAND

Barents
Sea

Svalbard

Bear I.

Greenland
Sea

N. Cape

White
Sea

Kola

Dvina

Scandinavia

Volga

Moscow

Leningrad

Caspian
Sea

EUROPE

Don

Dnepr

Caucasus

Black Sea

Ankara

Mississippi

L.
Michigan

Chicago

L. Superior

L. Huron

Moosonee

L. Erie

Toronto

Hudson Str.

Labrador

C. Farewell

30

Denmark Str.

Iceland

Jan Mayen I.

Arctic Circle

Faroe Is.

North
Sea

British
Isles

Edinburgh

Baltic Sea

Gulf of Bothnia

Hamburg

Berlin

Warsaw

Vienna

Belgrade

Danube

Istanbul

120

60

90

30

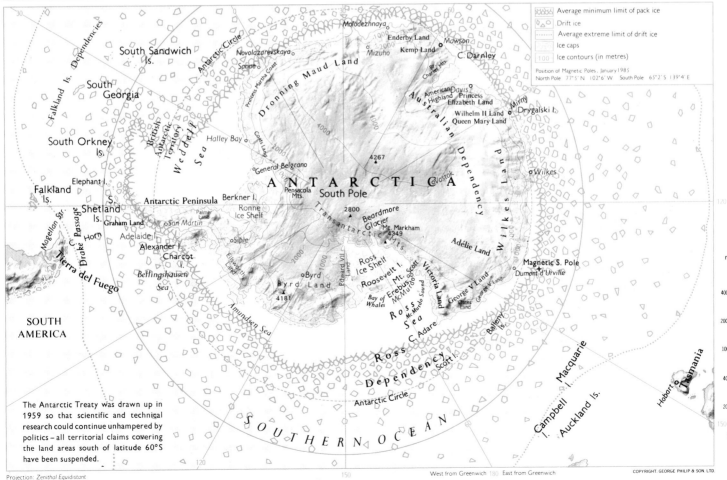

Average minimum limit of pack ice
Drift ice
Average extreme limit of drift ice
Ice caps
100   Ice contours (in metres)

Position of Magnetic Poles. January 1985
North Pole 77°5′N 102°6′W   South Pole 65°2′S 139°4′E

30

Falkland Is. Dependencies

South Sandwich
Is.

South
Georgia

South Orkney
Is.

Falkland
Is.

Elephant I.

S.
Shetland
Is.

Horn

Tierra del Fuego

SOUTH
AMERICA

Magellan Str.

Drake Passage

C.C.C.

Bellingshausen
Sea

Adelaide I.

Alexander I.
Charcot
I.

Graham Land

San Martin

Palmer
Land

Antarctic Peninsula

British
Antarctic
Territory

Weddell
Sea

Halley Bay

Coats Land

General Belgrano

Berkner I.

Ronne
Ice Shelf

Pensacola
Mts.

ANTARCTICA
South Pole

4267

Molodezhnaya

Enderby Land

Mawson

Novolazarevskaya

Sanae

Mizuho

Kemp Land

C. Darnley

Pr.
Charles Mts.

American
Highland

Davis

Princess
Elizabeth Land

Mirny

Drygalski I.

Wilhelm II Land

Queen Mary Land

Wilkes

Australian Dependency

Wilkes Land

Antarctic Circle

Princess Martha Coast

Dronning Maud Land

2000

1000

4000

2000

1000

Vostok

Byrd

4181

Byrd Land

Siple

Ellsworth
Land

Edward VII

2800

Transantarctic

Beardmore
Glacier

Mt. Markham
4349

Mts.

Ross
Ice Shelf

Roosevelt I.

Mt. Erebus
McMurdo

Bay of
Whales

Ross
Sea

McMurdo Sound

Victoria Land

George V Land

George's Land

Oates
Land

Adélie Land

Magnetic S. Pole

Dumont d'Urville

Scott I.

C. Adare

Balleny
Is.

Ross

Dependency

Antarctic Circle

Macquarie
I.

Campbell
I.   Auckland Is.

Hobart

Tasmania

SOUTHERN   OCEAN

Projection: Zenithal Equidistant

West from Greenwich   180   East from Greenwich

120

150

m

4000
2000
1000
400
200
150
0

180
80   160
140
120   100   80   60   40   20

Queen Elizabeth Is.   Ellesmere I.   G r e e n l a n d

Bering Str.   Victoria I.   North Magnetic Pole   Baffin
Yukon   Mackenzie   Island   Arctic Circle

60   Mt. McKinley   Gt. Bear L.   Davis Str.
Bering   6199   Gt. Slave L.   Hudson Str.   Iceland
Sea   Hudson   Labrador   C. Farewell

Aleutian Is.   Bay   British
L. Winnipeg   Isles

Vancouver I.   Great   St. Lawrence   Newfoundland
Lakes   C. Race

40   Rocky Mountains   Missouri   Appalachian Mts.   Py
Coast Ra.   Great plains   Ohio   Iberian
Cascade Ra.   Arkansas   Azores   Pen.
Mt. Whitney   Colorado   Mississippi   C. Hatteras   Str. of Gibraltar
4418   Sierra Nevada   Rio Grande   Bermuda   Canary Is.   Atlas Mts.

Lower   Gulf of   Bahama   A T L A N T I C   Tropic of Cancer
California   Mexico   Islands   S   a
20   Hawaiian Is.   Popocatepetl   Florida Str.   Cuba
Mauna Kea   5452   Yucatan   Greater   Hispaniola
4202   Citlaltepetl   Jamaica   Antilles   C.Verde   G u
5700   Caribbean Sea   Lesser   Is.   C. Verde
Antilles   G. of

P A C I F I C   Isthmus   Llanos   Orinoco   O C E A N   C. Palmas
Palmyra Is.   of Panama   Guiana Highlands
Tabuaeran   Roraima   Equator
Kiritimati   Galapagos   Chimborazo   2772
0   Is.   6267   Negro
Phoenix Is.   Amazon   C. de São Roque   Ascension
Selvas
Tokelau Is.   Marquesas Is.   Madeira   Tocantins   St. Helena
Samoa Is.   O C E A N   Mato Grosso
Society Is.   Tuamotu   Andes   Brazilian Highlands   Tropic of Capricorn
Cook Is.   Tahiti   Archipelago   L. Titicaca   C. Frio
20   Tonga   Tubuai Is.   Gran Chaco   Paraguay
Is.   Atacama   Tristan da Cunha
Desert   Pampas   Parana
Pitcairn I.   Ojos del Salado   R. de la Plata
Easter I.   6863   Negro
Aconcagua   Patagonia
40   6960
Kermadec Is.   Chatham Is.   Falkland Is.
Tierra del Fuego   S. Georgia
Magellan's Str.   C. Horn
Drake Passage
Antarctic
Graham   Peninsula   Antarctic Circle
60   Land   W e d d e l l   S e a
Palmer
Land   Caird Coast
Ellsworth Land   Coats Land
Ross Sea   Byrd Land   40   20   0
80   160   120   100   80   60
180   140   West from Greenwich

HEIGHT OF LAND
in metres
Above 6 000
4 000 – 6 000
2 000 – 4 000
1000 – 2 000
200 – 1000
0 – 200
Below Sea-Level

DEPTH OF SEA
in metres
0 – 200
200 – 4000
4000 – 8000
Below 8000

A R C T I C   O C E A N

Svalbard
N. Cape
Novaya Zemlya
Severnaya Zemlya
New Siberian Is.
Scandinavia
L. Ladoga
Ob
West Siberian Plain
Yenisey
Lr. Tunguska
Lena
Aldon
Stanovoy Ra.
Sea of Okhotsk
North Sea
Baltic Sea
North European Plain
Ural Mts.
S i b e r i a
Volga
Irtysh
Angara
L. Baikal
Amur
Sakhalin
Rhine
Carpathians
Danube
Don
L. Balkhash
Sayan Mts.
Altai
Hokkaido
t. Blanc Alps 4810
Apennines
Balkan Pen.
Black Sea
Caucasus
Elbrus 5633
Aral Sea
Caspian Sea
Syr Darya
Tian Shan
Gobi
Sea of Japan
40
es
Anatolia
Amu Darya
Pamirs
Nan Shan
Huang
North China Plain
Honshu
Mt. Fuji 3776
Mediterranean Sea
Elburz Mts.
Hindu Kush
Karakoram
Kunlun
Yellow Sea
East China Sea
PACIFIC
Euphrates
Tigris
Suleiman Ra.
Indus
Himalaya
Plateau of Tibet
Mt. Everest 8848
Yangtze
Xi
Libyan Desert
Nile
The Gulf
Thar Desert
Ganges
Schween
Taiwan
20
Hoggar
Tibesti
Red Sea
Arabia
Rub 'al Khali
Arabian Sea
W. Ghats
Deccan
E. Ghats
Bay of Bengal
Mekong
Hainan
Philippine Is.
OCEAN
Wake I.
Mariana Is.
Guam
h a r a
L. Chad
White Nile
Blue Nile
Socotra
C. Guardafui
South China Sea
Marshall Is.
Niger
Ethiopian Highlands
C. Comorin
Ceylon
Str. of Malacca
Sumatra
Kinabalu 4101
Caroline Islands
Gilbert Is.
0
Cameroon Pk. 4070
Uele
(Congo)
L. Turkana
Celebes Sea
Borneo
Moluccas
Nauru
Guinea
Zaïre
L. Victoria
Mt. Kenya 5199
Kilimanjaro 5895
Seychelles
I N D I A N
Sunda Is.
Celebes
Banda Sea
New Guinea
Bismarck Arch.
Solomon Is.
Ellice Is.
Kasai
L. Tanganyika
O C E A N
Java Sea
Java
Timor
Comoro Is.
Cocos or Keeling Is.
Torres Str.
C. York
Coral Sea
New Hebrides
Fiji Is.
Cubango
L. Malawi
Zambezi
Mozambique Chan.
Madagascar
Mauritius
Réunion
Gt. Barrier Reef
New Caledonia
20
Kalahari Desert
Hamersley Ra.
Macdonnell Ra.
Great Divide
Orange
Great Victoria Desert
Darling
Drakensberg
New
C. of Good Hope
Comoro Is.
C. Leeuwin
Great Australian Bight
Murray
Australian Alps
Mt. Kosciusko 2230
North I.
Crozet Is.
Bass Str.
Tasmania
New Zealand
Mt. Cook 3764
South I.
40
Kerguelen Is.

S O U T H E R N   O C E A N

60

Queen Maud Land
Enderby Land
Queen Mary Coast
Wilkes Land
Adélie Land
South Magnetic Pole
Victoria Land
20   40   60   80   100   120   140   160   180
East from Greenwich

STRUCTURE

1:95 000 000

Structural Regions of the Land

- Pre-Cambrian shields
- Sedimentary cover on Pre-Cambrian shields
- Palæozoic (Caledonian and Hercynian) folding
- Sedimentary cover on Palæozoic folding
- Mesozoic folding
- Sedimentary cover on Mesozoic folding
- Cainozoic folding
- Sedimentary cover on Cainozoic folding
- Intensive Mesozoic and Cainozoic vulcanism
- Oceanic-type crust raised above sea level

Structural Regions of the Oceans

- Regions of continental-type crust
- Limit of continental shelf
- Oceanic marginal troughs
- Mid-oceanic volcanic ridges
- Rift valleys in mid-oceanic ridges
- Principal faults
- ++++ Frontal line of overthrust folds

GEOLOGICAL TIME SCALE

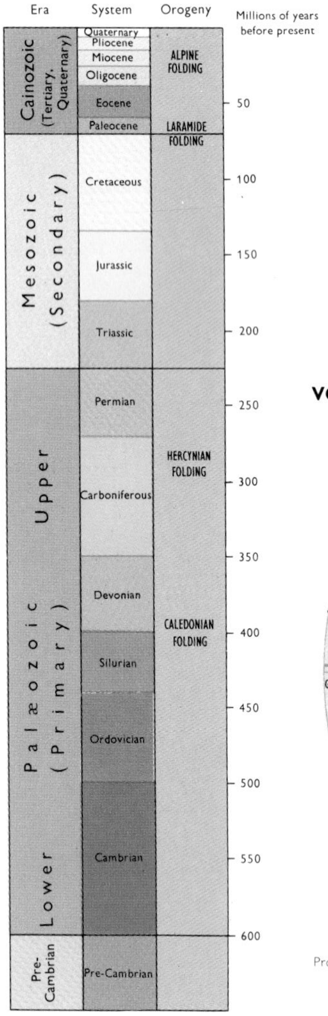

Era	System	Orogeny	Millions of years before present
Cainozoic (Tertiary, Quaternary)	Quaternary / Pliocene	ALPINE FOLDING	
	Miocene		
	Oligocene		
	Eocene	LARAMIDE FOLDING	50
	Paleocene		
Mesozoic (Secondary)	Cretaceous		100
	Jurassic		150
	Triassic		200
Palæozoic (Primary) Upper	Permian	HERCYNIAN FOLDING	250
	Carboniferous		300
	Devonian	CALEDONIAN FOLDING	350
	Silurian		400
Palæozoic (Primary) Lower	Ordovician		450
	Cambrian		500
			550
			600
Pre-Cambrian	Pre-Cambrian		

Map labels (Structure map): Canadian Shield, Rocky Mountains, Appalachians, Northern Mid-Atlantic, Sierra Madre, East Pacific Ridge, Pacific-Antarctic Ridge, Guiana Shield, Amazonian Shield

VOLCANOES

Equatorial Scale 1: 280 000 000

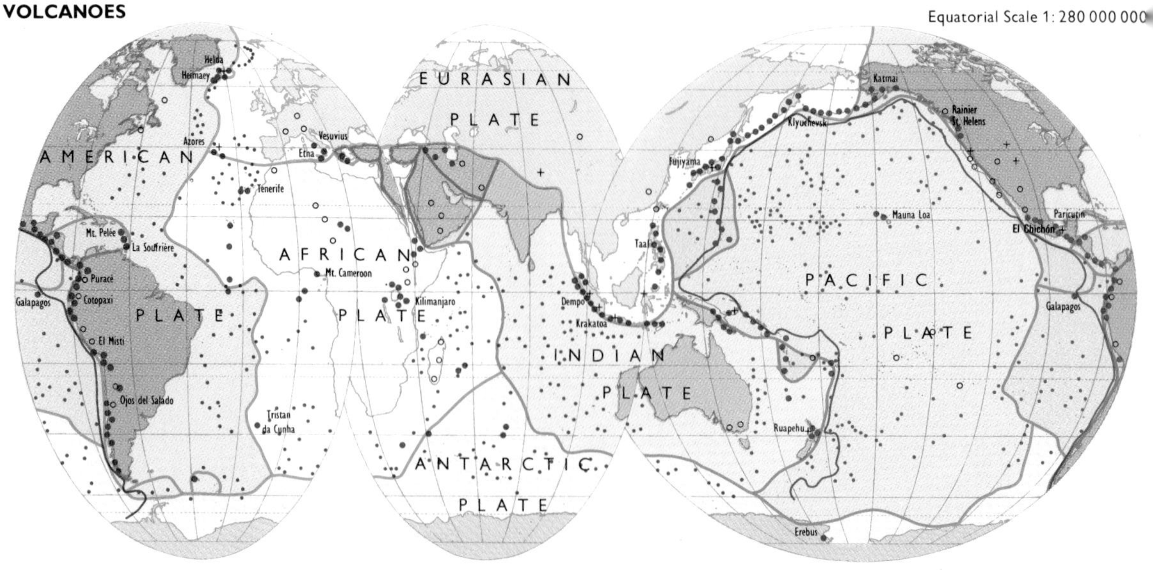

Map labels (Volcanoes map): EURASIAN PLATE, AMERICAN PLATE, AFRICAN PLATE, PACIFIC PLATE, INDIAN PLATE, ANTARCTIC PLATE, Hekla, Heimaey, Katmai, Kliuchevski, Rainier, Mt Helens, Azores, Vesuvius, Etna, Fujiyama, Tenerife, Mauna Loa, Paricutin, El Chichón, Mt Pelée, La Soufrière, Taal, Galapagos, Puracé, Cotopaxi, Mt Cameroon, Kilimanjaro, Dempo, Krakatoa, Galapagos, El Misti, Tristan da Cunha, Ruapehu, Ojos del Salado, Erebus

Projection: Interrupted Mollweide's Homolographic

- ● Land volcanoes active since 1700
- ○ Land volcanoes inactive since 1700
- ● Submarine volcanoes
- + Geysers
- ── Plate boundaries
- ── Andesite line (boundary between sial continental crust and sima oceanic crust in the Pacific)

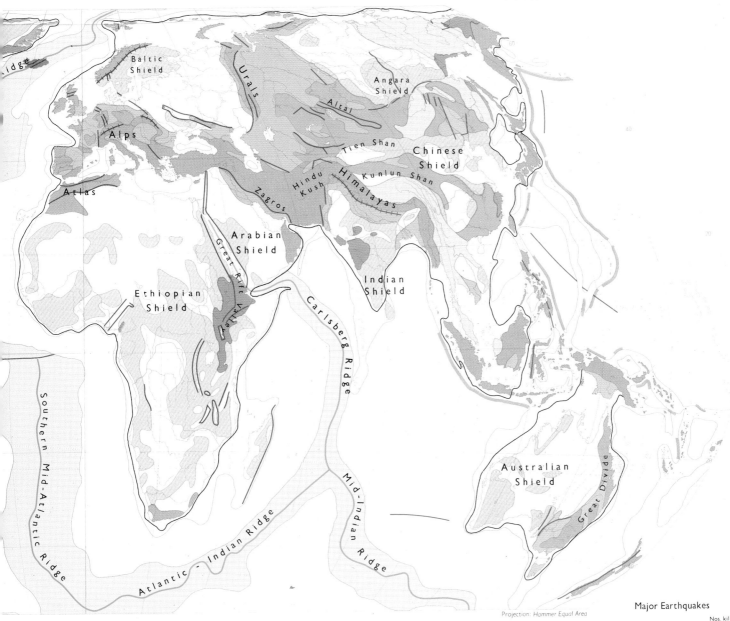

Baltic
Shield

Urals

Angara
Shield

Altai

Alps

Tien Shan

Chinese
Shield

Kunlun Shan

Atlas

Zagros

Hindu
Kush

Himalayas

Great Rift Valley

Arabian
Shield

Indian
Shield

Ethiopian
Shield

Carlsberg Ridge

Southern Mid-Atlantic Ridge

Atlantic - Indian Ridge

Mid-Indian Ridge

Australian
Shield

Great Divide

Projection: *Hammer Equal Area*

EARTHQUAKES

Equatorial Scale 1 : 280 000 000

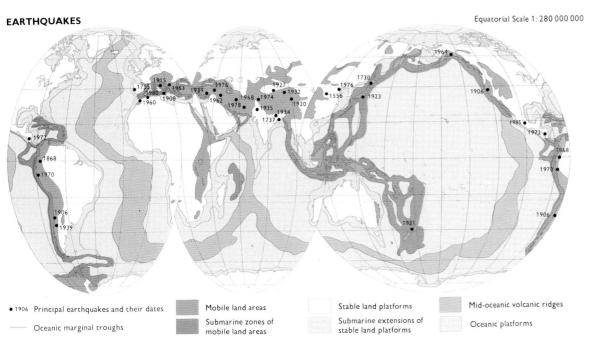

• 1906 Principal earthquakes and their dates

    Oceanic marginal troughs

    Mobile land areas

    Submarine zones of mobile land areas

    Stable land platforms

    Submarine extensions of stable land platforms

    Mid-oceanic volcanic ridges

    Oceanic platforms

Major Earthquakes

		Nos. killed
1556	Shaanxi, China	830 000
1730	Hokkaido, Japan	137 000
1737	Calcutta, India	300 000
1755	Lisbon, Portugal	60 000
1868	Ecuador and N. Peru	40 000
1906	Valparaiso, Chile	22 000
1906	San Francisco, U.S.A.	450
1908	Messina, Italy	77 000
1915	Avezzano, Italy	30 000
1920	Gansu, China	180 000
1923	Yokohama, Japan	143 000
1927	Nan Shan, China	200 000
1931	Napier, N. Zealand	250
1932	Gansu, China	70 000
1934	Nepal	11 700
1935	Quetta, Pakistan	30 000
1939	Erzincan, Turkey	30 000
1960	Agadir, Morocco	12 000
1962	Khorasan, Iran	10 000
1963	Skopje, Yugoslavia	1 000
1964	Anchorage, Alaska	100
1968	N.E. Iran	12 000
1970	N. Peru	67 000
1972	Managua, Nicaragua	7 000
1974	N. Pakistan	10 000
1976	Tangshan, China	650 000
1978	Tabas, Iran	11 000
1980	El Asnam, Algeria	20 000
1985	Mexico	20 000

CLIMATES

after Köppen

Climatic group	Climate		Temperature	Rainfall
A TROPICAL RAINY CLIMATES	**Af**	RAIN-FOREST CLIMATE	All mean monthly temperatures above 18°C	
	Am	MONSOON CLIMATE		
	Aw	SAVANNA CLIMATE		
B DRY CLIMATES	**BS**	STEPPE CLIMATE	Mean annual temperature **h** = above 18°C **k** = below 18°C	
	BW	DESERT CLIMATE		
C WARM TEMPERATE RAINY CLIMATES	**Cw**	DRY WINTER CLIMATE	Mean temperature of the coldest month between −3°C to 18°C	**a** Mean temperature of hottest month above 22°C, and with more than 4 months of over 10°C
	Cs	DRY SUMMER CLIMATE (Mediterranean)		**b** Mean temperature of hottest month below 22°C and with more than 4 months of over 10°C
	Cf	CLIMATE WITH NO DRY SEASON		**c** Mean temperature of hottest month below 22°C; but with less than 4 months of over 10°C
D COLD TEMPERATE RAINY CLIMATES	**Dw**	DRY WINTER CLIMATE	Mean temperature of the coldest month below −3°C	**d** Mean temperature of hottest month below 22°C, and of the coldest month below −38°C
	Df	CLIMATE WITH NO DRY SEASON		
E POLAR CLIMATES	**ET**	TUNDRA CLIMATE	Mean temperature of the hottest month below 10°C	Mean temperature of the hottest month between 0°C and 10°C
	EF	PERPETUAL FROST		Mean temperature of the hottest month between 0°C and 10°C

Rainfall temperature graph — **Af**, **Aw**, **Am**; Rainfall during the driest month (mm) 0–100; Annual rainfall (mm) 1000 2000 3000

BW/BS Boundary; **BW**, **BS**; BS/Wet Climates Boundary; Wet Climates A, C, D; Mean annual temperature (°C) 0–30; Annual rainfall (mm) 0 200 400 600
- - - summer rainfall
——— winter rainfall
—·—·— rainfall evenly distributed

w dry winter
Rainfall of the driest month of the cold season is one-tenth or less of the rainfall of the wettest month of the hot season

s dry summer
Rainfall of the driest month of the hot season is less than one-third of the rainfall of the wettest month of the cold season and less than 40mm.

f with no dry season
Rainfall does not correspond to w or s climates

H More than 1500m above sea level

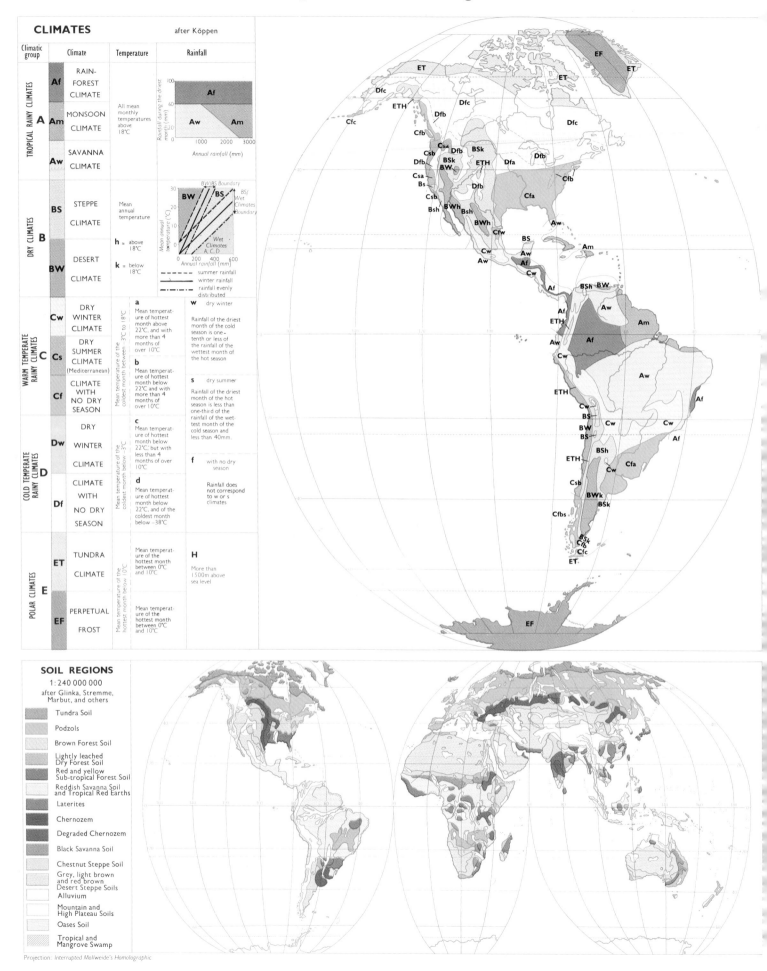

SOIL REGIONS

1:240 000 000

after Glinka, Stremme, Marbut, and others

- Tundra Soil
- Podzols
- Brown Forest Soil
- Lightly leached Dry Forest Soil
- Red and yellow Sub-tropical Forest Soil
- Reddish Savanna Soil and Tropical Red Earths
- Laterites
- Chernozem
- Degraded Chernozem
- Black Savanna Soil
- Chestnut Steppe Soil
- Grey, light brown and red brown Desert Steppe Soils
- Alluvium
- Mountain and High Plateau Soils
- Oases Soil
- Tropical and Mangrove Swamp

Projection: Interrupted Molliweide's Homolographic

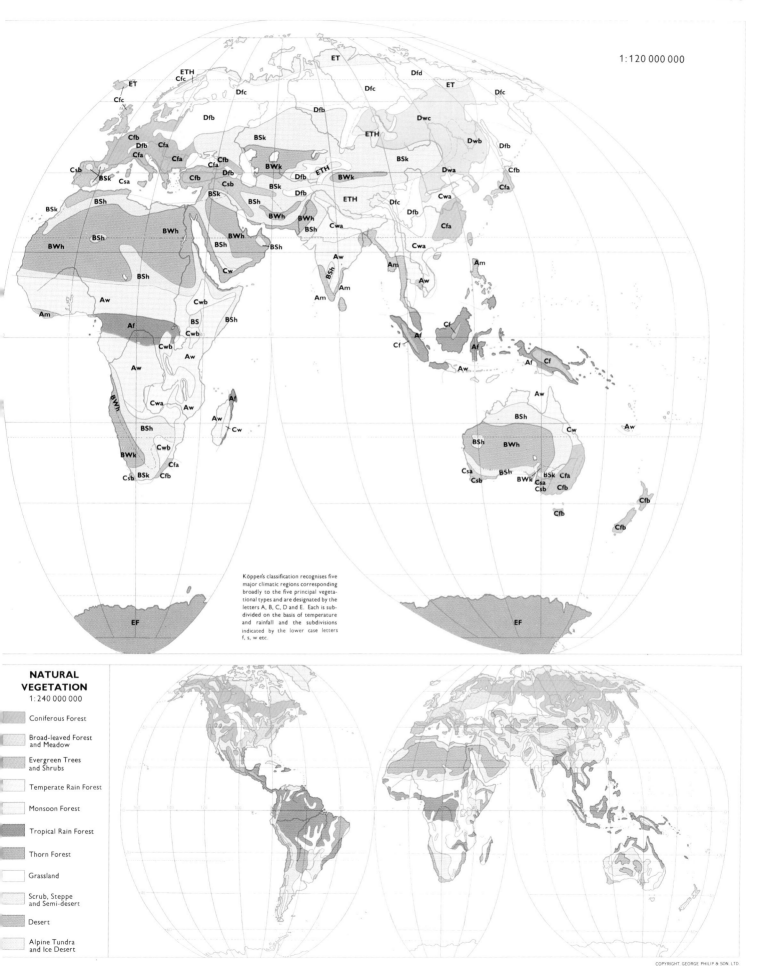

1:120 000 000

Köppen's classification recognises five major climatic regions corresponding broadly to the five principal vegetational types and are designated by the letters A, B, C, D and E. Each is subdivided on the basis of temperature and rainfall and the subdivisions indicated by the lower case letters f, s, w etc.

NATURAL VEGETATION

1:240 000 000

- Coniferous Forest
- Broad-leaved Forest and Meadow
- Evergreen Trees and Shrubs
- Temperate Rain Forest
- Monsoon Forest
- Tropical Rain Forest
- Thorn Forest
- Grassland
- Scrub, Steppe and Semi-desert
- Desert
- Alpine Tundra and Ice Desert

These four pages give temperature and precipitation statistics for over 80 stations, which are arranged by listing the continents and the places within each continent in alphabetical order. The elevation of each station, in metres above mean sea level, is stated beneath its name. The average monthly temperature, in degrees Celsius, and the average monthly precipitation, in millimetres, are given. To the right, the average yearly rainfall, the average yearly temperature, and the annual range of temperature (the difference between the warmest and the coldest months) are also stated.

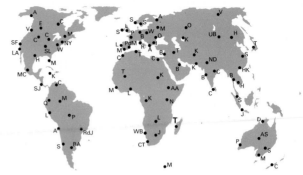

AFRICA

		Jan.	Feb.	Mar.	Apr.	May	June	July	Aug.	Sept.	Oct.	Nov.	Dec.	Year	Annual Range
Addis Ababa, Ethiopia	Precipitation	201	206	239	102	28	<3	0	<3	3	25	135	213	1 151	
2 450 m	Temperature	19	20	20	20	19	18	18	19	21	22	21	20	20	4
Cairo, Egypt	Precipitation	5	5	5	3	3	<3	0	0	<3	<3	3	5	28	
116 m	Temperature	13	15	18	21	25	28	28	28	26	24	20	15	22	15
Cape Town, South Africa	Precipitation	15	8	18	48	79	84	89	66	43	31	18	10	5û8	
17 m	Temperature	21	21	20	17	14	13	12	13	14	16	18	19	17	9
Casablanca, Morocco	Precipitation	53	48	56	36	23	5	0	<3	8	38	66	71	404	
50 m	Temperature	13	13	14	16	18	20	22	23	22	19	16	13	18	10
Johannesburg, South Africa	Precipitation	114	109	89	38	25	8	8	8	23	56	107	125	709	
1 665 m	Temperature	20	20	18	16	13	10	11	13	16	18	19	20	16	10
Khartoum, Sudan	Precipitation	<3	<3	<3	<3	3	8	53	71	18	5	<3	0	158	
390 m	Temperature	24	25	28	31	33	34	32	31	32	32	28	25	29	9
Kinshasa, Zaïre	Precipitation	135	145	196	196	158	8	3	3	31	119	221	142	1 354	
325 m	Temperature	26	26	27	27	26	24	23	24	25	26	26	26	25	4
Lagos, Nigeria	Precipitation	28	46	102	150	269	460	279	64	140	206	69	25	1 836	
3 m	Temperature	27	28	29	28	28	26	26	25	26	26	28	28	27	4
Lusaka, Zambia	Precipitation	231	191	142	18	3	<3	<3	0	<3	10	91	150	836	
1 277 m	Temperature	21	22	21	21	19	16	16	18	22	24	23	22	21	8
Monrovia, Liberia	Precipitation	31	56	97	216	516	973	996	373	744	772	236	130	5 138	
23 m	Temperature	26	26	27	27	26	25	24	25	25	25	26	26	26	3
Nairobi, Kenya	Precipitation	38	64	125	211	158	46	15	23	31	53	109	86	958	
1 820 m	Temperature	19	19	19	19	18	16	16	16	18	19	18	18	18	3
Tananarive, Madagascar	Precipitation	300	279	178	53	18	8	8	10	18	61	135	287	1 356	
1 372 m	Temperature	21	21	21	19	18	15	14	15	17	19	21	21	19	7
Timbuktu, Mali	Precipitation	<3	<3	3	<3	5	23	79	81	38	3	<3	<3	231	
301 m	Temperature	22	24	28	32	34	35	32	30	32	31	28	23	29	13
Tunis, Tunisia	Precipitation	64	51	41	36	18	8	3	8	33	51	48	61	419	
66 m	Temperature	10	11	13	16	19	23	26	27	25	20	16	11	18	17
Walvis Bay, South Africa	Precipitation	<3	5	8	3	3	<3	<3	3	<3	<3	<3	<3	23	
7 m	Temperature	19	19	19	18	17	16	15	14	14	15	17	18	18	5

AMERICA, NORTH

		Jan.	Feb.	Mar.	Apr.	May	June	July	Aug.	Sept.	Oct.	Nov.	Dec.	Year	Annual Range
Anchorage, Alaska, U.S.A.	Precipitation	20	18	15	10	13	18	41	66	66	56	25	23	371	
40 m	Temperature	−11	−8	−5	2	7	12	14	13	9	2	−5	−11	2	25
Cheyenne, Wyo., U.S.A.	Precipitation	10	15	25	48	61	41	53	41	31	25	13	13	376	
1 871 m	Temperature	−4	−3	1	5	10	16	19	19	14	7	1	−2	7	23
Chicago, Ill., U.S.A.	Precipitation	51	51	66	71	86	89	84	81	79	66	61	51	836	
251 m	Temperature	−4	−3	2	9	14	20	23	22	19	12	5	−1	10	27
Churchill, Man., Canada	Precipitation	15	13	18	23	32	44	46	58	51	43	39	21	402	
13 m	Temperature	−28	−26	−20	−10	−2	6	12	11	5	−2	−12	−22	−7	40

		Jan.	Feb.	Mar.	Apr.	May	June	July	Aug.	Sept.	Oct.	Nov.	Dec.	Year	Annual range
Edmonton, Alta., Canada															
	Precipitation	25	19	19	22	43	77	89	78	39	17	16	25	466	
676 m	Temperature	−15	−10	−5	4	11	15	17	16	11	6	−4	−10	3	32
Honolulu, Hawaii, U.S.A.															
	Precipitation	104	66	79	48	25	18	23	28	36	48	64	104	643	
12 m	Temperature	23	18	19	20	22	24	25	26	26	24	22	19	22	8
Houston, Tex., U.S.A.															
	Precipitation	89	76	84	91	119	117	99	99	104	94	89	109	1 171	
12 m	Temperature	12	13	17	21	24	27	28	29	26	22	16	12	21	17
Kingston, Jamaica															
	Precipitation	23	15	23	31	102	89	38	91	99	180	74	36	800	
34 m	Temperature	25	25	25	26	26	28	28	28	27	27	26	26	26	3
Los Angeles, Calif., U.S.A.															
	Precipitation	79	76	71	25	10	3	<3	<3	5	15	31	66	381	
95 m	Temperature	13	14	14	16	17	19	21	22	21	18	16	14	17	9
Mexico City, Mexico															
	Precipitation	13	5	10	20	53	119	170	152	130	51	18	8	747	
2 309 m	Temperature	12	13	16	18	19	19	17	18	18	16	14	13	16	7
Miami, Fla., U.S.A.															
	Precipitation	71	53	64	81	173	178	155	160	203	234	71	51	1 516	
8 m	Temperature	20	20	22	23	25	27	28	28	27	25	22	21	24	8
Montreal, Que., Canada															
	Precipitation	72	65	74	74	66	82	90	92	88	76	81	87	946	
57 m	Temperature	−10	−9	−3	−6	13	18	21	20	15	9	2	−7	6	31
New York, N.Y., U.S.A.															
	Precipitation	94	97	91	81	81	84	107	109	86	89	76	91	1 092	
96 m	Temperature	−1	−1	3	10	16	20	23	23	21	15	7	2	8	24
St. Louis, Mo., U.S.A.															
	Precipitation	58	64	89	97	114	114	89	86	81	74	71	64	1 001	
173 m	Temperature	0	1	7	13	19	24	26	26	22	15	8	2	14	26
San Francisco, Calif., U.S.A.															
	Precipitation	119	97	79	38	18	3	<3	<3	8	25	64	112	561	
16 m	Temperature	10	12	13	13	14	15	15	15	17	16	14	11	14	7
San José, Costa Rica															
	Precipitation	15	5	20	46	229	241	211	241	305	300	145	41	1 798	
1 146 m	Temperature	19	19	21	21	22	21	21	21	21	20	20	19	20	2
Vancouver, B.C., Canada															
	Precipitation	154	115	101	60	52	45	32	41	67	114	150	182	1113	
14 m	Temperature	3	5	6	9	12	15	17	17	14	10	6	4	10	14
Washington, D.C., U.S.A.															
	Precipitation	86	76	91	84	94	99	112	109	94	74	66	79	1 064	
22 m	Temperature	1	2	7	12	18	23	25	24	20	14	8	3	13	24

AMERICA, SOUTH

		Jan.	Feb.	Mar.	Apr.	May	June	July	Aug.	Sept.	Oct.	Nov.	Dec.	Year	Annual range
Antofagasta, Chile															
	Precipitation	0	0	0	<3	<3	3	5	3	<3	3	<3	0	13	
94 m	Temperature	21	21	20	18	16	15	14	14	15	16	18	19	17	7
Buenos Aires, Argentina															
	Precipitation	79	71	109	89	76	61	56	61	79	86	84	99	950	
27 m	Temperature	23	23	21	17	13	9	10	11	13	15	19	22	16	14
Caracas, Venezuela															
	Precipitation	23	10	15	33	79	102	109	109	107	109	94	46	836	
1 042 m	Temperature	19	19	20	21	22	21	21	21	21	21	20	20	21	3
Lima, Peru															
	Precipitation	3	<3	<3	<3	5	5	8	8	8	3	3	<3	41	
120 m	Temperature	23	24	24	22	19	17	17	16	17	18	19	21	20	8
Manaus, Brazil															
	Precipitation	249	231	262	221	170	84	58	38	46	107	142	203	1 811	
44 m	Temperature	28	28	28	27	28	28	28	28	29	29	29	28	28	2
Paraná, Brazil															
	Precipitation	287	236	239	102	13	<3	3	5	28	127	231	310	1 582	
260 m	Temperature	23	23	23	23	23	21	21	22	24	24	24	23	23	3
Quito, Ecuador															
	Precipitation	99	112	142	175	137	43	20	31	69	112	97	79	1 115	
2 879 m	Temperature	15	15	15	15	15	14	14	15	15	15	15	15	15	1
Rio de Janeiro, Brazil															
	Precipitation	125	122	130	107	79	53	41	43	66	79	104	137	1 082	
61 m	Temperature	26	26	25	24	22	21	21	21	21	22	23	25	23	5
Santiago, Chile															
	Precipitation	3	3	5	13	64	84	76	56	31	15	8	5	358	
520 m	Temperature	21	20	18	15	12	9	9	10	12	15	17	19	15	12

ASIA

		Jan.	Feb.	Mar.	Apr.	May	June	July	Aug.	Sept.	Oct.	Nov.	Dec.	Year	Annual range
Bahrain	Precipitation	8	18	13	8	<3	0	0	0	0	0	18	18	81	
5 m	Temperature	17	18	21	25	29	32	33	34	31	28	24	19	26	16
Bangkok, Thailand	Precipitation	8	20	36	58	198	160	160	175	305	206	66	5	1 397	
2 m	Temperature	26	28	29	30	29	29	28	28	28	28	26	25	28	5
Beirut, Lebanon	Precipitation	191	158	94	53	18	3	<3	<3	5	51	132	185	892	
34 m	Temperature	14	14	16	18	22	24	27	28	26	24	19	16	21	14
Bombay, India	Precipitation	3	3	3	<3	18	485	617	340	264	64	13	3	1 809	
11 m	Temperature	24	24	26	28	30	29	27	27	27	28	27	26	27	6
Calcutta, India	Precipitation	10	31	36	43	140	297	325	328	252	114	20	5	1 600	
6 m	Temperature	20	22	27	30	30	30	29	29	29	28	23	19	26	11
Colombo, Sri Lanka	Precipitation	89	69	147	231	371	224	135	109	160	348	315	147	2 365	
7 m	Temperature	26	26	27	28	28	27	27	27	27	27	26	26	27	2
Harbin, China	Precipitation	5	5	10	23	43	94	112	104	46	33	8	5	488	
160 m	Temperature	−18	−15	−5	6	13	19	22	21	14	4	−6	−16	3	40
Ho Chi Minh City, Vietnam	Precipitation	15	3	13	43	221	330	315	269	335	269	114	56	1 984	
9 m	Temperature	26	27	29	30	29	28	28	28	27	27	27	26	28	4
Jakarta, Indonesia	Precipitation	300	300	211	147	114	97	64	43	66	112	142	203	1 798	
8 m	Temperature	26	26	27	27	27	27	27	27	27	27	27	26	27	1
Hong Kong	Precipitation	33	46	74	137	292	394	381	361	257	114	43	31	2 162	
33 m	Temperature	16	15	18	22	26	28	28	28	27	25	21	18	23	13
Kabul, Afghanistan	Precipitation	31	36	94	102	20	5	3	3	<3	15	20	10	338	
1 815 m	Temperature	−3	−1	6	13	18	22	25	24	20	14	7	3	12	28
Karachi, Pakistan	Precipitation	13	10	8	3	3	18	81	41	13	<3	3	5	196	
4 m	Temperature	19	20	24	28	30	31	30	29	28	28	24	20	26	12
New Delhi, India	Precipitation	23	18	13	8	13	74	180	172	117	10	3	10	640	
218 m	Temperature	14	17	23	28	33	34	31	30	29	26	20	15	25	20
Shanghai, China	Precipitation	48	58	84	94	94	180	147	142	130	71	51	36	1 135	
7 m	Temperature	4	5	9	14	20	24	28	28	23	19	12	7	16	24
Singapore	Precipitation	252	173	193	188	173	173	170	196	178	208	254	257	2 413	
10 m	Temperature	26	27	28	28	28	28	28	27	27	27	27	27	27	2
Tehran, Iran	Precipitation	46	38	46	36	13	3	3	3	3	8	20	31	246	
1 220 m	Temperature	2	5	9	16	21	26	30	29	25	18	12	6	17	28
Tokyo, Japan	Precipitation	48	74	107	135	147	165	142	152	234	208	97	56	1 565	
6 m	Temperature	3	4	7	13	17	21	25	26	23	17	11	6	14	23
Ulan Bator, Mongolia	Precipitation	<3	<3	3	5	10	28	76	51	23	5	5	3	208	
1 325 m	Temperature	−26	−21	−13	−1	6	14	16	14	8	−1	−13	−22	−3	42

AUSTRALIA, NEW ZEALAND and ANTARCTICA

		Jan.	Feb.	Mar.	Apr.	May	June	July	Aug.	Sept.	Oct.	Nov.	Dec.	Year	Annual range
Alice Springs, Australia	Precipitation	43	33	28	10	15	13	8	8	8	18	31	38	252	
579 m	Temperature	29	28	25	20	15	12	12	14	18	23	26	28	21	17
Christchurch, New Zealand	Precipitation	56	43	48	48	66	66	69	48	46	43	48	56	638	
10 m	Temperature	16	16	14	12	9	6	6	7	9	12	14	16	11	10
Darwin, Australia	Precipitation	386	312	254	97	15	3	<3	3	13	51	119	239	1 491	
30 m	Temperature	29	29	29	29	28	26	25	26	28	29	30	29	28	5
Mawson, Antarctica	Precipitation	11	30	20	10	44	180	4	40	3	20	0	0	362	
14 m	Temperature	0	−5	−10	−14	−15	−16	−18	−18	−19	−13	−5	−1	−11	18

		Jan.	Feb.	Mar.	Apr.	May	June	July	Aug.	Sept.	Oct.	Nov.	Dec.	Year	Annual Range
Melbourne, Australia															
	Precipitation	48	46	56	58	53	53	48	48	58	66	58	58	653	
35 m	Temperature	20	20	18	15	13	10	9	11	13	14	16	18	15	11
Perth, Australia															
	Precipitation	8	10	20	43	130	180	170	149	86	56	20	13	881	
60 m	Temperature	23	23	22	19	16	14	13	13	15	16	19	22	18	10
Sydney, Australia															
	Precipitation	89	102	127	135	127	117	117	76	73	71	73	73	1 181	
42 m	Temperature	22	22	21	18	15	13	12	13	15	18	19	21	17	10

EUROPE and U.S.S.R.

		Jan.	Feb.	Mar.	Apr.	May	June	July	Aug.	Sept.	Oct.	Nov.	Dec.	Year	Annual Range
Archangel, U.S.S.R.															
	Precipitation	31	19	25	29	42	52	62	56	63	63	47	41	530	
13 m	Temperature	−16	−14	−9	0	7	12	15	14	8	2	−4	−11	0	31
Athens, Greece															
	Precipitation	62	37	37	23	23	14	6	7	15	51	56	71	402	
107 m	Temperature	10	10	12	16	20	25	28	28	24	20	15	11	18	18
Berlin, Germany															
	Precipitation	46	40	33	42	49	65	73	69	48	49	46	43	603	
55 m	Temperature	−1	0	4	9	14	17	19	18	15	9	5	1	9	20
Istanbul, Turkey															
	Precipitation	109	92	72	46	38	34	34	30	58	81	103	119	816	
114 m	Temperature	5	6	7	11	16	20	23	23	20	16	12	8	14	18
Kazalinsk, U.S.S.R.															
	Precipitation	10	10	13	13	15	5	5	8	8	10	13	15	125	
63 m	Temperature	−12	−11	−3	6	18	23	25	23	16	8	−1	−7	7	37
Lisbon, Portugal															
	Precipitation	111	76	109	54	44	16	3	4	33	62	93	103	708	
77 m	Temperature	11	12	14	16	17	20	22	23	21	18	14	12	17	12
London, U.K.															
	Precipitation	54	40	37	37	46	45	57	59	49	57	64	48	593	
5 m	Temperature	4	5	7	9	12	16	18	17	15	11	8	5	11	14
Málaga, Spain															
	Precipitation	61	51	62	46	26	5	1	3	29	64	64	62	474	
33 m	Temperature	12	13	15	17	19	29	25	26	23	20	16	13	18	17
Moscow, U.S.S.R.															
	Precipitation	39	38	36	37	53	58	88	71	58	45	47	54	624	
156 m	Temperature	−13	−10	−4	6	13	16	18	17	12	6	−1	−7	4	31
Odessa, U.S.S.R.															
	Precipitation	57	62	30	21	34	34	42	37	37	13	35	71	473	
64 m	Temperature	−3	−1	2	9	15	20	22	22	18	12	9	1	10	25
Omsk, U.S.S.R.															
	Precipitation	15	8	8	13	31	51	51	51	28	25	18	20	318	
85 m	Temperature	−22	−19	−12	−1	10	16	18	16	10	1	−11	−18	−1	40
Palma de Mallorca, Spain															
	Precipitation	39	34	51	32	29	17	3	25	55	77	47	40	449	
10 m	Temperature	10	11	12	15	17	21	24	25	23	18	14	11	17	15
Paris, France															
	Precipitation	56	46	35	42	57	54	59	64	55	50	51	50	619	
75 m	Temperature	3	4	8	11	15	18	20	19	17	12	7	4	12	17
Rome, Italy															
	Precipitation	71	62	57	51	46	37	15	21	63	99	129	93	744	
17 m	Temperature	8	9	11	14	18	22	25	25	22	17	13	10	16	17
Shannon, Irish Republic															
	Precipitation	94	67	56	53	61	57	77	79	86	86	96	117	929	
2 m	Temperature	5	5	7	9	12	14	16	16	14	11	8	6	10	11
Stavanger, Norway															
	Precipitation	93	56	45	70	49	84	93	118	142	129	125	126	1 130	
85 m	Temperature	1	1	3	6	10	13	15	15	13	9	6	3	8	14
Stockholm, Sweden															
	Precipitation	43	30	25	31	34	45	61	76	60	48	53	48	554	
44 m	Temperature	−3	−3	−1	5	10	15	18	17	12	7	3	0	7	21
Verkhoyansk, U.S.S.R.															
	Precipitation	5	5	3	5	8	23	28	25	13	8	8	5	134	
100 m	Temperature	−50	−45	−32	−15	0	12	14	9	2	−15	−38	−48	−17	64
Warsaw, Poland															
	Precipitation	27	32	27	37	46	69	96	65	43	38	31	44	555	
110 m	Temperature	−3	−3	2	7	14	17	19	18	14	9	3	0	8	22

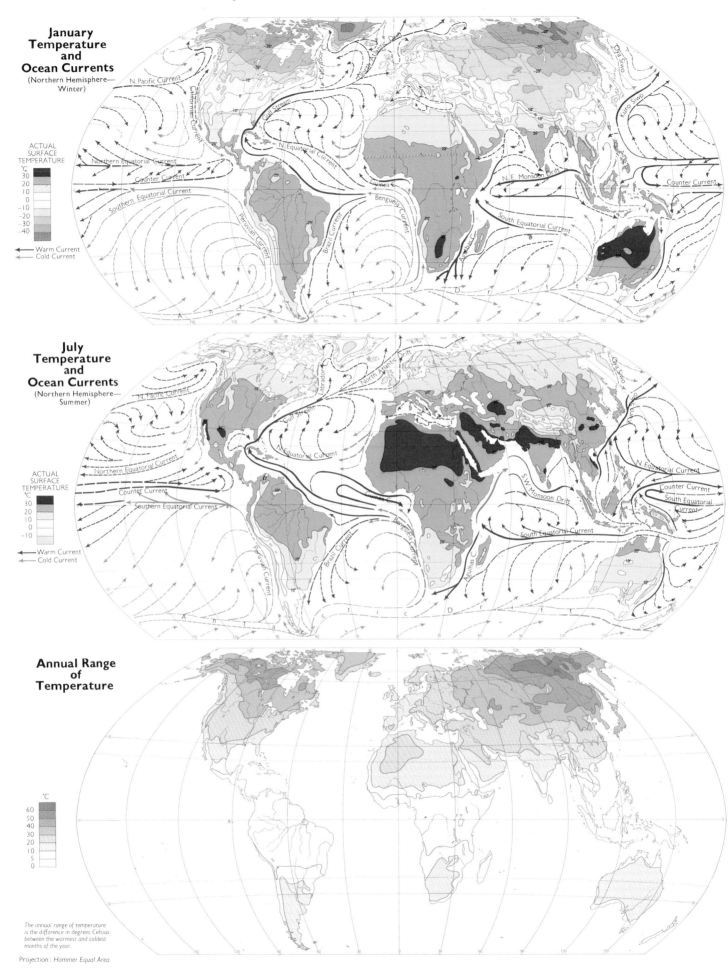

January Temperature and Ocean Currents
(Northern Hemisphere—Winter)

ACTUAL SURFACE TEMPERATURE
°C
30
20
10
0
-10
-20
-30
-40

→ Warm Current
→ Cold Current

July Temperature and Ocean Currents
(Northern Hemisphere—Summer)

ACTUAL SURFACE TEMPERATURE
°C
30
20
10
0
-10

→ Warm Current
→ Cold Current

Annual Range of Temperature

°C
60
50
40
30
20
10
5
0

The annual range of temperature is the difference in degrees Celsius between the warmest and coldest months of the year.

Projection: *Hammer Equal Area*

1:190 000 000

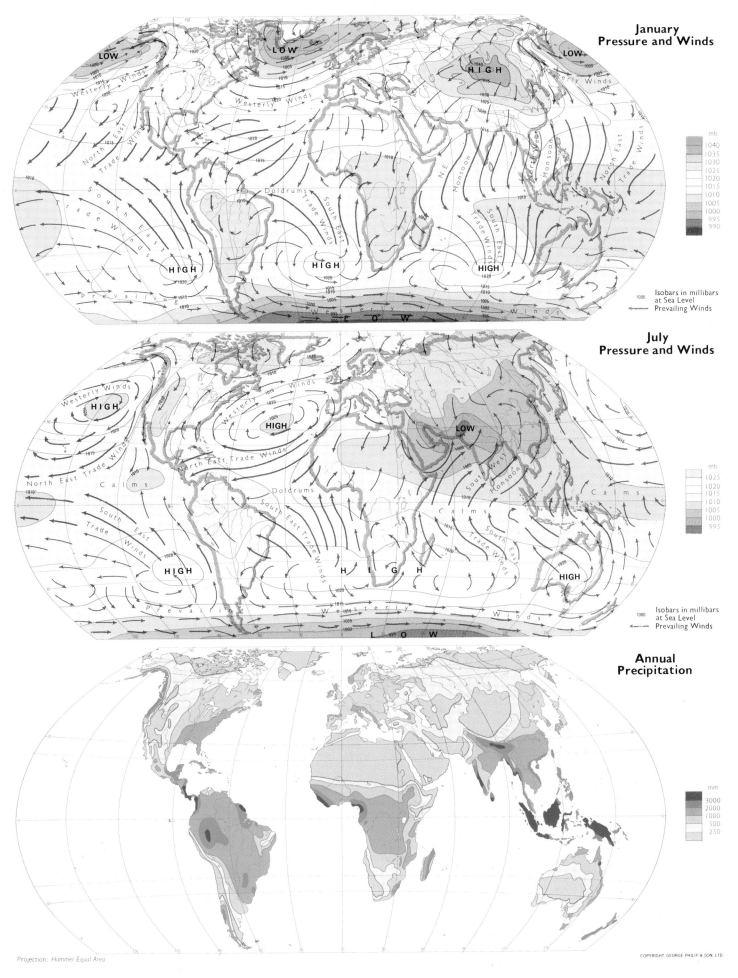

January Pressure and Winds

mb
1040
1035
1030
1025
1020
1015
1010
1005
1000
995
990

1000 Isobars in millibars at Sea Level
Prevailing Winds

July Pressure and Winds

mb
1025
1020
1015
1010
1005
1000
995

1000 Isobars in millibars at Sea Level
Prevailing Winds

Annual Precipitation

mm
3000
2000
1000
500
250

Projection: *Hammer Equal Area*

COPYRIGHT GEORGE PHILIP & SON. LTD

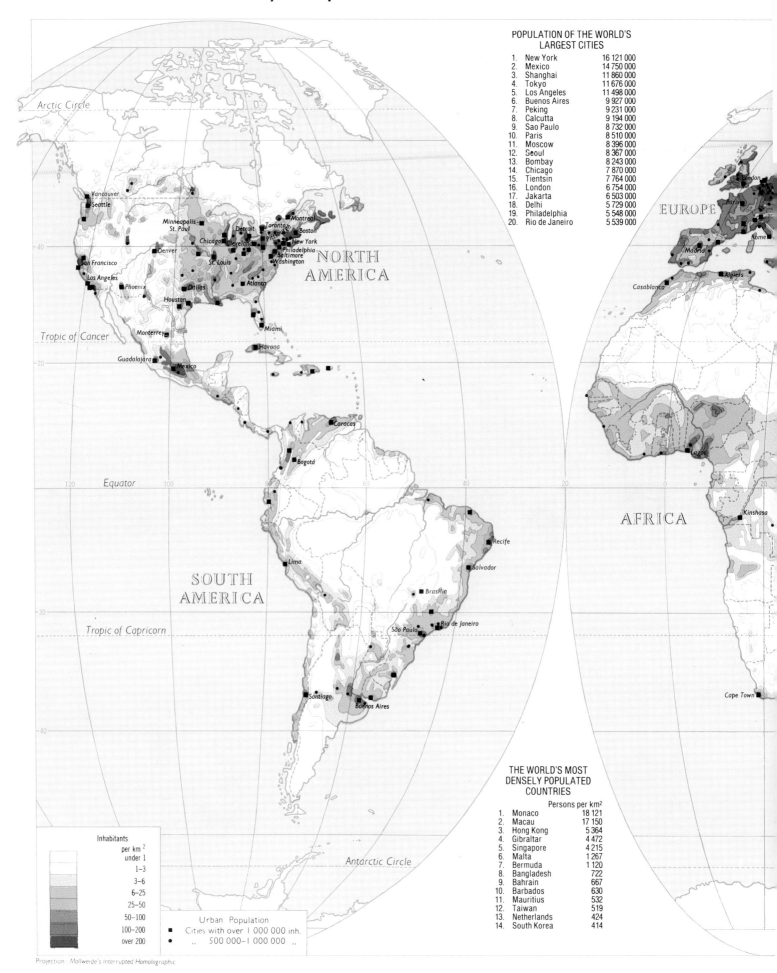

POPULATION OF THE WORLD'S
LARGEST CITIES

1.	New York	16 121 000
2.	Mexico	14 750 000
3.	Shanghai	11 860 000
4.	Tokyo	11 676 000
5.	Los Angeles	11 498 000
6.	Buenos Aires	9 927 000
7.	Peking	9 231 000
8.	Calcutta	9 194 000
9.	Sao Paulo	8 732 000
10.	Paris	8 510 000
11.	Moscow	8 396 000
12.	Seoul	8 367 000
13.	Bombay	8 243 000
14.	Chicago	7 870 000
15.	Tientsin	7 764 000
16.	London	6 754 000
17.	Jakarta	6 503 000
18.	Delhi	5 729 000
19.	Philadelphia	5 548 000
20.	Rio de Janeiro	5 539 000

THE WORLD'S MOST
DENSELY POPULATED
COUNTRIES

		Persons per km2
1.	Monaco	18 121
2.	Macau	17 150
3.	Hong Kong	5 364
4.	Gibraltar	4 472
5.	Singapore	4 215
6.	Malta	1 267
7.	Bermuda	1 120
8.	Bangladesh	722
9.	Bahrain	667
10.	Barbados	630
11.	Mauritius	532
12.	Taiwan	519
13.	Netherlands	424
14.	South Korea	414

Inhabitants
per km2
under 1
1–3
3–6
6–25
25–50
50–100
100–200
over 200

Urban Population
■ Cities with over 1 000 000 inh.
● ,,   500 000–1 000 000 ,,

Projection: Mollweide's interrupted Homolographic

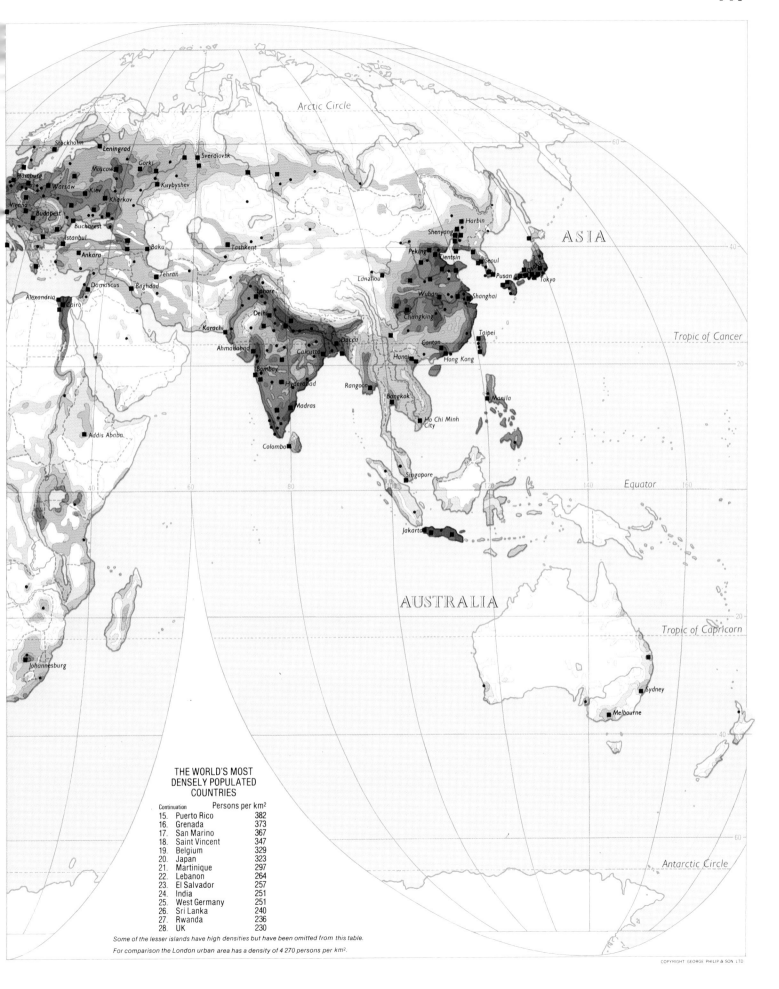

Arctic Circle

Stockholm
Leningrad
Sv(erdlovsk)
Hamburg
Moscow
Gorki
Warsaw
Kiev
Kuybyshev
Harbin
Vienna
Kharkov
ASIA
Budapest
Shenyang
Bucharest
Peking
Seoul
Istanbul
Baku
Tientsin
Pusan
Ankara
Tashkent
Tokyo
Tehran
Lanzhou
Damascus
Baghdad
Lahore
Wuhan
Shanghai
Alexandria
Delhi
Chungking
Tropic of Cancer
Cairo
Karachi
Taipei
Ahmadabad
Dacca
Canton
Hanoi
Hong Kong
Calcutta
Bombay
Hyderabad
Rangoon
Addis Ababa
Madras
Bangkok
Manila
Ho Chi Minh
City
Colombo
Equator
Singapore
Jakarta
AUSTRALIA
Tropic of Capricorn
Johannesburg
Sydney
Melbourne
Antarctic Circle

THE WORLD'S MOST DENSELY POPULATED COUNTRIES

Continuation		Persons per km^2
15.	Puerto Rico	382
16.	Grenada	373
17.	San Marino	367
18.	Saint Vincent	347
19.	Belgium	329
20.	Japan	323
21.	Martinique	297
22.	Lebanon	264
23.	El Salvador	257
24.	India	251
25.	West Germany	251
26.	Sri Lanka	240
27.	Rwanda	236
28.	UK	230

Some of the lesser islands have high densities but have been omitted from this table.

For comparison the London urban area has a density of 4 270 persons per km^2.

The population figures used are from censuses or more recent estimates and are given in thousands for towns and cities over 200,000 (over 250,000 in Brazil and Japan and 500,000 in China, India, U.S.A. and U.S.S.R.). Where possible the population of the metropolitan area is given e.g. Greater London.

AFRICA

ALGERIA (1977)
- Algiers 1 740
- Oran 543
- Constantine 379
- Annaba 246
- Tizi-Ouzou 224

ANGOLA (1982)
- Luanda 700

BENIN (1981)
- Cotonou 383

BURKINA FASO (1982)
- Ouagadougou 286

CAMEROON (1983)
- Douala 708
- Yaoundé 485

CANARY ISLANDS (1981)
- Las Palmas 360

CENTRAL AFRICAN REPUBLIC (1981)
- Bangui 387

CHAD (1979)
- Ndjamena 303

CONGO (1980)
- Brazzaville 422

EGYPT (1976)
- Cairo 5 074
- Alexandria 2 318
- El Giza 1 230
- Shubra el Kheima 394
- El Mahalla el Kubra 292
- Tanta 285
- Port Said 263
- El Mansûra 259
- Asyût 214
- Zagazig 203

ETHIOPIA (1983)
- Addis Ababa 1 478
- Asmera 491

GABON (1976)
- Libreville 186

GHANA (1970)
- Accra 738
- Kumasi 345

GUINEA (1980)
- Conakry 763

IVORY COAST (1976)
- Abidjan 850
- Bouaké 318

KENYA (1983)
- Nairobi 1 048
- Mombasa 410

LIBERIA (1981)
- Monrovia 306

LIBYA (1982)
- Tripoli 980
- Benghazi 650
- Misrātah 285

MADAGASCAR (1978)
- Antananarivo 400

MALAWI (1977)
- Blantyre 229

MALI (1976)
- Bamako 419

MOROCCO (1981)
- Casablanca 2 409
- Rabat-Salé 842
- Fès 562
- Marrakesh 549
- Meknès 487
- Oujda 470
- Kénitra 450
- Tétouan 372
- Tangier 304
- Safi 256
- Agadir 246
- Khouribga 229
- Béni-Mellal 204

MOZAMBIQUE (1970)
- Maputo 384

NIGER (1977)
- Niamey 225

NIGERIA (1975)
- Lagos 1 477
- Ibadan 847
- Ogbomosho 432
- Kano 399
- Oshogbo 282
- Ilorin 282
- Abeokuta 253
- Port Harcourt 242
- Zaria 224
- Ilesha 224
- Onitsha 220
- Iwo 214
- Ado-Ekiti 213
- Kaduna 202

SENEGAL (1976)
- Dakar 779

SIERRA LEONE (1974)
- Freetown 316

SOMALI REP. (1980)
- Mogadishu 400

SOUTH AFRICA (1980)
- Johannesburg 1 726
- Cape Town 1 491
- Durban 961
- Pretoria 739
- Port Elizabeth 585

SUDAN (1980)
- Khartoum 561
- Omdurman 454
- Khartoum North 249
- Port Sudan 205

TANZANIA (1978)
- Dar-es-Salaam 757

TOGO (1979)
- Lomé 247

TUNISIA (1984)
- Tunis 597
- Sfax 232

UGANDA (1975)
- Kampala 332

ZAIRE (1975)
- Kinshasa 2 242
- Lubumbashi 481
- Kananga 377
- Kisangani 298
- Mbuji Mayi 283

ZAMBIA (1980)
- Lusaka 641
- Kitwe 341
- Ndola 323

ZIMBABWE (1983)
- Harare 681
- Bulawayo 429
- Chitungwiza 202

ASIA

AFGHANISTAN (1979)
- Kābul 1 036

BANGLADESH (1982)
- Dacca 3 459
- Chittagong 1 388
- Khulna 623
- Narayanganj 298

BURMA (1977)
- Rangoon 2 276
- Mandalay 458
- Kanbe 254

CAMBODIA (KAMPUCHEA) (1981)
- Phnom Penh 400

CHINA (1970)
- Shanghai 11 860
- Peking 9 231
- Tientsin 7 764
- Shenyang 2 800
- Wuhan 2 560
- Canton 2 500
- Chungking 2 400
- Nanking 1 750
- Harbin 1 670
- Dalian 1 650
- Sian 1 600
- Lanzhou 1 450
- Taiyuan 1 350
- Qingdao 1 300
- Chengdu 1 250
- Changchun 1 200
- Kunming 1 100
- Jinan 1 100
- Fushun 1 000
- Anshan 1 050
- Zhengzhou 1 050
- Hangzhou 960
- Tangshan 950
- Baotou 920
- Zibo 850
- Changsha 825
- Shijiazhuang 800
- Qiqihar 760
- Suzhou 730
- Jilin 720
- Xuzhou 700
- Fuzhou 680
- Nanchang 675
- Guiyang 660
- Wuxi 650
- Hefei 630
- Huainan 600
- Benxi 600
- Luoyang 580
- Nanning 550
- Hohhot 530
- Xining 500
- Ürümqi 500

HONG KONG (1981)
- Kowloon 2 450
- Hong Kong 1 184
- Tsuen Wan 599

INDIA (1981)
- Calcutta 9 194
- Bombay 8 243
- Delhi 5 729
- Madras 4 289
- Bangalore 2 922
- Ahmadabad 2 548
- Hyderabad 2 546
- Pune 1 686
- Kanpur 1 639
- Nagpur 1 302
- Jaipur 1 015
- Lucknow 1 008
- Coimbatore 920
- Patna 919
- Surat 914
- Madurai 908
- Indore 829
- Varanasi 797
- Jabalpur 757
- Agra 747
- Vadodara 744
- Cochin 686
- Dhanbad 678
- Bhopal 671
- Jamshedpur 670
- Allahabad 650
- Ulhasnagar 649
- Tiruchchirappalli 610
- Ludhiana 606
- Srinagar 606
- Vishakhapatnam 604
- Amritsar 595
- Gwalior 556
- Calicut 546
- Vijayawada 543
- Meerut 537
- Dharwad 527
- Trivandrum 520
- Salem 519
- Solapur 515
- Jodhpur 506
- Ranchi 503

INDONESIA (1980)
- Jakarta 6 503
- Surabaya 2 028
- Bandung 1 462
- Medan 1 379
- Semarang 1 026
- Palembang 787
- Ujung Pandang 709
- Malang 512
- Padang 481
- Surakarta 470
- Yogyakarta 399
- Banjarmasin 381
- Pontianak 305
- Tanjung Karang 284
- Balikpapan 281
- Samarinda 265
- Bogor 247
- Jambi 230
- Cirebon 224
- Kediri 222
- Manado 217
- Ambon 209

IRAN (1976)
- Tehrān 4 496
- Esfahān 672
- Mashhad 670
- Tabrīz 599
- Shirāz 416
- Ahvāz 329
- Abadan 296
- Bākhtarān 291
- Qom 247

IRAQ (1970)
- Baghdād 2 969
- Basra 371
- Mosul 293
- Kirkūk 208

ISRAEL (1982)
- Jerusalem 424
- Tel Aviv-Jaffa 326
- Haifa 226

JAPAN (1982)
- Tōkyō 11 676
- Yokohama 2 848
- Ōsaka 2 623
- Nagoya 2 093
- Kyōto 1 480
- Sapporo 1 465
- Kobe 1 383
- Fukuoka 1 121
- Kitakyūshū 1 065
- Kawasaki 1 055
- Hiroshima 898
- Sakai 809
- Chiba 756
- Sendai 662
- Okayama 551
- Kumamoto 522
- Kagoshima 514
- Amagasaki 510
- Higashiōsaka 501
- Hamamatsu 500
- Funabashi 488
- Shizuoka 462
- Niigata 458
- Sagamihara 455
- Nagasaki 449
- Hameji 448
- Yokosuka 429
- Matsuyama 413
- Kanazawa 412
- Matsudo 411
- Nishinoyama 410
- Kurashiki 410
- Wakayama 404
- Toyonaka 397
- Hachiōji 395
- Kawaguchi 391
- Utsunomiya 389
- Ichikawa 374
- Hirakata 368
- Oita 367
- Urawa 366
- Omiya 361
- Asahikawa 359
- Fukuyama 353
- Iwaki 352
- Takatsuki 340
- Suita 333
- Nagano 328
- Hakodate 321
- Takamatsu 320
- Fujisawa 313
- Toyohashi 311
- Nara 309
- Toyama 308
- Kōchi 305
- Naha 302
- Machida 301
- Aomori 291
- Kōriyama 290
- Akita 290
- Toyota 287
- Maebashi 271
- Okazaki 269
- Miyazaki 267
- Yao 266
- Fukushima 265
- Kawagoe 265
- Yokkaichi 258
- Akashi 257
- Neyagawa 255
- Ichinomiya 253
- Sasebo 253
- Tokushima 251

JORDAN (1981)
- 'Ammān 681
- Az-Zarqā 234

KOREA, NORTH (1972)
- Pyŏngyang 1 500
- Hamhung 420
- Chongjin 265
- Kimchaek 265

KOREA, SOUTH (1980)
- Seoul 8 367
- Pusan 3 160
- Taegu 1 607
- Inchŏn 1 085
- Kwangju 728
- Taejon 652
- Masan 387
- Songnam 376
- Chonju 367
- Suwŏn 311
- Ulsan 253

KUWAIT (1975)
- Kuwait 775

LEBANON (1980)
- Beirut 702

MACAU (1981)
- Macau 250

MALAYSIA (1980)
- Kuala Lumpur 938
- Ipoh 301
- Pinang 251

MONGOLIA (1980)
- Ulan Bator 419

NEPAL (1971)
- Katmandu 210

PAKISTAN (1981)
- Karachi 5 103
- Lahore 2 922
- Faisalabad 1 092
- Rawalpindi 806
- Hyderabad 795
- Multan 730
- Gujranwala 597
- Peshawar 555
- Sialkot 296
- Sargodha 294
- Quetta 243
- Islamabad 201

PHILIPPINES (1981)
- Manila 1 630
- Quezon City 1 166
- Davao 610
- Cebu 490
- Caloocan 468
- Zamboanga 344
- Bacolod 262
- Iloilo 245
- Cagayan de Oro 227

SAUDI ARABIA (1974)
- Riyadh 667
- Jedda 561
- Mecca 367
- Taif 205

SINGAPORE (1983)
- Singapore 2 517

SRI LANKA (1981)
- Colombo 1 412

SYRIA (1982)
- Damascus 1 112
- Aleppo 985
- Homs 354

TAIWAN (1981)
- Taipei 2 271
- Kaohsiung 1 227
- Taichung 607
- Tainan 595
- Chilung 348
- Sanchung 335
- Chiai 252
- Hsinchu 243

THAILAND (1982)
- Bangkok 5 468

TURKEY (1982)
- İstanbul 2 949
- Ankara 2 276
- İzmir 1 083
- Adana 864
- Konya 691
- Bursa 658
- Gaziantep 526
- Igel 440
- Kayseri 394
- Diyarbakir 390
- Samsun 354
- Balikesir 352
- Eskişehir 352
- Kocaeli 328
- Zonguldak 321
- Erzurum 292
- Maras 292
- Antalya 290
- Urfa 285
- Sivas 279
- Malatya 245
- Denizli 211

UNITED ARAB EMIRATES (1980)
- Abu Dhabi 449
- Dubai 278

VIETNAM (1973-79)
- Ho Chi Minh City 3 420
- Hanoi 2 571
- Haiphong 1 279
- Da-Nang 492
- Nha-Trang 216
- Qui-Nhon 214
- Hue 209

YEMEN, SOUTH (1977)
- Aden 285

AUSTRALIA AND NEW ZEALAND

AUSTRALIA (1982)
- Sydney 3 310
- Melbourne 2 837
- Brisbane 1 124
- Adelaide 960
- Perth 948
- Newcastle 410
- Canberra 251
- Wollongong 234

NEW ZEALAND (1982)
- Auckland 839
- Wellington 343
- Christchurch 322

EUROPE

ALBANIA (1982)
- Tiranë 202

AUSTRIA (1981)
- Vienna 1 516
- Graz 243

BELGIUM (1983)
- Brussels 989
- Antwerp 491
- Ghent 237
- Charleroi 216
- Liège 207

BULGARIA (1982)
- Sofia 1 064
- Plovdiv 355
- Varna 292

CZECHOSLOVAKIA (1983)
Prague 1 186
Bratislava 401
Brno 381
Ostrava 323
Kosice 214

DENMARK (1981)
Copenhagen 1 382

FINLAND (1982)
Helsinki 922
Tampere 248
Turku 244

FRANCE (1982)
Paris 8 510
Lyons 1 170
Marseilles 1 080
Lille 935
Bordeaux 628
Toulouse 523
Nantes 465
Nice 449
Toulon 410
Grenoble 392
Rouen 380
Strasbourg 373
Valenciennes 337
Lens 323
St-Étienne 317
Grasse-Cannes 296
Nancy 278
Clermont-Ferrand ... 256
Le Havre 255
Tours 255
Rennes 234
Montpellier 221
Mulhouse 220
Orléans 220
Dijon 209
Douai 202

GERMANY, EAST (1982)
East Berlin 1 173
Leipzig 557
Dresden 521
Karl-Marx-Stadt 320
Magdeburg 288
Rostock 239
Halle 235
Erfurt 213

GERMANY, WEST (1980)
West Berlin 1 896
Hamburg 1 645
Munich 1 299
Cologne 977
Essen 648
Frankfurt 629
Dortmund 608
Düsseldorf 590
Stuttgart 581
Duisburg 558
Bremen 555
Hanover 535
Nuremberg 484
Bochum 401
Wuppertal 393
Bielefeld 313
Gelsenkirchen 304
Mannheim 304
Bonn 288
Wiesbaden 274
Karlsruhe 272
Munster 270
Braunschweig 261
Mönchengladbach ... 258
Kiel 250
Augsburg 248
Aachen 244
Oberhausen 229
Krefeld 224
Lübeck 221
Hagen 219

GREECE (1981)
Athens 3 027
Thessaloniki 706

HUNGARY (1983)
Budapest 2 067
Miskolc 210

IRISH REPUBLIC (1981)
Dublin 525

ITALY (1981)
Rome 2 831
Milan 1 635
Naples 1 211
Turin 1 104
Genoa 760
Palermo 700
Bologna 456
Florence 453
Catánia 379
Bari 371
Venice 333
Verona 261
Messina 256
Trieste 251
Táranto 243
Cágliari 233
Padua 231
Bréscia 206

NETHERLANDS (1983)
Rotterdam 1 025
Amsterdam 936
The Hague 674
Utrecht 499
Eindhoven 374
Arnhem 291
Heerlen-Kerkrade ... 265
Enschede-Hengelo .. 248
Nijmegen 229
Tilburg 221
Haarlem 219
Groningen 206

NORWAY (1980)
Oslo 624
Bergen 208

POLAND (1983)
Warsaw 1 641
Łodz 848
Kraków 735
Wrocław 631
Poznań 571
Gdansk 465
Szczecin 389
Katowice 361
Bydgoszcz 358
Lublin 320
Sosnowiec 252
Bytom 238
Częstochowa 244
Gdynia 240
Białystok 240
Gliwice 211
Radom 201

PORTUGAL (1981)
Lisbon 818
Oporto 330

ROMANIA (1982)
Bucharest 1 979
Braşov 334
Constanţa 307
Timişoara 302
Cluj-Napoca 301
Iaşi 295
Galaţi 279
Craiova 253
Ploieşti 228
Brăila 225
Oradea 201

SPAIN (1981)
Madrid 3 159
Barcelona 1 753
Valencia 745
Seville 646
Zaragoza 572
Málaga 502
Bilbao 433
Valladolid 320
Hospitalet 295
Palma de Mallorca .. 290
Murcia 285
Córdoba 279

Vigo 261
Gijón 256
Granada 247
Alicante 246
La Coruña 232
Badalona 230

SWEDEN (1983)
Stockholm 1 409
Göteborg 696
Malmö 454

SWITZERLAND (1982)
Zürich 705
Basle 363
Geneva 339
Bern 289
Lausanne 226

U.S.S.R. (1983)
Moscow 8 396
Leningrad 4 779
Kiev 2 355
Tashkent 1 944
Baku 1 638
Kharkov 1 519
Minsk 1 405
Gorki 1 382
Novosibirsk 1 370
Sverdlovsk 1 269
Kuybyshev 1 242
Dnepropetrovsk ... 1 128
Tbilisi 1 125
Odessa 1 097
Yerevan 1 095
Omsk 1 080
Chelyabinsk 1 077
Donetsk 1 055
Perm 1 037
Ufa 1 034
Kazan 1 031
Alma-Ata 1 023
Rostov 977
Volgograd 962
Saratov 887
Riga 867
Krasnoyarsk 845
Zaporozhye 835
Voronezh 831
Lvov 711
Krivoy Rog 674
Yaroslavl 619
Karaganda 600
Krasnodar 595
Ustinov 594
Vladivostok 584
Irkutsk 582
Kishinev 580
Frunze 577
Novokuznetsk 564
Barnaul 561
Khabarovsk 560
Dushanbe 530
Tula 527
Vilnius 525
Zhdanov 516
Penza 515
Ulyanovsk 509
Samarkand 505
Orenburg 505

UNITED KINGDOM (1983)
London 6 754
Birmingham 1 013
Glasgow 751
Leeds 714
Sheffield 543
Liverpool 502
Bradford 464
Manchester 458
Edinburgh 441
Bristol 399
Belfast 324
Coventry 316
Leicester 282
Cardiff 280
Nottingham 277
Hull 269
Wolverhampton ... 255
Plymouth 250
Stoke-on-Trent ... 250
Derby 215
Southampton 206

YUGOSLAVIA (1981)
Belgrade 1 407
Zagreb 1 175
Skopje 507
Sarajevo 449
Ljubljana 305
Novi Sad 258
Split 236
Niš 231
Priština 216

NORTH AMERICA

CANADA (1983)
Toronto 3 067
Montréal 2 862
Vancouver 1 311
Ottawa 738
Edmonton 699
Calgary 634
Winnipeg 601
Québec 580
Hamilton 548
St. Catherines 304
Kitchener 294
London 287
Halifax 281
Windsor 245
Victoria 240

COSTA RICA (1983)
San José 272

CUBA (1981)
Havana 1 925
Santiago de Cuba .. 563
Camagüey 480

DOMINICAN REP. (1981)
Santo Domingo ... 1 313
Santiago 279

EL SALVADOR (1978)
San Salvador 429

GUATEMALA (1979)
Guatemala 793

HAITI (1982)
Port-au-Prince 888

HONDURAS (1981)
Tegucigalpa 485
San Pedro Sula ... 319

JAMAICA (1980)
Kingston 671

MEXICO (1979)
Mexico 14 750
Guadalajara 2 468
Netzahualcóyotl .. 2 331
Monterrey 2 019
Puebla 711
Ciudad Juárez 625
León 625
Tijuana 566
Acapulco 462
Torreón 407
Tampico 390
Chihuahua 386
Mexicali 349
San Luis Potosi ... 327
Culiacán 324
Hermosillo 319
Veracruz 307
Mérida 270
Saltillo 258
Aguascalientes ... 257
Morelia 251
Toluca 242
Cuernavaca 241
Reynosa 231
Durango 229
Nuevo Laredo 224
Jalapa 201

NICARAGUA (1981)
Managua 820

PANAMA (1981)
Panama 655

PUERTO RICO (1980)
San Juan 1 086
Ponce 253
Bayamón 209

UNITED STATES (1980)
New York 16 121
Los Angeles 11 498
Chicago 7 870
Philadelphia 5 548
San Francisco ... 5 180
Detroit 4 618
Boston 3 448
Houston 3 101
Washington 3 061
Dallas 2 975
Cleveland 2 834
Miami 2 644
St. Louis 2 356
Pittsburgh 2 264
Baltimore 2 174
Minneapolis-St. Paul . 2 114
Seattle 2 093
Atlanta 2 030
San Diego 1 817
Cincinnati 1 660
Denver 1 621
Milwaukee 1 570
Tampa 1 569
Phoenix 1 509
Kansas City 1 327
Indianapolis 1 306
Portland 1 243
Buffalo 1 243
New Orleans ... 1 187
Providence 1 096
Columbus 1 093
San Antonio ... 1 072
Sacramento 1 014
Dayton 1 014
Rochester 971
Salt Lake City ... 936
Memphis 913
Louisville 906
Nashville 851
Birmingham 847
Oklahoma 834
Greensboro 827
Norfolk 807
Albany 795
Toledo 792
Honolulu 763
Jacksonville 738
Hartford 726
Orlando 700
Tulsa 689
Syracuse 643
Scranton 640
Charlotte 637
Allentown 635
Richmond 632
Grand Rapids 602
Omaha 570
Greenville 569
West Palm Beach ... 577
Austin 537
Tucson 531
Springfield 531
Youngstown 531
Raleigh 531
Flint 522
Fresno 515

SOUTH AMERICA

ARGENTINA (1980)
Buenos Aires 9 927
Córdoba 982
Rosario 955
Mendoza 597
La Plata 560
San Miguel de
Tucuman 497
Mar del Plata 407
San Juan 290
Santa Fé 287
Salta 260
Bahia Blanca 221
Resistencia 218

BOLIVIA (1982)
La Paz 881
Santa Cruz 377
Cochabamba 282

BRAZIL (1980)
São Paulo 8 732
Rio de Janeiro ... 5 539
Belo Horizonte ... 1 937
Salvador 1 502
Recife 1 433
Fortaleza 1 307
Brasilia 1 306
Pôrto Alegre ... 1 221
Nova Iguaçu ... 1 184
Curitiba 943
Belém 934
Goiánia 680
Duque de Caxias .. 666
São Gonçalo 660
Santo André 634
Campinas 587
Osasco 492
Manaus 483
Santos 453
São João de Meriti . 442
Niterói 433
São Luis 405
Guarulhos 404
Natal 401
Maceió 390
Campos 357
Londrina 349
Teresina 349
São Bernardo do
Campo 348
Juiz de Fora 334
João Pessoa 332
Jaboatao 321
Ribeirão Preto 309
Olinda 308
Feira de Santana .. 274
Aracaju 273
Campina Grande .. 266
Pelotas 256

CHILE (1983)
Santiago 4 132
Viña del Mar 299
Valparaiso 268
Talcahuano 213
Concepción 210

COLOMBIA (1978)
Bogotá 4 056
Medellin 1 507
Cali 1 316
Barranquilla 855
Cartagena 435
Bucaramanga 402
Cucuta 435
Ibagué 264
Pereira 252
Manizales 246

ECUADOR (1982)
Guayaquil 1 279
Quito 881

PARAGUAY (1978)
Asunción 602

PERU (1981)
Lima 4 601
Arequipa 447
Callao 441
Trujillo 355
Chiclayo 280
Chimbote 216

URUGUAY (1981)
Montevideo 1 173

VENEZUELA (1980)
Caracas 2 944
Maracaibo 901
Valencia 506
Barquisimento 489
Maracay 344
Barcelona-Puerto
La Cruz 275
San Cristóbal 272
Departamento Vargas . 246
Ciudad Guayana ... 206

1:105 000 000

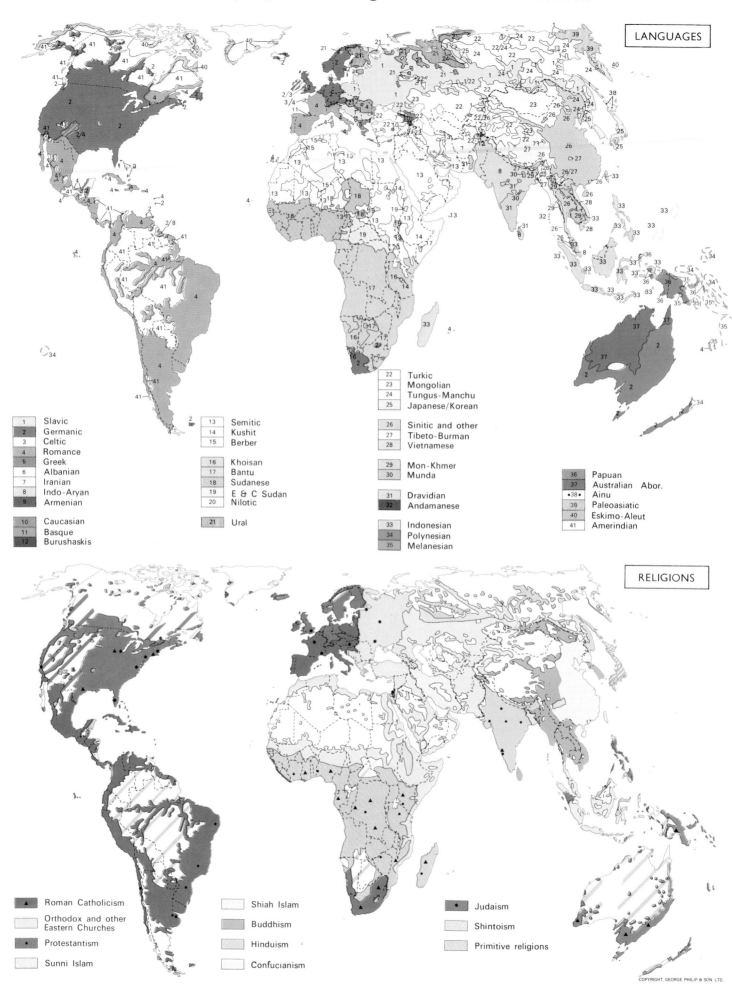

LANGUAGES

22	Turkic
23	Mongolian
24	Tungus-Manchu
25	Japanese/Korean

26	Sinitic and other
27	Tibeto-Burman
28	Vietnamese

29	Mon-Khmer
30	Munda

31	Dravidian
32	Andamanese

33	Indonesian
34	Polynesian
35	Melanesian

1	Slavic
2	Germanic
3	Celtic
4	Romance
5	Greek
6	Albanian
7	Iranian
8	Indo-Aryan
9	Armenian

10	Caucasian
11	Basque
12	Burushaskis

13	Semitic
14	Kushit
15	Berber

16	Khoisan
17	Bantu
18	Sudanese
19	E & C Sudan
20	Nilotic

21	Ural

36	Papuan
37	Australian Abor.
•38•	Ainu
39	Paleoasiatic
40	Eskimo-Aleut
41	Amerindian

RELIGIONS

▲	Roman Catholicism
	Orthodox and other Eastern Churches
•	Protestantism
	Sunni Islam

	Shiah Islam
	Buddhism
	Hinduism
	Confucianism

✳	Judaism
	Shintoism
	Primitive religions

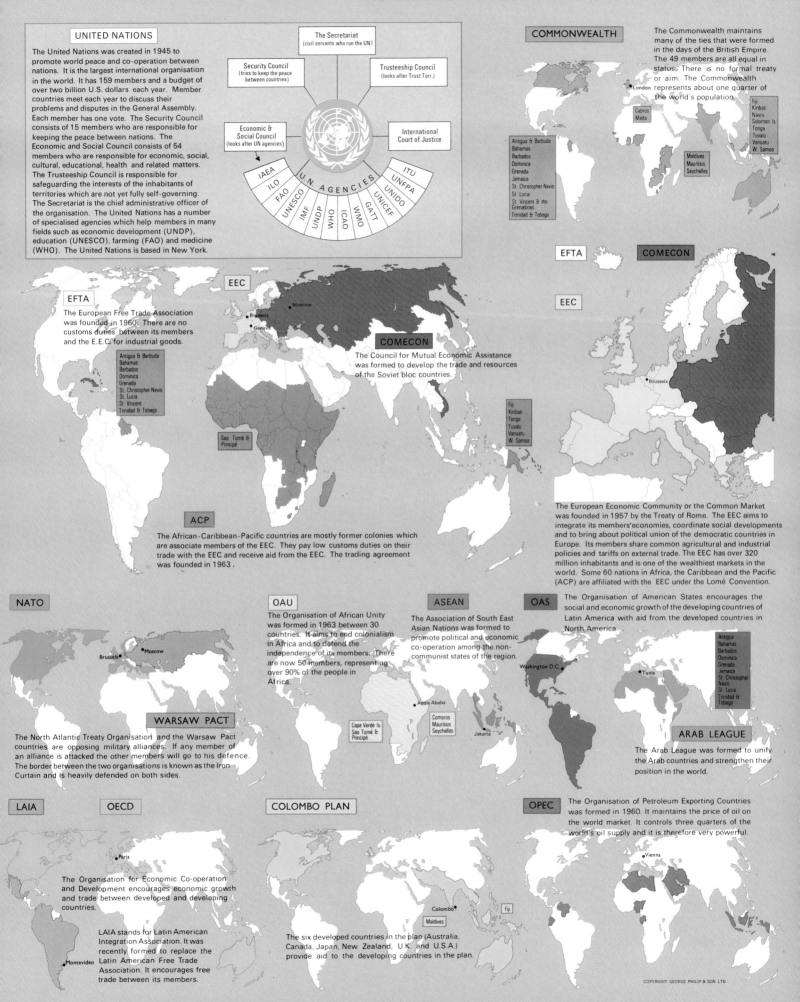

UNITED NATIONS

The United Nations was created in 1945 to promote world peace and co-operation between nations. It is the largest international organisation in the world. It has 159 members and a budget of over two billion U.S. dollars each year. Member countries meet each year to discuss their problems and disputes in the General Assembly. Each member has one vote. The Security Council consists of 15 members who are responsible for keeping the peace between nations. The Economic and Social Council consists of 54 members who are responsible for economic, social, cultural, educational, health and related matters. The Trusteeship Council is responsible for safeguarding the interests of the inhabitants of territories which are not yet fully self-governing. The Secretariat is the chief administrative officer of the organisation. The United Nations has a number of specialised agencies which help members in many fields such as economic development (UNDP), education (UNESCO), farming (FAO) and medicine (WHO). The United Nations is based in New York.

The Secretariat (civil servants who run the UN)

Security Council (tries to keep the peace between countries)

Trusteeship Council (looks after Trust Terr.)

Economic & Social Council (looks after UN agencies)

International Court of Justice

U.N. AGENCIES: IAEA, ILO, FAO, UNESCO, IMF, UNDP, OHM, ICAO, WMO, GATT, UNICEF, UNIDO, UNFPA, ITU

COMMONWEALTH

The Commonwealth maintains many of the ties that were formed in the days of the British Empire. The 49 members are all equal in status. There is no formal treaty or aim. The Commonwealth represents about one quarter of the world's population.

London

Cyprus, Malta

Fiji, Kiribati, Nauru, Solomon Is., Tonga, Tuvalu, Vanuatu, W. Samoa

Maldives, Mauritius, Seychelles

Antigua & Barbuda, Bahamas, Barbados, Dominica, Grenada, Jamaica, St. Christopher-Nevis, St. Lucia, St. Vincent & the Grenadines, Trinidad & Tobago

EFTA

The European Free Trade Association was founded in 1960. There are no customs duties between its members and the E.E.C. for industrial goods.

EEC

Moscow, Brussels, Geneva

Antigua & Barbuda, Bahamas, Barbados, Dominica, Grenada, St. Christopher-Nevis, St. Lucia, St. Vincent, Trinidad & Tobago

Sao Tomé & Principe

COMECON

The Council for Mutual Economic Assistance was formed to develop the trade and resources of the Soviet bloc countries.

EFTA

COMECON

EEC

Brussels

Fiji, Kiribati, Tonga, Tuvalu, Vanuatu, W. Samoa

The European Economic Community or the Common Market was founded in 1957 by the Treaty of Rome. The EEC aims to integrate its members' economies, coordinate social developments and to bring about political union of the democratic countries in Europe. Its members share common agricultural and industrial policies and tariffs on external trade. The EEC has over 320 million inhabitants and is one of the wealthiest markets in the world. Some 60 nations in Africa, the Caribbean and the Pacific (ACP) are affiliated with the EEC under the Lomé Convention.

ACP

The African-Caribbean-Pacific countries are mostly former colonies which are associate members of the EEC. They pay low customs duties on their trade with the EEC and receive aid from the EEC. The trading agreement was founded in 1963.

NATO

WARSAW PACT

The North Atlantic Treaty Organisation and the Warsaw Pact countries are opposing military alliances. If any member of an alliance is attacked the other members will go to his defence. The border between the two organisations is known as the Iron Curtain and is heavily defended on both sides.

Brussels, Moscow

OAU

The Organisation of African Unity was formed in 1963 between 30 countries. It aims to end colonialism in Africa and to defend the independence of its members. There are now 50 members, representing over 90% of the people in Africa.

Addis Ababa

Cape Verde Is., Sao Tomé & Principe

Comoros, Mauritius, Seychelles

ASEAN

The Association of South East Asian Nations was formed to promote political and economic co-operation among the non-communist states of the region.

Jakarta

OAS

The Organisation of American States encourages the social and economic growth of the developing countries of Latin America with aid from the developed countries in North America.

Washington D.C., Tunis

Antigua, Bahamas, Barbados, Dominica, Grenada, Jamaica, St. Christopher Nevis, St. Lucia, Trinidad & Tobago

ARAB LEAGUE

The Arab League was formed to unify the Arab countries and strengthen their position in the world.

LAIA

LAIA stands for Latin American Integration Association. It was recently formed to replace the Latin American Free Trade Association. It encourages free trade between its members.

Montevideo

OECD

The Organisation for Economic Co-operation and Development encourages economic growth and trade between developed and developing countries.

Paris

COLOMBO PLAN

The six developed countries in the plan (Australia, Canada, Japan, New Zealand, U.K. and U.S.A.) provide aid to the developing countries in the plan.

Colombo, Fiji, Maldives

OPEC

The Organisation of Petroleum Exporting Countries was formed in 1960. It maintains the price of oil on the world market. It controls three quarters of the world's oil supply and it is therefore very powerful.

Vienna

NATURAL INCREASE
The birth rates and death rates are the number of births and deaths per 1000 population each year.

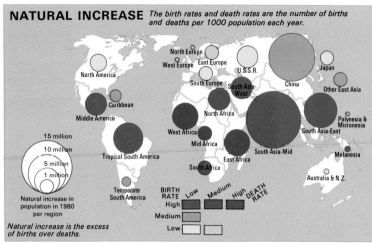

Natural increase in population in 1980 per region

15 million
10 million
5 million
1 million

Natural increase is the excess of births over deaths.

BIRTH RATE	Low	Medium	High	DEATH RATE
High				
Medium				
Low				

FAMILY SIZE
Family size is the total number of children an average woman will bear in her lifetime, for each region. In 1980 the world average was 3.6 children; in 2000 it is expected to be 2.8 children.

Family Size 1980
no. of children

4·2 Expected family size 2000

AGE DISTRIBUTION PYRAMIDS

The bars represent the percentage of the population in the age group shown. The blue bars represent the males, the red bars the females. The developing countries such as India tend to have a higher proportion of young people than the developed countries such as Canada.

See page 8 for age distribution pyramid of the U.K.

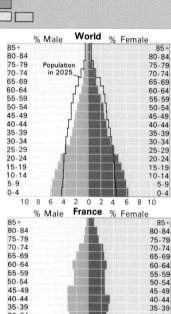

World
Population in 2025

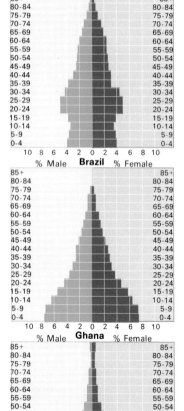

Canada

Brazil

Ghana

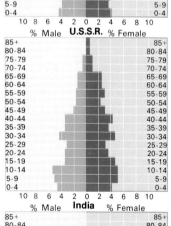

France

U.S.S.R.

India

LIFE EXPECTANCY
Life expectancy is the average number of years a newly-born baby can expect to live. The world average has risen from 47 years in 1950 to 58 years in 1980, and is expected to be 64 years in 2000.

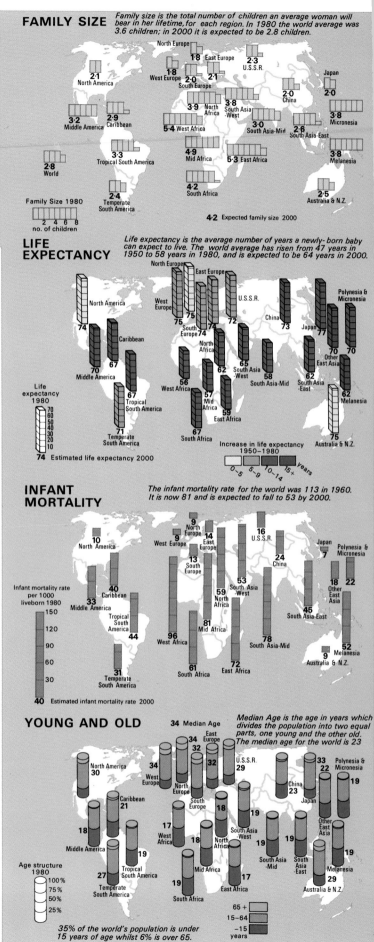

Life expectancy 1980

74 Estimated life expectancy 2000

Increase in life expectancy 1950–1980
0–5   5–9   10–14   15+   years

INFANT MORTALITY
The infant mortality rate for the world was 113 in 1960. It is now 81 and is expected to fall to 53 by 2000.

Infant mortality rate per 1000 liveborn 1980
150
120
90
60
30

40 Estimated infant mortality rate 2000

YOUNG AND OLD
34 Median Age

Median Age is the age in years which divides the population into two equal parts, one young and the other old. The median age for the world is 23

Age structure 1980
100%
75%
50%
25%

65 +
15–64
–15
years

35% of the world's population is under 15 years of age whilst 6% is over 65.

See page 125 for maps of Population Growth and Urbanisation

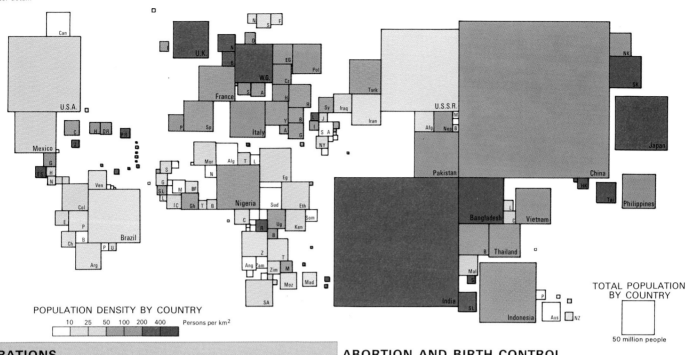

POPULATION BY COUNTRY

See map on pages 116-117 for greater detail.

The most populous country (China) contains a quarter of the world's population. The four most populous countries (China, India, U.S.S.R., and U.S.A.) contain half, and the first eighteen (all those countries named in larger type on the map) contain over three-quarters of the world's population. The remaining 150 countries contain only one quarter.

POPULATION DENSITY BY COUNTRY

| 10 | 25 | 50 | 100 | 200 | 400 | Persons per km² |

TOTAL POPULATION BY COUNTRY

50 million people

MIGRATIONS

← Direction of migrations

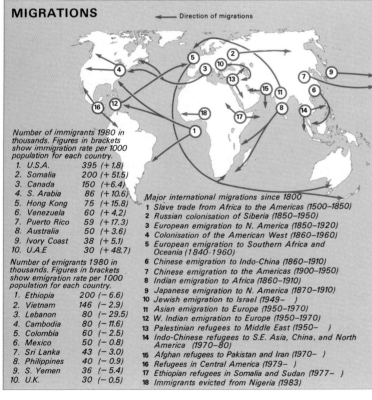

Number of immigrants 1980 in thousands. Figures in brackets show immigration rate per 1000 population for each country.

1. U.S.A.   395 (+1.8)
2. Somalia   200 (+51.5)
3. Canada   150 (+6.4)
4. S. Arabia   86 (+10.6)
5. Hong Kong   75 (+15.8)
6. Venezuela   60 (+4.2)
7. Puerto Rico   59 (+17.3)
8. Australia   50 (+3.6)
9. Ivory Coast   38 (+5.1)
10. U.A.E   30 (+48.7)

Number of emigrants 1980 in thousands. Figures in brackets show emigration rate per 1000 population for each country.

1. Ethiopia   200 (−6.6)
2. Vietnam   146 (−2.9)
3. Lebanon   80 (−29.5)
4. Cambodia   80 (−11.6)
5. Colombia   60 (−2.5)
6. Mexico   50 (−0.8)
7. Sri Lanka   43 (−3.0)
8. Philippines   40 (−0.9)
9. S. Yemen   36 (−5.4)
10. U.K.   30 (−0.5)

Major international migrations since 1800
1. Slave trade from Africa to the Americas (1500–1850)
2. Russian colonisation of Siberia (1850–1950)
3. European emigration to N. America (1850–1920)
4. Colonisation of the American West (1860–1960)
5. European emigration to Southern Africa and Oceania (1840–1960)
6. Chinese emigration to Indo-China (1860–1910)
7. Chinese emigration to the Americas (1900–1950)
8. Indian emigration to Africa (1860–1910)
9. Japanese emigration to N. America (1870–1910)
10. Jewish emigration to Israel (1949–)
11. Asian emigration to Europe (1950–1970)
12. W. Indian emigration to Europe (1950–1970)
13. Palestinian refugees to Middle East (1950–)
14. Indo-Chinese refugees to S.E. Asia, China, and North America (1970–80)
15. Afghan refugees to Pakistan and Iran (1970–)
16. Refugees in Central America (1979–)
17. Ethiopian refugees in Somalia and Sudan (1977–)
18. Immigrants evicted from Nigeria (1983)

Until comparatively recently there was little increase in the population of the world. It is thought there were about 200 million in 600 B.C., 300 million in 1000 A.D. and 500 million by 1600 A.D.. This diagram shows how the world's population has increased since then at an ever increasing rate. 90% of this increase has been in the less developed regions The world population of 1950 will have doubled by 1990 and if present trends continue it will have trebled by 2020.

POPULATION INCREASE SINCE 1650

ABORTION AND BIRTH CONTROL

Poland 75%
France 79%
China 69%
U.S.A. 65%
Mexico 39%
Egypt 24%
India 28%
Indonesia 53%
Nigeria 6%

Status of Abortion
- Abortion legal
- Legal only for certain medical or juridical reasons
- Abortions illegal
- No data

Percentage of married women using contraception, for selected countries.

Legally induced abortions per 1000 live births. Total abortions in thousands are in brackets.

Bulgaria	1216 (152)	Canada	175 (66)
U.S.A.	347 (1 158)	New Zealand	133 (7)
France	207 (171)	Tunisia	77 (16)
Poland	192 (141)	India	27 (346)
Great Britain	189 (137)		

POPULATION IN 2000 A.D.

Percentage of world total is given in brackets.

World	6 119		
South Asia	2 075 (34%)	U.S.S.R.	310 (5%)
East Asia	1 475 (24%)	Europe	512 (8.5%)
Oceania	30 (0.5%)		
Africa	853 (14%)		
South America	566 (9%)		
N. America	299 (5%)		

6000 m
5000 m
4000 m
3000 m
2000 m
1000 m

South Asia
Oceania
Africa
East Asia
South America
North America

Asia pre 1925
U.S.S.R.
Europe pre 1925
Europe

1700 1750 1800 1850 1900 1925 1950 1975 2000

NATURAL DISASTERS

EARTHQUAKES AND VOLCANOES

○ Major earthquakes with dates

▲ Major volcanoes

▧ Earthquake zones (land and sea)

STORMS AND FLOODS

✻ Major storms and floods with dates

⇨ Paths of winter blizzards

⇨ Paths of tropical storms

▨ Areas liable to flood

PESTS

⋯ Locust invasion areas

▨ Main tsetse fly areas

MAJOR FAMINES

◉ Sahel 1973

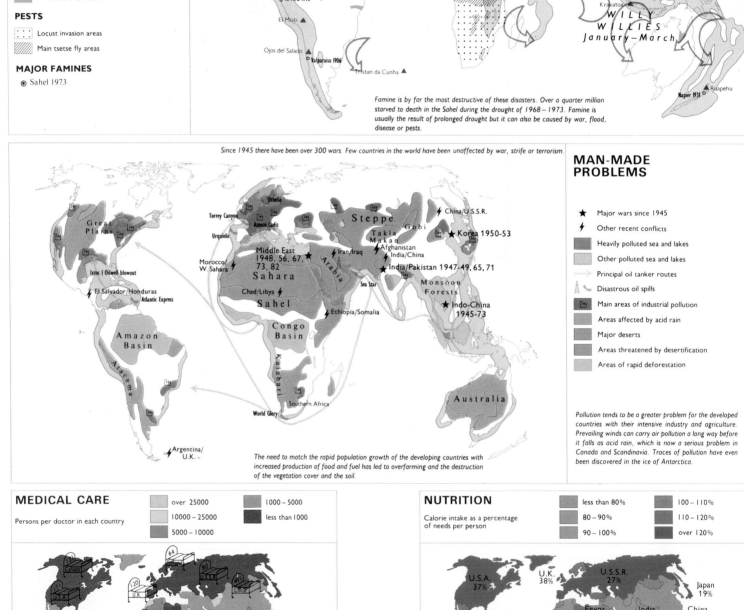

BLIZZARDS *November–March*

Anchorage 1964 ○ ▲ Katmai · Hekla · Klyuchevsk · Heimaey · Ireland 1845 ◉ · ▲ Rainier · St. Helens · ○ San Francisco 1906 · Ukraine 1920 ◉ · Northern China 1939 · Hokkaido 1730 · Tashkent 1966 · Tangshan 1976 · China 1876 · Fujiyama · Azores ▲ · Lisbon 1755 ○ · ▲ Vesuvius · Nan Shan 1927 · Shensi 1556 · Yokohama 1923 · Etna · Erzincan 1939 · Kansu 1920, 32 · Japan 1959 · El Asnam 1980 · Messina 1908 · Quetta 1935 · Hwang-ho 1087, 1931 · Yangtze 1911 · Tenerife ▲ · India 1837, 63, 1900 · Calcutta 1737 · Bangladesh 1960, 63, 65, 70, 85 · **HURRICANES** *August–October* · Central Mexico 1985 ✻ · W. Indies 1928, 63 ✻ · Sahel 1973 ◉ · Haiphong 1881 · ▲ Mt. Pelée · Tigre 1984 ◉ · Tai · Paricutin ▲ ✻ El Chichonal · Horn of Africa 1980 ◉ · Philippines 1970 ✻ · **TYPHOONS** *July–October* · Central America 1966, 74 · ▲ La Soufrière · **CYCLONES** *June–November* · Dempo · ▲ Purace · Nevado del Ruiz · Mt. Cameroon ▲ · ▲ Kilimanjaro · Krakatoa ▲ · Galapagos ▲ · ▲ Ecuador and N. Peru 1868 · **WILLY WILLIES** *January–March* · Cotopaxi ▲ · ▲ N. Peru 1970 · ○ N.E. Brazil 1877 · ▲ El Misti · Ojos del Salado ▲ · ▲ Ruapehu · Napier 1931 ✻ · Valparaiso 1906 ○ · Tristan da Cunha ▲

Famine is by far the most destructive of these disasters. Over a quarter million starved to death in the Sahel during the drought of 1968–1973. Famine is usually the result of prolonged drought but it can also be caused by war, flood, disease or pests.

Since 1945 there have been over 300 wars. Few countries in the world have been unaffected by war, strife or terrorism.

MAN-MADE PROBLEMS

★ Major wars since 1945

⚡ Other recent conflicts

▨ Heavily polluted sea and lakes

▨ Other polluted sea and lakes

→ Principal oil tanker routes

⛏ Disastrous oil spills

▨ Main areas of industrial pollution

▨ Areas affected by acid rain

▨ Major deserts

▨ Areas threatened by desertification

▨ Areas of rapid deforestation

Great Plains · Othello · Torrey Canyon · Amoco Cadiz · China/U.S.S.R. · **Steppe** · Takla Makan · Gobi · Urquiola · Korea 1950-53 · Ixtoc I Oilwell blowout · Middle East 1948, 56, 67, 73, 82 · Iran/Iraq · Afghanistan · India/China · Morocco/W. Sahara · **Sahara** · Arabia · India/Pakistan 1947-49, 65, 71 · El Salvador/Honduras · Atlantic Express · Sea Star · **Monsoon Forests** · Amazon Basin · Chad/Libya ⚡ · **Sahel** · Ethiopia/Somalia · Indo-China 1945-73 · Atacama · Congo Basin · Kalahari · Australia · World Glory · Southern Africa · Argentina/U.K.

Pollution tends to be a greater problem for the developed countries with their intensive industry and agriculture. Prevailing winds can carry air pollution a long way before it falls as acid rain, which is now a serious problem in Canada and Scandinavia. Traces of pollution have even been discovered in the ice of Antarctica.

The need to match the rapid population growth of the developing countries with increased production of food and fuel has led to overfarming and the destruction of the vegetation cover and the soil.

MEDICAL CARE

Persons per doctor in each country

▨ over 25000 · ▨ 1000 – 5000

▨ 10000 – 25000 · ▨ less than 1000

▨ 5000 – 10000

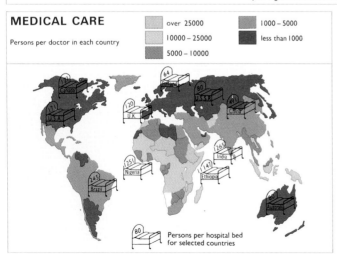

Canada 64 · Japan 80 · U.S.S.R. · U.K. 120 · China 41 · U.S.A. 11 · India 263 · Nigeria 125 · Ethiopia 147 · Brazil 245 · Australia 80

🛏 80 | Persons per hospital bed for selected countries

NUTRITION

Calorie intake as a percentage of needs per person

▨ less than 80% · ▨ 100 – 110%

▨ 80 – 90% · ▨ 110 – 120%

▨ 90 – 100% · ▨ over 120%

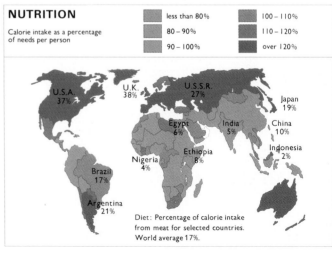

U.S.A. 37% · U.K. 38% · U.S.S.R. 27% · Japan 19% · Egypt 6% · India 5% · China 10% · Nigeria 4% · Ethiopia 8% · Indonesia 2% · Brazil 17% · Argentina 21%

Diet: Percentage of calorie intake from meat for selected countries. World average 17%.

STANDARDS OF LIVING

THE RICH

Countries with more than four times the world's average income

Countries with more than twice the world's average income

Countries with incomes just above the world's average

THE POOR

Countries with incomes just below the world's average

Countries with less than half of the world's average income

Countries with less than one quarter of the world's average income

Data not available

The world's average income is just under 2200 US$ per annum. The richest country on a per capita basis is Kuwait with an income over 200 times that of the poorest country, Mali.

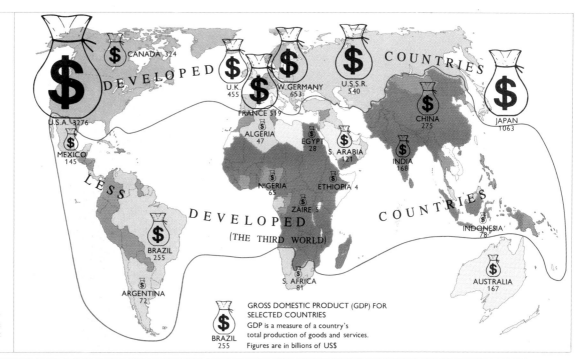

GROSS DOMESTIC PRODUCT (GDP) FOR SELECTED COUNTRIES

GDP is a measure of a country's total production of goods and services.

Figures are in billions of US$

BRAZIL 255

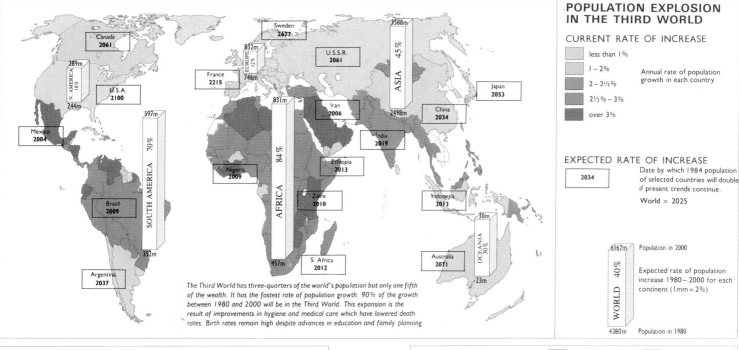

POPULATION EXPLOSION IN THE THIRD WORLD

CURRENT RATE OF INCREASE

less than 1%

1 – 2%

2 – 2½%

2½% – 3%

over 3%

Annual rate of population growth in each country

EXPECTED RATE OF INCREASE

2034

Date by which 1984 population of selected countries will double if present trends continue.

World = 2025

6167m   Population in 2000

WORLD 40%   Expected rate of population increase 1980 – 2000 for each continent (1mm = 2%)

4380m   Population in 1980

The Third World has three-quarters of the world's population but only one fifth of the wealth. It has the fastest rate of population growth. 90% of the growth between 1980 and 2000 will be in the Third World. This expansion is the result of improvements in hygiene and medical care which have lowered death rates. Birth rates remain high despite advances in education and family planning

---

URBANISATION

Percentage of population living in towns and cities in each country

75 – 100%   25 – 50%

50 – 75%   0 – 25%

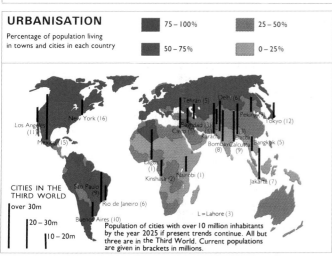

CITIES IN THE THIRD WORLD

over 30m

20 – 30m

10 – 20m

Population of cities with over 10 million inhabitants by the year 2025 if present trends continue. All but three are in the Third World. Current populations are given in brackets in millions.

L = Lahore (3)

ILLITERACY

Percentage of population in each country who are illiterate

80 – 100%   20 – 40%

60 – 80%   0 – 20%

40 – 60%

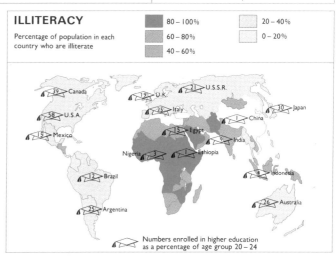

Numbers enrolled in higher education as a percentage of age group 20 – 24

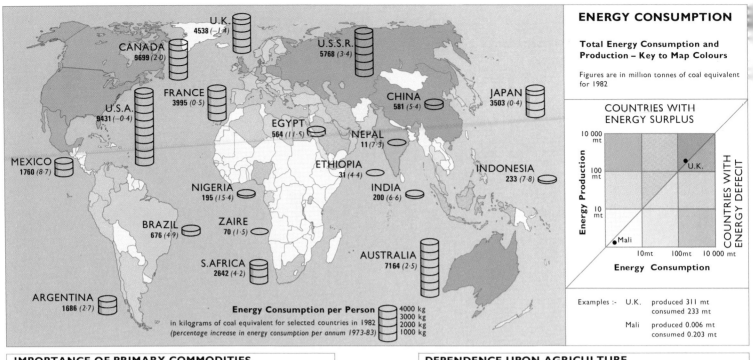

ENERGY CONSUMPTION

Total Energy Consumption and Production – Key to Map Colours

Figures are in million tonnes of coal equivalent for 1982

COUNTRIES WITH ENERGY SURPLUS

Examples :- U.K. produced 311 mt
consumed 233 mt

Mali produced 0.006 mt
consumed 0.203 mt

Energy Consumption per Person
in kilograms of coal equivalent for selected countries in 1982
(percentage increase in energy consumption per annum 1973-83)

4000 kg
3000 kg
2000 kg
1000 kg

IMPORTANCE OF PRIMARY COMMODITIES

Primary commodities as a percentage of total exports. Primary commodities are raw materials such as minerals, fuel, food and timber.

| 0-25% | 25-50% | 50-75% | 75-100% |

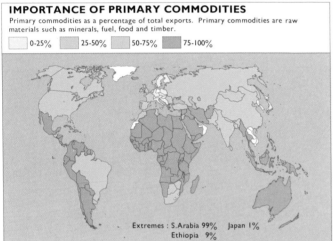

Extremes : S.Arabia 99%   Japan 1%
Ethiopia 9%

DEPENDENCE UPON AGRICULTURE

Value of agriculture as a percentage of G.D.P. (Gross Domestic Product)

| 0-10% | 10-20% | 20-30% | 30-40% | 40-50% | over 50% |

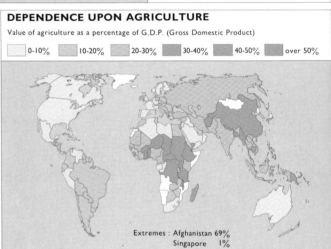

Extremes : Afghanistan 69%
Singapore 1%

FOOD PRODUCTION

Food production per person

Percentage change from 1974-6 to 1981-3 for each country

INCREASE
over 20%
15-20%
10-15%
5-10%
0-5%

DECREASE
0-5%
5-10%
10-15%
15-20%
over 20%

TRADE IN FOOD

Cereal imports per person for selected countries in 1983 (figures in kilograms)

Net exporters of food (value of food exports greater than food imports)

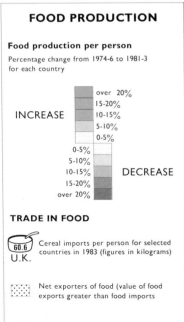

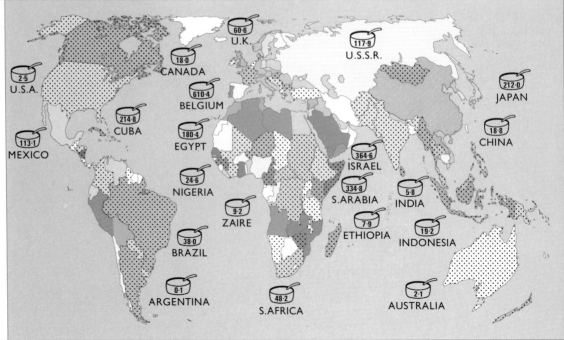

COPYRIGHT. GEORGE PHILIP & SON, LTD

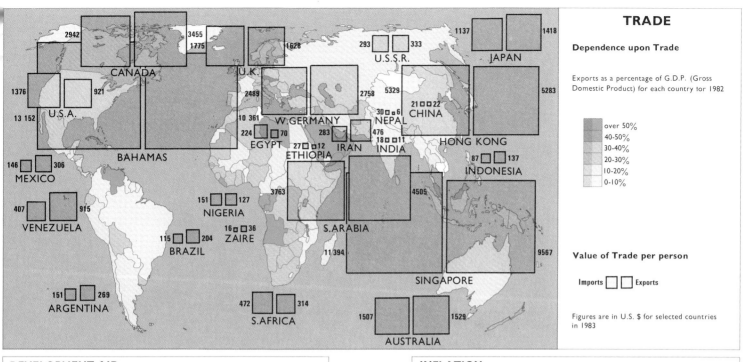

TRADE

Dependence upon Trade

Exports as a percentage of G.D.P. (Gross Domestic Product) for each country for 1982

over 50%
40-50%
30-40%
20-30%
10-20%
0-10%

Value of Trade per person

Imports ☐ ☐ Exports

Figures are in U.S. $ for selected countries in 1983

CANADA 2942 3455 1775 1628
U.K. 293 333 U.S.S.R. 1137 1418 JAPAN
U.S.A. 1376 921 13 152
2489 W.GERMANY 2758 5329 5283
10 361 224 ☐ 70 EGYPT 283 CHINA 21 ☐ 22 HONG KONG
ETHIOPIA 27 ☐ 12 30 ☐ 6 NEPAL
IRAN 476 18 ☐ 11 INDIA
BAHAMAS
MEXICO 146 306
VENEZUELA 407 915
NIGERIA 151 127 S.ARABIA 4505 87 ☐ 137 INDONESIA
ZAIRE 115 204 3763
BRAZIL 16 ☐ 36 11 394 9567 SINGAPORE
ARGENTINA 151 269
S.AFRICA 472 314
AUSTRALIA 1507 1529

DEVELOPMENT AID

Development aid received per person in U.S. $, 1979-81 average

0-10$ 10-20$ 20-50$ 50-100$ over 100$

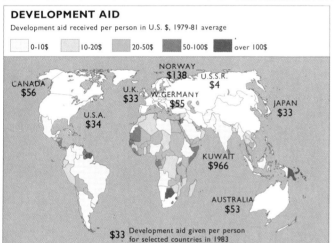

CANADA $56
U.K. $33
U.S.A. $34
NORWAY $138
W.GERMANY $55
U.S.S.R. $4
JAPAN $33
KUWAIT $966
AUSTRALIA $53

$33 Development aid given per person for selected countries in 1983

INFLATION

Annual average rate of increase 1973-83

0-5% 5-10% 10-15% 15-20% 20-50% 50-100% over 100%

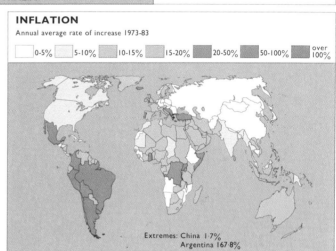

Extremes: China 1·7%
Argentina 167·8%

EMPLOYMENT

Employment by Sector in 1980
Key to Map Colours

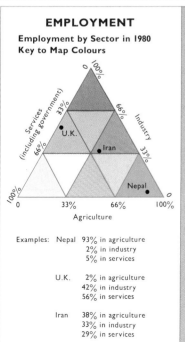

Services (including government)
Industry
Agriculture
U.K.
Iran
Nepal

Examples: Nepal 93% in agriculture
2% in industry
5% in services

U.K. 2% in agriculture
42% in industry
56% in services

Iran 38% in agriculture
33% in industry
29% in services

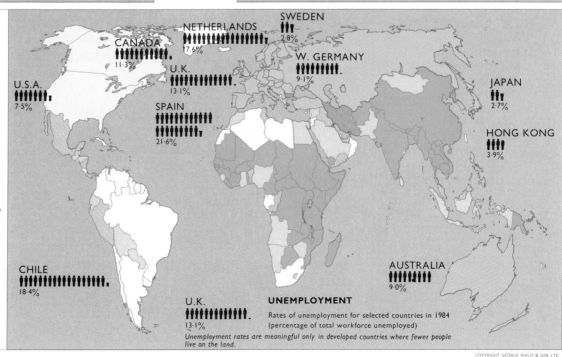

NETHERLANDS 7·6%
SWEDEN 2·8%
CANADA 11·3%
U.K. 13·1%
W. GERMANY 9·1%
U.S.A. 7·5%
SPAIN 21·6%
JAPAN 2·7%
HONG KONG 3·9%
CHILE 18·4%
AUSTRALIA 9·0%
U.K. 13·1%

UNEMPLOYMENT

Rates of unemployment for selected countries in 1984 (percentage of total workforce unemployed)

Unemployment rates are meaningful only in developed countries where fewer people live on the land.

Polar Routes

A

Pacific
Routes

Pacific
Routes

Principal Air Routes
Distances in km

Queen Elizabeth Is.

Victoria I.

Baffin I.

GREENLAND

ICELAND

Anchorage

Churchill

Hudson
Bay

Newfoundland

UNITED
KINGDOM Glasgow
IRELAND London

Vancouver

Edmonton

C   A   N   A   D   A

Calgary

Seattle

Winnipeg

Quebec

Montreal

Toronto

Chicago

Detroit

Boston

FRANCE

San Francisco

Denver

St. Louis

New York

Washington

PORTUGAL Madrid

Lisbon   SPAIN

UNITED   STATES

Azores

Los Angeles

Dallas

New Orleans

Casablanca MOROCCO

Houston

Canary Is.

ALG

Tropic of Cancer

MEXICO

Gulf of
Mexico

Miami

ATLANTIC

Hawaiian
Islands
(U.S.)

Mexico

Havana   CUBA

BAHAMAS

W. SAHARA

MAURITANIA

MAL

JAMAICA HAITI

West Indies

DOMINICAN REP.

PUERTO

BELIZE

RICO

GUATEMALA

HONDURAS

Caribbean

C. Verde Is.

SENEGAL

EL SALVADOR

Sea

GAMBIA

NICARAGUA

GUINEA-BISSAU

GUINEA

P   A   C   I   F   I   C

COSTA
RICA

PANAMA

Caracas

VENEZUELA

SIERRA
LEONE

IVORY
COAST

GHANA

Palmyra Is.
(U.S.)

Bogota

GUYANA

LIBERIA

Tabuaeran

COLOMBIA

SURINAM

FR.
GUIANA

OCEAN

Kiritimati

Equator

Quito

ECUADOR

Manaus

Belém

Galapagos Is.
(Ecuador)

Ascension
(Br.)

Phoenix Is.

O   C   E   A   N

B   R   A   Z   I   L

Recife

Tokelau Is.
(N.Z.)

PERU

St. Helena
(Br.)

Samoan Is.

Lima

Brasilia

Salvador

Tonga

Society Is.
(Fr.)

Tuamotu
Archipelago
(Fr.)

La Paz

BOLIVIA

Rio de Janeiro

PARAGUAY

Tubuai Is.
(Fr.)

Asunción

São Paulo

Tropic of Capricorn

Kermadec Is.
(N.Z.)

Easter I.

CHILE

ARGENTINA

URUGUAY

Montevideo

Santiago

Buenos
Aires

Tristan da
Cunha
(Br.)

Chatham Is.
(N.Z.)

Falkland Is.

S. Georgia

Tierra del Fuego

FALKLAND   IS.   DEPENDENCIES(Br.)

ROSS DEPENDENCY

BRITISH ANTARCTIC TERRITORY

NORWEG

West from Greenwich

Principal Sea Routes
Distances in km

ARCTIC OCEAN

Svalbard

Novaya Zemlya

NORWAY SWEDEN FINLAND

Arkhangelsk

Oslo Helsinki Leningrad UNION OF SOVIET SOCIALIST REPUBLICS Bering Sea

DEN. Stockholm

Copenhagen Moscow Sverdlovsk Novosibirsk

Brussels POLAND Warsaw

GERMANY Berlin Kiev Irkutsk Vladivostok Sapporo

Vienna Ulan Bator N.

Paris ITALY ROMANIA Bucharest MONGOLIA Peking KOREA JAPAN Tokyo

Rome YUGOSLAVIA Istanbul Baku Tashkent CHINA Dalian S. Osaka

BULGARIA GREECE TURKEY Tehran AFGHANISTAN Pusan Shanghai

Tunis Athens SYRIA Baghdad Kabul Islamabad Chungking

Algiers Mediterranean Sea Tripoli ISRAEL IRAQ IRAN Lahore TAIWAN

ERIA JORDAN KUWAIT Alexandria Cairo PAKISTAN NEPAL Delhi BANGLA- Dacca Hanoi Hong Kong

LIBYA EGYPT BAHRAIN Karachi DESH Calcutta BURMA

SAUDI U.A.E. INDIA Ahmadabad LAOS Manila

NIGER CHAD Mecca OMAN Bombay Madras Rangoon THAILAND VIETNAM PHILIPPINES

Niamey ARABIA Red Sea Bay of Bangkok CAM- BODIA

NIGERIA Khartoum YEMEN SOUTH Arabian Bengal Phnom Ho Chi Minh

Kano SUDAN YEMEN Sea Madras Penh City

Lagos Ndjamena DJIB. Addis Ababa SOMALI REP. Colombo SRI LANKA MALAYSIA BRUNEI

CAMEROON CENTRAL AFRICAN REPUBLIC ETHIOPIA Kuala Lumpur

EQUATORIAL GUINEA Douala UGANDA Mogadishu Maldives Singapore Borneo

GABON CONGO ZAIRE KENYA Nairobi INDIAN Padang Sumatra INDONESIA

RWANDA Seychelles

CABINDA BURUNDI Mombasa

Kinshasa TANZANIA Dar-es-Salaam OCEAN Jakarta Surabaya

Luanda

ANGOLA ZAMBIA

NAMIBIA MALAWI MOZAMBIQUE Darwin

Harare Antananarivo Coral

BOTSWANA ZIMBABWE MADAGASCAR Mauritius Sea

Johannesburg SWAZ. Alice Springs

SOUTH LES. AUSTRALIA

Cape Town AFRICA Durban Perth

Crozet Is. (Fr.) Adelaide Sydney

Kerguelen Is. (Fr.) Canberra Auckland

Melbourne NEW

Tasmania ZEALAND

Hobart Christchurch

Dunedin

SOUTHERN OCEAN

AN DEPENDENCY AUSTRALIAN DEPENDENCY ADELIE LAND

East from Greenwich

Copyright. George Philip & Son, Ltd.

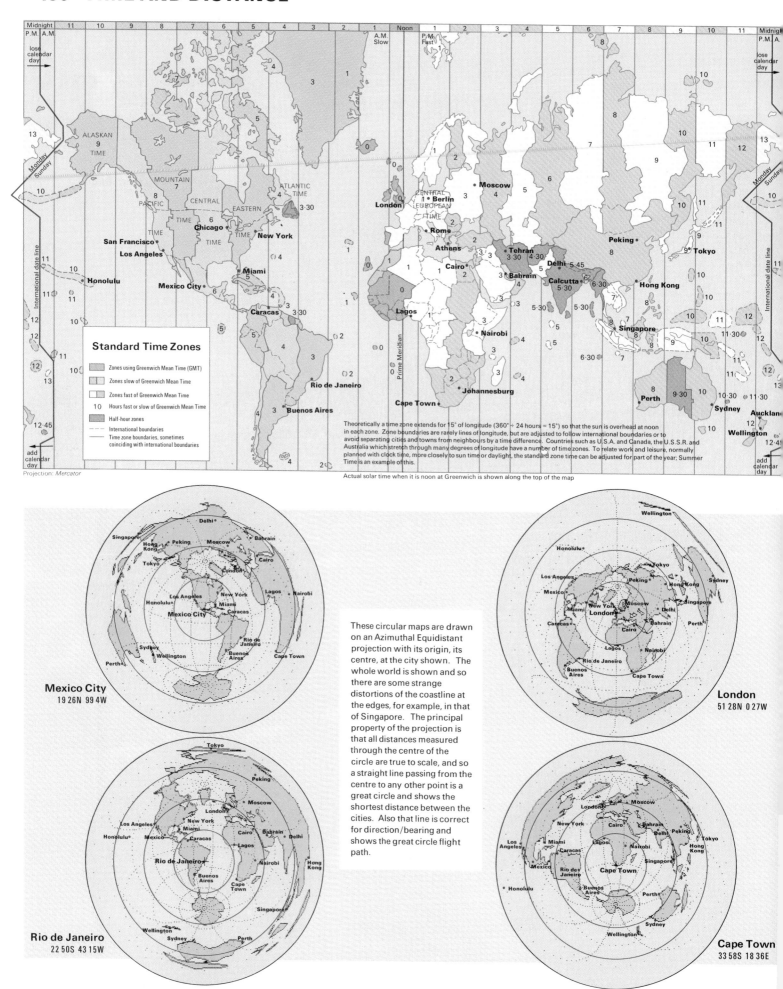

Projection: *Mercator*

Theoretically a time zone extends for 15° of longitude (360° ÷ 24 hours = 15°) so that the sun is overhead at noon in each zone. Zone boundaries are rarely lines of longitude, but are adjusted to follow international boundaries or to avoid separating cities and towns from neighbours by a time difference. Countries such as U.S.A. and Canada, the U.S.S.R. and Australia which stretch through many degrees of longitude have a number of time zones. To relate work and leisure, normally planned with clock time, more closely to sun time or daylight, the standard zone time can be adjusted for part of the year; Summer Time is an example of this.

Actual solar time when it is noon at Greenwich is shown along the top of the map

Standard Time Zones

Zones using Greenwich Mean Time (GMT)

Zones slow of Greenwich Mean Time

Zones fast of Greenwich Mean Time

10   Hours fast or slow of Greenwich Mean Time

Half-hour zones

--- International boundaries

— Time zone boundaries, sometimes coinciding with international boundaries

Mexico City
19 26N 99 4W

London
51 28N 0 27W

Rio de Janeiro
22 50S 43 15W

Cape Town
33 58S 18 36E

These circular maps are drawn on an Azimuthal Equidistant projection with its origin, its centre, at the city shown. The whole world is shown and so there are some strange distortions of the coastline at the edges, for example, in that of Singapore. The principal property of the projection is that all distances measured through the centre of the circle are true to scale, and so a straight line passing from the centre to any other point is a great circle and shows the shortest distance between the cities. Also that line is correct for direction/bearing and shows the great circle flight path.

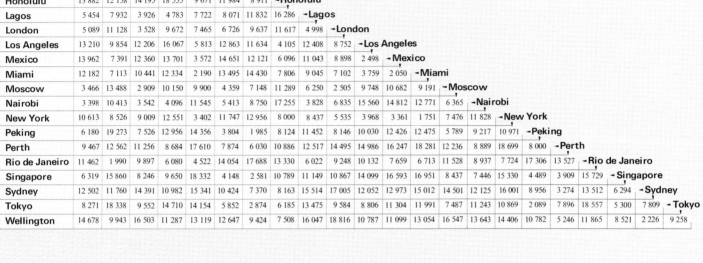

These distances are in kilometres and are the great circle distances between the cities (international airports). Great circle distances are the shortest distances between two points on the globe. They are the normal flight paths for aircraft where they are free from the restrictions of air corridors or national airspace.

	Bahrain	Buenos Aires	Cairo	Cape Town	Caracas	Delhi	Hong Kong	Honolulu	Lagos	London	Los Angeles	Mexico	Miami	Moscow	Nairobi	New York	Peking	Perth	Rio de Janeiro	Singapore	Sydney	Tokyo
Buenos Aires	13 291																					
Cairo	1 927	11 845																				
Cape Town	7 496	6 880	7 246																			
Caracas	12 121	5 124	10 200	10 254																		
Delhi	2 618	15 784	4 400	9 278	14 186																	
Hong Kong	6 387	18 442	8 121	11 852	16 340	3 768																
Honolulu	13 882	12 158	14 195	18 555	9 671	11 984	8 911															
Lagos	5 454	7 932	3 926	4 783	7 722	8 071	11 832	16 286														
London	5 089	11 128	3 528	9 672	7 465	6 726	9 637	11 617	4 998													
Los Angeles	13 210	9 854	12 206	16 067	5 813	12 863	11 634	4 105	12 408	8 752												
Mexico	13 962	7 391	12 360	13 701	3 572	14 651	12 121	6 096	11 043	8 898	2 498											
Miami	12 182	7 113	10 441	12 334	2 190	13 495	14 430	7 806	9 045	7 102	3 759	2 050										
Moscow	3 466	13 488	2 909	10 150	9 900	4 359	7 148	11 289	6 250	2 505	9 748	10 682	9 191									
Nairobi	3 398	10 413	3 542	4 096	11 545	5 413	8 750	17 255	3 828	6 835	15 560	14 812	12 771	6 365								
New York	10 613	8 526	9 009	12 551	3 402	11 747	12 956	8 000	8 437	5 535	3 968	3 361	1 751	7 476	11 828							
Peking	6 180	19 273	7 526	12 956	14 356	3 804	1 985	8 124	11 452	8 146	10 030	12 426	12 475	5 789	9 217	10 971						
Perth	9 467	12 562	11 256	8 684	17 610	7 874	6 030	10 886	12 517	14 495	14 986	16 247	18 281	12 236	8 889	18 699	8 000					
Rio de Janeiro	11 462	1 990	9 897	6 080	4 522	14 054	17 688	13 330	6 022	9 248	10 132	7 659	6 713	11 528	8 937	7 724	17 306	13 527				
Singapore	6 319	15 860	8 246	9 650	18 332	4 148	2 581	10 789	11 149	10 867	14 099	16 593	16 951	8 437	7 446	15 330	4 489	3 909	15 729			
Sydney	12 502	11 760	14 391	10 982	15 341	10 424	7 370	8 163	15 514	17 005	12 052	12 973	15 012	14 501	12 125	16 001	8 956	3 274	13 512	6 294		
Tokyo	8 271	18 338	9 552	14 710	14 154	5 852	2 874	6 185	13 475	9 584	8 806	11 304	11 991	7 487	11 243	10 869	2 089	7 896	18 557	5 300	7 809	
Wellington	14 678	9 943	16 503	11 287	13 119	12 647	9 424	7 508	16 047	18 816	10 787	11 099	13 054	16 547	13 643	14 406	10 782	5 246	11 865	8 521	2 226	9 258

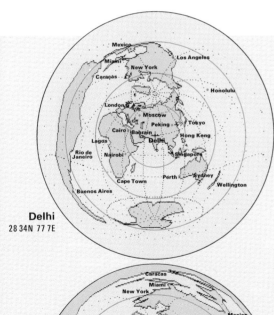

Delhi
28 34N 77 7E

The three circles are drawn at radius 5 000, 10 000 and 15 000 km from the central city

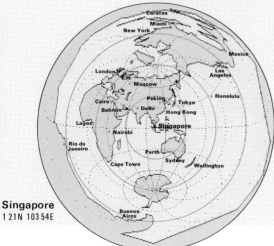

Singapore
1 21N 103 54E

· Cities shown on the distance table

The co-ordinates given are for the airport of each city

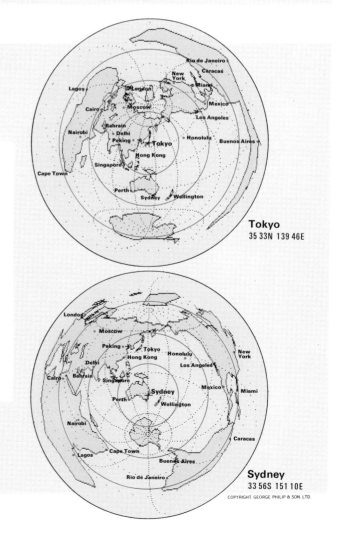

Tokyo
35 33N 139 46E

Sydney
33 56S 151 10E

INDEX

The number in bold type which follows each name in the index refers to the number of the page where that feature or place will be found.

The geographical co-ordinates which follow the place name are sometimes only approximate but are close enough for the place name to be located.

An open square □ signifies that the name refers to an administrative division of a country while a solid square ■ follows the name of a country.

Rivers have been indexed to their mouth or to their confluence.

The alphabetical order of names composed of two or more words is governed primarily by the first word and then by the second. This is an example of the rule:

> West Wyalong
> West Yorkshire
> Westbourne
> Westbury
> Westbury-on-Severn
> Western Australia

Names composed of a proper name (Gibraltar) and a description (Strait of) are positioned alphabetically by the proper name. All river names are followed by ➤. If the same word occurs in the name of a town and a geographical feature, the town name is listed first followed by the name or names of the geographical features.

Names beginning with M', Mc are all indexed as if they were spelled Mac.

If the same place name occurs twice or more in the index and the places are in different countries they will be followed by the country names and the latter in alphabetical order.

> Sydney, Australia
> Sydney, Canada

In the index each placename is followed by its geographical co-ordinates which allow the reader to find the place on the map. These co-ordinates give the latitude and longitude of a particular place.

The latitude (or parallel) is the distance of a point north or south of the Equator measured as an angle with the centre of the earth. The Equator is latitude 0°, the North Pole is 90°N and the South Pole 90°S. On a globe the lines could be drawn as concentric circles parallel to the Equator, decreasing in diameter from the Equator until they become a point at the Poles. On the maps these lines of latitude are usually represented as lines running across the map from East to West in smooth curves. They are numbered on the sides of the map; north of the Equator the numbers increase northwards, to the south they increase southwards. The degree interval between them depends on the scale of the map. On a large scale map (for example, 1:2 000 000) the interval is one degree, but on a small scale (for example 1:50 000 000) it will be ten degrees.

Lines of longitude (or meridians) cut the latitude lines at right angles on the globe and intersect with one another at the Poles. Longitude is measured by the angle at the centre of the earth between it and the meridian of origin which runs through Greenwich (0°). It may be a measurement East or West of this line and from 0° to 180° in each direction. The longitude line of 180° runs North – South through the Pacific Ocean. On a particular map the interval between the lines of longitude is always the same as that between the lines of latitude and normally they are drawn vertically. They are numbered in the top and bottom margins and a note states East or West from Greenwich.

The unit of measurement for latitude and longitude is the degree and it is subdivided into 60 minutes. An index entry states the position of a place in degrees and minutes, a space being left between the degrees and minutes. The latitude is followed by N(orth) or S(outh) and the longitude by E(ast) or W(est).

The diagram illustrates how the reader has to estimate the required distance from the nearest line of latitude or longitude. In the diagram there is one degree, or 60 minutes between the lines and so to find the position of Calais an estimate has to be made, 57 parts of 60 north of the 50 degree latitude line and 50 parts of 60, or 50 minutes east of the one degree longitude line.

Where the map is smaller in scale it is more difficult to calculate the position of a place because there are five or ten degree intervals between the lines.

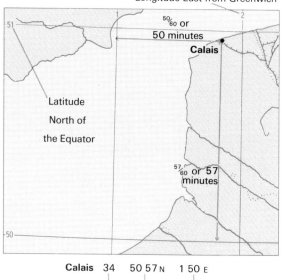

Scale 1:2 000 000

Calais	34	50 57N	1 50 E
	page	latitude	longitude

The following is a list of the principal abbreviations used in the Index.

Auxerre

A

Aachen, W. Ger. 36 50 47N 6 4 E
Aalborg, Den. 45 57 2N 9 54 E
Aalst, Belg. 36 50 56N 4 2 E
Aarhus, Den. 45 56 8N 10 11 E
Ābādān, Iran 56 30 22N 48 20 E
Abbey Town, U.K. 18 54 50N 3 18W
Abbots Bromley, U.K. 14 52 50N 1 52W
Abbots Langley, U.K. 15 51 43N 0 25W
Abbotsbury, U.K. 14 50 40N 2 36W
Abéché, Chad 79 13 50N 20 35 E
Aberaeron, U.K. 17 52 15N 4 16W
Aberdare, U.K. 17 51 43N 3 27W
Aberdeen, U.K. 23 57 9N 2 6W
Aberdour, U.K. 21 56 2N 3 18W
Aberdovey, U.K. 17 52 33N 4 3W
Aberfeldy, U.K. 23 56 37N 3 50W
Aberfoyle, U.K. 20 56 10N 4 23W
Abergavenny, U.K. 17 51 49N 3 1W
Abergele, U.K. 17 53 17N 3 35W
Aberlady, U.K. 21 56 0N 2 51W
Abernethy, U.K. 21 56 19N 3 18W
Aberporth, U.K. 17 52 8N 4 32W
Abersoch, U.K. 17 52 50N 4 30W
Abersychan, U.K. 17 51 44N 3 3W
Abertillery, U.K. 17 51 44N 3 9W
Aberystwyth, U.K. 17 52 25N 4 6W
Abidjan, Ivory C. 78 5 26N 3 58W
Abingdon, U.K. 14 51 40N 1 17W
Abington, U.K. 21 55 30N 3 42W
Aboyne, U.K. 23 57 4N 2 48W
Abū Dhabī, U.A.E. 57 24 28N 54 36 E
Acapulco, Mex. 94 16 51N 99 56W
Accra, Ghana 78 5 35N 0 6W
Accrington, U.K. 18 53 46N 2 22W
Achill Hd., Ire. 24 53 59N 10 15W
Achill I., Ire. 24 53 58N 10 5W
Achinsk, U.S.S.R. 49 56 20N 90 20 E
Achnasheen, U.K. 22 57 35N 5 5W
Acklins I., Baham. 95 22 30N 74 0W
Acle, U.K. 15 52 38N 1 32 E
Aconcagua, Cerro, Arg. 102 32 39S 70 0W
Acre, Isr. 57 32 55N 35 4 E
Acton Burnell, U.K. 14 52 37N 2 41W
Adamaoua Plateau, Cam. 80 7 20N 12 20 E
Adam's Bridge, Sri L. 58 9 15N 79 40 E
Adana, Turk. 47 37 0N 35 16 E
Adapazarı, Turk. 47 40 48N 30 25 E
Addis Ababa, Eth. 79 9 2N 38 42 E
Addlestone, U.K. 15 51 22N 0 30W
Adelaide, Austral. 67 34 52S 138 30 E
Adélie Land, Ant. 103 68 0S 140 0 E
Aden, S. Yem. 56 12 45N 45 0 E
Aden, G. of, Asia 56 13 0N 50 0 E
Adirondack Mts., U.S.A. 93 44 0N 74 15W
Admiralty Is., P.N.G. 64 2 0S 147 0 E
Adrar, Alg. 78 27 51N 0 11W
Adriatic Sea, Europe 40 43 0N 16 0 E
Adwick le Street, U.K. 19 53 35N 1 12W
Ægean Sea, Europe 41 37 0N 25 0 E
Afghanistan ■, Asia 57 33 0N 65 0 E
Agadès, Niger 78 16 58N 7 59 E
Agadir, Mor. 78 30 28N 9 35W
Agartala, India 59 23 50N 91 23 E
Agra, India 58 27 17N 77 58 E
Agrigento, It. 40 37 19N 13 33 E
Aguascalientes, Mex. 94 21 53N 102 12W
Ahmadabad, India 58 23 0N 72 40 E
Ahvāz, Iran 56 31 20N 48 40 E
Ahvenanmaa = Åland, Fin. 45 60 15N 20 0 E
Ailsa Craig, U.K. 20 55 15N 5 7W
Ainsdale, U.K. 18 53 37N 3 2W
Airdrie, U.K. 21 55 53N 3 57W
Aire →, U.K. 19 53 42N 0 55W
Aisgill, U.K. 18 54 23N 2 21W
Aix-en-Provence, Fr. 35 43 32N 5 27 E
Ajaccio, Fr. 35 41 55N 8 40 E
Akashi, Jap. 62 34 45N 135 0 E
Akita, Jap. 62 39 45N 140 7 E
Akranes, Ice. 44 64 19N 21 58W
Akron, U.S.A. 92 41 7N 81 31W
Aktyubinsk, U.S.S.R. 47 50 17N 57 10 E
Akure, Nig. 78 7 15N 5 5 E
Akureyri, Ice. 44 65 40N 18 6W
Al Ḥudaydah, Yem. 56 14 50N 43 0 E
Al Hūfuf, Si. Arab. 56 25 25N 49 45 E
Al Jawf, Si. Arab. 56 29 55N 39 40 E
Al Qaṭīf, Si. Arab. 56 26 35N 50 0 E
Al Qunaytirah, Syria 57 32 55N 35 45 E
Alabama □, U.S.A. 91 33 0N 87 0W
Åland, Fin. 45 60 15N 20 0 E
Alaska □, U.S.A. 88 65 0N 150 0W
Alaska, G. of, Pac. Oc. 88 58 0N 145 0W
Alaska Pen., U.S.A. 88 56 0N 160 0W
Alaska Range, U.S.A. 88 62 50N 151 0W
Alba Iulia, Rom. 43 46 8N 23 39 E
Albacete, Sp. 37 39 0N 1 50W
Albania ■, Europe 41 41 0N 20 0 E
Albany, Austral. 66 35 1S 117 58 E
Albany, Ga., U.S.A. 90 31 40N 84 10W
Albany, N.Y., U.S.A. 93 42 35N 73 47W
Albany →, Canada 89 52 17N 81 31W
Alberta □, Canada 88 54 40N 115 0W
Albrighton, U.K. 14 52 38N 2 17W
Albuquerque, U.S.A. 90 35 5N 106 47W
Albury, Austral. 70 36 3S 146 56 E
Alcalá de Henares, Sp. 37 40 28N 3 22W
Alcester, U.K. 14 52 13N 1 52W
Aldan →, U.S.S.R. 49 63 28N 129 35 E
Aldborough, U.K. 19 54 6N 1 21W
Aldbourne, U.K. 14 51 28N 1 38W
Aldbrough, U.K. 19 53 50N 0 7W
Aldeburgh, U.K. 15 52 9N 1 35 E
Alderbury, U.K. 14 51 4N 1 45W
Alderley Edge, U.K. 18 53 18N 2 15W
Alderney, U.K. 34 49 42N 2 12W
Aldershot, U.K. 15 51 15N 0 43W
Aldingham, U.K. 18 54 8N 3 3W
Aleppo, Syria 56 36 10N 37 15 E
Alessándria, It. 40 44 54N 8 37 E
Ålesund, Nor. 44 62 28N 6 12 E
Aleutian Is., Pac. Oc. 88 52 0N 175 0W
Alexander Arch., U.S.A. 88 57 0N 135 0W
Alexandria, Egypt 79 31 0N 30 0 E
Alexandria, U.K. 20 55 59N 4 40W
Alexandria, U.S.A. 90 31 20N 92 30W
Alford, Grampian, U.K. 23 57 13N 2 42W
Alford, Lincs., U.K. 19 53 16N 0 10 E
Alfreton, U.K. 19 53 6N 1 22W
Alfriston, U.K. 15 50 48N 0 10 E
Algarve, Port. 37 36 58N 8 20W
Algeciras, Sp. 37 36 9N 5 28W
Algeria ■, Africa 78 35 10N 3 11 E
Algiers, Alg. 78 36 42N 3 8 E
Alicante, Sp. 37 38 23N 0 30W
Alice Springs, Austral. 66 23 40S 133 50 E
Aligarh, India 58 27 55N 78 10 E
Alkmaar, Neth. 36 52 37N 4 45 E
Allahabad, India 59 25 25N 81 58 E
Allegheny Mts., U.S.A. 92 38 0N 80 0W
Allen →, U.K. 21 54 53N 2 13W
Allen, Bog of, Ire. 25 53 15N 7 0W
Allen, L., Ire. 24 54 12N 8 5W
Allendale, U.K. 21 54 55N 2 15W
Allenheads, U.K. 21 54 49N 2 12W
Allentown, U.S.A. 93 40 36N 75 30W
Alloa, U.K. 21 56 7N 3 49W
Allonby, U.K. 18 54 45N 3 27W
Alma Ata, U.S.S.R. 48 43 15N 76 57 E
Almelo, Neth. 36 52 22N 6 42 E
Almería, Sp. 37 36 52N 2 27W
Almond →, U.K. 21 56 27N 3 27W
Almondsbury, U.K. 14 51 33N 2 34W
Aln →, U.K. 21 55 27N 1 32W
Alness, U.K. 23 57 41N 4 15W
Alnmouth, U.K. 21 55 24N 1 37W
Alnwick, U.K. 19 55 25N 1 42W
Alphen, Neth. 36 51 29N 4 58 E
Alphington, U.K. 16 50 41N 3 32W
Alps, Europe 42 47 0N 8 0 E
Alrewas, U.K. 14 52 43N 1 44W
Alsager, U.K. 18 53 7N 2 20W
Alston, U.K. 18 54 48N 2 26W
Altai Mts., Asia 60 46 40N 92 45 E
Altarnun, U.K. 16 50 35N 4 30W
Altay, China 60 47 48N 88 10 E
Alton, U.K. 15 51 8N 0 59W
Altoona, U.S.A. 92 40 32N 78 24W
Altrincham, U.K. 18 53 25N 2 21W
Altun Shan, China 60 38 30N 88 0 E
Alva, U.K. 21 56 9N 3 49W
Alvechurch, U.K. 14 52 22N 1 58W
Alwinton, U.K. 21 55 20N 2 7W
Alyth, U.K. 23 56 38N 3 15W
Amadjuak L., Canada 89 65 0N 71 8W
Amagasaki, Jap. 62 34 42N 135 20 E
Amarillo, U.S.A. 90 35 14N 101 46W
Amazon →, S. Am. 100 0 5S 50 0W
Amazonas □, Brazil 101 4 0S 62 0W
Amble, U.K. 21 55 20N 1 36W
Ambleside, U.K. 18 54 26N 2 58W
Ambon, Indon. 63 3 35S 128 20 E
American Samoa ■, Pac. Oc. 65 14 20S 170 40W
Amersfoort, Neth. 36 52 9N 5 23 E
Amersham, U.K. 15 51 40N 0 38W
Amesbury, U.K. 14 51 10N 1 46W
Amiens, Fr. 34 49 54N 2 16 E
Amlwch, U.K. 17 53 24N 4 21W
'Ammān, Jord. 57 31 57N 35 52 E
Ammanford, U.K. 17 51 48N 4 0W
Amoy = Xiamen, China 61 24 25N 118 4 E
Ampleforth, U.K. 19 54 13N 1 8W
Ampthill, U.K. 15 52 3N 0 30W
Amravati, India 58 20 55N 77 45 E
Amritsar, India 58 31 35N 74 57 E
Amsterdam, Neth. 36 52 23N 4 54 E
Amudarya →, U.S.S.R. 48 43 40N 59 0 E
Amundsen Gulf, Canada 88 71 0N 124 0W
Amundsen Sea, Ant. 103 72 0S 115 0W
Amur →, U.S.S.R. 49 52 56N 141 10 E
An Nafūd, Si. Arab. 56 28 15N 41 0 E
An Najaf, Iraq 56 32 3N 44 15 E
An Uaimh, Ire. 24 53 39N 6 40W
Anadyr, G. of, U.S.S.R. 49 64 0N 180 0 E
Anaheim, U.S.A. 90 33 50N 118 0W
Anápolis, Brazil 101 16 15S 48 50W
Anatolia, Turk. 47 38 0N 30 0 E
Ancaster, U.K. 19 52 59N 0 32W
Ancholme →, U.K. 19 53 42N 0 32W
Anchorage, U.S.A. 88 61 10N 149 50W
Ancona, It. 40 43 37N 13 30 E
Ancrum, U.K. 21 55 31N 2 35W
Anda, China 61 46 24N 125 19 E
Andalusia, Reg., Sp. 37 37 35N 5 0W
Andaman Is., India 51 12 30N 92 30 E
Anderlecht, Belg. 36 50 50N 4 19 E
Andes, S. Am. 96 20 0S 68 0W
Andhra Pradesh □, India 58 16 0N 79 0 E
Andizhan, U.S.S.R. 48 41 10N 72 0 E
Andorra ■, Europe 35 42 30N 1 30 E
Andover, U.K. 14 51 13N 1 29W
Andreanof Is., Pac. Oc. 88 52 0N 178 0W
Andreas, U.K. 18 54 23N 4 25W
Ándria, It. 40 41 13N 16 17 E
Andropov, U.S.S.R. 46 58 5N 38 50 E
Andros I., Baham. 95 24 30N 78 0W
Angara →, U.S.S.R. 49 58 30N 97 0 E
Angarsk, U.S.S.R. 49 52 30N 104 0 E
Angers, Fr. 34 47 30N 0 35W
Anglesey, U.K. 17 53 17N 4 20W
Angmagssalik, Green. 89 65 40N 37 20W
Angmering, U.K. 15 50 48N 0 28W
Angola ■, Africa 81 12 0S 18 0 E
Angoulême, Fr. 35 45 39N 0 10 E
Anguilla, W. Ind. 94 18 14N 63 5W
Angus, Braes of, U.K. 23 56 51N 3 10W
Anhui □, China 61 32 0N 117 0 E
Anjou, Fr. 34 47 20N 0 15W
Ankara, Turk. 47 40 0N 32 54 E
Ann Arbor, U.S.A. 92 42 17N 83 45W
Annaba, Alg. 78 36 50N 7 46 E
Annalee →, Ire. 24 54 3N 7 15W
Annan, U.K. 21 55 0N 3 17W
Annan →, U.K. 21 54 58N 3 18W
Annandale, U.K. 21 55 10N 3 25W
Annecy, Fr. 35 45 55N 6 8 E
Annfield Plain, U.K. 19 54 52N 1 45W
Annobón, Atl. Oc. 73 1 25S 5 36 E
Anshan, China 61 41 5N 122 58 E
Anshun, China 60 26 18N 105 57 E
Anstey, U.K. 14 52 41N 1 14W
Anstruther, U.K. 21 56 14N 2 40W
Antalya, Turk. 47 36 52N 30 45 E
Antananarivo, Madag. 81 18 55S 47 31 E
Antarctic Pen., Ant. 103 67 0S 60 0W
Antarctica, Cont. 103 90 0S 0 0 E
Anticosti, I. d', Canada 93 49 30N 63 0W
Antigua & Barbuda ■, W. Ind. 94 17 20N 61 48W
Antofagasta, Chile 102 23 50S 70 30W
Antony, U.K. 16 50 22N 4 13W
Antrim, U.K. 24 54 43N 6 13W
Antrim □, U.K. 24 54 55N 6 20W
Antrim, Mts. of, U.K. 24 54 57N 6 8W
Antsiranana, Madag. 81 12 25S 49 20 E
Antwerp, Belg. 36 51 13N 4 25 E
Anyang, China 61 36 5N 114 21 E
Anzhero-Sudzhensk, U.S.S.R. 48 56 10N 86 0 E
Aomori, Jap. 62 40 45N 140 45 E
Apeldoorn, Neth. 36 52 13N 5 57 E
Apennines, It. 40 44 20N 10 20 E
Appalachian Mts., U.S.A. 91 38 0N 80 0W
Appleby, U.K. 18 54 35N 2 29W
Appledore, Devon, U.K. 16 51 3N 4 12W
Appledore, Kent, U.K. 15 51 2N 0 47 E
Arabia, Asia 50 25 0N 45 0 E
Arabian Desert, Egypt 79 26 0N 33 30 E
Arabian Sea, Ind. Oc. 50 16 0N 65 0 E
Aracaju, Brazil 101 10 55S 37 4W
Araçatuba, Brazil 101 21 10S 50 30W
Arad, Rom. 43 46 10N 21 20 E
Arafura Sea, E. Ind. 64 9 0S 135 0 E
Aragón □, Sp. 37 41 25N 1 0W
Araguaia →, Brazil 101 5 21S 48 41W
Arakan Yoma, Burma 59 20 0N 94 40 E
Aral Sea, U.S.S.R. 48 44 30N 60 0 E
Aralsk, U.S.S.R. 48 46 50N 61 20 E
Aran I., Ire. 24 55 0N 8 30W
Aran Is., Ire. 25 53 5N 9 42W
Arapiraca, Brazil 101 9 45S 36 39W
Ararat, Austral. 70 37 16S 143 0 E
Arbroath, U.K. 23 56 34N 2 35W
Arctic Ocean, Arctic 103 78 0N 160 0W
Arctic Red River, Canada 88 67 15N 134 0W
Ardbeg, U.K. 20 55 38N 6 6W
Ardchyle, U.K. 20 56 26N 4 24W
Ardee, Ire. 24 53 51N 6 32W
Ardennes, Belg. 36 50 0N 5 10 E
Ardentinny, U.K. 20 56 3N 4 56W
Ardgour, U.K. 22 56 45N 5 25W
Ardingly, U.K. 15 51 3N 0 3W
Ardlui, U.K. 20 56 19N 4 43W
Ardmore Pt., U.K. 20 55 40N 6 0W
Ardnamurchan, Pt. of, U.K. 22 56 44N 6 14W
Ardnave Pt., U.K. 20 55 54N 6 20W
Ardrishaig, U.K. 20 56 0N 5 27W
Ardrossan, U.K. 20 55 39N 4 50W
Ards □, U.K. 24 54 35N 5 30W
Ards Pen., U.K. 24 54 30N 5 25W
Ardvasar, U.K. 22 57 5N 5 52W
Arendal, Nor. 45 58 28N 8 46 E
Arequipa, Peru 100 16 20S 71 30W
Argentina ■, S. Am. 102 35 0S 66 0W
Argyll, U.K. 20 56 14N 5 10W
Arica, Chile 100 18 32S 70 20W
Arima, Trin. & Tob. 94 10 38N 61 17W
Arinagour, U.K. 20 56 38N 6 31W
Arisaig, U.K. 22 56 55N 5 50W
Arizona □, U.S.A. 90 34 20N 111 30W
Arkaig, L., U.K. 22 56 58N 5 10W
Arkansas □, U.S.A. 91 35 0N 92 30W
Arkansas →, U.S.A. 91 33 48N 91 4W
Arkhangelsk, U.S.S.R. 46 64 40N 41 0 E
Arkle →, U.K. 18 54 25N 1 55W
Arklow, Ire. 25 52 48N 6 10W
Arles, Fr. 35 43 41N 4 40 E
Arlon, Belg. 36 49 42N 5 49 E
Armadale, U.K. 21 55 54N 3 42W
Armagh, U.K. 24 54 22N 6 40W
Armagh □, U.K. 24 54 18N 6 37W
Armenia, Col. 100 4 35N 75 45W
Armenia □, U.S.S.R. 47 40 0N 41 0 E
Armidale, Austral. 67 30 30S 151 40 E
Arnhem, Neth. 36 51 58N 5 55 E
Arnhem Land, Austral. 66 13 10S 134 30 E
Arnold, U.K. 19 53 0N 1 8W
Arnside, U.K. 18 54 12N 2 49W
Arran, U.K. 20 55 34N 5 12W
Arras, Fr. 34 50 17N 2 46 E
Arrochar, U.K. 20 56 12N 4 45W
Arrow, L., Ire. 24 54 3N 8 20W
Arun →, U.K. 15 50 48N 0 33W
Arunachal Pradesh □, India 59 28 0N 95 0 E
Arundel, U.K. 15 50 52N 0 32W
Arusha, Tanz. 80 3 20S 36 40 E
As Salt, Jord. 57 32 2N 35 43 E
As Summān, Si. Arab. 56 25 0N 47 0 E
Asahigawa, Jap. 62 43 46N 142 22 E
Asansol, India 59 23 40N 87 1 E
Ascension I., Atl. Oc. 128 8 0S 14 15W
Ascot, U.K. 15 51 24N 0 41W
Asfordby, U.K. 15 52 45N 0 57W
Ash, Kent, U.K. 15 51 17N 1 16 E
Ash, Surrey, U.K. 15 51 14N 0 43W
Ashbourne, U.K. 19 53 2N 1 44W
Ashburton, N.Z. 71 43 53S 171 48 E
Ashburton, U.K. 16 50 31N 3 45W
Ashburton →, Austral. 66 21 40S 114 56 E
Ashby-de-la-Zouch, U.K. 14 52 45N 1 29W
Ashchurch, U.K. 14 52 0N 2 7W
Ashdown Forest, U.K. 15 51 4N 0 2 E
Ashford, Derby, U.K. 19 53 13N 1 43W
Ashford, Kent, U.K. 15 51 8N 0 53 E
Ashington, U.K. 21 55 12N 1 35W
Ashkhabad, U.S.S.R. 48 38 0N 57 50 E
Ashq'elon, Isr. 57 31 42N 34 35 E
Ashton-in-Makerfield, U.K. 18 53 29N 2 39W
Ashton-under-Lyne, U.K. 18 53 30N 2 8W
Ashurstwood, U.K. 15 51 6N 0 2 E
Ashwater, U.K. 16 50 43N 4 18W
Ashwick, U.K. 14 51 13N 2 31W
'Asīr □, Si. Arab. 56 18 40N 42 30 E
Asir, Ras, Som. 73 11 55N 51 10 E
Askrigg, U.K. 18 54 19N 2 6W
Aslackby, U.K. 19 52 53N 0 23W
Asmera, Eth. 79 15 19N 38 55 E
Aspatria, U.K. 18 54 45N 3 20W
Assam □, India 59 26 0N 93 0 E
Assen, Neth. 36 53 0N 6 35 E
Assynt, L., U.K. 22 58 25N 5 15W
Asti, It. 40 44 54N 8 11 E
Aston Clinton, U.K. 15 51 48N 0 44W
Astrakhan, U.S.S.R. 47 46 25N 48 5 E
Astwood Bank, U.K. 14 52 15N 1 55W
Asunción, Par. 102 25 10S 57 30W
Aswân, Egypt 79 24 4N 32 57 E
Atacama, Desierto de, Chile 102 24 0S 69 20W
Atbara, Sudan 79 17 42N 33 59 E
Athabasca, L., Canada 88 59 15N 109 15W
Athboy, Ire. 24 53 37N 6 55W
Athenry, Ire. 25 53 18N 8 45W
Athens, Greece 41 37 58N 23 46 E
Atherstone, U.K. 14 52 35N 1 32W
Atherton, U.K. 18 53 32N 2 30W
Athínai = Athens, Greece 41 37 58N 23 46 E
Athlone, Ire. 24 53 26N 7 57W
Atholl, Forest of, U.K. 23 56 51N 3 50W
Athy, Ire. 25 53 0N 7 0W
Atlanta, U.S.A. 91 33 50N 84 24W
Atlantic City, U.S.A. 93 39 25N 74 25W
Atlantic Ocean 128 0 0 20 0W
Atlas Mts., Mor. 72 32 30N 5 0W
Attleborough, U.K. 15 52 32N 1 1 E
Auchencairn, U.K. 21 54 51N 3 52W
Auchinleck, U.K. 20 55 28N 4 18W
Auchterarder, U.K. 21 56 18N 3 43W
Auchterderran, U.K. 21 56 8N 3 16W
Auchtermuchty, U.K. 21 56 18N 3 15W
Auchtertyre, U.K. 22 57 17N 5 35W
Auckland, N.Z. 71 36 52S 174 46 E
Audlem, U.K. 18 52 59N 2 31W
Aughnacloy, U.K. 24 54 25N 6 58W
Augsburg, W. Ger. 42 48 22N 10 54 E
Augusta, U.S.A. 90 33 29N 81 59W
Aurangabad, India 58 19 50N 75 23 E
Aurora, U.S.A. 92 41 42N 88 12W
Austin, U.S.A. 90 30 20N 97 45W
Australia ■, Oc. 66 23 0S 135 0 E
Australian Alps, Austral. 70 36 30S 148 30 E
Australian Cap. Terr. □, Austral. 70 35 30S 149 0 E
Austria ■, Europe 42 47 0N 14 0 E
Auxerre, Fr. 34 47 48N 3 32 E

Avebury

Avebury, *U.K.* **14** 51 25N 1 52W
Avellino, *It.* **40** 40 54N 14 46 E
Aveton Gifford, *U.K.* **16** 50 17N 3 51W
Avich, L., *U.K.* **20** 56 17N 5 25W
Aviemore, *U.K.* **23** 57 11N 3 50W
Avignon, *Fr.* **35** 43 57N 4 50 E
Ávila, *Sp.* **37** 40 39N 4 43W
Avoca, *Ire.* **25** 52 52N 6 13W
Avon □, *U.K.* **14** 51 30N 2 40W
Avon →, *Avon, U.K.* **14** 51 30N 2 43W
Avon →, *Hants., U.K.* **14** 50 44N 1 45W
Avon →, *Warwick, U.K.* **14** 52 0N 2 9W
Avonmouth, *U.K.* **14** 51 30N 2 42W
Awe, L., *U.K.* **20** 56 15N 5 15W
Axbridge, *U.K.* **14** 51 17N 2 50W
Axe →, *U.K.* **14** 51 17N 2 52W
Axe Edge, *U.K.* **18** 53 14N 1 59W
Axholme, Isle of, *U.K.* **19** 53 30N 0 55W
Axminster, *U.K.* **16** 50 47N 3 1W
Axmouth, *U.K.* **16** 50 43N 3 2W
Ayers Rock, *Austral.* **66** 25 23S 131 5 E
Aylesbury, *U.K.* **15** 51 48N 0 49W
Aylesford, *U.K.* **15** 51 18N 0 29 E
Aylsham, *U.K.* **15** 52 48N 1 16 E
Aynho, *U.K.* **14** 51 59N 1 15W
Ayr, *U.K.* **20** 55 28N 4 37W
Ayr →, *U.K.* **20** 55 29N 4 40W
Ayr, Heads of, *U.K.* **20** 55 25N 4 43W
Ayre, Pt. of, *U.K.* **18** 54 27N 4 21W
Aysgarth, *U.K.* **18** 54 18N 2 0W
Ayton, *Borders, U.K.* **21** 55 51N 2 6W
Ayton, *N. Yorks., U.K.* **19** 54 15N 0 29W
Az Zarqā, *Jord.* **57** 32 5N 36 4 E
Azores, *Atl. Oc.* **128** 38 44N 29 0W
Azov Sea, *U.S.S.R.* **47** 46 0N 36 30 E
Azuero, Pen. de, *Pan.* **95** 7 30N 80 30W

B

Bābol, *Iran* **56** 36 40N 52 50 E
Bacabal, *Brazil* **101** 4 15S 44 45W
Bacău, *Rom.* **43** 46 35N 26 55 E
Back, *U.K.* **22** 58 17N 6 20W
Bacolod, *Phil.* **63** 10 40N 122 57 E
Bacton, *U.K.* **15** 52 50N 1 29 E
Bacup, *U.K.* **18** 53 42N 2 12W
Badajoz, *Sp.* **37** 38 50N 6 59W
Badalona, *Sp.* **37** 41 26N 2 15 E
Baffin B., *Canada* **89** 72 0N 64 0W
Baffin I., *Canada* **89** 68 0N 75 0W
Bagenalstown = Muine Bheag, *Ire.* **25** 52 42N 6 57W
Baggy Pt., *U.K.* **16** 51 11N 4 12W
Baghdād, *Iraq* **56** 33 20N 44 30 E
Bagshot, *U.K.* **15** 51 22N 0 41W
Bahamas ■, *Atl. Oc.* **95** 24 0N 75 0W
Bahawalpur, *Pak.* **58** 29 24N 71 40 E
Bahía = Salvador, *Brazil* **101** 13 0S 38 30W
Bahía Blanca, *Arg.* **102** 38 35S 62 13W
Bahrain ■, *Asia* **56** 26 0N 50 35 E
Baia Mare, *Rom.* **43** 47 40N 23 35 E
Baildon, *U.K.* **19** 53 52N 1 46W
Baile Atha Cliath = Dublin, *Ire.* **24** 53 20N 6 18W
Bain →, *U.K.* **19** 53 10N 0 15W
Bainbridge, *U.K.* **18** 54 18N 2 7W
Bakersfield, *U.S.A.* **90** 35 25N 119 0W
Bakewell, *U.K.* **19** 53 13N 1 40W
Bākhtarān, *Iran* **56** 34 23N 47 0 E
Baku, *U.S.S.R.* **47** 40 25N 49 45 E
Bala, *U.K.* **17** 52 54N 3 36W
Bala, L. = Tegid, L., *U.K.* **17** 52 53N 3 38W
Balallan, *U.K.* **22** 58 5N 6 35W
Balaton, *Hung.* **43** 46 50N 17 40 E
Balbeggie, *U.K.* **21** 56 26N 3 19W
Balboa, *Pan.* **94** 9 0N 79 30W
Balbriggan, *Ire.* **24** 53 35N 6 10W
Balderton, *U.K.* **19** 53 3N 0 46W
Baldock, *U.K.* **15** 51 59N 0 11W
Balearic Is., *Sp.* **37** 39 30N 3 0 E
Balfron, *U.K.* **20** 56 4N 4 20W
Bali □, *Indon.* **63** 8 20S 115 0 E
Balikesir, *Turk.* **47** 39 35N 27 58 E
Balikpapan, *Indon.* **63** 1 10S 116 55 E
Balkan Mts., *Bulg.* **41** 43 15N 23 0 E
Balkan Pen., *Europe* **26** 42 0N 22 0 E
Balkhash, L., *U.S.S.R.* **48** 46 0N 74 50 E
Ballachulish, *U.K.* **22** 56 40N 5 10W
Ballantrae, *U.K.* **20** 55 6N 5 0W
Ballarat, *Austral.* **70** 37 33S 143 50 E
Ballasalla, *U.K.* **18** 54 7N 4 36W
Ballater, *U.K.* **23** 57 2N 3 2W
Ballaugh, *U.K.* **18** 54 20N 4 32W
Ballina, *Mayo, Ire.* **24** 54 7N 9 10W
Ballina, *Tipp., Ire.* **25** 52 49N 8 27W
Ballinasloe, *Ire.* **25** 53 20N 8 12W
Ballinrobe, *Ire.* **24** 53 36N 9 13W
Ballinskelligs B., *Ire.* **25** 51 46N 10 11W
Balloch, *U.K.* **20** 56 0N 4 35W
Ballycastle, *U.K.* **24** 55 12N 6 15W
Ballyclare, *U.K.* **24** 54 46N 6 0W
Ballymena, *U.K.* **24** 54 53N 6 18W
Ballymena □, *U.K.* **24** 54 53N 6 18W
Ballymoney, *U.K.* **24** 55 5N 6 30W
Ballymoney □, *U.K.* **24** 55 5N 6 23W
Ballynahinch, *U.K.* **24** 54 24N 5 55W
Ballyshannon, *Ire.* **24** 54 30N 8 10W
Balmaclellan, *U.K.* **21** 55 6N 4 5W
Balmoral, *U.K.* **23** 57 3N 3 13W
Balquhidder, *U.K.* **20** 56 22N 4 22W
Balsas →, *Mex.* **94** 17 55N 102 10W
Baltic Sea, *Europe* **45** 56 0N 20 0 E
Baltimore, *Ire.* **25** 51 29N 9 22W
Baltimore, *U.S.A.* **92** 39 18N 76 37W
Baluchistan □, *Pak.* **58** 27 30N 65 0 E
Balurghat, *India* **59** 25 15N 88 44 E
Balvicar, *U.K.* **20** 56 17N 5 38W
Bamako, *Mali* **78** 12 34N 7 55W
Bamberg, *W. Ger.* **42** 49 54N 10 53 E
Bamburgh, *U.K.* **21** 55 36N 1 42W
Bamenda, *Cam.* **80** 5 57N 10 11 E
Bamford, *U.K.* **19** 53 21N 1 41W
Bampton, *Devon, U.K.* **16** 50 59N 3 29W
Bampton, *Oxon., U.K.* **14** 51 44N 1 33W
Banaras = Varanasi, *India* **59** 25 22N 83 0 E
Banbridge, *U.K.* **24** 54 21N 6 17W
Banbridge □, *U.K.* **24** 54 21N 6 16W
Banbury, *U.K.* **14** 52 4N 1 21W
Banchory, *U.K.* **23** 57 3N 2 30W
Banda Aceh, *Indon.* **63** 5 35N 95 20 E
Banda Sea, *Indon.* **63** 6 0S 130 0 E
Bandār 'Abbās, *Iran* **57** 27 15N 56 15 E
Bandar Seri Begawan, *Brunei* **63** 4 52N 115 0 E
Bandon, *Ire.* **25** 51 44N 8 45W
Bandon →, *Ire.* **25** 51 40N 8 41W
Bandundu, *Zaïre* **80** 3 15S 17 22 E
Bandung, *Indon.* **63** 6 54S 107 36 E
Banff, *U.K.* **23** 57 40N 2 32W
Bangalore, *India* **58** 12 59N 77 40 E
Bangka, Selat, *Indon.* **63** 2 30S 105 30 E
Bangkok, *Thai.* **63** 13 45N 100 35 E
Bangladesh ■, *Asia* **59** 24 0N 90 0 E
Bangor, *N. Ireland, U.K.* **24** 54 40N 5 40W
Bangor, *Wales, U.K.* **17** 53 13N 4 9W
Bangor, *U.S.A.* **93** 44 48N 68 42W
Bangui, *C.A.R.* **80** 4 23N 18 35 E
Banham, *U.K.* **15** 52 27N 1 3 E
Banjarmasin, *Indon.* **63** 3 20S 114 35 E
Banjul, *Gambia* **78** 13 28N 16 40W
Bankend, *U.K.* **21** 55 2N 3 31W
Bankfoot, *U.K.* **21** 56 30N 3 31W
Banks I., *Canada* **88** 73 15N 121 30W
Banks Pen., *N.Z.* **71** 43 45S 173 15 E
Bann →, *Down, U.K.* **24** 54 30N 6 31W
Bann →, *Londonderry, U.K.* **24** 55 10N 6 34W
Bannockburn, *U.K.* **21** 56 5N 3 55W
Bantry, *Ire.* **25** 51 40N 9 28W
Bantry, B., *Ire.* **25** 51 35N 9 50W
Banwell, *U.K.* **14** 51 19N 2 51W
Baoding, *China* **61** 38 50N 115 28 E
Baoji, *China* **60** 34 20N 107 5 E
Baotou, *China* **61** 40 32N 110 2 E
Barbados ■, *W. Ind.* **94** 13 0N 59 30W
Barcaldine, *Austral.* **67** 23 43S 145 6 E
Barcelona, *Sp.* **37** 41 21N 2 10 E
Bardney, *U.K.* **19** 53 13N 0 19W
Bardsey I., *U.K.* **17** 52 46N 4 47W
Bareilly, *India* **58** 28 22N 79 27 E
Barents Sea, *Arctic* **48** 73 0N 39 0 E
Barford, *U.K.* **14** 52 15N 1 35W
Bargoed, *U.K.* **17** 51 42N 3 22W
Barham, *U.K.* **15** 51 12N 1 10 E
Bari, *It.* **40** 41 6N 16 52 E
Bari Doab, *Pak.* **58** 30 20N 73 0 E
Barisal, *Bangla.* **59** 22 45N 90 20 E
Barisan Mts., *Indon.* **63** 3 30S 102 15 E
Barking, *U.K.* **15** 51 31N 0 10 E
Barkly Tableland, *Austral.* **67** 17 50S 136 40 E
Barlborough, *U.K.* **19** 53 17N 1 17W
Barlby, *U.K.* **19** 53 48N 1 3W
Barletta, *It.* **40** 41 20N 16 17 E
Barmby Moor, *U.K.* **19** 53 55N 0 47W
Barmoor Castle, *U.K.* **21** 55 38N 2 0W
Barmouth, *U.K.* **17** 52 44N 4 3W
Barnard Castle, *U.K.* **18** 54 33N 1 55W
Barnaul, *U.S.S.R.* **48** 53 20N 83 40 E
Barnet, *U.K.* **15** 51 37N 0 15W
Barnetby le Wold, *U.K.* **19** 53 34N 0 24W
Barnoldswick, *U.K.* **18** 53 55N 2 11W
Barnsley, *U.K.* **19** 53 33N 1 29W
Barnstaple, *U.K.* **16** 51 5N 4 3W
Barnstaple B., *U.K.* **16** 51 5N 4 25W
Baroda = Vadodara, *India* **58** 22 20N 73 10 E
Barquísimeto, *Ven.* **100** 10 4N 69 19W
Barr, *U.K.* **20** 55 13N 4 44W
Barra, *U.K.* **22** 57 0N 7 30W
Barra, Sd. of, *U.K.* **22** 57 4N 7 25W
Barra Hd., *U.K.* **22** 56 47N 7 40W
Barrancabermeja, *Col.* **100** 7 0N 73 50W
Barranquilla, *Col.* **100** 11 0N 74 50W
Barrhead, *U.K.* **20** 55 48N 4 23W
Barrhill, *U.K.* **20** 55 7N 4 46W
Barrow →, *Ire.* **25** 52 10N 6 57W
Barrow-in-Furness, *U.K.* **18** 54 8N 3 15W
Barrow upon Humber, *U.K.* **19** 53 41N 0 22W
Barrowford, *U.K.* **18** 53 51N 2 14W
Barry, *S. Glam., U.K.* **17** 51 23N 3 19W
Barry, *Tayside, U.K.* **21** 56 29N 2 45W
Barton, *U.K.* **19** 54 28N 1 38W
Barton-upon-Humber, *U.K.* **19** 53 41N 0 27W
Barvas, *U.K.* **22** 58 21N 6 31W
Barwell, *U.K.* **14** 52 35N 1 22W
Basildon, *U.K.* **15** 51 34N 0 29 E
Basingstoke, *U.K.* **14** 51 15N 1 5W
Basle, *Switz.* **42** 47 35N 7 35 E
Basra, *Iraq* **56** 30 30N 47 50 E
Bass Rock, *U.K.* **21** 56 5N 2 40W
Bass Str., *Austral.* **67** 39 15S 146 30 E
Basse-Terre, *Guad.* **94** 16 0N 61 40W
Bassein, *Burma* **59** 16 45N 94 30 E
Bassenthwaite, L., *U.K.* **18** 54 40N 3 14W
Basseterre, *Guad.* **94** 17 17N 62 43W
Bastia, *Fr.* **35** 42 40N 9 30 E
Baston, *U.K.* **15** 52 43N 0 19W
Bata, *Eq. Guin.* **80** 1 57N 9 50 E
Batangas, *Phil.* **63** 13 35N 121 10 E
Bath, *U.K.* **14** 51 22N 2 22W
Bathford, *U.K.* **14** 51 23N 2 18W
Bathgate, *U.K.* **21** 55 54N 3 38W
Bathurst, *Austral.* **70** 33 25S 149 31 E
Bathurst, *Canada* **93** 47 37N 65 43W
Batley, *U.K.* **19** 53 43N 1 38W
Batna, *Alg.* **78** 35 34N 6 15 E
Baton Rouge, *U.S.A.* **91** 30 30N 91 5W
Battle, *U.K.* **15** 50 55N 0 30 E
Batumi, *U.S.S.R.* **47** 41 30N 41 30 E
Bauru, *Brazil* **101** 22 10S 49 0W
Bavaria □, *W. Ger.* **42** 49 7N 11 30 E
Bawdsey, *U.K.* **15** 52 1N 1 27 E
Bawtry, *U.K.* **19** 53 25N 1 1W
Bayamo, *Cuba* **95** 20 20N 76 40W
Bayan Har Shan, *China* **60** 34 0N 98 0 E
Bayeux, *Fr.* **34** 49 17N 0 42W
Baykal, L., *U.S.S.R.* **49** 53 0N 108 0 E
Bayonne, *Fr.* **35** 43 30N 1 28W
Beachley, *U.K.* **14** 51 37N 2 39W
Beachy Head, *U.K.* **15** 50 44N 0 16 E
Beaconsfield, *U.K.* **15** 51 36N 0 39W
Beadnell, *U.K.* **21** 55 33N 1 38W
Beagle, Canal, *S. Am.* **102** 55 0S 68 30W
Beaminster, *U.K.* **14** 50 48N 2 44W
Bear I., *Ire.* **25** 51 38N 9 50W
Beardmore Glacier, *Ant.* **103** 84 30S 170 0 E
Bearsden, *U.K.* **20** 55 55N 4 21W
Bearsted, *U.K.* **15** 51 15N 0 35 E
Beattock, *U.K.* **21** 55 19N 3 27W
Beaufort Sea, *Arctic* **103** 72 0N 140 0W
Beaulieu, *U.K.* **14** 50 49N 1 27W
Beauly, *U.K.* **23** 57 29N 4 27W
Beauly →, *U.K.* **23** 57 26N 4 28W
Beaumaris, *U.K.* **17** 53 16N 4 7W
Beaumont, *U.S.A.* **91** 30 5N 94 8W
Beauvais, *Fr.* **34** 49 25N 2 8 E
Bebington, *U.K.* **18** 53 23N 3 1W
Beccles, *U.K.* **15** 52 27N 1 33 E
Béchar, *Alg.* **78** 31 38N 2 18W
Beckermet, *U.K.* **18** 54 26N 3 31W
Beckfoot, *U.K.* **18** 54 50N 3 25W
Beckingham, *U.K.* **19** 53 24N 0 49W
Bedale, *U.K.* **19** 54 18N 1 35W
Beddgelert, *U.K.* **17** 53 2N 4 8W
Bedford, *U.K.* **15** 52 8N 0 29W
Bedford □, *U.K.* **15** 52 4N 0 28W
Bedford Level, *U.K.* **15** 52 25N 0 5 E
Bedlington, *U.K.* **21** 55 8N 1 35W
Bedworth, *U.K.* **14** 52 28N 1 29W
Beeford, *U.K.* **19** 53 58N 0 18W
Beer, *U.K.* **16** 50 41N 3 5W
Beersheba, *Isr.* **57** 31 15N 34 48 E
Beeston, *U.K.* **19** 52 55N 1 11W
Bei'an, *China* **61** 48 10N 126 20 E
Beighton, *U.K.* **19** 53 21N 1 21W
Beijing = Peking, *China* **61** 39 55N 116 20 E
Beira, *Mozam.* **81** 19 50S 34 52 E
Beira-Baixa, *Port.* **37** 40 2N 7 30W
Beirut, *Leb.* **57** 33 53N 35 31 E
Beith, *U.K.* **20** 55 45N 4 38W
Bejaïa, Golfe de, *Alg.* **78** 36 42N 5 13 E
Belbroughton, *U.K.* **14** 52 23N 2 5W
Belcher Is., *Canada* **89** 56 15N 78 45W
Belém, *Brazil* **101** 1 20S 48 30W
Belfast, *U.K.* **24** 54 35N 5 56W
Belfast □, *U.K.* **24** 54 35N 5 56W
Belfast, L., *U.K.* **24** 54 40N 5 50W
Belford, *U.K.* **21** 55 36N 1 50W
Belfort, *Fr.* **34** 47 38N 6 50 E
Belgium ■, *Europe* **36** 50 30N 5 0 E
Belgorod, *U.S.S.R.* **47** 50 35N 36 35 E
Belgrade, *Yug.* **41** 44 50N 20 37 E
Beliton, Is., *Indon.* **63** 3 10S 107 50 E
Belize ■, *Cent. Am.* **94** 17 0N 88 30W
Belize City, *Belize* **94** 17 25N 88 0W
Bell Rock = Inchcape Rock, *U.K.* **21** 56 26N 2 24W
Bellary, *India* **58** 15 10N 76 56 E
Belle-Ile, *Fr.* **34** 47 20N 3 10W
Belle Isle, Str. of, *Canada* **89** 51 30N 56 30W
Belleville, *Canada* **92** 44 10N 77 23W
Bellingham, *U.K.* **21** 55 9N 2 16W
Belmopan, *Belize* **94** 17 18N 88 30W
Belmullet, *Ire.* **24** 54 13N 9 58W
Belo Horizonte, *Brazil* **101** 19 55S 43 56W
Beloye More, *U.S.S.R.* **46** 66 30N 38 0 E
Belper, *U.K.* **19** 53 2N 1 29W
Belsay, *U.K.* **21** 55 6N 1 53W
Belton, *Humberside, U.K.* **19** 53 33N 0 49W
Belton, *Norfolk, U.K.* **15** 52 35N 1 39 E
Belturbet, *Ire.* **24** 54 6N 7 28W
Bembridge, *U.K.* **14** 50 41N 1 4W
Ben Bheigeir, *U.K.* **20** 55 43N 6 6W
Ben Chonzie, *U.K.* **21** 56 27N 4 0W
Ben Cruachan, *U.K.* **20** 56 26N 5 8W
Ben Dearg, *U.K.* **23** 57 47N 4 58W
Ben Dorain, *U.K.* **20** 56 30N 4 42W
Ben Hope, *U.K.* **23** 58 24N 4 36W
Ben Lawers, *U.K.* **23** 56 33N 4 13W
Ben Lomond, *U.K.* **20** 56 12N 4 39W
Ben Lui, *U.K.* **20** 56 24N 4 50W
Ben Macdhui, *U.K.* **23** 57 4N 3 40W
Ben Mhor, *U.K.* **22** 57 16N 7 21W
Ben More, *Central, U.K.* **20** 56 23N 4 31W
Ben More, *Strathclyde, U.K.* **20** 56 26N 6 2W
Ben More Assynt, *U.K.* **23** 58 7N 4 51W
Ben Nevis, *U.K.* **22** 56 48N 5 0W
Ben Venue, *U.K.* **20** 56 13N 4 28W
Ben Vorlich, *U.K.* **20** 56 22N 4 15W
Ben Wyvis, *U.K.* **23** 57 40N 4 35W
Benalla, *Austral.* **70** 36 30S 146 0 E
Benares = Varanasi, *India* **59** 25 22N 83 0 E
Benbecula, *U.K.* **22** 57 26N 7 21W
Bendigo, *Austral.* **70** 36 40S 144 15 E
Beneraird, *U.K.* **20** 55 4N 4 57W
Benevento, *It.* **40** 41 7N 14 45 E
Bengal, Bay of, *Ind. Oc.* **59** 18 0N 90 0 E
Bengbu, *China* **61** 32 58N 117 20 E
Benghazi, *Libya* **79** 32 11N 20 3 E
Beni Suef, *Egypt* **79** 29 5N 31 6 E
Benin ■, *Africa* **78** 10 0N 2 0 E
Benin, Bight of, *W. Afr.* **78** 5 0N 3 0 E
Benin City, *Nig.* **78** 6 20N 5 31 E
Benington, *U.K.* **19** 52 59N 0 5 E
Bennane Hd., *U.K.* **20** 55 9N 5 2W
Benoni, *S. Afr.* **81** 26 11S 28 18 E
Benson, *U.K.* **14** 51 37N 1 6W
Bentley, *Hants., U.K.* **15** 51 12N 0 52W
Bentley, *S. Yorks., U.K.* **19** 53 33N 1 9W
Benue →, *Nig.* **78** 7 48N 6 46 E
Benxi, *China* **61** 41 20N 123 48 E
Berbera, *Som.* **73** 10 30N 45 2 E
Berbérati, *C.A.R.* **80** 4 15N 15 40 E
Bere Alston, *U.K.* **16** 50 29N 4 11W
Bere Regis, *U.K.* **14** 50 45N 2 13W
Berezniki, *U.S.S.R.* **46** 59 24N 56 46 E
Bérgamo, *It.* **40** 45 42N 9 40 E
Bergen, *Nor.* **45** 60 23N 5 20 E
Bergen-op-Zoom, *Neth.* **36** 51 30N 4 18 E
Bergerac, *Fr.* **35** 44 51N 0 30 E
Bergisch-Gladbach, *W. Ger.* **36** 50 59N 7 9 E
Berhampore, *India* **59** 24 2N 88 27 E
Berhampur, *India* **59** 19 15N 84 54 E
Bering Sea, *Pac. Oc.* **88** 58 0N 167 0 E
Bering Str., *N. Am.* **103** 66 0N 170 0W
Berkeley, *U.K.* **14** 51 41N 2 28W
Berkhamsted, *U.K.* **15** 51 45N 0 33W
Berkshire □, *U.K.* **14** 51 30N 1 20W
Berkshire Downs, *U.K.* **15** 51 30N 1 30W
Berlin, *Ger.* **42** 52 32N 13 24 E
Bermuda ■, *Atl. Oc.* **95** 32 45N 65 0W
Bern, *Switz.* **42** 46 57N 7 28 E
Berry Hd., *U.K.* **16** 50 24N 3 29W
Berwick-upon-Tweed, *U.K.* **19** 55 47N 2 0W
Berwyn Mts., *U.K.* **17** 52 54N 3 26W
Besançon, *Fr.* **34** 47 15N 6 0 E
Bethesda, *U.K.* **17** 53 11N 4 3W
Bethlehem, *Jord.* **57** 31 43N 35 12 E
Bethlehem, *U.S.A.* **93** 40 39N 75 24W
Béthune, *Fr.* **34** 50 30N 2 38 E
Betws-y-Coed, *U.K.* **17** 53 4N 3 49W
Beverley, *U.K.* **19** 53 52N 0 26W
Beverwijk, *Neth.* **36** 52 28N 4 38 E
Bewdley, *U.K.* **14** 52 23N 2 19W
Bexhill, *U.K.* **15** 50 51N 0 29 E
Bexley, *U.K.* **15** 51 26N 0 10 E
Béziers, *Fr.* **35** 43 20N 3 12 E
Bhagalpur, *India* **59** 25 10N 87 0 E
Bhatinda, *India* **58** 30 15N 74 57 E
Bhatpara, *India* **59** 22 50N 88 25 E
Bhavnagar, *India* **58** 21 45N 72 10 E
Bhimavaram, *India* **59** 16 30N 81 30 E
Bhopal, *India* **58** 23 20N 77 30 E
Bhubaneshwar, *India* **59** 20 15N 85 50 E
Bhutan ■, *Asia* **59** 27 25N 90 30 E
Bialystok, *Pol.* **43** 53 10N 23 10 E
Biarritz, *Fr.* **34** 43 29N 1 33W
Bibury, *U.K.* **14** 51 46N 1 50W
Bicester, *U.K.* **14** 51 53N 1 9W
Bicton, *U.K.* **14** 52 43N 2 47W
Biddenden, *U.K.* **15** 51 7N 0 40 E
Biddulph, *U.K.* **18** 53 8N 2 11W
Bideford, *U.K.* **16** 51 1N 4 13W
Bideford Bay, *U.K.* **16** 51 5N 4 20W
Bidford on Avon, *U.K.* **14** 52 9N 1 53W
Bié Plateau, *Angola* **81** 12 0S 16 0 E
Biel, *Switz.* **42** 47 8N 7 14 E
Bielefeld, *W. Ger.* **42** 52 2N 8 31 E
Bigbury, *U.K.* **16** 50 17N 3 52W
Bigbury B., *U.K.* **16** 50 18N 3 58W
Biggar, *U.K.* **21** 55 38N 3 31W
Biggleswade, *U.K.* **15** 52 6N 0 16W
Bighorn Mts., *U.S.A.* **90** 44 30N 107 30W
Bihar □, *India* **59** 25 0N 86 0 E
Bikaner, *India* **58** 28 2N 73 18 E

Bundoran

Bikini Atoll, *Pac. Oc.* **64** 12 0N 167 30 E
Bilbao, *Sp.* **37** 43 16N 2 56W
Billericay, *U.K.* **15** 51 38N 0 25 E
Billesdon, *U.K.* **15** 52 38N 0 56W
Billingham, *U.K.* **19** 54 36N 1 18W
Billinghay, *U.K.* **19** 53 5N 0 17W
Billings, *U.S.A.* **90** 45 43N 108 29W
Billingshurst, *U.K.* **15** 51 2N 0 28W
Bilston, *U.K.* **14** 52 34N 2 5W
Binbrook, *U.K.* **19** 53 26N 0 9W
Bingham, *U.K.* **19** 52 57N 0 55W
Binghamton, *U.S.A.* **93** 42 9N 75 54W
Bingley, *U.K.* **18** 53 51N 1 50W
Bioko, *Eq. Guin.* **80** 3 30N 8 40 E
Birch, *U.K.* **15** 51 50N 0 54 E
Birchington, *U.K.* **15** 51 22N 1 18 E
Birdlip, *U.K.* **14** 51 50N 2 7W
Birkdale, *U.K.* **18** 53 38N 3 2W
Birkenhead, *U.K.* **18** 53 24N 3 1W
Birmingham, *U.K.* **14** 52 30N 1 55W
Birmingham, *U.S.A.* **91** 33 31N 86 50W
Birr, *Ire.* **25** 53 7N 7 55W
Birtley, *Northumberland, U.K.* **21** 55 5N 2 12W
Birtley, *Tyne & Wear, U.K.* **21** 54 53N 1 34W
Biscay, B. of, *Atl. Oc.* **35** 45 0N 2 0W
Bishop Auckland, *U.K.* **19** 54 40N 1 40W
Bishop's Castle, *U.K.* **14** 52 29N 3 0W
Bishop's Cleeve, *U.K.* **14** 51 56N 2 3W
Bishop's Frome, *U.K.* **14** 52 8N 2 29W
Bishops Lydeard, *U.K.* **14** 51 4N 3 12W
Bishop's Nympton, *U.K.* **16** 50 58N 3 44W
Bishop's Stortford, *U.K.* **15** 51 52N 0 11 E
Bishop's Waltham, *U.K.* **14** 50 57N 1 13W
Bishopsteignton, *U.K.* **16** 50 32N 3 32W
Bishopstoke, *U.K.* **14** 50 58N 1 19W
Biskra, *Alg.* **78** 34 50N 5 44 E
Bismarck Arch., *P.N.G.* **64** 2 30S 150 0 E
Bissau, *Guin.-Biss.* **78** 11 45N 15 45W
Bitola, *Yug.* **41** 41 5N 21 10 E
Bitton, *U.K.* **14** 51 25N 2 27W
Biwa-Ko, *Jap.* **62** 35 15N 136 10 E
Biysk, *U.S.S.R.* **48** 52 40N 85 0 E
Blaby, *U.K.* **14** 52 34N 1 10W
Black Combe, *U.K.* **18** 54 16N 3 20W
Black Esk →, *U.K.* **21** 55 14N 3 13W
Black Forest, Mts., *W. Ger.* **42** 48 0N 8 0 E
Black Hd., *U.K.* **16** 50 1N 5 6W
Black Mt. = Mynydd Du, *U.K.* **17** 51 45N 3 45W
Black Mts., *U.K.* **17** 51 52N 3 5W
Black Sea, *Europe* **47** 43 30N 35 0 E
Black Volta →, *Africa* **78** 8 41N 1 33W
Blackall, *Austral.* **67** 24 25S 145 45 E
Blackburn, *U.K.* **18** 53 44N 2 30W
Blackdown Hills, *U.K.* **14** 50 57N 3 15W
Blackford, *U.K.* **21** 56 15N 3 48W
Blackmoor Gate, *U.K.* **16** 51 9N 3 55W
Blackmoor Vale, *U.K.* **14** 50 54N 2 28W
Blackpool, *U.K.* **18** 53 48N 3 3W
Blacksod B., *Ire.* **24** 54 6N 10 0W
Blacktown, *Austral.* **70** 33 48S 150 55 E
Blackwater →, *Ire.* **25** 51 55N 7 50W
Blackwater →, *Essex, U.K.* **15** 51 44N 0 53 E
Blackwater →, *N. Ireland, U.K.* **24** 54 31N 6 35W
Blackwood, *U.K.* **21** 55 40N 3 56W
Blaenau Ffestiniog, *U.K.* **17** 53 0N 3 57W
Blaenavon, *U.K.* **17** 51 46N 3 5W
Blagdon, *U.K.* **14** 51 19N 2 42W
Blagoveshchensk, *U.S.S.R.* **49** 50 20N 127 30 E
Blair Athol, *Austral.* **67** 22 42S 147 31 E
Blair Atholl, *U.K.* **23** 56 46N 3 50W
Blairgowrie, *U.K.* **23** 56 36N 3 20W
Blakeney, *Gloucs., U.K.* **14** 51 45N 2 29W
Blakeney, *Norfolk, U.K.* **15** 52 57N 1 1 E
Blanc, Mont, *Europe* **35** 45 48N 6 50 E
Blandford Forum, *U.K.* **14** 50 52N 2 10W
Blantyre, *Malawi* **81** 15 45S 35 0 E
Blarney, *Ire.* **25** 51 57N 8 35W
Blaydon, *U.K.* **19** 54 56N 1 47W
Bleadon, *U.K.* **14** 51 18N 2 57W
Blean, *U.K.* **15** 51 18N 1 3 E
Bleasdale Moors, *U.K.* **18** 53 57N 2 40W
Blenheim, *N.Z.* **71** 41 38S 173 57 E
Bletchingdon, *U.K.* **14** 51 51N 1 16W
Bletchley, *U.K.* **15** 51 59N 0 44W
Blisworth, *U.K.* **15** 52 11N 0 56W
Blockley, *U.K.* **14** 52 1N 1 45W
Bloemfontein, *S. Afr.* **81** 29 6S 26 14 E
Blofield, *U.K.* **15** 52 38N 1 25 E
Blois, *Fr.* **34** 47 35N 1 20 E
Bloody Foreland, *Ire.* **24** 55 10N 8 18W
Bloxham, *U.K.* **14** 52 1N 1 22W
Blue Mts., *Austral.* **70** 33 40S 150 0 E
Blue Mts., *U.S.A.* **90** 45 15N 119 0W
Blue Nile →, *Sudan* **79** 12 30N 34 30 E
Blue Ridge Mts., *U.S.A.* **91** 36 30N 80 15W
Blue Stack Mts., *Ire.* **24** 54 46N 8 5W
Blumenau, *Brazil* **102** 27 0S 49 0W
Blundeston, *U.K.* **15** 52 33N 1 42 E
Blyth, *Northumberland, U.K.* **19** 55 8N 1 32W
Blyth, *Notts., U.K.* **19** 53 22N 1 2W
Blyth →, *U.K.* **21** 55 8N 1 30W
Blyth Bridge, *U.K.* **21** 55 41N 3 22W
Blyton, *U.K.* **19** 53 25N 0 42W
Bobo-Dioulasso, *B. Faso* **78** 11 8N 4 13W
Bocholt, *W. Ger.* **36** 51 50N 6 35 E
Bochum, *W. Ger.* **36** 51 28N 7 12 E
Bodenham, *U.K.* **14** 52 9N 2 41W
Bodensee, *W. Ger.* **42** 47 35N 9 25 E
Bodiam, *U.K.* **15** 51 1N 0 33 E
Bodinnick, *U.K.* **16** 50 20N 4 37W
Bodmin, *U.K.* **16** 50 28N 4 44W
Bodmin Moor, *U.K.* **16** 50 33N 4 36W
Bodø, *Nor.* **44** 67 17N 14 24 E
Bogan →, *Austral.* **67** 29 59S 146 17 E
Boggeragh Mts., *Ire.* **25** 52 2N 8 55W
Bognor Regis, *U.K.* **15** 50 47N 0 40W
Bogor, *Indon.* **63** 6 36S 106 48 E
Bogota, *Col.* **100** 4 34N 74 0W
Bohemian Forest, *Czech.* **42** 49 20N 13 0 E
Boise, *U.S.A.* **90** 43 43N 116 9W
Bolgatanga, *Ghana* **78** 10 44N 0 53W
Bolivia ■, *S. Am.* **100** 17 6S 64 0W
Bolivian Plateau, *S. Am.* **96** 20 0S 67 30W
Bollington, *U.K.* **18** 53 18N 2 8W
Bolney, *U.K.* **15** 50 59N 0 11W
Bologna, *It.* **40** 44 30N 11 20 E
Bolshevik, I., *U.S.S.R.* **49** 78 30N 102 0 E
Bolshezemelskaya Tundra, *U.S.S.R.* **46** 67 0N 56 0 E
Bolsover, *U.K.* **19** 53 14N 1 18W
Bolt Head, *U.K.* **16** 50 13N 3 48W
Bolt Tail, *U.K.* **16** 50 13N 3 55W
Bolton, *U.K.* **18** 53 35N 2 26W
Bolton Abbey, *U.K.* **18** 53 59N 1 53W
Bolton by Bowland, *U.K.* **18** 53 56N 2 21W
Bolton le Sands, *U.K.* **18** 54 7N 2 49W
Bolungavík, *Ice.* **44** 66 9N 23 15W
Bolzano, *It.* **40** 46 30N 11 20 E
Boma, *Zaïre* **80** 5 50S 13 4 E
Bombay, *India* **58** 18 55N 72 50 E
Bonaparte Archipelago, *Austral.* **66** 14 0S 124 30 E
Bonarbridge, *U.K.* **23** 57 53N 4 20W
Bonchester Bridge, *U.K.* **21** 55 23N 2 36W
Bonchurch, *U.K.* **14** 50 36N 1 11W
Bo'ness, *U.K.* **21** 56 0N 3 38W
Bonifacio, Str. of, *Fr.* **40** 41 12N 9 15 E
Bonn, *W. Ger.* **36** 50 43N 7 6 E
Bonnyrigg, *U.K.* **21** 55 52N 3 8W
Boot, *U.K.* **18** 54 24N 3 18W
Boothia, Gulf of, *Canada* **89** 71 0N 90 0W
Boothia Pen., *Canada* **88** 71 0N 94 0W
Bootle, *Cumbria, U.K.* **18** 54 17N 3 24W
Bootle, *Merseyside, U.K.* **18** 53 28N 3 1W
Borås, *Swed.* **45** 57 43N 12 56 E
Bordeaux, *Fr.* **35** 44 50N 0 36W
Borders □, *U.K.* **21** 55 35N 2 50W
Bordon, *U.K.* **15** 51 6N 0 52W
Borehamwood, *U.K.* **15** 51 40N 0 15W
Boreland, *U.K.* **21** 55 12N 3 16W
Borgarnes, *Ice.* **44** 64 32N 21 55W
Borneo, *E. Ind.* **63** 1 0N 115 0 E
Bornholm, *Den.* **45** 55 10N 15 0 E
Boroughbridge, *U.K.* **19** 54 6N 1 23W
Borrowdale, *U.K.* **18** 54 31N 3 10W
Borth, *U.K.* **17** 52 29N 4 3W
Bosbury, *U.K.* **14** 52 5N 2 27W
Boscastle, *U.K.* **16** 50 42N 4 42W
Bosham, *U.K.* **15** 50 50N 0 51W
Bosporus, *Turk.* **47** 41 10N 29 10 E
Boston, *U.K.* **19** 52 59N 0 2W
Boston, *U.S.A.* **93** 42 20N 71 0W
Botany Bay, *Austral.* **70** 34 0S 151 14 E
Bothel, *U.K.* **18** 54 43N 3 16W
Bothnia, G. of, *Europe* **44** 63 0N 20 0 E
Botswana ■, *Africa* **81** 22 0S 24 0 E
Bottesford, *U.K.* **19** 52 57N 0 48W
Bottrop, *W. Ger.* **36** 51 34N 6 59 E
Bouaké, *Ivory C.* **78** 7 40N 5 2W
Bouar, *C.A.R.* **80** 6 0N 15 40 E
Boulogne-sur-Mer, *Fr.* **34** 50 42N 1 36 E
Bourges, *Fr.* **34** 47 9N 2 25 E
Bourgogne, *Fr.* **34** 47 0N 4 50 E
Bourke, *Austral.* **67** 30 8S 145 55 E
Bourne, *U.K.* **15** 52 46N 0 22W
Bournemouth, *U.K.* **14** 50 43N 1 53W
Bourton-on-the-Water, *U.K.* **14** 51 53N 1 45W
Bovey Tracey, *U.K.* **16** 50 36N 3 40W
Bowen, *Austral.* **67** 20 0S 148 16 E
Bowes, *U.K.* **18** 54 31N 1 59W
Bowland, Forest of, *U.K.* **18** 54 0N 2 30W
Bowmore, *U.K.* **20** 55 45N 6 18W
Bowness, *Solway, U.K.* **18** 54 57N 3 13W
Bowness, *Windermere, U.K.* **18** 54 22N 2 56W
Box, *U.K.* **14** 51 24N 2 16W
Box Hill, *U.K.* **15** 51 16N 0 16W
Boxley, *U.K.* **15** 51 17N 0 34 E
Boyle, *Ire.* **24** 53 58N 8 19W
Boyne →, *Ire.* **24** 53 43N 6 15W
Bozeat, *U.K.* **15** 52 14N 0 41W
Bracadale, L., *U.K.* **22** 57 20N 6 30W
Bracebridge Heath, *U.K.* **19** 53 13N 0 32W
Brackley, *U.K.* **14** 52 3N 1 9W
Bracknell, *U.K.* **15** 51 24N 0 45W
Braco, *U.K.* **21** 56 16N 3 55W
Bradda Hd., *U.K.* **18** 54 6N 4 46W
Bradford, *U.K.* **19** 53 47N 1 45W
Bradford-on-Avon, *U.K.* **14** 51 20N 2 15W
Brading, *U.K.* **14** 50 41N 1 9W
Bradwell-on-Sea, *U.K.* **15** 51 44N 0 55 E
Bradworthy, *U.K.* **16** 50 54N 4 22W
Braemar, *U.K.* **23** 57 2N 3 20W
Braga, *Port.* **37** 41 35N 8 25W
Brahmaputra →, *India* **59** 24 2N 90 59 E
Braich-y-pwll, *U.K.* **17** 52 47N 4 46W
Brăila, *Rom.* **43** 45 19N 27 59 E
Brailsford, *U.K.* **19** 52 58N 1 35W
Braintree, *U.K.* **15** 51 53N 0 34 E
Bramford, *U.K.* **15** 52 5N 1 6 E
Brampton, *Canada* **92** 43 45N 79 45W
Brampton, *Cambs., U.K.* **15** 52 19N 0 13W
Brampton, *Cumbria, U.K.* **18** 54 56N 2 43W
Bramshott, *U.K.* **15** 51 5N 0 47W
Brancaster, *U.K.* **15** 52 58N 0 40 E
Branco →, *Brazil* **100** 1 20S 61 50W
Brander, Pass of, *U.K.* **20** 56 25N 5 10W
Brandon, *Canada* **88** 49 50N 99 57W
Brandon, *Durham, U.K.* **19** 54 46N 1 37W
Brandon, *Suffolk, U.K.* **15** 52 27N 0 37 E
Brandon, Mt., *Ire.* **25** 52 15N 10 15W
Brandon B., *Ire.* **25** 52 17N 10 8W
Branston, *U.K.* **19** 53 13N 0 28W
Brantford, *Canada* **92** 43 10N 80 15W
Brasília, *Brazil* **101** 15 47S 47 55 E
Braşov, *Rom.* **43** 45 38N 25 35 E
Brasted, *U.K.* **15** 51 16N 0 8 E
Bratislava, *Czech.* **43** 48 10N 17 7 E
Bratsk, *U.S.S.R.* **49** 56 10N 101 30 E
Braunton, *U.K.* **16** 51 6N 4 9W
Bray, *Ire.* **25** 53 12N 6 6W
Bray, *U.K.* **15** 51 30N 0 42W
Brazil ■, *S. Am.* **101** 10 0S 50 0W
Brazilian Highlands, *Brazil* **101** 18 0S 46 30W
Brazzaville, *Congo* **80** 4 9S 15 12 E
Breadalbane, *U.K.* **20** 56 30N 4 15W
Breage, *U.K.* **16** 50 6N 5 17W
Breamish →, *U.K.* **21** 55 30N 1 55W
Brechin, *U.K.* **23** 56 44N 2 40W
Breckland, *U.K.* **15** 52 30N 0 40 E
Brecon, *U.K.* **17** 51 57N 3 23W
Brecon Beacons, *U.K.* **17** 51 53N 3 27W
Brede, *U.K.* **15** 50 56N 0 37 E
Bredon Hill, *U.K.* **14** 52 3N 2 2W
Breiðafjörður, *Ice.* **44** 65 15N 23 15W
Bremen, *W. Ger.* **42** 53 4N 8 47 E
Bremerhaven, *W. Ger.* **40** 53 34N 8 35 E
Brendon Hills, *U.K.* **14** 51 6N 3 25W
Brenner Pass, *Alps* **42** 47 0N 11 30 E
Brent, *U.K.* **15** 51 33N 0 18W
Brentwood, *U.K.* **15** 51 37N 0 19 E
Bréscia, *It.* **40** 45 33N 10 13 E
Breslau = Wrocław, *Pol.* **43** 51 5N 17 5 E
Bressay I., *U.K.* **22** 60 10N 1 5W
Brest, *Fr.* **34** 48 24N 4 31W
Brest, *U.S.S.R.* **46** 52 10N 23 40 E
Bretagne, *Fr.* **34** 48 0N 3 0W
Brewood, *U.K.* **14** 52 41N 2 10W
Brezhnev, *U.S.S.R.* **46** 55 42N 52 19 E
Bride, *U.K.* **18** 54 24N 4 23W
Bridestowe, *U.K.* **16** 50 41N 4 7W
Bridge, *U.K.* **15** 51 14N 1 8 E
Bridge of Allan, *U.K.* **21** 56 9N 3 57W
Bridge of Earn, *U.K.* **21** 56 20N 3 25W
Bridge of Orchy, *U.K.* **20** 56 29N 4 48W
Bridge of Weir, *U.K.* **20** 55 51N 4 35W
Bridgend, *Islay, U.K.* **20** 55 46N 6 15W
Bridgend, *Mid Glam., U.K.* **17** 51 30N 3 35W
Bridgeport, *U.S.A.* **93** 41 12N 73 12W
Bridgetown, *Barb.* **94** 13 0N 59 30W
Bridgnorth, *U.K.* **14** 52 33N 2 25W
Bridgwater, *U.K.* **14** 51 7N 3 0W
Bridgwater B., *U.K.* **14** 51 15N 3 15W
Bridlington, *U.K.* **19** 54 6N 0 11W
Bridlington B., *U.K.* **19** 54 4N 0 10W
Bridport, *U.K.* **14** 50 43N 2 45W
Brierfield, *U.K.* **18** 53 49N 2 15W
Brierley Hill, *U.K.* **14** 52 29N 2 7W
Brigg, *U.K.* **19** 53 33N 0 30W
Brighouse, *U.K.* **19** 53 42N 1 47W
Brighstone, *U.K.* **15** 50 38N 1 36W
Brightlingsea, *U.K.* **15** 51 49N 1 1 E
Brighton, *U.K.* **15** 50 50N 0 9W
Brightstone, *U.K.* **14** 50 38N 1 23W
Brigstock, *U.K.* **15** 52 27N 0 38W
Brill, *U.K.* **14** 51 49N 1 3W
Brimfield, *U.K.* **14** 52 18N 2 42W
Bríndisi, *It.* **41** 40 39N 17 55 E
Brinklow, *U.K.* **14** 52 25N 1 22W
Brinkworth, *U.K.* **14** 51 33N 1 59W
Brisbane, *Austral.* **67** 27 25S 153 2 E
Bristol, *U.K.* **14** 51 26N 2 35W
Bristol Channel, *U.K.* **16** 51 18N 4 30W
Briston, *U.K.* **15** 52 52N 1 4 E
British Columbia □, *Canada* **88** 55 0N 125 15W
British Guiana = Guyana ■, *S. Am.* **100** 5 0N 59 0W
British Isles, *Europe* **4** 55 0N 4 0W
Brittany = Bretagne, *Fr.* **34** 48 0N 3 0W
Brixham, *U.K.* **16** 50 24N 3 31W
Brixworth, *U.K.* **15** 52 20N 0 54W
Brize Norton, *U.K.* **14** 51 46N 1 35W
Brno, *Czech.* **42** 49 10N 16 35 E
Broad B., *U.K.* **22** 58 14N 6 16W
Broad Chalke, *U.K.* **14** 51 2N 1 54W
Broad Clyst, *U.K.* **16** 50 46N 3 27W
Broad Haven, *Ire.* **24** 54 20N 9 55W
Broad Law, *U.K.* **21** 55 30N 3 22W
Broad Sd., *U.K.* **16** 49 56N 6 19W
Broadford, *U.K.* **22** 57 14N 5 55W
Broadhembury, *U.K.* **16** 50 49N 3 16W
Broads, The, *U.K.* **15** 52 45N 1 30 E
Broadstairs, *U.K.* **15** 51 21N 1 28 E
Broadway, *U.K.* **14** 52 2N 1 51W
Broadwindsor, *U.K.* **14** 50 49N 2 49W
Brockenhurst, *U.K.* **14** 50 49N 1 34W
Brockton, *U.S.A.* **93** 42 25N 79 26W
Brockworth, *U.K.* **14** 51 51N 2 9W
Brodick, *U.K.* **20** 55 34N 5 9W
Broken Hill, *Austral.* **70** 31 58S 141 29 E
Bromborough, *U.K.* **18** 53 20N 3 0W
Bromfield, *U.K.* **14** 52 25N 2 45W
Bromham, *U.K.* **14** 51 23N 2 3W
Bromley, *U.K.* **15** 51 20N 0 5 E
Brompton, *U.K.* **19** 54 22N 1 25W
Bromsgrove, *U.K.* **14** 52 20N 2 3W
Bromyard, *U.K.* **14** 52 12N 2 30W
Brooks, *Canada* **88** 50 35N 111 55W
Brooks Ra., *U.S.A.* **88** 68 40N 147 0W
Broom, L., *U.K.* **22** 57 55N 5 15W
Broomfield, *U.K.* **14** 51 46N 0 28 E
Broomhill, *U.K.* **21** 55 19N 1 36W
Brora, *U.K.* **23** 58 0N 3 50W
Brora →, *U.K.* **23** 58 4N 3 52W
Broseley, *U.K.* **14** 52 36N 2 30W
Brosna →, *Ire.* **25** 53 8N 8 0W
Brothertoft, *U.K.* **19** 53 0N 0 5W
Brotton, *U.K.* **19** 54 34N 0 55W
Brough, *Cumbria, U.K.* **18** 54 32N 2 19W
Brough, *Humberside, U.K.* **19** 53 44N 0 35W
Broughton, *Borders, U.K.* **21** 55 37N 3 25W
Broughton, *Humberside, U.K.* **19** 53 33N 0 36W
Broughton, *N. Yorks., U.K.* **19** 54 26N 1 8W
Broughton, *Northants., U.K.* **15** 52 22N 0 45W
Broughton-in-Furness, *U.K.* **18** 54 17N 3 12W
Broughty Ferry, *U.K.* **21** 56 29N 2 50W
Brown Willy, *U.K.* **16** 50 35N 4 34W
Brownhills, *U.K.* **14** 52 38N 1 57W
Broxburn, *U.K.* **21** 55 56N 3 23W
Bruay-en-Artois, *Fr.* **34** 50 29N 2 33 E
Bruce, Mt., *Austral.* **66** 22 37S 118 8 E
Brue →, *U.K.* **14** 51 10N 2 59W
Bruges, *Belg.* **36** 51 13N 3 13 E
Brunei ■, *E. Ind.* **63** 4 50N 115 0 E
Brunswick, *W. Ger.* **42** 52 17N 10 28 E
Brunton, *U.K.* **21** 55 2N 2 6W
Brussels, *Belg.* **36** 50 51N 4 21 E
Bruton, *U.K.* **14** 51 6N 2 28W
Bryansk, *U.S.S.R.* **46** 53 13N 34 25 E
Bryher I., *U.K.* **16** 49 57N 6 21W
Brynamman, *U.K.* **17** 51 49N 3 52W
Brynmawr, *U.K.* **17** 51 48N 3 11W
Bucaramanga, *Col.* **100** 7 0N 73 0W
Buchan, *U.K.* **23** 57 32N 2 8W
Buchan Ness, *U.K.* **23** 57 29N 1 48W
Bucharest, *Rom.* **43** 44 27N 26 10 E
Buchlyvie, *U.K.* **20** 56 7N 4 20W
Buckden, *U.K.* **15** 52 17N 0 16W
Buckfastleigh, *U.K.* **16** 50 28N 3 47W
Buckhaven, *U.K.* **21** 56 10N 3 2W
Buckie, *U.K.* **23** 57 40N 2 58W
Buckingham, *U.K.* **15** 52 0N 0 59W
Buckingham □, *U.K.* **15** 51 50N 0 55W
Buckland Brewer, *U.K.* **16** 50 56N 4 14W
Buckland Newton, *U.K.* **14** 50 45N 2 25W
Buckley, *U.K.* **17** 53 10N 3 5W
Budapest, *Hung.* **43** 47 29N 19 5 E
Buddon Ness, *U.K.* **21** 56 29N 2 42W
Bude, *U.K.* **16** 50 49N 4 33W
Bude Bay, *U.K.* **16** 50 50N 4 40W
Budle B., *U.K.* **21** 55 37N 1 45W
Budleigh Salterton, *U.K.* **16** 50 37N 3 19W
Buenaventura, *Col.* **100** 3 53N 77 4W
Buenos Aires, *Arg.* **102** 34 30S 58 20W
Buffalo, *U.S.A.* **92** 42 55N 78 50W
Bug →, *Pol.* **43** 52 31N 21 5 E
Bug →, *U.S.S.R.* **47** 46 59N 31 58 E
Buglawton, *U.K.* **18** 53 12N 2 11W
Bugle, *U.K.* **16** 50 23N 4 46W
Buie L., *U.K.* **20** 56 20N 5 55W
Builth Wells, *U.K.* **17** 52 10N 3 26W
Bujumbura, *Bur.* **80** 3 16S 29 18 E
Bukavu, *Zaïre* **80** 2 20S 28 52 E
Bukhara, *U.S.S.R.* **48** 39 48N 64 25 E
Bulawayo, *Zimb.* **81** 20 7S 28 32 E
Bulford, *U.K.* **14** 51 11N 1 45W
Bulgaria ■, *Europe* **41** 42 35N 25 30 E
Bulwell, *U.K.* **19** 53 1N 1 12W
Bunbury, *Austral.* **66** 33 20S 115 35 E
Buncrana, *Ire.* **24** 55 8N 7 28W
Bundaberg, *Austral.* **67** 24 54S 152 22 E
Bundoran, *Ire.* **24** 54 24N 8 17W

Bunessan, *U.K.*	20 56 18N	6 15W
Bungay, *U.K.*	15 52 27N	1 26 E
Buntingford, *U.K.*	15 51 57N	0 1W
Bunwell, *U.K.*	15 52 30N	1 9 E
Buraydah, *Si. Arab.*	56 26 20N	44 8 E
Burbage, *Derby, U.K.*	18 53 15N	1 55W
Burbage, *Leics., U.K.*	14 52 31N	1 20W
Burbage, *Wilts., U.K.*	14 51 21N	1 40W
Burdwan, *India*	59 23 14N	87 39 E
Bure →, *U.K.*	15 52 38N	1 45 E
Burford, *U.K.*	14 51 48N	1 38W
Burgas, *Bulg.*	41 42 33N	27 29 E
Burgess Hill, *U.K.*	15 50 57N	0 7W
Burgh-le-Marsh, *U.K.*	19 53 10N	0 15 E
Burgos, *Sp.*	37 42 21N	3 41W
Burgundy =		
Bourgogne, *Fr.*	34 47 0N	4 50 E
Burkina Faso ■, *Africa*	78 12 0N	1 0W
Burley, *Hants., U.K.*	14 50 49N	1 41W
Burley, *N. Yorks., U.K.*	19 53 55N	1 46W
Burlington, *U.S.A.*	93 44 27N	73 14W
Burma ■, *Asia*	59 21 0N	96 30 E
Burnham, *Essex, U.K.*	15 51 37N	0 50 E
Burnham, *Somerset,*		
U.K.	14 51 14N	3 0W
Burnham Market, *U.K.*	15 52 57N	0 43 E
Burnie, *Austral.*	67 41 4S 145 56 E
Burnley, *U.K.*	18 53 47N	2 15W
Burnmouth, *U.K.*	21 55 50N	2 4W
Burntisland, *U.K.*	21 56 4N	3 14W
Burrelton, *U.K.*	21 56 30N	3 16W
Burrow Hd., *U.K.*	20 54 40N	4 23W
Burry Port, *U.K.*	17 51 41N	4 17W
Bursa, *Turk.*	47 40 15N	29 5 E
Burstwick, *U.K.*	19 53 43N	0 6W
Burton, *U.K.*	18 54 10N	2 43W
Burton Agnes, *U.K.*	19 54 4N	0 18W
Burton Bradstock, *U.K.*	14 50 41N	2 43W
Burton Fleming, *U.K.*	19 54 8N	0 20W
Burton Latimer, *U.K.*	15 52 23N	0 41W
Burton upon Stather,		
U.K.	19 53 39N	0 41W
Burton-upon-Trent, *U.K.*	14 52 48N	1 39W
Burundi ■, *Africa*	80 3 15S	30 0 E
Burwash, *U.K.*	15 50 59N	0 24 E
Burwell, *U.K.*	15 52 17N	0 20 E
Bury, *U.K.*	18 53 36N	2 19W
Bury St. Edmunds, *U.K.*	15 52 15N	0 42 E
Buryat A.S.S.R. □,		
U.S.S.R.	49 53 0N 110 0 E
Bûshehr, *Iran*	56 28 20N	51 45 E
Bushey, *U.K.*	15 51 38N	0 20W
Bushmills, *U.K.*	24 55 14N	6 32W
Bute, *U.K.*	20 55 48N	5 2W
Bute, Kyles of, *U.K.*	20 55 55N	5 10W
Bute, Sd. of, *U.K.*	20 55 43N	5 8W
Buttermere, *U.K.*	18 54 32N	3 17W
Butuan, *Phil.*	63 8 57N 125 33 E
Buxton, *U.K.*	18 53 16N	1 54W
Buzău, *Rom.*	43 45 10N	26 50 E
Bydgoszcz, *Pol.*	43 53 10N	18 0 E
Byfield, *U.K.*	14 52 10N	1 15W
Byrd Land, *Ant.*	103 79 30S 125 0W
Byrrang Mts., *U.S.S.R.*	49 75 0N 100 0 E
Bytom, *Pol.*	43 50 25N	18 54 E

C

Cabimas, *Ven.*	100 10 23N	71 25W
Cabinda □, *Angola*	80 5 0S	12 30 E
Čačak, *Yug.*	41 43 54N	20 20 E
Cáceres, *Sp.*	37 39 26N	6 23W
Cachoeira do Sul, *Brazil*	102 30 3S	52 53W
Cader Idris, *U.K.*	17 52 43N	3 56W
Cádiz, *Sp.*	37 36 30N	6 20W
Caen, *Fr.*	34 49 10N	0 22W
Caenby Corner, *U.K.*	19 53 23N	0 32W
Caernarfon, *U.K.*	17 53 8N	4 17W
Caernarfon B., *U.K.*	17 53 4N	4 40W
Caerphilly, *U.K.*	17 51 34N	3 13W
Caersws, *U.K.*	17 52 32N	3 27W
Cagayan de Oro, *Phil.*	63 8 30N 124 40 E
Cágliari, *It.*	40 39 15N	9 6 E
Caha Mts., *Ire.*	25 51 45N	9 40W
Caher, *Ire.*	25 52 23N	7 56W
Cahersiveen, *Ire.*	25 51 57N	10 13W
Cahore Pt., *Ire.*	25 52 34N	6 11W
Caicos Is., *W. Ind.*	95 21 40N	71 40W
Cairn Gorm, *U.K.*	23 57 7N	3 40W
Cairn Table, *U.K.*	21 55 30N	4 0W
Cairn Toul, *U.K.*	23 57 3N	3 44W
Cairngorm Mts., *U.K.*	23 57 6N	3 42W
Cairnryan, *U.K.*	20 54 59N	5 0W
Cairns, *Austral.*	67 16 57S 145 45 E
Cairo, *Egypt*	79 30 1N	31 14 E
Caister-on-Sea, *U.K.*	15 52 38N	1 43 E
Caistor, *U.K.*	19 53 29N	0 20W
Caithness, Ord of, *U.K.*	23 58 9N	3 37W
Cajamarca, *Peru*	100 7 5S	78 28W
Calabar, *Nig.*	78 4 57N	8 20 E
Calábria □, *It.*	40 39 24N	16 30 E
Calais, *Fr.*	34 50 57N	1 50 E
Calbayog, *Phil.*	63 12 4N 124 38 E
Calcutta, *India*	59 22 36N	88 24 E
Caldbeck, *U.K.*	18 54 45N	3 3W
Calder →, *U.K.*	19 53 44N	1 21W
Calder Bridge, *U.K.*	18 54 27N	3 31W

Caldew →, *U.K.*	18 54 54N	2 59W
Caledonian Canal, *U.K.*	23 56 50N	5 6W
Calf of Man, *U.K.*	18 54 4N	4 48W
Calgary, *Canada*	88 51 0N 114 10W
Calgary, *U.K.*	20 56 34N	6 17W
Cali, *Col.*	100 3 25N	76 35W
Caliach Pt., *U.K.*	20 56 37N	6 20W
Calicut, *India*	58 11 15N	75 43 E
California □, *U.S.A.*	90 37 25N 120 0W
California, G. of, *N. Am.*	94 27 0N 111 0W
Callan, *Ire.*	25 52 33N	7 25W
Callander, *U.K.*	20 56 15N	4 14W
Callao, *Peru*	100 12 0S	77 0W
Calne, *U.K.*	14 51 26N	2 0W
Calshot, *U.K.*	14 50 49N	1 18W
Calstock, *U.K.*	16 50 30N	4 13W
Caltanissetta, *It.*	40 37 30N	14 3 E
Cam →, *U.K.*	15 52 21N	0 16 E
Camagüey, *Cuba*	95 21 20N	78 0W
Camargue, *Fr.*	35 43 34N	4 34 E
Cambay, G. of, *India*	58 20 45N	72 30 E
Camberley, *U.K.*	15 51 20N	0 44W
Cambo, *U.K.*	21 55 9N	1 57W
Cambodia ■, *Asia*	63 12 15N 105 0 E
Camborne, *U.K.*	16 50 13N	5 18W
Cambrian Mts., *U.K.*	17 52 25N	3 52W
Cambridge, *U.K.*	15 52 13N	0 8 E
Cambridge, *U.S.A.*	93 42 20N	71 8W
Cambridge Bay,		
Canada	88 69 10N 105 0W
Cambridgeshire □, *U.K.*	15 52 12N	0 7 E
Camden, *U.K.*	15 51 33N	0 10W
Camden, *U.S.A.*	93 39 57N	75 7W
Camel →, *U.K.*	16 50 28N	4 49W
Camelford, *U.K.*	16 50 37N	4 41W
Cameroon ■, *Africa*	80 6 0N	12 30 E
Campbellton, *Canada*	93 49 17N	54 56W
Campbelltown, *Austral.*	70 34 53S 138 40 E
Campbeltown, *U.K.*	20 55 25N	5 36W
Campeche, *Mex.*	94 19 50N	90 32W
Campeche, G. of, *Mex.*	94 19 30N	93 0W
Campina Grande, *Brazil*	101 7 20S	35 47W
Campinas, *Brazil*	102 22 50S	47 0W
Campo Grande, *Brazil*	101 20 25S	54 40W
Campos, *Brazil*	101 21 50S	41 20W
Campsie Fells, *U.K.*	20 56 2N	4 20W
Camrose, *Canada*	88 53 0N 112 50W
Can Tho, *Viet.*	63 10 2N 105 46 E
Canada ■, *N. Am.*	88 60 0N 100 0W
Canary Is., *Atl. Oc.*	78 29 30N	17 0W
Canaveral, C., *U.S.A.*	91 28 28N	80 31W
Canberra, *Austral.*	70 35 15S 149 8 E
Canik Mts., *Turk.*	47 40 30N	38 0 E
Canna, *U.K.*	22 57 3N	6 33W
Cannes, *Fr.*	35 43 32N	7 0 E
Cannington, *U.K.*	14 51 8N	3 4W
Cannock, *U.K.*	14 52 42N	2 2W
Cannock Chase, *U.K.*	14 52 43N	2 0W
Canonbie, *U.K.*	21 55 4N	2 58W
Cantabrian Mts., *Sp.*	37 43 0N	5 10W
Canterbury, *U.K.*	15 51 17N	1 5 E
Canterbury Plains, *N.Z.*	71 43 55S 171 22 E
Canton = Guangzhou,		
China	61 23 5N 113 10 E
Canton, *U.S.A.*	92 40 47N	81 22W
Canvey, *U.K.*	15 51 32N	0 35 E
Caoles, *U.K.*	20 56 32N	6 43W
Caolisport, Loch, *U.K.*	20 55 54N	5 40W
Cape Breton I., *Canada*	93 46 0N	60 30W
Cape Coast, *Ghana*	78 5 5N	1 15W
Cape Province □,		
S. Afr.	81 32 0S	23 0 E
Cape Town, *S. Afr.*	81 33 55S	18 22 E
Cape Verde Is. ■,		
Atl. Oc.	128 17 10N	25 20W
Cape York Peninsula,		
Austral.	67 12 0S 142 30 E
Capel, *U.K.*	15 51 8N	0 18W
Caracas, *Ven.*	100 10 30N	66 55W
Caratinga, *Brazil*	101 19 50S	42 10W
Carbost, *U.K.*	22 57 19N	6 21W
Cardiff, *U.K.*	17 51 28N	3 11W
Cardigan, *U.K.*	17 52 6N	4 41W
Cardigan B., *U.K.*	17 52 30N	4 30W
Cardington, *U.K.*	15 52 7N	0 23W
Carey, L., *Austral.*	66 29 0S 122 15 E
Caribbean Sea	95 15 0N	75 0W
Carisbrooke, *U.K.*	14 50 42N	1 19W
Cark, *U.K.*	18 54 11N	2 59W
Carleton Rode, *U.K.*	15 52 30N	1 6 E
Carlingford, L., *Ire.*	24 54 0N	6 5W
Carlisle, *U.K.*	18 54 54N	2 55W
Carlops, *U.K.*	21 55 47N	3 20W
Carlow, *Ire.*	25 52 50N	6 58W
Carlow □, *Ire.*	25 52 43N	6 50W
Carloway, *U.K.*	22 58 17N	6 48W
Carlton, *U.K.*	19 52 58N	1 6W
Carlton Colville, *U.K.*	15 52 27N	1 41 E
Carlton Miniott, *U.K.*	19 54 13N	1 22W
Carluke, *U.K.*	21 55 44N	3 50W
Carmarthen, *U.K.*	17 51 52N	4 20W
Carmarthen B., *U.K.*	17 51 40N	4 30W
Carnarvon, *Austral.*	66 24 51S 113 42 E
Carndonagh, *Ire.*	24 55 15N	7 16W
Carnegie, L., *Austral.*	66 26 5S 122 30 E
Carnforth, *U.K.*	18 54 8N	2 47W
Carno, *U.K.*	17 52 34N	3 31W
Carnoustie, *U.K.*	21 56 30N	2 41W
Carnsore Pt., *Ire.*	25 52 10N	6 20W
Carnwath, *U.K.*	21 55 42N	3 38W

Caroline Is., *Pac. Oc.*	64 8 0N 150 0 E
Carpathians, Mts.,		
Europe	43 49 50N	21 0 E
Carpentaria, G. of,		
Austral.	67 14 0S 139 0 E
Carradale, *U.K.*	20 55 35N	5 30W
Carrauntoohill, Mt., *Ire.*	25 52 0N	9 49W
Carrick, *U.K.*	20 55 12N	4 38W
Carrick-on-Shannon,		
Ire.	24 53 57N	8 7W
Carrick-on-Suir, *Ire.*	25 52 22N	7 30W
Carrickfergus, *U.K.*	24 54 43N	5 50W
Carrickfergus □, *U.K.*	24 54 43N	5 49W
Carrickmacross, *Ire.*	24 54 0N	6 43W
Carron →, *U.K.*	22 57 30N	5 30W
Carron, L., *U.K.*	22 57 22N	5 35W
Carronbridge, *U.K.*	21 55 16N	3 46W
Carse of Gowrie, *U.K.*	21 56 30N	3 10W
Carsphairn, *U.K.*	20 55 13N	4 15W
Carstairs, *U.K.*	21 55 42N	3 41W
Cartagena, *Col.*	100 10 25N	75 33W
Cartagena, *Sp.*	37 37 38N	0 59W
Cartmel, *U.K.*	18 54 13N	2 57W
Caruaru, *Brazil*	101 8 15S	35 55W
Carúpano, *Ven.*	100 10 39N	63 15W
Casablanca, *Mor.*	78 33 36N	7 36W
Cascade Ra., *U.S.A.*	90 47 0N 121 30W
Cashel, *Ire.*	25 52 31N	7 53W
Casper, *U.S.A.*	90 42 52N 106 20W
Caspian Sea, *U.S.S.R.*	47 43 0N	50 0 E
Castellón □, *Sp.*	37 40 15N	0 5W
Castle Acre, *U.K.*	15 52 42N	0 42W
Castle Cary, *U.K.*	14 51 5N	2 32W
Castle Donington, *U.K.*	14 52 50N	1 20W
Castle Douglas, *U.K.*	21 54 57N	3 57W
Castle Eden, *U.K.*	19 54 45N	1 20W
Castlebar, *Ire.*	24 53 52N	9 17W
Castlebay, *U.K.*	22 56 57N	7 30W
Castleblaney, *Ire.*	24 54 7N	6 44W
Castleford, *U.K.*	19 53 43N	1 21W
Castlereagh, *Ire.*	24 53 47N	8 30W
Castlereagh □, *U.K.*	24 54 33N	5 53W
Castlereagh →,		
Austral.	70 30 12S 147 32 E
Castleside, *U.K.*	18 54 50N	1 52W
Castleton, *Derby, U.K.*	19 53 20N	1 47W
Castleton, *N. Yorks.,*		
U.K.	19 54 27N	0 57W
Castletown, *U.K.*	18 54 4N	4 40W
Castletown Bearhaven,		
Ire.	25 51 40N	9 54W
Castries, *St. Lucia*	94 14 0N	60 50W
Catánia, *It.*	40 37 31N	15 4 E
Catanzaro, *It.*	40 38 54N	16 38 E
Catcleugh, *U.K.*	21 55 19N	2 22W
Caterham, *U.K.*	15 51 16N	0 4W
Caton, *U.K.*	18 54 5N	2 41W
Catrine, *U.K.*	20 55 30N	4 20W
Catsfield, *U.K.*	15 50 53N	0 28 E
Catterick, *U.K.*	19 54 23N	1 38W
Catterick Camp, *U.K.*	19 54 22N	1 43W
Catton, *U.K.*	21 54 56N	2 16W
Caucasus, *U.S.S.R.*	47 43 0N	44 0 E
Caulkerbush, *U.K.*	21 54 54N	3 40W
Cavan, *Ire.*	24 54 0N	7 22W
Cavan □, *Ire.*	24 53 58N	7 10W
Cawood, *U.K.*	19 53 50N	1 7W
Cawston, *U.K.*	15 52 47N	1 10 E
Caxias, *Brazil*	101 4 55S	43 20W
Caxias do Sul, *Brazil*	102 29 10S	51 10W
Cayenne, *Fr. G.*	101 5 0N	52 18W
Ceanannus Mor, *Ire.*	24 53 42N	6 53W
Cebu, *Phil.*	63 10 18N 123 54 E
Cedar Rapids, *U.S.A.*	90 42 0N	91 38W
Celbridge, *Ire.*	25 53 20N	6 33W
Celebes = Sulawesi □,		
Indon.	63 2 0S 120 0 E
Celebes Sea, *E. Ind.*	63 3 0N 123 0 E
Cemaes Bay, *U.K.*	17 53 24N	4 27W
Central □, *U.K.*	20 56 10N	4 30W
Central African		
Republic ■, *Africa*	80 7 0N	20 0 E
Central Russian		
Uplands, *U.S.S.R.*	26 54 0N	36 0 E
Central Siberian		
Plateau, *U.S.S.R.*	49 65 0N 105 0 E
Cephalonia = Kefallinía,		
Greece	41 38 20N	20 30 E
Ceram, *Indon.*	63 3 10S 129 0 E
Ceres, *U.K.*	21 56 18N	2 57W
Cerignola, *It.*	40 41 17N	15 53 E
Cerne Abbas, *U.K.*	14 50 49N	2 29W
Cerrig-y-drudion, *U.K.*	17 53 2N	3 34W
Cessnock, *Austral.*	70 32 50S 151 21 E
Ceuta, *Mor.*	78 35 52N	5 18W
Cévennes, *Fr.*	34 44 10N	3 50 E
Ceylon = Sri Lanka ■,		
Asia	58 7 30N	80 50 E
Chacewater, *U.K.*	16 50 15N	5 8W
Chad ■, *Africa*	78 15 0N	17 15 E
Chad, L., *Chad*	79 13 30N	14 30 E
Chagford, *U.K.*	16 50 40N	3 50W
Chale, *U.K.*	14 50 35N	1 19W
Chalfont St. Peter, *U.K.*	15 51 36N	0 33W
Châlons-sur-Marne, *Fr.*	34 48 58N	4 20 E
Chambéry, *Fr.*	35 45 34N	5 55 E
Champagne, *Fr.*	34 48 40N	4 20 E
Champlain, L., *U.S.A.*	93 44 30N	73 20W
Chandigarh, *India*	58 30 43N	76 47 E
Chandler's Ford, *U.K.*	14 50 59N	1 23W

Changchun, *China*	61 43 58N 125 19 E
Changde, *China*	61 29 4N 111 35 E
Changsha, *China*	61 28 5N 113 1 E
Changzhou, *China*	61 31 47N 119 58 E
Channel Is., *U.K.*	34 49 30N	2 40W
Chao Phraya →, *Thai.*	63 13 32N 100 36 E
Chapel-en-le-Frith, *U.K.*	18 53 19N	1 54W
Chapel St. Leonards,		
U.K.	19 53 13N	0 19 E
Chard, *U.K.*	14 50 52N	2 59W
Chardzhou, *U.S.S.R.*	48 39 6N	63 34 E
Charing, *U.K.*	15 51 12N	0 49 E
Charlbury, *U.K.*	14 51 52N	1 29W
Charleroi, *Belg.*	36 50 24N	4 27 E
Charleston, *U.S.A.*	91 32 47N	79 56W
Charleville = Rath		
Luirc, *Ire.*	25 52 21N	8 40W
Charleville, *Austral.*	67 26 24S 146 15 E
Charleville-Mézières, *Fr.*	34 49 44N	4 40 E
Charlotte, *U.S.A.*	91 35 16N	80 46W
Charlottenburg, *W. Ger.*	42 52 31N	13 15 E
Charlottetown, *Canada*	93 46 14N	63 8W
Charlton Kings, *U.K.*	14 51 52N	2 3W
Charlwood, *U.K.*	15 51 8N	0 12W
Charminster, *U.K.*	14 50 43N	2 28W
Charmouth, *U.K.*	14 50 45N	2 54W
Charnwood Forest, *U.K.*	14 52 43N	1 18W
Charters Towers,		
Austral.	67 20 5S 146 13 E
Chartham, *U.K.*	15 51 14N	1 1 E
Chartres, *Fr.*	34 48 29N	1 30 E
Châteauroux, *Fr.*	34 46 50N	1 40 E
Chatham, *U.K.*	15 51 22N	0 32 E
Chattanooga, *U.S.A.*	91 35 2N	85 17W
Chatteris, *U.K.*	15 52 27N	0 3 E
Chatton, *U.K.*	21 55 34N	1 55W
Cheadle,		
Gr. Manchester, U.K.	18 53 23N	2 14W
Cheadle, *Staffs., U.K.*	18 52 59N	1 59W
Cheadle Hulme, *U.K.*	18 53 22N	2 12W
Cheboksary, *U.S.S.R.*	46 56 8N	47 12 E
Cheddar, *U.K.*	14 51 16N	2 47W
Cheddleton, *U.K.*	18 53 5N	2 2W
Chelmarsh, *U.K.*	14 52 29N	2 25W
Chelmer →, *U.K.*	15 51 45N	0 42 E
Chelmsford, *U.K.*	15 51 44N	0 29 E
Cheltenham, *U.K.*	14 51 55N	2 5W
Chelyabinsk, *U.S.S.R.*	48 55 10N	61 24 E
Chenab →, *Pak.*	58 30 23N	71 2 E
Chengdu, *China*	60 30 38N 104 2 E
Chepstow, *U.K.*	17 51 38N	2 40W
Cherbourg, *Fr.*	34 49 39N	1 40W
Cheremkhovo, *U.S.S.R.*	49 53 8N 103 1 E
Cherepovets, *U.S.S.R.*	46 59 5N	37 55 E
Cheriton, *U.K.*	14 51 3N	1 9W
Cheriton Fitzpaine, *U.K.*	16 50 51N	3 38W
Cherkassy, *U.S.S.R.*	47 49 27N	32 4 E
Chernigov, *U.S.S.R.*	46 51 28N	31 20 E
Chernovtsy, *U.S.S.R.*	47 48 15N	25 52 E
Chertsey, *U.K.*	15 51 23N	0 30W
Cherwell →, *U.K.*	14 51 46N	1 18W
Chesapeake Bay,		
U.S.A.	92 38 0N	76 12W
Chesham, *U.K.*	15 51 42N	0 36W
Cheshire □, *U.K.*	18 53 14N	2 30W
Cheshunt, *U.K.*	15 51 42N	0 1W
Chesil Beach, *U.K.*	14 50 37N	2 33W
Chester, *U.K.*	18 53 12N	2 53W
Chester-le-Street, *U.K.*	19 54 53N	1 34W
Chesterfield, *U.K.*	19 53 14N	1 26W
Chesterfield Inlet,		
Canada	88 63 30N	90 45W
Cheviot, The, *U.K.*	19 55 29N	2 8W
Cheviot Hills, *U.K.*	19 55 20N	2 30W
Chew Magna, *U.K.*	14 51 21N	2 37W
Chiai, *China*	61 23 29N 120 25 E
Chiba, *Jap.*	62 35 30N 140 7 E
Chicago, *U.S.A.*	92 41 53N	87 40W
Chichester, *U.K.*	15 50 50N	0 47W
Chiclayo, *Peru*	100 6 42S	79 50W
Chicoutimi, *Canada*	93 48 28N	71 5W
Chiddingfold, *U.K.*	15 51 6N	0 37W
Chidley, C., *Canada*	89 60 23N	64 26W
Chieti, *It.*	40 42 22N	14 10 E
Chihli, G. of, *China*	61 38 30N 119 0 E
Chihuahua, *Mex.*	94 28 40N 106 3W
Chile ■, *S. Am.*	102 35 0S	72 0W
Chilham, *U.K.*	15 51 15N	0 59 E
Chillán, *Chile*	102 36 40S	72 10W
Chilpancingo, *Mex.*	94 17 30N	99 30W
Chiltern Hills, *U.K.*	15 51 44N	0 42W
Chilung, *Taiwan*	61 25 3N 121 45 E
Chimborazo, *Ecuad.*	100 1 29S	78 55W
Chimbote, *Peru*	100 9 0S	78 35W
Chimkent, *U.S.S.R.*	48 42 18N	69 36 E
China ■, *Asia*	60 30 0N 110 0 E
Chincha Alta, *Peru*	100 13 25S	76 7W
Chingola, *Zam.*	81 12 31S	27 53 E
Chipata, *Zam.*	81 13 38S	32 28 E
Chippenham, *U.K.*	14 51 27N	2 7W
Chipping Campden,		
U.K.	14 52 4N	1 48W
Chipping Norton, *U.K.*	14 51 56N	1 32W
Chipping Ongar, *U.K.*	15 51 43N	0 15 E
Chipping Sodbury, *U.K.*	14 51 31N	2 23W
Chirbury, *U.K.*	14 52 35N	3 6W
Chirnside, *U.K.*	21 55 47N	2 11W
Chisledon, *U.K.*	14 51 30N	1 44W
Chita, *U.S.S.R.*	49 52 0N 113 35 E
Chittagong, *Bangla.*	59 22 19N	91 48 E

Darent

Chollerton, *U.K.* 21 55 4N 2 7W
Cholsey, *U.K.* 14 51 34N 1 10W
Chongjin, *N. Kor.* 61 41 47N 129 50 E
Chongqing = Chungking, *China* 60 29 35N 106 25 E
Chorley, *U.K.* 18 53 39N 2 39W
Chorrera, La, *Pan.* 94 8 50N 79 50W
Chorzów, *Pol.* 43 50 18N 18 57 E
Choybalsan, *Mong.* 61 48 4N 114 30 E
Christchurch, *N.Z.* 71 43 33S 172 47 E
Christchurch, *U.K.* 14 50 44N 1 33W
Chudleigh, *U.K.* 16 50 35N 3 36W
Chulmleigh, *U.K.* 16 50 55N 3 52W
Chungking, *China* 60 29 35N 106 25 E
Chur, *Switz.* 42 46 52N 9 32 E
Church Stretton, *U.K.* 14 52 32N 2 49W
Churchdown, *U.K.* 14 51 53N 2 9W
Churchill →, *Canada* 88 58 47N 94 12W
Ciénaga, *Col.* 100 11 1N 74 15W
Cienfuegos, *Cuba* 95 22 10N 80 30W
Cincinnati, *U.S.A.* 92 39 10N 84 26W
Cinderford, *U.K.* 14 51 49N 2 30W
Cirencester, *U.K.* 14 51 43N 1 59W
Citlaltépetl, *Mex.* 94 19 0N 97 20W
Ciudad Bolívar, *Ven.* 100 8 5N 63 36W
Ciudad Guayana, *Ven.* 100 8 0N 62 30W
Ciudad Juárez, *Mex.* 94 31 40N 106 28W
Ciudad Madero, *Mex.* 94 22 19N 97 50W
Ciudad Obregón, *Mex.* 94 27 28N 109 59W
Ciudad Real, *Sp.* 37 38 59N 3 55W
Ciudad Victoria, *Mex.* 94 23 41N 99 9W
Clabhach, *U.K.* 20 56 38N 6 36W
Clach Leathad, *U.K.* 20 56 36N 7 52W
Clachan, *U.K.* 20 55 45N 5 35W
Clackmannan, *U.K.* 21 56 10N 3 50W
Clacton-on-Sea, *U.K.* 15 51 47N 1 10 E
Cladich, *U.K.* 20 56 21N 5 5W
Clara, *Ire.* 25 53 20N 7 38W
Clare, *U.K.* 15 52 5N 0 36 E
Clare □, *Ire.* 25 52 20N 9 0W
Clare →, *Ire.* 24 53 22N 9 5W
Clare I., *Ire.* 24 53 48N 10 0W
Claremorris, *Ire.* 24 53 45N 9 0W
Clarksville, *U.S.A.* 90 36 32N 87 20W
Clatteringshaws L., *U.K.* 20 55 3N 4 17W
Claverley, *U.K.* 14 52 32N 2 19W
Clay Cross, *U.K.* 19 53 11N 1 26W
Clay Hd., *U.K.* 18 54 13N 4 23W
Claydon, *U.K.* 15 52 6N 1 7 E
Clear, C., *Ire.* 25 51 26N 9 30W
Clear I., *Ire.* 25 51 26N 9 30W
Cleator Moor, *U.K.* 18 54 30N 3 32W
Clee Hills, *U.K.* 14 52 26N 2 35W
Cleethorpes, *U.K.* 19 53 33N 0 2W
Cleeve Cloud, *U.K.* 14 51 56N 2 0W
Clent, *U.K.* 14 52 25N 2 6W
Cleobury Mortimer, *U.K.* 14 52 23N 2 28W
Clermont-Ferrand, *Fr.* 34 45 46N 3 4 E
Clevedon, *U.K.* 14 51 26N 2 52W
Cleveland, *U.S.A.* 92 41 28N 81 43W
Cleveland □, *U.K.* 19 54 35N 1 8 E
Cleveland Hills, *U.K.* 19 54 25N 1 11W
Clew B., *Ire.* 24 53 54N 9 50W
Cley, *U.K.* 15 52 57N 1 3 E
Clifden, *Ire.* 24 53 30N 10 2W
Cliffe, *U.K.* 15 51 27N 0 31 E
Clifford, *U.K.* 14 52 6N 3 6W
Clipston, *U.K.* 15 52 26N 0 58W
Clitheroe, *U.K.* 18 53 52N 2 23W
Clonakilty, *Ire.* 25 51 37N 8 53W
Clonakilty B., *Ire.* 25 51 33N 8 50W
Cloncurry, *Austral.* 67 20 40S 140 28 E
Clones, *Ire.* 24 54 10N 7 13W
Clonmel, *Ire.* 25 52 22N 7 42W
Closeburn, *U.K.* 21 55 13N 3 45W
Cloughton, *U.K.* 19 54 20N 0 27W
Clovelly, *U.K.* 16 51 0N 4 25W
Clowne, *U.K.* 19 53 18N 1 16W
Cluj-Napoca, *Rom.* 43 46 47N 23 38 E
Clun, *U.K.* 14 52 26N 3 2W
Clun Forest, *U.K.* 14 52 27N 3 7W
Clunbury, *U.K.* 14 52 25N 2 55W
Clwyd □, *U.K.* 17 53 5N 3 20W
Clwyd →, *U.K.* 17 53 20N 3 30W
Clyde →, *U.K.* 20 55 56N 4 29W
Clyde, Firth of, *U.K.* 20 55 20N 5 0W
Clydebank, *U.K.* 20 55 54N 4 25W
Clydesdale, *U.K.* 21 55 42N 3 50W
Coalbrookdale, *U.K.* 14 52 38N 2 30W
Coalburn, *U.K.* 21 55 35N 3 55W
Coalville, *U.K.* 14 52 43N 1 21W
Coast Mts., *Canada* 88 55 0N 129 0W
Coast Ranges, *U.S.A.* 90 41 0N 123 0W
Coatbridge, *U.K.* 21 55 52N 4 2W
Coatzacoalcos, *Mex.* 94 18 7N 94 25W
Cóbh, *Ire.* 25 51 50N 8 18W
Cobourg Pen., *Austral.* 66 11 20S 132 15 E
Cochabamba, *Bol.* 100 17 26S 66 10W
Cochin, *India* 58 9 59N 76 22 E
Cockburnspath, *U.K.* 21 55 56N 2 23W
Cockenzie, *U.K.* 21 55 58N 2 59W
Cockerham, *U.K.* 18 53 58N 2 49W
Cockermouth, *U.K.* 18 54 40N 3 22W
Cockfield, *U.K.* 15 52 8N 0 47 E
Cod, C., *U.S.A.* 93 42 8N 70 10W
Coddenham, *U.K.* 15 52 8N 1 8 E
Coffs Harbour, *Austral.* 67 30 16S 153 5 E
Coggeshall, *U.K.* 15 51 53N 0 41 E
Coimbatore, *India* 58 11 2N 76 59 E
Coimbra, *Port.* 37 40 15N 8 27W
Colac, *Austral.* 70 38 21S 143 35 E
Colby, *U.K.* 18 54 6N 4 42W
Colchester, *U.K.* 15 51 54N 0 55 E
Cold Fell, *U.K.* 18 54 54N 2 40W
Coldingham, *U.K.* 21 55 53N 2 10W
Coldstream, *U.K.* 21 55 39N 2 14W
Colebrooke, *U.K.* 16 50 45N 3 44W
Coleford, *U.K.* 14 51 46N 2 38W
Coleraine, *U.K.* 24 55 8N 6 40W
Coleraine □, *U.K.* 24 55 8N 6 40 E
Coleshill, *U.K.* 14 52 30N 1 42W
Colima, *Mex.* 94 19 14N 103 43W
Colinton, *U.K.* 21 55 54N 3 17W
Coll, *U.K.* 20 56 40N 6 35W
Collie, *Austral.* 66 33 22S 116 8 E
Collier Law Pk., *U.K.* 18 54 47N 1 59W
Collin, *U.K.* 21 55 4N 3 30W
Collingbourne, *U.K.* 14 51 16N 1 39W
Collooney, *Ire.* 24 54 11N 8 28W
Colmar, *Fr.* 34 48 5N 7 20 E
Colmonel, *U.K.* 20 55 8N 4 55W
Colne, *U.K.* 18 53 51N 2 11W
Colne →, *Essex, U.K.* 15 51 55N 0 50 E
Colne →, *Herts., U.K.* 15 51 36N 0 30W
Cologne, *W. Ger.* 36 50 56N 6 58 E
Colombia ■, *S. Am.* 100 3 45N 73 0W
Colombo, *Sri L.* 58 6 56N 79 58 E
Colón, *Mex.* 94 20 48N 100 3W
Colonsay, *U.K.* 20 56 4N 6 12W
Colorado □, *U.S.A.* 90 37 40N 106 0W
Colorado →, *Calif., U.S.A.* 90 34 45N 114 40W
Colorado →, *Tex., U.S.A.* 90 28 36N 95 58W
Colorado Plateau, *U.S.A.* 90 36 40N 110 30W
Colorado Springs, *U.S.A.* 90 38 55N 104 50W
Colstorworth, *U.K.* 15 52 48N 0 37W
Coltishall, *U.K.* 15 52 44N 1 21 E
Columbia, *Miss., U.S.A.* 90 31 16N 89 50W
Columbia, *S.C., U.S.A.* 91 34 0N 81 0W
Columbia →, *N. Am.* 90 46 15N 124 5W
Columbus, *Ga., U.S.A.* 91 32 30N 84 58W
Columbus, *Ohio, U.S.A.* 92 39 57N 83 1W
Colwell, *U.K.* 21 55 4N 2 4W
Colwich, *U.K.* 14 52 48N 1 58W
Colwyn Bay, *U.K.* 17 53 17N 3 44W
Colyton, *U.K.* 16 50 44N 3 4W
Combe Martin, *U.K.* 16 51 12N 4 2W
Comber, *U.K.* 24 54 33N 5 45W
Comeragh Mts., *Ire.* 25 52 17N 7 35W
Comilla, *Bangla.* 59 23 28N 91 10 E
Comino, *Malta* 40 36 0N 14 20 E
Communism Pk., *U.S.S.R.* 48 38 40N 72 20 E
Como, *It.* 40 45 48N 9 5 E
Como, L., *It.* 40 46 5N 9 17 E
Comodoro Rivadavia, *Arg.* 102 45 50S 67 40W
Comorin, C., *India* 58 8 3N 77 40 E
Comoro Is. ■, *Ind. Oc.* 73 12 10S 44 15 E
Compiègne, *Fr.* 34 49 24N 2 50 E
Comrie, *U.K.* 21 56 22N 4 0W
Conakry, *Guin.* 78 9 29N 13 49W
Concepción, *Chile* 102 36 50S 73 0W
Conchos →, *Mex.* 94 29 32N 104 25W
Concordia, *Arg.* 102 31 20S 58 2W
Condover, *U.K.* 14 52 39N 2 46W
Congleton, *U.K.* 18 53 10N 2 12W
Congo = Zaïre →, *Africa* 80 6 4S 12 24 E
Congo ■, *Africa* 80 1 0S 16 0 E
Congo Basin, *Africa* 72 0 10S 24 30 E
Congresbury, *U.K.* 14 51 20N 2 49W
Coningsby, *U.K.* 19 53 7N 0 9W
Conisbrough, *U.K.* 19 53 29N 1 12W
Coniston, *U.K.* 18 54 22N 3 6W
Coniston Water, *U.K.* 18 54 20N 3 5W
Conn, L., *Ire.* 24 54 3N 9 15W
Connacht, *Ire.* 24 53 23N 8 40W
Connah's Quay, *U.K.* 17 53 13N 3 6W
Connecticut □, *U.S.A.* 93 41 40N 72 40W
Connecticut →, *U.S.A.* 93 41 17N 72 21W
Connel, *U.K.* 20 56 27N 5 24W
Connel Park, *U.K.* 20 55 22N 4 15W
Connemara, *Ire.* 24 53 29N 9 45W
Conon →, *U.K.* 23 57 33N 4 28W
Cononbridge, *U.K.* 23 57 32N 4 30W
Consett, *U.K.* 18 54 52N 1 50W
Constance, L. = Bodensee, *W. Ger.* 42 47 35N 9 25 E
Constanţa, *Rom.* 43 44 14N 28 38 E
Constantine, *Alg.* 78 36 25N 6 42 E
Conwy, *U.K.* 17 53 17N 3 50W
Conwy →, *U.K.* 17 53 18N 3 50W
Cook, Mt., *N.Z.* 71 43 36S 170 9 E
Cook Is., *Pac. Oc.* 65 17 0S 160 0W
Cook Strait, *N.Z.* 71 41 15S 174 29 E
Cookham, *U.K.* 15 51 33N 0 42W
Cookstown, *U.K.* 24 54 40N 6 43W
Cookstown □, *U.K.* 24 54 40N 6 43W
Coolgardie, *Austral.* 66 30 55S 121 8 E
Cootamundra, *Austral.* 70 34 36S 148 1 E
Cootehill, *Ire.* 24 54 5N 7 5W
Copenhagen, *Den.* 45 55 41N 12 34 E
Coppermine, *Canada* 88 67 50N 115 5W
Coppermine →, *Canada* 88 67 49N 116 4W
Copythorne, *U.K.* 14 50 56N 1 34W
Coquet →, *U.K.* 19 55 18N 1 45W
Coquet, I., *U.K.* 21 55 21N 1 30W
Coral Sea, *Pac. Oc.* 64 15 0S 150 0 E
Coral Sea Islands Terr., *Austral.* 67 20 0S 155 0 E
Corbridge, *U.K.* 21 54 58N 2 0W
Corby, *Lincs., U.K.* 15 52 49N 0 31W
Corby, *Northants., U.K.* 15 52 29N 0 41W
Córdoba, *Arg.* 102 31 20S 64 10W
Córdoba, *Sp.* 37 37 50N 4 50W
Cordova, *U.S.A.* 88 60 36N 145 45W
Corfe Castle, *U.K.* 14 50 37N 2 3W
Corfe Mullen, *U.K.* 14 50 45N 2 0W
Corfu = Kérkira, *Greece* 41 39 38N 19 50 E
Corinth, G. of, *Greece* 41 38 16N 22 30 E
Cork, *Ire.* 25 51 54N 8 30W
Cork □, *Ire.* 25 51 50N 8 50W
Cork Harbour, *Ire.* 25 51 46N 8 16W
Corner Brook, *Canada* 89 48 57N 57 58W
Cornforth, *U.K.* 19 54 42N 1 28W
Cornwall □, *U.K.* 16 50 26N 4 40W
Cornwall, C., *U.K.* 16 50 8N 5 42W
Coro, *Ven.* 100 11 25N 69 41W
Coromandel Coast, *India* 58 12 30N 81 0 E
Coronation Gulf, *Canada* 88 68 25N 110 0W
Corpus Christi, *U.S.A.* 90 27 50N 97 28W
Corrib, L., *Ire.* 24 53 5N 9 10W
Corrie, *U.K.* 20 55 39N 5 10W
Corrientes, *Arg.* 102 27 30S 58 45W
Corringham, *U.K.* 19 53 25N 0 42W
Corryvreckan, G. of, *U.K.* 20 56 10N 5 44W
Corsewall Pt., *U.K.* 20 55 0N 5 10W
Corsham, *U.K.* 14 51 25N 2 11W
Corsica, I., *Medit. S.* 35 42 0N 9 0 E
Corsley, *U.K.* 14 51 12N 2 14W
Corsock, *U.K.* 21 55 54N 3 56W
Corton, *U.K.* 15 52 31N 1 46 E
Corumbá, *Brazil* 100 19 0S 57 30W
Coruña, La, *Sp.* 37 43 20N 8 25W
Corve →, *U.K.* 14 52 22N 2 43W
Coseley, *U.K.* 14 52 33N 2 6W
Cosenza, *It.* 40 39 17N 16 14 E
Cosham, *U.K.* 14 50 51N 1 3W
Costa Rica ■, *Cent. Am.* 95 10 0N 84 0W
Costessey, *U.K.* 15 52 40N 1 11 E
Côte d'Or, *Fr.* 34 47 10N 4 50 E
Cotherstone, *U.K.* 18 54 34N 1 59W
Cotonou, *Benin* 78 6 20N 2 25 E
Cotopaxi, Vol., *Ecuad.* 100 0 40S 78 30W
Cotswold Hills, *U.K.* 14 51 42N 2 10W
Cottbus, *E. Ger.* 42 51 44N 14 20 E
Cottenham, *U.K.* 15 52 18N 0 8 E
Cottingham, *U.K.* 19 53 47N 0 29W
Coulport, *U.K.* 20 56 3N 4 53W
Council Bluffs, *U.S.A.* 90 41 20N 95 50W
Coupar Angus, *U.K.* 21 56 33N 3 17W
Coventry, *U.K.* 14 52 25N 1 31W
Cover →, *U.K.* 18 54 14N 1 45W
Coverack, *U.K.* 16 50 2N 5 6W
Covington, *U.S.A.* 92 39 5N 84 30W
Cowal, *U.K.* 20 56 5N 5 8W
Cowan, L., *Austral.* 66 31 45S 121 45 E
Cowbridge, *U.K.* 17 51 28N 3 28W
Cowdenbeath, *U.K.* 21 56 7N 3 20W
Cowes, *U.K.* 14 50 45N 1 18W
Cowfold, *U.K.* 15 50 58N 0 16W
Cowley, *U.K.* 14 51 43N 1 12W
Cowpen, *U.K.* 21 55 8N 1 34W
Cowra, *Austral.* 70 33 49S 148 42 E
Craigavon □, *U.K.* 24 54 30N 6 25W
Craighouse, *U.K.* 20 55 50N 5 58W
Craignish, L., *U.K.* 20 56 11N 5 32W
Crail, *U.K.* 21 56 16N 2 38W
Craiova, *Rom.* 43 44 21N 23 48 E
Cramlington, *U.K.* 21 55 5N 1 36W
Cranborne, *U.K.* 14 50 55N 1 55W
Cranborne Chase, *U.K.* 14 50 56N 2 6W
Cranbrook, *Canada* 88 49 30N 115 46W
Cranbrook, *U.K.* 15 51 6N 0 33 E
Cranleigh, *U.K.* 15 51 8N 0 29W
Cranshaws, *U.K.* 21 55 51N 2 30W
Cranwell, *U.K.* 19 53 4N 0 29W
Craven Arms, *U.K.* 14 52 27N 2 49W
Crawford, *U.K.* 21 55 28N 3 40W
Crawley, *U.K.* 15 51 7N 0 10W
Credenhill, *U.K.* 14 52 6N 2 49W
Crediton, *U.K.* 16 50 47N 3 39W
Cree →, *U.K.* 20 54 51N 4 24W
Creeside, *U.K.* 20 55 4N 4 41W
Creetown, *U.K.* 20 54 54N 4 23W
Cremona, *It.* 40 45 8N 10 2 E
Crete, I., *Greece* 41 35 15N 25 0 E
Creusot, Le, *Fr.* 34 46 48N 4 24 E
Crewe, *U.K.* 18 53 6N 2 28W
Crewkerne, *U.K.* 14 50 53N 2 48W
Crianlarich, *U.K.* 20 56 24N 4 37W
Criccieth, *U.K.* 17 52 55N 4 15W
Crick, *U.K.* 14 52 22N 1 9W
Crickhowell, *U.K.* 17 51 52N 3 8W
Cricklade, *U.K.* 14 51 38N 1 50W
Crieff, *U.K.* 21 56 22N 3 50W
Criffell, *U.K.* 21 54 56N 3 38W
Crimea, *U.S.S.R.* 47 45 0N 34 0 E
Crinan, *U.K.* 20 56 6N 5 34W
Crinan Canal, *U.K.* 20 56 4N 5 30W
Croaghpatrick, *Ire.* 24 53 46N 9 40W
Crocketford, *U.K.* 21 55 3N 3 49W
Croglin, *U.K.* 18 54 50N 2 37W
Cromarty, *U.K.* 23 57 40N 4 2W
Cromarty Firth, *U.K.* 23 57 40N 4 15W
Cromer, *U.K.* 15 52 56N 1 18 E
Crondall, *U.K.* 15 51 13N 0 51W
Crook, *U.K.* 19 54 43N 1 45W
Crooklands, *U.K.* 18 54 16N 2 43W
Crosby, *Cumbria, U.K.* 18 54 45N 3 25W
Crosby, *Merseyside, U.K.* 18 53 30N 3 2W
Crosby Ravensworth, *U.K.* 18 54 34N 2 35W
Cross Fell, *U.K.* 18 54 44N 2 29W
Crosshaven, *Ire.* 25 51 48N 8 19W
Crosshill, *U.K.* 20 55 19N 4 39W
Crouch →, *U.K.* 15 51 37N 0 53 E
Crow Hd., *Ire.* 25 51 34N 10 9W
Crow Sound, *U.K.* 16 49 56N 6 16W
Crowborough, *U.K.* 15 51 3N 0 9 E
Crowland, *U.K.* 15 52 41N 0 10W
Crowle, *U.K.* 19 53 36N 0 49W
Croyde, *U.K.* 16 51 7N 4 13W
Croydon, *U.K.* 15 51 18N 0 5W
Crudgington, *U.K.* 14 52 46N 2 33W
Crummock Water L., *U.K.* 18 54 33N 3 18W
Cruzeiro do Sul, *Brazil* 100 7 35S 72 35W
Cuba ■, *W. Ind.* 95 22 0N 79 0W
Cuckfield, *U.K.* 15 51 0N 0 8W
Cúcuta, *Col.* 100 7 54N 72 31W
Cudworth, *U.K.* 19 53 35N 1 25W
Cuenca, *Ecuad.* 100 2 50S 79 9W
Cuenca, *Sp.* 37 40 5N 2 10W
Cuernavaca, *Mex.* 94 18 55N 99 15W
Cuiabá, *Brazil* 101 15 30S 56 0W
Cuillin Hills, *U.K.* 22 57 14N 6 15W
Cuillin Sd., *U.K.* 22 57 12N 6 20W
Culiacán, *Mex.* 94 24 50N 107 23W
Cullen, *U.K.* 23 57 45N 2 50W
Culloden Moor, *U.K.* 23 57 29N 4 7W
Cullompton, *U.K.* 16 50 52N 3 23W
Culm →, *U.K.* 16 50 46N 3 31W
Culrain, *U.K.* 23 57 55N 4 25W
Culross, *U.K.* 21 56 4N 3 38W
Cumaná, *Ven.* 100 10 30N 64 5W
Cumberland Plateau, *U.S.A.* 91 36 0N 84 30W
Cumbrae Is., *U.K.* 20 55 46N 4 54W
Cumbria □, *U.K.* 18 54 35N 2 55W
Cumbrian Mts., *U.K.* 18 54 30N 3 0W
Cummertrees, *U.K.* 21 55 0N 3 20W
Cumnock, *U.K.* 20 55 27N 4 18W
Cumnor, *U.K.* 14 51 44N 1 20W
Cumwhinton, *U.K.* 18 54 51N 2 49W
Cúneo, *It.* 40 44 23N 7 31 E
Cunninghame, *U.K.* 20 55 38N 4 35W
Cupar, *U.K.* 21 56 20N 3 0W
Curitiba, *Brazil* 102 25 20S 49 10W
Currie, *U.K.* 21 55 53N 3 17W
Curry Rivel, *U.K.* 14 51 2N 2 52W
Cuttack, *India* 59 20 25N 85 57 E
Cuzco, *Peru* 100 13 32S 72 0W
Cwmbran, *U.K.* 17 51 39N 3 0W
Cyclades = Kikládhes, *Greece* 41 37 20N 24 30 E
Cyprus ■, *Medit. S.* 47 35 0N 33 0 E
Czechoslovakia ■, *Europe* 42 49 0N 17 0 E
Częstochowa, *Pol.* 43 50 49N 19 7 E

D

Da Lat, *Viet.* 63 11 56N 108 25 E
Da Nang, *Viet.* 63 16 4N 108 13 E
Dacca, *Bangla.* 59 23 43N 90 26 E
Daer →, *U.K.* 21 55 23N 3 39W
Dailly, *U.K.* 20 55 16N 4 44W
Daingean, *Ire.* 25 53 18N 7 15W
Dakar, *Sene.* 78 14 34N 17 29W
Dakhla, *W. Sah.* 78 23 50N 15 53W
Dalbeattie, *U.K.* 21 54 55N 3 50W
Dalian, *China* 61 38 50N 121 40 E
Dalkeith, *U.K.* 21 55 54N 3 5W
Dallas, *U.S.A.* 91 32 50N 96 50W
Dalmally, *U.K.* 20 56 25N 5 0W
Dalmatia, *Yug.* 41 43 20N 17 0 E
Dalmellington, *U.K.* 20 55 20N 4 25W
Daloa, *Ivory C.* 78 7 0N 6 30W
Dalry, *U.K.* 20 55 44N 4 42W
Dalrymple, *U.K.* 20 55 24N 4 36W
Dalton, *Cumbria, U.K.* 18 54 9N 3 11W
Dalton, *Dumf. & Gall., U.K.* 21 55 3N 3 22W
Dalton, *N. Yorks., U.K.* 19 54 28N 1 32W
Dalwhinnie, *U.K.* 23 56 56N 4 14W
Damascus, *Syria* 57 33 30N 36 18 E
Damerham, *U.K.* 14 50 57N 1 52W
Dampier, *Austral.* 66 20 41S 116 42 E
Dandenong, *Austral.* 70 38 0S 145 15 E
Dandong, *China* 61 40 10N 124 20 E
Dannevirke, *N.Z.* 71 40 12S 176 8 E
Danube →, *Europe* 42 45 20N 29 40 E
Dar-es-Salaam, *Tanz.* 80 6 50S 39 12 E
Dar'ā, *Syria* 57 32 36N 36 7 E
Dardanelles, *Turk.* 47 40 0N 26 0 E
Darent →, *U.K.* 15 51 22N 0 12 E

Gelderland

Elishaw, U.K. 21 55 16N 2 14W
Elizabeth, Austral. 67 34 42S 138 41 E
Elizabeth, U.S.A. 93 40 37N 74 12W
Elland, U.K. 19 53 41N 1 49W
Ellen →, U.K. 18 54 44N 3 30W
Eller Beck Bridge, U.K. 19 54 23N 0 40W
Ellesmere, U.K. 18 52 55N 2 53W
Ellesmere I., Canada 103 79 30N 80 0W
Ellesmere Port, U.K. 18 53 17N 2 55W
Ellice Is. = Tuvalu ■, Pac. Oc. 64 8 0S 178 0 E
Ellington, U.K. 21 55 14N 1 34W
Ellon, U.K. 23 57 21N 2 5W
Elmira, U.S.A. 92 42 8N 76 49W
Elmswell, U.K. 15 52 14N 0 53 E
Eluru, India 59 16 48N 81 8 E
Ely, U.K. 15 52 24N 0 16 E
Emāmrūd, Iran 56 36 30N 55 0 E
Embleton, U.K. 21 55 30N 1 38W
Emden, W. Ger. 36 53 22N 7 12 E
Emerald, Austral. 67 23 32S 148 10 E
Emmeloord, Neth. 36 52 44N 5 46 E
Emmen, Neth. 36 52 48N 6 57 E
Ems →, W. Ger. 36 52 37N 9 26 E
Enard B., U.K. 22 58 5N 5 20W
Enderbury I., Pac. Oc. 64 3 8S 171 5W
Enderby, U.K. 14 52 35N 1 15W
Enderby Land, Antarctica 103 66 0S 53 0 E
Enfield, U.K. 15 51 39N 0 4W
England □, U.K. 5 53 0N 2 0W
English Channel, Europe 15 50 0N 2 0W
Ennerdale Water, U.K. 18 54 32N 3 24W
Ennis, Ire. 25 52 51N 8 59W
Enniscorthy, Ire. 25 52 30N 6 35W
Enniskillen, U.K. 24 54 20N 7 40W
Ennistimon, Ire. 25 52 56N 9 18W
Enschede, Neth. 36 52 13N 6 53 E
Ensenada, Mex. 94 31 50N 116 50W
Enstone, U.K. 14 51 55N 1 25W
Entebbe, Uganda 80 0 4N 32 28 E
Enugu, Nig. 78 6 20N 7 30 E
Epping, U.K. 15 51 42N 0 8 E
Epping Forest, U.K. 15 51 40N 0 5 E
Epsom, U.K. 15 51 19N 0 16W
Epworth, U.K. 19 53 30N 0 50W
Equatorial Guinea ■, Africa 80 2 0S 8 0 E
Erebus, Mt., Ant. 103 77 35S 167 0 E
Erfurt, E. Ger. 42 50 58N 11 2 E
Eriboll, L., U.K. 23 58 28N 4 41W
Erie, U.S.A. 92 42 10N 80 7W
Erie, L., N. Am. 92 42 15N 81 0W
Eritrea □, Eth. 79 14 0N 41 0 E
Erlangen, W. Ger. 42 49 35N 11 0 E
Erne →, U.K. 24 54 30N 8 16W
Erne, Lough, U.K. 24 54 26N 7 46W
Erode, India 58 11 24N 77 45 E
Errigal, Mt., Ire. 24 55 2N 8 8W
Erris Hd., Ire. 24 54 19N 10 0W
Errol, U.K. 21 56 24N 3 13W
Erzurum, Turk. 47 39 57N 41 15 E
Esbjerg, Den. 45 55 29N 8 29 E
Esch, Neth. 36 51 37N 5 17 E
Eschweiler, W. Ger. 36 50 49N 6 14 E
Escrick, U.K. 19 53 53N 1 3W
Eşfahān, Iran 56 33 0N 53 0 E
Esk →, Cumbria, U.K. 18 54 23N 3 21W
Esk →, Dumf. & Gall., U.K. 21 54 58N 3 4W
Esk →, N. Yorks, U.K. 19 54 27N 0 36W
Eskdale, U.K. 21 55 12N 3 4W
Eskifjörður, Ice. 44 65 3N 13 55W
Eskilstuna, Swed. 45 59 22N 16 32 E
Eskimo Pt., Canada 88 61 10N 94 15W
Eskişehir, Turk. 47 39 50N 30 35 E
Esmeraldas, Ecuad. 100 1 0N 79 40W
Esperance, Austral. 66 33 45S 121 55 E
Espinhaço, Serra do, Brazil 101 17 30S 43 30W
Essen, W. Ger. 36 51 28N 6 59 E
Essex □, U.K. 15 51 48N 0 30 E
Eston, U.K. 19 54 33N 1 6W
Estonian S.S.R. □, U.S.S.R. 46 58 30N 25 30 E
Etchingham, U.K. 15 51 0N 0 27 E
Ethiopia ■, Africa 78 8 0N 40 0 E
Ethiopian Highlands, Eth. 72 10 0N 37 0 E
Etive, L., U.K. 20 56 30N 5 12W
Etna, It. 40 37 45N 15 0 E
Eton, U.K. 15 51 29N 0 37W
Ettington, U.K. 14 52 8N 1 38W
Ettrick Forest, U.K. 21 55 30N 3 0W
Ettrick Water, U.K. 21 55 31N 2 55W
Eugene, U.S.A. 90 44 0N 123 8W
Euphrates →, Asia 56 31 0N 47 25 E
Euston, Austral. 70 34 30S 142 46 E
Euxton, U.K. 18 53 41N 2 42W
Evansville, U.S.A. 92 38 0N 87 35W
Evercreech, U.K. 14 51 8N 2 30W
Everest, Mt., Nepal 60 28 5N 86 58 E
Evesham, U.K. 14 52 6N 1 57W
Évora, Port. 37 38 33N 7 57W
Évreux, Fr. 34 49 0N 1 8 E
Évvoia, Greece 41 38 30N 24 0 E
Ewe, L., U.K. 22 57 49N 5 38W
Ewell, U.K. 15 51 20N 0 15W
Ewhurst, U.K. 15 51 9N 0 25W
Exe →, U.K. 16 50 38N 3 27W
Exeter, U.K. 16 50 43N 3 31W
Exford, U.K. 14 51 8N 3 39W
Exminster, U.K. 16 50 40N 3 29W
Exmoor, U.K. 16 51 10N 3 59W
Exmouth, Austral. 66 21 54S 114 10 E
Exmouth, U.K. 16 50 37N 3 26W
Exmouth G., Austral. 66 22 15S 114 15 E
Exton, U.K. 15 52 42N 0 38W
Eyam, U.K. 19 53 17N 1 40W
Eye, Cambs., U.K. 15 52 36N 0 11W
Eye, Suffolk, U.K. 15 52 19N 1 9 E
Eye Pen., U.K. 22 58 13N 6 10W
Eyemouth, U.K. 21 55 53N 2 5W
Eynsham, U.K. 14 51 47N 1 21W
Eyre, L., Austral. 67 29 30S 137 26 E
Eyre Cr. →, Austral. 67 26 40S 139 0 E
Eyre Pen., Austral. 66 33 30S 137 17 E

F

Fair Hd., U.K. 24 55 14N 6 10W
Fairbanks, U.S.A. 88 64 50N 147 50W
Fairfield, Austral. 70 33 53S 150 57 E
Fairford, U.K. 14 51 42N 1 48W
Fairlie, N.Z. 71 44 5S 170 49 E
Fairlie, U.K. 20 55 44N 4 52W
Fairlight, U.K. 15 50 53N 0 40 E
Faisalabad, Pak. 58 31 30N 73 5 E
Faizabad, India 59 26 45N 82 10 E
Fakenham, U.K. 15 52 50N 0 51 E
Faldingworth, U.K. 19 53 21N 0 22W
Falkenberg, Swed. 45 56 54N 12 30 E
Falkirk, U.K. 21 56 0N 3 47W
Falkland, U.K. 21 56 15N 3 13W
Falkland Is., Atl. Oc. 102 51 30S 59 0W
Fall River, U.S.A. 93 41 45N 71 5W
Falmouth, U.K. 16 50 9N 5 5W
Falmouth B., U.K. 16 50 7N 5 3W
Falstone, U.K. 21 55 10N 2 26W
Falun, Swed. 45 60 37N 15 37 E
Famagusta, Cyprus 47 35 8N 33 55 E
Fannich, L., U.K. 22 57 40N 5 0W
Fareham, U.K. 14 50 52N 1 11W
Faringdon, U.K. 14 51 39N 1 34W
Farnborough, U.K. 15 51 17N 0 46W
Farne Is., U.K. 19 55 38N 1 37W
Farnham, U.K. 15 51 13N 0 49W
Farnworth, U.K. 18 53 33N 2 24W
Faroe Is., Atl. Oc. 26 62 0N 7 0W
Farrar →, U.K. 23 57 30N 4 30W
Faslane, U.K. 20 56 3N 4 49W
Fastnet Rock, Ire. 25 51 22N 9 37W
Fauldhouse, U.K. 21 55 50N 3 44W
Faversham, U.K. 15 51 18N 0 54 E
Fawley, U.K. 14 50 49N 1 20W
Faya-Largeau, Chad 79 17 58N 19 6 E
Fayetteville, U.S.A. 91 35 0N 78 58W
Fazeley, U.K. 14 52 36N 1 42W
Fdérik, Maurit. 78 22 40N 12 45W
Feale →, Ire. 25 52 26N 9 40W
Feilding, N.Z. 71 40 13S 175 35 E
Feira de Santana, Brazil 101 12 15S 38 57W
Felixstowe, U.K. 15 51 58N 1 22 E
Felpham, U.K. 15 50 47N 0 38W
Felton, U.K. 21 55 18N 1 42W
Feltwell, U.K. 15 52 29N 0 32 E
Fenit, Ire. 25 52 17N 9 51W
Fenny Bentley, U.K. 19 53 4N 1 43W
Fenny Compton, U.K. 14 52 9N 1 20W
Fenny Stratford, U.K. 15 51 59N 0 42W
Fens, The, U.K. 15 52 45N 0 2 E
Fenwick, U.K. 20 55 38N 4 25W
Fergana, U.S.S.R. 48 40 23N 71 19 E
Fermanagh □, U.K. 24 54 21N 7 40W
Fermoy, Ire. 25 52 4N 8 18W
Fernhurst, U.K. 15 51 3N 0 43W
Ferrara, It. 40 44 50N 11 36 E
Ferryhill, U.K. 19 54 42N 1 32W
Fès, Mor. 78 34 0N 5 0W
Fetlar, U.K. 22 60 36N 0 52W
Ffestiniog, U.K. 17 52 58N 3 56W
Fianarantsoa, Madag. 81 21 26S 47 5 E
Fife □, U.K. 21 56 13N 3 2W
Fife Ness, U.K. 21 56 17N 2 35W
Fiji ■, Pac. Oc. 64 17 20S 179 0 E
Filby, U.K. 15 52 40N 1 39 E
Filey, U.K. 19 54 13N 0 18W
Filey B., U.K. 19 54 12N 0 15W
Filton, U.K. 14 51 29N 2 34W
Fincham, U.K. 15 52 38N 0 30 E
Findhorn →, U.K. 23 57 38N 3 38W
Findon, U.K. 15 50 53N 0 24W
Finedon, U.K. 15 52 20N 0 40W
Fingest, U.K. 15 51 35N 0 52W
Finisterre, C., Sp. 37 42 50N 9 19W
Finland ■, Europe 44 63 0N 27 0 E
Finland, G. of, Europe 45 60 0N 26 0 E
Finn →, Ire. 24 54 50N 7 55W
Finnart, U.K. 20 56 7N 4 48W
Finnmark fylke □, Nor. 44 69 30N 25 0 E
Finstown, U.K. 23 59 0N 3 8W
Fionnphort, U.K. 20 56 19N 6 23W
Firozabad, India 58 27 10N 78 25 E
Fishguard, U.K. 17 51 59N 4 59W
Fishtoft, U.K. 19 52 27N 0 2 E
Fitzroy →, Austral. 66 17 31S 123 35 E
Flamborough, U.K. 19 54 7N 0 7W
Flamborough Hd., U.K. 19 54 8N 0 4W
Flanders, Belg. 34 51 10N 3 15 E
Flatey, Ice. 44 65 22N 22 56W
Fleet, U.K. 15 51 16N 0 50W
Fleetwood, U.K. 18 53 55N 3 1W
Flensburg, W. Ger. 42 54 46N 9 28 E
Fletton, U.K. 15 52 34N 0 13W
Flimby, U.K. 18 54 42N 3 31W
Flinders →, Austral. 67 17 36S 140 36 E
Flinders Ranges, Austral. 67 31 30S 138 30 E
Flint, U.K. 17 53 15N 3 7W
Flint, U.S.A. 92 43 5N 83 40W
Flint →, U.S.A. 91 30 52N 84 38W
Flitwick, U.K. 15 51 59N 0 30W
Flodden, U.K. 19 55 37N 2 8W
Florence, It. 40 43 47N 11 15 E
Flores, Indon. 63 8 35S 121 0 E
Flores Sea, Indon. 63 6 30S 124 0 E
Florianópolis, Brazil 102 27 30S 48 30W
Florida □, U.S.A. 91 28 30N 82 0W
Florida, Straits of, U.S.A. 95 25 0N 80 0W
Florida Keys, U.S.A. 91 25 0N 80 40W
Florissant, U.S.A. 90 38 48N 90 20W
Flushing = Vlissingen, Neth. 36 51 26N 3 34 E
Fóggia, It. 40 41 28N 15 31 E
Folkestone, U.K. 15 51 5N 1 11 E
Fontainebleau, Fr. 34 48 24N 2 40 E
Forbach, Fr. 34 49 10N 6 52 E
Ford, U.K. 20 56 10N 5 27W
Fordham, U.K. 15 52 19N 0 23 E
Fordingbridge, U.K. 14 50 56N 1 48W
Forest Row, U.K. 15 51 6N 0 3 E
Forfar, U.K. 23 56 40N 2 53W
Formby, U.K. 18 53 34N 3 4W
Formby Pt., U.K. 18 53 33N 3 7W
Formosa = Taiwan ■, Asia 61 23 30N 121 0 E
Formosa Strait, Asia 61 24 40N 120 0 E
Forres, U.K. 23 57 37N 3 38W
Fort Augustus, U.K. 23 57 9N 4 40W
Fort Collins, U.S.A. 90 40 30N 105 4W
Fort-de-France, Mart. 94 14 36N 61 2W
Fort George, Canada 89 53 50N 79 0W
Fort Lauderdale, U.S.A. 91 26 10N 80 5W
Fort McMurray, Canada 88 56 44N 111 7W
Fort Smith, U.S.A. 90 35 25N 94 25W
Fort Wayne, U.S.A. 92 41 5N 85 10W
Fort William, U.K. 22 56 48N 5 8W
Fort Worth, U.S.A. 90 32 45N 97 25W
Fortaleza, Brazil 101 3 45S 38 35W
Forth, U.K. 21 55 45N 3 42W
Forth, Firth of, U.K. 21 56 5N 2 55W
Forth Bridge, U.K. 21 56 0N 3 24W
Fortrose, U.K. 23 57 35N 4 10W
Foshan, China 61 23 4N 113 5 E
Fothergill, U.K. 18 54 43N 3 30W
Fotheringhay, U.K. 15 52 32N 0 28W
Foulness I., U.K. 15 51 36N 0 55 E
Foulness Pt., U.K. 15 51 36N 0 59 E
Foulsham, U.K. 15 52 48N 1 1 E
Fountainhall, U.K. 21 55 45N 2 55W
Fountains Abbey, U.K. 19 54 8N 1 35W
Fovant, U.K. 14 51 4N 2 0W
Foveaux Str., N.Z. 71 46 42S 168 10 E
Fowey, U.K. 16 50 20N 4 39W
Fowey →, U.K. 16 50 20N 4 39W
Fownhope, U.K. 14 52 0N 2 37W
Foxdale, U.K. 18 54 12N 4 38W
Foxe Chan., Canada 89 65 0N 80 0W
Foyle, Lough, U.K. 24 55 6N 7 8W
Foynes, Ire. 25 52 37N 9 5W
Fraddon, U.K. 16 50 22N 4 55W
Framlingham, U.K. 15 52 14N 1 20 E
France ■, Europe 34 47 0N 3 0 E
Frankfurt am Main, W. Ger. 42 50 7N 8 40 E
Frankston, Austral. 70 38 8S 145 8 E
Frant, U.K. 15 51 5N 0 17 E
Franz Josef Land, U.S.S.R. 48 82 0N 55 0 E
Fraser →, Canada 88 49 7N 123 11W
Fraser I., Austral. 67 25 15S 153 10 E
Fraserburgh, U.K. 23 57 41N 2 0W
Fredericton, Canada 93 45 57N 66 40W
Frederikshavn, Den. 45 57 28N 10 31 E
Fredrikstad, Nor. 45 59 13N 10 57 E
Freetown, Sa. Leone 78 8 30N 13 17W
Freiburg, W. Ger. 42 48 0N 7 52 E
Fremantle, Austral. 66 32 7S 115 47 E
French Guiana ■, S. Am. 101 4 0N 53 0W
French Polynesia □, Pac. Oc. 65 20 0S 145 0 E
Freshwater, U.K. 14 50 42N 1 31W
Fresnillo, Mex. 94 23 10N 103 0W
Fresno, U.S.A. 90 36 47N 119 50W
Freuchie, U.K. 21 56 14N 3 8W
Fridaythorpe, U.K. 19 54 2N 0 40W
Friesland □, Neth. 36 53 5N 5 50 E
Frimley, U.K. 15 51 18N 0 43W
Frinton-on-Sea, U.K. 15 51 50N 1 16 E
Frisa, Loch, U.K. 20 56 34N 6 5W
Frisian Is., Europe 36 53 30N 6 0 E
Frizington, U.K. 18 54 33N 3 30W
Frobisher B., Canada 89 62 30N 66 0W
Frodsham, U.K. 18 53 17N 2 45W
Frome, U.K. 14 51 16N 2 17W
Frome →, U.K. 14 50 44N 2 5W
Frome, L., Austral. 67 30 45S 139 45 E
Frunze, U.S.S.R. 48 42 54N 74 46 E
Fuji-San, Jap. 62 35 22N 138 44 E
Fujian □, China 61 26 0N 118 0 E
Fukui, Jap. 62 36 0N 136 10 E
Fukuoka, Jap. 62 33 39N 130 21 E
Fukushima, Jap. 62 37 44N 140 28 E
Fukuyama, Jap. 62 34 35N 133 20 E
Fulwood, U.K. 18 53 47N 2 41W
Fundy, B. of, Canada 93 45 0N 66 0W
Furneaux Group, Austral. 66 40 10S 147 50 E
Furness, Pen., U.K. 18 54 12N 3 10W
Fürth, W. Ger. 42 49 29N 11 0 E
Fury and Hecla Str., Canada 89 69 56N 84 0W
Fushun, China 61 41 50N 123 56 E
Fuxin, China 61 42 5N 121 48 E
Fuzhou, China 61 26 5N 119 16 E
Fylde, U.K. 18 53 50N 2 58W
Fylingdales Moor, U.K. 19 54 22N 0 32W
Fyn, Den. 45 55 20N 10 30 E
Fyne, L., U.K. 20 56 0N 5 20W
Fyvie, U.K. 23 57 26N 2 24W

G

Gabès, Tunisia 78 33 53N 10 2 E
Gabon ■, Africa 80 0 10S 10 0 E
Gaborone, Bots. 81 24 45S 25 57 E
Gabrovo, Bulg. 41 42 52N 25 19 E
Gainesville, U.S.A. 90 29 38N 82 20W
Gainford, U.K. 19 54 34N 1 44W
Gainsborough, U.K. 19 53 23N 0 46W
Gairdner L., Austral. 66 31 30S 136 0 E
Gairloch, U.K. 22 57 42N 5 40W
Gairloch, L., U.K. 22 57 43N 5 45W
Galápagos, Pac. Oc. 65 0 0 89 0W
Galashiels, U.K. 21 55 37N 2 50W
Galaţi, Rom. 43 45 27N 28 2 E
Galgate, U.K. 18 53 59N 2 47W
Galilee, Sea of = Kinneret, Lake, Isr. 57 32 45N 35 35 E
Galle, Sri L. 58 6 5N 80 10 E
Galley Hd., Ire. 25 51 32N 8 56W
Gällivare, Swed. 44 67 9N 20 40 E
Galloway, U.K. 20 55 0N 4 25W
Galloway, Mull of, U.K. 20 54 38N 4 50W
Galmpton, U.K. 16 50 23N 3 32W
Galston, U.K. 20 55 36N 4 22W
Galty Mts., Ire. 25 52 22N 8 10W
Galtymore, Ire. 25 52 22N 8 12W
Galveston, U.S.A. 91 29 15N 94 48W
Galway, Ire. 25 53 16N 9 4W
Galway □, Ire. 24 53 16N 9 3W
Galway B., Ire. 25 53 10N 9 20W
Gambia ■, W. Afr. 78 13 25N 16 0W
Gamboa, Pan. 94 9 8N 79 42W
Gamlingay, U.K. 15 52 9N 0 11W
Gan Jiang →, China 61 29 15N 116 0 E
Ganga →, India 59 23 20N 90 30 E
Ganganagar, India 58 29 56N 73 56 E
Ganges = Ganga →, India 59 23 20N 90 30 E
Gansu □, China 60 36 0N 104 0 E
Gao, Mali 78 16 15N 0 5W
Gap, Fr. 34 44 33N 6 5 E
Garboldisham, U.K. 15 52 24N 0 57 E
Garda, L. di, It. 40 45 40N 10 40 E
Gare, L., U.K. 20 56 1N 4 50W
Garelochhead, U.K. 20 56 7N 4 50W
Garforth, U.K. 19 53 48N 1 22W
Gargrave, U.K. 18 53 58N 2 7W
Garlieston, U.K. 20 54 47N 4 22W
Garonne →, Fr. 35 45 2N 0 36W
Garoua, Cam. 80 9 19N 13 21 E
Garry →, U.K. 23 56 47N 3 47W
Garsdale Head, U.K. 18 54 19N 2 19W
Garstang, U.K. 18 53 53N 2 47W
Garston, U.K. 18 53 21N 2 55W
Garvald, U.K. 21 55 55N 2 39W
Garvellachs, Is., U.K. 20 56 14N 5 48W
Gary, U.S.A. 92 41 35N 87 20W
Garzê, China 60 31 39N 99 58 E
Gascony, Fr. 35 43 45N 0 20 E
Gascoyne →, Austral. 66 24 52S 113 37 E
Gaspé, Pén. de, Canada 93 48 45N 65 40W
Gatehouse of Fleet, U.K. 20 54 53N 4 10W
Gateshead, U.K. 19 54 57N 1 37W
Gatley, U.K. 18 53 25N 2 15W
Gatun, Pan. 94 9 16N 79 55W
Gatun, L., Pan. 94 9 7N 79 56W
Gävle, Swed. 45 60 40N 17 9 E
Gawthwaite, U.K. 18 54 16N 3 6W
Gaya, India 59 24 47N 85 4 E
Gayton, U.K. 15 52 45N 0 35 E
Gaywood, U.K. 15 52 46N 0 26 E
Gaza, Egypt 57 31 30N 34 28 E
Gaziantep, Turk. 47 37 6N 37 23 E
Gdańsk, Pol. 43 54 22N 18 40 E
Gdańsk Bay, Pol. 43 54 30N 19 20 E
Gdynia, Pol. 43 54 35N 18 33 E
Gedney, U.K. 15 52 47N 0 5 E
Geelong, Austral. 70 38 10S 144 22 E
Gejiu, China 60 23 20N 103 10 E
Gelderland □, Neth. 36 52 5N 6 10 E

Gelsenkirchen

Gelsenkirchen, *W. Ger.* **36** 51 30N 7 5 E
Geneva, *Switz.* **42** 46 12N 6 9 E
Geneva, L., *Switz.* **42** 46 26N 6 30 E
Genk, *Belg.* **36** 50 58N 5 32 E
Gennargentu, Mti. del, *It.* **40** 40 0N 9 10 E
Genoa, *It.* **40** 44 24N 8 56 E
Geographe Chan., *Austral.* **66** 24 30S 113 0 E
George, *S. Afr.* **81** 33 58S 22 29 E
George Town, *Malay.* **63** 5 25N 100 15 E
Georgetown, *Guy.* **100** 6 50N 58 12W
Georgia □, *U.S.A.* **91** 32 0N 82 0W
Georgia □, *U.S.S.R.* **47** 42 0N 43 0 E
Georgian B., *Canada* **92** 45 15N 81 0W
Gera, *E. Ger.* **42** 50 53N 12 11 E
Geraldton, *Austral.* **66** 28 48S 114 32 E
Germiston, *S. Afr.* **81** 26 15S 28 10 E
Gerona, *Sp.* **37** 41 58N 2 46 E
Gerrans B., *U.K.* **16** 50 12N 4 57W
Gerrards Cross, *U.K.* **15** 51 35N 0 32W
Ghaghara →, *India* **59** 25 45N 84 40 E
Ghana ■, *W. Afr.* **78** 6 0N 1 0W
Ghaziabad, *India* **58** 28 42N 77 26 E
Ghent, *Belg.* **36** 51 2N 3 42 E
Giant's Causeway, *U.K.* **24** 55 15N 6 30W
Gibraltar, *Europe* **37** 36 7N 5 22W
Gibraltar, Str. of, *Medit. S.* **37** 35 55N 5 40W
Gibraltar Pt., *U.K.* **19** 53 6N 0 20 E
Gibson Desert, *Austral.* **66** 24 0S 126 0 E
Gifford, *U.K.* **21** 55 54N 2 45W
Gifu, *Jap.* **62** 35 30N 136 45 E
Giggleswick, *U.K.* **18** 54 5N 2 19W
Gigha, *U.K.* **20** 55 42N 5 45W
Gijón, *Sp.* **37** 43 32N 5 42W
Gilbert Is. = Kiribati ■, *Pac. Oc.* **65** 1 0N 176 0 E
Gillingham, *Dorset, U.K.* **14** 51 2N 2 15W
Gillingham, *Kent, U.K.* **15** 51 23N 0 34 E
Gilsland, *U.K.* **18** 55 0N 2 34W
Girdle Ness, *U.K.* **23** 57 9N 2 2W
Gironde →, *Fr.* **35** 45 32N 1 7W
Girvan, *U.K.* **20** 55 15N 4 50W
Girvan →, *U.K.* **20** 55 18N 4 51W
Gisborne, *N.Z.* **71** 38 39S 178 5 E
Gisburn, *U.K.* **18** 53 56N 2 16W
Gizhiga, *U.S.S.R.* **49** 62 3N 160 30 E
Gizhiga, G., *U.S.S.R.* **49** 61 0N 158 0 E
Gladstone, *Austral.* **67** 25 57S 114 17 E
Glanton, *U.K.* **21** 55 25N 1 54W
Glasgow, *U.K.* **20** 55 52N 4 14W
Glastonbury, *U.K.* **14** 51 9N 2 42W
Glemsford, *U.K.* **15** 52 6N 0 41 E
Glen →, *U.K.* **15** 52 50N 0 7W
Glen Affric, *U.K.* **22** 57 15N 5 0W
Glen Almond, *U.K.* **21** 56 28N 3 50W
Glen Coe, *U.K.* **19** 56 40N 5 0W
Glen Etive, *U.K.* **20** 56 37N 5 0W
Glen Garry, *U.K.* **22** 57 3N 5 7W
Glen Helen, *U.K.* **18** 54 14N 4 35W
Glen Mor, *U.K.* **23** 57 12N 4 37 E
Glen Moriston, *U.K.* **22** 57 10N 4 58W
Glen Orchy, *U.K.* **20** 56 27N 4 52W
Glen Spean, *U.K.* **23** 56 53N 4 40W
Glenbarr, *U.K.* **20** 55 34N 5 40W
Glendale, *U.S.A.* **90** 34 7N 118 18W
Gleneagles, *U.K.* **21** 56 16N 3 44W
Glengarriff, *Ire.* **25** 51 45N 9 33W
Glenkens, The, *U.K.* **20** 55 10N 4 15W
Glenluce, *U.K.* **20** 54 53N 4 50W
Glenmaye, *U.K.* **18** 54 11N 4 42W
Glenorchy, *Austral.* **67** 31 55S 139 46 E
Glenrothes, *U.K.* **20** 56 12N 3 11W
Glenties, *Ire.* **24** 54 48N 8 18W
Glentrool Village, *U.K.* **20** 55 5N 4 30W
Gliwice, *Pol.* **43** 50 22N 18 41 E
Glossop, *U.K.* **18** 53 27N 1 56W
Gloucester, *U.K.* **14** 51 52N 2 15W
Gloucestershire □, *U.K.* **14** 51 44N 2 10W
Gnosall, *U.K.* **14** 52 48N 2 15W
Goa □, *India* **58** 15 33N 73 59 E
Goat Fell, *U.K.* **20** 55 37N 5 11W
Gobi, *Asia* **60** 44 0N 111 0 E
Godalming, *U.K.* **15** 51 12N 0 37W
Godavari →, *India* **58** 16 25N 82 18 E
Godmanchester, *U.K.* **15** 52 19N 0 11W
Godshill, *U.K.* **14** 50 38N 1 13W
Godstone, *U.K.* **15** 51 15N 0 3W
Goiânia, *Brazil* **101** 16 43S 49 20W
Goil, L., *U.K.* **20** 56 8N 4 52W
Gold Coast, *Austral.* **67** 28 0S 153 25 E
Golden Vale, *Ire.* **25** 52 33N 8 17W
Golspie, *U.K.* **23** 57 58N 3 58W
Gomel, *U.S.S.R.* **46** 52 28N 31 0 E
Gometra I., *U.K.* **20** 56 30N 6 18W
Gómez Palacio, *Mex.* **94** 25 40N 104 0W
Gonder, *Eth.* **79** 12 39N 37 30 E
Good Hope, C. of, *S. Afr.* **81** 34 24S 18 30 E
Goodrich, *U.K.* **14** 51 52N 2 38W
Goodwood, *U.K.* **15** 50 53N 0 44W
Goole, *U.K.* **19** 53 42N 0 52W
Goondiwindi, *Austral.* **67** 28 30S 150 21 E
Gorakhpur, *India* **59** 26 47N 83 23 E
Gordon, *U.K.* **21** 55 41N 2 32W
Gorebridge, *U.K.* **21** 55 51N 3 2W
Gorey, *Ire.* **25** 52 41N 6 18W
Goring, *Oxon., U.K.* **14** 51 31N 1 8W
Goring, *W. Sussex, U.K.* **15** 50 49N 0 26W
Gorki, *U.S.S.R.* **46** 56 20N 44 0 E
Gorleston, *U.K.* **15** 52 35N 1 44 E
Görlitz, *E. Ger.* **42** 51 10N 14 59 E
Gort, *Ire.* **25** 53 4N 8 50W
Gorzów Wielkopolski, *Pol.* **42** 52 43N 15 15 E
Gosberton, *U.K.* **19** 52 52N 0 10W
Gosford, *Austral.* **70** 33 23S 151 18 E
Gosforth, *U.K.* **18** 54 24N 3 27W
Gosport, *U.K.* **14** 50 48N 1 8W
Göteborg, *Swed.* **45** 57 43N 11 59 E
Gotha, *E. Ger.* **42** 50 56N 10 42 E
Gotland, *Swed.* **45** 57 30N 18 33 E
Gouda, *Neth.* **36** 52 1N 4 42 E
Goudhurst, *U.K.* **15** 51 7N 0 28 E
Gouin, Rés., *Canada* **93** 48 35N 74 40W
Goulburn, *Austral.* **70** 34 44S 149 44 E
Gourock, *U.K.* **20** 55 58N 4 49W
Governador Valadares, *Brazil* **101** 18 15S 41 57W
Gower, The, *U.K.* **17** 51 35N 4 10W
Gowna, L., *Ire.* **24** 53 52N 7 35W
Gowrie, Carse of, *U.K.* **21** 56 30N 3 10W
Goya, *Arg.* **102** 29 10S 59 10W
Gozo, *Malta* **40** 36 0N 14 13 E
Grafham Water, *U.K.* **15** 52 18N 0 17W
Grafton, *Austral.* **67** 29 38S 152 58 E
Graham Bell, I., *U.S.S.R.* **48** 80 5N 70 0 E
Graham Land, *Ant.* **103** 65 0S 64 0W
Grainthorpe, *U.K.* **19** 53 27N 0 5 E
Grampian □, *U.K.* **23** 57 0N 3 0W
Grampian Mts., *U.K.* **23** 56 50N 4 0W
Gran Canaria, *Can. Is.* **78** 27 55N 15 35W
Gran Chaco, *S. Am.* **96** 25 0S 61 0W
Granada, *Sp.* **37** 37 10N 3 35W
Granard, *Ire.* **24** 53 47N 7 30W
Grand Bahama, *Baham.* **95** 26 40N 78 30W
Grand Canyon National Park, *U.S.A.* **90** 36 15N 112 20W
Grand Cayman, *W. Ind.* **95** 19 20N 81 20W
Grand Rapids, *U.S.A.* **92** 42 57N 86 40W
Grande de Santiago →, *Mex.* **94** 21 36N 105 26W
Grande Prairie, *Canada* **88** 55 10N 118 50W
Grange-over-Sands, *U.K.* **18** 54 12N 2 55W
Grangemouth, *U.K.* **21** 56 1N 3 43W
Grangetown, *U.K.* **19** 54 36N 1 7W
Grantham, *U.K.* **19** 52 55N 0 39W
Grantown-on-Spey, *U.K.* **23** 57 19N 3 36W
Grantshouse, *U.K.* **21** 55 53N 2 17W
Grasmere, *U.K.* **18** 54 28N 3 2W
Grassington, *U.K.* **18** 54 5N 2 0W
Gravesend, *U.K.* **15** 51 25N 0 22 E
Grayrigg, *U.K.* **18** 54 22N 2 40W
Grays, *U.K.* **15** 51 28N 0 23 E
Graz, *Austria* **42** 47 4N 15 27 E
Great Abaco I., *Baham.* **95** 26 25N 77 10W
Great Australian Bight, *Austral.* **66** 33 30S 130 0 E
Great Ayton, *U.K.* **19** 54 29N 1 8W
Great Baddow, *U.K.* **15** 51 43N 0 31 E
Great Barrier Reef, *Austral.* **67** 18 0S 146 50 E
Great Basin, *U.S.A.* **90** 40 0N 116 30W
Great Bear L., *Canada* **88** 65 30N 120 0W
Great Bentley, *U.K.* **15** 51 51N 1 5 E
Great Blasket I., *Ire.* **25** 52 5N 10 30W
Great Britain, *Europe* **5** 54 0N 2 15W
Great Chesterford, *U.K.* **15** 52 4N 0 11 E
Great Clifton, *U.K.* **18** 54 39N 3 29W
Great Divide, The, *Austral.* **70** 35 0S 149 17 E
Great Dividing Ra., *Austral.* **67** 23 0S 146 0 E
Great Dunmow, *U.K.* **15** 51 52N 0 22 E
Great Falls, *U.S.A.* **90** 47 27N 111 12W
Great Harwood, *U.K.* **18** 53 43N 2 30W
Great Inagua I., *Baham.* **95** 21 0N 73 20W
Great Indian Desert = Thar Desert, *India* **58** 28 0N 72 0 E
Great Malvern, *U.K.* **14** 52 7N 2 19W
Great Massingham, *U.K.* **15** 52 47N 0 41 E
Great Missenden, *U.K.* **15** 51 42N 0 42W
Great Orme's Head, *U.K.* **17** 53 20N 3 52W
Great Ouse →, *U.K.* **15** 52 47N 0 22 E
Great Plains, *N. Am.* **82** 47 0N 105 0W
Great Salt Lake, *U.S.A.* **90** 41 0N 112 30W
Great Sandy Desert, *Austral.* **66** 21 0S 124 0 E
Great Shefford, *U.K.* **14** 51 29N 1 27W
Great Shelford, *U.K.* **15** 52 9N 0 9 E
Great Shunner Fell, *U.K.* **18** 54 22N 2 16W
Great Slave L., *Canada* **88** 61 23N 115 38W
Great Stour = Stour →, *U.K.* **15** 51 15N 1 20 E
Great Torrington, *U.K.* **16** 50 57N 4 9W
Great Victoria Desert, *Austral.* **66** 29 30S 126 30 E
Great Waltham, *U.K.* **15** 51 47N 0 29 E
Great Whernside, *U.K.* **18** 54 9N 1 59W
Great Wyrley, *U.K.* **14** 52 40N 2 1W
Great Yarmouth, *U.K.* **15** 52 40N 1 45 E
Great Yeldham, *U.K.* **15** 52 1N 0 33 E
Greater Antilles, *W. Ind.* **95** 17 40N 74 0W
Greater London □, *U.K.* **15** 51 30N 0 5W
Greater Manchester □, *U.K.* **18** 53 30N 2 15W
Greater Sunda Is., *Indon.* **63** 7 0S 112 0 E
Greatham, *U.K.* **19** 54 38N 1 14W
Greece ■, *Europe* **41** 40 0N 23 0 E
Greeley, *U.S.A.* **90** 40 30N 104 40W
Green B., *U.S.A.* **92** 45 0N 87 30W
Green Bay, *U.S.A.* **92** 44 30N 88 0W
Green Hammerton, *U.K.* **19** 54 2N 1 17W
Green Lowther, *U.K.* **21** 55 22N 3 44W
Greenhead, *U.K.* **21** 54 58N 2 31W
Greenland ■, *N. Am.* **89** 66 0N 45 0W
Greenland Sea, *Arctic* **103** 73 0N 10 0W
Greenlaw, *U.K.* **21** 55 42N 2 28W
Greenock, *U.K.* **20** 55 57N 4 46W
Greenodd, *U.K.* **18** 54 14N 3 3W
Greenore, *Ire.* **24** 54 2N 6 8W
Greenore Pt., *Ire.* **25** 52 15N 6 20W
Greensboro, *U.S.A.* **91** 36 7N 79 46W
Greenwich, *U.K.* **15** 51 28N 0 0 E
Grenada ■, *W. Ind.* **94** 12 10N 61 40W
Grenoble, *Fr.* **35** 45 12N 5 42 E
Greta →, *U.K.* **18** 54 9N 2 36W
Gretna, *U.K.* **21** 54 59N 3 4W
Gretna Green, *U.K.* **21** 55 0N 3 3W
Gretton, *U.K.* **15** 52 33N 0 40W
Grey Range, *Austral.* **67** 27 0S 143 30 E
Greymouth, *N.Z.* **71** 42 29S 171 13 E
Greystoke, *U.K.* **18** 54 39N 2 52W
Gribbin Head, *U.K.* **16** 50 18N 4 41W
Griffith, *Austral.* **70** 34 18S 146 2 E
Grimsby, *U.K.* **19** 53 35N 0 5W
Gris-Nez, C., *Fr.* **34** 50 52N 1 35 E
Grizebeck, *U.K.* **18** 54 16N 3 10W
Grodno, *U.S.S.R.* **46** 53 42N 23 52 E
Groningen, *Neth.* **36** 53 15N 6 35 E
Groote Eylandt, *Austral.* **67** 14 0S 136 40 E
Groznyy, *U.S.S.R.* **47** 43 20N 45 45 E
Gruinard B., *U.K.* **22** 57 56N 5 35W
Guadalajara, *Mex.* **94** 20 40N 103 20W
Guadalajara, *Sp.* **37** 40 37N 3 12W
Guadalete →, *Sp.* **37** 36 35N 6 13W
Guadeloupe ■, *W. Ind.* **94** 16 20N 61 40W
Guadiana →, *Port.* **37** 37 14N 7 22W
Guadix, *Sp.* **37** 37 18N 3 11W
Gualeguay, *Arg.* **102** 33 10S 59 14W
Guam, *Pac. Oc.* **64** 13 27N 144 45 E
Guangdong □, *China* **61** 23 0N 113 0 E
Guangxi Zhuangzu Zizhiqu □, *China* **61** 24 0N 109 0 E
Guangzhou, *China* **61** 23 5N 113 10 E
Guantánamo, *Cuba* **95** 20 10N 75 14W
Guaporé →, *Brazil* **100** 11 55S 65 4W
Guard Bridge, *U.K.* **21** 56 21N 2 52W
Guardafui, C. = Asir, Ras, *Som.* **73** 11 55N 51 10 E
Guatemala, *Guat.* **94** 14 40N 90 22W
Guatemala ■, *Cent. Am.* **94** 15 40N 90 30W
Guaviare →, *Col.* **100** 4 3N 67 44W
Guayaquil, *Ecuad.* **100** 2 15S 79 52W
Guaymas, *Mex.* **94** 27 59N 110 54W
Guelph, *Canada* **92** 43 35N 80 20W
Guernsey, *U.K.* **34** 49 30N 2 35W
Guestling Green, *U.K.* **15** 50 53N 0 40 E
Guildford, *U.K.* **15** 51 14N 0 34W
Guilin, *China* **61** 25 18N 110 15 E
Guinea ■, *W. Afr.* **78** 10 20N 10 0W
Guinea, Gulf of, *Atl. Oc.* **72** 3 0N 2 30 E
Guinea-Bissau ■, *Africa* **78** 12 0N 15 0W
Guisborough, *U.K.* **19** 54 32N 1 2W
Guiyang, *China* **60** 26 32N 106 40 E
Guizhou □, *China* **60** 27 0N 107 0 E
Gujarat □, *India* **58** 23 20N 71 0 E
Gujranwala, *Pak.* **58** 32 10N 74 12 E
Gujrat, *Pak.* **58** 32 40N 74 2 E
Gulbarga, *India* **58** 17 20N 76 50 E
Gulf, The, *Asia* **56** 27 0N 50 0 E
Gullane, *U.K.* **21** 56 2N 2 50W
Guntur, *India* **59** 16 23N 80 30 E
Gurnard's Head, *U.K.* **16** 50 12N 5 37W
Guyana ■, *S. Am.* **100** 5 0N 59 0W
Gwalchmai, *U.K.* **17** 53 16N 4 23W
Gwalior, *India* **58** 26 12N 78 10 E
Gweebarra B., *Ire.* **24** 54 52N 8 21W
Gweedore, *Ire.* **24** 55 4N 8 15W
Gweek, *U.K.* **16** 50 6N 5 12W
Gwennap, *U.K.* **16** 50 12N 5 9W
Gwent □, *U.K.* **17** 51 45N 2 55W
Gweru, *Zimb.* **81** 19 28S 29 45 E
Gwynedd □, *U.K.* **17** 53 0N 4 0W
Gympie, *Austral.* **67** 26 11S 152 38 E
Györ, *Hung.* **43** 47 41N 17 40 E

H

Haarlem, *Neth.* **36** 52 23N 4 39 E
Hachinohe, *Jap.* **62** 40 30N 141 29 E
Hackney, *U.K.* **15** 51 33N 0 2W
Hackthorpe, *U.K.* **18** 54 37N 2 42W
Haddenham, *U.K.* **15** 51 46N 0 56W
Haddington, *U.K.* **21** 55 57N 2 48W
Hadleigh, *U.K.* **15** 52 3N 0 58 E
Hadley, *U.K.* **14** 52 42N 2 28W
Hadlow, *U.K.* **15** 51 12N 0 20 E
Hadrians Wall, *U.K.* **19** 55 0N 2 30W
Haeju, *N. Kor.* **61** 38 3N 125 45 E
Hafnarfjörður, *Ice.* **44** 64 4N 21 57W
Hagen, *W. Ger.* **36** 51 21N 7 29 E
Hags Hd., *Ire.* **25** 52 57N 9 30W
Haifa, *Isr.* **57** 32 46N 35 0 E
Haikou, *China* **61** 20 1N 110 16 E
Ḥā'il, *Si. Arab.* **56** 27 28N 41 45 E
Hailar, *China* **61** 49 12N 119 37 E
Hailsham, *U.K.* **15** 50 52N 0 17 E
Hainan, *China* **61** 19 0N 109 30 E
Hainton, *U.K.* **19** 53 21N 0 13W
Haiphong, *Viet.* **60** 20 47N 106 41 E
Haiti ■, *W. Ind.* **95** 19 0N 72 30W
Hakodate, *Jap.* **62** 41 45N 140 44 E
Halberton, *U.K.* **16** 50 55N 3 24W
Hale, *U.K.* **18** 53 24N 2 21W
Halesowen, *U.K.* **14** 52 27N 2 2W
Halesworth, *U.K.* **15** 52 21N 1 30 E
Halifax, *Canada* **93** 44 38N 63 35W
Halifax, *U.K.* **18** 53 43N 1 51W
Halifax B., *Austral.* **67** 18 50S 147 0 E
Halkirk, *U.K.* **23** 58 30N 3 30W
Halle, *Ger.* **42** 51 29N 12 0 E
Hallow, *U.K.* **14** 52 14N 2 15W
Hallworthy, *U.K.* **16** 50 38N 4 34W
Halmahera, *Indon.* **63** 0 40N 128 0 E
Halmstad, *Swed.* **45** 56 41N 12 52 E
Halstead, *U.K.* **15** 51 59N 0 39 E
Haltwhistle, *U.K.* **21** 54 58N 2 27W
Hamadān, *Iran* **56** 34 52N 48 32 E
Hamāh, *Syria* **56** 35 5N 36 40 E
Hamamatsu, *Jap.* **62** 34 45N 137 45 E
Hambledon, *U.K.* **14** 50 56N 1 6W
Hambleton Hills, *U.K.* **19** 54 17N 1 12W
Hamburg, *W. Ger.* **42** 53 32N 9 59 E
Hämeenlinna, *Fin.* **45** 61 0N 24 28 E
Hamersley Ra., *Austral.* **66** 22 0S 117 45 E
Hamilton, *Berm.* **95** 32 15N 64 45W
Hamilton, *Canada* **92** 43 15N 79 50W
Hamilton, *N.Z.* **71** 37 47S 175 19 E
Hamilton, *U.K.* **21** 55 47N 4 2W
Hamm, *W. Ger.* **36** 51 40N 7 49 E
Hammerfest, *Nor.* **44** 70 39N 23 41 E
Hammersmith, *U.K.* **15** 51 30N 0 15W
Hammond, *U.S.A.* **92** 41 40N 87 30W
Hampshire □, *U.K.* **14** 51 3N 1 20W
Hampshire Downs, *U.K.* **14** 51 10N 1 10W
Hampton in Arden, *U.K.* **14** 52 26N 1 42W
Hangzhou, *China* **61** 30 18N 120 11 E
Hanko, *Fin.* **45** 59 59N 22 57 E
Hanningfield Water, *U.K.* **15** 51 40N 0 30 E
Hanoi, *Viet.* **60** 21 5N 105 55 E
Hanover, *W. Ger.* **42** 52 23N 9 43 E
Haora, *India* **59** 22 37N 88 20 E
Happy Valley, *Canada* **89** 53 15N 60 20W
Harare, *Zimb.* **81** 17 43S 31 2 E
Harbin, *China* **61** 45 46N 126 51 E
Hardangerfjorden, *Nor.* **45** 60 15N 6 0 E
Harewood, *U.K.* **19** 53 54N 1 30W
Haringey, *U.K.* **15** 51 35N 0 7W
Harlech, *U.K.* **17** 52 52N 4 7W
Harleston, *U.K.* **15** 52 25N 1 18 E
Harlingen, *Neth.* **36** 53 11N 5 25 E
Harlow, *U.K.* **15** 51 47N 0 9 E
Harpenden, *U.K.* **15** 51 48N 0 20W
Harrietsham, *U.K.* **15** 51 15N 0 41 E
Harrington, *U.K.* **18** 54 37N 3 55W
Harris, *U.K.* **22** 57 50N 6 55W
Harris, Sd. of, *U.K.* **22** 57 44N 7 6W
Harrisburg, *U.S.A.* **93** 40 18N 76 52W
Harrogate, *U.K.* **19** 53 59N 1 32W
Harrow, *U.K.* **15** 51 35N 0 15W
Hartest, *U.K.* **15** 52 7N 0 41 E
Hartford, *U.S.A.* **93** 41 47N 72 41W
Harthill, *U.K.* **21** 55 52N 3 45W
Hartland, *U.K.* **16** 50 59N 4 29W
Hartland Pt., *U.K.* **16** 51 2N 4 32W
Hartlebury, *U.K.* **14** 52 20N 2 13W
Hartlepool, *U.K.* **19** 54 42N 1 11W
Hartley, *U.K.* **21** 55 5N 1 27W
Hartpury, *U.K.* **14** 51 55N 2 18W
Harwell, *U.K.* **14** 51 40N 1 17W
Harwich, *U.K.* **15** 51 56N 1 18 E
Harz, *Europe* **26** 51 40N 10 40 E
Hasa, *Si. Arab.* **56** 26 0N 49 0 E
Haslemere, *U.K.* **15** 51 5N 0 41W
Haslingden, *U.K.* **18** 53 43N 2 20W
Hasselt, *Belg.* **36** 50 56N 5 21 E
Hastings, *N.Z.* **71** 39 39S 176 52 E
Hastings, *U.K.* **15** 50 51N 0 36 E
Hatfield, *U.K.* **15** 51 46N 0 11W
Hatfield Broad Oak, *U.K.* **15** 51 48N 0 16 E
Hatherleigh, *U.K.* **16** 50 49N 4 4W
Hathersage, *U.K.* **19** 53 20N 1 39W
Hatteras, C., *U.S.A.* **91** 35 10N 75 30W
Haugh of Urr, *U.K.* **21** 55 0N 3 51W
Haughley, *U.K.* **15** 52 13N 0 59 E
Hauraki Gulf, *N.Z.* **71** 36 35S 175 5 E
Hauxley, *U.K.* **21** 55 21N 1 35W
Havana, *Cuba* **95** 23 8N 82 22W
Havant, *U.K.* **15** 50 51N 0 59W
Haverfordwest, *U.K.* **17** 51 48N 4 59W
Haverhill, *U.K.* **15** 52 6N 0 27 E
Haverigg, *U.K.* **18** 54 12N 3 16W
Havering, *U.K.* **15** 51 33N 0 20 E
Havre, Le, *Fr.* **34** 49 30N 0 5 E
Hawaiian Is., *Pac. Oc.* **90** 20 30N 156 0W
Hawera, *N.Z.* **71** 39 35S 174 19 E
Hawes, *U.K.* **18** 54 18N 2 12W
Haweswater, *U.K.* **18** 54 32N 2 48W
Hawick, *U.K.* **21** 55 25N 2 48W
Hawkchurch, *U.K.* **16** 50 47N 2 56W

Jersey, I.

Hawke B., N.Z. 71 39 25S 177 20 E
Hawkesbury Upton, U.K. 14 51 34N 2 19W
Hawkhurst, U.K. 15 51 2N 0 31 E
Hawkshead, U.K. 18 54 23N 3 0W
Haworth, U.K. 18 53 50N 1 57W
Hawsker, U.K. 19 54 27N 0 34W
Haxby, U.K. 19 54 1N 1 4W
Hay-on-Wye, U.K. 17 52 4N 3 9W
Hay River, Canada 88 60 51N 115 44W
Hayburn Wyke, U.K. 19 54 22N 0 28W
Haydon Bridge, U.K. 21 54 58N 2 15W
Hayle, U.K. 16 50 12N 5 25W
Hayton, U.K. 18 54 55N 2 45W
Hayward's Heath, U.K. 15 51 0N 0 5W
Heacham, U.K. 15 52 55N 0 30 E
Headcorn, U.K. 15 51 10N 0 39 E
Heanor, U.K. 19 53 1N 1 20W
Heathfield, U.K. 15 50 58N 0 18 E
Hebburn, U.K. 21 54 59N 1 30W
Hebden Bridge, U.K. 18 53 45N 2 0W
Hebei □, China 61 39 0N 116 0 E
Hebrides, U.K. 22 57 30N 7 0W
Hechuan, China 60 30 2N 106 12 E
Heckington, U.K. 19 52 59N 0 17W
Hedmark fylke □, Nor. 44 61 17N 11 40 E
Hednesford, U.K. 14 52 43N 2 0W
Hedon, U.K. 19 53 44N 0 11W
Heerlen, Neth. 36 50 55N 6 0 E
Hefei, China 61 31 52N 117 18 E
Hegang, China 61 47 20N 130 19 E
Heidelberg, W. Ger. 42 49 23N 8 41 E
Heilbronn, W. Ger. 42 49 8N 9 13 E
Heilongjiang □, China 61 48 0N 126 0 E
Hekla, Ice. 44 63 56N 19 35W
Helensburgh, U.K. 20 56 0N 4 44W
Heligoland, W. Ger. 42 54 10N 7 51 E
Hellifield, U.K. 18 54 0N 2 13W
Helmond, Neth. 36 51 29N 5 41 E
Helmsdale, U.K. 23 58 7N 3 40W
Helmsley, U.K. 19 54 15N 1 2W
Helperby, U.K. 19 54 8N 1 20W
Helsby, U.K. 18 53 16N 2 47W
Helsingborg, Swed. 45 56 3N 12 42 E
Helsingør, Den. 45 56 2N 12 35 E
Helsinki, Fin. 45 60 15N 25 3 E
Helston, U.K. 16 50 7N 5 17W
Helvellyn, U.K. 18 54 31N 3 1W
Hemel Hempstead, U.K. 15 51 45N 0 28W
Hempton, U.K. 15 52 50N 0 49 E
Hemsworth, U.K. 19 53 37N 1 21W
Hemyock, U.K. 16 50 50N 3 15W
Henan □, China 61 34 0N 114 0 E
Henfield, U.K. 15 50 56N 0 17W
Hengelo, Neth. 36 52 16N 6 48 E
Hengyang, China 61 26 51N 112 30 E
Henley-in-Arden, U.K. 14 52 18N 1 47W
Henley-on-Thames, U.K. 15 51 32N 0 53W
Henlow, U.K. 15 52 2N 0 18W
Henstridge, U.K. 14 50 59N 2 24W
Henzada, Burma 59 17 38N 95 26 E
Herāt, Afg. 57 34 20N 62 7 E
Hereford, U.K. 14 52 4N 2 42W
Hereford and Worcester □, U.K. 14 52 10N 2 30W
Hermosillo, Mex. 94 29 4N 110 58W
Herne, W. Ger. 36 51 33N 7 12 E
Herne Bay, U.K. 15 51 22N 1 8 E
Herning, Den. 45 56 8N 8 58 E
Herstmonceux, U.K. 15 50 53N 0 21 E
Hertford, U.K. 15 51 47N 0 4W
Hertford □, U.K. 15 51 51N 0 5W
's-Hertogenbosch, Neth. 36 51 42N 5 17 E
Hesse □, W. Ger. 42 50 40N 9 20 E
Hessle, U.K. 19 53 44N 0 28 E
Hethersett, U.K. 15 52 35N 1 10 E
Hetton-le-Hole, U.K. 21 54 49N 1 26W
Hexham, U.K. 21 54 58N 2 7W
Heybridge, U.K. 15 51 44N 0 42 E
Heysham, U.K. 18 54 5N 2 53W
Heytesbury, U.K. 14 51 11N 2 7W
Heywood, U.K. 18 53 36N 2 13W
High Atlas, Mor. 72 32 30N 5 0W
High Bentham, U.K. 18 54 8N 2 31W
High Borrow Bridge, U.K. 18 54 26N 2 43W
High Ercall, U.K. 14 52 46N 2 37W
High Hesket, U.K. 18 54 47N 2 49W
High Pike, U.K. 18 54 43N 3 4W
High Willhays, U.K. 16 50 41N 3 59W
High Wycombe, U.K. 15 51 37N 0 45W
Higham Ferrers, U.K. 15 52 18N 0 36W
Highbridge, U.K. 14 51 13N 2 59W
Highclere, U.K. 14 51 20N 1 22W
Highland □, U.K. 22 57 30N 5 0W
Highley, U.K. 14 52 25N 2 23W
Hightae, U.K. 21 55 5N 3 27W
Highworth, U.K. 14 51 38N 1 42W
Hilgay, U.K. 15 52 34N 0 23 E
Hillingdon, U.K. 15 51 33N 0 29W
Hillsborough, U.K. 24 54 28N 6 6W
Hilo, U.S.A. 90 19 44N 155 5W
Hilpsford Pt., U.K. 18 54 4N 3 12W
Hilversum, Neth. 36 52 14N 5 10 E
Himachal Pradesh □, India 58 31 30N 77 0 E
Himalaya, Mts., Asia 62 29 0N 84 0 E
Himeji, Jap. 62 34 50N 134 40 E
Hinckley, U.K. 14 52 33N 1 21W
Hinderwell, U.K. 19 54 32N 0 45W
Hindhead, U.K. 15 51 6N 0 42W
Hindley, U.K. 18 53 32N 2 35W
Hindu Kush, Asia 57 36 0N 71 0 E
Hingham, U.K. 15 52 35N 0 59 E
Hinkley Pt., U.K. 14 50 59N 3 32W
Hinstock, U.K. 14 52 50N 2 28W
Hiroshima, Jap. 62 34 24N 132 30 E
Hispaniola, W. Ind. 95 19 0N 71 0W
Histon, U.K. 15 52 15N 0 6 E
Hitchin, U.K. 15 51 57N 0 16W
Ho Chi Minh City, Viet. 63 10 58N 106 40 E
Hobart, Austral. 66 42 50S 147 21 E
Hodder →, U.K. 18 53 57N 2 27W
Hoddesdon, U.K. 15 51 45N 0 1W
Hodge →, U.K. 19 54 14N 0 55W
Hoff, U.K. 18 54 34N 2 31W
Hoggar, Mts., Alg. 78 23 0N 6 30 E
Hog's Back, U.K. 15 51 13N 0 40W
Hohhot, China 61 40 52N 111 40 E
Hokitika, N.Z. 71 42 42S 171 0 E
Hokkaidō □, Jap. 62 43 30N 143 0 E
Holbeach, U.K. 15 52 48N 0 1 E
Holbeach Marsh, U.K. 15 52 52N 0 5 E
Holderness, U.K. 19 53 45N 0 5W
Holguín, Cuba 95 20 50N 76 20W
Holkham, U.K. 15 52 57N 0 48 E
Holland Fen, U.K. 19 53 0N 0 8W
Holland-on-Sea, U.K. 15 51 48N 1 12 E
Holme, Humberside, U.K. 19 53 50N 0 48W
Holme, N. Yorks., U.K. 18 53 34N 1 50W
Holmes Chapel, U.K. 18 53 13N 2 21W
Holmfirth, U.K. 19 53 34N 1 48W
Holmwood, U.K. 15 51 12N 0 19W
Holsworthy, U.K. 16 50 48N 4 21W
Holt, U.K. 15 52 55N 1 4 E
Holy I., England, U.K. 19 55 42N 1 48W
Holy I., Scotland, U.K. 20 55 31N 5 4W
Holy I., Wales, U.K. 17 53 17N 4 37W
Holyhead, U.K. 17 53 18N 4 38W
Holywell, U.K. 17 53 16N 3 14W
Holywood, U.K. 24 54 38N 5 50W
Homs, Syria 56 34 40N 36 45 E
Honduras ■, Cent. Am. 94 14 40N 86 30W
Honduras, G. de, Cent. Am. 94 16 50N 87 0W
Hong →, Viet. 60 20 17N 106 34 E
Hong Kong ■, Asia 61 22 11N 114 14 E
Honington, U.K. 19 52 58N 0 35W
Honiton, U.K. 16 50 48N 3 11W
Honolulu, U.S.A. 90 21 19N 157 52W
Honshū, Jap. 62 36 0N 138 0 E
Hoo, U.K. 15 51 25N 0 33 E
Hook, U.K. 15 51 17N 0 55W
Hook Hd., Ire. 25 52 8N 6 57W
Hoorn, Neth. 36 52 38N 5 4 E
Horden, U.K. 19 54 45N 1 17W
Horley, U.K. 15 51 10N 0 10W
Horn, C., Chile 102 55 50S 67 30W
Horn Head, Ire. 24 55 13N 8 0W
Horncastle, U.K. 19 53 13N 0 8W
Horndean, U.K. 15 50 50N 0 59W
Horningsham, U.K. 14 51 11N 2 16W
Hornsby, Austral. 70 33 42S 151 2 E
Hornsea, U.K. 19 53 55N 0 10W
Horsens, Den. 45 55 52N 9 51 E
Horsforth, U.K. 19 53 50N 1 39W
Horsham, Austral. 70 36 44S 142 13 E
Horsham, U.K. 15 51 4N 0 20W
Horsham St. Faith, U.K. 15 52 41N 1 15 E
Horsted Keynes, U.K. 15 51 2N 0 1W
Horton-in-Ribblesdale, U.K. 18 54 9N 2 19W
Horwich, U.K. 18 53 37N 2 33W
Hospitalet de Llobregat, Sp. 37 41 21N 2 6 E
Hotan, China 60 37 25N 79 55 E
Houghton-le-Spring, U.K. 19 54 51N 1 28W
Houghton Regis, U.K. 15 51 54N 0 32W
Hounslow, U.K. 15 51 29N 0 20W
Houston, U.S.A. 91 29 50N 95 20W
Hovd, Mong. 60 48 2N 91 37 E
Hove, U.K. 15 50 50N 0 10W
Hoveton, U.K. 15 52 45N 1 23 E
Hovingham, U.K. 19 54 10N 0 59W
Hövsgöl Nuur, Mong. 60 51 0N 100 30 E
Howden, U.K. 19 53 45N 0 52W
Howth Hd., Ire. 24 53 21N 6 0W
Hoxne, U.K. 15 52 22N 1 11 E
Hoy I., U.K. 23 58 50N 3 15W
Hoylake, U.K. 18 53 24N 3 11W
Hrádec Králové, Czech. 42 50 15N 15 50 E
Hron →, Czech. 43 47 49N 18 45 E
Huainan, China 61 32 39N 117 2 E
Huambo, Angola 81 12 42S 15 54 E
Huancayo, Peru 100 12 5S 75 12W
Huang He →, China 60 37 55N 118 50 E
Huangshi, China 61 30 10N 115 3 E
Huánuco, Peru 100 9 55S 76 15W
Hubei □, China 61 31 0N 112 0 E
Hucknall, U.K. 19 53 3N 1 12W
Huddersfield, U.K. 19 53 38N 1 49W
Hudson →, U.S.A. 93 40 42N 74 2W
Hudson Bay, Canada 89 52 51N 102 23W
Hudson Str., Canada 89 62 0N 70 0W
Hue, Viet. 63 16 30N 107 35 E
Huelva, Sp. 37 37 18N 6 57W
Huesca, Sp. 37 42 8N 0 25W
Hugh Town, U.K. 16 49 55N 6 19W
Hughenden, Austral. 67 20 52S 144 10 E
Hughes, U.S.A. 88 66 0N 154 20W
Hull, Canada 93 45 25N 75 44W
Hull = Kingston-upon-Hull, U.K. 19 53 45N 0 20W
Hull →, U.K. 19 53 43N 0 25W
Hullavington, U.K. 14 51 31N 2 9W
Hulme End, U.K. 18 53 8N 1 51W
Humber →, U.K. 19 53 40N 0 10W
Humber, Mouth of the, U.K. 19 53 32N 0 8 E
Humberside □, U.K. 19 53 50N 0 30W
Humboldt →, U.S.A. 90 40 2N 118 31W
Hume, L., Austral. 70 36 0S 147 0 E
Humshaugh, U.K. 21 55 3N 2 8W
Húnaflói, Ice. 44 65 50N 20 50W
Hunan □, China 61 27 30N 111 30 E
Hungary ■, Europe 43 47 20N 19 20 E
Hungary, Plain of, Europe 26 47 0N 20 0 E
Hungerford, U.K. 14 51 25N 1 30W
Hŭngnam, N. Kor. 61 39 49N 127 45 E
Hunmanby, U.K. 19 54 12N 0 19W
Hunstanton, U.K. 15 52 57N 0 30 E
Hunter →, Austral. 70 32 52S 151 46 E
Hunterston, U.K. 20 55 43N 4 55W
Huntingdon, U.K. 15 52 20N 0 11W
Huntington, U.S.A. 92 38 20N 82 30W
Huntly, U.K. 23 57 27N 2 48W
Huntsville, U.S.A. 91 34 45N 86 35W
Hurlford, U.K. 20 55 35N 4 29W
Huron, L., N. Am. 92 45 0N 83 0W
Hursley, U.K. 14 51 1N 1 23W
Hurstbourne Tarrant, U.K. 14 51 17N 1 27W
Hurstpierpoint, U.K. 15 50 56N 0 11W
Húsavík, Ice. 44 66 3N 17 21W
Husband's Bosworth, U.K. 14 52 27N 1 3W
Huyton, U.K. 18 53 25N 2 52W
Hyde, U.K. 18 53 26N 2 6W
Hyderabad, India 58 17 22N 78 29 E
Hyderabad, Pak. 58 25 23N 68 24 E
Hynish, U.K. 20 56 27N 6 54W
Hynish B., U.K. 20 56 29N 6 40W
Hythe, U.K. 15 51 4N 1 5 E

I

Iaşi, Rom. 43 47 10N 27 40 E
Ibadan, Nig. 78 7 22N 3 58 E
Ibagué, Col. 100 4 20N 75 20W
Iberian Peninsula, Europe 26 40 0N 5 0W
Ibiza, Sp. 37 38 54N 1 26 E
Ibstock, U.K. 14 52 42N 1 23W
Icá, Peru 100 14 0S 75 48W
Iceland ■, Atl. Oc. 44 65 0N 19 0W
Ichinomiya, Jap. 62 35 18N 136 48 E
Idaho □, U.S.A. 90 44 10N 114 0W
Idar-Oberstein, W. Ger. 36 49 43N 7 19 E
Idle →, U.K. 19 53 27N 0 49W
Idmiston, U.K. 14 51 8N 1 43W
Idsworth, U.K. 15 50 56N 0 56W
Igarka, U.S.S.R. 49 67 30N 86 33 E
Iglésias, It. 40 39 19N 8 27 E
Iguaçu Falls, Brazil 102 25 41S 54 26W
IJsselmeer, Neth. 36 52 45N 5 20 E
Ilchester, U.K. 14 51 0N 2 41W
Île-de-France, Fr. 34 49 0N 2 20 E
Ilfracombe, U.K. 16 51 13N 4 8W
Ilhéus, Brazil 101 14 49S 39 2W
Ilkeston, U.K. 19 52 59N 1 19W
Ilkley, U.K. 18 53 56N 1 49W
Illinois □, U.S.A. 91 40 15N 89 30W
Ilminster, U.K. 14 50 55N 2 56W
Iloilo, Phil. 63 10 45N 122 33 E
Immingham, U.K. 19 53 37N 0 12W
Imphal, India 59 24 48N 93 56 E
Inari, Fin. 44 68 54N 27 5 E
Ince, U.K. 18 53 32N 2 38W
Inchcape Rock, U.K. 21 56 26N 2 24W
Inchkeith, I., U.K. 21 56 2N 3 8W
Inchon, S. Kor. 61 37 27N 126 40 E
Inchture, U.K. 21 56 26N 3 8W
Indaal, L., U.K. 20 55 44N 6 20W
India ■, Asia 58 20 0N 78 0 E
Indian Ocean 129 5 0S 75 0 E
Indiana □, U.S.A. 92 40 0N 86 0W
Indianapolis, U.S.A. 92 39 42N 86 10W
Indonesia ■, Asia 63 5 0S 115 0 E
Indore, India 58 22 42N 75 53 E
Indus →, Pak. 58 24 20N 67 47 E
Ingatestone, U.K. 15 51 40N 0 23W
Ingleborough, U.K. 18 54 11N 2 23W
Ingleton, U.K. 18 54 9N 2 29W
Ingoldmells, Pt., U.K. 19 53 11N 0 21 E
Inishbofin, Ire. 24 53 35N 10 12W
Inishmore, Ire. 25 53 8N 9 45W
Inishowen, Ire. 24 55 14N 7 15W
Inkberrow, U.K. 14 52 13N 1 59W
Inkpen Beacon, U.K. 14 51 22N 1 28W
Inn →, Austria 40 48 35N 13 28 E
Innellan, U.K. 20 55 54N 4 58W
Inner Hebrides, U.K. 22 57 0N 6 30W
Inner Mongolia □, China 61 42 0N 112 0 E
Inner Sound, U.K. 22 57 30N 5 55W
Innerleithen, U.K. 21 55 37N 3 4W
Innsbruck, Austria 42 47 16N 11 23 E
Inny →, Ire. 25 53 30N 7 50W
Interlaken, Switz. 42 46 41N 7 50 E
Inuvik, Canada 88 68 16N 133 40W
Inveraray, U.K. 20 56 13N 5 5W
Inverbervie, U.K. 23 56 50N 2 17W
Invercargill, N.Z. 71 46 24S 168 24 E
Inverell, Austral. 67 29 45S 151 8 E
Invergarry, U.K. 23 57 5N 4 48W
Invergordon, U.K. 23 57 41N 4 10W
Invergowrie, U.K. 21 56 29N 3 5W
Inverkeithing, U.K. 21 56 2N 3 24W
Invermoriston, U.K. 23 57 13N 4 38W
Inverness, U.K. 23 57 29N 4 12W
Inverurie, U.K. 23 57 15N 2 21W
Iona, U.K. 20 56 20N 6 25W
Ionian Is., Greece 41 38 40N 20 0 E
Ionian Sea, Greece 41 37 30N 17 30 E
Iowa □, U.S.A. 91 42 18N 93 30W
Iowa City, U.S.A. 90 41 40N 91 35W
Ipoh, Malay. 63 4 35N 101 5 E
Ipswich, U.K. 15 52 4N 1 9 E
Iquique, Chile 100 20 19S 70 5W
Iquitos, Peru 100 3 45S 73 10W
Iráklion, Greece 41 35 20N 25 12 E
Iran ■, Asia 57 33 0N 53 0 E
Irapuato, Mex. 94 20 40N 101 30W
Iraq ■, Asia 56 33 0N 44 0 E
Irchester, U.K. 15 52 17N 0 40W
Ireland ■, Europe 24 53 0N 8 0W
Ireland's Eye, Ire. 24 53 25N 6 4W
Irian Jaya □, Indon. 64 4 0S 137 0 E
Iringa, Tanz. 80 7 48S 35 43 E
Irish Republic ■, Europe 25 53 0N 8 0W
Irish Sea, Europe 18 54 0N 5 0W
Irkutsk, U.S.S.R. 49 52 18N 104 20 E
Irlam, U.K. 18 53 26N 2 27W
Ironbridge, U.K. 14 52 38N 2 29W
Irrawaddy →, Burma 59 15 50N 95 6 E
Irt →, U.K. 18 54 24N 3 25W
Irthing →, U.K. 21 54 55N 2 55W
Irthlingborough, U.K. 15 52 20N 0 37W
Irtysh →, U.S.S.R. 48 61 4N 68 52 E
Irvine, U.K. 20 55 37N 4 40W
Irvine →, U.K. 20 55 35N 4 40W
Irvinestown, U.K. 24 54 28N 7 38W
Isabela, Phil. 63 10 12N 122 59 E
Ísafjörður, Ice. 44 66 5N 23 9W
Ishim →, U.S.S.R. 48 57 45N 71 10 E
İskenderun, Turk. 47 36 32N 36 10 E
Isla →, U.K. 23 56 32N 3 20W
Islamabad, Pak. 58 33 40N 73 10 E
Islay, U.K. 20 55 46N 6 10W
Islay Sound, U.K. 20 55 45N 6 5W
Isle of Whithorn, U.K. 20 54 42N 4 22W
Isle of Wight □, U.K. 14 50 40N 1 20W
Isleham, U.K. 15 52 21N 0 24 E
Islip, U.K. 14 51 49N 1 12W
Ismâ'ilîya, Egypt 79 30 37N 32 18 E
Israel ■, Asia 57 32 0N 34 50 E
İstanbul, Turk. 47 41 0N 29 0 E
Itabuna, Brazil 101 14 48S 39 16W
Italy ■, Europe 40 42 0N 13 0 E
Itchen →, U.K. 14 50 57N 1 20W
Ivanovo, U.S.S.R. 46 52 7N 25 29 E
Ivinghoe, U.K. 15 51 50N 0 38W
Ivory Coast ■, Africa 78 7 30N 5 0W
Ivugivik, Canada 89 62 24N 77 55W
Ivybridge, U.K. 16 50 24N 3 56W
Iwaki, Jap. 62 37 3N 140 55 E
Ixworth, U.K. 15 52 18N 0 50 E
Izhevsk = Ustinov, U.S.S.R. 46 56 51N 53 14 E
İzmir, Turk. 47 38 25N 27 8 E

J

Jabalpur, India 58 23 9N 79 58 E
Jackson, U.S.A. 91 32 20N 90 10W
Jacksonville, U.S.A. 91 30 15N 81 38W
Jaén, Sp. 37 37 44N 3 43W
Jaffna, Sri L. 58 9 45N 80 2 E
Jaipur, India 58 27 0N 75 50 E
Jakarta, Indon. 63 6 9S 106 49 E
Jamaica ■, W. Ind. 94 18 10N 77 30W
Jambi, Indon. 63 1 38S 103 30 E
James B., Canada 89 51 30N 80 0W
Jammu, India 58 32 43N 74 54 E
Jammu & Kashmir □, India 58 34 25N 77 0 E
Jamnagar, India 58 22 30N 70 6 E
Jamshedpur, India 59 22 44N 86 12 E
Japan ■, Asia 62 36 0N 136 0 E
Japan, Sea of, Asia 62 40 0N 135 0 E
Japurá →, Brazil 100 3 8S 64 46W
Jarrow, U.K. 21 54 58N 1 28W
Java, I., Indon. 63 7 0S 110 0 E
Java Sea, E. Ind. 63 4 35S 107 15 E
Jedburgh, U.K. 21 55 28N 2 33W
Jedda, Si. Arab. 56 21 29N 39 10 E
Jena, E. Ger. 42 50 56N 11 33 E
Jequié, Brazil 101 13 51S 40 5W
Jerez de la Frontera, Sp. 37 36 41N 6 7W
Jericho, Jord. 57 31 52N 35 27 E
Jersey, I., U.K. 34 49 13N 2 7W

Jersey City

Jersey City, U.S.A. 93 40 41N 74 8W
Jerusalem, Asia 57 31 47N 35 10 E
Jervaulx, U.K. 19 54 19N 1 41W
Jervis Bay, Austral. 70 35 8S 150 43 E
Jhansi, India 58 25 30N 78 36 E
Jhelum →, Pak. 58 31 20N 72 10 E
Jiamusi, China 61 46 40N 130 26 E
Ji'an, China 61 27 6N 114 59 E
Jiangsu □, China 61 33 0N 120 0 E
Jiangxi □, China 61 27 30N 116 0 E
Jilin, China 61 43 44N 126 30 E
Jilin □, China 61 44 0N 124 0 E
Jima, Eth. 79 7 40N 36 47 E
Jinan, China 61 36 38N 117 1 E
Jinja, Uganda 80 0 25N 33 12 E
Jinzhou, China 61 41 5N 121 3 E
Jixi, China 61 45 20N 130 50 E
João Pessoa, Brazil 101 7 10S 34 52W
Johannesburg, S. Afr. 81 26 10S 28 2 E
John o' Groats, U.K. 23 58 39N 3 3W
Johnstone, U.K. 20 55 50N 4 31W
Johnstown, U.S.A. 92 40 19N 78 53W
Johor Baharu, Malay. 63 1 28N 103 46 E
Jönköping, Swed. 45 57 45N 14 10 E
Jonquière, Canada 93 48 27N 71 14W
Jordan ■, Asia 57 31 0N 36 0 E
Jordan →, Asia 57 31 48N 35 32 E
Jos, Nig. 78 9 53N 8 51 E
Joseph Bonaparte G., Austral. 66 14 35S 128 50 E
Jotunheimen, Nor. 44 61 35N 8 25 E
Juan de Fuca Str., Canada 90 48 15N 124 0W
Juàzeiro do Norte, Brazil 101 7 10S 39 18W
Juiz de Fora, Brazil 101 21 43S 43 19W
Juliaca, Peru 100 15 25S 70 10W
Julianehåb, Green. 89 60 43N 46 0W
Jullundur, India 58 31 20N 75 40 E
Jundiaí, Brazil 102 24 30S 47 0W
Juneau, U.S.A. 88 58 20N 134 20W
Jura, U.K. 20 56 0N 5 50W
Jura, Mts., Europe 42 46 40N 6 5 E
Jura, Paps of, U.K. 20 55 55N 6 0W
Jura, Sd. of, U.K. 20 55 57N 5 45W
Jurby Hd., U.K. 18 54 23N 4 31W
Juruá →, Brazil 100 2 37S 65 44W
Jutland = Jylland, Den. 45 56 25N 9 30 E
Jylland, Den. 45 56 25N 9 30 E
Jyväskylä, Fin. 44 62 14N 25 50 E

K

Kābul, Afg. 57 34 28N 69 11 E
Kabwe, Zam. 81 14 30S 28 29 E
Kaduna, Nig. 78 10 30N 7 21 E
Kaesŏng, N. Kor. 61 37 58N 126 35 E
Kagoshima, Jap. 62 31 35N 130 33 E
Kaifeng, China 61 34 49N 114 30 E
Kaiserslautern, W. Ger. 36 49 30N 7 43 E
Kaitaia, N.Z. 71 35 8S 173 17 E
Kajaani, Fin. 44 64 17N 27 46 E
Kakinada, India 59 16 57N 82 11 E
Kalahari, Africa 81 24 0S 21 30 E
Kalamazoo, U.S.A. 92 42 20N 85 35W
Kalemie, Zaïre 80 5 55S 29 9 E
Kalgoorlie-Boulder, Austral. 66 30 40S 121 22 E
Kalimantan, Indon. 63 0 0 114 0 E
Kalinin, U.S.S.R. 46 56 55N 35 55 E
Kaliningrad, U.S.S.R. 46 54 42N 20 32 E
Kaluga, U.S.S.R. 46 54 35N 36 10 E
Kamchatka Pen., U.S.S.R. 49 57 0N 160 0 E
Kamensk Uralskiy, U.S.S.R. 48 56 25N 62 2 E
Kames, U.K. 20 55 53N 5 15W
Kamina, Zaïre 80 8 45S 25 0 E
Kamloops, Canada 88 50 40N 120 20W
Kampala, Uganda 80 0 20N 32 30 E
Kampuchea = Cambodia ■, Asia 63 12 15N 105 0 E
Kananga, Zaïre 80 5 55S 22 18 E
Kanazawa, Jap. 62 36 30N 136 38 E
Kanchenjunga, Nepal 59 27 50N 88 10 E
Kandy, Sri L. 58 7 18N 80 43 E
Kangaroo I., Austral. 67 35 45S 137 0 E
Kanin, Pen., U.S.S.R. 46 68 0N 45 0 E
Kankan, Guin. 78 10 23N 9 15W
Kano, Nig. 78 12 2N 8 30 E
Kanpur, India 58 26 28N 80 20 E
Kansas □, U.S.A. 90 38 40N 98 0W
Kansas City, Kans., U.S.A. 91 39 0N 94 40W
Kansas City, Mo., U.S.A. 91 39 3N 94 30W
Kansk, U.S.S.R. 49 56 20N 95 37 E
Kanturk, Ire. 25 52 10N 8 55W
Kaohsiung, Taiwan 61 22 35N 120 16 E
Kaolack, Sene. 78 14 5N 16 8W
Kara Bogaz Gol, Zaliv, U.S.S.R. 47 41 0N 53 30 E
Kara Kalpak A.S.S.R. □, U.S.S.R. 48 43 0N 60 0 E
Kara Kum, U.S.S.R. 48 39 30N 60 0 E
Kara Sea, U.S.S.R. 48 75 0N 70 0 E
Karachi, Pak. 58 24 53N 67 0 E
Karaganda, U.S.S.R. 48 49 50N 73 10 E
Karakoram Ra., Asia 58 35 30N 77 0 E
Karbalā, Iraq 56 32 36N 44 3 E
Karl-Marx-Stadt, E. Ger. 42 50 50N 12 55 E
Karlskrona, Swed. 45 56 10N 15 35 E
Karlsruhe, W. Ger. 42 49 3N 8 23 E
Karlstad, Swed. 45 59 23N 13 30 E
Karratha, Austral. 66 20 53S 116 40 E
Karsakpay, U.S.S.R. 48 47 55N 66 40 E
Karshi, U.S.S.R. 48 38 53N 65 48 E
Kāshān, Iran 56 34 5N 51 30 E
Kashi, China 60 39 30N 76 2 E
Kassala, Sudan 79 16 0N 36 0 E
Kassel, W. Ger. 42 51 19N 9 32 E
Katmandu, Nepal 59 27 45N 85 20 E
Katoomba, Austral. 70 33 41S 150 19 E
Katowice, Pol. 43 50 17N 19 5 E
Katrine, L., U.K. 20 56 15N 4 30W
Katsina, Nig. 78 13 0N 7 32 E
Kattegatt, Den. 45 57 0N 11 20 E
Kauai, U.S.A. 90 22 0N 159 30W
Kaunas, U.S.S.R. 46 54 54N 23 54 E
Kaválla, Greece 41 40 57N 24 28 E
Kawagoe, Jap. 62 35 55N 139 29 E
Kawasaki, Jap. 62 35 35N 139 42 E
Kawthoolei □, Burma 59 18 0N 97 30 E
Kayes, Mali 78 14 25N 11 30W
Kayseri, Turk. 47 38 45N 35 30 E
Kazakhstan □, U.S.S.R. 48 50 0N 70 0 E
Kazan, U.S.S.R. 46 55 48N 49 3 E
Kea, U.K. 16 50 13N 5 4W
Keady, U.K. 24 54 15N 6 42W
Keal, Loch na, U.K. 20 56 30N 6 5W
Kecskemét, Hung. 43 46 57N 19 42 E
Kediri, Indon. 63 7 51S 112 1 E
Keelby, U.K. 19 53 34N 0 15W
Keele, U.K. 18 53 0N 2 17W
Keeper Hill, Ire. 25 52 46N 8 17W
Keewatin, Canada 88 49 46N 94 34W
Kefallinía, Greece 41 38 20N 20 30 E
Keflavík, Ice. 44 64 2N 22 35W
Kegworth, U.K. 14 52 50N 1 17W
Keighley, U.K. 18 53 52N 1 54W
Keith, U.K. 23 57 33N 2 58W
Keld, U.K. 18 54 24N 2 11W
Kellerberrin, Austral. 66 31 36S 117 38 E
Kells = Ceanannus Mor, Ire. 24 53 42N 6 53W
Kells, Rhinns of, U.K. 20 55 9N 4 22W
Kelowna, Canada 88 49 50N 119 25W
Kelsale, U.K. 15 52 15N 1 30 E
Kelsall, U.K. 18 53 14N 2 44W
Kelso, U.K. 21 55 36N 2 27W
Kelvedon, U.K. 15 51 50N 0 43 E
Kemble, U.K. 14 51 40N 2 1W
Kemerovo, U.S.S.R. 48 55 20N 86 5 E
Kemi, Fin. 44 65 44N 24 34 E
Kempsey, U.K. 14 52 8N 2 11W
Kempston, U.K. 15 52 7N 0 30W
Ken, L., U.K. 21 55 0N 4 8W
Kendal, U.K. 18 54 19N 2 44W
Kenilworth, U.K. 14 52 22N 1 35W
Kenitra, Mor. 78 34 15N 6 40W
Kenmare, Ire. 25 51 52N 9 35W
Kenmare →, Ire. 25 51 40N 10 0W
Kennet →, U.K. 14 51 24N 0 58W
Kenninghall, U.K. 15 52 26N 1 0 E
Kenora, Canada 88 49 47N 94 29W
Kent □, U.K. 15 51 12N 0 40 E
Kentisbeare, U.K. 16 50 51N 3 18W
Kenton, U.K. 16 50 37N 3 28W
Kentucky □, U.S.A. 91 37 20N 85 0W
Kenya ■, Africa 80 1 0N 38 0 E
Kerala □, India 58 11 0N 76 15 E
Kerch, U.S.S.R. 47 45 20N 36 20 E
Kérkira, Greece 41 39 38N 19 50 E
Kermān, Iran 57 30 15N 57 1 E
Kerrera I., U.K. 20 56 24N 5 32W
Kerry □, Ire. 25 52 7N 9 35W
Kerry Hd., Ire. 25 52 26N 9 56W
Kessingland, U.K. 15 52 25N 1 41 E
Keswick, U.K. 18 54 35N 3 9W
Ketchikan, U.S.A. 88 55 25N 131 40W
Kettering, U.K. 15 52 24N 0 44W
Kettle Ness, U.K. 19 54 32N 0 41W
Kettlewell, U.K. 18 54 8N 2 2W
Keweenaw Pen., U.S.A. 92 47 30N 88 0W
Kexby, U.K. 19 53 21N 0 41W
Key West, U.S.A. 91 24 33N 82 0W
Keyingham, U.K. 19 53 42N 0 7W
Keymer, U.K. 15 50 55N 0 5W
Keynsham, U.K. 14 51 25N 2 30W
Keyworth, U.K. 14 52 52N 1 8W
Khabarovsk, U.S.S.R. 49 48 30N 135 5 E
Khaniá, Greece 41 35 30N 24 4 E
Kharagpur, India 59 22 20N 87 25 E
Kharkov, U.S.S.R. 47 49 58N 36 20 E
Khartoum, Sudan 79 15 31N 32 35 E
Khaskovo, Bulg. 41 41 56N 25 30 E
Kherson, U.S.S.R. 47 46 35N 32 35 E
Khíos, I., Greece 41 38 20N 26 0 E
Khorrāmshahr, Iran 56 30 29N 48 15 E
Khouribga, Mor. 78 32 58N 6 57W
Khulna, Bangla. 59 22 45N 89 34 E
Khulna □, Bangla. 59 22 25N 89 35 E
Khurasan, Iran 57 34 0N 57 0 E
Kibworth Beauchamp, U.K. 15 52 33N 0 59W
Kicking Horse Pass, Canada 88 51 28N 116 16W
Kidderminster, U.K. 14 52 24N 2 13W
Kidlington, U.K. 14 51 49N 1 18W
Kidsgrove, U.K. 18 53 6N 2 15W
Kidstones, U.K. 18 54 15N 2 2W
Kidwelly, U.K. 17 51 44N 4 20W
Kiel, W. Ger. 42 54 16N 10 8 E
Kielce, Pol. 43 50 52N 20 42 E
Kielder, U.K. 21 55 14N 2 35W
Kiev, U.S.S.R. 47 50 30N 30 28 E
Kigali, Rwanda 80 1 59S 30 4 E
Kigoma-Ujiji, Tanz. 80 4 55S 29 36 E
Kikládhes, Greece 41 37 20N 24 30 E
Kikwit, Zaïre 80 5 5S 18 45 E
Kilbirnie, U.K. 20 55 46N 4 42W
Kilbrannan Sd., U.K. 20 55 40N 5 23W
Kilcreggan, U.K. 20 55 59N 4 50W
Kildare, Ire. 25 53 10N 6 50W
Kildare □, Ire. 25 53 10N 6 50W
Kildonan, U.K. 23 58 10N 3 50W
Kilfinan, U.K. 20 55 57N 5 19W
Kilham, U.K. 19 54 4N 0 22W
Kilimanjaro, Tanz. 80 3 7S 37 20 E
Kilkee, Ire. 25 52 41N 9 40W
Kilkeel, U.K. 24 54 4N 6 0W
Kilkenny, Ire. 25 52 40N 7 17W
Kilkenny □, Ire. 25 52 35N 7 15W
Kilkhampton, U.K. 16 50 53N 4 30W
Kilkieran B., Ire. 25 53 18N 9 45W
Killala, Ire. 24 54 13N 9 12W
Killala B., Ire. 24 54 20N 9 12W
Killaloe, Ire. 25 52 48N 8 28W
Killarney, Ire. 25 52 2N 9 30W
Killarney, Lakes of, Ire. 25 52 0N 9 30W
Killary Harbour, Ire. 24 53 38N 9 52W
Killchianaig, U.K. 20 56 2N 5 48W
Killean, U.K. 20 55 38N 5 40W
Killiecrankie, Pass of, U.K. 23 56 44N 3 46W
Killin, U.K. 20 56 28N 4 20W
Killinghall, U.K. 19 54 1N 1 33W
Killybegs, Ire. 24 54 38N 8 26W
Kilmacolm, U.K. 20 55 54N 4 39W
Kilmarnock, U.K. 20 55 36N 4 30W
Kilmartin, U.K. 20 56 8N 5 29W
Kilmaurs, U.K. 20 55 37N 4 33W
Kilmelford, U.K. 20 56 16N 5 30W
Kilninver, U.K. 20 56 20N 5 30W
Kilrenny, U.K. 21 56 15N 2 40W
Kilrush, Ire. 25 52 39N 9 30W
Kilsby, U.K. 14 52 20N 1 11W
Kilsyth, U.K. 21 55 58N 4 3W
Kilwinning, U.K. 20 55 40N 4 41W
Kimberley, Austral. 66 16 20S 127 0 E
Kimberley, S. Afr. 81 28 43S 24 46 E
Kimbolton, U.K. 15 52 17N 0 23W
Kincardine, U.K. 21 56 4N 3 43W
Kindu, Zaïre 80 2 55S 25 50 E
Kineton, U.K. 14 52 10N 1 30W
King Frederick VI Coast, Green. 89 63 0N 43 0W
King Sd., Austral. 66 16 50S 123 20 E
Kingarth, U.K. 20 55 45N 5 2W
Kinghorn, U.K. 21 56 4N 3 10W
King's Lynn, U.K. 15 52 45N 0 25 E
King's Sutton, U.K. 14 52 1N 1 16W
King's Worthy, U.K. 14 51 6N 1 18W
Kingsbarns, U.K. 21 56 18N 2 40W
Kingsbridge, U.K. 16 50 17N 3 46W
Kingsbury, U.K. 14 52 33N 1 41W
Kingscourt, Ire. 24 53 55N 6 48W
Kingskerswell, U.K. 16 50 30N 3 34W
Kingsland, U.K. 14 52 15N 2 49W
Kingsteignton, U.K. 16 50 32N 3 35W
Kingston, Canada 92 44 14N 76 30W
Kingston, Jam. 94 18 0N 76 50W
Kingston, U.K. 14 51 18N 1 40W
Kingston-upon-Hull, U.K. 19 53 45N 0 20W
Kingston-upon-Thames, U.K. 15 51 23N 0 20W
Kingstown, St. Vinc. 94 13 10N 61 10W
Kingswear, U.K. 16 50 21N 3 33W
Kingswood, U.K. 14 51 26N 2 31W
Kington, U.K. 14 52 12N 3 2W
Kingussie, U.K. 23 57 5N 4 2W
Kinlochewe, U.K. 22 57 37N 5 20W
Kinlochleven, U.K. 22 56 42N 4 59W
Kinnairds Hd., U.K. 23 57 40N 2 0W
Kinneret, Lake, Isr. 57 32 45N 35 35 E
Kinross, U.K. 21 56 13N 3 25W
Kinsale, Ire. 25 51 42N 8 31W
Kinsale, Old Hd. of, Ire. 25 51 37N 8 32W
Kinshasa, Zaïre 80 4 20S 15 15 E
Kintyre, U.K. 20 55 30N 5 35W
Kintyre, Mull of, U.K. 20 55 17N 5 55W
Kippen, U.K. 20 56 8N 4 12W
Kippure, Ire. 25 53 11N 6 23W
Kirensk, U.S.S.R. 49 57 50N 107 55 E
Kirgizia □, U.S.S.R. 48 42 0N 75 0 E
Kirgiziya Steppe, U.S.S.R. 47 50 0N 55 0 E
Kiribati ■, Pac. Oc. 65 1 0N 176 0 E
Kirk Michael, U.K. 18 54 17N 4 35W
Kirkbean, U.K. 21 54 56N 3 35W
Kirkbride, U.K. 18 54 54N 3 13W
Kirkburton, U.K. 19 53 36N 1 42W
Kirkby, U.K. 18 53 29N 2 54W
Kirkby-in-Ashfield, U.K. 19 53 6N 1 15W
Kirkby Lonsdale, U.K. 18 54 13N 2 36W
Kirkby Malzeard, U.K. 19 54 10N 1 38W
Kirkby Moorside, U.K. 19 54 16N 0 56W
Kirkby Stephen, U.K. 18 54 27N 2 23W
Kirkby Thore, U.K. 18 54 38N 2 34W
Kirkcaldy, U.K. 21 56 7N 3 10W
Kirkcolm, U.K. 20 54 59N 5 4W
Kirkconnel, U.K. 21 55 23N 4 0W
Kirkcowan, U.K. 20 54 53N 4 38W
Kirkcudbright, U.K. 21 54 50N 4 3W
Kirkcudbright B., U.K. 21 54 46N 4 0W
Kirkham, U.K. 18 53 47N 2 52W
Kirkinner, U.K. 20 54 49N 4 28W
Kirkintilloch, U.K. 21 55 57N 4 10W
Kirkland Lake, Canada 92 48 9N 80 2W
Kirkliston, U.K. 21 55 55N 3 27W
Kirkoswald, U.K. 18 54 46N 2 41W
Kirkoswold, U.K. 20 55 19N 4 48W
Kirkstone P., U.K. 18 54 29N 2 55W
Kirkūk, Iraq 56 35 30N 44 21 E
Kirkwall, U.K. 23 58 59N 2 59W
Kirkwhelpington, U.K. 21 55 9N 2 0W
Kirov, U.S.S.R. 46 58 35N 49 40 E
Kirovabad, U.S.S.R. 47 40 45N 46 20 E
Kirovograd, U.S.S.R. 47 48 35N 32 20 E
Kirovsk, U.S.S.R. 46 48 35N 38 30 E
Kirriemuir, U.K. 23 56 41N 3 0W
Kirtling, U.K. 15 52 11N 0 27 E
Kirtlington, U.K. 14 51 54N 1 9W
Kirton, U.K. 19 52 56N 0 3W
Kirton-in-Lindsey, U.K. 19 53 29N 0 35W
Kiruna, Swed. 44 67 52N 20 15 E
Kisangani, Zaïre 80 0 35N 25 15 E
Kishinev, U.S.S.R. 47 47 0N 28 50 E
Kismayu, Som. 73 0 22S 42 32 E
Kisumu, Kenya 80 0 3S 34 45 E
Kitakyūshū, Jap. 62 33 50N 130 50 E
Kitchener, Canada 92 43 27N 80 29W
Kithira, Greece 41 36 9N 23 0 E
Kitikmeot □, Canada 88 70 0N 110 0W
Kitimat, Canada 88 54 3N 128 38W
Kitwe, Zam. 81 12 54S 28 13 E
Klagenfurt, Austria 42 46 38N 14 20 E
Klerksdorp, S. Afr. 81 26 51S 26 38 E
Klondike, Canada 88 64 0N 139 26W
Knapdale, U.K. 20 55 55N 5 30W
Knaresborough, U.K. 19 54 1N 1 29W
Knebworth, U.K. 15 51 52N 0 11W
Knighton, U.K. 17 52 21N 3 2W
Knockmealdown Mts., Ire. 25 52 16N 8 0W
Knossos, Greece 41 35 16N 25 10 E
Knott End, U.K. 18 53 55N 3 0W
Knottingley, U.K. 19 53 42N 1 15W
Knowle, U.K. 14 52 23N 1 43W
Knoxville, U.S.A. 91 35 58N 83 57W
Knutsford, U.K. 18 53 18N 2 22W
Kōbe, Jap. 62 34 45N 135 10 E
København = Copenhagen, Den. 45 55 41N 12 34 E
Koblenz, W. Ger. 36 50 21N 7 36 E
Kodiak I., U.S.A. 88 57 30N 152 45W
Koforidua, Ghana 78 6 3N 0 17W
Kokand, U.S.S.R. 48 40 30N 70 57 E
Kokchetav, U.S.S.R. 48 53 20N 69 25 E
Kokkola, Fin. 44 63 50N 23 8 E
Kola Pen., U.S.S.R. 46 67 30N 38 0 E
Kolding, Den. 45 55 30N 9 29 E
Kolguyev, I., U.S.S.R. 46 69 20N 48 30 E
Kolomna, U.S.S.R. 46 55 8N 38 45 E
Kolwezi, Zaïre 80 10 40S 25 25 E
Kolyma →, U.S.S.R. 49 69 30N 161 0 E
Kolyma Ra., U.S.S.R. 49 63 0N 157 0 E
Komandorskiye, Is., U.S.S.R. 49 55 0N 167 0 E
Komsomolets I., U.S.S.R. 49 80 30N 95 0 E
Komsomolsk, U.S.S.R. 49 50 30N 137 0 E
Konya, Turk. 47 37 52N 32 35 E
Kópavogur, Ice. 44 64 6N 21 55W
Korce, Alb. 41 40 37N 20 50 E
Korea, North ■, Asia 61 40 0N 127 0 E
Korea, South ■, Asia 61 36 0N 128 0 E
Korea Strait, Asia 61 34 0N 129 30 E
Kōriyama, Jap. 62 37 24N 140 23 E
Korla, China 60 41 45N 86 4 E
Kortrijk, Belg. 36 50 50N 3 17 E
Koryak Range, U.S.S.R. 49 61 0N 171 0 E
Kos, Greece 41 36 50N 27 15 E
Košice, Czech. 43 48 42N 21 15 E
Kôstî, Sudan 79 13 8N 32 43 E
Kostroma, U.S.S.R. 46 57 50N 40 58 E
Kota, India 58 25 14N 75 49 E
Kota Baharu, Malay. 63 6 7N 102 14 E
Kota Kinabalu, Malay. 63 6 0N 116 4 E
Kotka, Fin. 45 60 28N 26 58 E
Kra, Isthmus of, Thai. 63 10 15N 99 30 E
Kragujevac, Yug. 41 44 2N 20 56 E
Krakatau, Indon. 63 6 10S 105 20 E
Kraków, Pol. 43 50 4N 19 57 E
Krasnodar, U.S.S.R. 47 45 5N 39 0 E
Krasnoturinsk, U.S.S.R. 46 59 46N 60 12 E
Krasnovodsk, U.S.S.R. 48 40 0N 52 52 E
Krasnoyarsk, U.S.S.R. 49 56 8N 93 0 E
Krefeld, W. Ger. 36 51 20N 6 32 E
Kremenchug, U.S.S.R. 47 49 5N 33 25 E
Krishna →, India 59 15 57N 80 59 E
Kristiansand, Nor. 45 58 9N 8 1 E
Kristianstad, Swed. 45 56 2N 14 9 E
Kristiansund, Nor. 44 63 7N 7 45 E
Krivoy Rog, U.S.S.R. 47 47 51N 33 20 E
Kroonstad, S. Afr. 81 27 43S 27 19 E
Krung Thep = Bangkok, Thai. 63 13 45N 100 35 E
Kruševac, Yug. 41 43 35N 21 28 E
Kuala Lumpur, Malay. 63 3 9N 101 41 E

Ludwigshafen

Kuala Trengganu, *Malay.* 63 5 20N 103 8 E
Kuangchou = Guangzhou, *China* 61 23 5N 113 10 E
Kuantan, *Malay.* 63 3 49N 103 20 E
Kucing, *Malay.* 63 1 33N 110 25 E
Kueiyang = Guiyang, *China* 60 26 32N 106 40 E
Kumanovo, *Yug.* 41 42 9N 21 42 E
Kumasi, *Ghana* 78 6 41N 1 38W
Kunlun Shan, *Asia* 60 36 0N 86 30 E
Kunming, *China* 60 25 1N 102 41 E
Kuopio, *Fin.* 44 62 53N 27 35 E
Kura →, *U.S.S.R.* 47 39 50N 49 20 E
Kurashiki, *Jap.* 62 34 40N 133 50 E
Kure, *Jap.* 62 34 14N 132 32 E
Kurgan, *U.S.S.R.* 48 55 26N 65 18 E
Kuria Maria Is., *Ind. Oc.* 57 17 30N 55 58 E
Kuril Is., *U.S.S.R.* 49 45 0N 150 0 E
Kurnool, *India* 58 15 45N 78 0 E
Kurri Kurri, *Austral.* 70 32 50S 151 28 E
Kursk, *U.S.S.R.* 46 51 42N 36 11 E
Kurume, *Jap.* 62 33 15N 130 30 E
Kushiro, *Jap.* 62 43 0N 144 25 E
Kustanay, *U.S.S.R.* 48 53 10N 63 35 E
Kütahya, *Turk.* 47 39 30N 30 2 E
Kutaisi, *U.S.S.R.* 47 42 19N 42 40 E
Kutch, Gulf of, *India* 58 22 50N 69 15 E
Kutch, Rann of, *India* 58 24 0N 70 0 E
Kuwait, *Kuw.* 56 29 30N 47 30 E
Kuwait ■, *Asia* 56 29 30N 47 30 E
Kuybyshev, *U.S.S.R.* 46 53 8N 50 6 E
Kwangju, *S. Kor.* 61 35 9N 126 54 E
Kyle, *U.K.* 20 55 32N 4 25W
Kyle of Lochalsh, *U.K.* 22 57 17N 5 43W
Kyōto, *Jap.* 62 35 0N 135 45 E
Kyūshū, *Jap.* 62 33 0N 131 0 E
Kzyl-Orda, *U.S.S.R.* 48 44 48N 65 28 E

L

Labe = Elbe →, *Ger.* 42 53 50N 9 0 E
Labé, *Guin.* 78 11 24N 12 16W
Labrador, Coast of □, *Canada* 89 53 20N 61 0W
Labrador City, *Canada* 89 52 57N 66 55W
Laccadive Is. = Lakshadweep Is., *Ind. Oc.* 51 10 0N 72 30 E
Laceby, *U.K.* 19 53 32N 0 10W
Lachlan →, *Austral.* 70 34 22S 143 55 E
Lacock, *U.K.* 14 51 24N 2 8W
Ladock, *U.K.* 16 50 19N 4 58W
Ladoga, L., *U.S.S.R.* 46 61 15N 30 30 E
Ladybank, *U.K.* 21 56 16N 3 8W
Lafayette, *U.S.A.* 90 30 18N 92 0W
Lagan →, *U.K.* 24 54 35N 5 55W
Lagg, *U.K.* 20 55 51N 5 50W
Laggan B., *U.K.* 20 55 40N 6 20W
Lagos, *Nig.* 78 6 25N 3 27 E
Lagos, *Port.* 37 37 5N 8 41W
Lahore, *Pak.* 58 31 32N 74 22 E
Lahti, *Fin.* 45 60 58N 25 40 E
Lairg, *U.K.* 23 58 1N 4 24W
Lake Charles, *U.S.A.* 90 30 15N 93 10W
Lake District, *U.K.* 18 54 30N 3 10W
Lakenheath, *U.K.* 15 52 25N 0 30 E
Lakewood, *U.S.A.* 92 41 28N 81 50W
Lakshadweep Is., *Ind. Oc.* 51 10 0N 72 30 E
Lambay I., *Ire.* 24 53 30N 6 0W
Lamberhurst, *U.K.* 15 51 5N 0 21 E
Lambeth, *U.K.* 15 51 27N 0 7W
Lambley, *U.K.* 21 54 56N 2 30W
Lambourn, *U.K.* 14 51 31N 1 31W
Lamlash, *U.K.* 20 55 32N 5 8W
Lammermuir, *U.K.* 21 55 50N 2 25W
Lammermuir Hills, *U.K.* 21 55 50N 2 40W
Lampeter, *U.K.* 17 52 6N 4 6W
Lanark, *U.K.* 21 55 40N 3 48W
Lancashire □, *U.K.* 18 53 40N 2 30W
Lancaster, *U.K.* 18 54 3N 2 48W
Lancaster Sd., *Canada* 89 74 13N 84 0W
Lanchester, *U.K.* 19 54 50N 1 44W
Lancing, *U.K.* 15 50 49N 0 19W
Landkey, *U.K.* 16 51 2N 4 0W
Land's End, *U.K.* 16 50 4N 5 43W
Langholm, *U.K.* 21 55 9N 2 59W
Langness, *U.K.* 18 54 3N 4 37W
Langport, *U.K.* 14 51 2N 2 51W
Langstrothdale Chase, *U.K.* 18 54 14N 2 13W
Langtoft, *U.K.* 15 52 42N 0 19W
Langtree, *U.K.* 16 50 55N 4 11W
Lansing, *U.S.A.* 92 42 47N 84 40W
Lanzhou, *China* 60 36 1N 103 52 E
Laoag, *Phil.* 63 18 7N 120 34 E
Laois □, *Ire.* 25 53 0N 7 20W
Laos ■, *Asia* 63 17 45N 105 0 E
Lapford, *U.K.* 16 50 52N 3 49W
Lapland, *Europe* 44 68 7N 24 0 E
Laptev Sea, *U.S.S.R.* 49 76 0N 125 0 E
Larbert, *U.K.* 21 56 2N 3 50W
Laredo, *U.S.A.* 90 27 34N 99 29W
Largs, *U.K.* 20 55 48N 4 51W
Lárisa, *Greece* 41 39 49N 22 28 E
Larkhall, *U.K.* 21 55 44N 4 0W
Larne, *U.K.* 24 54 52N 5 50W
Las Palmas, *Can. Is.* 78 28 7N 15 26W
Las Vegas, *U.S.A.* 90 36 10N 115 5W
Laskill, *U.K.* 19 54 19N 1 6W
Lasswade, *U.K.* 21 55 53N 3 8W
Latakia, *Syria* 56 35 30N 35 45 E
Latina, *It.* 40 41 26N 12 53 E
Latvia □, *U.S.S.R.* 46 56 50N 24 0 E
Lauder, *U.K.* 21 55 43N 2 45W
Lauderdale, *U.K.* 21 55 43N 2 44W
Launceston, *Austral.* 67 41 24S 147 8 E
Launceston, *U.K.* 16 50 38N 4 21W
Laune →, *Ire.* 25 52 5N 9 40W
Laurencekirk, *U.K.* 23 56 50N 2 30W
Laurentian Plateau, *Canada* 82 52 0N 70 0W
Laurieston, *U.K.* 21 54 57N 4 2W
Lausanne, *Switz.* 42 46 32N 6 38 E
Laval, *Fr.* 34 48 4N 0 48W
Lavendon, *U.K.* 15 52 11N 0 39W
Lavenham, *U.K.* 15 52 7N 0 48 E
Lawers, *U.K.* 21 56 31N 4 9W
Lawrence, *U.S.A.* 93 42 40N 71 9W
Laxey, *U.K.* 18 54 15N 4 23W
Laxfield, *U.K.* 15 52 18N 1 23 E
Laxford, L., *U.K.* 22 58 25N 5 10W
Lazonby, *U.K.* 18 54 45N 2 42W
Lea, *U.K.* 19 53 22N 0 45W
Lea →, *U.K.* 15 51 30N 0 10W
Leadenham, *U.K.* 19 53 5N 0 33W
Leadhills, *U.K.* 21 55 25N 3 47W
Leamington, *U.K.* 14 52 18N 1 32W
Leatherhead, *U.K.* 15 51 18N 0 20W
Lebanon ■, *Asia* 56 34 0N 36 0 E
Lecce, *It.* 41 40 20N 18 10 E
Lechlade, *U.K.* 14 51 42N 1 40W
Ledbury, *U.K.* 14 52 3N 2 25W
Leduc, *Canada* 88 53 15N 113 30W
Lee, *U.K.* 14 50 47N 1 11W
Lee →, *Ire.* 25 51 50N 8 30W
Leeds, *U.K.* 19 53 48N 1 34W
Leek, *U.K.* 18 53 7N 2 2W
Leer, *W. Ger.* 36 53 13N 7 29 E
Leeton, *Austral.* 70 34 33S 146 23 E
Leeuwarden, *Neth.* 36 53 15N 5 48 E
Leeuwin, C., *Austral.* 66 34 20S 115 9 E
Leghorn, *It.* 40 43 32N 10 18 E
Legnica, *Pol.* 42 51 12N 16 10 E
Leicester, *U.K.* 14 52 39N 1 9W
Leicester □, *U.K.* 14 52 40N 1 10W
Leiden, *Neth.* 36 52 9N 4 30 E
Leigh, *Gr. Manchester, U.K.* 18 53 29N 2 31W
Leigh, *Hereford & Worcs., U.K.* 14 52 10N 2 21W
Leighton Buzzard, *U.K.* 15 51 55N 0 39W
Leinster □, *Ire.* 25 53 0N 7 10W
Leinster, Mt., *Ire.* 25 52 38N 6 47W
Leintwardine, *U.K.* 14 52 22N 2 51W
Leipzig, *E. Ger.* 42 51 20N 12 23 E
Leiston, *U.K.* 15 52 13N 1 35 E
Leith, *U.K.* 21 55 59N 3 10W
Leith Hill, *U.K.* 15 51 10N 0 23W
Leitholm, *U.K.* 21 55 42N 2 16W
Leitrim, *Ire.* 24 54 0N 8 5W
Leitrim □, *Ire.* 24 54 8N 8 0W
Lek →, *Neth.* 36 51 54N 4 35 E
Lelant, *U.K.* 16 50 11N 5 26W
Lelystad, *Neth.* 36 52 30N 5 25 E
Lena →, *U.S.S.R.* 49 72 52N 126 40 E
Lendalfoot, *U.K.* 20 55 12N 4 55W
Lenham, *U.K.* 15 51 14N 0 44 E
Leninakan, *U.S.S.R.* 47 40 47N 43 50 E
Leningrad, *U.S.S.R.* 46 59 55N 30 20 E
Leninsk-Kuznetskiy, *U.S.S.R.* 48 54 44N 86 10 E
Lennox Hills, *U.K.* 20 56 3N 4 12W
Lennoxtown, *U.K.* 20 55 58N 4 14W
Lens, *Fr.* 34 50 26N 2 50 E
Leominster, *U.K.* 14 52 15N 2 43W
León, *Mex.* 94 21 7N 101 40W
León, *Sp.* 37 42 38N 5 34W
Lérida, *Sp.* 37 41 37N 0 39 E
Lerwick, *U.K.* 22 60 10N 1 10W
Lesbos, I. = Lésvos, *Greece* 41 39 10N 26 20 E
Lesbury, *U.K.* 21 55 25N 1 37W
Leskovac, *Yug.* 41 43 0N 21 58 E
Leslie, *U.K.* 21 56 12N 3 12W
Lesmahagow, *U.K.* 21 55 38N 3 55W
Lesotho ■, *Africa* 81 29 40S 28 0 E
Lésvos, *Greece* 41 39 10N 26 20 E
Leswalt, *U.K.* 20 54 56N 5 6W
Letchworth, *U.K.* 15 51 58N 0 13W
Lethbridge, *Canada* 88 49 45N 112 45W
Letterkenny, *Ire.* 24 54 57N 7 42W
Leuchars, *U.K.* 21 56 23N 2 53W
Leven, *Fife, U.K.* 21 56 12N 3 0W
Leven, *Humberside, U.K.* 19 53 54N 0 18W
Leven →, *U.K.* 19 54 27N 1 15W
Leven, L., *U.K.* 21 56 12N 3 22W
Leverburgh, *U.K.* 22 57 46N 7 0W
Leverkusen, *W. Ger.* 36 51 2N 6 59 E
Lewes, *U.K.* 15 50 53N 0 2 E
Lewis, *U.K.* 22 58 10N 6 40W
Lewis, Butt of, *U.K.* 22 58 30N 6 12W
Lewisham, *U.K.* 15 51 27N 0 1W
Lexington, *U.S.A.* 92 38 6N 84 30W
Leyburn, *U.K.* 19 54 19N 1 50W
Leyland, *U.K.* 18 53 41N 2 42W
Leysdown on Sea, *U.K.* 15 51 23N 0 57 E
Lhasa, *China* 60 29 50N 91 3 E
Liaodong, Gulf of, *China* 61 40 20N 121 10 E
Liaoning □, *China* 61 41 40N 122 30 E
Liaoyang, *China* 61 41 15N 123 10 E
Liaoyüan, *China* 61 42 55N 125 10 E
Liberia ■, *W. Afr.* 78 6 30N 9 30W
Libreville, *Gabon* 80 0 25N 9 26 E
Libya ■, *N. Afr.* 79 27 0N 17 0 E
Libyan Desert, *Africa* 79 25 0N 25 0 E
Lichfield, *U.K.* 14 52 40N 1 50W
Lichinga, *Mozam.* 81 13 13S 35 11 E
Liechtenstein ■, *Europe* 42 47 8N 9 35 E
Liège, *Belg.* 36 50 38N 5 35 E
Liepaja, *U.S.S.R.* 46 56 30N 21 0 E
Liffey →, *Ire.* 25 53 21N 6 20W
Lifford, *Ire.* 24 54 50N 7 30W
Ligurian Sea, *It.* 40 43 20N 9 0 E
Likasi, *Zaïre* 80 10 55S 26 48 E
Lille, *Fr.* 34 50 38N 3 3 E
Lille Bælt, *Den.* 45 55 20N 9 45 E
Lillehammer, *Nor.* 45 61 8N 10 30 E
Lilleshall, *U.K.* 14 52 45N 2 22W
Lilongwe, *Malawi* 81 14 0S 33 48 E
Lima, *Peru* 100 12 0S 77 0W
Limassol, *Cyprus* 47 34 42N 33 1 E
Limavady, *U.K.* 24 55 3N 6 58W
Limavady □, *U.K.* 24 55 0N 6 55W
Limburg □, *Neth.* 36 51 20N 5 55 E
Limerick, *Ire.* 25 52 40N 8 38W
Limerick □, *Ire.* 25 52 30N 8 50W
Límnos, *Greece* 41 39 50N 25 5 E
Limoges, *Fr.* 35 45 50N 1 15 E
Limpopo →, *Mozam.* 81 25 15S 33 30 E
Limpsfield, *U.K.* 15 51 15N 0 1 E
Linares, *Sp.* 37 38 10N 3 40W
Lincluden, *U.K.* 21 55 5N 3 40W
Lincoln, *U.K.* 19 53 14N 0 32W
Lincoln, *U.S.A.* 90 40 50N 96 42W
Lincoln □, *U.K.* 19 53 14N 0 32W
Lincoln Wolds, *U.K.* 19 53 20N 0 5W
Lindale, *U.K.* 18 54 14N 2 54W
Lingfield, *U.K.* 15 51 11N 0 1W
Linkinhorne, *U.K.* 16 50 31N 4 22W
Linköping, *Swed.* 45 58 28N 15 36 E
Linlithgow, *U.K.* 21 55 58N 3 38W
Linnhe, L., *U.K.* 20 56 36N 5 25W
Linslade, *U.K.* 15 51 55N 0 40W
Linton, *U.K.* 15 52 6N 0 19 E
Linxia, *China* 60 35 36N 103 10 E
Linz, *Austria* 42 48 18N 14 18 E
Lion, G. du, *Fr.* 35 43 0N 4 0 E
Lípari, Is., *It.* 40 38 30N 14 50 E
Lipetsk, *U.S.S.R.* 46 52 37N 39 35 E
Lisbon, *Port.* 37 38 42N 9 10W
Lisburn, *U.K.* 24 54 30N 6 9W
Liscannor, B., *Ire.* 25 52 57N 9 24W
Liskeard, *U.K.* 16 50 27N 4 29W
Lismore, *Austral.* 67 28 44S 153 21 E
Lismore, *Ire.* 25 52 8N 7 58W
Lismore I., *U.K.* 20 56 30N 5 30W
Liss, *U.K.* 15 51 3N 0 53W
Listowel, *Ire.* 25 52 27N 9 30W
Litcham, *U.K.* 15 52 43N 0 49 E
Litherland, *U.K.* 18 53 29N 3 0W
Lithgow, *Austral.* 70 33 25S 150 8 E
Lithuania □, *U.S.S.R.* 46 55 30N 24 0 E
Little Minch, *U.K.* 22 57 35N 6 45W
Little Ouse →, *U.K.* 15 52 25N 0 50 E
Little Rock, *U.S.A.* 91 34 41N 92 10W
Little Walsingham, *U.K.* 15 52 53N 0 51 E
Littleborough, *U.K.* 18 53 38N 2 8W
Littlehampton, *U.K.* 15 50 48N 0 32W
Littleport, *U.K.* 15 52 27N 0 18 E
Littlestone-on-Sea, *U.K.* 15 50 59N 0 59 E
Liuzhou, *China* 61 24 22N 109 22 E
Liverpool, *Austral.* 70 33 54S 150 58 E
Liverpool, *U.K.* 18 53 25N 3 0W
Liverpool Plains, *Austral.* 70 31 15S 150 15 E
Livingston, *U.K.* 21 55 52N 3 33W
Livingstone, *Zam.* 81 17 46S 25 52 E
Lizard, *U.K.* 16 49 58N 5 10W
Lizard Pt., *U.K.* 16 49 57N 5 11W
Ljubljana, *Yug.* 40 46 4N 14 33 E
Llandeilo, *U.K.* 17 51 53N 4 0W
Llandovery, *U.K.* 17 51 59N 3 49W
Llandrindod Wells, *U.K.* 17 52 15N 3 23W
Llandudno, *U.K.* 17 53 19N 3 51W
Llanelli, *U.K.* 17 51 41N 4 11W
Llanerchymedd, *U.K.* 17 53 20N 4 22W
Llanfair Caereinion, *U.K.* 17 52 39N 3 20W
Llanfair Talhaiarn, *U.K.* 17 53 13N 3 37W
Llanfairfechan, *U.K.* 17 53 15N 3 58W
Llangefni, *U.K.* 17 53 15N 4 20W
Llangollen, *U.K.* 17 52 58N 3 10W
Llanidloes, *U.K.* 17 52 28N 3 31W
Llanllyfni, *U.K.* 17 53 2N 4 18W
Llanos, *S. Am.* 100 5 0N 71 35W
Llanrhystyd, *U.K.* 17 52 19N 4 9W
Llantrisant, *U.K.* 17 51 33N 3 22W
Llantwit-Major, *U.K.* 17 51 24N 3 29W
Llanwrtyd Wells, *U.K.* 17 52 6N 3 39W
Llanyblodwel, *U.K.* 14 52 47N 3 8W
Llanymynech, *U.K.* 14 52 48N 3 6W
Lleyn Peninsula, *U.K.* 17 52 55N 4 35W
Loanhead, *U.K.* 21 55 53N 3 10W
Lobito, *Angola* 81 12 18S 13 35 E
Lochaber, *U.K.* 22 56 55N 5 0W
Lochans, *U.K.* 20 54 52N 5 1W
Lochboisdale, *U.K.* 22 57 10N 7 20W
Lochbuie, *U.K.* 20 56 21N 5 52W
Lochcarron, *U.K.* 22 57 25N 5 30W
Lochdonhead, *U.K.* 20 56 27N 5 40W
Lochearnhead, *U.K.* 20 56 24N 4 19W
Lochgelly, *U.K.* 21 56 7N 3 18W
Lochgilphead, *U.K.* 20 56 2N 5 37W
Lochgoilhead, *U.K.* 20 56 10N 4 54W
Lochinver, *U.K.* 22 58 9N 5 15W
Lochmaben, *U.K.* 21 55 8N 3 27W
Lochmaddy, *U.K.* 22 57 36N 7 10W
Lochnagar, *U.K.* 23 56 57N 3 14W
Lochranza, *U.K.* 20 55 42N 5 18W
Lochwinnoch, *U.K.* 20 55 47N 4 39W
Lochy →, *U.K.* 22 56 52N 5 3W
Lockerbie, *U.K.* 21 55 7N 3 21W
Lod, *Isr.* 57 31 57N 34 54 E
Loddon, *U.K.* 15 52 32N 1 29 E
Łódź, *Pol.* 43 51 45N 19 27 E
Lofoten, *Nor.* 44 68 30N 15 0 E
Loftus, *U.K.* 19 54 33N 0 52W
Logan, Mt., *Canada* 88 60 31N 140 22W
Logroño, *Sp.* 37 42 28N 2 27W
Loire →, *Fr.* 34 47 16N 2 10W
Lolland, *Den.* 45 54 45N 11 30 E
Lombardy □, *It.* 40 45 35N 9 45 E
Lomé, *Togo* 78 6 9N 1 20 E
Lomond, L., *U.K.* 20 56 8N 4 38W
Łomza, *Pol.* 43 53 10N 22 2 E
London, *Canada* 92 42 59N 81 15W
London, *U.K.* 15 51 30N 0 5W
London, Greater □, *U.K.* 15 51 30N 0 5W
Londonderry, *U.K.* 24 55 0N 7 20W
Londonderry □, *U.K.* 24 55 0N 7 20W
Londrina, *Brazil* 102 23 18S 51 10W
Long, L., *U.K.* 20 56 4N 4 50W
Long Beach, *U.S.A.* 90 33 46N 118 12W
Long Bennington, *U.K.* 19 52 59N 0 45W
Long Clawson, *U.K.* 15 52 51N 0 56W
Long Crendon, *U.K.* 15 51 47N 1 0W
Long Eaton, *U.K.* 19 52 54N 1 16W
Long I., *Baham.* 95 23 20N 75 10W
Long I., *U.S.A.* 93 40 50N 73 20W
Long Itchington, *U.K.* 14 52 16N 1 24W
Long Melford, *U.K.* 15 52 5N 0 44 E
Long Mynd, *U.K.* 14 52 35N 2 50W
Long Preston, *U.K.* 18 54 0N 2 16W
Long Sutton, *U.K.* 15 52 47N 0 9 E
Longford, *Ire.* 24 53 43N 7 50W
Longford, *U.K.* 14 51 53N 2 14W
Longford □, *Ire.* 24 53 42N 7 45W
Longforgan, *U.K.* 21 56 28N 3 8W
Longframlington, *U.K.* 21 55 18N 1 47W
Longhorsley, *U.K.* 21 55 15N 1 46W
Longhoughton, *U.K.* 21 55 26N 1 38W
Longridge, *U.K.* 18 53 50N 2 37W
Longton, *U.K.* 18 53 43N 2 48W
Longtown, *Cumbria, U.K.* 18 55 1N 2 59W
Longtown, *Hereford & Worcs., U.K.* 14 51 58N 2 59W
Löningen, *W. Ger.* 36 52 43N 7 44 E
Looe, *U.K.* 16 50 24N 4 25W
Loop Hd., *Ire.* 25 52 34N 9 55W
Lop Nor, *China* 60 40 20N 90 10 E
Lorca, *Sp.* 37 37 41N 1 42W
Lorient, *Fr.* 34 47 45N 3 23W
Lorn, *U.K.* 20 56 26N 5 10W
Lorn, Firth of, *U.K.* 20 56 20N 5 40W
Los Angeles, *Chile* 102 37 28S 72 23W
Los Angeles, *U.S.A.* 90 34 0N 118 10W
Los Mochis, *Mex.* 94 25 45N 108 57W
Lossiemouth, *U.K.* 23 57 43N 3 17W
Lostwithiel, *U.K.* 16 50 24N 4 41W
Lothian □, *U.K.* 21 55 50N 3 0W
Loughborough, *U.K.* 14 52 46N 1 11W
Loughrea, *Ire.* 25 53 11N 8 33W
Loughros More B., *Ire.* 24 54 48N 8 30W
Louisiana □, *U.S.A.* 91 30 50N 92 0W
Louisville, *U.S.A.* 92 38 15N 85 45W
Lourdes, *Fr.* 35 43 6N 0 3W
Louth, *Ire.* 24 53 47N 6 33W
Louth, *U.K.* 19 53 23N 0 0 E
Louth □, *Ire.* 24 53 55N 6 30W
Louvière, La, *Belg.* 36 50 27N 4 10 E
Lowell, *U.S.A.* 93 42 38N 71 19W
Lower Beeding, *U.K.* 15 51 2N 0 15W
Lower California, *Mex.* 94 31 10N 115 12W
Lower Hutt, *N.Z.* 71 41 10S 174 55 E
Lower Tunguska →, *U.S.S.R.* 49 64 20N 93 0 E
Lowes Water L., *U.K.* 18 54 35N 3 23W
Lowestoft, *U.K.* 15 52 29N 1 44 E
Lowick, *U.K.* 21 55 38N 1 57W
Lowther Hills, *U.K.* 21 55 20N 3 40W
Luanda, *Angola* 80 8 50S 13 15 E
Luanshya, *Zam.* 81 13 3S 28 28 E
Lubbock, *U.S.A.* 90 33 40N 101 53W
Lübeck, *W. Ger.* 42 53 52N 10 41 E
Lublin, *Pol.* 43 51 12N 22 38 E
Lubumbashi, *Zaïre* 81 11 40S 27 28 E
Luce Bay, *U.K.* 20 54 45N 4 48W
Lucknow, *India* 59 26 50N 81 0 E
Lüda = Dalian, *China* 61 38 50N 121 40 E
Ludgershall, *U.K.* 14 51 15N 1 38W
Ludgvan, *U.K.* 16 50 9N 5 30W
Ludhiana, *India* 58 30 57N 75 56 E
Ludlow, *U.K.* 14 52 23N 2 42W
Ludwigshafen, *W. Ger.* 42 49 27N 8 27 E

Lugano

Lugano, *Switz.* **42** 46 0N 8 57 E
Lugnaquilla, *Ire.* **25** 52 58N 6 28W
Lugo, *Sp.* **37** 43 2N 7 35W
Lugwardine, *U.K.* **14** 52 4N 2 38W
Luing I., *U.K.* **20** 56 15N 5 40W
Luleå, *Swed.* **44** 65 35N 22 10 E
Lundy, *U.K.* **16** 51 10N 4 41W
Lune →, *U.K.* **18** 54 0N 2 51W
Lünen, *W. Ger.* **36** 51 36N 7 31 E
Luoyang, *China* **61** 34 40N 112 26 E
Lurgan, *U.K.* **24** 54 28N 6 20W
Lusaka, *Zam.* **81** 15 28S 28 16 E
Luss, *U.K.* **20** 56 6N 4 40W
Luton, *U.K.* **15** 51 53N 0 24W
Lutterworth, *U.K.* **14** 52 28N 1 12W
Luxembourg, *Lux.* **36** 49 37N 6 9 E
Luxembourg ■, *Europe* **36** 50 0N 6 0 E
Luzern, *Switz.* **42** 47 3N 8 18 E
Luzhou, *China* **60** 28 52N 105 20 E
Luzon, *Phil.* **63** 16 0N 121 0 E
Lvov, *U.S.S.R.* **47** 49 50N 24 0 E
Lyakhov Is., *U.S.S.R.* **49** 73 40N 141 0 E
Lybster, *U.K.* **23** 58 18N 3 16W
Lydd, *U.K.* **15** 50 57N 0 56 E
Lydford, *U.K.* **16** 50 38N 4 7W
Lydham, *U.K.* **14** 52 31N 2 59W
Lyell Range, *N.Z.* **71** 41 38S 172 20 E
Lyme Bay, *U.K.* **16** 50 36N 2 55W
Lyme Regis, *U.K.* **16** 50 44N 2 57W
Lyminge, *U.K.* **15** 51 7N 1 6 E
Lymington, *U.K.* **14** 50 46N 1 32W
Lymm, *U.K.* **18** 53 23N 2 30W
Lympne, *U.K.* **15** 51 4N 1 2 E
Lynchburg, *U.S.A.* **92** 37 23N 79 10W
Lyndhurst, *U.K.* **14** 50 53N 1 33W
Lyneham, *U.K.* **14** 51 30N 1 57W
Lynemouth, *U.K.* **21** 55 15N 1 29W
Lynmouth, *U.K.* **16** 51 14N 3 50W
Lynn Lake, *Canada* **88** 56 51N 101 3W
Lynton, *U.K.* **16** 51 14N 3 50W
Lyons, *Fr.* **35** 45 46N 4 50 E
Lytchett Minster, *U.K.* **14** 50 44N 2 3W
Lytham St. Anne's, *U.K.* **18** 53 45N 2 58W
Lythe, *U.K.* **19** 54 30N 0 40W

M

Ma'ān, *Jord.* **56** 30 12N 35 44 E
Maarianhamina, *Fin.* **45** 60 5N 19 55 E
Maastricht, *Neth.* **36** 50 50N 5 40 E
Mablethorpe, *U.K.* **19** 53 21N 0 14 E
Macapá, *Brazil* **101** 0 5N 51 4W
Macau ■, *Asia* **61** 22 16N 113 35 E
Macclesfield, *U.K.* **18** 53 16N 2 9W
McClure Str., *Canada* **103** 75 0N 119 0W
Macdonnell Ranges, *Austral.* **66** 23 40S 133 0 E
Macduff, *U.K.* **23** 57 40N 2 30W
Macedonia □, *Greece* **41** 40 39N 22 0 E
Macedonia □, *Yug.* **41** 41 53N 21 40 E
Maceió, *Brazil* **101** 9 40S 35 41W
Macgillycuddy's Reeks, *Ire.* **25** 52 2N 9 45W
Machakos, *Kenya* **80** 1 30S 37 15 E
Machala, *Ecuad.* **100** 3 20S 79 57W
Machars, The, *U.K.* **20** 54 46N 4 30W
Machrihanish, *U.K.* **20** 55 25N 5 42W
Machynlleth, *U.K.* **17** 52 36N 3 51W
Macintyre →, *Austral.* **67** 28 37S 150 47 E
Mackay, *Austral.* **67** 21 8S 149 11 E
Mackay, L., *Austral.* **66** 22 30S 129 0 E
McKeesport, *U.S.A.* **92** 40 21N 79 50W
Mackenzie →, *Austral.* **67** 23 38S 149 46 E
Mackenzie →, *Canada* **88** 69 10N 134 20W
Mackenzie Mts., *Canada* **88** 64 0N 130 0W
McKinley, Mt., *U.S.A.* **88** 63 2N 151 0W
M'Clintock Chan., *Canada* **88** 72 0N 102 0W
Macon, *U.S.A.* **90** 32 50N 83 37W
Macquarie →, *Austral.* **70** 30 5S 147 30 E
Macquarie Harbour, *Austral.* **67** 42 15S 145 23 E
Macquarie Is., *S. Oc.* **64** 54 36S 158 55 E
Macroom, *Ire.* **25** 51 54N 8 57W
Madadeni, *S. Afr.* **81** 27 43S 30 3 E
Madagascar ■, *Africa* **81** 20 0S 47 0 E
Madeira, *Atl. Oc.* **78** 32 50N 17 0W
Madeira →, *Brazil* **100** 3 22S 58 45W
Madeley, *Salop, U.K.* **14** 52 38N 2 28W
Madeley, *Staffs., U.K.* **18** 52 59N 2 20W
Madhya Pradesh □, *India* **59** 21 50N 81 0 E
Madīnat ash Sha'b, *S. Yem.* **56** 12 50N 45 0 E
Madison, *U.S.A.* **92** 43 5N 89 25W
Madiun, *Indon.* **63** 7 38S 111 32 E
Madley, *U.K.* **14** 52 3N 2 51W
Madras, *India* **58** 13 8N 80 19 E
Madre, L., *U.S.A.* **91** 26 0N 97 40W
Madre, Sierra, *Mex.* **94** 16 0N 93 0W
Madrid, *Sp.* **37** 40 25N 3 45W
Madurai, *India* **58** 9 55N 78 10 E
Maesteg, *U.K.* **17** 51 36N 3 40W
Magadan, *U.S.S.R.* **49** 59 38N 150 50 E
Magdalena →, *Col.* **100** 11 6N 74 51W
Magdeburg, *E. Ger.* **42** 52 8N 11 36 E
Magee, I., *U.K.* **24** 54 48N 5 44W
Magelang, *Indon.* **63** 7 29S 110 13 E
Magellan's Str., *Chile* **102** 52 30S 75 0W
Maggiore, L., *It.* **40** 46 0N 8 35 E
Magherafelt, *U.K.* **24** 54 44N 6 37W
Maghull, *U.K.* **18** 53 31N 2 56W
Magnitogorsk, *U.S.S.R.* **46** 53 27N 59 4 E
Mahajanga, *Madag.* **81** 17 0S 47 0 E
Maiden Bradley, *U.K.* **14** 51 9N 2 18W
Maiden Newton, *U.K.* **14** 50 46N 2 35W
Maidenhead, *U.K.* **15** 51 31N 0 42W
Maidstone, *U.K.* **15** 51 16N 0 31 E
Maiduguri, *Nig.* **79** 12 0N 13 20 E
Main →, *U.K.* **24** 54 49N 6 20W
Maine □, *U.S.A.* **93** 45 20N 69 0W
Maine →, *Ire.* **25** 52 10N 9 40W
Mainland, *Orkney, U.K.* **23** 59 0N 3 10W
Mainland, *Shetland, U.K.* **22** 60 15N 1 22W
Mainz, *W. Ger.* **36** 50 0N 8 17 E
Maitland, *Austral.* **70** 32 33S 151 36 E
Majorca, I. = Mallorca, *Sp.* **37** 39 30N 3 0 E
Makasar, Str. of, *Indon.* **63** 1 0S 118 20 E
Maker, *U.K.* **16** 50 20N 4 10W
Makeyevka, *U.S.S.R.* **47** 48 0N 38 0 E
Makhachkala, *U.S.S.R.* **47** 43 0N 47 30 E
Makran Coast Range, *Pak.* **58** 25 40N 64 0 E
Mal B., *Ire.* **25** 52 50N 9 30W
Malabar Coast, *India* **58** 11 0N 75 0 E
Malacca, Str. of, *Indon.* **63** 3 0N 101 0 E
Málaga, *Sp.* **37** 36 43N 4 23W
Malang, *Indon.* **63** 7 59S 112 45 E
Malanje, *Angola* **80** 9 36S 16 17 E
Mälaren, *Swed.* **45** 59 30N 17 10 E
Malatya, *Turk.* **47** 38 25N 38 20 E
Malawi ■, *Africa* **81** 13 0S 34 0 E
Malay Pen., *Asia* **63** 7 25N 100 0 E
Malaysia ■, *Asia* **63** 5 0N 110 0 E
Maldives ■, *Ind. Oc.* **129** 7 0N 73 0 E
Maldon, *U.K.* **15** 51 43N 0 41 E
Malham Tarn, *U.K.* **18** 54 6N 2 11W
Mali ■, *Africa* **78** 15 0N 2 0W
Mallaig, *U.K.* **22** 57 0N 5 50W
Mallorca, *Sp.* **37** 39 30N 3 0 E
Mallow, *Ire.* **25** 52 8N 8 40W
Malmédy, *Belg.* **36** 50 25N 6 2 E
Malmesbury, *U.K.* **14** 51 35N 2 5W
Malmö, *Swed.* **45** 55 36N 12 59 E
Malpas, *U.K.* **18** 53 3N 2 47W
Malta ■, *Europe* **40** 35 50N 14 30 E
Maltby, *U.K.* **19** 53 25N 1 12W
Malton, *U.K.* **19** 54 9N 0 48W
Malvern, *U.K.* **14** 52 7N 2 19W
Malvern Hills, *U.K.* **14** 52 0N 2 19W
Malvern Wells, *U.K.* **14** 52 4N 2 19W
Malvinas, Is. = Falkland Is., *Atl. Oc.* **102** 51 30S 59 0W
Man, I. of, *U.K.* **18** 54 15N 4 30W
Manaar, Gulf of, *Asia* **58** 8 30N 79 0 E
Manacles, The, *U.K.* **16** 50 3N 5 5W
Manado, *Indon.* **63** 1 29N 124 51 E
Managua, *Nic.* **94** 12 6N 86 20W
Manaus, *Brazil* **100** 3 0S 60 0W
Manby, *U.K.* **19** 53 22N 0 6 E
Manchester, *U.K.* **18** 53 30N 2 15W
Manchester, *U.S.A.* **93** 42 58N 71 29W
Manchuria, *China* **61** 42 0N 125 0 E
Mandalay, *Burma* **59** 22 0N 96 4 E
Manea, *U.K.* **15** 52 29N 0 10 E
Mangalore, *India* **58** 12 55N 74 47 E
Mangotsfield, *U.K.* **14** 51 29N 2 29W
Manila, *Phil.* **63** 14 40N 121 3 E
Manitoba □, *Canada* **88** 55 30N 97 0W
Manizales, *Col.* **100** 5 5N 75 32W
Manly, *Austral.* **70** 33 48S 151 17 E
Mannheim, *W. Ger.* **42** 49 28N 8 29 E
Manningtree, *U.K.* **15** 51 56N 1 3 E
Mans, Le, *Fr.* **34** 48 0N 0 10 E
Mansfield, *U.K.* **19** 53 8N 1 12W
Mansfield, *U.S.A.* **92** 40 45N 82 30W
Mansfield Woodhouse, *U.K.* **19** 53 11N 1 11W
Mantes-la-Jolie, *Fr.* **34** 49 0N 1 41 E
Manton, *U.K.* **15** 52 37N 0 41W
Mantua, *It.* **40** 45 20N 10 42 E
Manukau, *N.Z.* **71** 37 1S 174 55 E
Manzhouli, *China* **61** 49 35N 117 25 E
Maoming, *China* **61** 21 50N 110 54 E
Maputo, *Mozam.* **81** 25 58S 32 32 E
Mar del Plata, *Arg.* **102** 38 0S 57 30W
Maracaibo, *Ven.* **100** 10 40N 71 37W
Maracaibo, L., *Ven.* **100** 9 40N 71 30W
Maracay, *Ven.* **100** 10 15N 67 28W
Marajó, I. de, *Brazil* **101** 1 0S 49 30W
Maranhão = São Luís, *Brazil* **101** 2 39S 44 15W
Marañón →, *Peru* **100** 4 30S 73 35W
Marazion, *U.K.* **16** 50 8N 5 29W
March, *U.K.* **15** 52 33N 0 5 E
Marden, *U.K.* **14** 52 7N 2 42W
Maree L., *U.K.* **22** 57 40N 5 30W
Mareeba, *Austral.* **67** 16 59S 145 28 E
Mareham le Fen, *U.K.* **19** 53 7N 0 3W
Marfleet, *U.K.* **19** 53 45N 0 15W
Margarita I., *Ven.* **100** 11 0N 64 0W
Margate, *U.K.* **15** 51 23N 1 24 E
Maribor, *Yug.* **40** 46 36N 15 40 E
Maricourt, *Canada* **89** 56 34N 70 49W
Marie-Galante, *W. Ind.* **94** 15 56N 61 16W
Marília, *Brazil* **101** 22 13S 50 0W
Maringá, *Brazil* **102** 23 26S 52 2W
Mark, *U.K.* **20** 55 2N 5 1W
Market Bosworth, *U.K.* **14** 52 37N 1 24W
Market Deeping, *U.K.* **15** 52 40N 0 20W
Market Drayton, *U.K.* **18** 52 55N 2 30W
Market Harborough, *U.K.* **15** 52 29N 0 55W
Market Lavington, *U.K.* **14** 51 17N 1 59W
Market Rasen, *U.K.* **19** 53 24N 0 20W
Market Weighton, *U.K.* **19** 53 52N 0 40W
Markfield, *U.K.* **14** 52 42N 1 18W
Markinch, *U.K.* **21** 56 12N 3 9W
Marks Tey, *U.K.* **15** 51 53N 0 48 E
Marlborough, *U.K.* **14** 51 26N 1 44W
Marlborough □, *N.Z.* **71** 41 45S 173 33 E
Marlborough Downs, *U.K.* **14** 51 25N 1 55W
Marlow, *U.K.* **15** 51 34N 0 47W
Marmara, Sea of, *Turk.* **47** 40 45N 28 15 E
Marne →, *Fr.* **34** 48 48N 2 24 E
Marnhull, *U.K.* **14** 50 58N 2 20W
Maroua, *Cam.* **80** 10 40N 14 20 E
Marple, *U.K.* **18** 53 23N 2 5W
Marquesas Is., *Pac. Oc.* **65** 9 30S 140 0W
Marrakech, *Mor.* **78** 31 9N 8 0W
Marseilles, *Fr.* **35** 43 18N 5 23 E
Marshall Is., *Pac. Oc.* **64** 9 0N 171 0 E
Marshfield, *U.K.* **14** 51 27N 2 18W
Marske by the Sea, *U.K.* **19** 54 35N 1 0W
Marston Moor, *U.K.* **19** 53 58N 1 17W
Martaban, G. of, *Burma* **59** 16 5N 96 30 E
Martham, *U.K.* **15** 52 42N 1 38 E
Martinique, *W. Ind.* **94** 14 40N 61 0W
Martley, *U.K.* **14** 52 14N 2 22W
Martock, *U.K.* **14** 50 58N 2 47W
Mary Kathleen, *Austral.* **67** 20 44S 139 48 E
Maryborough, *Austral.* **67** 37 0S 143 44 E
Maryland □, *U.S.A.* **93** 39 10N 76 40W
Maryport, *U.K.* **18** 54 43N 3 30W
Marytavy, *U.K.* **16** 50 34N 4 6W
Masan, *S. Kor.* **61** 35 11N 128 32 E
Maseru, *Les.* **81** 29 18S 27 30 E
Masham, *U.K.* **19** 54 15N 1 40W
Mashhad, *Iran* **57** 36 20N 59 35 E
Mask, L., *Ire.* **24** 53 36N 9 24W
Massachusetts □, *U.S.A.* **93** 42 25N 72 0W
Massif Central, *Fr.* **35** 45 30N 3 0 E
Masterton, *N.Z.* **71** 40 56S 175 39 E
Masvingo, *Zimb.* **81** 20 8S 30 49 E
Matadi, *Zaïre* **80** 5 52S 13 31 E
Matamoros, *Mex.* **94** 25 33N 103 15W
Matera, *It.* **40** 40 40N 16 37 E
Matlock, *U.K.* **19** 53 8N 1 32W
Mato Grosso □, *Brazil* **101** 14 0S 55 0W
Matsue, *Jap.* **62** 35 25N 133 10 E
Matsuyama, *Jap.* **62** 33 45N 132 45 E
Matterhorn, *Switz.* **42** 45 58N 7 39 E
Maturín, *Ven.* **100** 9 45N 63 11W
Maubeuge, *Fr.* **34** 50 17N 3 57 E
Mauchline, *U.K.* **20** 55 31N 4 23W
Maughold, *U.K.* **18** 54 18N 4 17W
Maughold Hd., *U.K.* **18** 54 18N 4 17W
Maui, *U.S.A.* **90** 20 45N 156 20 E
Mauna Loa, *U.S.A.* **90** 21 8N 157 10W
Mauritania ■, *Africa* **78** 20 50N 10 0W
Mauritius ■, *Ind. Oc.* **129** 20 0S 57 0 E
Mawgan, *U.K.* **16** 50 4N 5 10W
Mawlaik, *Burma* **59** 23 40N 94 26 E
Maxwellheugh, *U.K.* **21** 55 35N 2 23W
May, I. of, *U.K.* **21** 56 11N 2 32W
May Pen, *Jam.* **94** 17 58N 77 15W
Maybole, *U.K.* **20** 55 21N 4 41W
Mayfield, *Derby, U.K.* **19** 53 1N 1 47W
Mayfield, *E. Sussex, U.K.* **15** 51 1N 0 17 E
Maynooth, *Ire.* **24** 53 22N 6 38W
Mayo □, *Ire.* **24** 53 47N 9 7W
Mazar-e Sharīf, *Afg.* **57** 36 41N 67 0 E
Mazatlán, *Mex.* **94** 23 13N 106 25W
Mbabane, *Swaz.* **81** 26 18S 31 6 E
Mbandaka, *Zaïre* **80** 0 1N 18 18 E
Mbanza Ngungu, *Zaïre* **80** 5 12S 14 53 E
Mbeya, *Tanz.* **80** 8 54S 33 29 E
Mbini □, *Eq. Guin.* **80** 1 30N 10 0 E
Mbuji-Mayi, *Zaïre* **80** 6 9S 23 40 E
Mdantsane, *S. Afr.* **81** 32 56S 27 46 E
Mealsgate, *U.K.* **18** 54 46N 3 14W
Measham, *U.K.* **14** 52 43N 1 30W
Meath □, *Ire.* **24** 53 32N 6 40W
Mecca, *Si. Arab.* **56** 21 30N 39 54 E
Mechelen, *Belg.* **36** 50 58N 5 41 E
Medan, *Indon.* **63** 3 40N 98 38 E
Medellín, *Col.* **100** 6 15N 75 35W
Medicine Hat, *Canada* **88** 50 0N 110 45W
Medina, *Si. Arab.* **56** 24 35N 39 52 E
Mediterranean Sea, *Europe* **38** 35 0N 15 0 E
Medley, *Canada* **88** 54 25N 110 16W
Medstead, *U.K.* **14** 51 7N 1 4W
Medway →, *U.K.* **15** 51 28N 0 45 E
Meekatharra, *Austral.* **66** 26 32S 118 29 E
Meerut, *India* **58** 29 1N 77 42 E
Mei Xian, *China* **61** 24 16N 116 6 E
Meknès, *Mor.* **78** 33 57N 5 33W
Mekong →, *Asia* **63** 9 30N 106 15 E
Melanesia, *Pac. Oc.* **64** 4 0S 155 0 E
Melbourn, *U.K.* **15** 52 5N 0 1 E
Melbourne, *Austral.* **70** 37 50S 145 0 E
Melbourne, *U.K.* **14** 52 50N 1 25W
Melfort, Loch, *U.K.* **20** 56 13N 5 33W
Melitopol, *U.S.S.R.* **47** 46 50N 35 22 E
Melksham, *U.K.* **14** 51 22N 2 9W
Melmerby, *U.K.* **18** 54 44N 2 35W
Melrose, *U.K.* **21** 53 35N 2 44W
Melsonby, *U.K.* **19** 54 28N 1 41W
Melton, *U.K.* **15** 52 51N 1 1 E
Melton Constable, *U.K.* **15** 52 52N 1 1 E
Melton Mowbray, *U.K.* **15** 52 46N 0 52W
Melvich, *U.K.* **23** 58 33N 3 55W
Melville I., *Austral.* **66** 11 30S 131 0 E
Melville Pen., *Canada* **89** 68 0N 84 0W
Memphis, *U.S.A.* **91** 35 7N 90 0W
Menai Bridge, *U.K.* **17** 53 14N 4 11W
Menai Strait, *U.K.* **17** 53 14N 4 10W
Menan = Chao Phraya →, *Thai.* **63** 13 32N 100 36 E
Mendip Hills, *U.K.* **14** 51 17N 2 40W
Mendlesham, *U.K.* **15** 52 15N 1 4 E
Mendoza, *Arg.* **102** 32 50S 68 52W
Menindee, *Austral.* **70** 32 20S 142 25 E
Menorca, *Sp.* **37** 40 0N 4 0 E
Mere, *U.K.* **14** 51 5N 2 16W
Mérida, *Mex.* **94** 20 58N 89 37W
Mérida, *Ven.* **100** 8 24N 71 8W
Meriden, *U.K.* **14** 52 27N 1 36W
Merrick, *U.K.* **20** 55 8N 4 30W
Merse, *U.K.* **21** 55 40N 2 30W
Mersea I., *U.K.* **15** 51 48N 0 55 E
Mersey →, *U.K.* **18** 53 20N 2 56W
Merseyside □, *U.K.* **18** 53 25N 2 55W
Mersin, *Turk.* **47** 36 51N 34 36 E
Merthyr Tydfil, *U.K.* **17** 51 45N 3 23W
Merton, *U.K.* **15** 51 25N 0 13W
Meru, *Tanz.* **80** 3 15S 36 46 E
Mesa, *U.S.A.* **90** 33 20N 111 56W
Mesopotamia, *Asia* **56** 33 30N 44 0 E
Messina, *It.* **40** 38 10N 15 32 E
Messina, Str. of, *It.* **40** 38 5N 15 35 E
Metheringham, *U.K.* **19** 53 9N 0 22W
Methil, *U.K.* **21** 56 10N 3 1W
Methven, *U.K.* **21** 56 25N 3 35W
Methwold, *U.K.* **15** 52 30N 0 33 E
Metz, *Fr.* **34** 49 8N 6 10 E
Meuse →, *Europe* **34** 50 45N 5 41 E
Mevagissey, *U.K.* **16** 50 16N 4 48W
Mevagissey Bay, *U.K.* **16** 50 15N 4 40W
Mexborough, *U.K.* **19** 53 29N 1 18W
Mexicali, *Mex.* **94** 32 40N 115 29W
México, *Mex.* **94** 19 20N 99 10W
Mexico ■, *Cent. Am.* **94** 20 0N 100 0W
Mexico, G. of, *Cent. Am.* **94** 25 0N 90 0W
Miami, *U.S.A.* **91** 25 45N 80 15W
Micheldever, *U.K.* **14** 51 7N 1 17W
Michigan □, *U.S.A.* **92** 44 40N 85 40W
Michigan, L., *U.S.A.* **92** 44 0N 87 0W
Mickle Fell, *U.K.* **18** 54 38N 2 16W
Mickleover, *U.K.* **19** 52 55N 1 32W
Mickleton, *Durham, U.K.* **18** 54 36N 2 3W
Mickleton, *Oxon., U.K.* **14** 52 5N 1 45W
Micronesia, *Pac. Oc.* **64** 11 0N 160 0 E
Mid Calder, *U.K.* **21** 55 53N 3 23W
Mid Glamorgan □, *U.K.* **17** 51 40N 3 25W
Middle Zoy, *U.K.* **14** 51 5N 2 54W
Middleham, *U.K.* **19** 54 17N 1 49W
Middlemarsh, *U.K.* **14** 50 51N 2 29W
Middlesbrough, *U.K.* **19** 54 35N 1 14W
Middleton, *Gr. Manchester, U.K.* **18** 53 33N 2 12W
Middleton, *Norfolk, U.K.* **15** 52 43N 0 29 E
Middleton Cheney, *U.K.* **14** 52 4N 1 17W
Middleton-in-Teesdale, *U.K.* **18** 54 38N 2 5W
Middleton on the Wolds, *U.K.* **19** 53 56N 0 35W
Middlewich, *U.K.* **18** 53 12N 2 28W
Midhurst, *U.K.* **15** 50 59N 0 44W
Midland, *U.S.A.* **90** 32 0N 102 3W
Midleton, *Ire.* **25** 51 52N 8 12W
Midsomer Norton, *U.K.* **14** 51 17N 2 29W
Midway Is., *Pac. Oc.* **64** 28 13N 177 22W
Mieres, *Sp.* **37** 43 18N 5 48W
Mikkeli, *Fin.* **44** 61 43N 27 15 E
Milan, *It.* **40** 45 28N 9 10 E
Milborne Port, *U.K.* **14** 50 58N 2 28W
Mildenhall, *U.K.* **15** 52 20N 0 30 E
Mildura, *Austral.* **70** 34 13S 142 9 E
Milford Haven, *U.K.* **17** 51 43N 5 2W
Milford Haven, B., *U.K.* **17** 51 40N 5 10W
Milford on Sea, *U.K.* **14** 50 44N 1 36W
Milk →, *U.S.A.* **90** 48 5N 106 15W
Millbrook, *U.K.* **16** 50 19N 4 12W
Milleur Pt., *U.K.* **20** 55 2N 5 5W
Millom, *U.K.* **18** 54 13N 3 16W
Millport, *U.K.* **20** 55 45N 4 55W
Milltown Malbay, *Ire.* **25** 52 51N 9 25W
Milnathort, *U.K.* **21** 56 14N 3 25W
Milngavie, *U.K.* **20** 55 57N 4 20W
Milnthorpe, *U.K.* **18** 54 14N 2 47W
Milton, *Dumf. & Gall., U.K.* **20** 55 18N 4 50W
Milton, *Hants., U.K.* **14** 50 45N 1 40W
Milton, *Highland, U.K.* **23** 57 18N 4 32W
Milton Abbot, *U.K.* **16** 50 35N 4 16W
Milton Keynes, *U.K.* **15** 52 3N 0 42W

Nicoya, Pen. de

Milverton, U.K. 14 51 2N 3 15W
Milwaukee, U.S.A. 92 43 9N 87 58W
Minas Gerais □, Brazil 101 18 50S 46 0W
Minatitlán, Mex. 94 17 59N 94 31W
Minchinghampton, U.K. 14 51 42N 2 10W
Mindanao, Phil. 63 8 0N 125 0 E
Mindoro, Phil. 63 13 0N 121 0 E
Minehead, U.K. 14 51 12N 3 29W
Minneapolis, U.S.A. 91 44 58N 93 20W
Minnesota □, U.S.A. 91 46 40N 94 0W
Minnigaff, U.K. 20 54 58N 4 30W
Minorca = Menorca, Sp. 37 40 0N 4 0 E
Minsk, U.S.S.R. 46 53 52N 27 30 E
Minster, U.K. 15 51 20N 1 20 E
Minster-on-Sea, U.K. 15 51 25N 0 50 E
Minsterley, U.K. 14 52 38N 2 56W
Mirfield, U.K. 19 53 37N 1 54W
Mirzapur, India 59 25 10N 82 34 E
Miskolc, Hung. 43 48 7N 20 50 E
Misrātah, Libya 79 32 24N 15 3 E
Mississippi □, U.S.A. 91 33 0N 90 0W
Mississippi →, U.S.A. 91 29 0N 89 15W
Mississippi, Delta of the, U.S.A. 91 29 15N 90 30W
Missouri □, U.S.A. 91 38 25N 92 30W
Missouri →, U.S.A. 91 38 50N 90 8W
Misterton, Notts., U.K. 19 53 27N 0 49W
Misterton, Somerset, U.K. 14 50 51N 2 46W
Mitcheldean, U.K. 14 51 51N 2 29W
Mitchell →, Austral. 67 15 12S 141 35 E
Mitchelstown, Ire. 25 52 16N 8 18W
Mittelland Kanal, W. Ger. 36 52 23N 7 45 E
Mitumba, Mts., Zaïre 80 6 0S 29 0 E
Miyazaki, Jap. 62 31 56N 131 30 E
Mizen Hd., Cork, Ire. 25 51 27N 9 50W
Mizen Hd., Wicklow, Ire. 25 52 52N 6 4W
Mizoram □, India 59 23 30N 92 40 E
Mmabatho, S. Afr. 81 25 49S 25 30 E
Mo i Rana, Nor. 44 66 15N 14 7 E
Mobile, U.S.A. 91 30 41N 88 3W
Mobutu Sese Seko, L., Africa 80 1 30N 31 0 E
Moçâmedes = Namibe, Angola 81 15 7S 12 11 E
Modbury, U.K. 16 50 21N 3 53W
Módena, It. 40 44 39N 10 55 E
Moe, Austral. 70 38 12S 146 19 E
Moffat, U.K. 21 55 20N 3 27W
Mogadishu, Som. 73 2 2N 45 25 E
Mogilev, U.S.S.R. 46 53 55N 30 18 E
Moidart, L., U.K. 22 56 47N 5 40W
Mojave Desert, U.S.A. 90 35 0N 116 30W
Mold, U.K. 17 53 10N 3 10W
Moldavia □, U.S.S.R. 47 47 0N 28 0 E
Mole →, U.K. 15 51 13N 0 15W
Mollendo, Peru 100 17 0S 72 0W
Mölndal, Swed. 45 57 40N 12 3 E
Molokai, U.S.A. 90 21 8N 157 0W
Moluccas, Indon. 63 1 0S 127 0 E
Mombasa, Kenya 80 4 2S 39 43 E
Mona Passage, W. Ind. 95 18 0N 67 40W
Monach Is., U.K. 22 57 32N 7 40W
Monaco ■, Europe 35 43 46N 7 23 E
Monadhliath Mts., U.K. 23 57 10N 4 4W
Monaghan, Ire. 24 54 15N 6 58W
Monaghan □, Ire. 24 54 10N 7 0W
Monastir = Bitola, Yug. 41 41 5N 21 10 E
Monclova, Mex. 94 26 50N 101 30W
Moncton, Canada 93 46 7N 64 51W
Moneymore, U.K. 24 54 42N 6 40W
Monghyr, India 59 25 23N 86 30 E
Mongolia ■, Asia 60 47 0N 103 0 E
Mongu, Zam. 81 15 16S 23 12 E
Moniaive, U.K. 21 55 11N 3 55W
Monifieth, U.K. 21 56 30N 2 48W
Monkton, U.K. 20 55 30N 4 37W
Monmouth, U.K. 17 51 48N 2 43W
Monnow →, U.K. 14 51 54N 2 48W
Monroe, U.S.A. 90 32 32N 92 4W
Monrovia, Lib. 78 6 18N 10 47W
Mons, Belg. 36 50 27N 3 58 E
Montana □, U.S.A. 90 47 0N 110 0W
Montbéliard, Fr. 34 47 31N 6 48 E
Montceau-les-Mines, Fr. 34 46 40N 4 23 E
Monte-Carlo, Monaco 35 43 46N 7 23 E
Montego Bay, Jam. 94 18 30N 78 0W
Montería, Col. 100 8 46N 75 53W
Monterrey, Mex. 94 25 40N 100 30W
Montes Claros, Brazil 101 16 30S 43 50W
Montevideo, Urug. 102 34 50S 56 11W
Montgomery, U.K. 17 52 34N 3 9W
Montgomery, U.S.A. 91 32 20N 86 20W
Montluçon, Fr. 35 46 22N 2 36 E
Montpelier, U.S.A. 93 44 15N 72 38W
Montpellier, Fr. 35 43 37N 3 52 E
Montréal, Canada 93 45 31N 73 34W
Montrose, U.K. 23 56 43N 2 28W
Montserrat, W. Ind. 94 16 40N 62 10W
Moonie →, Austral. 67 29 19S 148 43 E
Moorfoot Hills, U.K. 21 55 44N 3 8W
Moose Jaw, Canada 88 50 24N 105 30W
Moosehead L., U.S.A. 93 45 34N 69 40W
Mopti, Mali 78 14 30N 4 0W
Moradabad, India 58 28 50N 78 50 E
Morar L., U.K. 22 56 57N 5 40W
Moray Firth, U.K. 23 57 50N 3 30W
Morebattle, U.K. 21 55 30N 2 20W
Morecambe, U.K. 18 54 5N 2 52W
Morecambe B., U.K. 18 54 7N 3 0W
Morelia, Mex. 94 19 42N 101 7W
Morena, Sierra, Sp. 37 38 20N 4 0W
Moreton-in-Marsh, U.K. 14 51 59N 1 42W
Moretonhampstead, U.K. 16 50 39N 3 45W
Morley, U.K. 19 53 45N 1 36W
Morocco ■, N. Afr. 78 32 0N 5 50W
Morogoro, Tanz. 80 6 50S 37 40 E
Morpeth, U.K. 19 55 11N 1 41W
Morte Bay, U.K. 16 51 10N 4 13W
Morte Pt., U.K. 16 51 13N 4 14W
Mortehoe, U.K. 16 51 21N 4 12W
Mortimer's Cross, U.K. 14 52 17N 2 50W
Morton Fen, U.K. 15 52 45N 0 23W
Morvern, U.K. 22 56 38N 5 44W
Morwell, Austral. 70 38 10S 146 22 E
Morwenstow, U.K. 16 50 53N 4 32W
Moscow, U.S.S.R. 46 55 45N 37 35 E
Moselle →, Europe 34 50 22N 7 36 E
Moshi, Tanz. 80 3 22S 37 18 E
Mossley, U.K. 18 53 31N 2 1W
Mossoró, Brazil 101 5 10S 37 15W
Mostaganem, Alg. 78 35 54N 0 5 E
Mostar, Yug. 41 43 22N 17 50 E
Mosul, Iraq 56 36 15N 43 5 E
Motcombe, U.K. 14 51 1N 2 12W
Motherwell, U.K. 21 55 48N 4 0W
Mottisfont, U.K. 14 51 22N 1 32W
Moulmein, Burma 59 16 30N 97 40 E
Moulton, U.K. 15 52 17N 0 51W
Mount Barker, Austral. 66 34 38S 117 40 E
Mount Gambier, Austral. 70 37 50S 140 46 E
Mount Isa, Austral. 67 20 42S 139 26 E
Mount Lofty Ra., Austral. 67 34 35S 139 5 E
Mountain Ash, U.K. 17 51 42N 3 22W
Mountmellick, Ire. 25 53 7N 7 20W
Mounts Bay, U.K. 16 50 3N 5 27W
Mountsorrel, U.K. 14 52 43N 1 9W
Mourne →, U.K. 24 54 45N 7 39W
Mourne Mts., U.K. 24 54 10N 6 0W
Mouscron, Belg. 36 50 45N 3 12 E
Moville, Ire. 24 55 11N 7 3W
Moy →, Ire. 24 54 5N 8 50W
Moyle □, U.K. 24 55 10N 6 15W
Mozambique ■, Africa 81 19 0S 35 0 E
Mozambique Chan., Africa 81 20 0S 39 0 E
Mu Us Shamo, China 61 39 0N 109 0 E
Mubarraz, Si. Arab. 56 25 29N 49 40 E
Much Dewchurch, U.K. 14 51 58N 2 45W
Much Marcle, U.K. 14 51 59N 2 27W
Much Wenlock, U.K. 14 52 36N 2 34W
Muck, U.K. 22 56 50N 6 15W
Mudanjiang, China 61 44 38N 129 30 E
Mudgee, Austral. 70 32 32S 149 31 E
Mufulira, Zam. 81 12 32S 28 15 E
Muine Bheag, Ire. 25 52 42N 6 57W
Muir of Ord, U.K. 23 57 30N 4 35W
Muirdrum, U.K. 21 56 31N 2 40W
Muirhead, U.K. 21 55 54N 4 5W
Muirkirk, U.K. 21 55 31N 4 6W
Mülheim, W. Ger. 36 51 26N 6 53 E
Mulhouse, Fr. 34 47 40N 7 20 E
Mull, U.K. 20 56 27N 6 0W
Mull, Ross of, U.K. 20 56 20N 6 15W
Mull, Sound of, U.K. 20 56 30N 5 50W
Mullet Pen., Ire. 24 54 10N 10 2W
Mullingar, Ire. 24 53 31N 7 20W
Mullion, U.K. 16 50 1N 5 15W
Multan, Pak. 58 30 15N 71 36 E
Mumbles Hd., U.K. 17 51 33N 4 0W
Munchen-Gladbach, W. Ger. 36 51 12N 6 23 E
Mundesley, U.K. 15 52 53N 1 24 E
Munich, W. Ger. 42 48 8N 11 33 E
Münster, W. Ger. 36 51 58N 7 37 E
Munster □, Ire. 25 52 20N 8 40W
Murchison →, Austral. 66 27 45S 114 0 E
Murcia, Sp. 37 38 20N 1 10W
Mureş →, Rom. 43 46 15N 20 13 E
Murmansk, U.S.S.R. 46 68 57N 33 10 E
Murray →, S. Austral., Austral. 70 35 20S 139 22 E
Murray →, W. Austral., Austral. 67 32 33S 115 45 E
Murrumbidgee →, Austral. 70 34 43S 143 12 E
Murton, U.K. 19 54 51N 1 22W
Murwillumbah, Austral. 67 28 18S 153 27 E
Muscat, Oman 57 23 40N 58 38 E
Musgrave Ras., Austral. 66 26 0S 132 0 E
Musselburgh, U.K. 21 55 57N 3 3W
Muswellbrook, Austral. 70 32 16S 150 56 E
Mutare, Zimb. 81 18 58S 32 38 E
Muthill, U.K. 21 56 20N 3 50W
Muzaffarpur, India 59 26 7N 85 23 E
Mwanza, Tanz. 80 2 30S 32 58 E
Mweelrea, Ire. 24 53 37N 9 48W
My Tho, Viet. 63 10 29N 106 23 E
Myddle, U.K. 14 52 49N 2 47W
Myitkyina, Burma 59 25 24N 97 26 E
Mymensingh, Bangla. 59 24 45N 90 24 E
Mynydd Du, U.K. 17 51 45N 3 45W
Mynydd Prescelly, U.K. 17 51 57N 4 48W
Mysore, India 58 12 17N 76 41 E

N

Naas, Ire. 25 53 12N 6 40W
Nābulus, Jord. 57 32 14N 35 15 E
Nafferton, U.K. 19 54 1N 0 24W
Nagaland □, India 59 26 0N 94 30 E
Nagano, Jap. 62 36 40N 138 10 E
Nagaoka, Jap. 62 37 27N 138 51 E
Nagasaki, Jap. 62 32 47N 129 50 E
Nagoya, Jap. 62 35 10N 136 50 E
Nagpur, India 58 21 8N 79 10 E
Naha, Jap. 62 26 13N 127 42 E
Nailsea, U.K. 14 51 25N 2 44W
Nailsworth, U.K. 14 51 41N 2 12W
Nairn, U.K. 23 57 35N 3 54W
Nairobi, Kenya 80 1 17S 36 48 E
Nakuru, Kenya 80 0 15S 36 4 E
Nalchik, U.S.S.R. 47 43 30N 43 33 E
Nam Co, China 60 30 30N 90 45 E
Namangan, U.S.S.R. 48 41 0N 71 40 E
Namib Desert, Nam. 81 22 30S 15 0 E
Namibe, Angola 81 15 7S 12 11 E
Namibia ■, Africa 81 22 0S 18 9 E
Nampula, Mozam. 81 15 6N 39 15 E
Namur, Belg. 36 50 27N 4 52 E
Nan Shan, China 60 38 30N 99 0 E
Nanaimo, Canada 88 49 10N 124 0W
Nanchang, China 61 28 42N 115 55 E
Nanchong, China 60 30 43N 106 2 E
Nancy, Fr. 34 48 42N 6 12 E
Nanda Devi, India 58 30 23N 79 59 E
Nanjing = Nanking, China 61 32 2N 118 47 E
Nanking, China 61 32 2N 118 47 E
Nanning, China 60 22 48N 108 20 E
Nanping, China 61 26 38N 118 10 E
Nantes, Fr. 34 47 12N 1 33W
Nantong, China 61 32 1N 120 52 E
Nantucket Sd., U.S.A. 93 41 30N 70 15W
Nantwich, U.K. 18 53 5N 2 31W
Napier, N.Z. 71 39 30S 176 56 E
Naples, It. 40 40 50N 14 17 E
Nappa, U.K. 18 53 58N 2 14W
Nara, Jap. 62 34 40N 135 49 E
Narayanganj, Bangla. 59 23 40N 90 33 E
Narberth, U.K. 17 51 48N 4 45W
Narborough, U.K. 14 52 34N 1 12W
Nare Head, U.K. 16 50 12N 4 55W
Narmada →, India 58 21 38N 72 36 E
Narrandera, Austral. 70 34 42S 146 31 E
Narrogin, Austral. 66 32 58S 117 14 E
Narromine, Austral. 70 32 12S 148 12 E
Narvik, Nor. 44 68 28N 17 26 E
Naseby, U.K. 15 52 24N 0 59W
Nashua, U.S.A. 93 42 50N 71 25W
Nashville, U.S.A. 91 36 12N 86 46W
Nasik, India 58 19 58N 73 50 E
Nassau, Baham. 95 25 0N 77 20W
Nasser, L., Egypt 79 23 0N 32 30 E
Nässjö, Swed. 45 57 39N 14 42 E
Natal, Brazil 81 5 47S 35 13W
Natal □, S. Afr. 101 28 30S 30 30 E
Nauru ■, Pac. Oc. 64 1 0S 166 0 E
Navan = An Uaimh, Ire. 24 53 39N 6 40W
Navenby, U.K. 19 53 7N 0 32W
Naver →, U.K. 23 58 34N 4 15W
Náxos, Greece 41 37 8N 25 25 E
Nazareth, Isr. 57 32 42N 35 17 E
Naze, The, U.K. 15 51 53N 1 19 E
Ndjamena, Chad 79 12 10N 14 59 E
Ndola, Zam. 81 13 0S 28 34 E
Neagh, L., U.K. 24 54 35N 6 25W
Neath, U.K. 17 51 39N 3 49W
Nebraska □, U.S.A. 90 41 30N 100 0W
Needham Market, U.K. 15 52 9N 1 2 E
Needles, The, U.K. 14 50 39N 1 35W
Negro →, Arg. 102 41 2S 62 47W
Negro →, Brazil 100 3 0S 60 0W
Negros, Phil. 63 9 30N 122 40 E
Neijiang, China 60 29 35N 104 55 E
Neilston, U.K. 20 55 47N 4 27W
Neiva, Col. 100 2 56N 75 18W
Nellore, India 58 14 27N 79 59 E
Nelson, N.Z. 71 41 18S 173 16 E
Nelson, U.K. 18 53 50N 2 14W
Nelson →, Canada 88 54 33N 98 2W
Nelspruit, S. Afr. 81 25 29S 30 59 E
Nenagh, Ire. 25 52 52N 8 11W
Nene →, U.K. 15 52 38N 0 13 E
Nepal ■, Asia 59 28 0N 84 30 E
Nephin, Ire. 24 54 1N 9 21W
Ness, Loch, U.K. 23 57 15N 4 30W
Neston, U.K. 18 53 17N 3 3W
Netanya, Isr. 57 32 20N 34 51 E
Nether Stowey, U.K. 14 51 0N 3 10W
Netherbury, U.K. 14 50 46N 2 45W
Netherlands ■, Europe 36 52 0N 5 30 E
Netley, U.K. 14 50 53N 1 21W
Netley Marsh, U.K. 14 50 55N 1 32W
Nettlebed, U.K. 15 51 34N 0 54W
Nettleham, U.K. 19 53 15N 0 28W
Neuchâtel, Switz. 42 47 0N 6 55 E
Neukirchen, W. Ger. 36 54 52N 8 44 E
Neuss, W. Ger. 36 51 12N 6 39 E
Neustadt, W. Ger. 36 49 21N 8 10 E
Neuwied, W. Ger. 36 50 26N 7 29 E
Nevada □, U.S.A. 90 39 20N 117 0W
Nevada, Sierra, Sp. 37 37 3N 3 15W
Nevada, Sierra, U.S.A. 90 39 0N 120 30W
Nevers, Fr. 34 47 0N 3 9 E
New Abbey, U.K. 21 54 59N 3 38W
New Alresford, U.K. 14 51 6N 1 10W
New Amsterdam, Guy. 101 6 15N 57 36W
New Bedford, U.S.A. 93 41 40N 70 52W
New Brighton, N.Z. 71 43 29S 172 43 E
New Brighton, U.K. 18 53 27N 3 2W
New Brunswick □, Canada 93 46 50N 66 30W
New Caledonia, Pac. Oc. 64 21 0S 165 0 E
New Castile, Sp. 37 39 45N 3 20W
New Cumnock, U.K. 20 55 24N 4 13W
New Forest, U.K. 14 50 53N 1 40W
New Galloway, U.K. 21 55 4N 4 10W
New Guinea, Pac. Oc. 64 4 0S 136 0 E
New Hampshire □, U.S.A. 93 43 40N 71 40W
New Haven, U.S.A. 93 41 20N 72 54W
New Hebrides = Vanuatu ■, Pac. Oc. 64 15 0S 168 0 E
New Holland, U.K. 19 53 42N 0 22W
New Jersey □, U.S.A. 93 40 30N 74 10W
New London, U.S.A. 93 41 23N 72 8W
New Luce, U.K. 20 54 57N 4 50W
New Mexico □, U.S.A. 90 34 30N 106 0W
New Mills, U.K. 18 53 22N 2 0W
New Orleans, U.S.A. 91 30 0N 90 5W
New Plymouth, N.Z. 71 39 4S 174 5 E
New Quay, U.K. 17 52 13N 4 21W
New Radnor, U.K. 17 52 15N 3 10W
New Romney, U.K. 15 50 59N 0 57 E
New Ross, Ire. 25 52 24N 6 58W
New Rossington, U.K. 19 53 30N 1 4W
New Siberian Is., U.S.S.R. 49 75 0N 142 0 E
New South Wales □, Austral. 70 33 0S 146 0 E
New York □, U.S.A. 93 42 40N 76 0W
New York City, U.S.A. 93 40 45N 74 0W
New Zealand ■, Pac. Oc. 71 40 0S 176 0 E
Newark, U.S.A. 93 40 41N 74 12W
Newark-on-Trent, U.K. 19 53 6N 0 48W
Newbiggin-by-the-Sea, U.K. 21 55 12N 1 31W
Newbigging, U.K. 21 55 42N 3 33W
Newburgh, U.K. 21 56 21N 3 15W
Newburn, U.K. 21 54 57N 1 45W
Newbury, U.K. 14 51 24N 1 19W
Newby Bridge, U.K. 18 54 16N 2 59W
Newcastle, Austral. 70 33 0S 151 46 E
Newcastle, U.K. 24 54 13N 5 54W
Newcastle Emlyn, U.K. 17 52 2N 4 29W
Newcastle-under-Lyme, U.K. 18 53 2N 2 15W
Newcastle-upon-Tyne, U.K. 19 54 59N 1 37W
Newcastleton, U.K. 21 55 10N 2 50W
Newent, U.K. 14 51 56N 2 24W
Newfoundland □, Canada 89 53 0N 58 0W
Newham, U.K. 15 51 31N 0 2 E
Newhaven, U.K. 15 50 47N 0 4 E
Newington, Kent, U.K. 15 51 5N 1 8 E
Newington, Kent, U.K. 15 51 21N 0 40 E
Newlyn, U.K. 16 50 6N 5 33W
Newlyn East, U.K. 16 50 22N 5 3W
Newman, Austral. 66 23 18S 119 45 E
Newmarket, Ire. 25 52 13N 9 0W
Newmarket, Lewis, U.K. 22 58 14N 6 24W
Newmarket, Suffolk, U.K. 15 52 15N 0 23 E
Newmilns, U.K. 20 55 36N 4 20W
Newnham, U.K. 14 51 48N 2 27W
Newport, Dyfed, U.K. 17 52 1N 4 53W
Newport, Essex, U.K. 15 51 58N 0 13 E
Newport, Gwent, U.K. 17 51 35N 3 0W
Newport, I. of W., U.K. 14 50 42N 1 18W
Newport, Salop, U.K. 14 52 47N 2 22W
Newport News, U.S.A. 91 37 2N 76 30W
Newport on Tay, U.K. 21 56 27N 2 56W
Newport Pagnell, U.K. 15 52 5N 0 42W
Newquay, U.K. 16 50 24N 5 6W
Newry, U.K. 24 54 10N 6 20W
Newry & Mourne □, U.K. 24 54 10N 6 15W
Newton Abbot, U.K. 16 50 32N 3 37W
Newton Arlosh, U.K. 18 54 53N 3 15W
Newton-Aycliffe, U.K. 19 54 36N 1 33W
Newton Ferrers, U.K. 16 50 19N 4 3W
Newton le Willows, U.K. 18 53 28N 2 40W
Newton St. Cyres, U.K. 16 50 46N 3 35W
Newton Stewart, U.K. 20 54 57N 4 30W
Newtongrange, U.K. 21 55 52N 3 4W
Newtonmore, U.K. 23 57 4N 4 7W
Newtown, Scotland, U.K. 21 55 34N 2 38W
Newtown, Wales, U.K. 17 52 31N 3 19W
Newtownabbey, Ire. 24 54 40N 5 55W
Newtownabbey □, U.K. 24 54 45N 6 0W
Newtownards, U.K. 24 54 37N 5 40W
Nha Trang, Viet. 63 12 16N 109 10 E
Niagara Falls, Canada 92 43 7N 79 5W
Niagara Falls, U.S.A. 92 43 5N 79 0W
Niamey, Niger 78 13 27N 2 6 E
Nicaragua ■, Cent. Am. 94 11 40N 85 30W
Nicaragua, L., Nic. 94 12 0N 85 30W
Nice, Fr. 35 43 42N 7 14 E
Nicobar Is., Ind. Oc. 51 9 0N 93 0 E
Nicosia, Cyprus 47 35 10N 33 25 E
Nicoya, Pen. de, C.R. 94 9 45N 85 40W

Nidd →, U.K. 19 54 1N 1 32W
Nidderdale, U.K. 19 54 5N 1 46W
Niger ■, W. Afr. 78 13 30N 10 0 E
Niger →, W. Afr. 78 5 33N 6 33 E
Nigeria ■, W. Afr. 78 8 30N 8 0 E
Niigata, Jap. 62 37 58N 139 0 E
Niihau, U.S.A. 90 21 55N 160 10W
Nijmegen, Neth. 36 51 50N 5 52 E
Nikolayev, U.S.S.R. 47 46 58N 32 0 E
Nikolayevsk, U.S.S.R. 49 50 0N 45 35 E
Nile →, Africa 79 30 10N 31 6 E
Nîmes, Fr. 35 43 50N 4 23 E
Ninety Mile Beach, The, Austral. 70 38 15S 147 24 E
Ninfield, U.K. 15 50 53N 0 26 E
Ningbo, China 61 29 51N 121 28 E
Ningxia Huizu Zizhiqu □, China 60 38 0N 106 0 E
Niort, Fr. 35 46 19N 0 29W
Nipigon, L., Canada 92 49 50N 88 30W
Niš, Yug. 41 43 19N 21 58 E
Niterói, Brazil 101 22 52S 43 0W
Nith →, U.K. 21 55 20N 3 5W
Nithsdale, U.K. 21 55 14N 3 50W
Niton, U.K. 14 50 35N 1 14W
Nizhniy Tagil, U.S.S.R. 46 57 55N 59 57 E
Nkongsamba, Cam. 80 4 55N 9 55 E
Nobeoka, Jap. 62 32 36N 131 41 E
Nogales, Mex. 94 31 20N 110 56W
Nordelph, U.K. 15 52 34N 0 18 E
Nordhorn, W. Ger. 36 52 27N 7 4 E
Nordvik, U.S.S.R. 49 74 2N 111 32 E
Nore →, Ire. 25 52 40N 7 20W
Norfolk, U.S.A. 91 36 40N 76 15W
Norfolk □, U.K. 15 52 39N 1 0 E
Norfolk Broads, U.K. 15 52 30N 1 15 E
Norfolk I., Pac. Oc. 64 28 58S 168 3 E
Norham, U.K. 21 55 44N 2 9W
Norilsk, U.S.S.R. 49 69 20N 88 6 E
Norman, U.S.A. 90 35 12N 97 30W
Normandy, Fr. 34 48 45N 0 10 E
Normanton, U.K. 19 53 41N 1 26W
Norrbotten □, Swed. 44 66 30N 22 30 E
Norrköping, Swed. 45 58 37N 16 11 E
Norrland □, Swed. 44 66 50N 18 0 E
Norseman, Austral. 66 32 8S 121 43 E
North Battleford, Canada 88 52 50N 108 17W
North Bay, Canada 92 46 20N 79 30W
North Berwick, U.K. 21 56 4N 2 44W
North Cape, Nor. 44 71 15N 25 40 E
North Carolina □, U.S.A. 91 35 30N 80 0W
North Cerney, U.K. 14 51 45N 1 58W
North Channel, U.K. 20 55 0N 5 30W
North Collingham, U.K. 19 53 8N 0 46W
North Dakota □, U.S.A. 90 47 30N 100 0W
North Dorset Downs, U.K. 14 50 50N 2 30W
North Down □, U.K. 24 54 40N 5 45W
North Downs, U.K. 15 51 17N 0 30 E
North Esk →, U.K. 23 56 44N 2 25W
North European Plain 26 55 0N 20 0 E
North Foreland, U.K. 15 51 22N 1 28 E
North Hill, U.K. 16 50 33N 4 26W
North Hykeham, U.K. 19 53 10N 0 35W
North I., N.Z. 71 38 0S 175 0 E
North Minch, U.K. 22 58 5N 5 55W
North Molton, U.K. 16 51 3N 3 48W
North Petherton, U.K. 14 51 6N 3 1W
North Pole, Arctic 103 90 0N 0 0 E
North Queensferry, U.K. 21 56 1N 3 22W
North Rhine Westphalia □, W. Ger. 42 51 55N 7 0 E
North Ronaldsay, U.K. 23 59 20N 2 30W
North Sea, Europe 26 56 0N 4 0 E
North Somercotes, U.K. 19 53 28N 0 9 E
North Sunderland, U.K. 21 55 35N 1 40W
North Tawton, U.K. 16 50 48N 3 55W
North Thoresby, U.K. 19 53 27N 0 3W
North Tidworth, U.K. 14 51 14N 1 40W
North Tyne →, U.K. 19 54 59N 2 7W
North Uist, U.K. 22 57 40N 7 15W
North Walsham, U.K. 15 52 49N 1 22 E
North West Highlands, U.K. 22 57 35N 5 2W
North West Territories □, Canada 89 67 0N 110 0W
North York Moors, U.K. 19 54 25N 0 50W
North Yorkshire □, U.K. 19 54 15N 1 25W
Northallerton, U.K. 19 54 20N 1 26W
Northam, Austral. 66 31 35S 116 42 E
Northam, U.K. 16 51 2N 4 13W
Northampton, U.K. 15 52 14N 0 54W
Northampton □, U.K. 15 52 16N 0 55W
Northern Ireland □, U.K. 24 54 45N 7 0W
Northern Marianas, Pac. Oc. 64 17 0N 145 0 E
Northern Territory □, Austral. 66 16 0S 133 0 E
Northfleet, U.K. 15 51 26N 0 20 E
Northiam, U.K. 15 50 59N 0 39 E
Northland □, N.Z. 71 35 30S 173 30 E
Northleach, U.K. 14 51 49N 1 50W
Northrepps, U.K. 15 52 53N 1 20 E
Northumberland □, U.K. 19 55 12N 2 0W
Northumberland Str., Canada 93 46 20N 64 0W
Northwich, U.K. 18 53 16N 2 30W
Northwold, U.K. 15 52 33N 0 37 E
Norton, N. Yorks., U.K. 19 54 9N 0 48W
Norton, Suffolk, U.K. 15 52 15N 0 52 E
Norton Fitzwarren, U.K. 14 51 1N 3 10W
Norway ■, Europe 44 63 0N 11 0 E
Norwegian Sea, Atl. Oc. 44 66 0N 1 0 E
Norwich, U.K. 15 52 38N 1 17 E
Noss Hd., U.K. 23 58 29N 3 4W
Nottingham, U.K. 19 52 57N 1 10W
Nottingham □, U.K. 19 53 10N 1 0W
Nouâdhibou, Maurit. 78 20 54N 17 0W
Nouakchott, Maurit. 78 18 9N 15 58W
Nouméa, N. Cal. 64 22 17S 166 30 E
Nova Scotia □, Canada 93 45 10N 63 0W
Novara, It. 40 45 27N 8 36 E
Novaya Zemlya, U.S.S.R. 48 75 0N 56 0 E
Novi Sad, Yug. 41 45 18N 19 52 E
Novocherkassk, U.S.S.R. 47 47 27N 40 5 E
Novokuznetsk, U.S.S.R. 48 53 45N 87 10 E
Novomoskovsk, U.S.S.R. 46 54 5N 38 15 E
Novorossiysk, U.S.S.R. 47 44 43N 37 46 E
Novoshakhtinsk, U.S.S.R. 47 47 46N 39 58 E
Novosibirsk, U.S.S.R. 48 55 0N 83 5 E
Nubian Desert, Sudan 79 21 30N 33 30 E
Nuevo Laredo, Mex. 94 27 30N 99 30W
Nullarbor Plain, Austral. 66 30 45S 129 0 E
Nuneaton, U.K. 14 52 32N 1 29W
Nunney, U.K. 14 51 13N 2 20W
Nuremburg, W. Ger. 42 49 26N 11 5 E
Nyasa, L., Africa 81 12 30S 34 30 E
Nyíregyháza, Hung. 43 47 58N 21 47 E
Nykøbing, Den. 45 56 48N 8 51 E

O

Oa, Mull of, U.K. 20 55 35N 6 20W
Oa, The, Pen., U.K. 20 55 36N 6 17W
Oadby, U.K. 14 52 37N 1 7W
Oahe L., U.S.A. 90 45 30N 100 25W
Oahu, U.S.A. 90 21 30N 158 0W
Oakengates, U.K. 14 52 42N 2 29W
Oakham, U.K. 15 52 40N 0 43W
Oakland, U.S.A. 90 37 50N 122 18W
Oakleigh, Austral. 70 37 54S 145 6 E
Oamaru, N.Z. 71 45 5S 170 59 E
Oaxaca, Mex. 94 17 2N 96 40W
Ob →, U.S.S.R. 48 66 45N 69 30 E
Ob, G. of, U.S.S.R. 48 70 0N 73 0 E
Oban, U.K. 20 56 25N 5 30W
Oberhausen, W. Ger. 36 51 28N 6 50 E
Ochil Hills, U.K. 21 56 14N 3 40W
Ochiltree, U.K. 20 55 26N 4 23W
October Revolution I., U.S.S.R. 49 79 30N 97 0 E
Odense, Den. 45 55 22N 10 23 E
Odessa, U.S.A. 90 31 51N 102 23W
Odessa, U.S.S.R. 47 46 30N 30 45 E
Odiham, U.K. 15 51 16N 0 56W
Odra →, Pol. 42 53 33N 14 38 E
Offaly □, Ire. 25 53 15N 7 30W
Offenbach, W. Ger. 42 50 6N 8 46 E
Ogbomosho, Nig. 78 8 1N 4 11 E
Ogden, U.S.A. 90 41 13N 112 1W
Ohio □, U.S.A. 92 40 20N 14 10 E
Ohio →, U.S.A. 92 38 0N 86 0W
Ōita, Jap. 62 33 14N 131 36 E
Okavango Swamps, Bots. 81 18 45S 22 45 E
Okayama, Jap. 62 34 40N 133 54 E
Okazaki, Jap. 62 34 57N 137 10 E
Okehampton, U.K. 16 50 44N 4 1W
Okhotsk, U.S.S.R. 49 59 20N 143 10 E
Okhotsk, Sea of, Asia 49 55 0N 145 0 E
Oklahoma □, U.S.A. 90 35 20N 97 30W
Oklahoma City, U.S.A. 91 35 25N 97 30W
Ólafsfjörður, Ice. 44 66 4N 18 39W
Öland, Swed. 45 56 45N 16 38 E
Old Basing, U.K. 14 51 16N 1 3W
Old Castile, Sp. 37 41 55N 4 0W
Old Castle, Ire. 24 53 46N 7 10W
Old Kilpatrick, U.K. 20 55 56N 4 34W
Old Leake, U.K. 19 53 2N 0 6 E
Oldbury, Gloucs., U.K. 14 51 38N 2 30W
Oldbury, W. Midlands, U.K. 14 52 30N 2 0W
Oldenburg, W. Ger. 36 53 10N 8 10 E
Oldham, U.K. 18 53 33N 2 8W
Oldmeldrum, U.K. 23 57 20N 2 19W
Olekminsk, U.S.S.R. 49 60 25N 120 30 E
Olinda, Brazil 101 8 1S 34 51W
Ollerton, U.K. 19 53 12N 1 1W
Olney, U.K. 15 52 9N 0 42W
Olomouc, Czech. 42 49 38N 17 12 E
Olsztyn, Pol. 43 53 48N 20 29 E
Olympia, Greece 41 37 39N 21 39 E
Olympus, Mt., Greece 41 40 6N 22 23 E
Omagh, U.K. 24 54 36N 7 20W
Omagh □, U.K. 24 54 35N 7 15W
Omaha, U.S.A. 91 41 15N 96 0W
Oman ■, Si. Arab. 57 23 0N 58 0 E
Oman, G. of, Asia 57 24 30N 58 30 E
Ombersley, U.K. 14 52 17N 2 12W
Omdurmân, Sudan 79 15 40N 32 28 E
Ōmiya, Jap. 62 35 54N 139 38 E
Omsk, U.S.S.R. 48 55 0N 73 12 E
Ōmuta, Jap. 62 33 0N 130 26 E
Onchan, U.K. 18 54 11N 4 27W
Onega →, U.S.S.R. 46 63 58N 37 55 E
Onega, G. of, U.S.S.R. 46 64 30N 37 0 E
Onega, L., U.S.S.R. 46 62 0N 35 30 E
Onehunga, N.Z. 71 36 55S 174 48 E
Onny →, U.K. 14 52 30N 2 50W
Ontario □, Canada 88 52 0N 88 10W
Ontario, L., N. Am. 92 43 40N 78 0W
Opole, Pol. 43 50 42N 17 58 E
Oporto, Port. 37 41 8N 8 40W
Oradea, Rom. 43 47 2N 21 58 E
Oran, Alg. 78 35 45N 0 39W
Orange, Austral. 70 33 15S 149 7 E
Orange →, S. Afr. 81 28 41S 16 28 E
Orange Free State □, S. Afr. 81 28 30S 27 0 E
Ord, Mt., Austral. 66 17 20S 125 34 E
Ordos = Mu Us Shamo, China 61 39 0N 109 0 E
Ordzhonikidze, U.S.S.R. 47 43 0N 44 35 E
Örebro, Swed. 45 59 20N 15 18 E
Oregon □, U.S.A. 90 44 0N 121 0W
Orekhovo-Zuyevo, U.S.S.R. 46 55 50N 38 55 E
Orel, U.S.S.R. 46 52 57N 36 3 E
Orenburg, U.S.S.R. 46 51 45N 55 6 E
Orense, Sp. 37 42 19N 7 55W
Orford, U.K. 15 52 6N 1 31 E
Orford Ness, U.K. 15 52 6N 1 31 E
Orinoco →, Ven. 100 9 15N 61 30W
Orissa □, India 59 20 0N 84 0 E
Oristano, It. 40 39 54N 8 35 E
Orizaba, Mex. 94 18 51N 97 6W
Orkney □, U.K. 23 59 0N 3 0W
Orkney Is., U.K. 23 59 0N 3 0W
Orlando, U.S.A. 91 28 30N 81 25W
Orléans, Fr. 34 47 54N 1 52 E
Ormesby St. Margaret, U.K. 15 52 39N 1 42 E
Ormskirk, U.K. 18 53 35N 2 53W
Örnsköldsvik, Swed. 44 63 17N 18 40 E
Oronsay, Pass of, U.K. 20 56 0N 6 10W
Oronsay I., U.K. 20 56 0N 6 14W
Orsk, U.S.S.R. 46 51 12N 58 34 E
Orton Tebay, U.K. 18 54 28N 2 35W
Oruro, Bol. 100 18 0S 67 9W
Orwell →, U.K. 15 52 2N 1 12 E
Ōsaka, Jap. 62 34 40N 135 30 E
Osh, U.S.S.R. 48 40 37N 72 49 E
Oshawa, Canada 92 43 50N 78 50W
Oshogbo, Nig. 78 7 48N 4 37 E
Osijek, Yug. 41 45 34N 18 41 E
Osizweni, S. Afr. 81 27 49S 30 7 E
Oslo, Nor. 45 59 55N 10 45 E
Oslo Fjord, Nor. 45 58 30N 10 0 E
Osmotherley, U.K. 19 54 22N 1 18W
Osnabrück, W. Ger. 36 52 16N 8 2 E
Osorno, Chile 102 40 25S 73 0W
Ossett, U.K. 19 53 40N 1 35W
Ostend, Belg. 36 51 15N 2 50 E
Östersund, Swed. 44 63 10N 14 38 E
Ostrava, Czech. 43 49 51N 18 18 E
Osumi, Is., Jap. 62 30 30N 130 45 E
Oswaldtwistle, U.K. 18 53 44N 2 27W
Oswestry, U.K. 14 52 52N 3 3W
Otago □, N.Z. 71 44 44S 169 10 E
Otaru, Jap. 62 43 10N 141 0 E
Otley, U.K. 19 53 54N 1 41W
Otranto, Str. of, It. 41 40 15N 18 40 E
Ōtsu, Jap. 62 35 0N 135 50 E
Ottawa, Canada 93 45 27N 75 42W
Ottawa →, Canada 93 45 27N 74 8W
Otter →, U.K. 16 50 47N 3 12W
Otter Ferry, U.K. 20 56 1N 5 20W
Otterburn, U.K. 21 55 14N 2 12W
Ottery St. Mary, U.K. 16 50 45N 3 16W
Ouagadougou, B. Faso 78 12 25N 1 30W
Oujda, Mor. 78 34 41N 1 55W
Oulton, U.K. 15 52 29N 1 40 E
Oulton Broad, U.K. 15 52 28N 1 43 E
Oulu, Fin. 44 65 1N 25 29 E
Oulu, L., Fin. 44 64 25N 27 0 E
Oundle, U.K. 15 52 28N 0 28W
Ouse →, E. Sussex, U.K. 15 50 43N 0 3 E
Ouse →, N. Yorks., U.K. 19 54 3N 0 7 E
Outer Hebrides, U.K. 22 57 30N 7 40W
Outwell, U.K. 15 52 36N 0 14 E
Over Wallop, U.K. 14 51 9N 1 35W
Overstand, U.K. 15 52 55N 1 20W
Overton, U.K. 14 51 14N 1 16W
Oviedo, Sp. 37 43 25N 5 50W
Owston Ferry, U.K. 19 53 28N 0 47W
Ox Mts., Ire. 24 54 6N 9 0W
Oxford, U.K. 14 51 45N 1 15W
Oxford □, U.K. 14 51 45N 1 15W
Oykel →, U.K. 23 57 55N 4 26W
Ozark Plateau, U.S.A. 91 37 20N 91 40W

P

Paarl, S. Afr. 81 33 45S 18 56 E
Pacaraima, Sierra, Ven. 100 4 0N 62 30W
Pachuca, Mex. 94 20 10N 98 40W
Pacific Ocean 64 10 0N 140 0W
Padang, Indon. 63 1 0S 100 20 E
Paddock Wood, U.K. 15 51 13N 0 24 E
Padiham, U.K. 18 53 48N 2 20W
Padstow, U.K. 14 50 33N 4 57W
Padstow Bay, U.K. 16 50 35N 4 58W
Padua, It. 40 45 24N 11 52 E
Pagalu = Annobón, Atl. Oc. 73 1 25S 5 36 E
Paignton, U.K. 16 50 26N 3 33W
Painswick, U.K. 14 51 47N 2 11W
Paisley, U.K. 20 55 51N 4 27W
Pakistan ■, Asia 58 30 0N 70 0 E
Palawan, Phil. 63 9 30N 118 30 E
Palembang, Indon. 63 3 0S 104 50 E
Palencia, Sp. 37 42 1N 4 34W
Palermo, It. 40 38 8N 13 20 E
Palgrave, U.K. 15 52 22N 1 7 E
Palk Strait, Asia 58 10 0N 79 45 E
Palma de Mallorca, Sp. 37 39 35N 2 39 E
Palmer →, Austral. 66 24 46S 133 25 E
Palmerston North, N.Z. 71 40 21S 175 39 E
Palmira, Col. 100 3 32N 76 16W
Pamirs, U.S.S.R. 48 37 40N 73 0 E
Pamlico Sd., U.S.A. 91 35 20N 76 0W
Pampas, Arg. 96 35 0S 63 0W
Pamplona, Sp. 37 42 48N 1 38W
Panamá, Pan. 94 9 0N 79 25W
Panama ■, Cent. Am. 95 8 48N 79 55W
Panamá, G. de, Pan. 95 8 4N 79 20W
Panama Canal, Pan. 94 9 10N 79 37W
Panay, Phil. 63 11 10N 122 30 E
Pančevo, Yug. 41 44 52N 20 41 E
Pangbourne, U.K. 14 51 28N 1 5W
Pantelleria, It. 40 36 52N 12 0 E
Papua New Guinea ■, Oc. 64 8 0S 145 0 E
Pará □, Brazil 101 3 20S 52 0W
Paraguay ■, S. Am. 102 23 0S 57 0W
Paraguay →, Par. 102 27 18S 58 38W
Paramaribo, Surinam 101 5 50N 55 10W
Paraná, Arg. 102 31 45S 60 30W
Paraná →, Arg. 102 33 43S 59 15W
Parecis, Serra dos, Brazil 100 13 0S 60 0W
Parepare, Indon. 63 4 0S 119 40 E
Paris, Fr. 34 48 50N 2 20 E
Parkes, Austral. 70 33 9S 148 11 E
Parma, It. 40 44 50N 10 20 E
Parnaíba →, Brazil 101 3 0S 41 50W
Parracombe, U.K. 16 51 11N 3 55W
Parramatta, Austral. 70 33 48S 151 1 E
Parrett →, U.K. 14 51 7N 2 58W
Partney, U.K. 19 53 12N 0 7 E
Parton, U.K. 18 54 34N 3 35W
Passage West, Ire. 25 51 52N 8 20W
Pasto, Col. 100 1 13N 77 17W
Patagonia, Arg. 102 45 0S 69 0W
Patcham, U.K. 15 50 52N 0 9W
Pateley Bridge, U.K. 19 54 5N 1 45W
Paterson, U.S.A. 93 40 55N 74 10W
Patna, India 59 25 35N 85 12 E
Patna, U.K. 20 55 21N 4 30W
Pátrai, Greece 41 38 14N 21 47 E
Patrick, U.K. 18 54 13N 4 41W
Patrington, U.K. 19 53 41N 0 1W
Patterdale, U.K. 18 54 33N 2 55W
Pau, Fr. 35 43 19N 0 25W
Paull, U.K. 19 53 42N 0 12W
Pavia, It. 40 45 10N 9 10 E
Pavlodar, U.S.S.R. 48 52 33N 77 0 E
Pawtucket, U.S.A. 93 41 51N 71 22W
Paz, La, Bol. 100 16 20S 68 10W
Pazardzhik, Bulg. 41 42 12N 24 20 E
Peace →, Canada 88 59 0N 111 25W
Peacehaven, U.K. 15 50 47N 0 1 E
Peak, The, U.K. 18 53 24N 1 53W
Peasenhall, U.K. 15 52 17N 1 24 E
Pechora →, U.S.S.R. 46 68 13N 54 15 E
Pécs, Hung. 43 46 5N 18 15 E
Peebles, U.K. 21 55 40N 3 12W
Peel, U.K. 18 54 14N 4 40W
Peel Fell, U.K. 21 55 17N 2 35W
Pegasus Bay, N.Z. 71 43 20S 173 10 E
Pegswood, U.K. 21 55 12N 1 38W
Pegu, Burma 59 17 20N 96 29 E
Pegu Yoma, Burma 59 19 0N 96 0 E
Pegwell Bay, U.K. 15 51 18N 1 22 E
Pekanbaru, Indon. 63 0 30N 101 15 E
Peking, China 61 39 55N 116 20 E
Peloponnese □, Greece 41 37 10N 22 0 E
Pelotas, Brazil 102 31 42S 52 23W
Pelvoux, Massif de, Fr. 35 44 52N 6 20 E
Pematangsiantar, Indon. 63 2 57N 99 5 E
Pemba, Tanz. 80 5 0S 39 45 E
Pembridge, U.K. 14 52 13N 2 54W
Pembroke, U.K. 17 51 41N 4 57W
Pembury, U.K. 15 51 8N 0 20 E
Pen-y-Ghent, U.K. 18 54 10N 2 15W
Pen-y-groes, U.K. 17 53 3N 4 18W
Penang = Pinang, Malay. 63 5 25N 100 15 E
Penarth, U.K. 17 51 26N 3 11W
Pendeen, U.K. 16 50 11N 5 39W
Pendle Hill, U.K. 18 53 53N 2 18W
Penicuik, U.K. 21 55 50N 3 14W
Peninsular Malaysia □, Malay. 63 4 0N 102 0 E
Penistone, U.K. 19 53 31N 1 38W
Penkridge, U.K. 14 52 44N 2 8W
Pennines, U.K. 18 54 50N 2 20W
Pennsylvania □, U.S.A. 92 40 50N 78 0W
Penpont, U.K. 21 55 14N 3 49W

Rhayader

Rhayader, U.K. 17 52 19N 3 30W
Rheidol →, U.K. 17 52 25N 4 5W
Rhein →, W. Ger. 36 51 52N 6 20 E
Rheine, W. Ger. 36 52 17N 7 25 E
Rhine = Rhein →, W. Ger. 36 51 52N 6 20 E
Rhineland-Palatinate □, W. Ger. 42 50 0N 7 0 E
Rhins, The, U.K. 20 54 52N 5 3W
Rhode Island □, U.S.A. 93 41 38N 71 37W
Rhodes = Ródhos, Greece 41 36 15N 28 10 E
Rhodesia = Zimbabwe ■, Africa 81 20 0S 30 0 E
Rhodope Mts., Bulg. 41 41 40N 24 20 E
Rhondda, U.K. 17 51 39N 3 30W
Rhône →, Fr. 35 43 28N 4 42 E
Rhosllanerchrugog, U.K. 17 53 3N 3 4W
Rhossili, U.K. 17 51 34N 4 18W
Rhum, U.K. 22 57 0N 6 20W
Rhyl, U.K. 17 53 19N 3 29W
Rhymney, U.K. 17 51 32N 3 7W
Ribble →, U.K. 18 54 13N 2 20W
Ribeirão Prêto, Brazil 101 21 10S 47 50W
Riccall, U.K. 19 53 50N 1 4W
Riccarton, N.Z. 71 43 32S 172 37 E
Riccarton Junc., U.K. 21 55 16N 2 43W
Richmond, N. Yorks., U.K. 19 54 24N 1 43W
Richmond, Surrey, U.K. 15 51 28N 0 18W
Richmond, U.S.A. 92 37 33N 77 27W
Rickmansworth, U.K. 15 51 38N 0 28W
Ridsdale, U.K. 21 55 9N 2 8W
Rievaulx, U.K. 19 54 16N 1 7W
Riga, U.S.S.R. 46 56 53N 24 8 E
Riga, G. of, U.S.S.R. 46 57 40N 23 45 E
Rijeka, Yug. 40 45 20N 14 21 E
Rijswijk, Neth. 36 52 4N 4 22 E
Rillington, U.K. 19 54 10N 0 41W
Rímini, It. 40 44 3N 12 33 E
Rîmnicu Vîlcea, Rom. 43 45 9N 24 21 E
Rimouski, Canada 93 48 27N 68 30W
Rineanna, Ire. 25 52 42N 85 7W
Ringford, U.K. 21 54 55N 4 3W
Ringmer, U.K. 15 50 53N 0 5 E
Ringwood, U.K. 14 50 50N 1 48W
Rio Branco, Brazil 100 9 58S 67 49W
Río Cuarto, Arg. 102 33 10S 64 25W
Rio de Janeiro, Brazil 101 23 0S 43 12W
Río Gallegos, Arg. 102 51 35S 69 15W
Rio Grande, Brazil 102 32 0S 52 20W
Rio Grande →, U.S.A. 90 25 57N 97 9W
Rio Grande do Norte □, Brazil 94 5 40S 36 0W
Río Muni = Mbini □, Eq. Guin. 80 1 30N 10 0 E
Ríobamba, Ecuad. 100 1 50S 78 45W
Ripley, Derby, U.K. 19 53 3N 1 24W
Ripley, N. Yorks., U.K. 19 54 3N 1 34W
Ripon, U.K. 19 54 8N 1 31W
Risca, U.K. 17 51 36N 3 6W
Rishton, U.K. 18 53 46N 2 26W
Riverside, U.S.A. 90 34 0N 117 22W
Riyadh, Si. Arab. 56 24 41N 46 42 E
Roade, U.K. 15 52 10N 0 53W
Roadhead, U.K. 18 55 4N 2 44W
Roag, L., U.K. 22 58 10N 6 55W
Roanne, Fr. 35 46 3N 4 4 E
Roanoke, U.S.A. 92 37 19N 79 55W
Robe →, Ire. 24 53 38N 9 10W
Roberton, U.K. 21 55 24N 2 53W
Robin Hood's Bay, U.K. 19 54 26N 0 31W
Rocester, U.K. 18 52 56N 1 50W
Rochdale, U.K. 18 53 36N 2 10W
Roche, U.K. 16 50 24N 4 50W
Rochelle, La, Fr. 35 46 10N 1 9W
Rochester, Kent, U.K. 15 51 22N 0 30 E
Rochester, Northumberland, U.K. 21 55 16N 2 16W
Rochester, Minn., U.S.A. 90 44 1N 92 28W
Rochester, N.Y., U.S.A. 92 43 10N 77 40W
Rochford, U.K. 15 51 36N 0 42 E
Rockall, Atl. Oc. 26 57 37N 13 42W
Rockcliffe, U.K. 18 54 58N 3 0W
Rockford, U.S.A. 92 42 20N 89 0W
Rockhampton, Austral. 67 23 22S 150 32 E
Rockingham, U.K. 15 52 32N 0 43W
Rockingham Forest, U.K. 15 52 28N 0 42W
Rocky Mts., N. Am. 90 55 0N 121 0W
Ródhos, Greece 41 36 15N 28 10 E
Roding →, U.K. 15 51 31N 0 7 E
Roe →, U.K. 24 55 10N 6 59W
Roeselare, Belg. 36 50 57N 3 7 E
Rogaland fylke □, Nor. 45 59 12N 6 20 E
Rogans Seat, U.K. 18 54 25N 2 10W
Rogate, U.K. 15 51 0N 0 51W
Roma, Austral. 67 26 32S 148 49 E
Roma = Rome, It. 40 41 54N 12 30 E
Romania ■, Europe 43 46 0N 25 0 E
Rome, It. 40 41 54N 12 30 E
Romney Marsh, U.K. 15 51 0N 1 0 E
Romsey, U.K. 14 51 0N 1 29W
Rona, U.K. 22 57 33N 6 0W
Ronse, Belg. 36 50 45N 3 35 E
Roosendaal, Neth. 36 51 32N 4 29 E
Roper →, Austral. 67 14 43S 135 27 E
Ropsley, U.K. 19 52 53N 0 31W
Roraima, Mt., Ven. 101 5 10N 60 40W
Rosario, Arg. 102 33 0S 60 40W
Roscommon, Ire. 24 53 38N 8 11W
Roscommon □, Ire. 24 53 40N 8 15W
Roscrea, Ire. 25 52 58N 7 50W
Roseau, Dom. 94 15 20N 61 24W
Rosedale Abbey, U.K. 19 54 22N 0 51W
Roskilde, Den. 45 55 38N 12 3 E
Rosneath, U.K. 20 56 1N 4 49W
Ross Ice Shelf, Ant. 103 80 0S 180 0 E
Ross on Wye, U.K. 14 51 55N 2 34W
Ross Sea, Ant. 103 74 0S 178 0 E
Rossall Pt., U.K. 18 53 55N 3 2W
Rossan Pt., Ire. 24 54 42N 8 47W
Rosslare, Ire. 25 52 17N 6 23W
Rostock, E. Ger. 42 54 4N 12 9 E
Rostov, U.S.S.R. 47 47 15N 39 45 E
Rosyth, U.K. 21 56 2N 3 26W
Rothbury, U.K. 21 55 19N 1 55W
Rothbury Forest, U.K. 21 55 19N 1 50W
Rother →, U.K. 15 50 59N 0 40 E
Rotherham, U.K. 19 53 26N 1 21W
Rothes, U.K. 23 57 31N 3 12W
Rothesay, U.K. 20 55 50N 5 3W
Rothwell, Northants., U.K. 15 52 25N 0 48W
Rothwell, W. Yorks., U.K. 19 53 46N 1 29W
Rotorua, N.Z. 71 38 9S 176 16 E
Rotorua, L., N.Z. 71 38 5S 176 18 E
Rotterdam, Neth. 36 51 55N 4 30 E
Rottingdean, U.K. 15 50 48N 0 3W
Roubaix, Fr. 34 50 40N 3 10 E
Rouen, Fr. 34 49 27N 1 4 E
Rousay, U.K. 23 59 10N 3 2W
Rowanburn, U.K. 21 55 5N 2 54W
Rowrah, U.K. 18 54 34N 3 26W
Roxburgh, U.K. 21 55 34N 2 30W
Roxby, U.K. 19 53 38N 0 37W
Royston, U.K. 15 52 3N 0 1W
Royton, U.K. 18 53 34N 2 7W
Ruahine Ra., N.Z. 71 39 55S 176 2 E
Rub' al Khali, Si. Arab. 56 18 0N 48 0 E
Rubery, U.K. 14 52 24N 1 59W
Rubh a' Mhail, U.K. 20 55 55N 6 10W
Rubha Hunish, U.K. 22 57 42N 6 20W
Rudgwick, U.K. 15 51 7N 0 54W
Rudston, U.K. 19 54 6N 0 19W
Rufford, U.K. 18 53 37N 2 50W
Rugby, U.K. 14 52 23N 1 16W
Rugeley, U.K. 14 52 47N 1 56W
Rum Jungle, Austral. 66 13 0S 130 59 E
Runcorn, U.K. 18 53 20N 2 44W
Ruse, Bulg. 41 43 48N 25 59 E
Rushden, U.K. 15 52 17N 0 37W
Ruskington, U.K. 19 53 5N 0 23W
Russian S.F.S.R. □, U.S.S.R. 46 62 0N 105 0 E
Rutherglen, U.K. 20 55 50N 4 11W
Ruthin, U.K. 17 53 7N 3 20W
Ruthwell, U.K. 21 55 0N 3 24W
Rwanda ■, Africa 80 2 0S 30 0 E
Ryan, L., U.K. 20 55 0N 5 2W
Ryazan, U.S.S.R. 46 54 40N 39 40 E
Rybinsk = Andropov, U.S.S.R. 46 58 5N 38 50 E
Rybinsk Res., U.S.S.R. 46 58 30N 38 0 E
Rydal, U.K. 18 54 28N 2 59W
Ryde, U.K. 14 50 44N 1 9W
Rye, U.K. 15 50 57N 0 46 E
Rye →, U.K. 19 54 12N 0 53W
Rye Bay, U.K. 15 50 50N 0 50 E
Ryhope, U.K. 21 54 52N 1 22W
Ryton, Tyne & Wear, U.K. 21 54 58N 1 44W
Ryton, Warwick, U.K. 14 52 23N 1 25W
Ryūkyū Is., Jap. 62 26 0N 128 0 E
Rzeszów, Pol. 43 50 5N 21 58 E

S

Saarbrücken, W. Ger. 36 49 15N 6 58 E
Saaremaa, U.S.S.R. 46 58 30N 22 30 E
Saarland □, W. Ger. 36 49 15N 7 0 E
Saba, W. Ind. 94 17 42N 63 26W
Sabadell, Sp. 37 41 28N 2 7 E
Sabah □, Malay. 63 6 0N 117 0 E
Sabhah, Libya 79 27 9N 14 29 E
Sacramento, U.S.A. 90 38 33N 121 30 E
Sacriston, U.K. 19 54 49N 1 38W
Saddell, U.K. 20 55 31N 5 30W
Saffron Walden, U.K. 15 52 2N 0 15 E
Safi, Mor. 78 32 18N 9 20W
Sagar, India 58 14 14N 75 6 E
Saginaw, U.S.A. 92 43 26N 83 55W
Saginaw B., U.S.A. 92 43 50N 83 40W
Sahara, Africa 78 23 0N 5 0 E
Saharan Atlas, Alg. 78 34 9N 3 29 E
Saharanpur, India 58 29 58N 77 33 E
Saigon = Ho Chi Minh City, Viet. 63 10 58N 106 40 E
St. Abb's, U.K. 21 55 54N 2 7W
St. Abb's Head, U.K. 21 55 55N 2 10W
St. Agnes, U.K. 16 50 18N 5 13W
St. Agnes Hd., U.K. 16 50 19N 5 14W
St. Agnes I., U.K. 16 49 53N 6 20W
St. Albans, U.K. 15 51 44N 0 19W
St. Alban's Head, U.K. 14 50 34N 2 3W
St. Andrews, U.K. 21 56 20N 2 48W
St. Ann's, U.K. 21 55 14N 3 28W
St. Asaph, U.K. 17 53 15N 3 27W
St. Austell, U.K. 16 50 20N 4 48W
St. Bees, U.K. 18 54 29N 3 36W
St. Bee's Hd., U.K. 18 54 30N 3 38 E
St. Blazey, U.K. 16 50 22N 4 48W
St. Boniface, Canada 88 49 53N 97 5W
St. Boswells, U.K. 21 55 34N 2 39W
St. Briavels, U.K. 14 51 44N 2 39W
St. Brides B., U.K. 17 51 48N 5 15W
St.-Brieuc, Fr. 34 48 30N 2 46W
St. Budeaux, U.K. 16 50 23N 4 10W
St. Buryan, U.K. 16 50 4N 5 34W
St. Catharines, Canada 92 43 10N 79 15W
St. Catherine's Pt., U.K. 14 50 34N 1 18W
St. Christopher-Nevis ■, W. Ind. 94 17 20N 62 40W
St. Clair, L., Canada 92 42 30N 82 45W
St.-Claude, Fr. 35 46 22N 5 52 E
St. Clears, U.K. 17 51 48N 4 30W
St. Columb Major, U.K. 16 50 26N 4 56W
St. David's, U.K. 17 51 54N 5 16W
St. David's Head, U.K. 17 51 55N 5 16W
St. Dennis, U.K. 16 50 23N 4 53W
St. Dominick, U.K. 16 50 28N 4 15W
St. Elias Mts., Canada 88 60 33N 139 28W
St. Endellion, U.K. 16 50 33N 4 49W
St. Enoder, U.K. 16 50 22N 4 57W
St. Erth, U.K. 16 50 10N 5 26W
St.-Étienne, Fr. 35 45 27N 4 22 E
St. Fillans, U.K. 21 56 25N 4 7W
St. Gallen, Switz. 42 47 25N 9 20 E
St. George's, Gren. 94 12 5N 61 43W
St. George's Channel, U.K. 25 52 0N 6 0W
St. Germans, U.K. 16 50 24N 4 19W
St. Helena, Atl. Oc. 128 15 55S 5 44W
St. Helena B., S. Afr. 81 32 40S 18 10 E
St. Helens, I. of W., U.K. 14 50 42N 1 6W
St. Helens, Merseyside, U.K. 18 53 28N 2 44W
St. Helier, U.K. 34 49 11N 2 6W
St-Hyacinthe, Canada 93 45 40N 72 58W
St. Issey, U.K. 16 50 30N 4 55W
St. Ives, Cambs., U.K. 15 52 20N 0 5W
St. Ives, Cornwall, U.K. 16 50 13N 5 29W
St. Ives Bay, U.K. 16 50 15N 5 27W
St-Jean, L., Canada 93 48 40N 72 0W
St-Jérôme, Canada 93 45 47N 74 0W
St. John, Canada 93 45 20N 66 8W
St. John's, Antigua 94 17 6N 61 51W
St. John's, Canada 89 47 35N 52 40W
St. John's, U.K. 18 54 13N 4 38W
St. Johns Chapel, U.K. 18 54 43N 2 10W
St. Joseph, U.S.A. 90 39 46N 94 50W
St. Just, U.K. 16 50 7N 5 41W
St. Keverne, U.K. 16 50 3N 5 5W
St. Kew, U.K. 16 50 34N 4 48W
St. Lawrence →, Canada 93 49 30N 66 0W
St. Lawrence, Gulf of, Canada 89 48 25N 62 0W
St. Leonards, U.K. 15 50 51N 0 34 E
St. Levan, U.K. 16 50 3N 5 36W
St.-Lô, Fr. 34 49 7N 1 5W
St-Louis, Sene. 78 16 8N 16 27W
St. Louis, U.S.A. 92 38 40N 90 12W
St. Lucia ■, W. Ind. 94 14 0N 60 50W
St. Maarten, W. Ind. 94 18 0N 63 5W
St. Mabyn, U.K. 16 50 30N 4 45W
St.-Malo, Fr. 34 48 39N 2 1W
St. Margaret's-at-Cliffe, U.K. 15 51 10N 1 23 E
St. Margaret's Hope, U.K. 23 58 49N 2 58W
St-Martin, I., W. Ind. 94 18 0N 63 0W
St. Martin's I., U.K. 16 49 58N 6 16W
St. Mary Bourne, U.K. 14 51 16N 1 24W
St. Mary's, U.K. 16 49 55N 6 17W
St. Mary's Sd., U.K. 16 49 53N 6 19W
St. Mawes, U.K. 16 50 10N 5 1W
St. Merryn, U.K. 16 50 31N 4 58W
St. Michael's Mt., U.K. 16 50 7N 5 30W
St. Minver, U.K. 16 50 34N 4 52W
St. Monance, U.K. 21 56 13N 2 46W
St.-Nazaire, Fr. 34 47 17N 2 12W
St. Neots, U.K. 15 52 14N 0 16W
St-Niklaas, Belg. 36 51 10N 4 8 E
St. Osyth, U.K. 15 51 47N 1 4 E
St. Paul, U.S.A. 91 44 54N 93 5W
St. Peter Port, U.K. 34 49 27N 2 31W
St. Petersburg, U.S.A. 91 27 45N 82 40W
St.-Pierre et Miquelon □, N. Am. 89 46 55N 56 10W
St.-Quentin, Fr. 34 49 50N 3 16 E
St. Stephen, U.K. 16 50 20N 4 52W
St. Teath, U.K. 16 50 34N 4 45W
St.-Tropez, Fr. 35 43 17N 6 38 E
St. Tudy, U.K. 16 50 33N 4 45W
St. Vincent and the Grenadines ■, W. Ind. 94 13 0N 61 10W
Saintfield, U.K. 24 54 28N 5 50W
Sakai, Jap. 62 34 30N 135 30 E
Sakhalin, U.S.S.R. 49 51 0N 143 0 E
Salado →, Arg. 102 31 40S 60 41W
Salamanca, Sp. 37 40 58N 5 39W
Salcombe, U.K. 16 50 14N 3 47W
Salcombe Regis, U.K. 16 50 41N 3 11W
Sale, Austral. 70 38 6S 147 6 E
Sale, U.K. 18 53 26N 2 19W
Salem, India 58 11 40N 78 11 E
Salen, U.K. 20 56 31N 5 57W
Salerno, It. 40 40 40N 14 44 E
Salford, U.K. 18 53 30N 2 17W
Salford Priors, U.K. 14 52 10N 1 52W
Salisbury = Harare, Zimb. 81 17 43S 31 2 E
Salisbury, U.K. 14 51 4N 1 48W
Salisbury Plain, U.K. 14 51 13N 1 50W
Salonica = Thessaloníki, Greece 41 40 38N 22 58 E
Salop = Shropshire □, U.K. 14 52 36N 2 45W
Salt Lake City, U.S.A. 90 40 45N 111 58W
Salta, Arg. 102 24 57S 65 25W
Saltash, U.K. 16 50 25N 4 13W
Saltburn by the Sea, U.K. 19 54 35N 0 58W
Saltcoats, U.K. 20 55 38N 4 47W
Saltee Is., Ire. 25 52 7N 6 37W
Saltergate, U.K. 19 54 20N 0 40W
Saltfleet, U.K. 19 53 25N 0 11 E
Saltfleetby, U.K. 19 53 23N 0 10 E
Saltillo, Mex. 94 25 25N 101 0W
Salto, Urug. 102 31 27S 57 50W
Saltwood, U.K. 15 51 4N 1 5 E
Salvador, Brazil 101 13 0S 38 30W
Salween →, Burma 59 16 31N 97 37 E
Salzburg, Austria 42 47 48N 13 2 E
Salzgitter, W. Ger. 42 52 13N 10 22 E
Samarinda, Indon. 63 0 30S 117 9 E
Samarkand, U.S.S.R. 48 39 40N 66 55 E
Sámos, Greece 41 37 45N 26 50 E
Sampford Courtenay, U.K. 16 50 47N 3 58W
Samsun, Turk. 47 41 15N 36 22 E
San Angelo, U.S.A. 90 31 30N 100 30W
San Antonio, U.S.A. 90 29 30N 98 30W
San Bernardino, U.S.A. 90 34 7N 117 18W
San Carlos, Phil. 63 15 55N 120 20 E
San Cristóbal, Ven. 100 16 50N 92 40W
San Diego, U.S.A. 90 32 43N 117 10W
San Fernando, Mex. 94 30 0N 115 10W
San Francisco, U.S.A. 90 37 47N 122 30W
San Jorge, G., Arg. 102 46 0S 66 0W
San José, C.R. 95 10 0N 84 2W
San Jose, U.S.A. 90 37 20N 121 53W
San Juan, Arg. 102 31 30S 68 30W
San Juan, P.R. 95 18 28N 66 8W
San Luis Potosí, Mex. 94 22 9N 100 59W
San Marino ■, Europe 40 43 56N 12 25 E
San Matías, G., Arg. 102 41 30S 64 0W
San Miguel de Tucumán, Arg. 102 26 50S 65 20W
San Pedro Sula, Hond. 94 15 30N 88 0W
San Salvador, El Salv. 94 13 40N 89 10W
San Salvador de Jujuy, Arg. 102 24 10S 64 48W
San Sebastián, Sp. 37 43 17N 1 58W
Sana', Yem. 56 15 27N 44 12 E
Sanda I., U.K. 20 55 17N 5 35W
Sanday, U.K. 23 59 15N 2 30W
Sandbach, U.K. 18 53 9N 2 23W
Sandbank, U.K. 20 55 58N 4 57W
Sandgate, U.K. 15 51 5N 1 9 E
Sandhead, U.K. 20 54 48N 4 58W
Sandhurst, U.K. 15 51 21N 0 48W
Sandness, U.K. 22 60 18N 1 38W
Sandown, U.K. 14 50 39N 1 9W
Sandringham, U.K. 15 52 50N 0 30 E
Sandwich, U.K. 15 51 16N 1 21 E
Sandy, U.K. 15 52 8N 0 18W
Sangli, India 58 16 55N 74 33 E
Sanquhar, U.K. 21 55 21N 3 56W
Santa Ana, Mex. 94 30 33N 111 7W
Santa Ana, U.S.A. 90 33 48N 117 55W
Santa Clara, Cuba 95 22 20N 80 0W
Santa Cruz, Bol. 100 17 43S 63 10W
Santa Cruz de Tenerife, Can. Is. 78 28 28N 16 15W
Santa Fe, Arg. 102 31 35S 60 41W
Santa Fe, U.S.A. 90 35 40N 106 0W
Santa Maria, Brazil 102 29 40S 53 48W
Santa Marta, Col. 100 11 15N 74 13W
Santander, Sp. 37 43 27N 3 51W
Santarém, Brazil 101 2 25S 54 42W
Santarém, Port. 37 39 12N 8 42W
Santiago, Chile 102 33 24S 70 40W
Santiago de Compostela, Sp. 37 42 52N 8 37W
Santiago de Cuba, Cuba 95 20 0N 75 49W
Santiago de los Cabelleros, Dom. Rep. 95 19 30N 70 40W
Santo André, Brazil 102 23 39S 46 29W
Santo Domingo, Dom. Rep. 95 18 30N 64 54W
Santos, Brazil 102 24 0S 46 20W
São Francisco →, Brazil 101 10 30S 36 24W
São José do Rio Prêto, Brazil 101 20 50S 49 20W
São Luís, Brazil 101 2 39S 44 15W
São Paulo, Brazil 102 23 32S 46 37W
São Roque, C. de, Brazil 101 5 30S 35 16W
São Tomé & Principe ■, Africa 73 0 12N 6 39 E
Saône →, Fr. 34 45 44N 4 50 E
Sapporo, Jap. 62 43 0N 141 21 E

Staffa

Staffa, *U.K.* **20** 56 26N 6 21W
Stafford, *U.K.* **14** 52 49N 2 9W
Stafford □, *U.K.* **14** 52 53N 2 10W
Staindrop, *U.K.* **19** 54 35N 1 49W
Staines, *U.K.* **15** 51 26N 0 30W
Stainforth, *U.K.* **19** 53 37N 0 59W
Stainmore For., *U.K.* **18** 54 29N 2 5W
Stainton, *U.K.* **19** 53 17N 0 23W
Staithes, *U.K.* **19** 54 33N 0 47W
Stalbridge, *U.K.* **14** 50 57N 2 22W
Stalham, *U.K.* **15** 52 46N 1 31 E
Stalingrad = Volgograd, *U.S.S.R.* **47** 48 40N 44 25 E
Stallingborough, *U.K.* **19** 53 36N 0 11W
Stalybridge, *U.K.* **18** 53 29N 2 4W
Stamford, *U.K.* **15** 52 39N 0 29W
Stamford, *U.S.A.* **93** 41 5N 73 30W
Stamford Bridge, *U.K.* **19** 53 59N 0 53W
Stamfordham, *U.K.* **21** 55 3N 1 53W
Standish, *U.K.* **18** 53 35N 2 39W
Standon, *U.K.* **15** 51 53N 0 2 E
Stanford on Teme, *U.K.* **14** 52 17N 2 26W
Stanhope, *U.K.* **18** 54 45N 2 0W
Stanley, *Falk.* **102** 51 40S 59 51W
Stanley, *Durham, U.K.* **19** 54 53N 1 42W
Stanley, *Tayside, U.K.* **21** 56 29N 3 28W
Stannington, *U.K.* **21** 55 7N 1 41W
Stanovoy Ra., *U.S.S.R.* **49** 55 0N 130 0 E
Stansted Mountfitchet, *U.K.* **15** 51 54N 0 13 E
Stanwix, *U.K.* **18** 54 54N 2 56W
Stapleford, *U.K.* **19** 52 56N 1 16W
Staplehurst, *U.K.* **15** 51 9N 0 35 E
Stara Zagora, *Bulg.* **41** 42 26N 25 39 E
Start Bay, *U.K.* **16** 50 15N 3 35W
Start Pt., *U.K.* **16** 50 13N 3 38W
Staunton, *U.K.* **14** 51 58N 2 19W
Stavanger, *Nor.* **45** 58 57N 5 40 E
Staveley, *Cumbria, U.K.* **18** 54 24N 2 49W
Staveley, *Derby, U.K.* **19** 53 16N 1 20W
Stavropol, *U.S.S.R.* **47** 45 5N 42 0 E
Stenhousemuir, *U.K.* **21** 56 2N 3 46W
Sterlitamak, *U.S.S.R.* **46** 53 40N 56 0 E
Stevenage, *U.K.* **15** 51 54N 0 11W
Stevenston, *U.K.* **20** 55 38N 4 46W
Stewart I., *N.Z.* **71** 46 58S 167 54 E
Stewarton, *U.K.* **20** 55 40N 4 30W
Steyning, *U.K.* **15** 50 54N 0 19W
Stillington, *U.K.* **19** 54 7N 1 5W
Stinchar →, *U.K.* **20** 55 10N 4 50W
Stiperstones Mt., *U.K.* **14** 52 36N 2 57W
Stirling, *U.K.* **21** 56 7N 3 57W
Stobo, *U.K.* **21** 55 38N 3 18W
Stockbridge, *U.K.* **14** 51 7N 1 30W
Stockholm, *Swed.* **45** 59 20N 18 3 E
Stockport, *U.K.* **18** 53 25N 2 11W
Stocksbridge, *U.K.* **19** 53 30N 1 36W
Stockton, *U.S.A.* **90** 38 0N 121 20W
Stockton-on-Tees, *U.K.* **19** 54 34N 1 20W
Stoke, *U.K.* **15** 51 26N 0 41 E
Stoke Ferry, *U.K.* **15** 52 34N 0 31 E
Stoke Fleming, *U.K.* **16** 50 19N 3 36W
Stoke Mandeville, *U.K.* **15** 51 46N 0 47W
Stoke-on-Trent, *U.K.* **18** 53 1N 2 11W
Stoke Prior, *U.K.* **14** 52 18N 2 5W
Stokenham, *U.K.* **16** 50 15N 3 40W
Stokesley, *U.K.* **19** 54 27N 1 12W
Stone, *Bucks., U.K.* **15** 51 48N 0 52W
Stone, *Staffs., U.K.* **18** 52 55N 2 10W
Stonehaven, *U.K.* **23** 56 58N 2 11W
Stonehouse, *Gloucs., U.K.* **14** 51 45N 2 18W
Stonehouse, *Strathclyde, U.K.* **21** 55 42N 4 0W
Stonham Aspall, *U.K.* **15** 52 11N 1 7 E
Stony Stratford, *U.K.* **15** 52 4N 0 51W
Storm B., *Austral.* **67** 43 10S 147 30 E
Stornoway, *U.K.* **22** 58 12N 6 23W
Stort →, *U.K.* **15** 51 50N 0 7 E
Stotfold, *U.K.* **15** 52 2N 0 13W
Stour →, *Dorset, U.K.* **14** 50 48N 2 7W
Stour →, *Hereford & Worcs., U.K.* **14** 52 25N 2 13W
Stour →, *Kent, U.K.* **15** 51 15N 1 20 E
Stour →, *Suffolk, U.K.* **15** 51 55N 1 5 E
Stourbridge, *U.K.* **14** 52 28N 2 8W
Stourport, *U.K.* **14** 52 21N 2 18W
Stow, *U.K.* **21** 55 41N 2 50W
Stow Bardolph, *U.K.* **15** 52 38N 0 24 E
Stow-on-the-Wold, *U.K.* **14** 51 55N 1 42W
Stowmarket, *U.K.* **15** 52 11N 1 0 E
Strabane, *U.K.* **24** 54 50N 7 28W
Strabane □, *U.K.* **24** 54 45N 7 25W
Strachur, *U.K.* **20** 56 10N 5 5W
Stradbroke, *U.K.* **15** 52 19N 1 16 E
Stralsund, *E. Ger.* **42** 54 17N 13 5 E
Strangford, L., *U.K.* **24** 54 30N 5 37W
Stranraer, *U.K.* **20** 54 54N 5 0W
Strasbourg, *Fr.* **34** 48 35N 7 42 E
Stratford-on-Avon, *U.K.* **14** 52 12N 1 42W
Stratford St. Mary, *U.K.* **15** 51 58N 0 59 E
Strath Earn, *U.K.* **21** 56 20N 3 50W
Strath Spey, *U.K.* **23** 57 15N 3 40W
Strathaven, *U.K.* **21** 55 40N 4 4W
Strathclyde □, *U.K.* **20** 56 0N 4 50W
Strathmore, *U.K.* **23** 56 40N 3 4W
Strathpeffer, *U.K.* **23** 57 35N 4 32W
Strathy Pt., *U.K.* **23** 58 35N 4 0W
Strathyre, *U.K.* **20** 56 14N 4 20W
Stratmiglo, *U.K.* **21** 56 16N 3 15W
Stratton, *Cornwall, U.K.* **16** 50 49N 4 31W
Stratton, *Wilts., U.K.* **14** 51 41N 1 45W
Stratton St. Margaret, *U.K.* **14** 51 35N 1 45W
Streatley, *U.K.* **14** 51 31N 1 9W
Street, *U.K.* **14** 51 7N 2 43W
Strensall, *U.K.* **19** 54 3N 1 2W
Stretford, *U.K.* **18** 53 27N 2 19W
Stretton, *U.K.* **18** 53 21N 2 34W
Strichen, *U.K.* **23** 57 35N 2 5W
Striven, L., *U.K.* **20** 55 58N 5 9W
Stromeferry, *U.K.* **22** 57 20N 5 33W
Stromness, *U.K.* **23** 58 58N 3 18W
Stronachlachar, *U.K.* **20** 56 15N 4 35W
Strone, *U.K.* **20** 55 59N 4 54W
Stronsay, *U.K.* **23** 59 8N 2 38W
Stroud, *U.K.* **14** 51 44N 2 12W
Studland, *U.K.* **14** 50 39N 1 58W
Studley, *U.K.* **14** 52 16N 1 54W
Sturminster Marshall, *U.K.* **14** 50 48N 2 4W
Sturminster Newton, *U.K.* **14** 50 56N 2 18W
Sturt Cr. →, *Austral.* **66** 20 8S 127 24 E
Sturton, *U.K.* **19** 53 22N 0 39W
Stuttgart, *W. Ger.* **42** 48 46N 9 10 E
Subotica, *Yug.* **41** 46 6N 19 49 E
Suck →, *Ire.* **25** 53 17N 8 18W
Sucre, *Bol.* **100** 19 0S 65 15W
Sudan ■, *Africa* **78** 15 0N 30 0 E
Sudbury, *Canada* **92** 46 30N 81 0W
Sudbury, *Derby, U.K.* **19** 52 53N 1 43W
Sudbury, *Suffolk, U.K.* **15** 52 2N 0 44 E
Suez, *Egypt* **79** 29 58N 32 31 E
Suffolk □, *U.K.* **15** 52 16N 1 0 E
Suir →, *Ire.* **25** 52 15N 7 10W
Sukkur, *Pak.* **58** 27 42N 68 54 E
Sulawesi □, *Indon.* **63** 2 0S 120 0 E
Sulby, *U.K.* **18** 54 18N 4 29W
Sullom Voe, *U.K.* **22** 60 30N 1 20W
Sulu Sea, *E. Ind.* **63** 8 0N 120 0 E
Sumatra □, *Indon.* **63** 0 40N 100 20 E
Sumbawa, *Indon.* **63** 8 26S 117 30 E
Sumburgh Hd., *U.K.* **22** 59 52N 1 17W
Summer Is., *U.K.* **22** 58 0N 5 27W
Sumy, *U.S.S.R.* **47** 50 57N 34 50 E
Sunart, L., *U.K.* **22** 56 42N 5 43W
Sunda Str., *Indon.* **63** 6 20S 105 30 E
Sundarbans, The, *Asia* **59** 22 0N 89 0 E
Sunderland, *U.K.* **19** 54 54N 1 22W
Sundsvall, *Swed.* **44** 62 23N 17 17 E
Sunk Island, *U.K.* **19** 53 38N 0 7W
Sunninghill, *U.K.* **15** 51 25N 0 40W
Sunshine, *Austral.* **70** 37 48S 144 52 E
Superior, L., *N. Am.* **92** 47 40N 87 0W
Sūr, *Leb.* **57** 33 19N 35 16 E
Surabaya, *Indon.* **63** 7 17S 112 45 E
Surakarta, *Indon.* **63** 7 35S 110 48 E
Surat, *India* **58** 21 12N 72 55 E
Surgut, *U.S.S.R.* **48** 61 14N 73 20 E
Surinam ■, *S. Am.* **101** 4 0N 56 0W
Surrey □, *U.K.* **15** 51 16N 0 30W
Surtsey, *Ice.* **44** 63 20N 20 30W
Sutlej →, *Pak.* **58** 29 23N 71 3 E
Sutterton, *U.K.* **19** 52 54N 0 8W
Sutton, *U.K.* **15** 51 22N 0 13W
Sutton Bridge, *U.K.* **15** 52 46N 0 12 E
Sutton Coldfield, *U.K.* **14** 52 33N 1 50W
Sutton Courtenay, *U.K.* **14** 51 39N 1 16W
Sutton-in-Ashfield, *U.K.* **19** 53 7N 1 20W
Sutton-on-Sea, *U.K.* **19** 53 18N 0 18 E
Sutton Scotney, *U.K.* **14** 51 9N 1 20W
Suva, *Fiji* **64** 18 6S 178 30 E
Suzhou, *China* **61** 31 19N 120 38 E
Svalbard, *Arctic* **103** 78 0N 17 0 E
Svendborg, *Den.* **45** 55 4N 10 35 E
Sverdlovsk, *U.S.S.R.* **46** 56 50N 60 30 E
Sverdrup Is., *Canada* **103** 79 0N 97 0W
Swadlincote, *U.K.* **14** 52 47N 1 34W
Swaffham, *U.K.* **15** 52 38N 0 42 E
Swale →, *U.K.* **19** 54 5N 1 20W
Swan Hill, *Austral.* **70** 35 20S 143 33 E
Swanage, *U.K.* **14** 50 36N 1 59W
Swansea, *U.K.* **17** 51 37N 3 57W
Swaziland ■, *Africa* **81** 26 30S 31 30 E
Sweden ■, *Europe* **44** 57 0N 15 0 E
Swift Current, *Canada* **88** 50 20N 107 45W
Swilly, L., *Ire.* **24** 55 12N 7 35W
Swindon, *U.K.* **15** 51 33N 1 47W
Swineshead, *U.K.* **19** 52 56N 0 11W
Swinton, *Borders, U.K.* **21** 55 43N 2 14W
Swinton, *Gr. Manchester, U.K.* **18** 53 31N 2 21W
Swinton, *S. Yorks., U.K.* **19** 53 28N 1 20W
Switzerland ■, *Europe* **42** 46 30N 8 0 E
Swords, *Ire.* **24** 53 27N 6 15W
Sydney, *Austral.* **70** 33 53S 151 10 E
Sydney, *Canada* **93** 46 7N 60 7W
Syktyvkar, *U.S.S.R.* **46** 61 45N 50 40 E
Symington, *U.K.* **21** 55 35N 3 36W
Symonds Yat, *U.K.* **14** 51 50N 2 38W
Syracuse, *U.S.A.* **93** 43 4N 76 11W
Syrdarya →, *U.S.S.R.* **48** 46 3N 61 0 E
Syria ■, *Asia* **56** 35 0N 38 0 E
Syrian Desert, *Asia* **56** 31 0N 40 0 E
Syston, *U.K.* **14** 52 42N 1 5W
Syzran, *U.S.S.R.* **46** 53 12N 48 30 E
Szczecin, *Pol.* **42** 53 27N 14 27 E
Szeged, *Hung.* **43** 46 16N 20 10 E
Székesfehérvár, *Hung.* **43** 47 15N 18 25 E

T

Tabora, *Tanz.* **80** 5 2S 32 50 E
Tabrīz, *Iran* **56** 38 7N 46 20 E
Tabūk, *Si. Arab.* **56** 28 23N 36 36 E
Tacna, *Peru* **100** 18 0S 70 20W
Tacoma, *U.S.A.* **90** 47 15N 122 30W
Tacuarembó, *Urug.* **102** 31 45S 56 0W
Tadcaster, *U.K.* **19** 53 53N 1 16W
Tadley, *U.K.* **14** 51 21N 1 8W
Tadzhikistan □, *U.S.S.R.* **48** 35 30N 70 0 E
Taegu, *S. Kor.* **61** 35 50N 128 37 E
Taejŏn, *S. Kor.* **61** 36 20N 127 28 E
Taganrog, *U.S.S.R.* **47** 47 12N 38 50 E
Tagus = Tajo →, *Sp.* **37** 38 40N 9 24W
Tahiti, *Pac. Oc.* **65** 17 37S 149 27W
Taichung, *Taiwan* **61** 24 10N 120 35 E
Taimyr Pen., *U.S.S.R.* **49** 75 0N 100 0 E
Tain, *U.K.* **23** 57 49N 4 4W
Tainan, *Taiwan* **61** 23 17N 120 18 E
Taipei, *Taiwan* **61** 25 2N 121 30 E
Taiwan ■, *Asia* **61** 23 30N 121 0 E
Taiyuan, *China* **61** 37 52N 112 33 E
Ta'izz, *Yem.* **56** 13 35N 44 2 E
Tajo →, *Sp.* **37** 38 40N 9 24W
Tak, *Thai.* **59** 16 52N 99 8 E
Takamatsu, *Jap.* **62** 34 20N 134 5 E
Takaoka, *Jap.* **62** 36 47N 137 0 E
Takapuna, *N.Z.* **71** 36 47S 174 47 E
Takasaki, *Jap.* **62** 36 20N 139 0 E
Takeley, *U.K.* **15** 51 52N 0 16 E
Takla Makan, *China* **60** 39 0N 83 0 E
Talca, *Chile* **102** 35 28S 71 40W
Talcahuano, *Chile* **102** 36 40S 73 10W
Talgarth, *U.K.* **17** 51 59N 3 15W
Tallahassee, *U.S.A.* **91** 30 25N 84 15W
Tallinn, *U.S.S.R.* **46** 59 22N 24 48 E
Tamar →, *U.K.* **16** 50 33N 4 15W
Tambov, *U.S.S.R.* **46** 52 45N 41 28 E
Tame →, *U.K.* **14** 52 43N 1 45W
Tamerton Foliot, *U.K.* **16** 50 25N 4 10W
Tamil Nadu □, *India* **58** 11 0N 77 0 E
Tampa, *U.S.A.* **91** 27 57N 82 38W
Tampere, *Fin.* **44** 61 30N 23 50 E
Tampico, *Mex.* **94** 22 20N 97 50W
Tamworth, *Austral.* **67** 31 7S 150 58 E
Tamworth, *U.K.* **14** 52 38N 1 41W
Tana, L., *Eth.* **79** 13 5N 37 30 E
Tanami Desert, *Austral.* **66** 18 50S 132 0 E
Tandragee, *U.K.* **24** 54 22N 6 23W
Tanga, *Tanz.* **80** 5 5S 39 2 E
Tanganyika, L., *E. Afr.* **80** 6 40S 30 0 E
Tangier, *Mor.* **78** 35 50N 5 49W
Tangshan, *China* **61** 39 38N 118 10 E
Tanworth, *U.K.* **14** 52 20N 1 50W
Tanzania ■, *E. Afr.* **80** 6 40S 34 0 E
Tapajós →, *Brazil* **101** 2 24S 54 41W
Tarābulus, *Leb.* **56** 34 31N 35 50 E
Tarābulus, *Libya* **79** 32 49N 13 7 E
Taranaki □, *N.Z.* **71** 39 5S 174 51 E
Táranto, *It.* **40** 40 30N 17 11 E
Táranto, G. di, *It.* **40** 40 0N 17 15 E
Tarbat Ness, *U.K.* **23** 57 52N 3 48W
Tarbert, *Strathclyde, U.K.* **20** 55 55N 5 25W
Tarbert, *W. Isles, U.K.* **22** 57 54N 6 49W
Tarbes, *Fr.* **35** 43 15N 0 3 E
Tarbet, *U.K.* **20** 56 13N 4 44W
Tarbolton, *U.K.* **20** 55 30N 4 30W
Taree, *Austral.* **70** 31 50S 152 30 E
Tarija, *Bol.* **100** 21 30S 64 40W
Tarim Basin, *China* **60** 40 0N 84 0 E
Tarleton, *U.K.* **18** 53 41N 2 50W
Tarnów, *Pol.* **43** 50 3N 21 0 E
Tarporley, *U.K.* **18** 53 10N 2 42W
Tarragona, *Sp.* **37** 41 5N 1 17 E
Tarrasa, *Sp.* **37** 41 34N 2 1 E
Tashkent, *U.S.S.R.* **48** 41 20N 69 10 E
Tasman B., *N.Z.* **71** 40 59S 173 25 E
Tasman Sea, *Pac. Oc.* **71** 36 0S 160 0 E
Tasmania □, *Austral.* **67** 42 0S 146 30 E
Tatar A.S.S.R. □, *U.S.S.R.* **46** 55 30N 51 30 E
Tattenhall, *U.K.* **18** 53 7N 2 47W
Taunton, *U.K.* **14** 51 1N 3 7W
Taupo, *N.Z.* **71** 38 41S 176 7 E
Taupo, L., *N.Z.* **71** 38 46S 175 55 E
Tauranga, *N.Z.* **71** 37 42S 176 11 E
Taurus Mts., *Turk.* **47** 37 0N 35 0 E
Tavistock, *U.K.* **16** 50 33N 4 9W
Tavoy, *Burma* **59** 14 2N 98 12 E
Taw →, *U.K.* **16** 17 37S 177 55 E
Tay →, *U.K.* **21** 56 37N 3 38W
Tay, Firth of, *U.K.* **21** 56 25N 3 8W
Tay, L., *U.K.* **21** 56 30N 4 10W
Tay Bridge, *U.K.* **21** 56 28N 3 0W
Taynuilt, *U.K.* **20** 56 25N 5 15W
Tayport, *U.K.* **21** 56 27N 2 52W
Tayside □, *U.K.* **21** 56 25N 3 30W
Tbilisi, *U.S.S.R.* **47** 41 43N 44 50 E
Te Anau, L., *N.Z.* **71** 45 15S 167 45 E
Te Aroha, *N.Z.* **71** 37 32S 175 44 E
Tebay, *U.K.* **18** 54 25N 2 35W
Tees →, *U.K.* **19** 54 36N 1 25W
Teesdale, *U.K.* **18** 54 37N 2 10W
Teesside, *U.K.* **19** 54 37N 1 13W
Tegid, L., *U.K.* **17** 52 53N 3 38W
Tegucigalpa, *Hond.* **94** 14 5N 87 14W
Tehrān, *Iran* **56** 35 44N 51 30 E
Tehuantepec, Gulf of, *Mex.* **94** 15 50N 95 0W
Tehuantepec, Isthmus of, *Mex.* **94** 17 0N 94 30W
Teifi →, *U.K.* **17** 52 4N 4 14W
Teign →, *U.K.* **16** 50 41N 3 42W
Teignmouth, *U.K.* **16** 50 33N 3 30W
Tejo →, *Port.* **37** 38 40N 9 24W
Tel Aviv-Jaffa, *Isr.* **57** 32 4N 34 48 E
Telemark fylke □, *Nor.* **45** 59 25N 8 30 E
Telford, *U.K.* **14** 52 42N 2 31W
Teluk Betung, *Indon.* **63** 5 20S 105 10 E
Tema, *Ghana* **78** 5 41N 0 0 E
Teme →, *U.K.* **14** 52 23N 2 15W
Temirtau, *U.S.S.R.* **48** 50 5N 72 56 E
Temora, *Austral.* **70** 34 30S 147 30 E
Temple Combe, *U.K.* **14** 51 0N 2 25W
Temple Ewell, *U.K.* **15** 51 9N 1 15 E
Temple Sowerby, *U.K.* **18** 54 38N 2 33W
Templemore, *Ire.* **25** 52 48N 7 50W
Tenbury, *U.K.* **14** 52 18N 2 35W
Tenby, *U.K.* **17** 51 40N 4 42W
Tenerife, *Can. Is.* **78** 28 15N 16 35W
Tennessee □, *U.S.A.* **91** 36 0N 86 30W
Tennessee →, *U.S.A.* **91** 37 4N 88 34W
Tenterden, *U.K.* **15** 51 4N 0 42 E
Teófilo Otoni, *Brazil* **101** 17 50S 41 30W
Tepic, *Mex.* **94** 21 30N 104 54W
Téramo, *It.* **40** 42 40N 13 40 E
Teresina, *Brazil* **101** 5 9S 42 45W
Terni, *It.* **40** 42 34N 12 38 E
Terre Haute, *U.S.A.* **92** 39 28N 87 24W
Teruel, *Sp.* **37** 40 22N 1 8W
Test →, *U.K.* **14** 51 7N 1 30W
Tetbury, *U.K.* **14** 51 37N 2 9W
Tetlin, *U.S.A.* **88** 63 14N 142 50W
Tetney, *U.K.* **19** 53 30N 0 1W
Tétouan, *Mor.* **78** 35 35N 5 21W
Tetovo, *Yug.* **41** 42 1N 21 2 E
Tettenhall, *U.K.* **14** 52 35N 2 7W
Teviot →, *U.K.* **21** 55 21N 2 51W
Teviotdale, *U.K.* **21** 55 25N 2 50W
Teviothead, *U.K.* **21** 55 19N 2 55W
Tewkesbury, *U.K.* **14** 51 59N 2 8W
Texas □, *U.S.A.* **90** 31 40N 98 30W
Texel, *Neth.* **36** 53 5N 4 50 E
Teynham, *U.K.* **15** 51 19N 0 50 E
Thailand ■, *Asia* **63** 16 0N 102 0 E
Thailand, G. of, *Asia* **63** 11 30N 101 0 E
Thal Desert, *Pak.* **58** 31 10N 71 30 E
Thame, *U.K.* **15** 51 44N 0 58W
Thame →, *U.K.* **15** 51 35N 1 8W
Thames →, *U.K.* **15** 51 30N 0 35 E
Thanet, I. of, *U.K.* **15** 51 21N 1 20 E
Thar Desert, *India* **58** 28 0N 72 0 E
Thatcham, *U.K.* **14** 51 24N 1 17W
Thaxted, *U.K.* **15** 51 57N 0 20 E
The Entrance, *Austral.* **70** 33 21S 151 30 E
The Grenadines, Is., *W. Ind.* **94** 12 40N 61 20W
The Hague, *Neth.* **36** 52 7N 4 17 E
The Pas, *Canada* **88** 53 45N 101 15W
Theale, *U.K.* **14** 51 26N 1 5W
Thessaloníki, *Greece* **41** 40 38N 22 58 E
Thessaloniki, Gulf of, *Greece* **41** 40 15N 22 45 E
Thessaly □, *Greece* **41** 39 30N 22 0 E
Thetford, *U.K.* **15** 52 25N 0 44 E
Thies, *Sene.* **78** 14 50N 16 51W
Thimphu, *Bhutan* **59** 27 31N 89 45 E
Thionville, *Fr.* **34** 49 20N 6 10 E
Thirlmere, L., *U.K.* **18** 54 32N 3 4W
Thirsk, *U.K.* **19** 54 15N 1 20W
Thirston, *U.K.* **21** 55 20N 1 34W
Thisted, *Den.* **45** 56 58N 8 40 E
Thompson →, *Canada* **88** 50 15N 121 24W
Thornaby on Tees, *U.K.* **19** 54 36N 1 19W
Thornbury, *U.K.* **14** 51 36N 2 31W
Thorndon, *U.K.* **15** 52 16N 1 8 E
Thorne, *U.K.* **19** 53 36N 0 56W
Thorney, *U.K.* **15** 52 37N 0 8W
Thornham, *U.K.* **15** 52 59N 0 35 E
Thornhill, *U.K.* **21** 55 15N 3 46W
Thornthwaite, *U.K.* **18** 54 36N 3 13W
Thornton, *U.K.* **18** 53 52N 3 1W
Thornton Dale, *U.K.* **19** 54 14N 0 41W
Thorpe, *U.K.* **15** 52 38N 1 20 E
Thorpe le Soken, *U.K.* **15** 51 50N 1 11 E
Thrace □, *Greece* **41** 41 9N 25 30 E
Thrapston, *U.K.* **15** 52 24N 0 32W
Threlkeld, *U.K.* **18** 54 37N 3 2W
Threshfield, *U.K.* **18** 54 5N 2 2W
Thule, *Green.* **103** 77 40N 69 0W
Thunder Bay, *Canada* **92** 48 20N 89 15W
Thurlby, *U.K.* **15** 52 45N 0 21W
Thurles, *Ire.* **25** 52 40N 7 53W
Thurmaston, *U.K.* **14** 52 40N 1 8W
Thursby, *U.K.* **18** 54 40N 3 3W
Thurso, *U.K.* **23** 58 34N 3 31W
Tian Shan, *China* **60** 43 0N 84 0 E
Tianshui, *China* **60** 34 32N 105 40 E
Tiber →, *It.* **40** 41 44N 12 14 E
Tiberias, *Isr.* **57** 32 47N 35 32 E
Tibesti, *Chad* **79** 21 0N 17 30 E
Ticehurst, *U.K.* **15** 51 2N 0 23 E
Tickhill, *U.K.* **19** 53 25N 1 8W
Tideswell, *U.K.* **19** 53 17N 1 46W
Tientsin, *China* **61** 39 10N 117 15 E
Tierra del Fuego □, *Arg.* **102** 54 0S 67 45W
Tighnabruaich, *U.K.* **20** 55 55N 5 13W
Tigris →, *Iraq* **56** 37 0N 42 30 E

Waddingham

Waddingham, *U.K.* **19** 53 28N 0 31W
Waddington, *U.K.* **19** 53 10N 0 31W
Waddington, Mt., *Canada* **88** 51 23N 125 15W
Wadebridge, *U.K.* **16** 50 31N 4 51W
Wadhurst, *U.K.* **15** 51 3N 0 21 E
Wagga Wagga, *Austral.* **70** 35 7S 147 24 E
Wagin, *Austral.* **66** 33 17S 117 25 E
Wainfleet All Saints, *U.K.* **19** 53 7N 0 16 E
Waipara, *N.Z.* **71** 43 3S 172 46 E
Waitaki →, *N.Z.* **71** 44 56S 171 7 E
Wakatipu, L., *N.Z.* **71** 45 5S 168 33 E
Wakayama, *Jap.* **62** 34 15N 135 15 E
Wakefield, *U.K.* **19** 53 41N 1 31W
Walberswick, *U.K.* **15** 52 18N 1 39 E
Wałbrzych, *Pol.* **42** 50 45N 16 18 E
Walbury Hill, *U.K.* **14** 51 22N 1 28W
Waldron, *U.K.* **15** 50 56N 0 13 E
Wales □, *U.K.* **17** 52 30N 3 30W
Walgett, *Austral.* **67** 30 0S 148 5 E
Wallachia, *Rom.* **43** 44 35N 25 0 E
Wallasey, *U.K.* **18** 53 26N 3 2W
Wallingford, *U.K.* **14** 51 40N 1 15W
Wallis & Futuna, *Pac. Oc.* **64** 13 18S 176 10W
Wallsend, *U.K.* **19** 54 59N 1 30W
Walmer, *U.K.* **15** 51 12N 1 23 E
Walney, Isle of, *U.K.* **18** 54 5N 3 15W
Walpole, *U.K.* **15** 52 44N 0 13 E
Walsall, *U.K.* **14** 52 36N 1 59W
Walsoken, *U.K.* **15** 52 41N 0 12 E
Waltham, *U.K.* **19** 53 32N 0 6W
Waltham Abbey, *U.K.* **15** 51 40N 0 1 E
Waltham Forest, *U.K.* **15** 51 37N 0 2 E
Waltham on the Wolds, *U.K.* **15** 52 49N 0 48W
Walton-on-the-Naze, *U.K.* **15** 51 52N 1 17 E
Walvis Bay, *S. Afr.* **81** 23 0S 14 28 E
Wanborough, *U.K.* **14** 51 33N 1 40W
Wandsworth, *U.K.* **15** 51 28N 0 15W
Wanganui, *N.Z.* **71** 39 56S 175 3 E
Wangaratta, *Austral.* **70** 36 21S 146 19 E
Wansbeck, *U.K.* **21** 55 12N 1 28W
Wantage, *U.K.* **14** 51 35N 1 25W
Warboys, *U.K.* **15** 52 25N 0 5W
Warburton →, *Austral.* **67** 28 4S 137 28 E
Wardington, *U.K.* **14** 52 8N 1 17W
Wardle, *U.K.* **18** 53 7N 2 35W
Ward's Stone, *U.K.* **18** 54 2N 2 39W
Ware, *U.K.* **15** 51 48N 0 2W
Wareham, *U.K.* **14** 50 41N 2 8W
Wark, *U.K.* **21** 55 5N 2 14W
Warkworth, *U.K.* **21** 55 22N 1 38W
Warley, *U.K.* **14** 52 30N 2 0W
Warminster, *U.K.* **14** 51 12N 2 11W
Warracknabeal, *Austral.* **70** 36 9S 142 26 E
Warrego →, *Austral.* **67** 30 24S 145 21 E
Warrenpoint, *U.K.* **24** 54 7N 6 15W
Warrington, *U.K.* **18** 53 25N 2 38W
Warrnambool, *Austral.* **70** 38 25S 142 30 E
Warsaw, *Pol.* **43** 52 13N 21 0 E
Warsop, *U.K.* **19** 53 13N 1 9W
Warta →, *Pol.* **43** 52 35N 14 39 E
Warthe = Warta →, *Pol.* **43** 52 35N 14 39 E
Warwick, *Austral.* **67** 28 10S 152 1 E
Warwick, *U.K.* **14** 52 17N 1 36W
Warwick □, *U.K.* **14** 52 20N 1 30W
Wasatch Ra., *U.S.A.* **90** 40 30N 111 15W
Wash, The, *U.K.* **19** 52 58N 0 20 E
Washford, *U.K.* **14** 51 9N 3 22W
Washington, *U.K.* **21** 54 55N 1 30W
Washington, *U.S.A.* **92** 38 52N 77 0W
Washington □, *U.S.A.* **90** 47 45N 120 30W
Wast Water, L., *U.K.* **18** 54 26N 3 18W
Watchet, *U.K.* **14** 51 10N 3 20W
Waterbeach, *U.K.* **15** 52 16N 0 11 E
Waterbury, *U.S.A.* **93** 41 32N 73 0W
Waterford, *Ire.* **25** 52 16N 7 8W
Waterford □, *Ire.* **25** 52 10N 7 40W
Waterford Harb., *Ire.* **25** 52 10N 6 58W
Watergate Bay, *U.K.* **16** 50 26N 5 4W
Waterloo, *U.K.* **18** 53 29N 3 2W
Watford, *U.K.* **15** 51 38N 0 23W
Wath, *U.K.* **19** 53 29N 1 20W
Watlington, *Norfolk, U.K.* **15** 52 40N 0 24 E
Watlington, *Oxon., U.K.* **15** 51 38N 1 0W
Watton, *U.K.* **15** 52 35N 0 50 E
Waveney →, *U.K.* **15** 52 24N 1 20 E
Waver →, *U.K.* **18** 54 50N 3 15W
Weald, The, *U.K.* **15** 51 7N 0 9 E
Wear →, *U.K.* **19** 54 55N 1 22W
Weardale, *U.K.* **18** 54 44N 2 5W
Wearhead, *U.K.* **18** 54 45N 2 14W
Weaver →, *U.K.* **18** 53 17N 2 35W
Weaverham, *U.K.* **18** 53 15N 2 30W
Weddell Sea, *Ant.* **103** 72 30S 40 0W
Wedmore, *U.K.* **14** 51 14N 2 50W
Wednesbury, *U.K.* **14** 52 33N 2 1W
Wednesfield, *U.K.* **14** 52 36N 2 3W
Weedon Bec, *U.K.* **14** 52 14N 1 6W
Weifang, *China* **61** 36 47N 119 10 E
Weldon, *U.K.* **21** 55 16N 1 46W
Welford, *Berks., U.K.* **14** 51 28N 1 24W
Welford, *Northants., U.K.* **14** 52 26N 1 5W
Welkom, *S. Afr.* **81** 28 0S 26 50 E
Welland →, *U.K.* **15** 52 43N 0 10W
Wellesley Is., *Austral.* **67** 16 42S 139 30 E
Wellingborough, *U.K.* **15** 52 18N 0 41W
Wellington, *Austral.* **70** 32 35S 148 59 E
Wellington, *N.Z.* **71** 41 19S 174 46 E
Wellington, *Salop, U.K.* **14** 52 42N 2 31W
Wellington, *Somerset, U.K.* **14** 50 58N 3 13W
Wellow, *U.K.* **14** 51 20N 2 22W
Wells, *Norfolk, U.K.* **15** 52 57N 0 51 E
Wells, *Somerset, U.K.* **14** 51 12N 2 39W
Welney, *U.K.* **15** 52 31N 0 15 E
Wels, *Austria* **42** 48 9N 14 1 E
Welshpool, *U.K.* **17** 52 40N 3 9W
Welton, *U.K.* **19** 53 19N 0 29W
Welwyn Garden City, *U.K.* **15** 51 49N 0 11W
Wem, *U.K.* **14** 52 52N 2 45W
Wembury, *U.K.* **16** 50 19N 4 6W
Wemyss Bay, *U.K.* **20** 55 52N 4 54W
Wendover, *U.K.* **15** 51 46N 0 45W
Wenhaston, *U.K.* **15** 52 17N 1 35 E
Wenlock Edge, *U.K.* **14** 52 30N 2 43W
Wensleydale, *U.K.* **18** 54 18N 2 0W
Wensum →, *U.K.* **15** 52 35N 1 20 E
Wenzhou, *China* **61** 28 0N 120 38 E
Weobley, *U.K.* **14** 52 9N 2 52W
Werribee, *Austral.* **70** 37 54S 144 40 E
Werrington, *U.K.* **16** 50 40N 4 22W
Weser →, *W. Ger.* **42** 53 33N 8 30 E
West Auckland, *U.K.* **19** 54 38N 1 42W
West Bengal □, *India* **59** 23 0N 88 0 E
West Bridgford, *U.K.* **19** 52 56N 1 8W
West Bromwich, *U.K.* **14** 52 32N 2 1W
West Calder, *U.K.* **21** 55 51N 3 34W
West Coker, *U.K.* **14** 50 55N 2 40W
West Fen, *U.K.* **19** 53 5N 0 5W
West Germany ■, *Europe* **42** 52 0N 9 0 E
West Glamorgan □, *U.K.* **17** 51 40N 3 55W
West Grinstead, *U.K.* **15** 50 58N 0 19W
West Haddon, *U.K.* **14** 52 21N 1 5W
West Kilbride, *U.K.* **20** 55 41N 4 50W
West Kirby, *U.K.* **18** 53 22N 3 11W
West Linton, *U.K.* **21** 55 45N 3 24W
West Lulworth, *U.K.* **14** 50 37N 2 14W
West Malling, *U.K.* **15** 51 16N 0 25 E
West Meon, *U.K.* **14** 51 2N 1 3W
West Mersea, *U.K.* **15** 51 46N 0 55 E
West Midlands □, *U.K.* **14** 52 30N 1 55W
West Moors, *U.K.* **14** 50 49N 1 50W
West Parley, *U.K.* **14** 50 46N 1 52W
West Rasen, *U.K.* **19** 53 23N 0 23W
West Schelde →, *Neth.* **36** 51 23N 3 50 E
West Siberian Plain, *U.S.S.R.* **48** 62 0N 75 0 E
West Sussex □, *U.K.* **15** 50 55N 0 30W
West Tarbert, L., *U.K.* **20** 55 58N 5 30W
West Virginia □, *U.S.A.* **92** 39 0N 81 0W
West Wyalong, *Austral.* **70** 33 56S 147 10 E
West Yorkshire □, *U.K.* **19** 53 45N 1 40W
Westbourne, *U.K.* **15** 50 53N 0 55W
Westbury, *Salop, U.K.* **14** 52 40N 2 57W
Westbury, *Wilts., U.K.* **14** 51 16N 2 11W
Westbury-on-Severn, *U.K.* **14** 51 49N 2 24W
Westerham, *U.K.* **15** 51 16N 0 5 E
Western Australia □, *Austral.* **66** 25 0S 118 0 E
Western Ghats, *India* **58** 14 0N 75 0 E
Western Isles □, *U.K.* **22** 57 30N 7 10W
Western Sahara ■, *Africa* **78** 25 0N 13 0W
Western Samoa ■, *Pac. Oc.* **64** 14 0S 172 0W
Westfield, *U.K.* **15** 50 53N 0 30 E
Westhoughton, *U.K.* **18** 53 34N 2 30W
Westland Bight, *N.Z.* **71** 42 55S 170 5 E
Westmeath □, *Ire.* **24** 53 30N 7 30W
Weston, *U.K.* **14** 52 51N 2 2W
Weston-super-Mare, *U.K.* **14** 51 20N 2 59W
Westport, *Ire.* **24** 53 44N 9 31W
Westport, *N.Z.* **71** 41 46S 171 37 E
Westray, *U.K.* **23** 59 18N 3 0W
Westruther, *U.K.* **21** 55 45N 2 34W
Westward Ho!, *U.K.* **16** 51 2N 4 16W
Wetherby, *U.K.* **19** 53 56N 1 23W
Wetwang, *U.K.* **19** 54 2N 0 35W
Wexford, *Ire.* **25** 52 20N 6 28W
Wexford □, *Ire.* **25** 52 20N 6 25W
Wexford Harb., *Ire.* **25** 52 20N 6 25W
Wey →, *U.K.* **15** 51 19N 0 29W
Weybourne, *U.K.* **15** 52 57N 1 9 E
Weybridge, *U.K.* **15** 51 22N 0 28W
Weymouth, *U.K.* **14** 50 36N 2 28W
Whakatane, *N.Z.* **71** 37 57S 177 1 E
Whaley Bridge, *U.K.* **18** 53 20N 2 0W
Whalley, *U.K.* **18** 53 49N 2 25W
Whalsay, *U.K.* **22** 60 22N 1 0W
Whalton, *U.K.* **21** 55 7N 1 46W
Whangarei, *N.Z.* **71** 35 43S 174 21 E
Whaplode, *U.K.* **15** 52 42N 0 3W
Wharfe →, *U.K.* **19** 53 55N 1 30W
Wharfedale, *U.K.* **18** 54 7N 2 4W
Whauphill, *U.K.* **20** 54 48N 4 31W
Wheatley Hill, *U.K.* **19** 54 45N 1 23W
Whernside, *U.K.* **18** 54 14N 2 24W
Whichham, *U.K.* **18** 54 14N 3 22W
Whimple, *U.K.* **16** 50 46N 3 21W
Whipsnade, *U.K.* **15** 51 51N 0 32W
Whissendine, *U.K.* **15** 52 43N 0 46W
Whiston, *U.K.* **18** 53 25N 2 45W
Whitburn, *U.K.* **21** 55 52N 3 41W
Whitby, *U.K.* **19** 54 29N 0 37W
Whitchurch, *Devon, U.K.* **16** 50 31N 4 7W
Whitchurch, *Hants., U.K.* **14** 51 14N 1 20W
Whitchurch, *Hereford & Worcs., U.K.* **14** 51 51N 2 41W
Whitchurch, *Salop, U.K.* **18** 52 58N 2 42W
White Esk →, *U.K.* **21** 55 14N 3 11W
White Horse Hill, *U.K.* **14** 51 35N 1 35W
White Nile →, *Sudan* **79** 15 38N 32 31 E
White Russia □, *U.S.S.R.* **46** 53 30N 27 0 E
White Sea, *U.S.S.R.* **46** 66 30N 38 0 E
Whiteadder Water →, *U.K.* **21** 55 47N 2 20W
Whitehaven, *U.K.* **18** 54 33N 3 35W
Whitehead, *U.K.* **24** 54 45N 5 42W
Whitehorse, *Canada* **88** 60 43N 135 3W
Whitehorse, Vale of, *U.K.* **14** 51 37N 1 30W
Whitekirk, *U.K.* **21** 56 2N 2 36W
Whitesand B., *U.K.* **16** 50 18N 4 20W
Whithorn, *U.K.* **20** 54 44N 4 25W
Whitley Bay, *U.K.* **21** 55 4N 1 28W
Whitney, Mt., *U.S.A.* **90** 36 35N 118 14W
Whitstable, *U.K.* **15** 51 21N 1 2 E
Whittington, *Derby, U.K.* **19** 53 17N 1 26W
Whittington, *Salop, U.K.* **14** 52 53N 3 0W
Whittlesey, *U.K.* **15** 52 34N 0 8W
Whittlesford, *U.K.* **15** 52 6N 0 9 E
Whitton, *U.K.* **19** 53 42N 0 39W
Whitwell, *Derby, U.K.* **19** 53 16N 1 11W
Whitwell, *I. of W., U.K.* **14** 50 35N 1 19W
Whitwick, *U.K.* **14** 52 45N 1 23W
Whitworth, *U.K.* **18** 53 40N 2 11W
Whixley, *U.K.* **19** 54 2N 1 19W
Whyalla, *Austral.* **67** 33 2S 137 30 E
Wichita, *U.S.A.* **91** 37 40N 97 20W
Wichita Falls, *U.S.A.* **90** 33 57N 98 30W
Wick, *U.K.* **23** 58 26N 3 5W
Wickford, *U.K.* **15** 51 37N 0 31 E
Wickham, *U.K.* **14** 50 54N 1 11W
Wickham Market, *U.K.* **15** 52 9N 1 21 E
Wicklow, *Ire.* **25** 53 0N 6 2W
Wicklow □, *Ire.* **25** 52 59N 6 25W
Wicklow Mts., *Ire.* **25** 53 0N 6 30W
Wickwar, *U.K.* **14** 51 35N 2 23W
Widdrington, *U.K.* **21** 55 15N 1 35W
Widecombe, *U.K.* **16** 50 34N 3 48W
Widemouth, *U.K.* **16** 50 45N 4 34W
Widnes, *U.K.* **18** 53 22N 2 44W
Wiesbaden, *W. Ger.* **36** 50 7N 8 17 E
Wigan, *U.K.* **18** 53 33N 2 38W
Wight, I. of, *U.K.* **14** 50 40N 1 20W
Wigmore, *U.K.* **14** 52 19N 2 51W
Wigston, *U.K.* **14** 52 35N 1 6W
Wigton, *U.K.* **18** 54 50N 3 9W
Wigtown, *U.K.* **20** 54 52N 4 27W
Wigtown B., *U.K.* **20** 54 46N 4 15W
Wilhelm II Land, *Ant.* **103** 68 0S 90 0 E
Wilhelmshaven, *W. Ger.* **42** 53 30N 8 9 E
Wilkes Barre, *U.S.A.* **93** 41 15N 75 52W
Wilkes Land, *Ant.* **103** 69 0S 120 0 E
Willemstad, *Cur.* **94** 12 5N 69 0W
Willenhall, *U.K.* **14** 52 36N 2 3W
Willesborough, *U.K.* **15** 51 8N 0 55 E
Williamstown, *Austral.* **70** 37 51S 144 52 E
Willingdon, *U.K.* **15** 50 47N 0 17 E
Williton, *U.K.* **14** 51 9N 3 20W
Willoughby, *U.K.* **19** 53 14N 0 12 E
Wilmington, *U.K.* **16** 50 46N 3 8W
Wilmington, *U.S.A.* **93** 39 45N 75 32W
Wilmslow, *U.K.* **18** 53 19N 2 14W
Wilnecote, *U.K.* **14** 52 36N 1 40W
Wilsons Promontory, *Austral.* **70** 38 55S 146 25 E
Wilton, *U.K.* **14** 51 5N 1 52W
Wiltshire □, *U.K.* **14** 51 20N 2 0W
Wimblington, *U.K.* **15** 52 31N 0 5 E
Wimborne Minster, *U.K.* **14** 50 48N 2 0W
Wimmera →, *Austral.* **70** 36 8S 141 56 E
Wincanton, *U.K.* **14** 51 3N 2 24W
Winchelsea, *U.K.* **15** 50 55N 0 43 E
Winchester, *U.K.* **14** 51 4N 1 19W
Windermere, *U.K.* **18** 54 24N 2 56W
Windermere, L., *U.K.* **18** 54 20N 2 57W
Windhoek, *Nam.* **81** 22 35S 17 4 E
Windrush →, *U.K.* **14** 51 48N 1 35W
Windsor, *Canada* **92** 42 18N 83 0W
Windsor, *U.K.* **15** 51 28N 0 36W
Windward Passage, *W. Ind.* **95** 20 0N 74 0W
Windygates, *U.K.* **21** 56 12N 3 1W
Wing, *U.K.* **15** 51 54N 0 41W
Wingham, *Austral.* **70** 31 48S 152 22 E
Wingham, *U.K.* **15** 51 16N 1 12 E
Winkleigh, *U.K.* **16** 50 49N 3 57W
Winnipeg, *Canada* **88** 49 54N 97 9W
Winnipeg, L., *Canada* **88** 52 0N 97 0W
Winsford, *U.K.* **18** 53 12N 2 31W
Winslow, *U.K.* **15** 51 57N 0 52W
Winster, *U.K.* **19** 53 9N 1 42W
Winston-Salem, *U.S.A.* **91** 36 7N 80 15W
Winterborne Abbas, *U.K.* **14** 50 43N 2 30W
Winterthur, *Switz.* **42** 47 30N 8 44 E
Winterton, *Humberside, U.K.* **19** 53 39N 0 37W
Winterton, *Norfolk, U.K.* **15** 52 43N 1 43 E
Wirksworth, *U.K.* **19** 53 5N 1 34W
Wirral, *U.K.* **18** 53 25N 3 0W
Wisbech, *U.K.* **15** 52 39N 0 10 E
Wisborough Green, *U.K.* **15** 51 2N 0 30W
Wisconsin □, *U.S.A.* **92** 44 30N 90 0W
Wishaw, *U.K.* **21** 55 46N 3 55W
Wiske →, *U.K.* **19** 54 26N 1 27W
Wisła →, *Pol.* **43** 54 22N 18 55 E
Witbank, *S. Afr.* **81** 25 51S 29 14 E
Witham, *U.K.* **15** 51 48N 0 39 E
Witham →, *U.K.* **19** 53 3N 0 8W
Withern, *U.K.* **19** 53 19N 0 9 E
Withernsea, *U.K.* **19** 53 43N 0 2 E
Witley, *U.K.* **15** 51 9N 0 39W
Witney, *U.K.* **14** 51 47N 1 29W
Witten, *W. Ger.* **36** 51 26N 7 19 E
Wittersham, *U.K.* **15** 51 1N 0 42 E
Wiveliscombe, *U.K.* **14** 51 2N 3 20W
Wivenhoe, *U.K.* **15** 51 51N 0 59 E
Włocławek, *Pol.* **43** 52 40N 19 3 E
Woburn, *U.K.* **15** 51 59N 0 37W
Woburn Sands, *U.K.* **15** 52 1N 0 38W
Wodonga, *Austral.* **70** 36 5S 146 50 E
Woking, *U.K.* **15** 51 18N 0 33W
Wokingham, *U.K.* **15** 51 25N 0 50W
Wolf Rock, *U.K.* **16** 49 56N 5 50W
Wolfsburg, *W. Ger.* **42** 52 27N 10 49 E
Wollongong, *Austral.* **70** 34 25S 150 54 E
Wolsingham, *U.K.* **18** 54 44N 1 52W
Wolverhampton, *U.K.* **14** 52 35N 2 6W
Wolverton, *U.K.* **15** 52 3N 0 48W
Wolviston, *U.K.* **19** 54 39N 1 25W
Wombwell, *U.K.* **19** 53 31N 1 23W
Wŏnsan, *N. Kor.* **61** 39 11N 127 27 E
Wonston, *U.K.* **14** 51 9N 1 18W
Woodbridge, *U.K.* **15** 52 6N 1 19 E
Woodbury, *U.K.* **16** 50 40N 3 24W
Woodhall Spa, *U.K.* **19** 53 10N 0 12W
Woodhouse, *U.K.* **19** 53 23N 1 21W
Woodley, *U.K.* **15** 51 26N 0 54W
Woods, L. of the, *Canada* **88** 49 15N 94 45W
Woodstock, *U.K.* **14** 51 51N 1 20W
Wookey, *U.K.* **14** 51 13N 2 41W
Wookey Hole, *U.K.* **14** 51 13N 2 41W
Wool, *U.K.* **14** 50 41N 2 13W
Woolacombe, *U.K.* **16** 51 10N 4 12W
Wooler, *U.K.* **21** 55 33N 2 0W
Wootton Bassett, *U.K.* **14** 51 32N 1 55W
Wootton Wawen, *U.K.* **14** 52 16N 1 47W
Worcester, *S. Afr.* **81** 33 39S 19 27 E
Worcester, *U.K.* **14** 52 12N 2 12W
Worcester, *U.S.A.* **93** 42 14N 71 49W
Worfield, *U.K.* **14** 52 34N 2 22W
Workington, *U.K.* **18** 54 39N 3 34W
Worksop, *U.K.* **19** 53 19N 1 9W
Wormit, *U.K.* **21** 56 26N 2 59W
Worms, *W. Ger.* **42** 49 37N 8 21 E
Worplesdon, *U.K.* **15** 51 16N 0 36W
Wortham, *U.K.* **15** 52 22N 1 3 E
Worthing, *U.K.* **15** 50 49N 0 21W
Wotton-under-Edge, *U.K.* **14** 51 37N 2 20W
Woy Woy, *Austral.* **70** 33 30S 151 19 E
Wragby, *U.K.* **19** 53 17N 0 18W
Wrangel I., *U.S.S.R.* **49** 71 0N 180 0 E
Wrangle, *U.K.* **19** 53 3N 0 9 E
Wrath, C., *U.K.* **22** 58 38N 5 0W
Wrekin, The, *U.K.* **14** 52 41N 2 35W
Wrentham, *U.K.* **15** 52 24N 1 39 E
Wrexham, *U.K.* **17** 53 5N 3 0W
Writtle, *U.K.* **15** 51 44N 0 27 E
Wrocław, *Pol.* **43** 51 5N 17 5 E
Wrotham, *U.K.* **15** 51 18N 0 20 E
Wroughton, *U.K.* **14** 51 31N 1 47W
Wroxham, *U.K.* **15** 52 42N 1 23 E
Wuhan, *China* **61** 30 31N 114 18 E
Wuhu, *China* **61** 31 22N 118 21 E
Wuppertal, *W. Ger.* **36** 51 15N 7 8 E
Würzburg, *W. Ger.* **42** 49 46N 9 55 E
Wutongqiao, *China* **60** 29 22N 103 50 E
Wuxi, *China* **61** 31 30N 120 30 E
Wuzhou, *China* **61** 23 30N 111 18 E
Wye, *U.K.* **15** 51 11N 0 56 E
Wye →, *U.K.* **14** 51 36N 2 40W
Wylye →, *U.K.* **14** 51 8N 1 53W
Wymondham, *Leics., U.K.* **15** 52 45N 0 42W
Wymondham, *Norfolk, U.K.* **15** 52 34N 1 7 E
Wyndham, *Austral.* **66** 15 33S 128 3 E
Wyoming □, *U.S.A.* **90** 42 48N 109 0W
Wyre →, *U.K.* **18** 53 52N 2 57W
Wyre Forest, *U.K.* **14** 52 24N 2 24W

X

Xiaguan, *China* **60** 25 32N 100 16 E
Xiamen, *China* **61** 24 25N 118 4 E
Xiangfan, *China* **61** 32 2N 112 8 E
Xiangtan, *China* **61** 27 51N 112 54 E
Xiangyang, *China* **61** 32 1N 112 8 E
Xingu →, *Brazil* **101** 1 30S 51 53W
Xining, *China* **60** 36 34N 101 40 E
Xinjiang Uygur Zizhiqu □, *China* **60** 42 0N 86 0 E
Xuzhou, *China* **61** 34 18N 117 10 E

Y

Yablonovy Ra., *U.S.S.R.*	**49** 53 0N	114 0 E
Yakut A.S.S.R. □, *U.S.S.R.*	**49** 62 0N	130 0 E
Yakutsk, *U.S.S.R.*	**49** 62 5N	129 50 E
Yamagata, *Jap.*	**62** 38 15N	140 15 E
Yamal, Peninsula, *U.S.S.R.*	**48** 71 0N	70 0 E
Yambol, *Bulg.*	**41** 42 30N	26 36 E
Yamuna →, *India*	**59** 25 30N	81 53 E
Yana →, *U.S.S.R.*	**49** 71 30N	136 0 E
Yangtze Kiang →, *China*	**60** 31 40N	122 0 E
Yanji, *China*	**61** 42 59N	129 30 E
Yantai, *China*	**61** 37 34N	121 22 E
Yaoundé, *Cam.*	**80** 3 50N	11 35 E
Yarcombe, *U.K.*	**16** 50 51N	3 6W
Yare →, *U.K.*	**15** 52 36N	1 28 E
Yarm, *U.K.*	**19** 54 31N	1 21W
Yarmouth, *U.K.*	**14** 50 42N	1 29W
Yaroslavl, *U.S.S.R.*	**46** 57 35N	39 55 E
Yarrow, *U.K.*	**21** 55 32N	3 0W
Yate, *U.K.*	**14** 51 32N	2 26W
Yatsushiro, *Jap.*	**62** 32 30N	130 40 E
Yatton, *U.K.*	**14** 51 23N	2 50W
Yaxley, *U.K.*	**15** 52 31N	0 14W
Yazd, *Iran*	**56** 31 55N	54 27 E
Yealmpton, *U.K.*	**16** 50 21N	4 0W
Yell, *U.K.*	**22** 60 35N	1 5W
Yell Sd., *U.K.*	**22** 60 33N	1 15W

Yellow Sea, *China*	**61** 35 0N	123 0 E
Yellowknife, *Canada*	**88** 62 27N	114 29W
Yellowstone →, *U.S.A.*	**90** 47 58N	103 59W
Yellowstone National Park, *U.S.A.*	**90** 44 35N	110 0W
Yemen ■, *Si. Arab.*	**56** 15 0N	44 0 E
Yenisey →, *U.S.S.R.*	**48** 71 50N	82 40 E
Yeo →, *U.K.*	**14** 51 10N	3 0W
Yeovil, *U.K.*	**14** 50 57N	2 38W
Yerevan, *U.S.S.R.*	**47** 40 10N	44 31 E
Yes Tor, *U.K.*	**16** 50 41N	3 59W
Yibin, *China*	**60** 28 45N	104 32 E
Yichang, *China*	**61** 30 40N	111 20 E
Yichuan, *China*	**60** 36 2N	110 10 E
Yining, *China*	**60** 43 58N	81 10 E
Yogyakarta, *Indon.*	**63** 7 49S	110 22 E
Yokkaichi, *Jap.*	**62** 35 0N	136 38 E
Yokohama, *Jap.*	**62** 35 27N	139 28 E
Yokosuka, *Jap.*	**62** 35 20N	139 40 E
Yonkers, *U.S.A.*	**93** 40 57N	73 51W
York, *U.K.*	**19** 53 58N	1 7W
York, *U.S.A.*	**92** 39 57N	76 43W
York, Vale of, *U.K.*	**19** 54 15N	1 25W
Yorkshire Wolds, *U.K.*	**19** 54 0N	0 30W
Yosemite National Park, *U.S.A.*	**90** 38 0N	119 30W
Yoshkar Ola, *U.S.S.R.*	**46** 56 38N	47 55 E
Youghal, *Ire.*	**25** 51 58N	7 51W
Youghal B., *Ire.*	**25** 51 55N	7 50W
Youlgreave, *U.K.*	**19** 53 12N	1 50W
Youngstown, *U.S.A.*	**92** 41 7N	80 41W

Yoxall, *U.K.*	**14** 52 45N	1 49W
Yoxford, *U.K.*	**15** 52 16N	1 30 E
Ypres, *Belg.*	**36** 50 51N	2 53 E
Ystalyfera, *U.K.*	**17** 51 46N	3 48W
Ythan →, *U.K.*	**23** 57 26N	2 12W
Yuan Jiang →, *China*	**61** 28 55N	111 50 E
Yucatán, Península de, *Mex.*	**94** 19 30N	89 0W
Yucatan Str., *Carib.*	**94** 22 0N	86 30W
Yugoslavia ■, *Europe*	**41** 44 0N	20 0 E
Yukon →, *N. Am.*	**88** 65 30N	150 0W
Yukon Territory □, *Canada*	**88** 63 0N	135 0W
Yunnan □, *China*	**60** 25 0N	102 30 E
Yuzhno-Sakhalinsk, *U.S.S.R.*	**49** 46 58N	142 45 E

Z

Zaandam, *Neth.*	**36** 52 26N	4 49 E
Zabrze, *Pol.*	**43** 50 18N	18 50 E
Zagorsk, *U.S.S.R.*	**46** 56 20N	38 10 E
Zagreb, *Yug.*	**40** 45 50N	16 0 E
Zagros Mts., *Iran*	**56** 33 45N	47 0 E
Zahlah, *Leb.*	**57** 33 52N	35 50 E
Zaïre ■, *Africa*	**80** 3 0S	23 0 E
Zaïre →, *Africa*	**80** 6 4S	12 24 E

Zákinthos, *Greece*	**41** 37 47N	20 57 E
Zambezi →, *Africa*	**81** 18 55S	36 4 E
Zambia ■, *Africa*	**81** 15 0S	28 0 E
Zamboanga, *Phil.*	**63** 6 59N	122 3 E
Zamora, *Sp.*	**37** 41 30N	5 45W
Zante = Zákinthos, *Greece*	**41** 37 47N	20 57 E
Zanzibar, *Tanz.*	**80** 6 12S	39 12 E
Zaporozhye, *U.S.S.R.*	**47** 47 50N	35 10 E
Zaragoza, *Sp.*	**37** 41 39N	0 53W
Zaria, *Nig.*	**78** 11 0N	7 40 E
Zeebrugge, *Belg.*	**36** 51 19N	3 12 E
Zeist, *Neth.*	**36** 52 5N	5 15 E
Zhangjiakou, *China*	**61** 40 48N	114 55 E
Zhangzhou, *China*	**61** 24 30N	117 35 E
Zhanjiang, *China*	**61** 21 15N	110 20 E
Zhdanov, *U.S.S.R.*	**47** 47 5N	37 31 E
Zhejiang □, *China*	**61** 29 0N	120 0 E
Zhengzhou, *China*	**61** 34 45N	113 34 E
Zhitomir, *U.S.S.R.*	**47** 50 20N	28 40 E
Zibo, *China*	**61** 36 47N	118 3 E
Zielona Góra □, *Pol.*	**42** 51 57N	15 30 E
Zigong, *China*	**60** 29 15N	104 48 E
Ziguinchor, *Sene.*	**78** 12 35N	16 20W
Žilina, *Czech.*	**43** 49 12N	18 42 E
Zimbabwe ■, *Africa*	**81** 20 0S	30 0 E
Zion Nat. Park, *U.S.A.*	**90** 37 25N	112 50W
Zlatoust, *U.S.S.R.*	**46** 55 10N	59 40 E
Zonguldak, *Turk.*	**47** 41 28N	31 50 E
Zrenjanin, *Yug.*	**41** 45 22N	20 23 E
Zug, *Switz.*	**42** 47 10N	8 31 E

MAP PROJECTIONS

MAP PROJECTIONS

A map projection is the systematic depiction on a plane surface of the imaginary lines of latitude or longitude from a globe of the earth. This network of lines is called the graticule and forms the framework upon which an accurate depiction of the earth is made. The map graticule, which is the basis of any map, is constructed sometimes by graphical means, but often by using mathematical formulae to give the intersections of the graticule plotted as x and y co-ordinates. The choice between projections is based upon which properties the cartographer wishes the map to possess, the map scale and also the extent of the area to be mapped. Since the globe is three dimensional, it is not possible to depict its surface on a two dimensional plane without distortion. Preservation of one of the basic properties listed below can only be secured at the expense of the others and the choice of projection is often a compromise solution.

Correct Area

In these projections the areas from the globe are to scale on the map. For example, if you look at the diagram at the top right, areas of 10° x 10° are shown from the equator to the poles. The proportion of this area at the extremities are approximately 11:1. An equal area projection will retain that proportion in its portrayal of those areas. This is particularly useful in the mapping of densities and distributions. Projections with this property are termed **Equal Area, Equivalent or Homolographic.**

Correct Distance

In these projections the scale is correct along the meridians, or in the case of the Azimuthal Equidistant scale is true along any line drawn from the centre of the projection. They are called **Equidistant.**

Correct Shape

This property can only be true within small areas as it is achieved only by having a uniform scale distortion along both x and y axes of the projection. The projections are called **Conformal** or **Orthomorphic.**

In order to minimise the distortions at the edges of some projections, central portions of them are often selected for atlas maps. Below are listed some of the major types of projection.

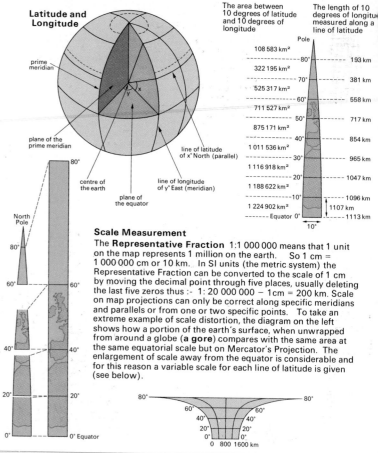

Latitude and Longitude

prime meridian — plane of the prime meridian — centre of the earth — plane of the equator — line of latitude of x° North (parallel) — line of longitude of y° East (meridian)

The area between 10 degrees of latitude and 10 degrees of longitude

108 583 km²	—80°
322 195 km²	—70°
525 317 km²	—60°
711 527 km²	—50°
875 171 km²	—40°
1 011 536 km²	—30°
1 116 918 km²	—20°
1 188 622 km²	—10°
1 224 902 km²	Equator 0°

The length of 10 degrees of longitude measured along a line of latitude

Pole	
—80°	193 km
—70°	381 km
—60°	558 km
—50°	717 km
—40°	854 km
—30°	965 km
—20°	1047 km
—10°	1096 km
	1107 km
	1113 km

Scale Measurement

The **Representative Fraction** 1:1 000 000 means that 1 unit on the map represents 1 million on the earth. So 1 cm = 1 000 000 cm or 10 km. In SI units (the metric system) the Representative Fraction can be converted to the scale of 1 cm by moving the decimal point through five places, usually deleting the last five zeros thus :- 1: 20 000 000 − 1cm = 200 km. Scale on map projections can only be correct along specific meridians and parallels or from one or two specific points. To take an extreme example of scale distortion, the diagram on the left shows how a portion of the earth's surface, when unwrapped from around a globe (**a gore**) compares with the same area at the same equatorial scale but on Mercator's Projection. The enlargement of scale away from the equator is considerable and for this reason a variable scale for each line of latitude is given (see below).

0 800 1600 km

AZIMUTHAL OR ZENITHAL PROJECTIONS

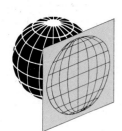

These are constructed by the projection of part of the graticule from the globe onto a plane tangential to any single point on it. This plane may be tangential to the equator (**equatorial case**), the poles (**polar case**) or any other point (**oblique case**). Any straight line drawn from the point at which the plane touches the globe is the shortest distance from that point and is known as a **great circle**. In its **Gnomonic** construction *any* straight line on the map is a great circle, but there is great exaggeration towards the edges and this reduces its general uses. There are five different ways of transferring the graticule onto the plane and these are shown on the right. The central diagram below shows how the graticules vary, using the polar case as the example.

Equidistant	Equal-Area	Orthographic	Gnomonic	Stereographic (conformal)

Oblique Case

The plane touches the globe at any point between the equator and poles. The oblique orthographic uses the distortion in azimuthal projections away from the centre to give a graphic depiction of the earth as seen from any desired point in space. It can also be used in both Polar and Equatorial cases. It is used not only for the earth but also for the moon and planets.

Polar Case

The polar case is the simplest to construct and the diagram below shows the differing effects of all five methods of construction comparing their coverage, distortion etc., using North America as the example.

Equatorial Case

The example shown here is Lambert's Equivalent Azimuthal. It is the only projection which is both equal area and where bearing is true from the centre.

Equidistant

Stereographic

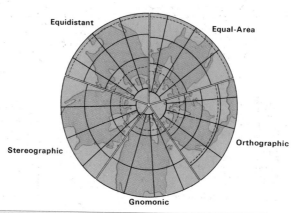

Equidistant — Equal-Area — Orthographic — Gnomonic